CORRECTNESS

D1537290

BS

Buffalo State

BS Buffalo State

I Stand Here Writing
Nancy Sommers

I stand in my kitchen, wiping the cardamom, coriander, and cayenne off my fingers. My head is abuzz with words, with bits and pieces of conversation. I hear a phrase I have read recently, something about "a radical loss of certainty." But, I wonder, how did the sentence begin? I search the air for the rest of the sentence, can't find it, shake some more cardamom, and a bit of coriander. Then, by some play of mind, I am back home again in Indiana with my family, sitting around the kitchen table. Two people are talking, and there are three opinions; three people are talking, and there are six opinions. Opinions grow exponentially. I fight my way back to that sentence. Writing, that's how it begins: "Writing is a radical loss of certainty." (Or is it uncertainty?) It isn't so great for the chicken when all these voices start showing up, with all these sentences hanging in mid-air, but the voices keep me company. I am a writer, not a cook, and the truth is I don't care much about the chicken. Stories beget stories. Writing emerges from writing.

The truth. Has truth anything to do with the facts? All I know is that no matter how many facts I might clutter my life with, I am as bound to the primordial drama of my family as the earth is to the sun. This year my father, the son of a severe Prussian matriarch, watched me indulge my daughters, and announced to me that he wished I had been his mother. This year, my thirtyninth, my last year to be thirty-something, my mother — who has a touch of magic, who can walk into the middle of a field of millions of clovers and find the one with four leaves — has begun to think I need help. She sends me cards monthly with four-leaf clovers taped inside. Two words neatly printed in capital letters — GOOD LUCK!! I look at these clovers and hear Reynolds Price's words: "Nobody under forty can believe how nearly everything's inherited." I wonder what my mother knows, what she is trying to tell me about the facts of my life.

When I was in high school studying French, laboring to conjugate verbs, the numerous four-leaf clovers my mother had carefully pressed inside her French dictionary made me imagine her in a field of clovers lyrically conjugating verbs of love. This is the only romantic image I have of my mother, a shy and conservative woman whose own mother died when she was five, whose grandparents were killed by the Nazis, who fled Germany at age thirteen with her father and sister. Despite the sheer facts of her life, despite the accumulation of grim knowable data, the truth is my mother is an optimistic person. She has the curious capacity always to be looking for luck, putting her faith in four-leaf clovers, ladybugs, pennies, and other amulets of fortune. She has a vision different from mine, one the facts alone can't explain. I, her daughter, was left, for a long time, seeing only the ironies; they were my defense against the facts of my life.

In this world of my inheritance in which daughters can become their fathers' mothers and mothers know their daughters are entering into a world where only sheer good luck will guide them, I hear from my own daughters that I am not in tune with their worlds, that I am just like a 50s mom, that they are 90s children, and I should stop acting so primitive. My children laugh uproariously at my autograph book, a 1959 artifact they unearthed in the basement of my parents' home. "Never kiss by the garden gate. Love is blind, but the neighbors ain't," wrote one friend. And my best friend, who introduced herself to me on the first day of first grade, looking me straight in the eye — and whispering through her crooked little teeth "the Jews killed Jesus" — wrote in this autograph book: "Mary had a little lamb. Her father shot it dead. Now she carries it to school between two slices of bread."

My ten-year-old daughter, Rachel, writes notes to me in hieroglyphics and tapes signs on the refrigerator in Urdu. "Salaam Namma Man Rachaal Ast" reads one sign. Simply translated it means "Hello, my name is Rachel." Alex, my seven-year-old daughter, writes me lists, new lists each month, visibly reminding me of the many things I need to buy or do for her. This month's list includes a little refrigerator filled with Coke and candy; ears pierced; a new toilet; neon nail polish and *real* adult make-up.

How do I look at these facts? How do I embrace these experiences, these texts of my life, and translate them into ideas? How do I make sense of them and the conversations they engender in my head? I look at Alex's list and wonder what kind of feminist daughter I am raising whose deepest desires include neon nail polish and *real* adult make-up. Looking at her lists a different way, I wonder if this second child of mine is asking me for something larger, something more permanent and real than adult make-up. Maybe I got that sentence wrong. Maybe it is that "Love (as well as writing) involves a radical loss of certainty."

Love is blind, but the neighbors ain't. Mary's father shot her little lamb dead, and now she carries it to school between two slices of bread. I hear these rhymes today, and they don't say to me what they say to my daughters. They don't seem so innocent. I hear them and think about the ways in which my neighbors in Indiana could only see my family as Jews from Germany, exotic strangers who ate tongue, outsiders who didn't celebrate Christmas. I wonder if my daughter Rachel needs to tell me her name in Urdu because she thinks we don't share a common language.

These sources change meaning when I ask the questions in a different way. They introduce new ironies, new questions.

I want to understand these living, breathing, primary sources all around me. I want to be, in Henry James's words, "a person upon whom nothing is lost." These sources speak to me of love and loss, of memory and desire, of the ways in which we come to understand something through difference and opposition. Two years ago I learned the word *segue* from one of my students. At first the word seemed peculiar. Segue sounded like something you did only on the Los Angeles freeway. Now I hear that word everywhere, and I have begun using it. I want to know how to segue from one idea to the next, from one thought to the fragment lying beside it. But the connections don't always come with four-leaf clovers and the words GOOD LUCK neatly printed beside them.

My academic need to find connections sends me to the library. There are eleven million books in my University's libraries. Certainly these sanctioned voices, these authorities, these published sources can help me find the connections. Someone, probably some three thousand someones, has studied what it is like to be the child of survivors. Someone has written a manual on how the granddaughter of a severe Prussian matriarch and the daughter of a collector of amulets ought to raise feminist daughters. I want to walk into the fields of writing, into those eleven million books, and find the one book that will explain it all. But I've learned to expect less from such sources. They seldom have the answers. And the answers they do have reveal themselves to me at the most unexpected times. I have been led astray more than once while searching books for the truth.

Once I learned a lesson about borrowing someone else's words and losing my own.

I was fourteen, light-years away from thirty-something. High school debate teams across the nation were arguing the pros and cons of the United States Military Aid Policy. It all came back to me as I listened to the news of the Persian Gulf War, as I listened to Stormin' Norman giving his morning briefings, an eerie resonance, all our arguments, the millions of combative words — sorties — fired back and forth. In my first practice debate, not having had enough time to assemble my own sources, I borrowed quote cards from my teammates. I attempted to bolster my position that the U.S. should limit its military aid by reading a quote in my best debate style: "W. W. Rostow says: 'We should not give military aid to India because it will exacerbate endemic rivalries.' "

Under cross-examination, my nemesis, Bobby Rosenfeld, the neighbor kid, who always knew the right answers, began firing a series of questions at me without stopping to let me answer:

"Nancy, can you tell me who W. W. Rostow is? And can you tell me why he might say this? Nancy, can you tell me what 'exacerbate' means?

Can you tell me what 'endemic rivalries' are? And exactly what does it mean to 'exacerbate endemic rivalries'?"

I didn't know. I simply did not know who W. W. Rostow was, why he might have said that, what "exacerbate" meant, or what an "endemic rivalry" was. Millions of four-leaf clovers couldn't have helped me. I might as well have been speaking Urdu. I didn't know who my source was, the context of the source, nor the literal meaning of the words I had read. Borrowing words from authorities had left me without any words of my own.

My debate partner and I went on that year to win the Indiana state championship and to place third in the nationals. Bobby Rosenfeld never cross-examined me again, but for twenty years he has appeared in my dreams. I am not certain why I would dream so frequently about this scrawny kid whom I despised. I think, though, that he became for me what the Sea Dyak tribe of Borneo calls a *ngarong*, a dream guide, someone guiding me to understanding. In this case, Bobby guided me to understand the endemic rivalries within myself. The last time Bobby appeared in a dream he had become a woman.

I learned a more valuable lesson about sources as a college senior. I was the kind of student who loved words, words out of context, words that swirled around inside my mouth, words like *exacerbate*, *undulating*, *lugubrious*, and *zeugma*. "She stained her honour or her new brocade," wrote Alexander Pope. I would try to write zeugmas whenever I could, exacerbating my already lugubrious prose. Within the English department, I was known more for my long hair, untamed and untranslatable, and for my long distance bicycle rides than for my scholarship.

For my senior thesis, I picked Emerson's essay "Eloquence." Harrison Hayford, my advisor, suggested that I might just get off my bicycle, get lost in the library, and read all of Emerson's essays, journals, letters. I had picked one of Emerson's least distinguished essays, an essay that the critics mentioned only in passing, and if I were not entirely on my own, I had at least carved out new territory for myself.

I spent weeks in the library reading Emerson's journals, reading newspaper accounts from Rockford and Peoria, Illinois, where he had first delivered "Eloquence" as a speech. Emerson stood at the podium, the wind blowing his papers hither and yon, calmly picking them up, and proceeding to read page 8 followed by page 3, followed by page 6, followed by page 2. No one seemed to know the difference. Emerson's Midwestern audience was overwhelmed by this strange man from Concord, Massachusetts, this eloquent stranger whose unit of expression was the sentence.

As I sat in the library, wearing my QUESTION AUTHORITY T-shirt, I could admire this man who delivered his Divinity School Address in 1838, speaking words so repugnant to the genteel people of Cambridge that it was almost thirty years before Harvard felt safe having him around again. I could understand the Midwestern audience's awe and adulation as they listened but didn't quite comprehend Emerson's stunning oratory. I had joined the debate team not to argue the U.S. Military Aid Policy, but to learn how to be an orator who could stun audiences, to learn a personal eloquence I could never learn at home. Perhaps only children of immigrant parents can understand the embarrassing moments of inarticulateness, the missed connections that come from learning to speak a language from parents who claim a different mother tongue.

As an undergraduate, I wanted to free myself from that mother tongue. Four-leaf clovers and amulets of oppression weighed heavy on my mind, and I could see no connection whatsoever between those facts of my life and the untranslatable side of myself that set me in opposition to authority. And then along came Emerson. Like his Midwest audience, I didn't care about having him whole. I liked the promise and the rhapsodic freedom I found in his sentences, in his invitation to seize life as our dictionary, to believe that "Life was not something to be learned but to be lived." I loved his insistence that "the one thing of value is the active soul." I read that "Books are for the scholar's idle time," and I knew that he had given me permission to explore the world. Going into Emerson was like walking into a revelation; it was the first time I had gone into the texts not looking for a specific answer, and it was the first time the texts gave me the answers I needed. Never mind that I got only part of what Emerson was telling me. I got inspiration, I got insight, and I began to care deeply about my work.

Today I reread the man who set me off on a new road, and I find a different kind of wisdom. Today I reread "The American Scholar," and I don't underline the sentence "Books are for the scholar's idle time." I continue to the next paragraph, underlining the sentence "One must be an inventor to read well." The second sentence doesn't contradict the one I read twenty years ago, but it means more today. I bring more to it, and I know that I can walk into text after text, source after source, and they will give me insight, but not answers. I have learned too that my sources can surprise me. Like my mother, I find myself sometimes surrounded by a field of four-leaf clovers, there for the picking, waiting to see what I can make of them. But I must be an inventor if I am to read those sources well, if I am to imagine the connections.

As I stand in my kitchen, the voices that come to me come by way of a lifetime of reading, they come on the waves of life, and they seem to be helping me translate the untranslatable. They come, not at my bidding, but when I least expect them, when I am receptive enough to listen to their voices. They come when I am open.

If I could teach my students one lesson about writing it would be to see themselves as sources, as places from which ideas originate, to see themselves as Emerson's transparent eyeball, all that they have read and experienced — the dictionaries of their lives — circulating through them. I want them to learn how sources thicken, complicate, enlarge writing, but I want them to know too how it is always the writer's voice, vision, and argument that create the new source. I want my students to see that nothing reveals itself straight out, especially the sources all around them. But I know enough by now that this Emersonian ideal can't be passed on in one lesson or even a semester of lessons.

Many of the students who come to my classes have been trained to collect facts; they act as if their primary job is to accumulate enough authorities so that there is no doubt about the "truth" of their thesis. They most often disappear behind the weight and permanence of their borrowed words, moving their pens, mouthing the words of others, allowing sources to speak through them unquestioned, unexamined.

At the outset, many of my students think that personal writing is writing about the death of their grandmother. Academic writing is reporting what Elizabeth Kübler-Ross has written about death and dying. Being personal, I want to show my students, does not mean being autobiographical. Being academic does not mean being remote, distant, imponderable. Being personal means bringing their judgments and interpretation to bear on what they read and. write, learning that they never leave themselves behind even when they write academic essays.

Last year, David Gray came into my essay class disappointed about everything. He didn't like the time of the class, didn't like the reading list, didn't seem to like me. Nothing pleased him. "If this is a class on the essay," he asked the first day, "why aren't we reading real essayists like Addison, Steele, and Lamb?" On the second day, after being asked to read Annie Dillard's "Living Like Weasels," David complained that a weasel wasn't a fit subject for an essay. "Writers need big subjects. Look at Melville. He needed a whale for *Moby-Dick*. A weasel — that's nothing but a rodent." And so it continued for a few weeks.

I kept my equanimity in class, but at home I'd tell my family about this kid who kept testing me, seizing me like Dillard's weasel, and not letting go. I secretly wanted him out of my class. But then again, I sensed in him a kindred spirit, someone else who needed to question authority.

I wanted my students to write exploratory essays about education, so I asked them to think of a time when they had learned something, and then a time when they had tried to learn something but couldn't. I wanted them to see what ideas and connections they could find between these two very different experiences and the other essays they were reading for the class. I wanted the various sources to work as catalysts. I wanted my students to find a way to talk back to those other writers. The assigned texts were an odd assortment with few apparent connections. I hoped my students would find the common ground, but also the moments of tension, the contradictions, and the ambiguities in those sources.

David used the assigned texts as a catalyst for his thinking, but as was his way, he went beyond the texts I offered and chose his own. He begins his essay, "Dulcis Est Sapientia," with an account of his high school Latin class, suggesting that he once knew declensions, that he had a knack for conjugations, but has forgotten them. He tells us that if his teacher were to appear suddenly today and demand the perfect subjunctive of venire, he would stutter hopelessly.

About that Latin class, David asks, "What is going on here? Did I once know Latin and forget it through disuse? Perhaps I never learned Latin at all. What I learned was a bunch of words which, with the aid of various ending sounds, indicated that Gaius was either a good man delivering messages to the lieutenant or a general who struck camp at the seventh hour. I may have known it once, but I never learned it." The class never gave David the gift of language. There was something awry in the method.

What is learning? That's what David explores in his essay as he moves from his Latin lesson to thinking about surrealist paintings, to thinking about barriers we create, to Plato, to an airplane ride in which he observed a mother teaching her child concepts of color and number, all the time taking his readers along with him on his journey, questioning sources, reflecting, expanding, and enriching his growing sense that learning should stress ideas rather than merely accumulating facts and information.

David draws his essay to a close with an analysis of a joke: A man goes to a cocktail party and gets soused. He approaches his host and asks, "Pardon me, but do lemons whistle?"

The host looks at him oddly and answers, "No, lemons don't whistle."

"Oh dear," says the guest, "then I'm afraid I just squeezed your canary into my gin and tonic."

David reflects about the significance of this joke: "One need not be an ornithologist to get the joke, but one must know that canaries are yellow and that they whistle. . . . What constitutes the joke is a connection made between two things . . . which have absolutely nothing in common except for their yellowness. It would never occur to us to make a comparison between the two, let alone to confuse one with the other. But this is the value of the joke, to force into our consciousness the ideas which we held but never actively considered. . . . This knocking down of barriers between ideas is parallel to the process that occurs in all learning. The barriers that we set . . . suddenly crumble; the boundaries . . . are extended to include other modes of thought." Learning, like joking, David argues, gives us pleasure by satisfying our innate capacity to recognize coherence, to discern patterns and connections.

David's essay, like any essay, does not intend to offer the last word on its subject. The civilizing influence of an essay is that it keeps the conversation going, chronicling an intellectual journey, reflecting conversations with sources. I am confident that when David writes for his philosophy course he won't tell a joke anywhere in his essay. But if the joke — if any of his sources — serves him as a catalyst for his thinking, if he makes connections among the sources that circulate within him, between Plato and surrealism, between Latin lessons and mother-child lessons — the dictionaries of *his* life — then he has learned something valuable about writing.

I say to myself that I don't believe in luck. And yet. Not too long ago Rachel came home speaking with some anxiety about an achievement test that she had to take at school. Wanting to comfort her, I urged her to take my rabbit's foot to school the next day. Always alert to life's ironies, Rachel said, "Sure, Mom, a rabbit's foot will really help me find the answers. And even if it did, how would I know the answer the next time when I didn't have that furry little claw?" The next day, proud of her ease in taking the test, she remained perplexed by the one question that seized her and wouldn't let go. She tried it on me: "Here's the question," she said. "Can you figure out which of these sentences cannot be true?"

(a) We warmed our hands by the fire.
(b) The rain poured in and around the windows.
(c) The wind beckoned us to open the door.

Only in the mind of someone who writes achievement tests, and wants to close the door on the imagination, could the one false sentence be "The wind beckoned us to open the door." Probably to this kind of mind, Emerson's sentence "Life is our dictionary" is also not a true sentence.

But life *is* our dictionary, and that's how we know that the wind can beckon us to open the door. Like Emerson, we let the wind blow our pages hither and yon, forcing us to start in the middle, moving from page 8 to page 2, forward to page 7, moving back and forth in time, losing our certainty.

Like Emerson, I love basic units, the words themselves, words like cardamom, coriander, words that play around in my head, swirl around in my mouth. The challenge, of course, is not to be a ventriloquist — not to be a mouther of words — but to be open to other voices, untranslatable as they might be. Being open to the unexpected, we can embrace complexities: canaries and lemons, amulets and autograph books, fathers who want their daughters to be their mothers, and daughters who write notes in Urdu — all those odd, unusual conjunctions can come together and speak through us.

The other day, I called my mother and told her about this essay, told her that I had been thinking about the gold bracelet she took with her as one of her few possessions from Germany — a thin gold chain with three amulets: a mushroom, a lady bug, and, of course, a four-leaf clover. Two other charms fell off years ago — she lost one, I the other. I used to worry over the missing links, thinking only of the loss, of what we could never retrieve. When I look at the bracelet now, I think about the Prussian matriarch, my grandmother, and my whole primordial family drama. I think too of Emerson and the pages that blew in the wind and the gaps that seemed not to matter. The bracelet is but one of many sources that intrigues me. Considering them in whatever order they appear, with whatever gaps, I want to see where they will lead me, what they tell me.

With writing and with teaching, as well as with love, we don't know how the sentence will begin and, rarely ever, how it will end. Having the courage to live with uncertainty, ambiguity, even doubt, we can walk into all of those fields of writing, knowing that we will find volumes upon volumes bidding *us* enter. We need only be inventors, we need only give freely and abundantly to the texts, imagining even as we write that we too will be a source from which other readers can draw sustenance.

Writing Skills Rubric

RATING	EXCEEDS	MEETS	DOES NOT MEET
Attention to Task	Writer effectively addresses all parts of the writing prompt.	Writer adequately addresses all parts of the writing prompt.	Writer neglects to address some or all parts of the writing prompt or does so inadequately.
Thesis/ Controlling Idea	Thesis/controlling idea is easily identifiable, focused, and thought-provoking.	Thesis/controlling idea is identifiable and focused.	Thesis/controlling idea is wandering, vague, unfocused, or absent.
Critical Thinking and Development	Writer presents pertinent evidence, examples, and/or logical reasoning to support conclusions or point of view. Writer identifies relevant qualifications or objections or alternative points of view and prioritizes evidence and/or reasons in support of the conclusion. Writer describes the broader relevance, significance or context of the issue.	Writer presents accurate examples and evidence to support conclusions or point of view. Writer identifies some qualifications, objections, or alternative points of view. Writer describes the broader relevance, significance or context of the issue.	Writer either fails to present examples/ evidence or examples/ evidence provided lack relevance, are inaccurate, or do not clearly support conclusions or point of view. Writer does not clearly identify or respond to relevant objections or alternative points of view. Writer fails to describe or inadequately describes the broader relevance, significance, or context of the issue.
Organization	Paper is effectively organized.	Paper is coherently organized.	Paper is not divided into paragraphs, or basic paragraphing exists but paper is ineffectively or inconsistently organized.
Introduction	Writer provides context and relevance.	Writer clearly introduces topic or issue at hand.	Introduction is absent, lacks focus, or includes too little or too much information.

Writing Skills Rubric *(continued)*

RATING	EXCEEDS	MEETS	DOES NOT MEET
Conclusion	Conclusion is well demonstrated.	Conclusion clearly summarizes or closes paper.	Conclusion doesn't adequately represent the body of the paper, or the last paragraph of the paper does not serve as a conclusion.
Tone and Diction	Writer demonstrates solid command of word choice. Tone and diction are appropriate for the subject and implied audience.	Writer demonstrates some degree of control over tone and diction, Both are appropriate for the subject and implied audience.	Tone and diction are often inconsistent and/or inappropriate for the subject and implied audience.
Sentence Structure	Sentence structure displays sophistication and variety.	For the most part, sentences are clear, concise, and well constructed.	Sentences are often wordy, awkward, and/or unclear. Problems exist with sentence combining, parallel construction, misplaced modifiers, fragments, and/or run-on sentences.
Mechanics (Grammar, Punctuation, and Spelling)	Mechanics are nearly flawless.	Mechanics are mostly accurate and do not obscure meaning.	Mechanics are not well executed and may, at times, obscure meaning.
OVERALL RATING			

Research Rubric

RATING	EXCEEDS	MEETS	DOES NOT MEET
Analysis and Integration of Source Material	Writer responds creatively to the issue under discussion. Evidence is drawn from carefully selected sources and documented in an accepted style. Conclusions are based on thoughtful integration of the writer's own thinking and careful analysis of outside sources.	Writer responds intelligently to the issue under discussion. Evidence is drawn from appropriately selected sources and documented in an accepted style. Conclusions demonstrate the writer's conscious attempts to integrate his or her own thinking with an analysis of outside sources.	Writer fails to address or ineffectively addresses the issue under discussion. Outside sources may be inappropriate to the topic, or information from sources may be presented without careful analysis and/or inadequately documented. Conclusions may demonstrate little evidence of the writer's own thinking, presenting mainly a summary or restatement of the main sources.
Documentation	Writer effectively uses the assigned citation method.	Writer adequately uses the assigned citation method. There are only minor errors in formatting that would not be considered plagiarism.	Writer ineffectively uses the assigned citation method. There are errors in formatting that may be considered plagiarism.
OVERALL RATING			

Revision Rubric

RATING	EXCEEDS	MEETS	DOES NOT MEET
Global Revision	Student consistently demonstrates a sophisticated ability to revise by altering content and approach, by reorganizing material, or by clarifying and strengthening the coherence of ideas of all drafts.	Student demonstrates the ability to revise by refining content, sharpening focus, and improving structure, clarity, and coherence of all drafts.	Student demonstrates a lack of ability or inconsistent ability to revise in any substantial way. Student did not engage in revision process, or revision attempts were either infrequent or insufficient to improve the content, focus, structure, clarity, and coherence of earlier drafts.
Sentence-Level Revision	The mechanics of final drafts are nearly flawless.	The mechanics of final drafts are mostly accurate and rarely impede meaning.	Mechanics either did not improve or appear to be the only focus of student's revisions.
OVERALL RATING			

College Writing Program Assessment Rubric

RATING	EXCEEDS	MEETS	DOES NOT MEET
Attention to Task	Writer effectively addresses all parts of the writing prompt.	Writer adequately addresses all parts of the writing prompt.	Writer neglects to address some or all parts of the writing prompt or does so inadequately.
Critical Thinking and Development	Writer presents pertinent evidence, examples, and/or logical reasoning to support conclusion or point of view. Writer describes the broader relevance, significance, or context of the issue.	Writer presents accurate examples and evidence to support conclusion or point of view. Writer describes the broader relevance, significance, or context of the issue.	Writer states a conclusion or point of view but examples and/or evidence may lack relevance, may be inaccurate, or may not clearly support ideas Writer does not adequately describe the broader relevance, significance, or context of the issue.
Organization	Paper is effectively organized.	Paper is coherently organized.	Paper is not divided into paragraphs, or basic paragraphing exists but paper is ineffectively or inconsistently organized.
Sentence Structure	Sentence structure displays sophistication and variety.	For the most part, sentences are clear, concise, and well constructed.	Sentences are often wordy, awkward, and/or unclear. Problems exist with sentence combining, parallel construction, misplaced modifiers, fragments, and/or run-on sentences.
Mechanics (Grammar, Punctuation, and Spelling)	Mechanics are nearly flawless.	Mechanics are mostly accurate and do not obscure meaning.	Mechanics are not well executed and may, at times, obscure meaning.
OVERALL RATING			

A Writer's Reference

SEVENTH EDITION

A Writer's Reference

Diana Hacker

Nancy Sommers
Harvard University

Contributing ESL Specialist
Marcy Carbajal Van Horn
St. Edward's University

BEDFORD / ST. MARTIN'S   BOSTON ◆ NEW YORK

For Bedford/St. Martin's

Executive Editor: Michelle M. Clark
Senior Development Editor: Barbara G. Flanagan
Development Editor: Mara Weible
Associate Editor: Alicia Young
Senior Production Editor: Rosemary R. Jaffe
Assistant Production Editor: Lindsay DiGianvittorio
Assistant Production Manager: Joe Ford
Marketing Manager: Marjorie Adler
Editorial Assistant: Kylie Paul
Copyeditor: Linda McLatchie
Indexer: Ellen Kuhl Repetto
Permissions Manager: Kalina Ingham Hintz
Senior Art Director: Anna Palchik
Text Design: Claire Seng-Niemoeller
Cover Design: Donna Lee Dennison
Composition: Nesbitt Graphics, Inc.
Printing and Binding: RR Donnelley and Sons

President: Joan E. Feinberg
Editorial Director: Denise B. Wydra
Editor in Chief: Karen S. Henry
Director of Marketing: Karen R. Soeltz
Director of Production: Susan W. Brown
Associate Director, Editorial Production: Elise S. Kaiser
Managing Editor: Elizabeth M. Schaaf

Library of Congress Control Number: 2010920402

Manufactured in the United States of America.

6   5   4
g

For information, write: Bedford/St. Martin's, 75 Arlington Street, Boston, MA 02116   (617-399-4000)

ISBN-10: 0-312-60143-3 ISBN-13: 978-0-312-60143-0 (Student Edition)
         0-312-60146-8   978-0-312-60146-1 (Instructor's Edition)

How to use this book
and its companion Web site

A *Writer's Reference* is designed to save you time and will answer most of the questions you are likely to ask as you plan, draft, revise, and edit a piece of writing: How do I choose and narrow a topic? How do I know when to begin a new paragraph? Should I write *each was* or *each were*? When should I place a comma before *and*? What is counterargument? How do I cite a source from the Web?

The book's companion Web site extends the book beyond its covers. See pages x–xi for details.

How to find information with an instructor's help

When you are revising an essay that your instructor has marked, tracking down information is simple. If your instructor uses a code such as S1-a or MLA-2b to indicate a problem, you can turn directly to the appropriate section of the handbook. Just flip through the tabs at the tops of the pages until you find the code in question.

If your instructor uses an abbreviation such as *w* or *dm*, consult the list of abbreviations and revision symbols on the next-to-last page of the book. There you will find the name of the problem (*wordy; dangling modifier*) and the number of the section to consult.

If your instructor provides advice without codes or abbreviations, use the index at the back of the book to look up specific terms. (See pp. ix and xii for more about the index.)

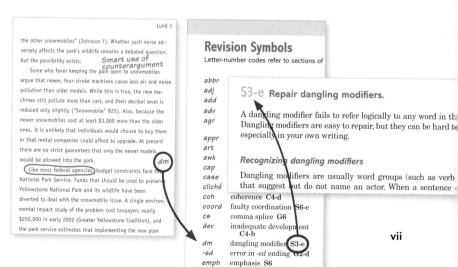

How to find information on your own

This handbook is designed to allow you to find information quickly without an instructor's help—usually by consulting the main menu inside the front cover. At times, you may also consult the detailed menu inside the back cover, the index, the glossary of usage, the list of revision symbols, or one of the directories to documentation models. The tutorials on pages xii–xv give you opportunities to practice finding information in different ways.

THE MAIN MENU   The main menu inside the front cover displays the handbook's contents briefly and simply. Each of the twelve sections in the main menu leads you to a color-coded tabbed divider (such as C/Composing and Revising), where you can find a more detailed menu.

Let's say that you want to find out how to make your sentences parallel. Your first step is to scan the main menu for the appropriate topic—in this case, S1, "Parallelism." Then you can browse the section numbers at the tops of the pages to find section S1.

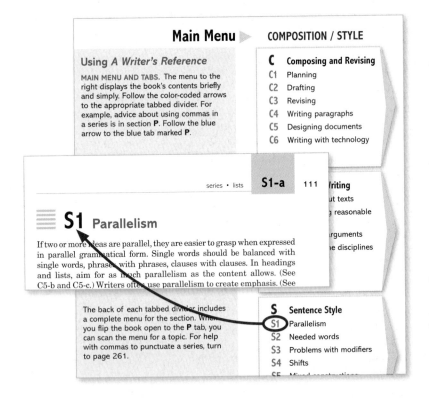

THE DETAILED MENU   The detailed menu appears inside the back cover. When the section you're looking for is broken up into quite a few subsections, try consulting this menu. For instance, if you have a question about the proper use of commas after introductory elements, this menu will quickly lead you from P/Punctuation to P1, "The comma" to P1-b, "Introductory elements."

Once you find the right subsection in the book, you will see three kinds of advice to help you edit your writing—a rule, an explanation, and one or more examples that show editing.

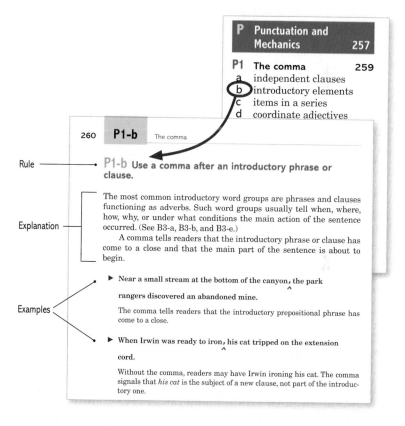

P   **Punctuation and Mechanics**   257

P1   **The comma**   259
a   independent clauses
b   introductory elements
c   items in a series
d   coordinate adjectives

260   **P1-b**   The comma

Rule ————→   P1-b **Use a comma after an introductory phrase or clause.**

Explanation ——   The most common introductory word groups are phrases and clauses functioning as adverbs. Such word groups usually tell when, where, how, why, or under what conditions the main action of the sentence occurred. (See B3-a, B3-b, and B3-e.)

A comma tells readers that the introductory phrase or clause has come to a close and that the main part of the sentence is about to begin.

Examples

▶ Near a small stream at the bottom of the canyon, the park

rangers discovered an abandoned mine.

The comma tells readers that the introductory prepositional phrase has come to a close.

▶ When Irwin was ready to iron, his cat tripped on the extension

cord.

Without the comma, readers may have Irwin ironing his cat. The comma signals that *his cat* is the subject of a new clause, not part of the introductory one.

THE INDEX   If you aren't sure which topic to choose from one of the menus, consult the index at the back of the book. For example, you may not realize that the question of whether to use *have* or *has* is a matter of subject-verb agreement (section G1). In that case, simply look up *"has* vs. *have"* in the index. You will be directed to specific pages covering subject-verb agreement.

MAKING THE MOST OF YOUR HANDBOOK You will find your way to helpful advice by using the index, the menus, or the tabbed dividers. Once you get to the page with the advice you are looking for, you may also find a "Making the most of your handbook" box that pulls together additional related advice and models for your assignment.

> drilling, for example, imagine a jury that represents those who have a stake in the matter: environmentalists, policymakers, oil company executives, and consumers.
>
> At times, you can deliberately narrow your audience. If you are working within a word limit, for example, you might not have the space in which to address all the concerns surrounding the offshore drilling debate. Or you might be primarily interested in reaching one segment of a general
>
> **Making the most of your handbook**
>
> You may need to consider a specific audience for your argument.
>
> ▶ Writing in a particular discipline, such as business or psychology: A4

THE GLOSSARY OF USAGE When in doubt about the correct use of a particular word (such as *affect* and *effect*), consult the glossary of usage, section W1. This glossary explains the difference between commonly confused words; it also includes words that are inappropriate in formal written English.

MORE ONLINE

Using the book's companion Web site: hackerhandbooks.com/writersref

Throughout *A Writer's Reference*, Seventh Edition, you will see references to more advice and help on the book's Web site. These are labeled PRACTICE (for interactive exercises), MODELS (for model papers and other documents), and THE WRITING CENTER (for tips on getting help with your assignments). Here is a complete list of resources on the site. Your instructor may use some of this material in class; each area of the site, however, has been developed for you to use on your own whenever you need it.

> Practice exercises
>   More than 1,800 interactive writing, grammar, and research/documentation exercise items, all with immediate feedback. Research exercises include topics such as integrating quotations and documenting sources in MLA, APA, and CMS (*Chicago*) styles.
> Model papers
>   Annotated sample papers, organized by style (MLA, APA, CMS [*Chicago*], CSE) and by genre (research paper, argument paper, review of the literature, and so on)
> *Research and Documentation Online*
>   Advice on finding sources in a variety of academic disciplines and up-to-date guidelines for documenting print and online sources in MLA, APA, CMS (*Chicago*), and CSE styles

DIRECTORIES TO DOCUMENTATION MODELS   When you are documenting sources in a research paper with MLA, APA, or CMS (*Chicago*) style, you can find documentation models by consulting the appropriate color-coded directories.

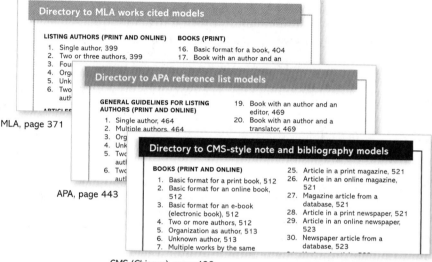

MLA, page 371

Directory to MLA works cited models

LISTING AUTHORS (PRINT AND ONLINE)
1. Single author, 399
2. Two or three authors, 399
3. Fou
4. Org
5. Unk
6. Two
   auth

BOOKS (PRINT)
16. Basic format for a book, 404
17. Book with an author and an

APA, page 443

Directory to APA reference list models

GENERAL GUIDELINES FOR LISTING
AUTHORS (PRINT AND ONLINE)
1. Single author, 464
2. Multiple authors, 464
3. Org
4. Unk
5. Two
   auth
6. Two
   auth

19. Book with an author and an editor, 469
20. Book with an author and a translator, 469

Directory to CMS-style note and bibliography models

BOOKS (PRINT AND ONLINE)
1. Basic format for a print book, 512
2. Basic format for an online book, 512
3. Basic format for an e-book (electronic book), 512
4. Two or more authors, 512
5. Organization as author, 513
6. Unknown author, 513
7. Multiple works by the same

25. Article in a print magazine, 521
26. Article in an online magazine, 521
27. Magazine article from a database, 521
28. Article in a print newspaper, 521
29. Article in an online newspaper, 523
30. Newspaper article from a database, 523

CMS (*Chicago*), page 498

> Multilingual/ESL
  Resources, strategies, model papers, and exercises to help multilingual students improve their college writing skills
> Revision
  Papers in progress and models of global and sentence-level revisions
> Writing center resources
  Revision checklists and helpsheets for common writing problems
> Language Debates
  Mini-essays exploring controversial issues of grammar and usage
> Exercise PDFs, diagnostics, and test prep
  Print-format practice exercises, interactive diagnostic tests, and links to additional online resources for every part of the book
> Nancy Sommers videos
  From the book's coauthor, advice on revising, reading and responding to texts, working with teacher comments, and developing an argument
> Re:Writing
  A free collection of resources for composition and other college classes: help with preparing presentation slides, avoiding plagiarism, evaluating online sources, and more
> E-book
  An online version of the book with interactive exercises, audio commentary on model papers, and short movies that teach essential college skills such as integrating sources in a research paper and revising with peer comments (This area of the Web site requires an activation code.)

Tutorials

The following tutorials will give you practice using the book's menus, index, glossary of usage, and MLA directory. Answers to the tutorials begin on page xiv.

TUTORIAL 1: Using the menus

Each of the following "rules" violates the principle it expresses. Using the main menu inside the front cover or the detailed menu inside the back cover, find the section in *A Writer's Reference* that explains the principle. Then fix the problem. Example:

> *Tutors in*
> ▶ ~~In~~ the writing center/~~they~~ say that vague pronoun reference is
> ^
> unacceptable. *G3-b*

1. A verb have to agree with its subject.
2. About sentence fragments. You should avoid them.
3. Its important to use apostrophe's correctly.
4. If your sentence begins with a long introductory word group use a comma to separate the word group from the rest of the sentence.

TUTORIAL 2: Using the index

Assume that you have written the following sentences and want to know the answers to the questions in brackets. Use the index at the back of the book to locate the information you need, and edit the sentences if necessary.

1. Each of the candidates have decided to participate in tonight's debate. [Should the verb be *has* or *have* to agree with *Each*?]
2. We had intended to go surfing but spent most of our vacation lying on the beach. [Should I use *lying* or *laying*?]
3. In some cultures, it is considered ill mannered for you to accept a gift. [Is it OK to use *you* to mean "anyone in general"?]
4. In Canada, Joanne picked up several bottles of maple syrup for her sister and me. [Should I write *for her sister and I*?]

TUTORIAL 3: Using the menus or the index

Imagine that you are in the following situations. Using either the menus or the index, find the information you need.

1. You are a student studying health administration, and you're editing a report you've just written on the benefits of community-based urgent

care clinics. You recall learning to put a comma between all items in a series except the last two. But you have noticed that most writers use a comma between all items. You're curious about the rule. Which section of *A Writer's Reference* will you consult?

2. You are tutoring in your university's writing center. A composition student comes to you for help with her first college essay. She is revising a draft and struggling with her use of articles (*a*, *an*, and *the*). You know how to use articles, but you aren't able to explain the complicated rules on their correct use. Which section in *A Writer's Reference* will you and the student, a multilingual writer, consult?

3. You have been assigned to write a response to an essay you read for your composition class. Your instructor has asked that you use at least three quotations from the text in your response, which must be written in MLA style. You aren't quite sure how to integrate words from another source in your own writing. Which section in this handbook will help?

4. You supervise interns at a housing agency. Two of your interns have trouble with the -*s* endings on verbs. One tends to drop -*s* endings; the other tends to add them where they don't belong. You suspect that both problems stem from dialects spoken at home. The interns are in danger of losing their jobs because your boss thinks that anyone who writes "the tenant refuse . . ." or "the landlords insists . . ." is beyond hope. You disagree. Where can you direct your interns for help in *A Writer's Reference*?

TUTORIAL 4: Using the glossary of usage

Consult the glossary of usage to see if the italicized words are used correctly. Then edit any sentences containing incorrect usage. Example:

>   *an*
> ▶ The pediatrician gave my daughter ~~a~~ injection for her allergy.
>   ^

1. Changing attitudes toward alcohol have *effected* the beer industry.
2. It is *mankind's* nature to think wisely and act foolishly.
3. Our goal this year is to *grow* our profits by 9 percent.
4. Most sleds are pulled by no *less* than two dogs and no more than ten.

TUTORIAL 5: Using the directory to MLA works cited models

Let's say that you have written a short research essay on the origins of hip-hop music. You have cited the following four sources in your essay, using MLA style, and you are ready to type your list of works cited. Turn to pages 371–72 and use the MLA directory to locate the appropriate models. Then write a correct entry for each source and arrange the entries in a properly formatted list of works cited.

A book by Jeff Chang titled *Can't Stop, Won't Stop: A History of the Hip-Hop Generation*. The book was published in New York by St. Martin's Press in 2005.

An online article by Kay Randall called "Studying a Hip Hop Nation." The article appeared on the University of Texas at Austin Web site. The title of the site is *University of Texas at Austin*. You accessed the site on April 13, 2010; the last update was October 9, 2008.

A sound recording entitled "Rapper's Delight" performed by the Sugarhill Gang on the CD *Sugarhill Gang*. The CD was released in 2008 by DBK Works.

A magazine article accessed online through the database *Expanded Academic ASAP*. The article, "The Roots Redefine Hip-Hop's Past," was written by Kimberly Davis and published in *Ebony* magazine in June 2003. The article appears on pages 162–64. You found this article on April 13, 2010.

Answers to the Tutorials

TUTORIAL 1

1. A verb has to agree with its subject. (G1-a)
2. Avoid sentence fragments. (G5)
3. It's important to use apostrophes correctly. (P4)
4. If your sentence begins with a long introductory word group, use a comma to separate the word group from the rest of the sentence. (P1-b)

TUTORIAL 2

1. The index entry *"each"* mentions that the word is singular, so you might not need to look further to realize that the verb should be *has*, not *have*. The first page reference takes you to the entry for *each* in the glossary of usage (W1), which directs you to G1-e and G3-a for details about why *has* is correct. The index entry *"has* vs. *have"* leads you to the chart in G1.
2. The index entry *"lying* vs. *laying"* takes you to section G2-b, where you will learn that *lying* (meaning "reclining or resting on a surface") is correct.
3. Looking up *"you*, inappropriate use of" leads you to the glossary of usage (W1) and section G3-b, which explain that *you* should not be used to mean "anyone in general." You can revise the sentence by using *a person* or *one* instead of *you*, or you can restructure the sentence completely: *In some cultures, accepting a gift is considered ill mannered.*
4. The index entries *"I* vs. *me"* and *"me* vs. *I"* take you to section G3-c, which explains why *for her sister and me* is correct.

TUTORIAL 3

1. Section P1-c states that, although usage varies, most experts advise using a comma between all items in a series—to prevent possible misreadings or ambiguities. To find this section, you would probably use the menu system.
2. You and the student would consult section M2, on articles. This section is easy to locate in the menu system.

3. In the menu system, you will find "MLA papers" and then section MLA-3, "Integrating sources."
4. You can send your interns to sections G1 and G2-c, which you can find in the menu system if you know to look under "Subject-verb agreement" or "Verb forms, tenses, and moods." If you aren't sure about the grammatical terminology, you can look in the index under "-*s*, as verb ending" or "Verbs, -*s* form of."

TUTORIAL 4

1. Changing attitudes toward alcohol have *affected* the beer industry.
2. It is *human* nature to think wisely and act foolishly.
3. Our goal this year is to *increase* our profits by 9 percent.
4. Most sleds are pulled by no *fewer* than two dogs and no more than ten.

TUTORIAL 5

Chang, Jeff. *Can't Stop, Won't Stop: A History of the Hip-Hop Generation*. New York: St. Martin's, 2005. Print.

Davis, Kimberly. "The Roots Redefine Hip-Hop's Past." *Ebony* June 2003: 162-64. *Expanded Academic ASAP*. Web. 13 Apr. 2010.

Randall, Kay. "Studying a Hip Hop Nation." *University of Texas at Austin*. U of Texas at Austin, 9 Oct. 2008. Web. 13 Apr. 2010.

Sugarhill Gang. "Rapper's Delight." *Sugarhill Gang*. DBK Works, 2008. CD.

Preface for instructors

Everywhere I travel, instructors tell me that they love *A Writer's Reference*—its clear, concise explanations and respectful tone and its ease of use inside and outside the classroom. I understand why *A Writer's Reference* inspires such affection; it is the book I too have always loved, the book my students trust and keep, and the one that teaches one patient lesson at a time. Over the last six editions, millions of students and instructors have turned to *A Writer's Reference* for the straightforward, reliable, and comprehensive support that Diana Hacker always offered. It has been one of the great pleasures of my own teaching career to build on that foundation as the coauthor of *A Writer's Reference*.

Many people have asked, *How do you revise the most successful handbook in the country—the handbook that everyone loves?* To prepare for the seventh edition, I traveled to more than forty-five colleges and universities to learn how students use their handbooks and how instructors teach from them. I listened, everywhere, for clues about how to make the handbook an even more helpful companion for students throughout their academic careers and an even stronger resource for the teachers guiding their development as writers. Throughout my travels, I heard students puzzle out the unfamiliar elements of academic writing, particularly those related to working with sources. I watched creative instructors show their students how to build arguments, synthesize sources, and strengthen their ideas through revision. I observed writing center tutors responding to students' questions about thesis statements and counterargument. And I listened to librarians expertly explain how to approach research assignments and evaluate sources. I wanted the seventh edition to capture the vibrant energy and creativity that surround conversations about student writing, wherever they take place.

As you look through the seventh edition, you'll discover many innovations inspired by these conversations. One of the new features I'm most excited about is "Revising with comments." During my travels, I asked students about the comments they receive most frequently and asked instructors to show me the comments they write most frequently on their students' drafts. The answers to these questions, combined with my own research on responding to student writers, shaped this feature, which helps students and instructors make the most of reviewing and commenting. In keeping with the Hacker tradition, this new feature teaches one lesson at a time—how to revise an unclear thesis or how to consider opposing viewpoints, for instance—and directs students to specific sections of the handbook to guide their revision strategies.

In *A Writer's Reference*, Diana Hacker created the most innovative and practical college reference—the one that responds most directly to student writers' questions and challenges. The seventh edition carries on that tradition. You'll find that the book you've always loved now includes a new argument paper, a stepped-out approach to writing and revising thesis statements, new coverage of synthesizing sources, expanded attention to writing assignments across the disciplines, and many more practical innovations. As a classroom teacher, I know how much a trusted and reliable handbook can help students make the most of their writing experiences in college and beyond. And now as the coauthor of the seventh edition, I am eager to share this book with you, knowing that you'll find everything you and your students love and trust about *A Writer's Reference*.

Nancy Sommers

Features of the seventh edition

What's new

TARGETED CONTENT FOR TODAY'S STUDENTS: ACADEMIC WRITING AND RESEARCH

- *Synthesis.* Many of today's college writing assignments require that students synthesize—analyze sources and work them into a conversation that helps develop an argument. New coverage of synthesis, with annotated examples in MLA and APA styles, helps students work with sources to meet the demands of academic writing. (See MLA-3c and APA-3c.)

- *A new sample argument paper* shows students how to state and support an argumentative thesis, address counterarguments, integrate visuals, and document sources. (See pp. 87–91.)

- *A new annotated advertisement* illustrates how one student analyzes key elements of a visual to begin building an interpretation. (See p. 70.)

- *A new case study* follows one student's research and writing process, providing an illustrated model for strategizing about a research assignment, using search tools and techniques, evaluating search results and sources, taking notes, thinking critically about how best to use sources in a paper, and integrating a source responsibly. This self-contained section (MLA-5b) directs students to more detailed information throughout the book. (See pp. 432–35.)

- *New advice for distinguishing scholarly and popular sources.* (See pp. 350–51.)

- *Integrating evidence in analytical papers.* New coverage in section A1-d, "Using interpretation in an analysis," shows—at the sentence level—how to introduce, include, and interpret a passage in an analytical paper. (See p. 74.)

- *More help with writing assignments in other disciplines and in various genres.* For students who work with evidence in disciplines other than English, we have included annotated assignments and excerpts from model papers in psychology, business, biology, and nursing. (See pp. 105-08.)

- *New documentation models, many annotated.* Eighty-six new models across the three styles (MLA, APA, CMS [*Chicago*]) include sources students are using today—podcasts, online videos, blogs, and DVD features. Detailed annotations for many models help students see at a glance how to gather information about their sources and format their citations. (See p. 419 for an example.)

- *New chart on avoiding plagiarism.* (See pp. 364–65.)

CONCRETE STRATEGIES FOR REVISING

- *New coverage of portfolio keeping.* For students who are asked to maintain and submit a writing portfolio, a new section, C3-e, "Prepare a portfolio; reflect on your writing," covers types of portfolios, offers tips for writing a reflective cover document, and provides a sample reflective essay. (See pp. 28-31.)

- *Revising with comments.* Based on research with sixty-five students at colleges and universities across the country, this new feature helps students understand common instructor comments such as "unclear thesis," "develop more," or "cite your source" and gives students revision strategies they can apply to their own work. (See pp. 23–27.)

- *Specific strategies for revising thesis statements.* We know that college writers often need help reworking thesis statements, in whatever discipline they are writing. A new stepped-out approach helps students identify a problem in a draft thesis, ask relevant questions, and use their own responses to revise. (See pp. 16–18.)

NEW EXAMPLES, RELEVANT GRAMMAR COVERAGE

- *Academic examples that reflect the types of sentences students are expected to write in college.* A new type of hand-edited example ("Writing with sources") shows typical errors students make — and how they can correct them — when they integrate sources in MLA, APA, and CMS (*Chicago*) papers. (See p. 270 for an example.)

- *More ESL coverage.* Part M, Multilingual Writers and ESL Challenges, offers more accessible advice and more support for multilingual writers across the disciplines.

- *Basic grammar content that is more straightforward than ever.* Tabbed section B, Basic Grammar, the handbook's reference within a reference, now teaches with everyday example sentences.

NAVIGATION HELP THAT MAKES SENSE TO STUDENTS

- *Making the most of your handbook.* These new boxes, running throughout the book, help students pull together the advice they need to complete writing assignments in any class. The boxes teach students to use their handbook as a reference by prompting them to consult related advice and examples from different parts of the book as they write and revise. (See p. 347 for an example.)

- *Plain-language navigation for quick and easy reference.* In the upper right-hand corner of every page, terms like *main idea, flow,* and *presenting the other side* will help students see at a glance the exact page they need.

A NEW COLLECTION OF RESOURCES THAT HELPS INSTRUCTORS MAKE THE MOST OF THEIR HANDBOOK

- *Teaching with Hacker Handbooks*, by Marcy Carbajal Van Horn, offers practical advice on common topics such as designing a composition course, crafting writing assignments, and teaching multilingual writers. Ten lesson plans, each including strategies and materials that are ready to use or customize, support common course goals, like teaching argument, teaching paragraphs, and teaching with peer review. The collection also includes a wealth of handouts, syllabi, and other resources for integrating a Hacker handbook into your course. Available in print and online (hackerhandbooks.com/teaching).

What's the same

The features that have made *A Writer's Reference* work so well for so many students and instructors are still here.

Color-coded main menu and tabbed dividers. The main menu directs students to yellow, blue, and green tabbed dividers; the color coding makes it easy for students to identify and flip to the section they need. The documentation sections are further color-coded: orange for MLA, dark green for APA, and purple for CMS (*Chicago*).

User-friendly index. Even students who are unsure of grammar terminology will find help fast by consulting the user-friendly index. When facing a choice between *I* and *me*, for example, students may not know to look for "Case" or "Pronoun case." They are more likely to look up "*I*" or "*me*," so the index includes entries for "*I* vs. *me*" and "*me* vs. *I*." Similar entries appear throughout the index.

Citation at a glance. Annotated visuals show students where to find the publication information they need to cite common types of sources in MLA, APA, and CMS (*Chicago*) styles. (See p. 416 for an example.)

Quick-access charts and an uncluttered design. The seventh edition has what instructors and students have come to expect of a Hacker handbook: a clear and navigable presentation of information, with charts that summarize key content.

What's on the companion Web site?
hackerhandbooks.com/writersref

See page xxi for a list of resources available on the handbook's companion Web site.

Grammar, writing, and research exercises with feedback for every item. More than 1,800 items offer students plenty of extra practice, and our new scorecard gives instructors flexibility in viewing students' results.

Annotated model papers in MLA, APA, CMS (*Chicago*), and CSE styles. Student writers can see formatting conventions and effective writing in traditional college essays and in other common genres: annotated bibliographies, literature reviews, lab reports, business proposals, and clinical documents.

Research and Documentation Online. Written by a college librarian, this award-winning resource gives students a jump start with research in thirty academic disciplines. In addition to coverage of MLA, APA, and CMS (*Chicago*) styles of documentation, the site includes complete documentation advice for writing in the sciences (CSE style).

Resources for writers and tutors. Checklists, hints, tips, and helpsheets are available in downloadable format.

Resources for multilingual writers and ESL. Writers will find advice and strategies for understanding college expectations and completing writing assignments. Also included are charts, exercises, activities, and an annotated student essay in draft and final form.

Language Debates. Twenty-two brief essays provide opportunities for critical thinking about grammar and usage issues.

Access to premium content. New copies of the print handbook can be packaged with a free activation code for premium content: the e-book, a series of online video tutorials, and a collection of games, activities, readings, guides, and more.

Supplements for instructors

PRACTICAL

Teaching with Hacker Handbooks (in print and online at hackerhandbooks.com/teaching)

A Writer's Reference instructor resources (on the companion Web site at hackerhandbooks.com/writersref)

PROFESSIONAL

Teaching Composition: Background Readings

The Bedford Guide for Writing Tutors, Fifth Edition

The Bedford Bibliography for Teachers of Writing, Sixth Edition

Supplements for students

PRINT

Exercises for A Writer's Reference

Developmental Exercises for A Writer's Reference

Working with Sources: Exercises for A Writer's Reference

Research and Documentation in the Electronic Age

Resources for Multilingual Writers and ESL

Writing in the Disciplines: Advice and Models

Writing about Literature

Strategies for Online Learners

ONLINE

A Writer's Reference e-Book

CompClass for A Writer's Reference

Acknowledgments

I am grateful for the expertise, enthusiasm, and classroom wisdom that so many individuals brought to the seventh edition.

Reviewers

For their participation in a focus group on *A Writer's Reference* at the 2010 Conference on College Composition and Communication, I would like to thank Jennifer Cellio, Northern Kentucky University; Robert Cummings, University of Mississippi; Karen Gardiner, University of Alabama; Letizia Guglielmo, Kennesaw State College; Liz Kleinfeld, Metropolitan State College of Denver; and Melinda Knight, Montclair State University.

I thank those professors whose meticulous feedback helped shape *Strategies for Online Learners*: Jill Dahlman, University of Hawaii; Dana Del George, Santa Monica College; Larry Giddings, Pikes Peak Community College; David Hennessy, Broward College; Neil Plakcy, Broward College; and Rolando Regino, Riverside Community College.

I am indebted to the members of our Librarian Advisory Board: Barbara Fister, Gustavus Adolphus College; Susan Gilroy, Harvard University; John Kupersmith, University of California, Berkeley; and Monica Wong, El Paso Community College.

For their invaluable input, I would like to thank an insightful group of reviewers who answered detailed questionnaires about the sixth edition: Susan Achziger, Community College of Aurora; Michelle Adkerson, Nashville State Community College; Chanon Adsanatham, Community College of Aurora; Martha Ambrose, Edison Community College; Kimberley Aslett, Lake Superior State University; Laurel Barlow, Weber State University; Cynthia Bates, University of California, Davis; Fiona C. Brantley, Kennesaw State University; Max Brzezinski, Wake Forest University; Ken A. Bugajski, University of Saint Francis; Jeff Calkins, Tacoma Community College; Erin E. Campbell, Abraham Baldwin Agricultural College; Elizabeth Canfield, Virginia Commonwealth University; Eric Cash, Abraham Baldwin College; Michael Chamberlain, Azusa Pacific University; Deborah Chedister, SUNY Orange County Community College; Rong Chen, SUNY at Stony Brook; Michele J. Cheung, University of Southern Maine; Denise-Marie Coulter, Atlantic Cape Community College; Meriah Crawford, Virginia Commonwealth University; Tony Cruz, SUNY Orange County Community College; Janet Dean, Bryant College; Jeffrey L. Decker, University of California, Los Angeles; Sarah Doetschman, University of Alaska, Fairbanks; Elizabeth Evans, Wake Forest University; Martin Fertig, Montgomery County Community College; Christina D. French, Diablo Valley College; Marilyn Gilbert, The Art Institute of Seattle; William Gorski, West Los Angeles College; Ann H. Gray, Scott Community College; Jeanette Gregory, Cloud County Community College; Wendy Harrison, Abraham Baldwin Agricultural College; Catherine Hutcheson, Troy University; Melissa Jenkins, Wake Forest University; Elizabeth C. Jones, Wor-Wic Community College; Kristen Katzin-Nystrom, SUNY Orange County Community College; Lolann A. King, Trinity Valley Community College; Jamison Klagmann, University of Alaska, Fairbanks; Cheryl Laz, University of Southern Maine; Mark Leidner, Abraham Baldwin Agricultural College; Lindsay Lewan, Arapahoe Community College; Keming Liu, Medgar Evers College; Jeanette Lonia, Delaware Technical & Community College; Stefanie Low, Brooklyn College; Angie Macri, Pulaski Technical College; Edward W. Maine, California State University, Fullerton; Diane McDonald, Montgomery County Community College; Vickie Melograno, Atlantic Cape Community College; Priya Menon, Troy University; Gayla Mills, Randolph-Macon College; Frank Nigro, Shasta College; Diana Palmer, Montgomery County Community College; Peter J. Pellegrin, Cloud County Community College; Brenton Phillips, Cloud County Community College; J. Andrew Prall, University of Saint Francis; Mary Jean Preston, Carthage College; Molly Pulda, Brooklyn College; Tiffany A. Rayl, Montgomery County Community College; Jessica Richard, Wake Forest University; S. Randall Rightmire, University of California, Santa Barbara; Charles Riley, Baruch College/CUNY;

Rekha Rosha, Wake Forest University; Mitchell Rowat, University of Western Ontario; Kirsti Sandy, Keene State College; Robert M. Sanford, University of Southern Maine; Su Senapati, Abraham Baldwin Agricultural College; Shant Shahoian, Glendale Community College; Michele Singletary, Nashville State Community College; Michel Small, Shasta College; Matt Smith, University of Saint Francis; Marcia A. Sol, Cloud Community College; Stephen E. Sullivan, University of Saint Francis; Judith K. Taylor, Northern Kentucky University; Matt Theado, Gardner-Webb University; Jennifer Thomas, Azusa Pacific University; Matthew A. Thomas, Azusa Pacific University; Katherine E. Tirabassi, Keene State College; Cliff Toliver, Missouri Southern State University; Elaine Torda, SUNY Orange County Community College; Monica Trent, Montgomery College, Rockville; Ellen Vance, Art Institute of Seattle; Travis Wagner, University of Southern Maine; Karen Woods Weierman, Worcester State College; and Kelli Wood, El Paso Community College. We would also like to thank our anonymous reviewers from Brooklyn College, the University of Colorado at Denver, Glendale Community College, Ithaca College, Northern Kentucky University, Pulaski Technical College, and Wake Forest University.

Contributors

I am grateful to the following individuals, fellow teachers of writing, for their smart revisions of two key supplements: Joe Bizup, Boston University, updated *Writing about Literature* with fresh selections and relevant advice; and Jon Cullick, Northern Kentucky University, and Terry Myers Zawacki, George Mason University, tackled *Writing in the Disciplines*, expanding the advice to cover nine disciplines with the addition of music, engineering, and criminology. I am enormously grateful to Marcy Carbajal Van Horn, ESL specialist, experienced composition instructor, and former online writing lab director, who lent her expertise on several projects: She served as lead author for two brand-new resources, *Teaching with Hacker Handbooks* and *Strategies for Online Learners*, and she improved our coverage for multilingual writers both in the handbook and on the companion Web site.

Student contributors

A number of bright and willing students helped identify which instructor comments provide the best guidance for revision. From Green River Community College: Kyle Baskin, Josué Cardona, Emily Dore, Anthony Hines, Stephanie Humphries, Joshua Kin, Jessica Llapitan, James Mitchell, Derek Pegram, Charlie Piehler, Lindsay

Allison Rae Richards, Kristen Saladis, Jacob Simpson, Christina Starkey, Ariana Stone, and Joseph Vreeburg. From Northern Kentucky University: Sarah Freidhoff, Marisa Hempel, Sarah Laughlin, Sean Moran, Laren Reis, and Carissa Spencer. From Palm Beach Community College: Alexis Day, Shawn Gibbons, Zachary Jennison, Jean Lacz, Neshia Neal, Sarah Reich, Jude Rene, and Sam Smith. And from the University of Maine at Farmington: Nicole Carr, Hannah Courtright, Timothy Doyle, Janelle Gallant, Amy Hobson, Shawn Menard, Jada Molton, Jordan Nicholas, Nicole Phillips, Tessa Rockwood, Emily Rose, Nicholas Tranten, and Ashley Wyman. I also thank the students who have let us use and adapt their papers as models in the handbook and on its companion Web site: Ned Bishop, Lucy Bonilla, Jamal Hammond, Sam Jacobs, Albert Lee, Luisa Mirano, Anna Orlov, Emilia Sanchez, and Matt Watson.

Bedford/St. Martin's

A handbook is truly a collaborative writing project, and it is a pleasure to acknowledge and thank the enormously talented Bedford/ St. Martin's editorial team, whose deep commitment to students informs each new feature of *A Writer's Reference.* Joan Feinberg, Bedford's president and Diana Hacker's first editor, offers her superb judgment on every aspect of the book. Joan's graceful and generous leadership, both within Bedford and in the national composition community, is a never-ending source of inspiration for those who work closely with her. Michelle Clark, executive editor; Mara Weible, lead development editor; and Barbara Flanagan, senior editor, are treasured friends and colleagues, the kind of editors every author dreams of having. Michelle, an endless source of creativity and joy, combines wisdom with patience, imagination with practicality, and hard work with good cheer. Mara's brilliant, close, and careful attention to each detail of the handbook comes from her teacher's sensibility and editor's unerring eye. And Barbara, who has worked on Diana Hacker's handbooks for more than twenty-five years, brings to the seventh edition her unrelenting insistence on both clarity and precision as well as her editorial patience and perseverance. Thanks to Alicia Young, associate editor, for expertly managing the review process, preparing documents, and editing several ancillaries. Thanks also to Kylie Paul, editorial assistant and newest member of the handbook team, for managing many small details related to both our Web and print projects.

The passionate commitment to *A Writer's Reference* of many Bedford colleagues — Denise Wydra, editorial director; Karen Henry, editor in chief; Marjorie Adler, marketing manager; and John Swanson, senior executive marketing manager—ensures that the seventh edition remains the most innovative and practical handbook on the market. Special thanks go to Jimmy Fleming, senior English specialist, for his abundant contributions, always wise and judicious, and for his enthusiasm and support as we traveled to colleges near and far. Many thanks to Rosemary Jaffe, senior production editor, who kept us on schedule and efficiently and gracefully turned a manuscript into a handbook. And thanks to Linda McLatchie, copyeditor, for her thoroughness and attention to detail; to Claire Seng-Niemoeller, text designer, who always has clarity and ease of use in mind as she designs *A Writer's Reference*; to Donna Dennison, art director, who has given the book a strikingly beautiful cover; and to Sarah Ferguson, new media editor, who developed the book's companion Web site and e-book.

Most important, I want to thank Diana Hacker. To create the best writing help for her students at Prince George's Community College, she studied their practices and puzzled out their challenges. What she learned inspired her to create the best reference for all students of academic writing. I'm honored to acknowledge her work, her legacy, and her innovative spirit—and pleased to continue in the tradition of this brilliant teacher and writer.

And last, but never least, I offer thanks to Maxine Rodburg, Laura Saltz, and Kerry Walk, friends and colleagues, for sustaining conversations about teaching writing; to Joshua Alper, an attentive reader of life and literature, for his steadfastness across the drafts; to Sam and Kate for lively conversations about writing; and to Rachel and Alexandra, whose good-natured and humorous observations about their real lives as college writers are a constant source of instruction and inspiration.

Nancy Sommers

Writing is a process of figuring out what you think, not a matter of recording already developed thoughts. Since it's not possible to think about everything all at once, most experienced writers handle a piece of writing in stages. You will generally move from planning to drafting to revising, but be prepared to return to earlier stages as your ideas develop.

C1 Planning

C1-a Assess the writing situation.

Begin by taking a look at your writing situation. Consider your subject, your purpose, your audience, available sources of information, and any assignment requirements such as length, document design, and deadlines (see the checklist on p. 6). It is likely that you will make final decisions about all of these matters later in the writing process—after a first draft, for example—but you can save yourself time by thinking about as many of them as possible in advance.

In many writing situations, part of your challenge will be determining your purpose, or your reason, for writing. The wording of an assignment may suggest its purpose. If no guidelines are given, you may need to ask yourself, "Why am I communicating with my readers?" or "What do I want to accomplish?" College writers most often write for the following purposes:

to inform	to analyze
to explain	to synthesize
to summarize	to propose
to recommend	to call readers to action
to evaluate	to change attitudes
to persuade	to express feelings

Audience analysis can often help you determine how to accomplish your purpose—how much detail or explanation to provide, what kind of tone and language to use, and what potential objections to address. You may need to consider multiple audiences. The audience for a business report, for example, might include readers who want details and those who prefer a quick overview. For a service learning course, the audience for a proposal might include both your instructor and the supervisor at the organization at which you volunteered. The checklist on page 6 includes questions that will help you analyze your audience and develop an effective strategy for reaching your readers.

Academic English   What counts as good writing varies from culture to culture and even among groups within cultures. In some situations, you will need to become familiar with the writing styles—such as direct or indirect, personal or impersonal, plain or embellished—that are valued by the culture or discipline for which you are writing.

C1-b Experiment with ways to explore your subject.

Instead of just plunging into a first draft, experiment with one or more techniques for exploring your subject: talking and listening, reading and annotating texts, listing, clustering, freewriting, asking questions, keeping a journal, blogging. Whatever technique you turn to, the goal is the same: to generate ideas that will lead you to a question, a problem, or a topic that you want to explore. At this early stage of the writing process, don't censor yourself. Sometimes an idea that initially seems trivial or far-fetched will turn out to be worthwhile.

Talking and listening

Because writing is a process of figuring out what you think about a subject, it can be useful to try out your ideas on other people. Conversation can deepen and refine your ideas before you even begin to set them down on paper. By talking and listening to others, you can also discover what they find interesting, what they are curious about, and where they disagree with you. If you are planning to advance an argument, you can try it out on listeners with other points of view.

Many writers begin a writing project by brainstorming ideas in a group, debating a point with friends, or chatting with an instructor. Others prefer to record themselves talking through their own thoughts. Some writers exchange ideas by sending e-mails or instant messages or by posting to discussion boards or blogs. You may be encouraged to share ideas with your classmates and instructor in an online workshop, where you can begin to refine your thoughts before starting a draft.

THE WRITING CENTER   hackerhandbooks.com/writersref
> Resources for writers and tutors > Tips from writing tutors:
Invention strategies

Understanding an assignment

Determining the purpose of the assignment

Usually the wording of an assignment will suggest its purpose. You might be expected to do one of the following in a college writing assignment:

- summarize information from books, lectures, or research (See A1-c.)
- analyze ideas and concepts (See A1-d.)
- take a position and defend it with evidence (See A2.)
- synthesize (combine ideas from) several sources and create an original argument (See MLA-3.)

Understanding how to answer an assignment's questions

Many assignments will ask you to answer a *how* or *why* question. Such questions cannot be answered using only facts; instead, you will need to take a position. For example, the question "*What* are the survival rates for leukemia patients?" can be answered by reporting facts. The question "*Why* are the survival rates for leukemia patients in one state lower than they are in a neighboring state?" must be answered with both facts and interpretation.

If a list of prompts appears in the assignment, be careful—instructors rarely expect you to answer all of the questions in order. Look instead for topics, themes, or ideas that will help you ask your own questions.

Recognizing implied questions

When you are asked to *discuss*, *analyze*, *argue*, or *consider*, your instructor will often expect you to answer a *how* or *why* question.

Discuss the effects of the No Child Left Behind Act on special education programs.	=	How has the No Child Left Behind Act affected special education programs?
Consider the recent rise of autism diagnoses.	=	Why are diagnoses of autism rising?

Recognizing disciplinary expectations

When you are asked to write in a specific discipline, pay attention to the expectations and features of the writing in that discipline. Look closely at the key terms and specialized vocabulary of the assignment and the kinds of evidence and citation style your instructor expects. (See A4.)

Checklist for assessing the writing situation

Subject

- Has the subject (or a range of possible subjects) been given to you, or are you free to choose your own?
- What interests you about your subject? What questions would you like to explore?
- Why is your subject worth writing about? How might readers benefit from reading about it?
- Do you need to narrow your subject to a more specific topic (because of length restrictions, for instance)?

Purpose and audience

- Why are you writing: To inform readers? To persuade them? To entertain them? To call them to action? Some combination of these?
- Who are your readers? How well informed are they about the subject? What do you want them to learn?
- How interested and attentive are they likely to be? Will they resist any of your ideas?
- What is your relationship to your readers: Student to instructor? Employee to supervisor? Citizen to citizen? Expert to novice?

Sources of information

- Where will your information come from: Reading? Personal experience? Research? Direct observation? Interviews? Questionnaires?
- What kinds of evidence will best serve your subject, purpose, and audience?
- What sort of documentation style is required: MLA? APA? CMS?

Length and document design

- Do you have any length specifications? If not, what length seems appropriate, given your subject, purpose, and audience?
- Does the assignment call for a particular kind of paper: A report? A proposal? An essay? An analysis of data? A reflection?
- Is a particular format required? If so, do you have guidelines to follow or examples to consult?
- How might visuals—charts, graphs, tables, images—help you convey information?

Reviewers and deadlines

- Who will be reviewing your draft in progress: Your instructor? A writing center tutor? Your classmates?
- What are your deadlines? How much time will you need for each stage, including proofreading and printing the final draft?

Reading and annotating texts

Reading is an important way to deepen your understanding of a topic and expand your perspective. Annotating a text, written or visual, encourages you to read actively—to highlight key concepts, to note possible contradictions in an argument, or to raise questions for further research and investigation. Here, for example, is a paragraph from an essay on medical ethics as one student annotated it:

> **Making the most of your handbook**
>
> Read critically and take notes before you write.
> ▶ Guidelines for active reading: **page 68**
> ▶ Taking notes: R3-c
> ▶ Analyzing texts: A1-d

What break-throughs? Do all breakthroughs have the same consequences?

Stem cell research

Is everyone really uneasy? Is something a breakthrough if it creates a predicament?

Breakthroughs in genetics present us with a promise and a predicament. The promise is that we may soon be able to treat and prevent a host of debilitating diseases. The predicament is that our newfound genetic knowledge may also enable us to manipulate our own nature—to enhance our muscles, memories, and moods; to choose the sex, height, and other genetic traits of our children; to make ourselves "better than well." When science moves faster than moral understanding, as it does today, men and women struggle to articulate their unease. In liberal societies they reach first for the language of autonomy, fairness, and individual rights. But this part of our moral vocabulary is ill equipped to address the hardest questions posed by genetic engineering. The genomic revolution has induced a kind of moral vertigo.
— Michael Sandel, "The Case against Perfection"

Sandel's key dilemma

What does he mean by "moral understanding"?

Which questions? He doesn't seem to be taking sides.

Listing

Listing ideas—a technique sometimes known as *brainstorming*—is a good way to figure out what you know and what questions you have.

Here is a list one student jotted down for an essay about community service requirements for college students:

- Volunteered in high school.
- Teaching adults to read motivated me to study education.
- "The best way to find yourself is to lose yourself in the service of others."   —Gandhi

- Volunteering helps students find interests and career paths.
- Volunteering as requirement? Contradiction?
- Many students need to work to pay college tuition.
- Enough time to study, work, and volunteer?
- Can't students volunteer for their own reasons?
- What schools have community service requirements?
- What do students say about community service requirements?

Listing questions and ideas helped the writer narrow her subject and identify her position. In other words, she treated her early list as a record of her thoughts and a springboard to new ideas, not as an outline.

Clustering

Unlike listing, clustering highlights relationships among ideas. To cluster ideas, write your subject in the center of a sheet of paper, draw a circle around it, and surround the circle with related ideas connected to it with lines. If some of the satellite ideas lead to more specific clusters, write them down as well. The writer of the following cluster diagram was exploring ideas for an essay on obesity in children.

CLUSTER DIAGRAM

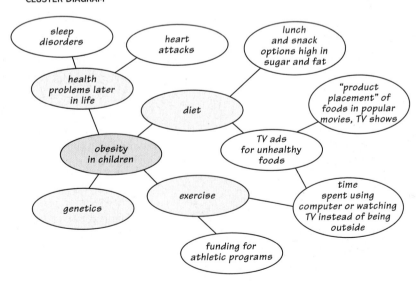

Freewriting

In its purest form, freewriting is simply nonstop writing. You set aside ten minutes or so and write whatever comes to mind, without pausing to think about word choice, spelling, or even meaning. If you get stuck, you can write about being stuck, but you should keep your fingers moving. If nothing much happens, you have lost only ten minutes. It's more likely, though, that something interesting will emerge—perhaps an eloquent sentence, a genuine expression of curiosity, or an idea worth further investigation.

To explore ideas on a particular topic, consider using a technique called *focused freewriting*. Again, you write quickly and freely, but this time you focus on a subject and pay attention to the connections among your ideas.

Asking questions

When gathering material for a story, journalists routinely ask themselves Who? What? When? Where? Why? and How? In addition to helping journalists get started, these questions ensure that they will not overlook an important fact.

Whenever you are writing about events, whether current or historical, asking the journalist's questions is one way to get started. One student, whose topic was the negative reaction in 1915 to D. W. Griffith's silent film *The Birth of a Nation*, began exploring her topic with this set of questions:

Who objected to the film?

What were the objections?

When were the protests first voiced?

Where were protests most strongly expressed?

Why did protesters object to the film?

How did protesters make their views known?

In the academic world, scholars often generate ideas by posing questions related to a specific discipline: one set of questions for analyzing short stories, another for evaluating experiments in social psychology, still another for reporting field experiences in criminal justice.

If you are writing in a particular discipline, you might begin your writing process by finding out which questions scholars in that discipline typically explore.

> **Making the most of your handbook**
>
> Effective college writers begin by asking questions.
>
> ▶ Asking questions in academic disciplines: A4-b

Keeping a journal

A journal is a collection of informal, exploratory, sometimes experimental writing. In a journal, often meant for your eyes only, you can take risks. You might freewrite, pose questions, comment on an interesting idea from one of your classes, or keep a list of questions that occur to you while reading and researching. You might imagine a conversation between yourself and your readers or stage a debate to understand opposing positions. A journal can also serve as a sourcebook of ideas to draw on in future essays.

Blogging

Although a blog (Weblog) is a type of journal, it is a public writing space rather than a private one. In a blog, you might express opinions, make observations, recap events, have fun with language, or interpret an image. Since most blogs have a commenting feature, you can create a conversation by inviting readers to give you feedback—ask questions, pose counterarguments, or suggest other readings on a topic.

C1-c Draft a working thesis.

As you explore your topic and identify questions to investigate, you will begin to see possible ways to focus your material. At this point, try to settle on a tentative central idea. The more complex your topic, the more your focus will change as your drafts evolve. For many types of writing, you will be able to assert your central idea in a sentence or two. Such a statement, which ordinarily appears in the opening paragraph of your finished essay, is called a *thesis statement* (see also C2-a).

A thesis is often one or more of the following:

- the answer to a question you have posed
- the solution for a problem you have identified
- a statement that takes a position on a debatable topic

A tentative or working thesis will help you organize your draft. Don't worry about the exact wording because your main point may change as you refine and focus your ideas. Here, for example, are one student's efforts to pose a question and draft a thesis statement for an essay in his film course.

QUESTION

In *Rebel without a Cause,* how does the filmmaker show that the main character becomes alienated from his family and friends?

Testing a working thesis

Once you have come up with a working thesis, you can use the following questions to evaluate it.

- Does your thesis answer a question, propose a solution to a problem, or take a position in a debate?
- Does the thesis require an essay's worth of development? Or will you run out of points too quickly?
- Is the thesis too obvious? If you cannot come up with interpretations that oppose your own, consider revising your thesis.
- Can you support your thesis with the evidence available?
- Can you explain why readers will want to read an essay with this thesis? Can you respond when a reader asks "So what?"

WORKING THESIS

In *Rebel without a Cause*, Jim Stark, the main character, is often seen literally on the edge of physical danger, suggesting that he is becoming more and more agitated by family and society.

The working thesis will need to be revised as the student thinks through and revises his paper, but it provides a useful place to start writing.

Here another student identifies a problem to focus an argument paper.

PROBLEM

Americans who earn average incomes cannot run effective national political campaigns.

WORKING THESIS

Congress should pass legislation that would make it possible for Americans who are not wealthy to be viable candidates in national political campaigns.

The student has roughed out language for how to solve the problem—enacting federal legislation. As she learns more about her topic, she will be able to refine her thesis and suggest a more specific solution, such as federal restriction of campaign spending.

Keep in mind as you draft your working thesis that an effective thesis is a promise to a reader; it points both the writer and the reader in a definite direction. For a more detailed discussion of thesis, see C2-a.

C1-d Sketch a plan.

Once you have drafted a working thesis, listing and organizing your supporting ideas is a good next step. Creating outlines, whether formal or informal, can help you make sure your writing is credible and logical.

When to use an informal outline

You might want to sketch an informal outline to see how you will support your thesis and to figure out a tentative structure for your ideas. Informal outlines can take many forms. Perhaps the most common is simply the thesis followed by a list of major ideas.

> Working thesis: Television advertising should be regulated to help prevent childhood obesity.
>
> - Children watch more television than ever.
> - Snacks marketed to children are often unhealthy and fattening.
> - Childhood obesity can cause sleeping disorders and other health problems.
> - Addressing these health problems costs taxpayers billions of dollars.
> - Therefore, these ads are actually costing the public money.
> - But if advertising is free speech, do we have the right to regulate it?
> - We regulate alcohol and cigarette ads on television, so why not advertisements for soda and junk food?

If you began by jotting down a list of ideas (see pp. 7–8), you can turn that list into a rough outline by crossing out some ideas, adding others, and putting the ideas in a logical order.

When to use a formal outline

Early in the writing process, rough outlines have certain advantages: They can be produced quickly, they are obviously tentative, and they can be revised easily. However, a formal outline may be useful later in the writing process, after you have written a rough draft, especially if your topic is complex. It can help you see whether the parts of your essay work together and whether your essay's structure is logical.

The following formal outline brought order to the research paper that appears in MLA-5c, on Internet surveillance in the workplace. The student's thesis is an important part of the outline. Everything else in the outline supports it, directly or indirectly.

FORMAL OUTLINE

Thesis: Although companies often have legitimate concerns that lead them to monitor employees' Internet usage—from expensive security breaches to reduced productivity—the benefits of electronic surveillance are outweighed by its costs to employees' privacy and autonomy.

I.   Although employers have always monitored employees, electronic surveillance is more efficient.

    A. Employers can gather data in large quantities.

    B. Electronic surveillance can be continuous.

    C. Electronic surveillance can be conducted secretly, with keystroke logging programs.

II. Some experts argue that employers have legitimate reasons to monitor employees' Internet usage.

    A. Unmonitored employees could accidentally breach security.

    B. Companies are legally accountable for the online actions of employees.

III. Despite valid concerns, employers should value employee morale and autonomy and avoid creating an atmosphere of distrust.

    A. Setting the boundaries for employee autonomy is difficult in the wired workplace.

        1. Using the Internet is the most popular way of wasting time at work.

        2. Employers can't tell easily if employees are working or surfing the Web.

    B. Surveillance can create resentment among employees.

        1. Web surfing can relieve stress, and restricting it can generate tension between managers and workers.

        2. Enforcing Internet usage can seem arbitrary.

IV. Surveillance may not increase employee productivity, and trust may benefit productivity.

    A. A company shouldn't care how many hours salaried employees work as long as they get the job done.

    B. Casual Internet use can actually benefit companies.

        1. The Internet may spark business ideas.

        2. The Internet may suggest ideas about how to operate more efficiently.

V.   Employees' rights to privacy are not well defined by the law.

    A. Few federal guidelines on electronic surveillance exist.

    B. Employers and employees are negotiating the boundaries without legal guidance.

    C. As technological capabilities increase, the need to define boundaries will also increase.

Guidelines for constructing an outline

1. Put the thesis at the top.
2. Make items at the same level parallel grammatically (see S1).
3. Use sentences unless phrases are clear.
4. Use the conventional system of numbers, letters, and indents:

   I.
     A.
     B.
        1.
        2.
           a.
           b.
   II.
     A.
     B.
        1.
        2.
           a.
           b.

5. Always include at least two items at each level.
6. Limit the number of major sections in the outline; if the list of roman numerals (at the first level) gets too long, try clustering the items into fewer major categories with more subcategories.

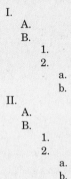

C2 Drafting

Generally, the introduction to a piece of writing announces the main point; the body develops it, usually in several paragraphs; the conclusion drives it home. You can begin drafting, however, at any point. If you find it difficult to introduce a paper that you have not yet written, try drafting the body first and saving the introduction for later.

C2-a For most types of writing, draft an introduction that includes a thesis.

Drafting an introduction

Your introduction will usually be a paragraph of 50 to 150 words (in a longer paper, it may be more than one paragraph). Perhaps the most common strategy is to open the paragraph with a few sentences that

THE WRITING CENTER hackerhandbooks.com/writersref
> Resources for writers and tutors > Tips from writing tutors: Writing
introductions and conclusions

engage the reader and establish your purpose for writing and then state your main point. The statement of your main point is called the *thesis*. (See also C1-c.)

In the following introductions, the thesis is highlighted.

> Credit card companies love to extend credit to college students, especially those just out of high school. Ads for credit cards line campus bulletin boards, flash across commercial Web sites for students, and get stuffed into shopping bags at college bookstores. Why do the companies market their product so vigorously to a population that lacks a substantial credit history and often has no steady source of income? The answer is that significant profits can be earned through high interest rates and assorted penalties and fees. By granting college students liberal lending arrangements, credit card companies often hook them on a cycle of spending that can ultimately lead to financial ruin.   — Matt Watson, student

> As the United States industrialized in the nineteenth century, using immigrant labor, social concerns took a backseat to the task of building a prosperous nation. The government did not regulate industries and did not provide an effective safety net for the poor or for those who became sick or injured on the job. Immigrants and the poor did have a few advocates, however. Settlement houses such as Hull-House in Chicago provided information, services, and a place for reform-minded individuals to gather and work to improve the conditions of the urban poor. Alice Hamilton was one of these reformers. Hamilton's efforts helped to improve the lives of immigrants and drew attention and respect to the problems and people that until then had been ignored.   — Laurie McDonough, student

Ideally, the introductory sentences leading to the thesis should hook the reader, perhaps with one of the following:

- a startling statistic or an unusual fact
- a vivid example
- a description or an image
- a paradoxical statement
- a quotation or a bit of dialogue
- a question
- an analogy
- an anecdote

Whether you are writing for a scholarly audience, a professional audience, or a general audience, you cannot assume your readers' interest in the topic. The hook should spark curiosity and offer readers a reason to continue.

Although the thesis frequently appears at the end of the introduction, it can also appear at the beginning. Much work-related writing, for example, requires a straightforward approach and commonly begins with the thesis.

> Flextime scheduling, which has proved effective at the Library of Congress, should be introduced on a trial basis at the main branch of the Montgomery County Public Library. By offering flexible work hours, the library can boost employee morale, cut down on absenteeism, and expand its hours of operation.   —David Warren, student

For some types of writing, it may be difficult or impossible to express the central idea in a thesis statement; or it may be unwise or unnecessary to include a thesis statement in the essay. A personal narrative, for example, may have a focus that is too subtle to be distilled in a single statement. Strictly informative writing, like that found in many business memos, may be difficult to summarize in a thesis. In such instances, do not try to force the central idea into a thesis sentence. Instead, think in terms of an overriding purpose, which may or may not be stated directly.

Making the most of your handbook

The thesis statement is central to many types of writing.

▶ Writing about texts: A1

▶ Constructing reasonable arguments: A2

▶ Writing research papers: MLA-1, APA-1, CMS-1

Academic English   If you come from a culture that prefers an indirect approach in writing, you may feel that asserting a thesis early in an essay sounds unrefined or even rude. In the United States, however, readers appreciate a direct approach; when you state your point as directly as possible, you show that you understand your topic and value your readers' time.

Writing effective thesis statements

An effective thesis statement is a central idea that requires supporting evidence; its scope is appropriate for the required length of the essay; and it is sharply focused. It should answer a question you have posed, resolve a problem you have identified, or take a position in a debate.

When constructing a thesis statement, ask yourself whether you can successfully develop it with the sources available to you and for the purposes you've identified. Also ask if you can explain why readers should be interested in reading an essay that explores this thesis.

A thesis must require proof or further development through facts and details; it cannot itself be a fact or a description.

| DRAFT THESIS | The first polygraph was developed by Dr. John A. Larson in 1921. |

PROBLEM The thesis is *too factual.* A reader could not disagree with it or debate it; no further development of this idea is required.

STRATEGY *Enter a debate* by posing a question about your topic that has more than one possible answer. For example: Should the polygraph be used by private employers? Your thesis should be your answer to the question.

| REVISED THESIS | Because the polygraph has not been proved reliable, even under controlled conditions, its use by employers should be banned. |

A thesis should be an answer to a question, not a question itself.

| DRAFT THESIS | Would John F. Kennedy have continued to escalate the war in Vietnam if he had lived? |

PROBLEM The thesis is a *question*, not an answer to a question.

STRATEGY *Take a position* on your topic by answering the question you have posed. Your thesis should be your answer to the question.

| REVISED THESIS | Although John F. Kennedy sent the first American troops to Vietnam before he died, an analysis of his foreign policy suggests that he would not have escalated the war had he lived. |

A thesis should be of sufficient scope for your assignment; it should not be too broad.

| DRAFT THESIS | Mapping the human genome has many implications for health and science. |

PROBLEM The thesis is *too broad.* Even in a very long research paper, you would not be able to discuss all the implications of mapping the human genome.

STRATEGY *Consider subtopics of your original topic.* Once you have chosen a subtopic, take a position in an ongoing debate and pose a question that has more than one answer. For example: Should people be tested for genetic diseases? Your thesis should be your answer to the question.

| REVISED THESIS | Although scientists can now detect genetic predisposition for specific diseases, policymakers should establish guidelines about whom to test and under what circumstances. |

A thesis also should not be too narrow.

DRAFT THESIS A person who carries a genetic mutation linked to a particular disease might or might not develop that disease.

PROBLEM The thesis is *too narrow.* It does not suggest any argument or debate about the topic.

STRATEGY *Identify challenging questions* that readers might have about your topic. Then pose a question that has more than one answer. For example: Do the risks of genetic testing outweigh its usefulness? Your thesis should be your answer to this question.

REVISED THESIS Though positive results in a genetic test do not guarantee that the disease will develop, such results can cause psychological trauma; genetic testing should therefore be avoided in most cases.

A thesis should be sharply focused, not too vague. Avoid fuzzy, hard-to-define words such as *interesting, good,* or *disgusting.*

DRAFT THESIS The Vietnam Veterans Memorial is an interesting structure.

PROBLEM This thesis is *too fuzzy and unfocused.* It's difficult to define *interesting*, and the sentence doesn't give the reader any cues about where the essay is going.

STRATEGY *Focus your thesis with concrete language and a clear plan.* Pose a question about the topic that has more than one answer. For example: How does the physical structure of the Vietnam Veterans Memorial shape the experience of visitors? Your thesis—your answer to the question—should use specific language that engages readers to follow your argument.

REVISED THESIS By inviting visitors to see their own reflections in the wall, the Vietnam Veterans Memorial creates a link between the present and the past.

C2-b Draft the body.

The body of your essay develops support for your thesis, so it's important to have at least a working thesis before you start writing. What does your thesis promise readers? Try to keep your response to that question in mind as you draft the body.

You may already have written an introduction that includes your working thesis. If not, as long as you have a draft thesis, you can begin developing the body and return later to the introduction. If your thesis suggests a plan or if you have sketched a preliminary outline, try to block out your paragraphs accordingly. Draft the body of your essay by writing at least a paragraph about each supporting point you listed in the planning stage. If you do not have a plan, pause for a few moments and sketch one (see C1-d).

Keep in mind that often you might not know what you want to say until you have written a draft. It is possible to begin without a plan — assuming you are prepared to treat your first attempt as a "discovery draft" that will be radically rewritten once you discover what you really want to say. Whether or not you have a plan when you begin drafting, you can often figure out a workable order for your ideas by stopping each time you start a new paragraph, to think about what your readers will need to know to follow your train of thought.

For more detailed advice about paragraphs in the body of an essay, see C4. For specific help with drafting paragraphs, see C4-b.

TIP: As you draft, keep careful notes and records of any sources you read and consult. (See R3.) If you quote, paraphrase, or summarize a source, include a citation, even in your draft. You will save time and avoid plagiarism if you follow the rules of citation and documentation while drafting.

C2-c Draft a conclusion.

A conclusion should remind readers of the essay's main idea without repeating it. Often the concluding paragraph can be relatively short. By the end of the essay, readers should already understand your main point; your conclusion drives it home and, perhaps, gives readers something larger to consider.

In addition to echoing your main idea, a conclusion might

- briefly summarize your essay's key points
- propose a course of action
- offer a recommendation
- discuss the topic's wider significance or implications
- pose a question for future study

To conclude an essay analyzing the shifting roles of women in the military services, one student discusses her topic's implications for society as a whole:

As the military continues to train women in jobs formerly reserved for men, our understanding of women's roles in society will no doubt continue to change. As news reports of women training for and taking part in combat operations become commonplace, reports of women becoming CEOs, police chiefs, and even president of the United States will cease to surprise us. Or perhaps we have already reached this point.   —Rosa Broderick, student

To make the conclusion memorable, you might include a detail, an example, or an image from the introduction to bring readers full circle; a quotation or a bit of dialogue; an anecdote; or a witty or ironic comment.

Whatever concluding strategy you choose, keep in mind that an effective conclusion is decisive and unapologetic. Avoid introducing wholly new ideas at the end of an essay. And because the conclusion is so closely tied to the rest of the essay in both content and tone, be prepared to rework it (or even replace it) as you revise your draft.

C3 Revising

Revising is rarely a one-step process. Global matters—focus, purpose, organization, content, and overall strategy—generally receive attention first. Improvements in sentence structure, word choice, grammar, punctuation, and mechanics come later.

C3-a Make global revisions.

Many of us resist global revisions because we find it difficult to view our work from our audience's perspective. To distance yourself from a draft, put it aside for a while, preferably overnight or even longer. When you return to it, try to play the role of your audience as you read. If possible, enlist friends or family to be the audience for your draft. Or visit your school's writing center to go over your draft with a writing tutor. Ask your reviewers to focus on the larger issues of

> **Making the most of your handbook**
>
> Seeking and using feedback are critical steps in revising a college paper.
> ▶ Guidelines for peer reviewers: **page 22**
> ▶ Revising with comments: **C3-c**

writing, such as purpose and organization, not on word- or sentence-level issues. The checklist for global revision on the next page may help you and your reviewers get started.

PRACTICE AND MODELS hackerhandbooks.com/writersref
  > Composing and revising > C3–1 and C3–2
  > Revising > Sample global revision
    > Sample sentence-level revision

Checklist for global revision

Purpose and audience

- Does the draft address a question, a problem, or an issue that readers care about?
- Is the draft appropriate for its audience? Does it account for the audience's knowledge of and possible attitudes toward the subject?

Focus

- Is the thesis clear? Is it prominently placed?
- If there is no thesis, is there a good reason for omitting one?
- Are any ideas obviously off the point?

Organization and paragraphing

- Are there enough organizational cues for readers (such as topic sentences or headings)?
- Are ideas presented in a logical order?
- Are any paragraphs too long or too short for easy reading?

Content

- Is the supporting material relevant and persuasive?
- Which ideas need further development?
- Are the parts proportioned sensibly? Do major ideas receive enough attention?
- Where might material be deleted?

Point of view

- Is the dominant point of view—first person (*I* or *we*), second person (*you*), or third person (*he, she, it, one,* or *they*)—appropriate for your purpose and audience? (See S4-a.)

C3-b Revise and edit sentences.

Much of this book offers advice on revising sentences for clarity and on editing them for grammar, punctuation, and mechanics. Some writers handle sentence-level revisions directly at the computer, experimenting with a variety of possible improvements. Other writers prefer to print out a hard copy of the draft and mark it up before making changes in the file. Here is a rough-draft paragraph as one student edited it on-screen for a variety of sentence-level problems.

Although some cities have found creative ways to improve access to public transportation for passengers with physical disabilities, ~~and to fund other programs, there have been problems in~~ our city has struggled with ~~due to the need to address~~ budget constraints and competing ~~needs~~ priorities. ~~This~~ The budget crunch has led citizens to question how funds are distributed.~~?~~ For example, last year ~~when~~ city officials voted to use available funds to support ~~had to choose between allocating funds for accessible transportation or allocating funds to~~ after-school programs rather than transportation upgrades. ~~, they voted for the after-school programs.~~ It is not clear to some citizens why ~~these~~ after-school programs are more important.

The original paragraph was flawed by wordiness, a problem that can be addressed through any number of revisions. The following revision would also be acceptable:

> Some cities have funded improved access to public transportation for passengers with physical disabilities. Because of budget constraints, our city chose to fund after-school programs rather than transportation programs. As a result, citizens have begun to question how funds are distributed and why certain programs are more important than others.

Some of the paragraph's improvements do not involve choice and must be fixed in any revision. The hyphen in *after-school programs* is necessary; a noun must be substituted for the pronoun *these* in the last sentence; and the question mark in the second sentence must be changed to a period.

C3-c Revising with comments

To revise is to "re-see," and the comments you receive from your instructors, peers, and writing center tutors will help you re-see your draft from your readers' point of view. Sometimes these comments are written as shorthand commands—"Be specific!"—and sometimes as questions—"What is your main point?" Such comments don't immediately show you *how* to revise, but they do identify places where global and sentence-level revisions can improve your draft.

When instructors, peers, and writing tutors comment on your work, you won't be able to incorporate everyone's advice. Sort through the comments you receive with your purpose and audience in mind.

You may also want to keep a revision and editing log, a list of the global and sentence-level concerns that come up repeatedly in your reviewers' comments. When you apply lessons from one assignment to another, comments can help you become a more effective writer.

Remember not to take criticism personally. Your readers are responding to your essay, not to you. It may be frustrating to hear that you still have more work to do, but taking feedback seriously—and revising accordingly—will make your essay stronger. This section addresses common types of comments an instructor or peer might make in response to your writing.

THE COMMENT: **Unclear thesis**

SIMILAR COMMENTS: **Vague thesis · State your position · What is your main point?**

UNDERSTANDING THE COMMENT When readers point out that your thesis is unclear, the comment often signals that they have a hard time identifying your essay's main point.

> the mother or other relatives.
> drives to dance lessons,
> eball team, hosts birthday
> omework help. Do more   **Unclear thesis**
> r hinder the development of

STRATEGIES FOR REVISING

- *Ask questions.*   What is the thesis, position, or main point of the draft? Can you support it with the available evidence? (See C1-c, A2-c, and A2-d.)

- *Reread your entire draft.*   Because ideas develop as you write, you may find that your conclusion contains a clearer statement of your main point than does your working thesis. Or you may find your thesis elsewhere in your draft. (See C-2a.)

- *Try framing your thesis* as an answer to a question you pose, the resolution of a problem you identify, or a position you take in a debate. And put your thesis to the "So what?" test: Why would a reader be interested in this thesis? (See C1-c and p. 11.)

THE COMMENT: **Narrow your introduction**

SIMILAR COMMENTS: **Unfocused intro · Too broad**

UNDERSTANDING THE COMMENT   When readers point out that your introduction needs to be "narrowed," the comment often signals that the beginning sentences of your essay are not specific or focused.

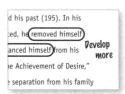

even believe that rituals
actions influence the outcome
fans go beyond cheering, and
ssment, and chanted slurs
rts.

Narrow your introduction

STRATEGIES FOR REVISING

- *Reread your introduction and ask questions.* Are the sentences leading to your thesis specific enough to engage readers and communicate your purpose? Do these sentences lead logically to your thesis? Do they spark your readers' curiosity and offer them a reason to continue reading? (See C-2a.)

- *Try engaging readers with a "hook"* in your introduction—a question, quotation, paradoxical statement, vivid example, or an image. (See p. 15.)

THE COMMENT: **Develop more**

SIMILAR COMMENTS: **Undeveloped · Give examples · Explain**

UNDERSTANDING THE COMMENT   When readers suggest that you "develop more," the comment often signals that you stopped short of providing a full and detailed discussion of your idea.

d his past (195). In his
ed, he removed himself
anced himself from his
e Achievement of Desire,"
e separation from his family

Develop more

STRATEGIES FOR REVISING

- *Read your paragraph to a peer or a tutor* and ask specific questions. What's missing? Do readers need more background information or examples to understand your point? Do they need more evidence to be convinced? Is it clear what point you're making with your details? (See A2-d.)

- *Keep your purpose in mind.* Your assignment probably asks you to do more than summarize sources or list examples and evidence. Make sure you discuss the examples and illustrations you provide and analyze your evidence. (See A2-e.)

- *Think about why your main point matters to your readers.* Take another look at your points and support and answer the question "So what?" (See p. 11.)

THE COMMENT: **Be specific**

SIMILAR COMMENTS: **Need examples • Evidence?**

UNDERSTANDING THE COMMENT When readers say that you need to "be specific," the comment often signals that you could strengthen your writing with additional details.

> cultural differences between the
> Italy. Italian citizens do not share
> **Be specific**
> attitudes or values as American
> rences make it hard for some
> feel comfortable coming to the

STRATEGIES FOR REVISING

- *Reread your topic sentence* to understand the focus of the paragraph. (See C4-a.)
- *Ask questions.* Does the paragraph contain claims that need support? Have you provided evidence—specific examples, vivid details and illustrations, statistics and facts—to help readers understand your ideas and find them persuasive? (See A2-e.)
- *Interpret your evidence.* Remember that details and examples don't speak for themselves. You'll need to show readers how evidence supports your claims. (See A1-d and A2-e.)

THE COMMENT: **Consider opposing viewpoints**

SIMILAR COMMENTS: **What about the other side?** • **Counterargument?**

UNDERSTANDING THE COMMENT When readers suggest that you "consider opposing viewpoints," the comment often signals that you need to recognize and respond to possible objections to your argument.

> stile work environment
> chers Shepard and Clifton
> es using drug-testing **Consider**
> ave lower productivity **opposing**
> **viewpoints**
> ve not adopted such

STRATEGIES FOR REVISING

- *Read more* to learn about the debates surrounding the topic. (See p. 7.)
- *Ask questions:* Are there other sides to the issue? Would a reasonable person offer an alternative explanation for the evidence or provide counterevidence? (See p. 85.)
- *Be open-minded.* Although it might seem illogical to introduce opposing arguments, you'll show your knowledge of the topic by

recognizing that not everyone draws the same conclusion. (See A2-f, A2-g, and p. 376.)

- *Introduce and counter objections* with phrases like these: "Some readers might point out that . . ." or "Critics of this view argue that. . . . " (See p. 85.)

- *Revise your thesis*, if necessary, to account for other points of view.

THE COMMENT: **Summarize less, analyze more**

SIMILAR COMMENTS: **Too much summary · Show, don't tell · Go deeper**

UNDERSTANDING THE COMMENT   When readers point out that you need to include more analysis and less summary, the comment often signals that they are looking for your interpretation of the text.

> ...ages she speaks with
>
> For example, she speaks **Summarize** ...ano Texas Spanish with her **less,** ...s English at school (327). **analyze more** ...r experience with speaking

STRATEGIES FOR REVISING

- *Reread your paragraph and highlight the sentences that summarize.* Then, in a different color, highlight the sentences that contain your analysis. (Summary describes what the text says; analysis offers a judgment or interpretation of the text.) (See A1-c and A1-d.)

- *Reread the text* (or passages of the text) that you are analyzing. Pay attention to how the language and structure of the text contribute to its meaning. (See A1-a.)

- *Ask questions.* What strategies does the author use and how do those strategies help convey the author's message? What insights about the text can you share with your readers? How can you deepen your reader's understanding of the author's main points? (See A3 and A1-d.)

THE COMMENT: **More than one point in this paragraph**

SIMILAR COMMENTS: **Unfocused · Lacks unity · Hard to follow**

UNDERSTANDING THE COMMENT   When readers tell you that you have "more than one point in this paragraph," the comment often signals that not all sentences in your paragraph support the topic sentence.

> ...he believes the social
>
> ...omic benefits. Many **More than** ...Most important, casino **one point** ...reas of the state that **in this** ...ecent years. **paragraph**

STRATEGIES FOR REVISING

- *Reread your paragraph and ask questions.* What is the main point of the paragraph? Is there a topic sentence that signals to readers what to expect in the rest of the paragraph? Have you included sentences that perhaps belong elsewhere in your draft? (See C4-a.)

- *Revisit your topic sentence.* It should serve as an important sign-post for readers. Make sure the wording of your topic sentence is precise and that you have enough evidence to support it in the paragraph. (See C4-b.)

THE COMMENT: **Your words?**

SIMILAR COMMENTS: **Source?** · **Who's talking here?**

UNDERSTANDING THE COMMENT   When readers ask "Your words?" the comment often signals that it is unclear whether you are using only your own words or are mixing in some words of your sources.

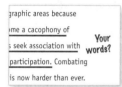

STRATEGIES FOR REVISING

- *Check that you have clearly marked the boundaries* between your source material and your own words. Have you borrowed words from sources without properly acknowledging them? (See MLA-2, APA-2, and CMS-2.)

- *Use a signal phrase* to introduce each source and provide context. Doing so prepares readers for a source's words. (See MLA-3b, APA-3b, and CMS-3b.)

- *Use quotation marks* to enclose language that you borrow word-for-word from a source and follow each quotation with a parenthetical citation. (See MLA-2b, APA-2b, and CMS-2b.)

- *Put summaries and paraphrases in your own words* and always cite your sources. (See MLA-2c, APA-2c, and CMS-2c.)

As you revise your paper, you might request feedback or clarification from instructors or peers by e-mail. Because e-mail communication can be quick and convenient, it's natural to think of it as informal, but be sure to keep your audience in mind. You should usually use a formal greeting for an instructor (*Dear Professor Brink*) instead of a casual one (*Hey!*) and use standard formatting and language (avoiding emoticons, abbreviations like *LOL,* and unconventional capitalization). You can often be more flexible with peers, but use a more formal style at the beginning of the semester, until you get to know them. And make sure you have a clear purpose in mind: Are you trying to share an observation? Asking for another perspective on your topic? Requesting feedback on a particular paragraph? For more on using e-mail in business and academic contexts, see C5-f.

C3-d Proofread the final manuscript.

After revising and editing, you are ready to prepare the final manuscript. (See C5-e for guidelines.) Make sure to allow yourself enough time for proofreading—the final and most important step in manuscript preparation.

Proofreading is a special kind of reading: a slow and methodical search for misspellings, typographical mistakes, and omitted words or word endings. Such errors can be difficult to spot in your own work because you may read what you intended to write, not what is actually on the page. To fight this tendency, try proofreading out loud, articulating each word as it is actually written. You might also try proofreading your sentences in reverse order, a strategy that takes your attention away from the meanings you intended and forces you to focus on one word at a time.

Although proofreading may be slow, it is crucial. Errors strewn throughout an essay are distracting and annoying. If the writer doesn't care about this piece of writing, the reader might wonder, why should I? A carefully proofread essay, however, sends a positive message that you value your writing and respect your readers.

C3-e Prepare a portfolio; reflect on your writing.

At the end of the semester, your instructor may ask you to submit a portfolio, or collection, of your writing. A writing portfolio often consists of drafts, revisions, and reflections that demonstrate a writer's thinking and learning processes or showcase the writer's best work. Your instructor may give you the choice of submitting a paper portfolio or an e-portfolio.

Reflection—the process of stepping back periodically to examine your decisions, preferences, strengths, and challenges as a writer—is the backbone of portfolio keeping. Your instructor may ask you to submit a reflective document in which you introduce or comment on the pieces in your portfolio and discuss your development as a writer throughout the course. This reflection may take the form of an essay, a cover letter, or some other kind of statement—often, but not always, placed as an introductory piece. You might try one or more of the following strategies:

- Discuss, in depth, your best entry. Explain why it is your best and how it represents what you learned in the course.

- Describe in detail the revisions you've made to one key piece and the improvements and changes you want readers to notice. Include specific passages from the piece.

- Demonstrate what this portfolio illustrates about you as a writer, student, researcher, or critical thinker.

- Reflect on what you've learned about writing and reading throughout the course.

- Reflect on how you plan to use the skills and experiences from your writing course in other courses where writing will be assigned.

SAMPLE REFLECTIVE LETTER FOR A PORTFOLIO

December 11, 2010
Professor Todd Andersen
Humanities Department
Johnson State College

Dear Professor Andersen,

   This semester has been more challenging than I had anticipated. I have always been a good writer, but I discovered this semester that I had to stretch myself in ways that weren't always comfortable. I learned that if I wanted to reach my readers, I needed to understand that not everyone sees the world the way I do. I needed to work with my peers and write multiple drafts to understand that a first draft is just a place to start. I have chosen three pieces of writing for my portfolio: "Negi and the Other Girl: Nicknames and Identity," "School Choice Is a Bad Choice," and "Flat-footed Advertising." Each shows my growth as a writer in different ways, and the final piece was my favorite assignment of the semester.

   The peer review sessions that our class held in October helped me with my analytical response paper. My group and I chose to write about

Reflective writing can take various forms. Bonilla wrote her reflection as a letter.

Reflective writing often calls for first person ("I").

Bonilla lists the pieces included in her portfolio by title.

"Jíbara," by Esmeralda Santiago, for the Identity unit. My first and second drafts were unfocused. I spent my first draft basically retelling the events of the essay. I think I got stuck doing that because the details of Santiago's essay are so interesting—the biting termites, the burning metal, and the *jíbara* songs on the radio—and because I didn't understand the differences between summary and analysis. My real progress came when I decided to focus the essay on one image—the mirror hanging in Santiago's small house, a mirror that was hung too high for her to look into. Finding a focus helped me move from listing the events of the essay to interpreting those events. I thought my peers would love my first draft, but they found it confusing. Some of their comments were hard to take, but their feedback (and all the peer feedback I received this semester) helped me see my words through a reader's eyes.

Bonilla comments on a specific area of growth.

While my Identity paper shows my struggle with focus, my next paper shows my struggle with argument. For my argument essay, I wrote about charter schools. My position is that the existence of charter schools weakens the quality of public schools. In my first draft, my lines of argument were not in the best order. When I revised, I ended the paper with my most powerful argument: Because they refuse to adopt open enrollment policies and are unwilling to admit students with severe learning or behavior problems, charter schools are elitist. While revising, I also introduced a counterargument in my final draft because our class discussion showed me that many of my peers disagree with me. To persuade them, I needed to address their arguments in favor of charter schools. My essay is stronger because I acknowledged that both the proponents and opponents of abandoning charters want improved education for America's children. It took me a while to understand that including counterarguments would actually make my argument more convincing, especially to readers who don't already agree with me. Understanding the importance of counterargument helped me with other writing I did in this course, and it will help me in the writing I do for my major, political science.

Even in the reflective document, Bonilla includes elements of good college writing, such as using transitions.

Bonilla reflects on how skills from her writing course will carry over to other courses.

Another stretch for me this semester was seeing visuals as texts that are worth more than a five-second response. The final assignment was my favorite because it involved a number of surprises. I wasn't so much surprised by the idea that ads make arguments because I understand that they are designed to persuade. What was surprising was being able to see all the elements of a visual and write about how they work together to convey a clear message. For my essay "Flat-footed Advertising," I chose the EAS Performance Nutrition ad "The New Theory of Evolution for Women." In my summary of the ad, I noted that the woman who follows the EAS program for twelve weeks and "evolves" is compared to modern humans and our evolution from apes as shown in the classic 1966 *March of Progress* illustration (Howell 41). It was these familiar poses of "Nicolle," the woman in the image, that drew me to study this ad. In my first draft, I made all of the obvious points, looking only literally at the comparison and almost congratulating the company on such a clever use of a classic scientific drawing. Your comments on my draft were a little unsettling because you asked me "So what?"—why would my ideas matter to a reader? You pushed me to consider the ad's assumptions and to question the meaning of the word *evolve*. In my revised essay, I argue that even though Nicolle is portrayed as powerful, satisfied, and "fully evolved," the ad campaign rests on the assumption that performance is best measured by physical milestones. In the end, an ad that is meant to pay homage to woman's strength is in fact demeaning. My essay evolved from draft to draft because I allowed my thinking to change and develop as I revised. I've never revised as much as I did with this final assignment. I cared about this paper and wanted to show my readers why my argument mattered.

Bonilla mentions how comments on her draft helped her revise.

The expectations for college writing are different from those for high school writing. I believe that my portfolio pieces show that I finished this course as a stronger writer. I have learned to take risks in my writing and to use the feedback from you and my peers, and now I know how to acknowledge the points of view of my audience to be more persuasive. I'm glad to have had the chance to write a reflection at the end of the course. I hope you enjoy reading this portfolio and seeing the evolution of my work this semester.

In her conclusion, Bonilla summarizes her growth in the course.

Sincerely,

Lucy Bonilla

Lucy Bonilla

C4 Writing paragraphs

Except for special-purpose paragraphs, such as introductions and conclusions (see C2-a and C2-c), paragraphs are clusters of information supporting an essay's main point (or advancing a story's action). Aim for paragraphs that are clearly focused, well developed, organized, coherent, and neither too long nor too short for easy reading.

C4-a Focus on a main point.

A paragraph should be unified around a main point. The main point should be clear to readers, and every sentence in the paragraph should relate to it.

Stating the main point in a topic sentence

As a rule, you should state the main point of a paragraph in a topic sentence — a one-sentence summary that tells readers what to expect as they read on. Usually the topic sentence (highlighted in the following example) comes first in the paragraph.

> All living creatures manage some form of communication. The dance patterns of bees in their hive help to point the way to distant flower fields or announce successful foraging. Male stickleback fish regularly swim upside-down to indicate outrage in a courtship contest. Male deer and lemurs mark territorial ownership by rubbing their own body secretions on boundary stones or trees. Everyone has seen a frightened dog put his tail between his legs and run in panic. We, too, use gestures, expressions, postures, and movement to give our words point.   — Olivia Vlahos, *Human Beginnings*

In college writing, topic sentences are often necessary for advancing or clarifying the lines of an argument or reporting the research in a field. In business writing, topic sentences (along with headings) are essential because readers often scan for information and summary statements. Sometimes the topic sentence is introduced by a transitional sentence linking the paragraph to earlier material, and occasionally the topic sentence is withheld until the end of the paragraph.

> **Making the most of your handbook**
>
> Topic sentences let your reader know how a body paragraph relates to your essay's thesis.
>
> ▶ Effective thesis statements: **page 16**

Sticking to the point

Sentences that do not support the topic sentence destroy the unity of a paragraph. If the paragraph is otherwise focused, such sentences can simply be deleted or perhaps moved elsewhere. In the following paragraph describing the inadequate facilities in a high school, the information about the chemistry instructor (highlighted) is clearly off the point.

> As the result of tax cuts, the educational facilities of Lincoln High School have reached an all-time low. Some of the books date back to 1990 and have long since shed their covers. The few computers in working order must share one printer. The lack of lab equipment makes it necessary for four or five students to work at one table, with most watching rather than performing experiments. Also, the chemistry instructor left to have a baby at the beginning of the semester, and most of the students don't like the substitute. As for the furniture, many of the upright chairs have become recliners, and the desk legs are so unbalanced that they play seesaw on the floor.

Sometimes the solution for a disunified paragraph is not as simple as deleting or moving material. Writers often wander into uncharted territory because they cannot think of enough evidence to support a topic sentence. Feeling that it is too soon to break into a new paragraph, they move on to new ideas for which they have not prepared the reader. When this happens, the writer is faced with a choice: Either find more evidence to support the topic sentence or adjust the topic sentence to mesh with the evidence that is available.

C4-b Develop the main point.

Though an occasional short paragraph is fine, particularly if it functions as a transition or emphasizes a point, a series of brief paragraphs suggests inadequate development. How much development is enough? That varies, depending on the writer's purpose and audience.

For example, when health columnist Jane Brody wrote a paragraph attempting to convince readers that it is impossible to lose fat quickly, she knew that she would have to present a great deal of evidence because many dieters want to believe the opposite. She did *not* write only the following:

> When you think about it, it's impossible to lose — as many diets suggest — 10 pounds of *fat* in ten days, even on a total fast. Even a moderately active person cannot lose so much weight so fast. A less active person hasn't a prayer.

This three-sentence paragraph is too skimpy to be convincing. But the paragraph that Brody did write contains enough evidence to convince even skeptical readers.

> When you think about it, it's impossible to lose — as many . . . diets suggest — 10 pounds of *fat* in ten days, even on a total fast. A pound of body fat represents 3,500 calories. To lose 1 pound of fat, you must expend 3,500 more calories than you consume. Let's say you weigh 170 pounds and, as a moderately active person, you burn 2,500 calories a day. If your diet contains only 1,500 calories, you'd have an energy deficit of 1,000 calories a day. In a week's time that would add up to a 7,000-calorie deficit, or 2 pounds of real fat. In ten days, the accumulated deficit would represent nearly 3 pounds of lost body fat. Even if you ate nothing at all for ten days and main-tained your usual level of activity, your caloric deficit would add up to 25,000 calories. . . . At 3,500 calories per pound of fat, that's still only 7 pounds of lost fat.
>
> —Jane Brody, *Jane Brody's Nutrition Book*

C4-c Choose a suitable pattern of organization.

Although paragraphs (and indeed whole essays) may be patterned in any number of ways, certain patterns of organization occur frequently, either alone or in combination:

- examples and illustrations (p. 34)
- narration (p. 35)
- description (p. 36)
- process (p. 36)
- comparison and contrast (p. 36)
- analogy (p. 37)
- cause and effect (p. 38)
- classification and division (p. 38)
- definition (p. 39)

These patterns (sometimes called *methods of development*) have different uses, depending on the writer's subject and purpose.

Examples and illustrations

Providing examples, perhaps the most common method of develop-ment, is appropriate whenever the reader might be tempted to ask, "For example?"

Normally my parents abided scrupulously by "The Budget," but several times a year Dad would dip into his battered black strongbox and splurge on some irrational, totally satisfying luxury. Once he bought over a hundred comic books at a flea market, doled out to us thereafter at the tantalizing rate of two a week. He always got a whole flat of pansies, Mom's favorite flower, for us to give her on Mother's Day. One day a boy stopped at our house selling fifty-cent raffle tickets on a sailboat, and Dad bought every ticket the boy had left—three books' worth.   —Connie Hailey, student

Illustrations are extended examples, frequently presented in story form. When well selected, they can be a vivid and effective means of developing a point.

Part of [Harriet Tubman's] strategy of conducting was, as in all battle-field operations, the knowledge of how and when to retreat. Numerous allusions have been made to her moves when she suspected that she was in danger. When she feared the party was closely pursued, she would take it for a time on a train southward bound. No one seeing Negroes going in this direction would for an instant suppose them to be fugitives. Once on her return she was at a railroad station. She saw some men reading a poster and she heard one of them reading it aloud. It was a description of her, offering a reward for her capture. She took a southbound train to avert suspicion. At another time when Harriet heard men talking about her, she pretended to read a book which she carried. One man remarked, "This can't be the woman. The one we want can't read or write." Harriet devoutly hoped the book was right side up.

—Earl Conrad, *Harriet Tubman*

Narration

A paragraph of narration tells a story or part of a story. The following paragraph recounts one of the author's experiences in the African wild.

One evening when I was wading in the shallows of the lake to pass a rocky outcrop, I suddenly stopped dead as I saw the sinuous black body of a snake in the water. It was all of six feet long, and from the slight hood and the dark stripes at the back of the neck I knew it to be a Storm's water cobra—a deadly reptile for the bite of which there was, at that time, no serum. As I stared at it an incoming wave gently deposited part of its body on one of my feet. I remained motionless, not even breathing, until the wave rolled back into the lake, drawing the snake with it. Then I leaped out of the water as fast as I could, my heart hammering.

—Jane Goodall, *In the Shadow of Man*

Description

A descriptive paragraph sketches a portrait of a person, place, or thing by using concrete and specific details that appeal to one or more of the senses—sight, sound, smell, taste, and touch. Consider, for example, the following description of the grasshopper invasions that devastated the midwestern landscape in the late 1860s.

> They came like dive bombers out of the west. They came by the millions with the rustle of their wings roaring overhead. They came in waves, like the rolls of the sea, descending with a terrifying speed, breaking now and again like a mighty surf. They came with the force of a williwaw and they formed a huge, ominous, dark brown cloud that eclipsed the sun. They dipped and touched earth, hitting objects and people like hailstones. But they were not hail. These were *live* demons. They popped, snapped, crackled, and roared. They were dark brown, an inch or longer in length, plump in the middle and tapered at the ends. They had transparent wings, slender legs, and two black eyes that flashed with a fierce intelligence.
>
> —Eugene Boe, "Pioneers to Eternity"

Process

A process paragraph is structured in chronological order. A writer may choose this pattern either to describe how something is made or done or to explain to readers, step by step, how to do something. The following paragraph explains how to perform a "roll cast," a popular fly-fishing technique.

> Begin by taking up a suitable stance, with one foot slightly in front of the other and the rod pointing down the line. Then begin a smooth, steady draw, raising your rod hand to just above shoulder height and lifting the rod to the 10:30 or 11:00 position. This steady draw allows a loop of line to form between the rod top and the water. While the line is still moving, raise the rod slightly, then punch it rapidly forward and down. The rod is now flexed and under maximum compression, and the line follows its path, bellying out slightly behind you and coming off the water close to your feet. As you power the rod down through the 3:00 position, the belly of line will roll forward. Follow through smoothly so that the line unfolds and straightens above the water.
>
> —*The Dorling Kindersley Encyclopedia of Fishing*

Comparison and contrast

To compare two subjects is to draw attention to their similarities, although the word *compare* also has a broader meaning that includes a consideration of differences. To contrast is to focus only on differences.

Whether a paragraph stresses similarities or differences, it may
be patterned in one of two ways. The two subjects may be presented
one at a time, as in the following paragraph of contrast.

> So Grant and Lee were in complete contrast, representing two
> diametrically opposed elements in American life. Grant was the
> modern man emerging; beyond him, ready to come on the stage, was
> the great age of steel and machinery, of crowded cities and a rest-
> less, burgeoning vitality. Lee might have ridden down from the old
> age of chivalry, lance in hand, silken banner fluttering over his head.
> Each man was the perfect champion of his cause, drawing both his
> strengths and his weaknesses from the people he led.
> — Bruce Catton, "Grant and Lee: A Study in Contrasts"

Or a paragraph may proceed point by point, treating the two subjects together, one aspect at a time. The following paragraph uses the
point-by-point method to contrast speeches given by Abraham Lincoln
in 1860 and Barack Obama in 2008.

> Two men, two speeches. The men, both lawyers, both from
> Illinois, were seeking the presidency, despite what seemed their
> crippling connection with extremists. Each was young by modern
> standards for a president. Abraham Lincoln had turned fifty-one
> just five days before delivering his speech. Barack Obama was
> forty-six when he gave his. Their political experience was mainly
> provincial, in the Illinois legislature for both of them, and they had
> received little exposure at the national level—two years in the
> House of Representatives for Lincoln, four years in the Senate for
> Obama. Yet each was seeking his party's nomination against a New
> York senator of longer standing and greater prior reputation—
> Lincoln against Senator William Seward, Obama against Senator
> Hillary Clinton. They were both known for having opposed an ini-
> tially popular war—Lincoln against President Polk's Mexican War,
> raised on the basis of a fictitious provocation; Obama against
> President Bush's Iraq War, launched on false claims that Saddam
> Hussein possessed WMDs [weapons of mass destruction] and had
> made an alliance with Osama bin Laden.
> — Garry Wills, "Two Speeches on Race"

Analogy

Analogies draw comparisons between items that appear to have little
in common. Writers can use analogies to make something abstract or
unfamiliar easier to grasp or to provoke fresh thoughts about a common subject. In the following paragraph, physician Lewis Thomas
draws an analogy between the behavior of ants and that of humans.

Ants are so much like human beings as to be an embarrassment. They farm fungi, raise aphids as livestock, launch armies into wars, use chemical sprays to alarm and confuse enemies, capture slaves. The families of weaver ants engage in child labor, holding their larvae like shuttles to spin out the thread that sews the leaves together for their fungus gardens. They exchange information ceaselessly. They do everything but watch television.

— Lewis Thomas, "On Societies as Organisms"

Cause and effect

A paragraph may move from cause to effects or from an effect to its causes. The topic sentence in the following paragraph mentions an effect; the rest of the paragraph lists several causes.

The fantastic water clarity of the Mount Gambier sinkholes results from several factors. The holes are fed from aquifers holding rainwater that fell decades — even centuries — ago, and that has been filtered through miles of limestone. The high level of calcium that limestone adds causes the silty detritus from dead plants and animals to cling together and settle quickly to the bottom. Abundant bottom vegetation in the shallow sinkholes also helps bind the silt. And the rapid turnover of water prohibits stagnation.

— Hillary Hauser, "Exploring a Sunken Realm in Australia"

Classification and division

Classification is the grouping of items into categories according to some consistent principle. The following paragraph classifies species of electric fish.

Scientists sort electric fishes into three categories. The first comprises the strongly electric species like the marine electric rays or the freshwater African electric catfish and South American electric eel. Known since the dawn of history, these deliver a punch strong enough to stun a human. In recent years, biologists have focused on a second category: weakly electric fish in the South American and African rivers that use tiny voltages for communication and navigation. The third group contains sharks, nonelectric rays, and catfish, which do not emit a field but possess sensors that enable them to detect the minute amounts of electricity that leak out of other organisms.

— Anne and Jack Rudloe, "Electric Warfare:
The Fish That Kill with Thunderbolts"

Division takes one item and divides it into parts. As with classification, division should be made according to some consistent principle.

The following paragraph describes the components that make up a baseball.

> Like the game itself, a baseball is composed of many layers. One of the delicious joys of childhood is to take apart a baseball and examine the wonders within. You begin by removing the red cotton thread and peeling off the leather cover—which comes from the hide of a Holstein cow and has been tanned, cut, printed, and punched with holes. Beneath the cover is a thin layer of cotton string, followed by several hundred yards of woolen yarn, which makes up the bulk of the ball. Finally, in the middle is a rubber ball, or "pill," which is a little smaller than a golf ball. Slice into the rubber and you'll find the ball's heart—a cork core. The cork is from Portugal, the rubber from southeast Asia, the covers are American, and the balls are assembled in Costa Rica.
>
> —Dan Gutman, *The Way Baseball Works*

Definition

A definition puts a word or concept into a general class and then provides enough details to distinguish it from other members in the same class. In the following paragraph, the writer defines *envy* as a special kind of desire.

> Envy is so integral and so painful a part of what animates behavior in market societies that many people have forgotten the full meaning of the word, simplifying it into one of the synonyms of desire. It is that, which may be why it flourishes in market societies: democracies of desire, they might be called, with money for ballots, stuffing permitted. But envy is more or less than desire. It begins with an almost frantic sense of emptiness inside oneself, as if the pump of one's heart were sucking on air. One has to be blind to perceive the emptiness, of course, but that's just what envy is, a selective blindness. *Invidia*, Latin for envy, translates as "non-sight," and Dante has the envious plodding along under cloaks of lead, their eyes sewn shut with leaden wire. What they are blind to is what they have, God-given and humanly nurtured, in themselves.
>
> —Nelson W. Aldrich Jr., *Old Money*

C4-d Make paragraphs coherent.

When sentences and paragraphs flow from one to another without discernible bumps, gaps, or shifts, they are said to be coherent. Coherence can be improved by strengthening the ties between old information and new. A number of techniques for strengthening those ties are detailed in this section.

Linking ideas clearly

Readers expect to learn a paragraph's main point in a topic sentence early in the paragraph. Then, as they move into the body of the paragraph, they expect to encounter specific details, facts, or examples that support the topic sentence—either directly or indirectly. In the following paragraph, all of the sentences following the topic sentence directly support it.

> A passenger list of the early years [of the Orient Express] would read like a *Who's Who of the World*, from art to politics. Sarah Bernhardt and her Italian counterpart Eleonora Duse used the train to thrill the stages of Europe. For musicians there were Toscanini and Mahler. Dancers Nijinsky and Pavlova were there, while lesser performers like Harry Houdini and the girls of the Ziegfeld Follies also rode the rails. Violinists were allowed to practice on the train, and occasionally one might see trapeze artists hanging like bats from the baggage racks.   —Barnaby Conrad III, "Train of Kings"

If a sentence does not support the topic sentence directly, readers expect it to support another sentence in the paragraph and therefore to support the topic sentence indirectly. The following paragraph begins with a topic sentence. The highlighted sentences are direct supports, and the rest of the sentences are indirect supports.

> Though the open-space classroom works for many children, it is not practical for my son, David. First, David is hyperactive. When he was placed in an open-space classroom, he became distracted and confused. He was tempted to watch the movement going on around him instead of concentrating on his own work. Second, David has a tendency to transpose letters and numbers, a tendency that can be overcome only by individual attention from the instructor. In the open classroom, he was moved from teacher to teacher, with each one responsible for a different subject. No single teacher worked with David long enough to diagnose the problem, let alone help him with it. Finally, David is not a highly motivated learner. In the open classroom, he was graded "at his own level," not by criteria for a certain grade. He could receive a B in reading and still be a grade level behind, because he was doing satisfactory work "at his own level."
> —Margaret Smith, student

Repeating key words

Repetition of key words is an important technique for gaining coherence. To prevent repetitions from becoming dull, you can use variations of the key word (*hike, hiker, hiking*), pronouns referring to the word (*gamblers . . . they*), and synonyms (*run, spring, race, dash*). In the following paragraph describing plots among indentured servants in the seventeenth century, historian Richard Hofstadter binds sentences together by repeating the key word *plots* and echoing it with a variety of synonyms (which are highlighted).

> Plots hatched by several servants to run away together occurred mostly in the plantation colonies, and the few recorded servant uprisings were entirely limited to those colonies. Virginia had been forced from its very earliest years to take stringent steps against mutinous plots, and severe punishments for such behavior were recorded. Most servant plots occurred in the seventeenth century: a contemplated uprising was nipped in the bud in York County in 1661; apparently led by some left-wing offshoots of the Great Rebellion, servants plotted an insurrection in Gloucester County in 1663, and four leaders were condemned and executed; some discontented servants apparently joined Bacon's Rebellion in the 1670's. In the 1680's the planters became newly apprehensive of discontent among the servants "owing to their great necessities and want of clothes," and it was feared they would rise up and plunder the storehouses and ships; in 1682 there were plant-cutting riots in which servants and laborers, as well as some planters, took part.
>
> —Richard Hofstadter, *America at 1750*

Using parallel structures

Parallel structures are frequently used within sentences to underscore the similarity of ideas (see S1). They may also be used to bind together a series of sentences expressing similar information. In the following passage describing folk beliefs, anthropologist Margaret Mead presents similar information in parallel grammatical form.

> Actually, almost every day, even in the most sophisticated home, something is likely to happen that evokes the memory of some old folk belief. The salt spills. A knife falls to the floor. Your nose tickles. Then perhaps, with a slightly embarrassed smile, the person who spilled the salt tosses a pinch over his left shoulder. Or someone recites the old rhyme, "Knife falls, gentleman calls." Or as you rub your nose you think, That means a letter. I wonder who's writing?
>
> —Margaret Mead, "New Superstitions for Old"

Maintaining consistency

Coherence suffers whenever a draft shifts confusingly from one point of view to another or from one verb tense to another. In addition, coherence can suffer when new information is introduced with the subject of each sentence. For advice on avoiding shifts, see S4.

Providing transitions

Transitions are bridges between what has been read and what is about to be read. Transitions help readers move from sentence to sentence; they also alert readers to more global connections of ideas—those between paragraphs or even larger blocks of text.

Academic English   Choose transitions carefully and vary them appropriately. Each transition has a different meaning; if you use a transition with an inappropriate meaning, you might confuse your reader.

▶ Although taking eight o'clock classes may seem

unappealing, coming to school early has its advan-
                  For example,
tages. ~~Moreover~~, students who arrive early typically

avoid the worst traffic and find the best parking spaces.

SENTENCE-LEVEL TRANSITIONS   Certain words and phrases signal connections between (or within) sentences. Frequently used transitions are included in the chart on page 43.

Skilled writers use transitional expressions with care, making sure, for example, not to use *consequently* when *also* would be more precise. They are also careful to select transitions with an appropriate tone, perhaps preferring *so* to *thus* in an informal piece, *in summary* to *in short* for a scholarly essay.

In the following paragraph, an excerpt from an argument that dinosaurs had the "'right-sized' brains for reptiles of their body size," biologist Stephen Jay Gould uses transitions (highlighted) to guide readers from one idea to the next.

I don't wish to deny that the flattened, minuscule head of large bodied Stegosaurus houses little brain from our subjective, top-heavy perspective, but I do wish to assert that we should not expect more of the beast. First of all, large animals have relatively smaller brains than related, small animals. The correlation of brain size with body size among kindred animals (all reptiles, all mammals, for example) is remarkably regular. As we move from small to large

Common transitions

TO SHOW ADDITION	and, also, besides, further, furthermore, in addition, moreover, next, too, first, second
TO GIVE EXAMPLES	for example, for instance, to illustrate, in fact, specifically
TO COMPARE	also, similarly, likewise
TO CONTRAST	but, however, on the other hand, in contrast, nevertheless, still, even though, on the contrary, yet, although
TO SUMMARIZE OR CONCLUDE	in other words, in short, in conclusion, to sum up, therefore
TO SHOW TIME	after, as, before, next, during, later, finally, meanwhile, since, then, when, while, immediately
TO SHOW PLACE OR DIRECTION	above, below, beyond, farther on, nearby, opposite, close, to the left
TO INDICATE LOGICAL RELATIONSHIP	if, so, therefore, consequently, thus, as a result, for this reason, because, since

animals, from mice to elephants or small lizards to Komodo dragons, brain size increases, but not so fast as body size. In other words, bodies grow faster than brains, and large animals have low ratios of brain weight to body weight. In fact, brains grow only about two-thirds as fast as bodies. Since we have no reason to believe that large animals are consistently stupider than their smaller relatives, we must conclude that large animals require relatively less brain to do as well as smaller animals. If we do not recognize this relationship, we are likely to underestimate the mental power of very large animals, dinosaurs in particular.

—Stephen Jay Gould, "Were Dinosaurs Dumb?"

PARAGRAPH-LEVEL TRANSITIONS Paragraph-level transitions usually link the *first* sentence of a new paragraph with the *first* sentence of the previous paragraph. In other words, the topic sentences signal global connections.

Look for opportunities to allude to the subject of a previous paragraph (as summed up in its topic sentence) in the topic sentence of the next one. In his essay "Little Green Lies," Jonathan H. Alder uses this strategy in the topic sentences of the following paragraphs, which appear in a passage describing the benefits of plastic packaging.

Consider aseptic packaging, the synthetic packaging for the "juice boxes" so many children bring to school with their lunch. One criticism of aseptic packaging is that it is nearly impossible to recycle, yet on almost every other count, aseptic packaging is environmentally preferable to the packaging alternatives. Not only do aseptic containers not require refrigeration to keep their contents from spoiling, but their manufacture requires less than one-10th the energy of making glass bottles.

What is true for juice boxes is also true for other forms of synthetic packaging. The use of polystyrene, which is commonly (and mistakenly) referred to as "Styrofoam," can reduce food waste dramatically due to its insulating properties. (Thanks to these properties, polystyrene cups are much preferred over paper for that morning cup of coffee.) Polystyrene also requires significantly fewer resources to produce than its paper counterpart.

TRANSITIONS BETWEEN BLOCKS OF TEXT   In long essays, you will need to alert readers to connections between blocks of text that are more than one paragraph long. You can do this by inserting transitional sentences or short paragraphs at key points in the essay. Here, for example, is a transitional paragraph from a student research paper. It announces that the first part of the paper has come to a close and the second part is about to begin.

Although the great apes have demonstrated significant language skills, one central question remains: Can they be taught to use that uniquely human language tool we call grammar, to learn the difference, for instance, between "ape bite human" and "human bite ape"? In other words, can an ape create a sentence?

C4-e If necessary, adjust paragraph length.

Most readers feel comfortable reading paragraphs that range between one hundred and two hundred words. Shorter paragraphs can require too much starting and stopping, and longer ones can strain the reader's attention span. There are exceptions to this guideline, however. Paragraphs longer than two hundred words frequently appear in scholarly writing, where writers explore complex ideas. Paragraphs shorter than one hundred words occur in business writing and on Web sites, where readers routinely skim for main ideas; in newspapers because of narrow columns; and in informal essays to quicken the pace.

In an essay, the first and last paragraphs will ordinarily be the introduction and the conclusion. These special-purpose paragraphs are likely to be shorter than those in the body of the essay. Typically, the body paragraphs will follow the essay's outline: one paragraph per point in short essays, several per point in longer ones. Some ideas require more development than others, however, so it is best to be flexible. If an idea stretches to a length unreasonable for a paragraph, you should divide the paragraph, even if you have presented comparable points in the essay in single paragraphs.

Paragraph breaks are not always made for strictly logical reasons. Writers use them for all of the following reasons.

REASONS FOR BEGINNING A NEW PARAGRAPH

- to mark off the introduction and the conclusion
- to signal a shift to a new idea
- to indicate an important shift in time or place
- to emphasize a point (by placing it at the beginning or the end, not in the middle, of a paragraph)
- to highlight a contrast
- to signal a change of speakers (in dialogue)
- to provide readers with a needed pause
- to break up text that looks too dense

Beware of using too many short, choppy paragraphs, however. Readers want to see how your ideas connect, and they become irritated when you break their momentum by forcing them to pause every few sentences. Here are some reasons you might have for combining some of the paragraphs in a rough draft.

REASONS FOR COMBINING PARAGRAPHS

- to clarify the essay's organization
- to connect closely related ideas
- to bind together text that looks too choppy

C5 Designing documents

The term *document* is broad enough to describe anything you might write in a college class, in the business world, or in everyday life. How you design a document (format it for the printed page or for a computer screen) will affect how readers respond to it.

Good document design promotes readability, but what *readability* means depends on your purpose and audience and perhaps on other elements of your writing situation, such as your subject and any length restrictions. All of your design choices—formatting options, headings, and lists—should be made with your writing situation in mind. Likewise, visuals—tables, charts, and images—can support your writing if they are used appropriately.

C5-a Determine layout and format to suit your purpose and audience.

Similar documents share common design features. Together, these features—layout, margins and line spacing, alignment, fonts, and font styles—can help guide readers through a document.

Layout

Most readers have set ideas about how different kinds of documents should look. Advertisements, for example, have a distinctive appearance, as do newsletters and brochures. Instructors have expectations about how a college paper should look (see C5-e). Employers, too, expect documents such as letters, résumés, memos, and e-mail messages to be presented in standard ways (see C5-f).

Unless you have a compelling reason to stray from convention, it's best to choose a document layout that conforms to your readers' expectations. If you're not sure what readers expect, look at examples of the kind of document you are producing.

Margins and line spacing

Margins help control the look of a page. For most academic and business documents, leave a margin of one to one and a half inches on all sides. These margins create a visual frame for the text and provide room for annotations, such as an instructor's comments or a peer's suggestions. Tight margins generally make a page crowded and difficult to read.

Most manuscripts in progress are double-spaced to allow room for editing. Final copy is often double-spaced as well, since single-spaced text is less inviting to read. If you are unsure about margin and spacing requirements for your document, check with your instructor or consult documents similar to the one you are writing. At times, the advantages of wide margins and double-spaced lines are offset by other considerations. For example, most business and technical documents are single-spaced, with double-spacing between paragraphs, to save paper and to promote quick scanning. Keep your purpose and audience in mind as you determine appropriate margins and line spacing for your document.

Planning a document: Design checklist for purpose and audience

- What is the purpose of your document? How can your document design help you achieve this purpose?
- Who are your readers? What are their expectations?
- What format is required? What format options—layout, margins, line spacing, and font styles—will readers expect?
- How can you use visuals—charts, graphs, tables, images—to help you convey information and achieve your purpose?

Fonts

If you have a choice, select a font that fits your writing situation in an easy-to-read size (usually 10–12 points). Although offbeat fonts may seem attractive, they slow readers down and can distract them from your ideas. For example, using Comic Sans, a font with a handwritten, childish feel, can make an essay seem too informal or unpolished, regardless of how well it's written. Fonts that are easy to read and appropriate for college and workplace documents include the following: Arial, Courier, Georgia, Times New Roman, and Verdana. Check with your instructor; he or she may expect or prefer a particular font.

Font styles

Font styles—such as **boldface,** *italics,* and underlining—can be useful for calling attention to parts of a document. On the whole, it is best to use restraint when selecting styles. Applying too many different styles within a document can result in busy-looking pages and can confuse readers.

TIP: Never write an academic document in all capital or all lower-case letters. Although some readers have become accustomed to instant messages and e-mails that omit capital letters entirely, their absence makes a piece of writing too informal and difficult to read.

C5-b Use headings when appropriate.

In short essays, you will have little need for headings, especially if you use paragraphing and clear topic sentences to guide readers. In more complex documents, however, such as longer essays, research papers, business reports, and Web sites, headings can be a useful visual cue for readers.

Headings help readers see at a glance the organization of a document. If more than one level of heading is used, the headings also indicate the hierarchy of ideas—as they do throughout this book.

Headings serve a number of functions for your readers, depending on the needs of different readers. When readers are looking for specific information and don't want to read the entire document, headings can guide them to the right place quickly. When readers are scanning, hoping to pick up a document's meaning or message, headings can provide an overview. Even when readers are committed enough to read every word, headings can help them preview a document before they begin reading or easily revisit a specific section after they've read through the document once.

> **Making the most of your handbook**
>
> Headings can help writers plan and readers understand a document.
>
> ▶ Papers organized with headings: pages 485 and 530

TIP: While headings can be useful, they cannot substitute for transitions between paragraphs (see p. 43).

Phrasing headings

Headings should be as brief and as informative as possible. Certain styles of headings—the most common being *-ing* phrases, noun phrases, questions, and imperative sentences—work better for some purposes, audiences, and subjects than for others.

Whatever style you choose, use it consistently. Headings on the same level of organization should be written in parallel structure (see S1), as in the following examples from a report, a history textbook, a financial brochure, and a nursing manual, respectively.

-*ING* PHRASES AS HEADINGS

Safeguarding Earth's atmosphere

Charting the path to sustainable energy

Conserving global forests

NOUN PHRASES AS HEADINGS

The civil rights movement

The antiwar movement

The feminist movement

QUESTIONS AS HEADINGS

How do I buy shares?

How do I redeem shares?

How has the fund performed in the past three years?

IMPERATIVE SENTENCES AS HEADINGS

Ask the patient to describe current symptoms.

Take a detailed medical history.

Record the patient's vital signs.

Placing and formatting headings

Headings on the same level of organization should be placed and formatted in a consistent way. If you have more than one level of heading, you might center your first-level headings and make them boldface; then you might make the second-level headings left-aligned and italicized, like this:

First-level heading
Second-level heading

A college paper with headings typically has only one level, and the headings are often centered, as in the sample paper on pages 488–96. In a report or a brochure, important headings can be highlighted by using white space above and below them. Less important headings can be downplayed by using less white space or by running them into the text.

C5-c Use lists to guide readers.

Lists are easy to read or scan when they are displayed, item by item, rather than run into your text. You might choose to display the following kinds of lists:

- steps in a process
- advice or recommendations
- items to be discussed
- criteria for evaluation (as in checklists)
- parts of an object

Lists are usually introduced with an independent clause followed by a colon (*All mammals share the following five characteristics:*).

Periods are not used after items in a list unless the items are complete sentences. Lists should be in parallel grammatical form (see S1).

Use bullets (circles or squares) or dashes to draw readers' eyes to a list and to emphasize individual items. If you are describing a sequence or a set of steps, number your list with arabic numerals (1, 2, 3) followed by periods.

Although lists can be useful visual cues, don't overdo them. Too many will clutter a document.

C5-d Add visuals to support your purpose.

Visuals can convey information concisely and powerfully. Charts, graphs, and tables, for example, can simplify complex numerical information. Images—including photographs and diagrams—often express an idea more vividly than words can. With access to the Internet, digital photography, and word processing or desktop publishing software, you can download or create your own visuals to enhance your document. Keep in mind that if you download a visual—or use published information to create your own visual—you must credit your source (see R3).

Choosing appropriate visuals

Use visuals to supplement your writing, not to substitute for it. Always consider how a visual supports your purpose and how your audience might respond to it. A student writing about online news used two screen shots to illustrate a point about hyperlinked text (see A2-h). Another student, writing about treatments for childhood obesity, created a table to display data she had found in two different sources and discussed in her paper (see APA-5b).

In many cases, the same information can be presented visually in different formats. When deciding whether to display data in a table or a graph, for example, think about the message you want to convey and the information your readers need. (See the examples on p. 51.) If your discussion refers to specific numbers, a table will be more useful to readers. If, however, you want readers to grasp at a glance that sales of hybrid electric vehicles increased from 2001 to 2007 and then declined, a line graph will be more effective.

As you draft and revise a document, carefully choose the visuals that support your main point, and avoid overloading your text with too many images. The chart on pages 52–53 describes eight types of visuals and their purposes.

INFORMATION DISPLAYED IN TWO TYPES OF VISUALS These visuals present the same information in two different ways. The table provides exact numbers for comparison. The line graph allows readers to see the trend in sales.

Hybrid electric vehicle sales by year in the United States

Year	Number of vehicles sold
2001	20,282
2002	36,035
2003	47,600
2004	84,199
2005	209,711
2006	252,636
2007	352,274
2008	312,386

Source: US Dept. of Energy (2009).

Hybrid electric vehicle sales by year in the United States

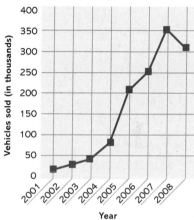

Placing and labeling visuals

A visual may be placed in the text of a document, near a discussion to which it relates, or it can be put in an appendix, labeled, and referred to in the text. Placing visuals in the text of a document can be tricky. Usually you will want a visual to appear close to the sentences that relate to it, but page breaks won't always allow this placement. At times, you may need to insert the visual at a later point and tell readers where it can be found; sometimes you can make the text flow, or wrap, around the visual. No matter where you place a visual, refer to it in your text. Don't expect visuals to speak for themselves.

> **Making the most of your handbook**
>
> Guidelines for using visuals may vary by academic discipline.
>
> ▶ English and other humanities: MLA-5a
> ▶ Social sciences: APA-5a
> ▶ History: CMS-5a

Most of the visuals you include in a document will require some sort of label. A label, which is typically placed above or below the visual, should be brief but descriptive. Most commonly, a visual is labeled with the word "Figure" or the abbreviation "Fig.," followed by a number: *Fig. 4.* Sometimes a title might be included to explain how the visual relates to the text: *Fig. 4. Voter turnout by age.*

Choosing visuals to suit your purpose

Pie chart

Pie charts compare a part or parts to the whole. Segments of the pie represent percentages of the whole (and always total 100 percent).

Health insurance coverage in the United States (2007)

Uninsured 15%   Medicaid 13%
Medicare 12%
Individual 5%
Other public insurance 1%
Employer-insured 54%

Line graph

Line graphs highlight trends over a period of time or compare numerical data.

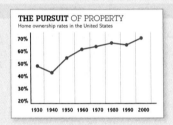

THE PURSUIT OF PROPERTY
Home ownership rates in the United States

(line graph with y-axis 20%–70%, x-axis 1930 1940 1950 1960 1970 1980 1990 2000)

Bar graph

Bar graphs, like line graphs, show trends or comparisons at a glance. This bar graph displays the same data as in the line graph above.

THE PURSUIT OF PROPERTY
Home ownership rates in the United States

(bar graph with y-axis 20%–70%, x-axis 1930 1940 1950 1960 1970 1980 1990 2000)

Table

Tables display numbers and words in columns and rows. They can be used to organize complicated numerical information into an easily understood format.

Prices of daily doses of AIDS drugs ($US)

Drug	Brazil	Uganda	Côte d'Ivoire	US
3TC (Lamuvidine)	1.66	3.26	2.95	8.70
ddC (Zalcitabine)	0.24	4.17	3.75	8.80
Didanosine	2.04	5.26	3.48	7.25
Efavirenz	6.96	n/a	6.41	13.13
Indinavir	10.32	12.79	9.07	14.93
Nelfinavir	4.14	4.45	4.39	6.47
Nevirapine	5.04	n/a	n/a	8.46
Saquinavir	6.24	7.37	5.52	6.50
Stavudine	0.56	6.19	4.10	9.07
ZDV/3TC	1.44	7.34	n/a	18.78
Zidovudine	1.08	4.34	2.43	10.12

Source: UNAIDS, 2000

Sources [top to bottom]: Kaiser Foundation; US Census Bureau; US Census Bureau; UNAIDS.

Photograph

Photographs can be used to vividly depict people, scenes, or objects discussed in a text.

Diagram

Diagrams, useful in scientific and technical writing, concisely illustrate processes, structures, or interactions.

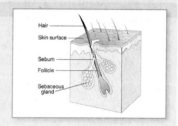

Flowchart

Flowcharts show structures (the hierarchy of employees at a company, for example) or steps in a process and their relation to one another. (For another example, see p. 122.)

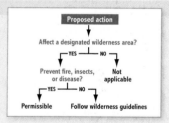

Map

Maps illustrate distances, historical information, or demographics and often use symbols for geographic features and points of interest.

Sources [top to bottom]: Fred Zwicky; NIAMS; Arizona Board of Regents; Lynn Hunt et al.

Using visuals responsibly

Most word processing and spreadsheet software will allow you to produce your own visuals. If you create a chart, a table, or a graph using information from your research, you must cite the source of the information even though the visual is your own. The visual at the right credits the source of its data.

If you download a photograph from the Web or scan an image from a magazine or book, you must credit the person or organization that created it, just as you would cite any other source you use in a college paper (see R3). Make sure any cropping or other changes you make to the visual do not distort the meaning of the original. If your document is written for publication outside the classroom, you will need to request permission to use any visual you borrow.

VISUAL WITH A SOURCE CREDITED

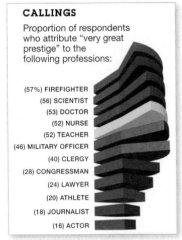

CALLINGS

Proportion of respondents who attribute "very great prestige" to the following professions:

(57%) FIREFIGHTER
(56) SCIENTIST
(53) DOCTOR
(52) NURSE
(52) TEACHER
(46) MILITARY OFFICER
(40) CLERGY
(28) CONGRESSMAN
(24) LAWYER
(20) ATHLETE
(18) JOURNALIST
(16) ACTOR

Source: The New York Times Company, September 21, 2008, from data by the Harris Poll, July 2008.

C5-e Use standard academic formatting.

Instructors have certain expectations about how a college paper should look. If your instructor provides guidelines for formatting an essay, a report, a research paper, or another document, you should follow them. Otherwise, use the manuscript format that is recommended for your academic discipline.

In most English and other humanities classes, you will be asked to use MLA (Modern Language Association) format (see pp. 55–56 and MLA-5). In most social science classes, such as psychology and sociology, and in most education, business, and health-related classes, you will be asked to use APA (American Psychological Association) format (see APA-5). In history and some other humanities classes, you will be asked to use CMS (*Chicago*) format (see CMS-5).

MLA PAPER FORMAT

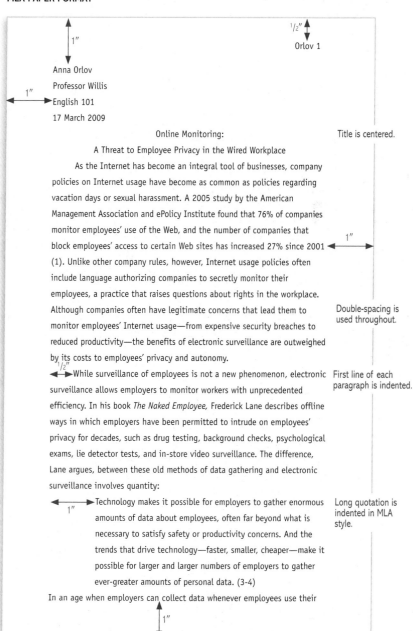

1″

¹/₂″
Orlov 1

1″

Anna Orlov
Professor Willis
English 101
17 March 2009

Online Monitoring: Title is centered.
A Threat to Employee Privacy in the Wired Workplace

As the Internet has become an integral tool of businesses, company
policies on Internet usage have become as common as policies regarding
vacation days or sexual harassment. A 2005 study by the American
Management Association and ePolicy Institute found that 76% of companies
monitor employees' use of the Web, and the number of companies that   1″
block employees' access to certain Web sites has increased 27% since 2001
(1). Unlike other company rules, however, Internet usage policies often
include language authorizing companies to secretly monitor their
employees, a practice that raises questions about rights in the workplace.
Although companies often have legitimate concerns that lead them to   Double-spacing is
monitor employees' Internet usage—from expensive security breaches to   used throughout.
reduced productivity—the benefits of electronic surveillance are outweighed
by its costs to employees' privacy and autonomy.

¹/₂″
While surveillance of employees is not a new phenomenon, electronic   First line of each
surveillance allows employers to monitor workers with unprecedented   paragraph is indented.
efficiency. In his book *The Naked Employee,* Frederick Lane describes offline
ways in which employers have been permitted to intrude on employees'
privacy for decades, such as drug testing, background checks, psychological
exams, lie detector tests, and in-store video surveillance. The difference,
Lane argues, between these old methods of data gathering and electronic
surveillance involves quantity:

Technology makes it possible for employers to gather enormous   Long quotation is
1″   amounts of data about employees, often far beyond what is   indented in MLA
necessary to satisfy safety or productivity concerns. And the   style.
trends that drive technology—faster, smaller, cheaper—make it
possible for larger and larger numbers of employers to gather
ever-greater amounts of personal data. (3-4)

In an age when employers can collect data whenever employees use their

1″

Marginal annotations indicate MLA-style formatting.

MLA PAPER FORMAT (continued)

1/2″

1″

Orlov 5

Heading is centered.

Works Cited

Adams, Scott. *Dilbert and the Way of the Weasel.* New York: Harper, 2002.
Print.

American Management Association and ePolicy Institute. "2005 Electronic
Monitoring and Surveillance Survey." *American Management
Association.* Amer. Management Assn., 2005. Web. 15 Feb. 2009.

"Automatically Record Everything They Do Online! Spector Pro 5.0
FAQ's." *Netbus.org.* Netbus.Org, n.d. Web. 17 Feb. 2009.

Flynn, Nancy. "Internet Policies." *ePolicy Institute.* ePolicy Inst., n.d.
Web. 15 Feb. 2009.

1″

Frauenheim, Ed. "Stop Reading This Headline and Get Back to Work."
CNET News.com. CNET Networks, 11 July 2005. Web. 17 Feb.
2009.

1″

Gonsalves, Chris. "Wasting Away on the Web." *eWeek.com.* Ziff Davis
Enterprise Holdings, 8 Aug. 2005. Web. 16 Feb. 2009.

Kesan, Jay P. "Cyber-Working or Cyber-Shirking? A First Principles
Examination of Electronic Privacy in the Workplace." *Florida
Law Review* 54.2 (2002): 289-332. Print.

1/2″

Double-spacing is
used throughout;
no extra space
between entries.

Lane, Frederick S., III. *The Naked Employee: How Technology Is
Compromising Workplace Privacy.* New York: Amer. Management
Assn., 2003. Print.

Tam, Pui-Wing, et al. "Snooping E-Mail by Software Is Now a Workplace
Norm." *Wall Street Journal* 9 Mar. 2005: B1+. Print.

Tynan, Daniel. "Your Boss Is Watching." *PC World.* PC World
Communications, 6 Oct. 2004. Web. 17 Sept. 2009.

Verespej, Michael A. "Inappropriate Internet Surfing." *Industry Week.*
Penton Media, 7 Feb. 2000. Web. 16 Feb. 2009.

C5-f Use standard business formatting.

This section provides guidelines for preparing business letters, résumés, and memos.

BUSINESS LETTER IN FULL BLOCK STYLE

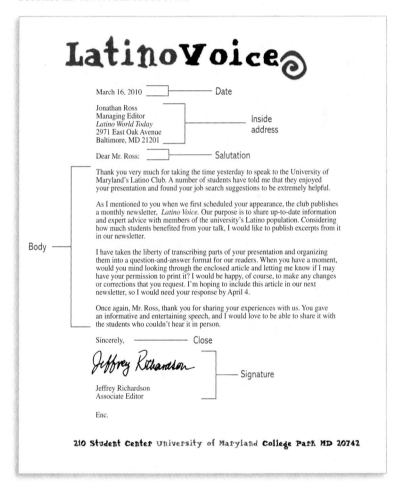

LatinoVoice

March 16, 2010 ———————— Date

Jonathan Ross
Managing Editor
Latino World Today   Inside
2971 East Oak Avenue   address
Baltimore, MD 21201

Dear Mr. Ross: ————— Salutation

Thank you very much for taking the time yesterday to speak to the University of Maryland's Latino Club. A number of students have told me that they enjoyed your presentation and found your job search suggestions to be extremely helpful.

As I mentioned to you when we first scheduled your appearance, the club publishes a monthly newsletter, *Latino Voice.* Our purpose is to share up-to-date information and expert advice with members of the university's Latino population. Considering how much students benefited from your talk, I would like to publish excerpts from it in our newsletter.

Body

I have taken the liberty of transcribing parts of your presentation and organizing them into a question-and-answer format for our readers. When you have a moment, would you mind looking through the enclosed article and letting me know if I may have your permission to print it? I would be happy, of course, to make any changes or corrections that you request. I'm hoping to include this article in our next newsletter, so I would need your response by April 4.

Once again, Mr. Ross, thank you for sharing your experiences with us. You gave an informative and entertaining speech, and I would love to be able to share it with the students who couldn't hear it in person.

Sincerely, ——————— Close

Jeffrey Richardson

Jeffrey Richardson   Signature
Associate Editor

Enc.

210 Student Center University of Maryland College Park MD 20742

Business letters

In writing a business letter, be direct, clear, and courteous. State your purpose or request at the beginning of the letter and include only relevant information in the body. By being as direct and concise as possible, you show that you value your reader's time.

For the format of the letter, use established business conventions. A sample business letter in full block style appears on page 57.

Résumés and cover letters

An effective résumé gives relevant information in a clear, concise form. You may be asked to produce a traditional résumé, a scannable résumé, or a Web résumé. The cover letter gives a prospective employer a reason to look at your résumé. The goal is to present yourself in a favorable light without including unnecessary details.

COVER LETTERS　Always include a cover letter to introduce yourself, state the position you seek, and tell where you learned about it. The letter should also highlight past experiences that qualify you for the position and emphasize what you can do for the employer (not what the job will do for you). End the letter with a suggestion for a meeting, and tell your prospective employer when you will be available.

TRADITIONAL RÉSUMÉS　Traditional résumés are produced on paper, and they are screened by people, not by computers. Because screeners often face stacks of applications, they may spend very little time looking at each résumé. Therefore, you need to make your résumé as reader-friendly as possible. Here are a few guidelines:

- Limit your résumé to one page if possible, two pages at most.

- Organize your information into clear categories—Education, Experience, and so on.

- Present the information in each category in reverse chronological order to highlight your most recent accomplishments.

- Use bulleted lists or some other simple, clear visual device to organize information.

- Use strong, active verbs to emphasize your accomplishments. For current activities, use present-tense verbs, such as *manage*; for past activities, use past-tense verbs, such as *managed*.

TRADITIONAL RÉSUMÉ

Jeffrey Richardson
121 Knox Road, #6
College Park, MD 20740
301-555-2651
jrichardson@example.net

OBJECTIVE	To obtain an editorial internship with a magazine
EDUCATION Fall 2007– present	University of Maryland • BA expected in June 2011 • Double major: English and Latin American studies • GPA: 3.7 (on a 4-point scale)
EXPERIENCE Fall 2009– present	Associate editor, *Latino Voice*, newsletter of Latino Club • Assign and edit feature articles • Coordinate community outreach
Fall 2008– present	Photo editor, *The Diamondback*, college paper • Shoot and organize photos for print and online publication • Oversee photo staff assignments; evaluate photos
Summer 2009	Intern, *The Globe,* Fairfax, Virginia • Wrote stories about local issues and personalities • Interviewed political candidates • Edited and proofread copy • Coedited "The Landscapes of Northern Virginia: A Photoessay"
Summers 2008, 2009	Tutor, Fairfax County ESL Program • Tutored Latino students in English as a Second Language • Trained new tutors
ACTIVITIES	Photographers' Workshop, Latino Club
PORTFOLIO	Available at http://jrichardson.example.net/jrportfolio.htm
REFERENCES	Available on request

SCANNABLE RÉSUMÉS Scannable résumés can be submitted on paper, by e-mail, or through an online employment service. The résumés are scanned and searched electronically, and a database matches keywords in the employer's job description with keywords in the résumés. A human screener then looks through the résumés selected by the database.

A scannable résumé must be formatted simply so that the scanner can accurately pick up its content. In general, follow these guidelines when preparing a scannable résumé:

- Include a Keywords section that lists words likely to be searched by a scanner. Use nouns, such as *manager*, not verbs, such as *manage*.
- Use standard résumé headings (for example, Education, Experience, References).
- Avoid special characters, graphics, or font styles.
- Avoid formatting such as tabs, indents, columns, or tables.

WEB RÉSUMÉS Posting your résumé on a Web site is an easy way to provide recent information about your employment goals and accomplishments. Most guidelines for traditional résumés apply to Web résumés. You may want to include a downloadable version of your résumé and link to an electronic portfolio. Always list the date that you last updated your résumé.

Memos

Usually brief and to the point, a memo reports information, makes a request, or recommends an action. The format of a memo, which varies from company to company, is designed for easy distribution, quick reading, and efficient filing.

Most memos display the date, the name of the recipient, the name of the sender, and the subject on separate lines at the top of the page. Many companies have preprinted forms for memos, and most word processing programs have memo templates.

The subject line of a memo should describe the topic as clearly and concisely as possible, and the introductory paragraph should get right to the point. In addition, the body of the memo should be well organized and easy to skim. To promote skimming, use headings where possible and set off any items that deserve special attention (in a list, for example, or in boldface).

E-mail

In business and academic contexts, you will want to show readers that you value their time. Your e-mail message may be just one of many that your readers have to wade through. Here are some strategies for writing effective e-mails:

- Use a meaningful, concise subject line to help readers sort through messages and set priorities.

BUSINESS MEMO

COMMONWEALTH PRESS

MEMORANDUM

February 25, 2010

To:	Editorial assistants, Advertising Department
cc:	Stephen Chapman
From:	Helen Brown
Subject:	New database software

The new database software will be installed on your computers next week. I have scheduled a training program to help you become familiar with the software and with our new procedures for data entry and retrieval.

Training program
A member of our IT staff will teach in-house workshops on how to use the new software. If you try the software before the workshop, please be prepared to discuss any problems you encounter.

We will keep the training groups small to encourage hands-on participation and to provide individual attention. The workshops will take place in the training room on the third floor from 10:00 a.m. to 2:00 p.m.

Lunch will be provided in the cafeteria.

Sign-up
Please sign up by March 1 for one of the following dates by adding your name in the department's online calendar:

- Wednesday, March 3
- Friday, March 5
- Monday, March 8

If you will not be in the office on any of those dates, please let me know by March 1.

- Put the most important part of your message at the beginning so that your reader sees it without scrolling.
- For long, detailed messages, provide a summary at the beginning.
- Write concisely, and keep paragraphs fairly short.
- Avoid writing in all capital letters or all lowercase letters.
- Be sparing with boldface, italics, and special characters; not all e-mail systems handle such elements consistently.
- Proofread for typos and obvious errors that are likely to slow down readers.

You will also want to use e-mail responsibly by following conventions of good etiquette and not violating standards of academic integrity. Here are some strategies for writing responsible e-mails:

- Remember that your messages can easily be forwarded to others and reproduced. Do not write anything that you would not want attributed to you. And do not forward another person's message without asking his or her consent.
- If you write an e-mail message that includes someone else's words — opinions, statistics, song lyrics, and so forth — it's best to let your reader know where any borrowed material begins and ends and the source for that material.
- Remember to choose your words carefully and judiciously because e-mail messages can easily be misread. Without your voice, facial gestures, or body language, a message can be misunderstood. Pay careful attention to tone and avoid writing anything that you wouldn't be comfortable saying directly to a reader.

C6 Writing with technology

C6-a Use software tools wisely.

Grammar checkers, spell checkers, and autoformatting are software tools designed to help you avoid errors and save time. These tools can alert you to possible errors in words, sentence structures, or formatting. But they're not always right. If a program suggests or makes a change, be sure the change is one you really want to make. Familiarizing yourself with your software's settings can help you use these tools effectively.

Grammar checkers

Grammar checkers can help with some of the sentence-level problems in a typical draft. But they will often misdiagnose errors, especially because they cannot account for your intended meaning. When the grammar checker makes a suggestion for revision, you must decide whether the change is more effective than your original.

It's just as important to be aware of what your grammar checker isn't picking up on. If you count on your grammar checker to identify trouble spots, you might overlook problems with coordination and subordination (see S6), sentence variety (see S7), sexist language (see W4-e), and passive verbs (see W3-a), for example.

Spell checkers

Spell checkers flag words not found in their dictionaries; they will suggest a replacement for any word they don't recognize. They can help you spot many errors, but don't let them be your only proof-reader. If you're writing about the health benefits of a Mediterranean diet, for example, don't let your software change *briam* (a vegetable dish) to *Brian*. Even if your spell checker identifies a real misspelling, the replacement word it suggests might carry a different connotation or even be nonsensical. After misspelling *probably*, you might end up with *portly*. Consider changes carefully before accepting them. If you're not sure what word or spelling you need, consult a dictionary, such as *Merriam-Webster's Collegiate Dictionary*. (See also W6-a.)

Because spell checkers flag only unrecognized words, they won't catch misused words, such as *accept* when you mean *except*. For help with commonly confused or misused words and with avoiding informal speech and jargon, consult the glossary of usage (W1).

Autoformatting

As you write, your software may attempt to save you effort with auto-formatting. It might recognize that you've typed a URL and turn it into a link. Or if you're building a list, it might add numbering for you. Be aware of such changes and make sure they are appropriate for your paper and applied to the right text.

C6-b Manage your files.

Your instructor may ask you to complete assignments in stages, including notes, outlines, annotated bibliographies, rough drafts, and a final draft. Keeping track of all of these documents can be challenging. Be sure to give your files distinct names that reflect the appropriate stage of your writing process, and store them in a logical place.

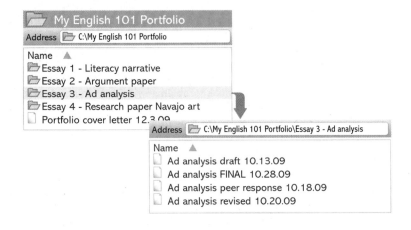

Writing online or in a word processing program can make writing and revising easier. You can undo changes or return to an earlier draft if a revision misfires. Applying the following steps can help you explore revision possibilities with little risk.

- Create folders and subfolders for each assignment. Save notes, outlines, and drafts together.

- Label revised drafts with different file names and dates.

- Print hard copies, make backup copies, and press the Save button early and often. Save work every five to ten minutes.

- Always record complete bibliographic information about sources, including images.

- Use a comment function to make notes to yourself or to respond to the drafts of peers.

When you write in college, you pose questions, explore ideas, and engage in scholarly debates and conversations. To join in those conversations, you will analyze and respond to texts, evaluate other people's arguments, and put forth your own ideas.

 # A1 Writing about texts

The word *texts* can refer to a variety of works, including essays, articles, government reports, books, Web sites, advertisements, and photographs. Most assignments that ask you to respond to a text call for a summary or an analysis or both.

> **Making the most of your handbook**
>
> Knowing the expectations for a writing assignment is a key first step in drafting.
>
> ▶ Understanding writing assignments: A4-f

A summary is neutral in tone and demonstrates that you have understood the author's key ideas. Assignments calling for an analysis of a text vary widely, but they usually ask you to look at how the text's parts contribute to its central argument or purpose, often with the aim of judging its evidence or overall effect.

When you write about a text, you will need to read it—or, in the case of a visual text, view it—several times to discover meaning. Two techniques will help you move beyond a superficial first reading: (1) annotating the text with your observations and questions and (2) outlining the text's key points. These techniques will help you analyze both written and visual texts.

A1-a Read actively: Annotate the text.

Read actively by jotting down your questions and thoughts in a notebook or in the margins of the text or visual. Use a pencil instead of a highlighter; with a pencil you can underline key concepts, mark points, or circle elements that intrigue you. If you change your mind, you can erase your early annotations and replace them with new ones. To annotate an electronic document, take notes in a separate file or use software features to highlight, underline, or insert comments.

THE WRITING CENTER hackerhandbooks.com/writersref
> Resources for writers and tutors > Tips from writing tutors:
Benefits of reading

Guidelines for active reading

Familiarize yourself with the basic features and structure of a text.

- What kind of text are you reading: An essay? An editorial? A scholarly article? An advertisement? A photograph? A Web site?
- What is the author's purpose: To inform? To persuade? To call to action?
- Who is the audience? How does the author appeal to the audience?
- What is the author's thesis? What question does the text attempt to answer?
- What evidence does the author provide to support the thesis?
- What key terms does the author define?

Note details that surprise, puzzle, or intrigue you.

- Has the author revealed a fact or made a point that counters your assumptions? Is anything surprising?
- Has the author made a generalization you disagree with? Can you think of evidence that would challenge the generalization?
- Do you see any contradictions or inconsistencies in the text?
- Does the text contain words, statements, or phrases that you don't understand? If so, what reference materials do you need to consult?

Read and reread to discover meaning.

- What do you notice on a second or third reading that you didn't notice earlier?
- Does the text raise questions that it does not resolve?
- If you could address the author directly, what questions would you pose? Where do you agree and disagree with the author? Why?

Apply additional critical thinking strategies to visual texts.

- What first strikes you about the visual text? What elements do you notice immediately?
- Who or what is the main subject of the visual text?
- What colors and textures dominate?
- What is in the background? In the foreground?
- What role, if any, do words or numbers play in the text?
- When was the visual created or the information collected?

On this page and on page 70 are an article from *CQ Researcher*, a newsletter about social and political issues, and an advertisement, both annotated by students. The students, Emilia Sanchez and Ren Yoshida, were assigned to analyze these texts. They began by reading actively.

ANNOTATED ARTICLE

Big Box Stores Are Bad for Main Street
BETSY TAYLOR

There is plenty of reason to be concerned about the proliferation of Wal-Marts and other so-called "big box" stores. The question, however, is not whether or not these types of stores create jobs (although several studies claim they produce a net job loss in local communities) or whether they ultimately save consumers money. The real concern about having a 25-acre slab of concrete with a 100,000 square foot box of stuff land on a town is whether it's good for a community's soul.

> *Opening strategy— the problem is not x, it's y.*
>
> *Sentimental— what is a community's soul?*

The worst thing about "big boxes" is that they have a tendency to produce Ross Perot's famous "big sucking sound"—sucking the life out of cities and small towns across the country. On the other hand, small businesses are great for a community. They offer more personal service; they won't threaten to pack up and leave town if they don't get tax breaks, free roads and other blandishments; and small-business owners are much more responsive to a customer's needs. (Ever try to complain about bad service or poor quality products to the president of Home Depot?)

> *Lumps all big boxes together.*
>
> *Assumes all small businesses are attentive.*
>
> *Logic problem? Why couldn't customer complain to store manager?*

Yet, if big boxes are so bad, why are they so successful? One glaring reason is that (we've become a nation of hyper-consumers,) and the big-box boys know this. Downtown shopping districts comprised of small businesses take some of the efficiency out of overconsumption. There's all that hassle of having to travel from store to store, and having to pull out your credit card so many times. Occasionally, we even find ourselves chatting with the shopkeeper, wandering into a coffee shop to visit with a friend or otherwise wasting precious time that could be spent on acquiring more stuff.

> *True?*
>
> *Taylor wishes for a time that is long gone or never was.*

But let's face it—bustling, thriving city centers are fun. They breathe life into a community. They allow cities and towns to stand out from each other. They provide an atmosphere for people to interact with each other that just cannot be found at Target, or Wal-Mart or Home Depot.

> *Community vs. economy. What about prices?*

Is it anti-American to be against having a retail giant set up shop in one's community? Some people would say so. On the other hand, if you board up Main Street, what's left of America?

> *Ends with emotional appeal.*

ANNOTATED ADVERTISEMENT

When you choose Equal Exchange fairly traded coffee, tea or chocolate, you join a network that empowers farmers in Latin America, Africa, and Asia to:

- **Stay on their land**
- **Care for the environment**
- **Farm organically**
- **Support their family**
- **Plan for the future**

www.equalexchange.coop

Photo: Jesus Choqueheranca de Quevero, Coffee farmer & CEPICAFE Cooperative member, Peru

What is being exchanged?

"Empowering" — why in an elegant font? Who is empowering farmers?

"Farmers" in all capital letters — shows strength?

Straightforward design and not much text.

Outstretched hands. Is she giving a gift? Inviting a partnership?

Raw coffee is red: earthy, natural, warm.

Positive verbs: consumers choose, join, empower; farmers stay, care, farm, support, plan.

Source: Equal Exchange.

A1-b Sketch a brief outline of the text.

After reading, rereading, and annotating a text, try to outline it. Seeing how the author has constructed a text can help you understand it. As you sketch an outline, pay special attention to the text's thesis (central idea) and its topic sentences. The thesis of a written text usually appears in the introduction, often in the first or second paragraph. Topic sentences can be found at the beginnings of most body paragraphs, where they announce a shift to a new topic. (See C2-a and C4-a.)

In your outline, put the author's thesis and key points in your own words. Here, for example, is the outline that Emilia Sanchez developed as she prepared to write her summary and analysis of the text on page 69. Notice that Sanchez's informal outline does not trace the author's ideas paragraph by paragraph; instead, it sums up the article's central points.

OUTLINE OF "BIG BOX STORES ARE BAD FOR MAIN STREET"

Thesis: Whether or not they take jobs away from a community or offer low prices to consumers, we should be worried about "big-box" stores like Wal-Mart, Target, and Home Depot because they harm communities by taking the life out of downtown shopping districts.

I. Small businesses are better for cities and towns than big-box stores are.
   A. Small businesses offer personal service, but big-box stores do not.
   B. Small businesses don't make demands on community resources as big-box stores do.
   C. Small businesses respond to customer concerns, but big-box stores do not.
II. Big-box stores are successful because they cater to consumption at the expense of benefits to the community.
   A. Buying everything in one place is convenient.
   B. Shopping at small businesses may be inefficient, but it provides opportunities for socializing.
   C. Downtown shopping districts give each city or town a special identity.

Conclusion: Although some people say that it's anti-American to oppose big-box stores, actually these stores threaten the communities that make up America by encouraging buying at the expense of the traditional interactions of Main Street.

A visual often doesn't state an explicit thesis or an explicit line of reasoning. Instead, you must sometimes infer the meaning beneath the image's surface and interpret its central point and supporting ideas from the elements of its design. One way to outline a visual text is to try to define its purpose and sketch a list of its key elements. Here, for example, are the key features that Ren Yoshida identified for the advertisement printed on page 70.

OUTLINE OF EQUAL EXCHANGE ADVERTISEMENT

Purpose: To persuade readers that they can improve the lives of organic farmers and their families by purchasing Equal Exchange coffee.

Key features:

- The farmer's heart-shaped hands are outstretched, offering the viewer partnership and the product of her hard work.
- The coffee beans are surprisingly red, fruitlike, and fresh—natural and healthy looking.
- Words above and below the photograph describe the equal exchange between farmers and consumers.
- Consumer support leads to a higher quality of life for the farmers and for all people, since these farmers care for the environment and plan for the future.
- The simplicity of the design echoes the simplicity of the exchange. The consumer only has to buy a cup of coffee to make a difference.
- Equal Exchange is selling more than a product—coffee. It is selling the idea that together farmers and consumers hold the future of land, environment, farms, and family in their hands.

A1-c Summarize to demonstrate your understanding.

Your goal in summarizing a text is to state the work's main ideas and key points simply, briefly, and accurately in your own words. Writing a summary does not require you to judge the author's ideas. If you have sketched a brief outline of the text (see A1-b), refer to it as you draft your summary.

To summarize a written text, first find the author's central idea—the thesis. Then divide the whole piece into a few major and perhaps minor ideas. Since a summary

Making the most of your handbook

Summarizing is a key research skill.

▶ Summarizing without plagiarizing: R3-c
▶ Putting summaries and paraphrases in your own words: MLA-2c, APA-2c, CMS-2c

Guidelines for writing a summary

- In the first sentence, mention the title of the text, the name of the author, and the author's thesis or the visual's central point.
- Maintain a neutral tone; be objective.
- Use the third-person point of view and the present tense: *Taylor argues. . . .*
- Keep your focus on the text. Don't state the author's ideas as if they were your own.
- Put all or most of your summary in your own words; if you borrow a phrase or a sentence from the text, put it in quotation marks and give the page number in parentheses.
- Limit yourself to presenting the text's key points.
- Be concise; make every word count.

must be fairly short, you must make judgments about what is most important.

To summarize a visual text, begin with essential information such as who created the visual, who the intended audience is, where the visual appeared, and when it was created. Briefly explain the visual's main point or purpose and identify its key features (see p. 72).

Following is Emilia Sanchez's summary of the article that is printed on page 69.

> In her essay "Big Box Stores Are Bad for Main Street," Betsy Taylor argues that chain stores harm communities by taking the life out of downtown shopping districts. Explaining that a community's "soul" is more important than low prices or consumer convenience, she argues that small businesses are better than stores like Home Depot and Target because they emphasize personal interactions and don't place demands on a community's resources. Taylor asserts that big-box stores are successful because "we've become a nation of hyper-consumers" (1011), although the convenience of shopping in these stores comes at the expense of benefits to the community. She concludes by suggesting that it's not "anti-American" to oppose big-box stores because the damage they inflict on downtown shopping districts extends to America itself.
>
> — Emilia Sanchez, student

A1-d Analyze to demonstrate your critical thinking.

Whereas a summary most often answers the question of *what* a text says, an analysis looks at *how* a text makes its point.

Typically, an analysis takes the form of an essay that makes its own argument about a text. Include an introduction that briefly summarizes the text, a thesis that states your own judgment about the text, and body paragraphs that support your thesis with evidence. If you are analyzing a visual, examine it as a whole and then reflect on how the individual elements contribute to its overall meaning. If you have written a summary of the text or visual, you may find it useful to refer to the main points of the summary as you write your analysis.

> **Making the most of your handbook**
>
> When you analyze a text, you weave words and ideas from the source into your own writing.
>
> ▶ Guidelines for using quotation marks: R3-c
>
> ▶ Quoting or paraphrasing: MLA-2, APA-2, CMS-2
>
> ▶ Using signal phrases: MLA-3b, APA-3b, CMS-3b

Using interpretation in an analysis

Student writer Emilia Sanchez begins her essay about Betsy Taylor's article (see p. 69) by summarizing Taylor's argument. She then states her own thesis, or claim, which offers her judgment of Taylor's article, and begins her analysis. In her first body paragraph, Sanchez interprets Taylor's use of language.

Topic sentence includes Sanchez's claim.

Quoted material shows Taylor's language and is placed in quotation marks.

Transition to Sanchez's next point.

Taylor's use of colorful language reveals that she has a sentimental view of American society and does not understand economic realities. In her first paragraph, Taylor refers to a big-box store as a "25-acre slab of concrete with a 100,000 square foot box of stuff" that "land[s] on a town," evoking images of a powerful monster crushing the American way of life (1011). But she oversimplifies a complex issue. Taylor does not consider. . . .

Signal phrase introduces a quotation from the text.

Quotation is followed by Sanchez's interpretation of Taylor's language.

A1-e Sample student essay: Analysis of an article

Beginning on the next page is Emilia Sanchez's analysis of the article by Betsy Taylor (see p. 69). Sanchez used Modern Language Association (MLA) style to format her paper and cite the source.

MODELS hackerhandbooks.com/bedhandbook
> Model papers > MLA analysis papers: Sanchez; Lee; Lopez

Sanchez 1

Emilia Sanchez

Professor Goodwin

English 10

23 October 2009

Rethinking Big-Box Stores

In her essay "Big Box Stores Are Bad for Main Street," Betsy Taylor focuses not on the economic effects of large chain stores but on the effects these stores have on the "soul" of America. She argues that stores like Home Depot, Target, and Wal-Mart are bad for America because they draw people out of downtown shopping districts and cause them to focus on consumption. In contrast, she believes that small businesses are good for America because they provide personal attention, encourage community interaction, and make each city and town unique. But Taylor's argument is unconvincing because it is based on sentimentality—on idealized images of a quaint Main Street—rather than on the roles that businesses play in consumers' lives and communities. By ignoring the complex economic relationship between large chain stores and their communities, Taylor incorrectly assumes that simply getting rid of big-box stores would have a positive effect on America's communities.

Taylor's use of colorful language reveals that she has a sentimental view of American society and does not understand economic realities. In her first paragraph, Taylor refers to a big-box store as a "25-acre slab of concrete with a 100,000 square foot box of stuff" that "land[s] on a town," evoking images of a powerful monster crushing the American way of life (1011). But she oversimplifies a complex issue. Taylor does not consider that many downtown business districts failed long before chain stores moved in, when factories and mills closed and workers lost their jobs. In cities with struggling economies, big-box stores can actually provide much-needed jobs. Similarly, while Taylor blames big-box stores for harming local economies by asking for tax breaks, free roads, and other perks, she doesn't acknowledge that these stores also enter into economic partnerships with the surrounding communities by offering financial benefits to schools and hospitals.

Opening briefly summarizes the article's purpose and thesis.

Sanchez begins to analyze Taylor's argument.

Thesis expresses Sanchez's judgment of Taylor's article.

Signal phrase introduces quotations from the source; Sanchez uses an MLA in-text citation.

Sanchez begins to identify and challenge Taylor's assumptions.

Transition to another point in Sanchez's analysis.

Marginal annotations indicate MLA-style formatting **and** effective writing.

Sanchez 2

Clear topic sentence announces a shift to a new topic.

Taylor's assumption that shopping in small businesses is always better for the customer also seems driven by nostalgia for an old-fashioned Main Street rather than by the facts. While she may be right that many small businesses offer personal service and are responsive to customer complaints, she does not consider that many customers appreciate the service at big-box stores. Just as customer service is better at some small businesses than at others, it is impossible to generalize about service at all big-box stores. For example, customers depend on the lenient return policies and the wide variety of products at stores like Target and Home Depot.

Sanchez refutes Taylor's claim.

Taylor blames big-box stores for encouraging American "hyper-consumerism," but she oversimplifies by equating big-box stores with bad values and small businesses with good values. Like her other points, this claim ignores the economic and social realities of American society today. Big-box stores do not force Americans to buy more. By offering lower prices in a convenient setting, however, they allow consumers to save time and purchase goods they might not be able to afford from small businesses. The existence of more small businesses would not change what most Americans can afford, nor would it reduce their desire to buy affordable merchandise.

Sanchez treats the author fairly.

Conclusion returns to the thesis and shows the wider significance of Sanchez's analysis.

Taylor may be right that some big-box stores have a negative impact on communities and that small businesses offer certain advantages. But she ignores the economic conditions that support big-box stores as well as the fact that Main Street was in decline before the big-box store arrived. Getting rid of big-box stores will not bring back a simpler America populated by thriving, unique Main Streets; in reality, Main Street will not survive if consumers cannot afford to shop there.

Sanchez 3

Work Cited

Work cited page is in MLA style.

Taylor, Betsy. "Big Box Stores Are Bad for Main Street." *CQ Researcher* 9.44 (1999): 1011. Print.

Guidelines for analyzing a text

Written texts

Instructors who ask you to analyze an essay or an article often expect you to address some of the following questions.

- What is the author's thesis or central idea? Who is the audience?
- What questions (stated or unstated) does the author address?
- How does the author structure the text? What are the key parts, and how do they relate to one another and to the thesis?
- What strategies has the author used to generate interest in the argument and to persuade readers of its merit?
- What evidence does the author use to support the thesis? How persuasive is the evidence? (See A2-d and A2-e.)
- Does the author anticipate objections and counter opposing views? (See A2-f.)
- Does the author use any faulty reasoning? (See A3-a.)

Visual texts

If you are analyzing a visual text, the following additional questions will help you evaluate an image's purpose and meaning.

- What confuses, surprises, or intrigues you about the image?
- What is the source of the visual, and who created it? What is its purpose?
- What clues suggest the visual text's intended audience? How does the image appeal to its audience?
- If the text is an advertisement, what product is it selling? Does it attempt to sell an idea or a message as well?
- If the visual text includes words, how do the words contribute to the meaning?
- How do design elements—colors, shapes, perspective, background, foreground—help convey the visual text's meaning or serve its purpose?

A2 Constructing reasonable arguments

In writing an argument, you take a stand on a debatable issue. The question being debated might be a matter of public policy:

> Should religious groups be allowed to meet on public school property?
>
> What is the least dangerous way to dispose of hazardous waste?
>
> Should motorists be banned from texting while driving?
>
> Should a state limit the number of charter schools?

On such questions, reasonable people may disagree.

Reasonable men and women also disagree about many scholarly issues. Psychologists debate the role of genes and environment in determining behavior; historians interpret the causes of the Civil War quite differently; biologists challenge one another's predictions about the effects of global warming.

When you construct a *reasonable* argument, your goal is not simply to win or to have the last word. Your aim is to explain your understanding of the truth about a subject or to propose the best solution to

---

Academic English   Some cultures value writers who argue with force; other cultures value writers who argue subtly or indirectly. Academic audiences in the United States will expect your writing to be assertive and confident—neither aggressive nor passive. You can create an assertive tone by acknowledging different positions and supporting your ideas with specific evidence.

TOO AGGRESSIVE	Of course only registered organ donors should be eligible for organ transplants. It's selfish and shortsighted to think otherwise.
TOO PASSIVE	I might be wrong, but I think that maybe people should have to register as organ donors if they want to be considered for a transplant.
ASSERTIVE	If only registered organ donors are eligible for transplants, more people will register as donors.

If you are uncertain about the tone of your work, ask for help at your school's writing center.

a problem—without being needlessly combative. In constructing your argument, you join a conversation with other writers and readers. Your aim is to convince readers to reconsider their positions by offering new reasons to question existing viewpoints.

A2-a Examine your issue's social and intellectual contexts.

Arguments appear in social and intellectual contexts. Public policy debates arise in social contexts and are conducted among groups with competing values and interests. For example, the debate over offshore oil drilling has been renewed in the United States in light of skyrocketing energy costs and terrorism concerns—with environmentalists, policymakers, oil company executives, and consumers all weighing in on the argument. Most public policy debates also have intellectual dimensions that address scientific or theoretical questions. In the case of the drilling issue, geologists, oceanographers, and economists all contribute their expertise.

Scholarly debates play out in intellectual contexts, but they have a social dimension as well. For example, scholars respond to the contributions of other specialists in the field, often building on others' views and refining them, but at times challenging them.

Because many of your readers will be aware of the social and intellectual contexts in which your issue is grounded, you will be at a disadvantage if you are not informed. That's why it is a good idea to conduct some research before preparing your argument; consulting even a few sources can deepen your understanding of the debates surrounding your topic. For example, the student whose paper appears on pages 87–91

> **Making the most of your handbook**
>
> Supporting your claims with evidence from sources can strengthen your argument.
>
> ▶ Conducting research: R1

became more knowledgeable about his issue—the shift from print to online news—after reading and annotating a few sources.

A2-b View your audience as a panel of jurors.

Do not assume that your audience already agrees with you; instead, envision skeptical readers who, like a panel of jurors, will make up their minds after listening to all sides of the argument. If you are arguing a public policy issue, aim your paper at readers who represent a variety of positions. In the case of the debate over offshore drilling, for example, imagine a jury that represents those who have a stake in the matter: environmentalists, policymakers, oil company executives, and consumers.

At times, you can deliberately narrow your audience. If you are working within a word limit, for example, you might not have the space in which to address all the concerns surrounding the offshore drilling debate. Or you might be primarily interested in reaching one segment of a general audience, such as consumers. In such instances, you can still view your audience as a panel of jurors; the jury will simply be a less diverse group.

In the case of scholarly debates, you will be addressing readers who share your interest in a discipline, such as literature or psychology. Such readers belong to a group with an agreed-upon way of investigating and talking about issues. Though they generally agree about disciplinary methods of asking questions and share specialized vocabulary, scholars in an academic discipline often disagree about particular issues. Once you see how they disagree about your issue, you should be able to imagine a jury that reflects the variety of positions they hold.

A2-c In your introduction, establish credibility and state your position.

When you are constructing an argument, make sure your introduction contains a thesis that states your position on the issue you have chosen to debate (see also C2-a). In the sentences leading up to the thesis, establish your credibility with readers by showing that you are knowledgeable and fair-minded. If possible, build common ground with readers who may not at first agree with your views and show them why they should consider your thesis.

In the following introduction, student Kevin Smith presents himself as someone worth listening to. Because Smith introduces both sides of the debate, readers are likely to approach his essay with an open mind.

Smith shows that he is familiar with the legal issues surrounding school prayer.

Although the Supreme Court has ruled against prayer in public schools on First Amendment grounds, many people still feel that prayer should be allowed. Such people value prayer as a practice central to their faith and believe that prayer is a way for schools to reinforce moral principles. They also compellingly point out a paradox in the First Amendment itself: at what point does the separation of church and state restrict the freedom of those who wish to practice their religion? What proponents of school prayer fail to realize, however, is that the Supreme Court's decision, although it was made on legal grounds, makes sense on religious grounds as well. Prayer is too important to be trusted to our public schools.

Smith is fair-minded, presenting the views of both sides.

Smith's thesis builds common ground.

—Kevin Smith, student

TIP: A good way to test a thesis while drafting and revising is to imagine a counterargument to your argument (see A2-f). If you can't think of an opposing point of view, rethink your thesis and ask a classmate or writing center tutor to respond to your argument.

A2-d Back up your thesis with persuasive lines of argument.

Arguments of any complexity contain lines of argument that, when taken together, might reasonably persuade readers that the thesis has merit. The following, for example, are the main lines of argument that Sam Jacobs used in his paper about the shift from print to online news (see pp. 87–91).

CENTRAL CLAIM	Thesis: The shift from print to online news provides unprecedented opportunities for readers to become more engaged with the news, to hold journalists accountable, and to participate as producers, not simply as consumers.
SUPPORTING CLAIMS	• Print news has traditionally had a one-sided relationship with its readers, delivering information for passive consumption.

(continued)

THE WRITING CENTER   hackerhandbooks.com/writersref
    > Resources for writers and tutors   > Tips from writing tutors:
                                            Writing assignments;
                                            Writing essays in English

SUPPORTING CLAIMS (continued)	• Online news invites readers to participate in a collaborative process—to question and even contribute to the content.
	• Links within news stories provide transparency, allowing readers to move easily from the main story to original sources, related articles, or background materials.
	• Technology has made it possible for readers to become news producers—posting text, audio, images, and video of news events.
	• Citizen journalists can provide valuable information, sometimes more quickly than traditional journalists can.

If you sum up your main lines of argument, as Jacobs did, you will have a rough outline of your essay. In your paper, you will provide evidence for each of your claims.

A2-e Support your claims with specific evidence.

You will need to support your central claim and any subordinate claims with evidence: facts, statistics, examples and illustrations, visuals, expert opinion, and so on. Most debatable topics require that you consult some written sources. As you read through the sources, you will learn more about the arguments and counterarguments at the center of your debate.

Remember that you must document your sources. Documentation gives credit to the authors and shows readers how to locate a source in case they want to assess its credibility or explore the issues further.

> **Making the most of your handbook**
>
> Sources, when used responsibly, can provide evidence to support an argument.
>
> ▶ Paraphrasing, summarizing, and quoting sources: R3-c
> ▶ Punctuating direct quotations: P5-a
> ▶ Citing sources: MLA-2, APA-2, CMS-2

Using facts and statistics

A fact is something that is known with certainty because it has been objectively verified: The capital of Wyoming is Cheyenne. Carbon has an atomic weight of 12. John F. Kennedy was assassinated on

November 22, 1963. Statistics are collections of numerical facts: Alcohol abuse is a factor in nearly 40 percent of traffic fatalities. More than four in ten businesses in the United States are owned by women.

Most arguments are supported at least to some extent by facts and statistics. For example, in the following passage the writer uses statistics to show that college students are granted unreasonably high credit limits.

> A 2009 study by Sallie Mae revealed that undergraduates are carrying record-high credit card balances and are relying on credit cards more than ever, especially in the economic downturn. The average credit card debt per college undergraduate is $3,173, and 82 percent of undergraduates carry balances and incur finance charges each month (Sallie Mae).

Writers often use statistics in selective ways to bolster their own positions. If you suspect that a writer's handling of statistics is not quite fair, track down the original sources for those statistics or read authors with opposing views, who may give you a fuller understanding of the numbers.

Using examples and illustrations

Examples and illustrations (extended examples, often in story form) rarely prove a point by themselves, but when used in combination with other forms of evidence they flesh out an argument with details and specific instances and bring it to life. Because examples are often concrete and sometimes vivid, they can reach readers in ways that statistics and abstract ideas cannot.

In a paper arguing that online news provides opportunities for readers that print news does not, Sam Jacobs describes how regular citizens armed with only cell phones and laptops helped save lives during Hurricane Katrina by relaying critical news updates.

Using visuals

Visuals—charts, graphs, diagrams, photographs—can support your argument by providing vivid and detailed evidence and by capturing your readers' attention. Bar or line graphs, for instance, describe and organize complex statistical data; photographs can immediately and evocatively convey abstract ideas. Writers in almost every academic field use visual evidence to support their arguments or to counter opposing arguments. For example, to explain a conflict among Southeast Asian countries, a historian might choose a map to illustrate the geographical situation and highlight particular issues. Or to refute another scholar's hypothesis about the dangers of a vegetarian diet, a nutritionist might support her claims by using a table to organize and highlight detailed numerical information. (See C5-d.)

As you consider using visual evidence, ask yourself the following questions:

- Is the visual accurate, credible, and relevant?

- How will the visual appeal to readers? Logically? Ethically? Emotionally?

- How will the visual evidence function? Will it provide background information? Present complex numerical information or an abstract idea? Lend authority? Anticipate or refute counterarguments?

> **Making the most of your handbook**
>
> Integrating visuals can strengthen your writing.
>
> ▶ Choosing appropriate visuals: **page 50**
> ▶ Placing and labeling visuals: **page 51**
> ▶ Using visuals responsibly: **page 54**

Like all forms of evidence, visuals don't speak for themselves; you'll need to analyze and interpret the evidence to show readers how the visuals inform and support your argument.

Citing expert opinion

Although they are no substitute for careful reasoning of your own, the views of an expert can contribute to the force of your argument. For example, to help him make the case that print journalism has a one-sided relationship with its readers, Sam Jacobs integrates an expert's key description:

> With the rise of the Internet, however, this one-sided relationship has been criticized by journalists such as Dan Gillmor, founder of the Center for Citizen Media, who argues that traditional print journalism treats "news as a lecture," whereas online news is "more of a conversation" (xxiv).

When you rely on expert opinion, make sure that your source is an expert in the field you are writing about. In some cases, you may need to provide credentials showing why your source is worth listening to. When including expert testimony in your paper, you can summarize or paraphrase the expert's opinion or you can quote the expert's exact words. You will of course need to document the source, as Jacobs did in the example just given.

Anticipating and countering opposing arguments

To anticipate a possible objection to your argument, consider the following questions:

- Could a reasonable person draw a different conclusion from your facts or examples?
- Might a reader question any of your assumptions?
- Could a reader offer an alternative explanation of this issue?
- Is there any evidence that might weaken your position?

The following questions may help you respond to a reader's potential objection:

- Can you concede the point to the opposition but challenge the point's importance or usefulness?
- Can you explain why readers should consider a new perspective or question a piece of evidence?
- Should you explain how your position responds to contradictory evidence?
- Can you suggest a different interpretation of the evidence?

When you write, use phrasing to signal to readers that you're about to present an objection. Often the signal phrase can go in the lead sentence of a paragraph:

Critics of this view argue that. . . .

Some readers might point out that. . . .

Researchers challenge these claims by. . . .

A2-f Anticipate objections; counter opposing arguments.

Readers who already agree with you need no convincing, but indifferent or skeptical readers may resist your arguments. To be willing to give up a position that seems reasonable, a reader has to see that there is an even more reasonable one. In addition to presenting your own case, therefore, you should consider the opposing arguments and attempt to counter them.

It might seem at first that drawing attention to an opposing point of view or contradictory evidence would weaken your argument. But by anticipating and countering objections, you show yourself as a reasonable and well-informed writer. You also establish your purpose, demonstrate the significance of the issue you are debating, and ultimately strengthen your argument.

There is no best place in an essay to deal with opposing views. Often it is useful to summarize the opposing position early in your essay. After stating your thesis but before developing your own arguments, you might have a paragraph that addresses the most important counterargument. Or you can anticipate objections paragraph by paragraph as you develop your case. Wherever you decide to address opposing arguments, you will enhance your credibility if you explain the arguments of others accurately and fairly.

A2-g Build common ground.

As you counter opposing arguments, try to seek out one or two assumptions you might share with readers who do not initially agree with your views. If you can show that you share their concerns, your readers may be more likely to acknowledge the validity of your argument. For example, to persuade people opposed to controlling the deer population with a regulated hunting season, a state wildlife commission would have to show that it too cares about preserving deer and does not want them to die needlessly. Having established these values in common, the commission might be able to persuade critics that reducing the total number of deer prevents starvation caused by overpopulation.

People believe that intelligence and decency support their side of an argument. To be persuaded, they must see these qualities in your argument. Otherwise they will persist in their opposition.

A2-h Sample argument paper

In the paper that begins on the next page, student Sam Jacobs argues that the shift from print to online news benefits readers by providing them with opportunities to become more engaged with the news, to hold journalists accountable, and to participate as producers, not simply as consumers. Notice that he is careful to present opposing views fairly before providing his counterarguments.

In writing the paper, Jacobs consulted both print and online sources. When he quotes or uses information from a source, he cites the source with an MLA (Modern Language Association) in-text citation. Citations in the paper refer readers to the list of works cited at the end of the paper. (For more details about citing sources, see MLA-4.)

MODELS hackerhandbooks.com/writersref
> Model papers > MLA argument papers: Jacobs; Hammond; Lund; Sanghvi
> MLA papers: Orlov; Daly; Levi

Jacobs 1

Sam Jacobs

Professor Alperini

English 101

March 19, 2010

From Lecture to Conversation: Redefining What's "Fit to Print"

"All the news that's fit to print," the motto of the *New York Times* since 1896, plays with the word *fit*, asserting that a news story must be newsworthy and must not exceed the limits of the printed page. The increase in online news consumption, however, challenges both meanings of the word *fit*, allowing producers and consumers alike to rethink who decides which topics are worth covering and how extensive that coverage should be. Any cultural shift usually means that something is lost, but in this case there are clear gains. The shift from print to online news provides unprecedented opportunities for readers to become more engaged with the news, to hold journalists accountable, and to participate as producers, not simply as consumers.

Guided by journalism's code of ethics—accuracy, objectivity, and fairness—print news reporters have gathered and delivered stories according to what editors decide is fit for their readers. Except for op-ed pages and letters to the editor, print news has traditionally had a one-sided relationship with its readers. The print news media's reputation for objective reporting has been held up as "a stop sign" for readers, sending a clear message that no further inquiry is necessary (Weinberger). With the rise of the Internet, however, this model has been criticized by journalists such as Dan Gillmor, founder of the Center for Citizen Media, who argues that traditional print journalism treats "news as a lecture," whereas online news is "more of a conversation" (xxiv). Print news arrives on the doorstep every morning as a fully formed lecture, a product created without participation from its readership. By contrast, online news invites readers to participate in a collaborative process—to question and even help produce the content.

One of the most important advantages online news offers over print news is the presence of built-in hyperlinks, which carry readers from one electronic document to another. If readers are curious about the definition of a term, the roots of a story, or other perspectives on a topic, links provide a path. Links help readers become more critical consumers of

Jacobs provides background in opening sentences for his thesis.

Thesis states the main point.

Jacobs does not need a citation for common knowledge.

Transition moves from Jacobs's main argument to specific examples.

Marginal annotations indicate MLA-style formatting and effective writing.

Jacobs 2

information by engaging them in a totally new way. For instance, the link embedded in the story "Window into Fed Debate over a Crucial Program" (Healy) allows readers to find out more about the trends in consumer spending and to check the journalist's handling of an original source (see Fig. 1). This kind of link gives readers the opportunity to conduct their own evaluation of the evidence and verify the journalist's claims.

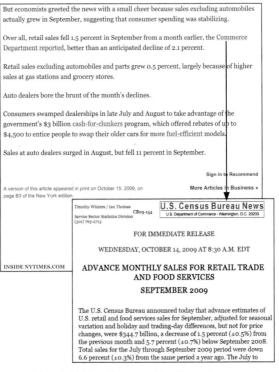

Fig. 1. Links embedded in online news articles allow readers to move from the main story to original sources, related articles, or background materials. The link in this online article (Healy) points to a government report, the original source of the author's data on consumer spending.

Jacobs 3

Links provide a kind of transparency impossible in print because they allow readers to see through online news to the "sources, disagreements, and the personal assumptions and values" that may have influenced a news story (Weinberger). The International Center for Media and the Public Agenda underscores the importance of news organizations letting "customers in on the often tightly held little secrets of journalism." To do so, they suggest, will lead to "accountability and accountability leads to credibility" ("Openness"). These tools alone don't guarantee that news producers will be responsible and trustworthy, but they encourage an open and transparent environment that benefits news consumers.

Not only has technology allowed readers to become more critical news consumers, but it also has helped some to become news producers. The Web gives ordinary people the power to report on the day's events. Anyone with an Internet connection can publish on blogs and Web sites, engage in online discussion forums, and contribute video and audio recordings. Citizen journalists with laptops, cell phones, and digital camcorders have become news producers alongside large news organizations.

Not everyone embraces the spread of unregulated news reporting online. Critics point out that citizen journalists are not necessarily trained to be fair or ethical, for example, nor are they subject to editorial oversight. Acknowledging that citizen reporting is more immediate and experimental, critics also question its accuracy and accountability: "While it has its place . . . it really isn't journalism at all, and it opens up information flow to the strong probability of fraud and abuse. . . . Information without journalistic standards is called gossip," writes David Hazinski in the *Atlanta Journal-Constitution* (23A). In his book *Losing the News*, media specialist Alex S. Jones argues that what passes for news today is in fact "pseudo news" and is "far less reliable" than traditional print news (27). Even a supporter like Gillmor is willing to agree that citizen journalists are "nonexperts," but he argues that they are "using technology to make a profound contribution, and a real difference" (140).

Citizen reporting made a difference in the wake of Hurricane Katrina in 2005. Armed with cell phones and laptops, regular citizens relayed critical news updates in a rapidly developing crisis, often before traditional journalists were even on the scene. In 2006, the enormous contributions of

*Jacobs clarifies key terms (*transparency *and* accountability*).*

Source is cited in MLA style.

Jacobs develops the thesis.

Opposing views are presented fairly.

Jacobs counters opposing arguments.

A vivid example helps Jacobs make his point.

citizen journalists were recognized when the New Orleans *Times-Picayune* received the Pulitzer Prize in public service for its online coverage—largely citizen-generated—of Hurricane Katrina. In recognizing the paper's "meritorious public service," the Pulitzer Prize board credited the newspaper's blog for "heroic, multi-faceted coverage of [the storm] and its aftermath" ("2006 Pulitzer"). Writing for the *Online Journalism Review*, Mark Glaser emphasizes the role that blog updates played in saving storm victims' lives. Further, he calls the *Times-Picayune*'s partnership with citizen journalists a "watershed for online journalism."

The Internet has enabled consumers to participate in a new way in reading, questioning, interpreting, and reporting the news. Decisions about appropriate content and coverage are no longer exclusively in the hands of news editors. Ordinary citizens now have a meaningful voice in the conversation—a hand in deciding what's "fit to print." Some skeptics worry about the apparent free-for-all and loss of tradition. But the expanding definition of news provides opportunities for consumers to be more engaged with events in their communities, their nations, and the world.

Jacobs uses specific evidence for support.

Conclusion echoes the thesis without dully repeating it.

Jacobs 5

Works Cited

Gillmor, Dan. *We the Media: Grassroots Journalism by the People, for the People*. Sebastopol: O'Reilly, 2006. Print.

Glaser, Mark. "NOLA.com Blogs and Forums Help Save Lives after Katrina." *OJR: The Online Journalism Review*. Knight Digital Media Center, 13 Sept. 2005. Web. 2 Mar. 2010.

Hazinski, David. "Unfettered 'Citizen Journalism' Too Risky." *Atlanta Journal-Constitution* 13 Dec. 2007: 23A. *General OneFile*. Web. 2 Mar. 2010.

Healy, Jack. "Window into Fed Debate over a Crucial Program." *New York Times*. New York Times, 14 Oct. 2009. Web. 4 Mar. 2010.

Jones, Alex S. *Losing the News: The Future of the News That Feeds Democracy*. New York: Oxford UP, 2009. Print.

"Openness and Accountability: A Study of Transparency in Global Media Outlets." *ICMPA: International Center for Media and the Public Agenda*. Intl. Center for Media and the Public Agenda, 2006. Web. 26 Feb. 2010.

"The 2006 Pulitzer Prize Winners: Public Service." *The Pulitzer Prizes*. Columbia U, n.d. Web. 2 Mar. 2010.

Weinberger, David. "Transparency Is the New Objectivity." *Joho the Blog*. David Weinberger, 19 July 2009. Web. 26 Feb. 2010.

Works cited page uses MLA style.

List is alphabetized by authors' last names (or by title when a work has no author).

Abbreviation "n.d." indicates that the online source has no update date.

A3 Evaluating arguments

In your reading and in your own writing, evaluate all arguments for logic and fairness. Many arguments can stand up to critical scrutiny. Sometimes, however, a line of argument that at first seems reasonable turns out to be illogical, unfair, or both.

A3-a Distinguish between reasonable and fallacious argumentative tactics.

A number of unreasonable argumentative tactics are known as *logical fallacies*. Most of the fallacies—such as hasty generalizations and false analogies—are misguided or dishonest uses of legitimate argumentative strategies. The examples in this section suggest when such strategies are reasonable and when they are not.

Generalizing (inductive reasoning)

Writers and thinkers generalize all the time. We look at a sample of data and conclude that data we have not observed will most likely conform to what we have seen. From a spoonful of soup, we conclude just how salty the whole bowl will be. After numerous unpleasant experiences with an airline, we decide to book future flights with a competitor.

When we draw a conclusion from an array of facts, we are engaged in inductive reasoning. Such reasoning deals in probability, not certainty. For a conclusion to be highly probable, it must be based on evidence that is sufficient, representative, and relevant. (See the chart on p. 94.)

The fallacy known as *hasty generalization* is a conclusion based on insufficient or unrepresentative evidence.

> **HASTY GENERALIZATION**
>
> In a single year, scores on standardized tests in California's public schools rose by ten points. Therefore, more children than ever are succeeding in America's public school systems.

Data from one state do not justify a conclusion about the whole United States.

A *stereotype* is a hasty generalization about a group. Here are a few examples.

STEREOTYPES

Women are bad bosses.

All politicians are corrupt.

Athletes are never strong students.

Stereotyping is common because of our tendency to perceive selectively. We tend to see what we want to see; we notice evidence confirming our already formed opinions and fail to notice evidence to the contrary. For example, if you have concluded that all politicians are corrupt, this stereotype will be confirmed by news reports of legislators being indicted — even though every day the media describe conscientious officials serving the public honestly and well.

> **Academic English**   Many hasty generalizations contain words such as *all*, *ever*, *always*, and *never*, when qualifiers such as *most*, *many*, *usually*, and *seldom* would be more accurate.

Drawing analogies

An analogy points out a similarity between two things that are otherwise different. Analogies can be an effective means of arguing a point. Our system of judicial decision making, or case law, which relies heavily on previous decisions, makes extensive use of reasoning by analogy. One lawyer may point out, for example, that specific facts or circumstances resemble those from a previous case and will thus argue for a similar result or decision. In response, the opposing lawyer may maintain that such facts or circumstances bear only a superficial resemblance to those in the previous case and that in legally relevant respects they are quite different and thus require a different result or decision.

It is not always easy to draw the line between a reasonable and an unreasonable analogy. At times, however, an analogy is clearly off base, in which case it is called a *false analogy*.

FALSE ANALOGY

If we can send a spacecraft to Pluto, we should be able to find a cure for the common cold.

The writer has falsely assumed that because two things are alike in one respect, they must be alike in others. Exploring the outer reaches of the solar system and finding a cure for the common cold are both scientific challenges, but the problems confronting medical researchers are quite different from those solved by space scientists.

Testing inductive reasoning

Though inductive reasoning leads to probable and not absolute truth, you can assess a conclusion's likely probability by asking three questions. This chart shows how to apply those questions to a sample conclusion based on a survey.

CONCLUSION The majority of students on our campus would volunteer at least five hours a week in a community organization if the school provided a placement service for volunteers.

EVIDENCE In a recent survey, 723 of 1,215 students questioned said they would volunteer at least five hours a week in a community organization if the school provided a placement service for volunteers.

1. Is the evidence sufficient?

   That depends. On a small campus (say, 3,000 students), the pool of students surveyed would be sufficient for market research, but on a large campus (say, 30,000), 1,215 students are only 4 percent of the population. If that 4 percent were known to be truly representative of the other 96 percent, however, even such a small sample would be sufficient (see question 2).

2. Is the evidence representative?

   The evidence is representative if those responding to the survey reflect the characteristics of the entire student population: age, sex, race, field of study, overall number of extracurricular commitments, and so on. If most of those surveyed are majors in a field like social work, however, the researchers would be wise to question the survey's conclusion.

3. Is the evidence relevant?

   Yes. The results of the survey are directly linked to the conclusion. Evidence based on a survey about the number of hours students work for pay, by contrast, would not be relevant because it would not be about *choosing to volunteer*.

Tracing causes and effects

Demonstrating a connection between causes and effects is rarely simple. For example, to explain why a chemistry course has a high failure rate, you would begin by listing possible causes: inadequate preparation of students, poor teaching, lack of qualified tutors, and so on. Next you would investigate each possible cause. Only after investigating the possible causes would you be able to weigh the relative impact of each cause and suggest appropriate remedies.

Because cause-and-effect reasoning is so complex, it is not surprising that writers frequently oversimplify it. In particular, writers sometimes assume that because one event follows another, the first is the cause of the second. This common fallacy is known as *post hoc*, from the Latin *post hoc, ergo propter hoc*, meaning "after this, therefore because of this."

> **POST HOC FALLACY**
>
> Since Governor Cho took office, unemployment of minorities in the state has decreased by 7 percent. Governor Cho should be applauded for reducing unemployment among minorities.

The writer must show that Governor Cho's policies are responsible for the decrease in unemployment; it is not enough to show that the decrease followed the governor's taking office.

Weighing options

Especially when reasoning about problems and solutions, writers must weigh options. To be fair, a writer should mention the full range of options, showing why one is superior to the others or might work well in combination with others.

It is unfair to suggest that there are only two alternatives when in fact there are more. When writers set up a false choice between their preferred option and one that is clearly unsatisfactory, they create an *either . . . or* fallacy.

> **EITHER . . . OR FALLACY**
>
> Our current war against drugs has not worked. Either we should legalize drugs or we should turn the drug war over to our armed forces and let them fight it.

Clearly there are other options, such as increased funding for drug abuse prevention and treatment.

Making assumptions

An assumption is a claim that is taken to be true—without the need of proof. Most arguments are based to some extent on assumptions, since writers rarely have the time and space to prove all the conceivable claims on which an argument is based. For example, someone arguing about the best means of limiting population growth in developing countries might well assume that the goal of limiting population growth is worthwhile. For most audiences, there would be no need to articulate this assumption or to defend it.

There is a danger, however, in failing to spell out and prove a claim that is clearly controversial. Consider the following short argument, in which a key claim is missing.

ARGUMENT WITH MISSING CLAIM

Violent crime is increasing. Therefore, we should vigorously enforce the death penalty.

The writer seems to be assuming that the death penalty deters violent criminals—and that most audiences will agree. The writer also assumes that the death penalty is a fair punishment for violent crimes. These are not safe assumptions; the writer will need to state and support both claims.

When a missing claim is an assertion that few would agree with, we say that a writer is guilty of a *non sequitur* (Latin for "it does not follow").

NON SEQUITUR

Leah loves good food; therefore, she will be an excellent chef.

Few people would agree with the missing claim—that lovers of good food always make excellent chefs.

Deducing conclusions (deductive reasoning)

When we deduce a conclusion, we—like Sherlock Holmes—put things together. We establish that a general principle is true, that a specific case is an example of that principle, and that therefore a particular conclusion about that case is a certainty. In real life, such absolute reasoning rarely happens. Approximations of it, however, sometimes occur.

Deductive reasoning can often be structured in a three-step argument called a *syllogism*. The three steps are the major premise, the minor premise, and the conclusion.

1. Anything that increases radiation in the environment is dangerous to public health. (Major premise)
2. Nuclear reactors increase radiation in the environment. (Minor premise)
3. Therefore, nuclear reactors are dangerous to public health. (Conclusion)

The major premise is a generalization. The minor premise is a specific case. The conclusion follows from applying the generalization to the specific case.

Deductive arguments break down if one of the premises is not true or if the conclusion does not logically follow from the premises. In the following argument, the major premise is very likely untrue.

UNTRUE PREMISE

The police do not give speeding tickets to people driving less than five miles per hour over the limit. Dominic is driving fifty-nine miles per hour in a fifty-five-mile-per-hour zone. Therefore, the police will not give Dominic a speeding ticket.

The conclusion is true only if the premises are true. If the police sometimes give speeding tickets for driving less than five miles per hour over the limit, Dominic cannot safely conclude that he will avoid a ticket.

In the following argument, both premises might be true, but the conclusion does not follow logically from them.

CONCLUSION DOES NOT FOLLOW

All members of our club ran in this year's Boston Marathon. Jay ran in this year's Boston Marathon. Therefore, Jay is a member of our club.

The fact that Jay ran the marathon is no guarantee that he is a member of the club. Presumably, many marathon runners are nonmembers.

Assuming that both premises are true, the following argument holds up.

CONCLUSION FOLLOWS

All members of our club ran in this year's Boston Marathon. Jay is a member of our club. Therefore, Jay ran in this year's Boston Marathon.

A3-b Distinguish between legitimate and unfair emotional appeals.

There is nothing wrong with appealing to readers' emotions. After all, many issues worth arguing about have an emotional as well as a logical dimension. Even the Greek logician Aristotle lists *pathos* (emotion) as a legitimate argumentative tactic. For example, in an essay criticizing big-box stores, writer Betsy Taylor has a good reason for tugging at readers' emotions: Her subject is the decline of city and town life. In her conclusion, Taylor appeals to readers' emotions by invoking their national pride.

LEGITIMATE EMOTIONAL APPEAL

Is it anti-American to be against having a retail giant set up shop in one's community? Some people would say so. On the other hand, if you board up Main Street, what's left of America?

As we all know, however, emotional appeals are frequently misused. Many of the arguments we see in the media, for instance, strive to win our sympathy rather than our intelligent agreement. A TV commercial suggesting that you will be thin and sexy if you drink a certain diet beverage is making a pitch to emotions. So is a political speech that recommends electing a candidate because he is a devoted husband and father who serves as a volunteer firefighter.

The following passage illustrates several types of unfair emotional appeals.

UNFAIR EMOTIONAL APPEALS

This progressive proposal to build a ski resort in the state park has been carefully researched by Western Trust, the largest bank in the state; furthermore, it is favored by a majority of the local merchants. The only opposition comes from narrow-minded, hippie environmentalists who care more about trees than they do about people; one of their leaders was actually arrested for disturbing the peace several years ago.

Words with strong positive or negative connotations, such as *progressive* and *hippie,* are examples of *biased language*. Attacking the people who hold a belief (environmentalists) rather than refuting their argument is called *ad hominem*, a Latin term meaning "to the man." Associating a prestigious name (Western Trust) with the writer's side is called *transfer*. Claiming that an idea should be accepted because a large number of people (the majority of merchants) are in favor is called the *bandwagon appeal*. Bringing in irrelevant issues (the arrest) is a *red herring*, named after a trick used in fox hunts to mislead the dogs by dragging a smelly fish across the trail.

A3-c Judge how fairly a writer handles opposing views.

The way in which a writer deals with opposing views is revealing. Some writers address the arguments of the opposition fairly, conceding points when necessary and countering others, all in a civil spirit. Other writers will do almost anything to win an argument: either ignoring opposing views altogether or misrepresenting such views and attacking their proponents.

In your own writing, you build credibility by addressing opposing arguments fairly. (See also A2-f.) In your reading, you can assess the credibility of your sources by looking at how they deal with views not in agreement with their own.

Describing the views of others

Writers and politicians often deliberately misrepresent the views of others. One way they do this is by setting up a "straw man," a character so weak that he is easily knocked down. The *straw man* fallacy consists of an oversimplification or outright distortion of opposing views. For example, in a California debate over attempts to control the mountain lion population, pro-lion groups characterized their opponents as trophy hunters bent on shooting harmless lions and sticking them on the walls of their dens. In truth, such hunters were only one faction of those who saw a need to control the lion population.

During the District of Columbia's struggle for voting representation, some politicians set up a straw man, as shown in the following example.

STRAW MAN FALLACY

Washington, DC, residents are lobbying for statehood. Giving a city such as the District of Columbia the status of a state would be unfair.

The straw man wanted statehood. In fact, most District citizens lobbied for voting representation in any form, not necessarily through statehood.

Quoting opposing views

Writers often quote the words of writers who hold opposing views. In general, this is a good idea, for it assures some level of fairness and accuracy. At times, though, both the fairness and the accuracy are an illusion.

A source may be misrepresented when it is quoted out of context. All quotations are to some extent taken out of context, but a fair writer will explain the context to readers. To select a provocative sentence from a source and to ignore the more moderate sentences surrounding it is both unfair and misleading. Sometimes a writer deliberately distorts a source through the device of ellipsis dots. Ellipsis dots tell readers that words have been omitted from the original source. When those words are crucial to an author's meaning, omitting them is obviously unfair. (See P6-c.)

ORIGINAL SOURCE

Johnson's *History of the American West* is riddled with inaccuracies and astonishing in its blatantly racist description of the Indian wars.   —B. R., reviewer

MISLEADING QUOTATION

According to B. R., Johnson's *History of the American West* is "astonishing in its . . . description of the Indian wars."

A4 Writing in the disciplines

College courses expose you to the thinking of scholars in many disciplines, such as the humanities (literature, music, art), the social sciences (psychology, anthropology, sociology), the sciences (biology, physics, chemistry), and the professions and applied sciences (nursing, education, forestry). Writing in any discipline provides opportunities to practice the methods used by scholars in these fields and to enter into their debates. Each field has its own questions, evidence, language, and conventions, but all disciplines share certain expectations for good writing.

A4-a Find commonalities across disciplines.

A good paper in any field needs to communicate a writer's purpose to an audience and to explore an engaging question about a subject. Effective writers make an argument and support their claims with evidence. Writers in most fields need to show the thesis they're developing (or, in the sciences, the hypothesis they're testing) and counter opposition from other writers. All disciplines require writers to document where they found their evidence and from whom they borrowed ideas.

A4-b Recognize the questions writers in a discipline ask.

Disciplines are characterized by the kinds of questions their scholars attempt to answer. Historians, for example, often ask questions about the causes and effects of events and about the connections between current and past events. One way to understand how disciplines ask different questions is to look at assignments on the same subject in

Writing advice for all your college courses

When writing for any course in any discipline, keeping the following steps in mind can help you write a strong academic paper. Consult sections of this handbook that are appropriate to your assignment.

- Understand the writing assignment: C1-b, A4-f
- Determine and communicate a purpose: C1-a, C1-b
- Consider your audience: C1-a, C1-b
- Ask questions appropriate to the field: A4-b
- Formulate a thesis: C2-a, MLA-1a, APA-1a, CMS-1a
- Determine what types of evidence to gather: A4-c, C5-d
- Conduct research: R1
- Support your claim: A2-d, A2-e, MLA-1c, APA-1c, CMS-1c
- Counter opposing arguments or objections: A2-f
- Identify the appropriate documentation style: A4-e, R4
- Integrate sources: MLA-3, APA-3, CMS-3
- Document your sources: MLA-4, APA-4, CMS-4
- Design and format your document: C5, MLA-5a, APA-5a, CMS-5a

various fields. In many disciplines, for example, writers might discuss disasters. The following are some questions that writers in different fields might ask about this subject.

EDUCATION	Should the elementary school curriculum teach students how to cope in disasters?
FILM	How has the disaster film genre changed since the advent of computer-generated imagery (CGI) in the early 1970s?
HISTORY	How did the formation of the American Red Cross reshape disaster relief in the United States?
ENGINEERING	What recent innovations in levee design are most promising?
PSYCHOLOGY	What are the most effective ways to identify and treat post-traumatic stress disorder (PTSD) in disaster survivors?

The questions you ask in any discipline will form the basis of the thesis for your paper. The questions themselves don't communicate a central idea, but they may lead you to one. For an education paper, for example, you might begin with the question "Should the elementary school curriculum teach students how to cope in disasters?" After considering the issues involved, you might draft the following working thesis.

> School systems should adopt age-appropriate curriculum units that introduce children to the risks of natural and human-made disasters and that allow children to practice coping strategies.

Whenever you write for a college course, try to determine the kinds of questions scholars in the field might ask about a topic. You can find clues in assigned readings, lecture or discussion topics, e-mail discussion groups, and the paper assignment itself.

A4-c Understand the kinds of evidence writers in a discipline use.

Regardless of the discipline in which you're writing, you must support any claims you make with evidence — facts, statistics, examples and illustrations, visuals, expert opinion, and so on.

The kinds of evidence used in different disciplines commonly overlap. Students of geography, media studies, and political science, for example, might use census data to explore different topics. The evidence that one discipline values, however, might not be sufficient to support an interpretation or a conclusion in another field. You might use anecdotes or interviews in an anthropology paper, for example, but such evidence would be irrelevant in a biology lab report. The chart on page 103 lists the kinds of evidence typically used in various disciplines.

A4-d Become familiar with a discipline's language conventions.

Every discipline has a specialized vocabulary. As you read the articles and books in a field, you'll notice certain words and phrases that come up repeatedly. Sociologists, for example, use terms such as *independent variables*, *political opportunity resources*, and *dyads* to describe social phenomena; computer scientists might refer to *algorithm design* and *loop invariants* to describe programming methods. Practitioners in health fields such as nursing use terms like *treatment plan* and *systemic assessment* to describe patient care. Use discipline-specific terms only when you are certain that you and your readers fully understand their meaning.

In addition to vocabulary, many fields of study have developed specialized conventions for point of view and verb tense. See the chart on page 104.

Evidence typically used in various disciplines

Humanities: Literature, art, film, music, philosophy

- Passages of text or lines of a poem
- Details from an image, a film, or a work of art
- Passages of a musical composition
- Critical essays that analyze original works

Humanities: History

- Primary sources such as photographs, letters, maps, and government documents
- Scholarly books and articles that interpret evidence

Social sciences: Psychology, sociology, political science, anthropology

- Data from original experiments
- Results of field research such as interviews, observations, or surveys
- Statistics from government agencies
- Scholarly books and articles that interpret data from original experiments and from other researchers' studies

Sciences: Biology, chemistry, physics

- Data from original experiments
- Scholarly articles that report findings from experiments

A4-e Use a discipline's preferred citation style.

In any discipline, you must give credit to those whose ideas or words you have borrowed. Avoid plagiarism by citing sources honestly and accurately (see R3).

While all disciplines emphasize careful documentation, each follows a particular system of citation that its members have agreed on. Writers in the humanities usually use the system established by the Modern Language Association (MLA). Scholars in some social sciences, such as psychology and anthropology, follow the style guidelines of the American Psychological Association (APA); scholars in history and some humanities typically follow *The Chicago Manual of Style*. For guidance on using the MLA, APA, or *Chicago* (CMS) format, see MLA-4, APA-4, or CMS-4, respectively. (For CSE [Council of Science Editors] style, see hackerhandbooks.com/resdoc.)

Point of view and verb tense in academic writing

Point of view

- Writers of analytical or research essays in the humanities usually use the third-person point of view: *Austen presents . . .* or *Castel describes the battle as. . . .*

- Scientists and most social scientists, who depend on quantitative research to present findings, tend to use the third-person point of view: *The results indicated. . . .*

- Writers in the humanities and in some social sciences occasionally use the first person in discussing their own experience or in writing a personal narrative: *After spending two years interviewing families affected by the war, I began to understand that . . .* or *Every July as we approached the Cape Cod Canal, we could sense. . . .*

Present or past tense

- Literature scholars use the present tense to discuss a text: *Hughes effectively dramatizes different views of minority assertiveness.* (See MLA-3.)

- Science and social science writers use the past tense to describe experiments and the present tense to discuss the findings: *In 2003, Berkowitz released the first double-blind placebo study. . . . These results paint a murky picture.* (See APA-3.)

- Writers in history use the present tense or the present perfect tense to discuss a text: *Shelby Foote describes the scene like this . . .* or *Shelby Foote has described the scene like this. . . .* (See CMS-3.)

A4-f Understand writing assignments in the disciplines.

When you are asked to write in a specific discipline, become familiar with the distinctive features of the writing in that discipline. Then read the assignment carefully and identify the purpose of the assignment and the types of evidence you are expected to use.

On the following pages are examples of assignments in four disciplines—psychology, business, biology, and nursing—along with excerpts from student papers that were written in response to the assignments.

MODELS　hackerhandbooks.com/writersref
> Model papers > APA literature review: Charat
> APA business proposal: Ratajczak
> CSE laboratory report: Johnson and Arnold
> APA nursing practice paper: Riss

Psychology

ASSIGNMENT: LITERATURE REVIEW

```
       ┌──────── 1 ────────┐      ┌─── 2 ───┐
```
Write a literature review in which you report on and
```
┌── 2 ──┐   ┌──────── 3 ────────┐    ┌──────── 1 ────────┐
```
evaluate the published research on a behavioral disorder.

1 Key terms
2 Purpose: to report on and evaluate a body of evidence
3 Evidence: research of other psychologists

ADHD IN BOYS VS. GIRLS   3

Always Out of Their Seats (and Fighting):

Why Are Boys Diagnosed with ADHD More Often Than Girls?

Attention deficit hyperactivity disorder (ADHD) is a commonly

diagnosed disorder in children that affects social, academic, or occupational

functioning. As the name suggests, its hallmark characteristics are

hyperactivity and lack of attention as well as impulsive behavior. For

decades, studies have focused on the causes, expression, prevalence, and

outcome of the disorder, but until recently very little research investigated

gender differences. In fact, until the early 1990s most research focused

exclusively on boys (Brown, Madan-Swain, & Baldwin, 1991), perhaps

because many more boys than girls are diagnosed with ADHD. Researchers

have speculated on the possible explanations for the disparity, citing

reasons such as true sex differences in the manifestation of the disorder's

symptoms, gender biases in those who refer children to clinicians, and

possibly even the diagnostic procedures themselves (Gaub & Carlson, 1997).

But the most persuasive reason is that ADHD is often a comorbid

condition—that is, it coexists with other behavior disorders that are not

diagnosed properly and that do exhibit gender differences.

It has been suggested that in the United States children are often

misdiagnosed as having ADHD when they actually suffer from a behavior

disorder such as conduct disorder (CD) or a combination of ADHD and

another behavior disorder (Disney, Elkins, McGue, & Iancono, 1999;

Lilienfeld & Waldman, 1990). Conduct disorder is characterized by negative

and criminal behavior in children and is highly correlated with adult

diagnoses of antisocial personality disorder (ASPD). This paper first

considers research that has dealt only with gender difference in the

Marginal annotations:

Background and explanation of writer's purpose.

Evidence from research the writer has reviewed.

APA citations and specialized language (*ADHD, comorbid*).

Thesis: writer's argument.

Two sources in one parenthetical citation are separated by a semicolon.

Marginal annotations indicate appropriate formatting and effective writing.

Business

ASSIGNMENT: PROPOSAL

[—— 2 ——] [— 1 —] [———— 1 ————]
Write a proposal, as a memo, for improving or adding a service
[—— 2 ——]
at a company where you have worked. Address the pros and
[—— 3 ——] [— 3 —]
cons of your proposal; draw on relevant studies, research, and
[—— 3 ——]
your knowledge of the company.

1 Key terms
2 Purpose: to analyze certain evidence and make a proposal based on that analysis
3 Appropriate evidence: relevant studies, research, personal experience

---

MEMORANDUM

To: Jay Crosson, Senior Vice President, Human Resources
From: Kelly Ratajczak, Intern, Purchasing Department
Subject: Proposal to Add a Wellness Program
Date: April 24, 2009

Writer's main idea.

Health care costs are rising. In the long run, implementing a wellness program in our corporate culture will decrease the company's health care costs.

Data from recent study as support for claim.

APA citation style, typical in business.

Business terms familiar to readers (costs, productivity, absenteeism).

Research indicates that nearly 70% of health care costs are from common illnesses related to high blood pressure, overweight, lack of exercise, high cholesterol, stress, poor nutrition, and other preventable health issues (Hall, 2006). Health care costs are a major expense for most businesses, and they do not reflect costs due to the loss of productivity or absenteeism. A wellness program would address most, if not all, of these health care issues and related costs.

Headings define sections of proposal.

Benefits of Healthier Employees

Not only would a wellness program substantially reduce costs associated with employee health care, but our company would prosper through many other benefits. Businesses that have wellness programs show a lower cost in production, fewer sick days, and healthier employees ("Workplace Health," 2006). Our healthier employees will help to cut not only our production and absenteeism costs but also potential costs such as higher

Biology

ASSIGNMENT: LABORATORY REPORT

Write a report on an experiment you conduct on the distribution pattern of a plant species indigenous to the Northeast. Describe your methods for collecting data and interpret your experiment's results.

1 Key terms
2 Purpose: to describe and interpret the results of an experiment
3 Evidence: data collected during the experiment

Distribution Pattern of Dandelion 1

Distribution Pattern of Dandelion (*Taraxacum officinale*)
on an Abandoned Golf Course

ABSTRACT

This paper reports our study of the distribution pattern of the common dandelion (*Taraxacum officinale*) on an abandoned golf course in Hilton, NY, on 10 July 2005. An area of 6 ha was sampled with 111 randomly placed 1×1 m^2 quadrats. The dandelion count from each quadrat was used to test observed frequencies against expected frequencies based on a hypothesized random distribution. [Abstract continues.]

INTRODUCTION

Theoretically, plants of a particular species may be aggregated, random, or uniformly distributed in space [1]. The distribution type may be determined by many factors, such as availability of nutrients, competition, distance of seed dispersal, and mode of reproduction [2].

The purpose of this study was to determine if the distribution pattern of the common dandelion (*Taraxacum officinale*) on an abandoned golf course was aggregated, random, or uniform.

METHODS

The study site was an abandoned golf course in Hilton, NY. The vegetation was predominantly grasses, along with dandelions, broad-leaf plantain (*Plantago major*), and bird's-eye speedwell (*Veronica chamaedrys*). We sampled an area of approximately 6 ha on 10 July 2005, approximately two weeks after the golf course had been mowed.

CSE style, typical in sciences.

Abstract: an overview of hypothesis, experiment, and results.

Specialized language (*aggregated, random, uniformly distributed*).

Introduction: context and purpose of experiment. Instead of a thesis in the introduction, a lab report interprets the data in a later Discussion section.

Scientific names for plant species.

Nursing

ASSIGNMENT: NURSING PRACTICE PAPER

1 —— 2 —— 1 ——

Write a client history, a nursing diagnosis, recommendations

—— 2 ——   —— 1 ——

for care, your rationales, and expected and actual outcomes.

—— 3 ——   —— 3 ——

Use interview notes, the client's health records, and relevant

—— 3 ——

research findings.

1   Key terms
2   Purpose: to provide client history, diagnosis, recommendations, and outcomes
3   Evidence: interviews, health records, and research findings

---

ALL AND HTN IN ONE CLIENT   1

Acute Lymphoblastic Leukemia and Hypertension in One Client:

A Nursing Practice Paper

Physical History

Evidence from client's medical chart for overall assessment.

E.B. is a 16-year-old white male 5'10" tall weighing 190 lb. He was admitted to the hospital on April 14, 2006, due to decreased platelets and a need for a PRBC transfusion. He was diagnosed in October 2005 with T-cell acute lymphoblastic leukemia (ALL), after a 2-week period of decreased energy, decreased oral intake, easy bruising, and petechia. The client had experienced a 20-lb weight loss in the previous 6 months. At the time of diagnosis, his CBC showed a WBC count of 32, an H & H of 13/38, and a platelet count of 34,000. His initial chest X-ray showed an anterior

Specialized nursing language (echocardiogram, chemotherapy, and so on).

mediastinal mass. Echocardiogram showed a structurally normal heart. He began induction chemotherapy on October 12, 2005, receiving vincristine, 6-mercaptopurine, doxorubicin, intrathecal methotrexate, and then high-dose methotrexate per protocol. During his hospital stay, he

Instead of a thesis, or main claim, the writer gives a diagnosis, recommendations for care, and expected outcomes, all supported by evidence from observations and client records.

required packed red cells and platelets on two different occasions. He was diagnosed with hypertension (HTN) due to systolic blood pressure readings consistently ranging between 130s and 150s and was started on nifedipine. E.B. has a history of mild ADHD, migraines, and deep vein thrombosis (DVT). He has tolerated the induction and consolidation phases of chemotherapy well and is now in the maintenance phase, in which he receives a daily dose of mercaptopurine, weekly doses of methotrexate, and intermittent doses of steroids.

S1 Parallelism

If two or more ideas are parallel, they are easier to grasp when expressed in parallel grammatical form. Single words should be balanced with single words, phrases with phrases, clauses with clauses. In headings and lists, aim for as much parallelism as the content allows. (See C5-b and C5-c.) Writers often use parallelism to create emphasis. (See p. 134.)

A kiss can be a comma, a question mark, or an exclamation point.

—Mistinguett

This novel is not to be tossed lightly aside, but to be hurled with great force.

—Dorothy Parker

In matters of principle, stand like a rock; in matters of taste, swim with the current.

—Thomas Jefferson

S1-a Balance parallel ideas in a series.

Readers expect items in a series to appear in parallel grammatical form. When one or more of the items violate readers' expectations, a sentence will be needlessly awkward.

▶ Children who study music also learn confidence, discipline, and creativity.
~~they are creative.~~
^

The revision presents all the items in the series as nouns: *confidence, discipline,* and *creativity.*

▶ Impressionist painters believed in focusing on ordinary subjects, capturing the effects of light on those subjects, and ~~to use~~ short
using
^
brushstrokes.

The revision uses *-ing* forms for all the items in the series: *focusing, capturing,* and *using.*

▶ **Racing to get to work on time, Sam drove down the middle of the**
ignored
road, ran one red light, and ~~two stop signs.~~
^

The revision adds a verb to make the three items parallel: *drove, ran,* and
ignored.

S1-b Balance parallel ideas presented as pairs.

When pairing ideas, underscore their connection by expressing them
in similar grammatical form. Paired ideas are usually connected in
one of these ways:

- with a coordinating conjunction such as *and, but,* or *or*
- with a pair of correlative conjunctions such as *either . . . or*
  or *not only . . . but also*
- with a word introducing a comparison, usually *than* or *as*

Parallel ideas linked with coordinating conjunctions

Coordinating conjunctions (*and, but, or, nor, for, so,* and *yet*) link
ideas of equal importance. When those ideas are closely parallel in
content, they should be expressed in parallel grammatical form.

▶ **Emily Dickinson's poetry features the use of dashes and**
the capitalization of
~~capitalizing~~ common words.
^

The revision balances the nouns *use* and *capitalization.*

▶ **Many states are reducing property taxes for home owners**
extending
and ~~extend~~ financial aid in the form of tax credits to renters.
^

The revision balances the verb *reducing* with the verb *extending.*

Parallel ideas linked with correlative conjunctions

Correlative conjunctions come in pairs: *either . . . or, neither . . . nor,
not only . . . but also, both . . . and, whether . . . or.* Make sure that the
grammatical structure following the second half of the pair is the
same as that following the first half.

▶ Thomas Edison was not only a prolific inventor but also ~~was~~

a successful entrepreneur.

The words *a prolific inventor* immediately follow *not only*, so *a successful entrepreneur* should follow *but also*. Repeating *was* after *also* creates an unbalanced effect.

to
▶ The clerk told me either to change my flight or ^ take the train.

To change, which follows *either*, should be balanced with *to take*, which follows *or*.

Comparisons linked with *than* or *as*

In comparisons linked with *than* or *as*, the elements being compared should be expressed in parallel grammatical structure.

to ground
▶ It is easier to speak in abstractions than ~~grounding~~ ^ one's

thoughts in reality.

To speak is balanced with *to ground*.

writing
▶ In Pueblo culture, according to Silko, ~~to write~~ ^ down the

stories of a tribe is not the same as "keeping track of all the

stories" (290).

Writing with sources

MLA-style citation

When you are quoting from a source, parallel grammatical structure—such as *writing . . . keeping*—helps create continuity between your sentence and the words from the source.

Comparisons should also be logical and grammatically complete. (See S2-c.)

S1-c Repeat function words to clarify parallels.

Function words such as prepositions (*by*, *to*) and subordinating conjunctions (*that*, *because*) signal the grammatical nature of the word groups to follow. Although you can sometimes omit such function words, be sure to include them whenever they signal parallel structures that readers might otherwise miss.

▶ Our study revealed that left-handed students were more likely
that
to have trouble with classroom desks and rearranging desks
^
for exam periods was useful.

A second subordinating conjunction helps readers sort out the two parallel ideas: *that* left-handed students have trouble with classroom desks and *that* rearranging desks was useful.

≡ **S2** Needed words

Sometimes writers leave out words intentionally, and the meaning of the sentence is not affected. But leaving out words can occasionally cause confusion for readers or make the sentence ungrammatical. Readers need to see at a glance how the parts of a sentence are connected.

> **ESL**   Languages sometimes differ in the need for certain words. In particular, be alert for missing articles, verbs, subjects, or expletives. See M2, M3-a, and M3-b.

S2-a Add words needed to complete compound structures.

In compound structures, words are often left out for economy: *Tom is a man who means what he says and* [who] *says what he means.* Such omissions are acceptable as long as the omitted words are common to both parts of the compound structure.

If a sentence defies grammar or idiom because an omitted word is not common to both parts of the compound structure, the simplest solution is to put the word back in.

▶ Successful advertisers target customers whom they identify through
who
demographic research or have purchased their product in the past.
^
The word *who* must be included because *whom . . . have purchased* is not grammatically correct.

accepted
▶ Mayor Davis never has and never will accept a bribe.
^
Has . . . accept is not grammatically correct.

PRACTICE   hackerhandbooks.com/writersref
  > Sentence style > S2–2 to S2–4

compounds • verbs • prepositions •
who • that • comparisons
S2-c   115

> *in*
▶ Many South Pacific islanders still believe and live by ancient laws.
>   ^

Believe . . . by is not idiomatic in English. (For a list of common idioms, see W5-d.)

NOTE: Even when the omitted word is common to both parts of the compound structure, occasionally it must be repeated to avoid ambiguity.

My favorite *professor* and *mentor* influenced my choice of a career. [Professor and mentor are the same person.]

My favorite *professor* and *my mentor* influenced my choice of a career. [Professor and mentor are two different people; *my* must be repeated.]

S2-b Add the word *that* if there is any danger of misreading without it.

If there is no danger of misreading, the word *that* may be omitted when it introduces a subordinate clause. *The value of a principle is the number of things [that] it will explain.* Occasionally, however, a sentence might be misread without *that.*

▶ In his famous obedience experiments, psychologist Stanley
>   *that*
Milgram discovered ordinary people were willing to inflict
>   ^

physical pain on strangers.

Milgram didn't discover ordinary people; he discovered that ordinary people were willing to inflict pain on strangers. The word *that* tells readers to expect a clause, not just *ordinary people*, as the direct object of *discovered.*

S2-c Add words needed to make comparisons logical and complete.

Comparisons should be made between items that are alike. To compare unlike items is illogical and distracting.

▶ The forests of North America are much more extensive than
> *those of*
Europe.
> ^

Forests must be compared with forests, not with all of Europe.

► ~~The death rate of~~ *I*nfantry soldiers in the Vietnam War ~~was~~
at a   rate   *died*
much higher than the other combat troops.

The death rate cannot logically be compared with troops. The writer could revise the sentence by inserting *that of* after *than*, but the revision shown here is more concise.

► Some say that Ella Fitzgerald's renditions of Cole Porter's songs
are better than any other ~~singer.~~ *singer's.*

Ella Fitzgerald's renditions cannot logically be compared with a singer. The revision uses the possessive form *singer's*, with the word *renditions* being implied.

Sometimes the word *other* must be inserted to make a comparison logical.

► Jupiter is larger than any *other* planet in our solar system.

Jupiter is a planet, and it cannot be larger than itself.

Sometimes the word *as* must be inserted to make a comparison grammatically complete.

► The city of Lowell is as old, *as* if not older than, the neighboring city of Lawrence.

The construction *as old* is not complete without a second *as: as old as . . . the neighboring city of Lawrence.*

Comparisons should be complete enough to ensure clarity. The reader should understand what is being compared.

INCOMPLETE   Brand X is less salty.

COMPLETE   Brand X is less salty than Brand Y.

Finally, comparisons should leave no ambiguity for readers. If more than one interpretation is possible, revise the sentence to state clearly which interpretation you intend. In the following ambiguous sentence, two interpretations are possible.

AMBIGUOUS   Ken helped me more than my roommate.

CLEAR   Ken helped me more than *he helped* my roommate.

CLEAR   Ken helped me more than my roommate *did*.

S2-d **Add the articles *a*, *an*, and *the* where necessary for grammatical completeness.**

It is not always necessary to repeat articles with paired items: *We bought a computer and printer.* However, if one of the items requires *a* and the other requires *an*, both articles must be included.

▶ We bought a computer and ^an^ antivirus program.

    Articles are sometimes omitted in recipes and other instructions that are meant to be followed while they are being read. In nearly all other forms of writing, whether formal or informal, such omissions are inappropriate.

> **ESL**   Choosing and using articles can be challenging for multilingual writers. See M2.

S3 Problems with modifiers

Modifiers, whether they are single words, phrases, or clauses, should point clearly to the words they modify. As a rule, related words should be kept together.

S3-a **Put limiting modifiers in front of the words they modify.**

Limiting modifiers such as *only*, *even*, *almost*, *nearly*, and *just* should appear in front of a verb only if they modify the verb: *At first, I couldn't even touch my toes, much less grasp them.* If modifiers limit the meaning of some other word in the sentence, they should be placed in front of that word.

▶ St. Vitus Cathedral, commissioned by Charles IV in the
                                                almost
    mid-fourteenth century, ~~almost~~ ^ took six centuries to complete.

    Almost limits the meaning of *six centuries*, not *took*.

> *just*
> ▶ If you ~~just~~ interview chemistry majors, your picture of the
>   ^
> student body's response to the new grading policies will be
>
> incomplete.

The adverb *just* limits the meaning of *chemistry majors*, not *interview*.

When the limiting modifier *not* is misplaced, the sentence usually suggests a meaning the writer did not intend.

> *not*
> ▶ In the United States in 1860, all black southerners were ~~not~~ slaves.
>   ^
> The original sentence says that no black southerners were slaves. The revision makes the writer's real meaning clear: Some (but not all) black southerners were slaves.

S3-b Place phrases and clauses so that readers can see at a glance what they modify.

Although phrases and clauses can appear at some distance from the words they modify, make sure your meaning is clear. When phrases or clauses are oddly placed, absurd misreadings can result.

MISPLACED   The soccer player returned to the clinic where he had undergone emergency surgery in 2009 in a limousine sent by Adidas.

REVISED   Traveling in a limousine sent by Adidas, the soccer player returned to the clinic where he had undergone emergency surgery in 2009.

The revision corrects the false impression that the soccer player underwent emergency surgery in a limousine.

> *On the walls*
> ▶ ~~There~~ are many pictures of comedians who have performed at
>   ^
> Gavin's. ~~on the walls.~~
>   ^
> The comedians weren't performing on the walls; the pictures were on the walls.

> *170-pound,*
> ▶ The robber was described as a six-foot-tall man with a heavy
>   ^
> mustache. ~~weighing 170 pounds.~~
>   ^
> The robber, not the mustache, weighed 170 pounds.

Occasionally the placement of a modifier leads to an ambiguity — a squinting modifier. In such a case, two revisions will be possible, depending on the writer's intended meaning.

AMBIGUOUS   The exchange students we met for coffee occasionally questioned us about our latest slang.

CLEAR   The exchange students we occasionally met for coffee questioned us about our latest slang.

CLEAR   The exchange students we met for coffee questioned us occasionally about our latest slang.

In the original version, it was not clear whether the meeting or the questioning happened occasionally. Both revisions eliminate the ambiguity.

S3-c Move awkwardly placed modifiers.

As a rule, a sentence should flow from subject to verb to object, without lengthy detours along the way. When a long adverbial word group separates a subject from its verb, a verb from its object, or a helping verb from its main verb, the result is often awkward.

▶ ~~Hong Kong,~~ ^A^ after more than 150 years of British rule, ^Hong Kong^ was

transferred back to Chinese control in 1997.

There is no reason to separate the subject, *Hong Kong*, from the verb, *was transferred*, with a long phrase.

▶ ~~Jeffrey Meyers discusses,~~ ^I^ in his biography of F. Scott

Fitzgerald, the writer's "fascination with the superiority,
Jeffrey Meyers discusses

the selfishness, and the emptiness of the rich" (166).

Writing
with
sources

MLA-style
citation

When you quote from a source, the phrase or clause that you use to introduce the source should be as straightforward as possible. There is no reason to separate the verb, *discusses*, from its object, *fascination*, with two prepositional phrases.

ESL   English does not allow an adverb to appear between a verb and its object. See M3-f.

▶ Yolanda lifted ~~easily~~ the fifty-pound weight.
easily

S3-d Avoid split infinitives when they are awkward.

An infinitive consists of *to* plus the base form of a verb: *to think, to run, to dance.* When a modifier appears between *to* and the verb, an infinitive is said to be "split": *to carefully balance, to completely understand.*

When a long word or a phrase appears between the parts of the infinitive, the result is usually awkward.

▶ ~~The~~ patient should try to ~~if possible~~ avoid putting weight on
  If possible, the
  his foot.

Attempts to avoid split infinitives can result in equally awkward sentences. When alternative phrasing sounds unnatural, most experts allow—and even encourage—splitting the infinitive.

AWKWARD   We decided actually to enforce the law.

BETTER   We decided to actually enforce the law.

At times, neither the split infinitive nor its alternative sounds particularly awkward. In such situations, it is usually better to unsplit the infinitive, especially in formal writing.

▶ Nursing students learn to ~~accurately~~ record a patient's vital
  signs/
        accurately.

S3-e Repair dangling modifiers.

A dangling modifier fails to refer logically to any word in the sentence. Dangling modifiers are easy to repair, but they can be hard to recognize, especially in your own writing.

Recognizing dangling modifiers

Dangling modifiers are usually word groups (such as verbal phrases) that suggest but do not name an actor. When a sentence opens with such a modifier, readers expect the subject of the next clause to name the actor. If it doesn't, the modifier dangles.

▶ Understanding the need to create checks and balances on power,
  the framers of
  the Constitution divided the government into three branches.

The framers of the Constitution (not the document itself) understood the need for checks and balances.

▶ After completing seminary training, ~~women's~~ *women have often been denied* access to the

priesthood. ~~has often been denied.~~

Women (not their access to the priesthood) complete the training.

The following sentences illustrate four common kinds of dangling modifiers.

DANGLING   *Deciding to join the navy*, the recruiter enthusiastically pumped Joe's hand. [Participial phrase]

DANGLING   *Upon entering the doctor's office*, a skeleton caught my attention. [Preposition followed by a gerund phrase]

DANGLING   *To satisfy her mother*, the piano had to be practiced every day. [Infinitive phrase]

DANGLING   *Though not eligible for the clinical trial*, the doctor was willing to prescribe the drug for Ethan on compassionate grounds. [Elliptical clause with an understood subject and verb]

These dangling modifiers falsely suggest that the recruiter decided to join the navy, that the skeleton entered the doctor's office, that the piano intended to satisfy the mother, and that the doctor was not eligible for the clinical trial.

Although most readers will understand the writer's intended meaning in such sentences, the inadvertent humor can be distracting.

Repairing dangling modifiers

To repair a dangling modifier, you can revise the sentence in one of two ways:

- Name the actor in the subject of the sentence.
- Name the actor in the modifier.

Depending on your sentence, one of these revision strategies may be more appropriate than the other.

Checking for dangling modifiers

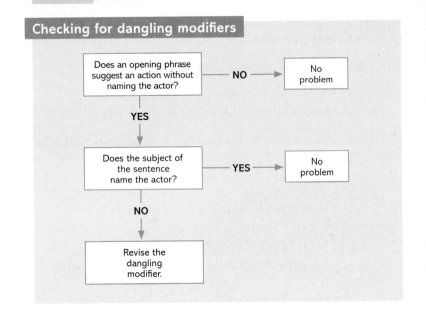

ACTOR NAMED IN SUBJECT

                           I noticed
▶ Upon entering the doctor's office, a skeleton. ~~caught my attention.~~
                     ^   ^

                      Jing-mei had to practice
▶ To satisfy her mother, the piano ~~had to be practiced~~ every day.
                          ^

ACTOR NAMED IN MODIFIER

When Joe decided
▶ ~~Deciding~~ to join the navy, the recruiter enthusiastically pumped
 ^
his
~~Joe's~~ hand.
^

        Ethan was
▶ Though not eligible for the clinical trial, the doctor was willing to
        ^   *him*
prescribe the drug for ~~Ethan~~ on compassionate grounds.
                     ^

NOTE: You cannot repair a dangling modifier just by moving it. Consider, for example, the sentence about the skeleton. If you put the modifier at the end of the sentence (*A skeleton caught my attention upon entering the doctor's office*), you are still suggesting—absurdly, of course—that the skeleton entered the office. The only way to avoid the problem is to put the word *I* in the sentence, either as the subject or in the modifier.

> *I noticed*
> ▶ Upon entering the doctor's office, a skeleton. ~~caught my attention.~~
>   ^   ^

> *As I entered*
> ▶ ~~Upon entering~~ the doctor's office, a skeleton caught my attention.
>   ^

S4 Shifts

The following sections can help you avoid unnecessary shifts that might distract or confuse your readers: shifts in point of view, in verb tense, in mood or voice, or from indirect to direct questions or quotations.

S4-a Make the point of view consistent in person and number.

The point of view of a piece of writing is the perspective from which it is written: first person (*I* or *we*), second person (*you*), or third person (*he, she, it, one, they*, or any noun).

The *I* (or *we*) point of view, which emphasizes the writer, is a good choice for informal letters and writing based primarily on personal experience. The *you* point of view, which emphasizes the reader, works well for giving advice or explaining how to do something. The third-person point of view, which emphasizes the subject, is appropriate in formal academic and professional writing.

Writers who are having difficulty settling on an appropriate point of view sometimes shift confusingly from one to another. The solution is to choose a suitable perspective and then stay with it.

> ▶ Our class practiced rescuing a victim trapped in a wrecked car.
>   *We*
>   We learned to dismantle the car with the essential tools. ~~You~~ were
>   *our*   *our*   ^
>   graded on ~~your~~ speed and ~~your~~ skill in freeing the victim.
>   ^   ^

The writer should have stayed with the *we* point of view. *You* is inappropriate because the writer is not addressing readers directly. *You* should not be used in a vague sense meaning "anyone." (See G3-b.)

> *You need*
> ▶ ~~One needs~~ a password and a credit card number to access the
>   ^
>   database. You will be billed at an hourly rate.

You is appropriate because the writer is giving advice directly to readers.

PRACTICE hackerhandbooks.com/writersref
> Sentence style > S4–5

▶ According to the National Institute of Mental Health (2007),
   children
   ~~a child~~ with attention deficit hyperactivity disorder may have trouble
   ^
   sitting still and may gradually stop paying attention to their teachers

(Symptoms section, para. 2).

In describing reports or results of studies, writers are often tempted to generalize with singular nouns, such as *child*, and then later in the passage find
themselves shifting from singular to plural. Here the writer might have
changed *their* to the singular *his or her* to agree with *child*, but the revision
making both terms plural is more concise. (See also W4-e and G3-a.)

S4-b Maintain consistent verb tenses.

Consistent verb tenses clearly establish the time of the actions being described. When a passage begins in one tense and shifts without warning
and for no reason to another, readers are distracted and confused.

▶ There was no way I could fight the current and win. Just as I was
                          jumped   *swam*
   losing hope, a stranger ~~jumps~~ off a passing boat and ~~swims~~
                           ^   ^
   toward me.

The writer thought that the present tense (*jumps, swims*) would convey
immediacy and drama. But having begun in the past tense (*could fight, was
losing*), the writer should follow through in the past tense.

Writers often encounter difficulty with verb tenses when writing
about literature. Because fictional events occur outside the time frames
of real life, the past tense and the present tense may seem equally
appropriate. The literary convention, however, is to describe fictional
events consistently in the present tense. (See p. 192.)

▶ The scarlet letter is a punishment sternly placed on Hester's
                                                is
   breast by the community, and yet it ~~was~~ a fanciful and
                                       ^
   imaginative product of Hester's own needlework.

S4-c Make verbs consistent in mood and voice.

Unnecessary shifts in the mood of a verb can be distracting and confusing
to readers. There are three moods in English: the *indicative*, used for facts,
opinions, and questions; the *imperative*, used for orders or advice; and the

subjunctive, used in certain contexts to express wishes or conditions contrary to fact (see G2-g).

The following passage shifts confusingly from the indicative to the imperative mood.

▶ The counselor advised us to spread out our core requirements over
She also suggested that we
two or three semesters. ~~Also,~~ pay attention to prerequisites for
                        ^

elective courses.

The writer began by reporting the counselor's advice in the indicative mood (*counselor advised*) and switched to the imperative mood (*pay attention*); the revision puts both sentences in the indicative.

A verb may be in either the active voice (with the subject doing the action) or the passive voice (with the subject receiving the action). (See W3-a.) If a writer shifts without warning from one to the other, readers may be left wondering why.

gives it
▶ Each student completes a self-assessment./ ~~The self-assessment~~
                                           ^
exchanges
~~is then given~~ to the teacher, and a copy ~~is exchanged~~ with a
                               ^   ^

classmate.

Because the passage began in the active voice (*student completes*) and then switched to the passive (*self-assessment is given, copy is exchanged*), readers are left wondering who gives the self-assessment to the teacher and the classmate. The active voice, which is clearer and more direct, leaves no ambiguity.

S4-d Avoid sudden shifts from indirect to direct questions or quotations.

An indirect question reports a question without asking it: *We asked whether we could visit Miriam.* A direct question asks directly: *Can we visit Miriam?* Sudden shifts from indirect to direct questions are awkward. In addition, sentences containing such shifts are impossible to punctuate because indirect questions must end with a period and direct questions must end with a question mark. (See P6-a.)

whether she reported
▶ I wonder whether Karla knew of the theft and, if so, ~~did she report~~ it
                                                     ^

to the police~~?~~.
            ^

The revision poses both questions indirectly. The writer could also ask both questions directly: *Did Karla know of the theft, and, if so, did she report it to the police?*

An indirect quotation reports someone's words without quoting word for word: *Annabelle said that she is a Virgo.* A direct quotation presents the exact words of a speaker or writer, set off with quotation marks: *Annabelle said, "I am a Virgo."* Unannounced shifts from indirect to direct quotations are distracting and confusing, especially when the writer fails to insert the necessary quotation marks, as in the following example.

▶ The patient said she had been experiencing heart palpitations and
   asked me to   *was*
   ~~please~~ run as many tests as possible to find out what̶'̶s̶ wrong.
   ^   ^

The revision reports the patient's words indirectly. The writer also could quote the words directly: *The patient said, "I have been experiencing heart palpitations. Please run as many tests as possible to find out what's wrong."*

S5 Mixed constructions

A mixed construction contains sentence parts that do not sensibly fit together. The mismatch may be a matter of grammar or of logic.

S5-a Untangle the grammatical structure.

Once you begin a sentence, your choices are limited by the range of grammatical patterns in English. (See B2 and B3.) You cannot begin with one grammatical plan and switch without warning to another. Often you must rethink the purpose of the sentence and revise.

> **MIXED**   For most drivers who have a blood alcohol level of
>   .05 percent double their risk of causing an accident.

The writer begins the sentence with a long prepositional phrase and makes it the subject of the verb *double*. But a prepositional phrase can serve only as a modifier; it cannot be the subject of a sentence.

> **REVISED**   For most drivers who have a blood alcohol level of
>   .05 percent, the risk of causing an accident is doubled.

> **REVISED**   Most drivers who have a blood alcohol level of
>   .05 percent double their risk of causing an accident.

PRACTICE   hackerhandbooks.com/writersref
   > Sentence style > S5–2 to S5–4

In the first revision, the writer begins with the prepositional phrase and finishes the sentence with a proper subject and verb (*risk . . . is doubled*). In the second revision, the writer stays with the original verb (*double*) and heads into the sentence another way, making *drivers* the subject of *double*.

▶ *Electing*
~~When the country elects~~ a president is the most important
　　　　　　　　　^

responsibility in a democracy.

The adverb clause *When the country elects a president* cannot serve as the subject of the verb *is*. The revision replaces the adverb clause with a gerund phrase, a word group that can function as a subject. (See B3-e and B3-b.)

▶ Although the United States is one of the wealthiest nations in the

world, ~~but~~ more than twelve million of our children live in poverty.

The coordinating conjunction *but* cannot link a subordinate clause (*Although the United States . . .*) with an independent clause (*more than twelve million of our children live in poverty*).

Occasionally a mixed construction is so tangled that it defies grammatical analysis. When this happens, back away from the sentence, rethink what you want to say, and then rewrite the sentence.

MIXED   In the whole-word method, children learn to recognize entire words rather than by the phonics method in which they learn to sound out letters and groups of letters.

REVISED   The whole-word method teaches children to recognize entire words; the phonics method teaches them to sound out letters and groups of letters.

ESL   English does not allow double subjects, nor does it allow an object or an adverb to be repeated in an adjective clause. Unlike some other languages, English does not allow a noun and a pronoun to be repeated in a sentence if they have the same grammatical function. See M3-c and M3-d.

▶ My father ~~he~~ moved to Peru before he met my mother.

　　　　　　　　　　　　　　　　　　the final exam
▶ ~~The final exam~~ I should really study for ~~it~~ to pass the course.
　　　　　　　　　　　　　　　　　　　　　^

S5-b Straighten out the logical connections.

The subject and the predicate (the verb and its modifiers) should make sense together; when they don't, the error is known as *faulty predication*.

▶ We decided that ~~Tiffany's welfare~~ would not be safe living
  _^*Tiffany*

  with her mother.

  Tiffany, not her welfare, would not be safe.

▶ Under the revised plan, the elderly/~~who now receive a double~~
  double personal exemption for the
  _^

  ~~personal exemption,~~ will be abolished.

  The exemption, not the elderly, will be abolished.

An appositive is a noun that renames a nearby noun. When an appositive and the noun it renames are not logically equivalent, the error is known as *faulty apposition*. (See B3-c.)

▶ ~~The tax accountant,~~ a very lucrative profession, requires intelligence,
  Tax accounting,
  _^

  patience, and attention to mathematical detail.

  The tax accountant is a person, not a profession.

S5-c Avoid *is when*, *is where*, and *reason . . . is because* constructions.

In formal English, readers sometimes object to *is when*, *is where*, and *reason . . . is because* constructions on grammatical or logical grounds.

▶ The ~~reason the~~ experiment failed ~~is~~ because conditions in the lab

  were not sterile.

  Grammatically, the verb *is* should not be followed by an adverb clause beginning with *because*. (See B2-b and B3-e.) The writer might have changed *because* to *that* (*The reason the experiment failed is that conditions in the lab were not sterile*), but the preceding revision is more concise.

▶ Anorexia nervosa is ~~where people~~ think they are too fat and diet
  a disorder suffered by people who
  _^

  to the point of starvation.

  Where refers to places. Anorexia nervosa is a disorder, not a place.

S6 Sentence emphasis

Within each sentence, emphasize your point by expressing it in the subject and verb of an independent clause, the words that receive the most attention from readers (see S6-a to S6-e).

Within longer stretches of prose, you can draw attention to ideas that deserve special emphasis by using a variety of techniques, often involving an unusual twist or some element of surprise (see S6-f).

S6-a Coordinate equal ideas; subordinate minor ideas.

When combining two or more ideas in one sentence, you have two choices: coordination or subordination. Choose coordination to indicate that the ideas are equal or nearly equal in importance. Choose subordination to indicate that one idea is less important than another.

Coordination

Coordination draws attention equally to two or more ideas. To coordinate single words or phrases, join them with a coordinating conjunction or with a pair of correlative conjunctions: bananas *and* strawberries; *not only* a lackluster plot *but also* inferior acting (see B1-g).

To coordinate independent clauses—word groups that express a complete thought and that can stand alone as a sentence—join them with a comma and a coordinating conjunction (*and, but, or, nor, for, so, yet*) or with a semicolon. The semicolon is often accompanied by a conjunctive adverb such as *moreover, furthermore, therefore,* or *however* or by a transitional phrase such as *for example, in other words,* or *as a matter of fact.* (For longer lists, see P3-a.)

> Social networking Web sites offer ways for people to connect in the virtual world, but they do not replace face-to-face social interaction.

> Social networking Web sites offer ways for people to connect in the virtual world; however, they do not replace face-to-face social interaction.

Subordination

To give unequal emphasis to two or more ideas, express the major idea in an independent clause and place any minor ideas in subordinate clauses or phrases. (See B3.) Subordinate clauses, which cannot stand alone, typically begin with one of the following subordinating conjunctions or relative pronouns.

after	since	whether
although	so that	which
as	that	while
as if	though	who
because	unless	whom
before	until	whose
even though	when	
if	where	

Let your intended meaning determine which idea you emphasize. Consider the two ideas about social networking Web sites.

Social networking Web sites offer ways for people to connect in the virtual world. They do not replace face-to-face social interaction.

If your purpose is to stress the ways that people can connect in the virtual world rather than the limitations of these connections, subordinate the idea about the limitations.

Although they do not replace face-to-face social interaction, social networking Web sites offer ways for people to connect in the virtual world.

To focus on the limitations of the virtual world, subordinate the idea about the Web sites.

Although social networking Web sites offer ways for people to connect in the virtual world, they do not replace face-to-face social interaction.

S6-b Combine choppy sentences.

Short sentences demand attention, so you should use them primarily for emphasis. Too many short sentences, one after the other, make for a choppy style.

If an idea is not important enough to deserve its own sentence, try combining it with a sentence close by. Put any minor ideas in subordinate structures such as phrases or subordinate clauses. (See B3.)

▶ The Parks Department keeps the use of insecticides to a minimum/
  because the
  ~~The~~ city is concerned about the environment.
  ^

The writer wanted to emphasize that the Parks Department minimizes its use of chemicals, so she put the reason in a subordinate clause beginning with *because.*

▶ The Chesapeake and Ohio Canal, ~~is~~ a 184-mile waterway

constructed in the 1800s. ~~It~~ was a major source of transportation

for goods during the Civil War.

A minor idea is now expressed in an appositive phrase (*a 184-mile waterway constructed in the 1800s*).

▶ ~~Sister Consilio was~~ *E*nveloped in a black robe with only her face and
Sister Consilio
hands visible, ~~She~~ was an imposing figure.

Because Sister Consilio's overall impression was more important to the writer's purpose, the writer put the description of the clothing in a participial phrase beginning with *Enveloped.*

Although subordination is ordinarily the most effective technique for combining short, choppy sentences, coordination is appropriate when the ideas are equal in importance.

▶ At 3:30 p.m., Forrest displayed a flag of truce, *and* ~~Forrest~~ sent in a

demand for unconditional surrender.

Combining two short sentences by joining their predicates (*displayed . . . sent*) is an effective coordination technique.

ESL   Unlike some other languages, English does not repeat objects or adverbs in adjective clauses. The relative pronoun (*that, which, whom*) or relative adverb (*where*) in the adjective clause represents the object or adverb. See M3-d.

▶ The apartment that we rented ~~it~~ needed repairs.

The pronoun *it* cannot repeat the relative pronoun *that.*

▶ The small town where my grandfather was born ~~there~~ is now

a big city.

The adverb *there* cannot repeat the relative adverb *where.*

S6-c Avoid ineffective or excessive coordination.

Coordinate structures are appropriate only when you intend to draw readers' attention equally to two or more ideas: *Professor Sakellarios praises loudly, and she criticizes softly.* If one idea is more important than another—or if a coordinating conjunction does not clearly signal the relationship between the ideas—you should subordinate the less important idea.

INEFFECTIVE COORDINATION	Closets were taxed as rooms, and most colonists stored their clothes in chests or clothespresses.
IMPROVED WITH SUBORDINATION	Because closets were taxed as rooms, most colonists stored their clothes in chests or clothespresses.

Because it is so easy to string ideas together with *and*, writers often rely too heavily on coordination in their rough drafts. Revising for excessive coordination is important: Look for opportunities to tuck minor ideas into subordinate clauses or phrases.

> *After four hours,*
> ► ~~Four hours went by, and~~ a rescue truck finally arrived, but by that
>   ^
>   time we had been evacuated in a helicopter.

Three independent clauses were excessive. The least important idea has become a prepositional phrase.

S6-d Do not subordinate major ideas.

If a sentence buries its major idea in a subordinate construction, readers may not give the idea enough attention. Make sure to express your major idea in an independent clause and to subordinate any minor ideas.

> *defeated Thomas E. Dewey,*
> ► Harry S. Truman, who was the unexpected winner of the 1948
>   ^
>   presidential election/. ~~defeated Thomas E. Dewey.~~
>   ^

The writer wanted to focus on Truman's unexpected victory, but the original sentence buried this information in an adjective clause. The revision puts the more important idea in an independent clause and tucks the less important idea into an adjective clause (*who defeated Thomas E. Dewey*).

> *As*
> ► I was driving home from my new job, heading down Ranchitos
>   ^
>   Road, ~~when~~ my car suddenly overheated.

The writer wanted to emphasize that the car overheated, not the fact of driving home. The revision expresses the major idea in an independent clause and places the less important idea in an adverb clause (*As I was driving home from my new job*).

S6-e Do not subordinate excessively.

In attempting to avoid short, choppy sentences, writers sometimes go to the opposite extreme, putting more subordinate ideas into a sentence than its structure can bear. Sentences that become too complicated can sometimes be restructured. More often, however, such sentences must be divided.

> ▶ In *Animal Liberation*, Peter Singer argues that animals possess
>
> nervous systems and can feel pain. ~~and that~~ H̶e therefore believes
>
> that "the ethical principle on which human equality rests requires
>
> us to extend equal consideration to animals" (1).

Writing with sources

MLA-style citation

Excessive subordination makes it difficult for the reader to focus on the quoted passage. By splitting the original sentence into two separate sentences, the writer draws attention to Peter Singer's main claim, that animals should be given "equal consideration" to humans.

S6-f Experiment with techniques for gaining special emphasis.

By experimenting with certain techniques, usually involving some element of surprise, you can draw attention to ideas that deserve special emphasis. Use such techniques sparingly, however, or they will lose their punch. The writer who tries to emphasize everything ends up emphasizing nothing.

Using sentence endings for emphasis

You can highlight an idea simply by withholding it until the end of a sentence. The technique works something like a punch line. In the following example, the sentence's meaning is not revealed until its very last word.

> The only completely consistent people are the dead.
>
> — Aldous Huxley

Using parallel structure for emphasis

Parallel grammatical structure draws special attention to paired ideas or to items in a series. (See S1.) When parallel ideas are paired, the emphasis falls on words that underscore comparisons or contrasts, especially when they occur at the end of a phrase or clause.

> We must *stop talking* about the *American dream* and *start listening* to the *dreams of Americans.*   —Reubin Askew

In a parallel series, the emphasis falls at the end, so it is generally best to end with the most dramatic or climactic item in the series.

> Sister Charity enjoyed passing out writing punishments: translate the Ten Commandments into Latin, type a thousand-word essay on good manners, copy the New Testament with a quill pen.
>   —Marie Visosky, student

Using an occasional short sentence for emphasis

Too many short sentences in a row will fast become monotonous (see S6-b), but an occasional short sentence, when played off against longer sentences in the same passage, will draw attention to an idea.

> The great secret, known to internists and learned early in marriage by internists' wives [or husbands], but still hidden from the general public, is that most things get better by themselves. Most things, in fact, are better by morning.   —Lewis Thomas

S7 Sentence variety

When a rough draft is filled with too many sentences that begin the same way or have the same structure, try injecting some variety—as long as you can do so without sacrificing clarity or ease of reading.

S7-a Use a variety of sentence structures.

A writer should not rely too heavily on simple sentences and compound sentences, for the effect tends to be both monotonous and choppy. (See S6-b and S6-c.) Too many complex or compound-complex sentences, however, can be equally monotonous. If your style tends to one or the other extreme, try to achieve a better mix of sentence types.

For a discussion of sentence types, see B4-a.

S7-b Vary your sentence openings.

Most sentences in English begin with the subject, move to the verb, and continue to the object, with modifiers tucked in along the way or put at the end. For the most part, such sentences are fine. Put too many of them in a row, however, and they become monotonous.

Adverbial modifiers are easily movable when they modify verbs; they can often be inserted ahead of the subject. Such modifiers might be single words, phrases, or clauses.

▶ *Eventually a*
  A few drops of sap ~~eventually~~ began to trickle into the bucket.
  ^

Like most adverbs, *eventually* does not need to appear close to the verb it modifies (*began*).

▶ *Just as the sun was coming up, a*
  A pair of black ducks flew over the pond. ~~just as the sun was~~
  ^   ^
  ~~coming up.~~

The adverb clause, which modifies the verb *flew*, is as clear at the beginning of the sentence as it is at the end.

Adjectives and participial phrases can frequently be moved to the beginning of a sentence without loss of clarity.

▶ *Dejected and withdrawn,*
  Edward/~~dejected and withdrawn,~~ nearly gave up his search
  ^
  for a job.

▶   *A*   *John and I*
  ~~John and I,~~ anticipating a peaceful evening, sat down at the
                ^   ^
  campfire to brew a cup of coffee.

TIP: When beginning a sentence with an adjective or a participial phrase, make sure that the subject of the sentence names the person or thing described in the introductory phrase. If it doesn't, the phrase will dangle. (See S3-e.)

S7-c Try inverting sentences occasionally.

A sentence is inverted if it does not follow the normal subject-verb-object pattern. Many inversions sound artificial and should be avoided except in the most formal contexts. But if an inversion sounds natural, it can provide a welcome touch of variety.

► *Opposite the produce section is a*
  A refrigerated case of cheeses. ~~is opposite the produce section.~~
    ^   ^

The revision inverts the normal subject-verb order by moving the verb, *is*, ahead of its subject, *case*.

► *Placed at the top two corners of the stage were huge*
  ~~Huge~~ lavender hearts outlined in bright white lights. ~~were~~
    ^   ^

  ~~at the top two corners of the stage.~~

In the revision, the subject, *hearts*, appears after the verb, *were placed*. The two parts of the verb are also inverted—and separated from each other (*Placed . . . were*)—without any awkwardness or loss of meaning.

Inverted sentences are used for emphasis as well as for variety (see S6-f).

W1 Glossary of usage

This glossary includes words commonly confused (such as *accept* and *except*), words commonly misused (such as *aggravate*), and words that are nonstandard (such as *hisself*). It also lists colloquialisms and jargon. Colloquialisms are casual expressions that may be appropriate in informal speech but are inappropriate in formal writing. Jargon is needlessly technical or pretentious language that is inappropriate in most contexts. If an item is not listed here, consult the index. For irregular verbs (such as *sing, sang, sung*), see G2-a. For idiomatic use of prepositions, see W5-d.

a, an Use *an* before a vowel sound, *a* before a consonant sound: *an apple, a peach.* Problems sometimes arise with words beginning with *h* or *u*. If the *h* is silent, the word begins with a vowel sound, so use *an: an hour, an honorable deed.* If the *h* is pronounced, the word begins with a consonant sound, so use *a: a hospital, a historian, a hotel.* Words such as *university* and *union* begin with a consonant sound (a *y* sound), so use *a: a union.* Words such as *uncle* and *umbrella* begin with a vowel sound, so use *an: an underground well.* When an abbreviation or an acronym begins with a vowel sound, use *an: an EKG, an MRI, an AIDS prevention program.*

accept, except *Accept* is a verb meaning "to receive." *Except* is usually a preposition meaning "excluding." *I will accept all the packages except that one. Except* is also a verb meaning "to exclude." *Please except that item from the list.*

adapt, adopt *Adapt* means "to adjust or become accustomed"; it is usually followed by *to. Adopt* means "to take as one's own." *Our family adopted a Vietnamese child, who quickly adapted to his new life.*

adverse, averse *Adverse* means "unfavorable." *Averse* means "opposed" or "reluctant"; it is usually followed by *to. I am averse to your proposal because it could have an adverse impact on the economy.*

advice, advise *Advice* is a noun, *advise* a verb. *We advise you to follow John's advice.*

affect, effect *Affect* is usually a verb meaning "to influence." *Effect* is usually a noun meaning "result." *The drug did not affect the disease, and it had adverse side effects. Effect* can also be a verb meaning "to bring about." *Only the president can effect such a dramatic change.*

aggravate *Aggravate* means "to make worse or more troublesome." *Overgrazing aggravated the soil erosion.* In formal writing, avoid the use of *aggravate* meaning "to annoy or irritate." *Her babbling annoyed* (not *aggravated*) *me.*

agree to, agree with   *Agree to* means "to give consent to." *Agree with* means "to be in accord with" or "to come to an understanding with." *He agrees with me about the need for change, but he won't agree to my plan.*

ain't   *Ain't* is nonstandard. Use *am not, are not (aren't),* or *is not (isn't). I am not* (not *ain't) going home for spring break.*

all ready, already   *All ready* means "completely prepared." *Already* means "previously." *Susan was all ready for the concert, but her friends had already left.*

all right   *All right* is written as two words. *Alright* is nonstandard.

all together, altogether   *All together* means "everyone or everything in one place." *Altogether* means "entirely." *We were not altogether certain that we could bring the family all together for the reunion.*

allude   To *allude* to something is to make an indirect reference to it. Do not use *allude* to mean "to refer directly." *In his lecture, the professor referred* (not *alluded) to several pre-Socratic philosophers.*

allusion, illusion   An *allusion* is an indirect reference. An *illusion* is a misconception or false impression. *Did you catch my allusion to Shakespeare? Mirrors give the room an illusion of depth.*

a lot   *A lot* is two words. Do not write *alot. Sam lost a lot of weight.* See also *lots, lots of.*

among, between   See *between, among.*

amongst   In American English, *among* is preferred.

amoral, immoral   *Amoral* means "neither moral nor immoral"; it also means "not caring about moral judgments." *Immoral* means "morally wrong." *Until recently, most business courses were taught from an amoral perspective. Murder is immoral.*

amount, number   Use *amount* with quantities that cannot be counted; use *number* with those that can. *This recipe calls for a large amount of sugar. We have a large number of toads in our garden.*

an   See *a, an.*

and etc.   *Et cetera (etc.)* means "and so forth"; *and etc.* is redundant. See also *etc.*

and/or   Avoid the awkward construction *and/or* except in technical or legal documents.

angry at, angry with   Use *angry with,* not *angry at,* when referring to a person. *The coach was angry with the referee.*

ante-, anti-   The prefix *ante-* means "earlier" or "in front of"; the prefix *anti-* means "against" or "opposed to." *William Lloyd Garrison was a leader of the antislavery movement during the antebellum period. Anti-* should be used with a hyphen when it is followed by a capital letter or a word beginning with *i*.

anxious *Anxious* means "worried" or "apprehensive." In formal writing, avoid using *anxious* to mean "eager." *We are eager* (not *anxious*) *to see your new house.*

anybody, anyone *Anybody* and *anyone* are singular. (See G1-e and G3-a.)

anymore Use the adverb *anymore* in a negative context to mean "any longer" or "now." *The factory isn't producing shoes anymore.* Using *anymore* in a positive context is colloquial; in formal writing, use *now* instead. *We order all our food online now* (not *anymore*).

anyone See *anybody, anyone.*

anyone, any one *Anyone*, an indefinite pronoun, means "any person at all." *Any one*, the pronoun *one* preceded by the adjective *any*, refers to a particular person or thing in a group. *Anyone from the winning team may choose any one of the games on display.*

anyplace In formal writing, use *anywhere*.

anyways, anywheres *Anyways* and *anywheres* are nonstandard. Use *anyway* and *anywhere*.

as Do not use *as* to mean "because" if there is any chance of ambiguity. *We canceled the picnic because* (not *as*) *it began raining. As* here could mean either "because" or "when."

as, like See *like, as.*

as to *As to* is jargon for *about. He inquired about* (not *as to*) *the job.*

averse See *adverse, averse.*

awful The adjective *awful* and the adverb *awfully* are not appropriate in formal writing.

awhile, a while *Awhile* is an adverb; it can modify a verb, but it cannot be the object of a preposition such as *for*. The two-word form *a while* is a noun preceded by an article and therefore can be the object of a preposition. *Stay awhile. Stay for a while.*

back up, backup *Back up* is a verb phrase. *Back up the car carefully. Be sure to back up your hard drive. Backup* is a noun meaning "a copy of electronically stored data." *Keep your backup in a safe place. Backup* can also be used as an adjective. *I regularly create backup disks.*

bad, badly *Bad* is an adjective, *badly* an adverb. *They felt bad about ruining the surprise. Her arm hurt badly after she slid into second base.* (See G4-a and G4-b.)

being as, being that *Being as* and *being that* are nonstandard expressions. Write *because* instead. *Because* (not *Being as*) *I slept late, I had to skip breakfast.*

USAGE hackerhandbooks.com/writersref
> Language Debates > Pronoun-antecedent agreement
> *bad* versus *badly*

beside, besides   *Beside* is a preposition meaning "at the side of" or "next to." *Annie Oakley slept with her gun beside her bed. Besides* is a preposition meaning "except" or "in addition to." *No one besides Terrie can have that ice cream. Besides* is also an adverb meaning "in addition." *I'm not hungry; besides, I don't like ice cream.*

between, among   Ordinarily, use *among* with three or more entities, *between* with two. *The prize was divided among several contestants. You have a choice between carrots and beans.*

bring, take   Use *bring* when an object is being transported toward you, *take* when it is being moved away. *Please bring me a glass of water. Please take these forms to Mr. Scott.*

burst, bursted; bust, busted   *Burst* is an irregular verb meaning "to come open or fly apart suddenly or violently." Its past tense is *burst.* The past-tense form *bursted* is nonstandard. *Bust* and *busted* are slang for *burst* and, along with *bursted*, should not be used in formal writing.

can, may   The distinction between *can* and *may* is fading, but some writers still observe it in formal writing. *Can* is traditionally reserved for ability, *may* for permission. *Can you speak French? May I help you?*

capital, capitol   *Capital* refers to a city, *capitol* to a building where lawmakers meet. *Capital* also refers to wealth or resources. *The residents of the state capital protested plans to close the streets surrounding the capitol.*

censor, censure   *Censor* means "to remove or suppress material considered objectionable." *Censure* means "to criticize severely." *The administration's policy of censoring books has been censured by the media.*

cite, site   *Cite* means "to quote as an authority or example." *Site* is usually a noun meaning "a particular place." *He cited the zoning law in his argument against the proposed site of the gas station.* Locations on the Internet are usually referred to as *sites. The library's Web site improves every week.*

climactic, climatic   *Climactic* is derived from *climax*, the point of greatest intensity in a series or progression of events. *Climatic* is derived from *climate* and refers to meteorological conditions. *The climactic period in the dinosaurs' reign was reached just before severe climatic conditions brought on an ice age.*

coarse, course   *Coarse* means "crude" or "rough in texture." *The coarse weave of the wall hanging gave it a three-dimensional quality. Course* usually refers to a path, a playing field, or a unit of study; the expression *of course* means "certainly." *I plan to take a course in car repair this summer. Of course, you are welcome to join me.*

compare to, compare with   *Compare to* means "to represent as similar." *She compared him to a wild stallion. Compare with* means "to examine similarities and differences." *The study compared the language ability of apes with that of dolphins.*

complement, compliment *Complement* is a verb meaning "to go with or complete" or a noun meaning "something that completes." As a verb, *compliment* means "to flatter"; as a noun, it means "flattering remark." *Her skill at rushing the net complements his skill at volleying. Martha's flower arrangements receive many compliments.*

conscience, conscious *Conscience* is a noun meaning "moral principles." *Conscious* is an adjective meaning "aware or alert." *Let your conscience be your guide. Were you conscious of his love for you?*

continual, continuous *Continual* means "repeated regularly and frequently." *She grew weary of the continual telephone calls. Continuous* means "extended or prolonged without interruption." *The broken siren made a continuous wail.*

could care less *Could care less* is nonstandard. Write *couldn't care less* instead. *He couldn't* (not *could*) *care less about his psychology final.*

could of *Could of* is nonstandard for *could have. We could have* (not *could of*) *taken the train.*

council, counsel A *council* is a deliberative body, and a *councilor* is a member of such a body. *Counsel* usually means "advice" and can also mean "lawyer"; a *counselor* is one who gives advice or guidance. *The councilors met to draft the council's position paper. The pastor offered wise counsel to the troubled teenager.*

criteria *Criteria* is the plural of *criterion*, which means "a standard or rule or test on which a judgment or decision can be based." *The only criterion for the scholarship is ability.*

data *Data* is a plural noun technically meaning "facts or results." But *data* is increasingly being accepted as a singular noun. *The new data suggest* (or *suggests*) *that our theory is correct.* (The singular *datum* is rarely used.)

different from, different than Ordinarily, write *different from. Your sense of style is different from Jim's.* However, *different than* is acceptable to avoid an awkward construction. *Please let me know if your plans are different than* (to avoid *from what*) *they were six weeks ago.*

differ from, differ with *Differ from* means "to be unlike"; *differ with* means "to disagree with." *My approach to the problem differed from hers. She differed with me about the wording of the agreement.*

disinterested, uninterested *Disinterested* means "impartial, objective"; *uninterested* means "not interested." *We sought the advice of a disinterested counselor to help us solve our problem. Mark was uninterested in anyone's opinion but his own.*

don't *Don't* is the contraction for *do not. I don't want any. Don't* should not be used as the contraction for *does not*, which is *doesn't. He doesn't* (not *don't*) *want any.*

due to *Due to* is an adjective phrase and should not be used as a preposition meaning "because of." *The trip was canceled because of* (not *due to*) *lack of interest. Due to* is acceptable as a subject complement and usually follows a form of the verb *be. His success was due to hard work.*

each *Each* is singular. (See G1-e and G3-a.)

effect See *affect, effect.*

e.g. In formal writing, replace the Latin abbreviation *e.g.* with its English equivalent: *for example* or *for instance.*

either *Either* is singular. (See G1-e and G3-a.) For *either . . . or* constructions, see G1-d and G-3a.

elicit, illicit *Elicit* is a verb meaning "to bring out" or "to evoke." *Illicit* is an adjective meaning "unlawful." *The reporter was unable to elicit any information from the police about illicit drug traffic.*

emigrate from, immigrate to *Emigrate* means "to leave one country or region to settle in another." *In 1903, my great-grandfather emigrated from Russia to escape the religious pogroms. Immigrate* means "to enter another country and reside there." *More than fifty thousand Bosnians immigrated to the United States in the 1990s.*

eminent, imminent *Eminent* means "outstanding" or "distinguished." *We met an eminent professor of Greek history. Imminent* means "about to happen." *The snowstorm is imminent.*

enthused Many people object to the use of *enthused* as an adjective. Use *enthusiastic* instead. *The children were enthusiastic* (not *enthused*) *about going to the circus.*

etc. Avoid ending a list with *etc.* It is more emphatic to end with an example, and in most contexts readers will understand that the list is not exhaustive. When you don't wish to end with an example, *and so on* is more graceful than *etc.* (See also *and etc.*)

eventually, ultimately Often used interchangeably, *eventually* is the better choice to mean "at an unspecified time in the future," and *ultimately* is better to mean "the furthest possible extent or greatest extreme." *He knew that eventually he would complete his degree. The existentialists considered suicide the ultimately rational act.*

everybody, everyone *Everybody* and *everyone* are singular. (See G1-e and G3-a.)

everyone, every one *Everyone* is an indefinite pronoun. *Every one*, the pronoun *one* preceded by the adjective *every*, means "each individual or thing in a particular group." *Every one* is usually followed by *of. Everyone wanted to go. Every one of the missing books was found.*

except See *accept, except.*

expect Avoid the informal use of *expect* meaning "to believe, think, or suppose." *I think* (not *expect*) *it will rain tonight.*

explicit, implicit *Explicit* means "expressed directly" or "clearly defined"; *implicit* means "implied, unstated." *I gave him explicit instructions not to go swimming. My mother's silence indicated her implicit approval.*

farther, further *Farther* usually describes distances. *Further* usually suggests quantity or degree. *Chicago is farther from Miami than I thought. I would be grateful for further suggestions.*

fewer, less Use *fewer* for items that can be counted; use *less* for items that cannot be counted. *Fewer people are living in the city. Please put less sugar in my tea.*

finalize *Finalize* is jargon meaning "to make final or complete." Use ordinary English instead. *The architect prepared final drawings* (not *finalized the drawings*).

firstly *Firstly* sounds pretentious, and it leads to the ungainly series *firstly, secondly, thirdly,* and so on. Write *first, second, third* instead.

further See *farther, further.*

get *Get* has many colloquial uses. In writing, avoid using *get* to mean the following: "to evoke an emotional response" (*That music always gets to me*); "to annoy" (*After a while his sulking got to me*); "to take revenge on" (*I got back at her by leaving the room*); "to become" (*He got sick*); "to start or begin" (*Let's get going*). Avoid using *have got to* in place of *must. I must* (not *have got to*) *finish this paper tonight.*

good, well *Good* is an adjective, *well* an adverb. (See G4-a and G4-b.) *He hasn't felt good about his game since he sprained his wrist last season. She performed well on the uneven parallel bars.*

graduate Both of the following uses of *graduate* are standard: *My sister was graduated from UCLA last year. My sister graduated from UCLA last year.* It is nonstandard, however, to drop the word *from: My sister graduated UCLA last year.* Though this usage is common in informal English, many readers object to it.

grow Phrases such as *to grow the economy* and *to grow a business* are jargon. Usually the verb *grow* is intransitive (it does not take a direct object). *Our business has grown very quickly.* Use *grow* in a transitive sense, with a direct object, to mean "to cultivate" or "to allow to grow." *We plan to grow tomatoes this year. John is growing a beard.*

hanged, hung *Hanged* is the past-tense and past-participle form of the verb *hang* meaning "to execute." *The prisoner was hanged at dawn. Hung* is the past-tense and past-participle form of the verb *hang* meaning "to fasten or suspend." *The stockings were hung by the chimney with care.*

hardly   Avoid expressions such as *can't hardly* and *not hardly*, which are considered double negatives. *I can* (not *can't*) *hardly describe my surprise at getting the job.* (See G4-d.)

has got, have got   *Got* is unnecessary and awkward in such constructions. It should be dropped. *We have* (not *have got*) *three days to prepare for the opening.*

he   At one time *he* was commonly used to mean "he or she." Today such usage is inappropriate. (See W4-e and G3-a.)

he/she, his/her   In formal writing, use *he or she* or *his or her*. For alternatives to these wordy constructions, see W4-e and G3-a.

hisself   *Hisself* is nonstandard. Use *himself*.

hopefully   *Hopefully* means "in a hopeful manner." *We looked hopefully to the future.* Some usage experts object to the use of *hopefully* as a sentence adverb, apparently on grounds of clarity. To be safe, avoid using *hopefully* in sentences such as the following: *Hopefully, your son will recover soon.* Instead, indicate who is doing the hoping: *I hope that your son will recover soon.*

however   In the past, some writers objected to the conjunctive adverb *however* at the beginning of a sentence, but current experts allow placing the word according to the intended meaning and emphasis. All of the following sentences are correct. *Pam decided, however, to attend the lecture. However, Pam decided to attend the lecture.* (She had been considering other activities.) *Pam, however, decided to attend the lecture.* (Unlike someone else, Pam chose to attend the lecture.) (See P1-f.)

hung   See *hanged, hung*.

i.e.   In formal writing, replace the Latin abbreviation *i.e.* with its English equivalent: *that is*.

if, whether   Use *if* to express a condition and *whether* to express alternatives. *If you go on a trip, whether to Nebraska or Italy, remember to bring traveler's checks.*

illusion   See *allusion, illusion*.

immigrate   See *emigrate from, immigrate to*.

imminent   See *eminent, imminent*.

immoral   See *amoral, immoral*.

implement   *Implement* is a pretentious way of saying "do," "carry out," or "accomplish." Use ordinary language instead. *We carried out* (not *implemented*) *the director's orders.*

imply, infer   *Imply* means "to suggest or state indirectly"; *infer* means "to draw a conclusion." *John implied that he knew all about computers, but the interviewer inferred that John was inexperienced.*

USAGE   **hackerhandbooks.com/writersref**
   > Language Debates   > Sexist language
            > *however* at the beginning of a sentence

in, into   *In* indicates location or condition; *into* indicates movement or a change in condition. *They found the lost letters in a box after moving into the house.*

in regards to   *In regards to* confuses two different phrases: *in regard to* and *as regards*. Use one or the other. *In regard to* (or *As regards*) *the contract, ignore the first clause.*

irregardless   *Irregardless* is nonstandard. Use *regardless*.

is when, is where   These mixed constructions are often incorrectly used in definitions. *A run-off election is a second election held to break a tie* (not *is when a second election is held to break a tie*). (See S5-c.)

its, it's   *Its* is a possessive pronoun; *it's* is a contraction for *it is*. (See P4-a and P4-b.) *It's always fun to watch a dog chase its tail.*

kind(s)   *Kind* is singular and should be treated as such. Don't write *These kind of chairs are rare*. Write instead *This kind of chair is rare*. *Kinds* is plural and should be used only when you mean more than one kind. *These kinds of chairs are rare.*

kind of, sort of   Avoid using *kind of* or *sort of* to mean "somewhat." *The movie was somewhat* (not *sort of*) *boring.* Do not put *a* after either phrase. *That kind of* (not *kind of a*) *salesclerk annoys me.*

lay, lie   See *lie, lay*.

lead, led   *Lead* is a metallic element; it is a noun. *Led* is the past tense of the verb *lead*. *He led me to the treasure.*

learn, teach   *Learn* means "to gain knowledge"; *teach* means "to impart knowledge." *I must teach* (not *learn*) *my sister to read.*

leave, let   *Leave* means "to exit." Avoid using it with the nonstandard meaning "to permit." *Let* (not *Leave*) *me help you with the dishes.*

less   See *fewer, less*.

let, leave   See *leave, let*.

liable   *Liable* means "obligated" or "responsible." Do not use it to mean "likely." *You're likely* (not *liable*) *to trip if you don't tie your shoelaces.*

lie, lay   *Lie* is an intransitive verb meaning "to recline or rest on a surface." Its forms are *lie, lay, lain*. *Lay* is a transitive verb meaning "to put or place." Its forms are *lay, laid, laid*. (See G2-b.)

like, as   *Like* is a preposition, not a subordinating conjunction. It can be followed only by a noun or a noun phrase. *As* is a subordinating conjunction that introduces a subordinate clause. In casual speech, you may say *She looks like she hasn't slept* or *You don't know her like I do*. But in formal writing, use *as*. *She looks as if she hasn't slept. You don't know her as I do.* (See also B1-f and B1-g.)

loose, lose   *Loose* is an adjective meaning "not securely fastened." *Lose* is a verb meaning "to misplace" or "to not win." *Did you lose your only loose pair of work pants?*

lots, lots of   *Lots* and *lots of* are informal substitutes for *many, much,* or *a lot.* Avoid using them in formal writing.

mankind   Avoid *mankind* whenever possible. It offends many readers because it excludes women. Use *humanity, humans, the human race,* or *humankind* instead. (See W4-e.)

may   See *can, may.*

maybe, may be   *Maybe* is an adverb meaning "possibly." *Maybe the sun will shine tomorrow. May be* is a verb phrase. *Tomorrow may be brighter.*

may of, might of   *May of* and *might of* are nonstandard for *may have* and *might have. We might have* (not *might of*) *had too many cookies.*

media, medium   *Media* is the plural of *medium. Of all the media that cover the Olympics, television is the medium that best captures the spectacle of the events.*

most   *Most* is informal when used to mean "almost" and should be avoided. *Almost* (not *Most*) *everyone went to the parade.*

must of   See *may of.*

myself   *Myself* is a reflexive or intensive pronoun. Reflexive: *I cut myself.* Intensive: *I will drive you myself.* Do not use *myself* in place of *I* or *me. He gave the flowers to Melinda and me* (not *myself*). (See also G3-c.)

neither   *Neither* is singular. (See G1-e and G3-a.) For *neither . . . nor* constructions, see G1-d and G3-a.

none   *None* may be singular or plural. (See G1-e.)

nowheres   *Nowheres* is nonstandard. Use *nowhere* instead.

number   See *amount, number.*

of   Use the verb *have,* not the preposition *of,* after the verbs *could, should, would, may, might,* and *must. They must have* (not *must of*) *left early.*

off of   *Off* is sufficient. Omit *of. The ball rolled off* (not *off of*) *the table.*

OK, O.K., okay   All three spellings are acceptable, but avoid these expressions in formal speech and writing.

parameters   *Parameter* is a mathematical term that has become jargon for "fixed limit," "boundary," or "guideline." Use ordinary English instead. *The task force worked within certain guidelines* (not *parameters*).

passed, past   *Passed* is the past tense of the verb *pass. Ann passed me another slice of cake. Past* usually means "belonging to a former time" or "beyond a time or place." *Our past president spoke until past midnight. The hotel is just past the next intersection.*

percent, per cent, percentage *Percent* (also spelled *per cent*) is always used with a specific number. *Percentage* is used with a descriptive term such as *large* or *small*, not with a specific number. *The candidate won 80 percent of the primary vote. A large percentage of registered voters turned out for the election.*

phenomena *Phenomena* is the plural of *phenomenon*, which means "an observable occurrence or fact." *Strange phenomena occur at all hours of the night in that house, but last night's phenomenon was the strangest of all.*

plus *Plus* should not be used to join independent clauses. *This raincoat is dirty; moreover* (not *plus*), *it has a hole in it.*

precede, proceed *Precede* means "to come before." *Proceed* means "to go forward." *As we proceeded up the mountain path, we noticed fresh tracks in the mud, evidence that a group of hikers had preceded us.*

principal, principle *Principal* is a noun meaning "the head of a school or an organization" or "a sum of money." It is also an adjective meaning "most important." *Principle* is a noun meaning "a basic truth or law." *The principal expelled her for three principal reasons. We believe in the principle of equal justice for all.*

proceed, precede See *precede, proceed.*

quote, quotation *Quote* is a verb; *quotation* is a noun. Avoid using *quote* as a shortened form of *quotation*. *Her quotations* (not *quotes*) *from current movies intrigued us.*

raise, rise *Raise* is a transitive verb meaning "to move or cause to move upward." It takes a direct object. *I raised the shades. Rise* is an intransitive verb meaning "to go up." *Heat rises.*

real, really *Real* is an adjective; *really* is an adverb. *Real* is sometimes used informally as an adverb, but avoid this use in formal writing. *She was really* (not *real*) *angry.* (See G4-b.)

reason . . . is because Use *that* instead of *because*. *The reason she's cranky is that* (not *because*) *she didn't sleep last night.* (See S5-c.)

reason why The expression *reason why* is redundant. *The reason* (not *The reason why*) *Jones lost the election is clear.*

relation, relationship *Relation* describes a connection between things. *Relationship* describes a connection between people. *There is a relation between poverty and infant mortality. Our business relationship has cooled over the years.*

respectfully, respectively *Respectfully* means "showing or marked by respect." *Respectively* means "each in the order given." *He respectfully* *submitted his opinion to the judge. John, Tom, and Larry were a butcher, a baker, and a lawyer, respectively.*

sensual, sensuous   *Sensual* means "gratifying the physical senses," especially those associated with sexual pleasure. *Sensuous* means "pleasing to the senses," especially those involved in the experience of art, music, and nature. *The sensuous music and balmy air led the dancers to more sensual movements.*

set, sit   *Set* is a transitive verb meaning "to put" or "to place." Its past tense is *set*. *Sit* is an intransitive verb meaning "to be seated." Its past tense is *sat*. *She set the dough in a warm corner of the kitchen. The cat sat in the doorway.*

shall, will   *Shall* was once used in place of the helping verb *will* with *I* or *we*: *I shall, we shall*. Today, however, *will* is generally accepted even when the subject is *I* or *we*. The word *shall* occurs primarily in polite questions (*Shall I find you a pillow?*) and in legalistic sentences suggesting duty or obligation (*The applicant shall file form A by December 31*).

should of   *Should of* is nonstandard for *should have*. *They should have* (not *should of*) *been home an hour ago.*

since   Do not use *since* to mean "because" if there is any chance of ambiguity. *Because* (not *Since*) *we won the game, we have been celebrating with a pitcher of root beer. Since* here could mean "because" or "from the time that."

sit   See *set, sit*.

site   See *cite, site*.

somebody, someone   *Somebody* and *someone* are singular. (See G1-e and G3-a.)

something   *Something* is singular. (See G1-e.)

sometime, some time, sometimes   *Sometime* is an adverb meaning "at an indefinite or unstated time." *Some time* is the adjective *some* modifying the noun *time* and means "a period of time." *Sometimes* is an adverb meaning "at times, now and then." *I'll see you sometime soon. I haven't lived there for some time. Sometimes I see him at the library.*

suppose to   Write *supposed to*.

sure and   Write *sure to*. *We were all taught to be sure to* (not *sure and*) *look both ways before crossing a street.*

take   See *bring, take*.

than, then   *Than* is a conjunction used in comparisons; *then* is an adverb denoting time. *That pizza is more than I can eat. Tom laughed, and then we recognized him.*

that   See *who, which, that*.

that, which Many writers reserve *that* for restrictive clauses, *which* for nonrestrictive clauses. (See P1-e.)

theirselves *Theirselves* is nonstandard for *themselves. The crash victims pushed the car out of the way themselves* (not *theirselves*).

them The use of *them* in place of *those* is nonstandard. *Please take those* (not *them*) *flowers to the patient in room 220.*

then, than See *than, then.*

there, their, they're *There* is an adverb specifying place; it is also an expletive (placeholder). Adverb: *Sylvia is lying there unconscious.* Expletive: *There are two plums left. Their* is a possessive pronoun. *Fred and Jane finally washed their car. They're* is a contraction of *they are. They're later than usual today.*

they The use of *they* to indicate possession is nonstandard. Use *their* instead. *Cindy and Sam decided to sell their* (not *they*) *1975 Corvette.*

they, their The use of the plural pronouns *they* and *their* to refer to singular nouns or pronouns is nonstandard. *No one handed in his or her* (not *their*) *draft on time.* (See G3-a.)

this kind See *kind(s).*

to, too, two *To* is a preposition; *too* is an adverb; *two* is a number. *Too many of your shots slice to the left, but the last two were just right.*

toward, towards *Toward* and *towards* are generally interchangeable, although *toward* is preferred in American English.

try and *Try and* is nonstandard for *try to. The teacher asked us all to try to* (not *try and*) *write an original haiku.*

ultimately, eventually See *eventually, ultimately.*

unique Avoid expressions such as *most unique, more straight, less perfect, very round.* Either something is unique or it isn't. It is illogical to suggest degrees of uniqueness. (See G4-c.)

usage The noun *usage* should not be substituted for *use* when the meaning is "employment of." *The use* (not *usage*) *of insulated shades has cut fuel costs dramatically.*

use to Write *used to.*

utilize *Utilize* means "to make use of." It often sounds pretentious; in most cases, *use* is sufficient. *I used* (not *utilized*) *the laser printer.*

wait for, wait on *Wait for* means "to be in readiness for" or "to await." *Wait on* means "to serve." *We're only waiting for* (not *waiting on*) *Ruth to take us to the museum.*

ways *Ways* is colloquial when used to mean "distance." *The city is a long way* (not *ways*) *from here.*

USAGE hackerhandbooks.com/writersref
 > Language Debates > *that* versus *which*
 > Absolute concepts such as *unique*

weather, whether The noun *weather* refers to the state of the atmosphere. *Whether* is a conjunction referring to a choice between alternatives. *We wondered whether the weather would clear.*

well, good See *good, well.*

where Do not use *where* in place of *that. I heard that* (not *where*) *the crime rate is increasing.*

which See *that, which* and *who, which, that.*

while Avoid using *while* to mean "although" or "whereas" if there is any chance of ambiguity. *Although* (not *While*) *Gloria lost money in the slot machine, Tom won it at roulette.* Here *While* could mean either "although" or "at the same time that."

who, which, that Do not use *which* to refer to persons. Use *who* instead. *That,* though generally used to refer to things, may be used to refer to a group or class of people. *The player who* (not *that* or *which*) *made the basket at the buzzer was named MVP. The team that scores the most points in this game will win the tournament.*

who, whom *Who* is used for subjects and subject complements; *whom* is used for objects. (See G3-d.)

who's, whose *Who's* is a contraction of *who is; whose* is a possessive pronoun. *Who's ready for more popcorn? Whose coat is this?* (See P4-b and P4-a.)

will See *shall, will.*

would of *Would of* is nonstandard for *would have. She would have* (not *would of*) *had a chance to play if she had arrived on time.*

you In formal writing, avoid *you* in an indefinite sense meaning "anyone." (See G3-b.) *Any spectator* (not *You*) *could tell by the way John caught the ball that his throw would be too late.*

your, you're *Your* is a possessive pronoun; *you're* is a contraction of *you are. Is that your new bike? You're in the finals.* (See P4-a and P4-b.)

USAGE hackerhandbooks.com/writersref
> Language Debates > *who* versus *which* or *that*
> *who* versus *whom*
> *you*

W2 Wordy sentences

Long sentences are not necessarily wordy, nor are short sentences always concise. A sentence is wordy if it can be tightened without loss of meaning.

W2-a Eliminate redundancies.

Writers often repeat themselves unnecessarily, thinking that expressions such as *cooperate together*, *yellow in color*, or *basic essentials* add emphasis to their writing. In reality, such redundancies do just the opposite. There is no need to say the same thing twice.

▶ Daniel ~~is now employed~~ at a private rehabilitation center ^works^

~~working~~ as a registered physical therapist.

Though modifiers ordinarily add meaning to the words they modify, occasionally they are redundant.

▶ Sylvia ~~very hurriedly~~ scribbled her name, address, and phone

number on a greasy napkin.

The word *scribbled* already suggests that Sylvia wrote very hurriedly.

▶ Gabriele Muccino's film *The Pursuit of Happyness* tells the story

of a single father determined ~~in his mind~~ to pull himself and his

son out of homelessness.

The word *determined* contains the idea that his resolution formed in his mind.

W2-b Avoid unnecessary repetition of words.

Though words may be repeated deliberately, for effect, repetitions will seem awkward if they are clearly unnecessary. When a more concise version is possible, choose it.

▶ Our fifth patient, in room six, is ∧ mentally ill. ~~patient.~~
                                      ^

Writing
with
sources

APA-style
citation

▶ A study by the Henry J. Kaiser Family Foundation (2004)
     measured
     ~~studied~~ the effects of diet and exercise on childhood
     ^

  obesity.

The repetition of *study . . . studied* is awkward and redundant. By using the
descriptive verb *measured* instead, the writer conveys more precisely the
purpose of the study and suggests its function in the paper.

W2-c Cut empty or inflated phrases.

An empty phrase can be cut with little or no loss of meaning. Common
examples are introductory word groups that weaken the writer's authority by apologizing or hedging: *in my opinion, I think that, it seems that,
one must admit that,* and so on.

                    O
▶ ~~In my opinion,~~ ∅ur current immigration policy is misguided.
                    ^

Inflated phrases can be reduced to a word or two without loss of
meaning.

INFLATED	CONCISE
along the lines of	like
as a matter of fact	in fact
at all times	always
at the present time	now, currently
at this point in time	now, currently
because of the fact that	because
by means of	by
by virtue of the fact that	because
due to the fact that	because
for the purpose of	for
for the reason that	because
have the ability to	be able to, can
in light of the fact that	because
in order to	to
in spite of the fact that	although, though
in the event that	if
in the final analysis	finally
in the nature of	like
in the neighborhood of	about
until such time as	until

> *now.*
> ► We are unable to provide funding ~~at this point in time.~~
>   ^

W2-d Simplify the structure.

If the structure of a sentence is needlessly indirect, try simplifying it. Look for opportunities to strengthen the verb.

> ► The financial analyst claimed that because of volatile market
>
> conditions she could not ~~make an~~ estimate ~~of~~ the company's
>
> future profits.
>
> The verb *estimate* is more vigorous and concise than *make an estimate of.*

The colorless verbs *is*, *are*, *was*, and *were* frequently generate excess words. (See also W3-b.)

> *examined*
> ► Investigators ~~were involved in examining~~ the effect of classical
>   ^
> music on unborn babies.
>
> The revision is more direct and concise. The action (*examining*), originally appearing in a subordinate structure, has become a strong verb, *examined.*

The expletive constructions *there is* and *there are* (or *there was* and *there were*) can also generate excess words. The same is true of expletive constructions beginning with *it.*

> *A*
> ► ~~There is~~ another module ~~that~~ tells the story of Charles Darwin
>   ^
> and introduces the theory of evolution.

> *A*   *must*
> ► ~~It is imperative that~~ all night managers follow strict procedures
>   ^   ^
> when locking the safe.

Finally, verbs in the passive voice may be needlessly indirect. When the active voice expresses your meaning as effectively, use it. (See also W3-a.)

> *our coaches have recruited*
> ► All too often, athletes with marginal academic skills. ~~have~~
>   ^   ^
> ~~been recruited by our coaches.~~

W2-e Reduce clauses to phrases, phrases to single words.

Word groups functioning as modifiers can often be made more compact. Look for any opportunities to reduce clauses to phrases or phrases to single words.

▶ We took a side trip to Monticello, ~~which was~~ the home of

Thomas Jefferson.

▶ In ~~the~~ essay, ~~that follows,~~ I argue against Immanuel Kant's
      this
  problematic
  claim that we should not lie under any circumstances/. ~~which~~

  ~~is a problematic assertion.~~

W3 Active verbs

As a rule, choose an active verb and pair it with a subject that names the person or thing doing the action. Active verbs express meaning more emphatically and vigorously than their weaker counterparts—forms of the verb *be* or verbs in the passive voice.

PASSIVE	The pumps *were destroyed* by a surge of power.
BE VERB	A surge of power *was* responsible for the destruction of the pumps.
ACTIVE	A surge of power *destroyed* the pumps.

Verbs in the passive voice lack strength because their subjects receive the action instead of doing it. Forms of the verb *be* (*be, am, is, are, was, were, being, been*) lack vigor because they convey no action.

    Although passive verbs and the forms of *be* have legitimate uses, choose an active verb if it can carry your meaning. Even among active verbs, some convey action more vigorously than others. Carefully selected verbs can energize a piece of writing.

▶ The goalie crouched low, ~~reached~~ out his stick, and ~~sent~~ the
                        swept   *hooked*
  rebound away from the mouth of the net.

> **Academic English**   Although you may be tempted to avoid the pas-
> sive voice completely, keep in mind that some writing situations call
> for it, especially scientific writing. For appropriate uses of the passive
> voice, see pages 157 and 158; for advice about forming the passive voice,
> see M1-b and B2-b.

W3-a Use the active voice unless you have a good reason for choosing the passive.

In the active voice, the subject of the sentence does the action; in the
passive voice, the subject receives the action. Although both voices
are grammatically correct, the active voice is usually more effective
because it is clearer and more direct.

ACTIVE   Hernando *caught* the fly ball.

PASSIVE   The fly ball *was caught* by Hernando.

Passive sentences often identify the actor in a phrase beginning with
by, as in the preceding example. Sometimes, however, that phrase is
omitted, and who or what is responsible for the action becomes unclear:
The fly ball was caught.

Most of the time, you will want to emphasize the actor, so you
should use the active voice. To replace a passive verb with an active
one, make the actor the subject of the sentence.

> The settlers stripped the land of timber before realizing
> ▶ ~~The land was stripped of timber before the settlers realized~~
> the consequences of their actions.

The revision emphasizes the actors (*settlers*) by naming them in the
subject.

> The contractor removed the
> ▶ ~~The~~ debris ~~was removed~~ from the construction site.

Sometimes the actor does not appear in a passive-voice sentence. To turn
such a sentence into the active voice, the writer must determine an
appropriate subject, in this case *contractor*.

The passive voice is appropriate if you wish to emphasize the
receiver of the action or to minimize the importance of the actor.

APPROPRIATE
PASSIVE
Many Hawaiians *were forced* to leave their homes after the earthquake.

APPROPRIATE
PASSIVE
As the time for harvest approaches, the tobacco plants *are sprayed* with a chemical to retard the growth of suckers.

The writer of the first sentence wished to emphasize the receiver of the action, *Hawaiians*. The writer of the second sentence wished to focus on the tobacco plants, not on the people spraying them.

In much scientific writing, the passive voice properly emphasizes the experiment or process being described, not the researcher. Check with your instructor for the preference in your discipline.

APPROPRIATE
PASSIVE
The solution *was heated* to the boiling point, and then it was reduced in volume by 50%.

W3-b Replace *be* verbs that result in dull or wordy sentences.

Not every *be* verb needs replacing. The forms of *be* (*be, am, is, are, was, were, being, been*) work well when you want to link a subject to a noun that clearly renames it or to an adjective that describes it: *Orchard House was the home of Louisa May Alcott. The harvest will be bountiful after the summer rains.* And *be* verbs are essential as helping verbs before present participles (*is flying, are disappearing*) to express ongoing action: *Derrick was fighting the fire when his wife went into labor.* (See G2-f.)

If using a *be* verb makes a sentence needlessly dull and wordy, however, consider replacing it. Often a phrase following the verb will contain a noun or an adjective (such as *violation, resistant*) that suggests a more vigorous, active verb (*violate, resist*).

▶ Burying nuclear waste in Antarctica would ~~be in violation of~~ *violate* an international treaty.

Violate is less wordy and more vigorous than *be in violation of*.

▶ When Rosa Parks ~~was resistant to~~ *resisted* giving up her seat on the bus, she became a civil rights hero.

Resisted is stronger than *was resistant to*.

W4 Appropriate language

Language is appropriate when it suits your subject, engages your audience, and blends naturally with your own voice.

W4-a Stay away from jargon.

Jargon is specialized language used among members of a trade, profession, or group. Use jargon only when readers will be familiar with it; even then, use it only when plain English will not do as well.

JARGON   We outsourced the work to a firm in Ohio because we didn't have the bandwidth to tackle it in-house.

REVISED   We hired a company in Ohio because we had too few employees to do the work.

Broadly defined, jargon includes puffed-up language designed more to impress readers than to inform them. The following are common examples from business, government, higher education, and the military, with plain English alternatives in parentheses.

ameliorate (improve)   indicator (sign)
commence (begin)   optimal (best, most favorable)
components (parts)   parameters (boundaries, limits)
endeavor (try)   peruse (read, look over)
facilitate (help)   prior to (before)
impact (v.) (affect)   utilize (use)

Sentences filled with jargon are hard to read and often wordy.

▶ All ~~employees functioning in the capacity of~~ work-study students *must prove that they are currently enrolled.* ~~are required to give evidence of current enrollment.~~

▶ The CEO should ~~dialogue~~ *talk* with investors about ~~partnering~~ *working* with clients to buy land in ~~economically deprived zones.~~ *poor neighborhoods.*

W4-b Avoid pretentious language, most euphemisms, and "doublespeak."

Hoping to sound profound or poetic, some writers embroider their thoughts with large words and flowery phrases. Such pretentious language is so ornate and wordy that it obscures the writer's meaning.

▶ Taylor's ~~employment of multihued means of expression draws~~ *use of colorful language reveals that she has a* ^
~~back the curtains and lets slip the~~ sentimental ~~vantage point from~~ *view of*
~~which she observes~~ American society ~~as well as her lack of~~ *and does not understand* ^

~~comprehension of~~ economic realities.

Euphemisms — nice-sounding words or phrases substituted for words thought to sound harsh or ugly — are sometimes appropriate. Many cultures, for example, accept euphemisms when speaking or writing about excretion (*I have to go to the bathroom*), sexual intercourse (*They did not sleep together*), and the like.

Most euphemisms, however, are needlessly evasive or even deceitful. Like pretentious language, they obscure the intended meaning.

EUPHEMISM	PLAIN ENGLISH
adult entertainment	pornography
preowned automobile	used car
economically deprived	poor
strategic withdrawal	retreat or defeat
revenue enhancers	taxes
chemical dependency	drug addiction
downsize	lay off, fire
correctional facility	prison

The term *doublespeak* applies to any deliberately evasive or deceptive language, including euphemisms. Doublespeak is especially common in politics and business. A military retreat is described as *tactical redeployment*, *enhanced interrogation* is a euphemism for "torture," and *downsizing* really means "firing employees."

W4-c In most contexts, avoid slang, regional expressions, and nonstandard English.

Slang is an informal and sometimes private vocabulary that expresses the solidarity of a group such as teenagers, rock musicians, or football fans; it is subject to more rapid change than standard English. For example, the slang teenagers use to express approval changes every few years; *cool*, *groovy*, *neat*, *awesome*, *phat*, and *sick* have replaced one another within the last four decades. Sometimes slang becomes so widespread that it is accepted as standard vocabulary. *Jazz*, for example, started out as slang but is now a standard term for a style of music.

Although slang has a certain vitality, it is a code that not every-one understands, and it is very informal. Therefore, it is inappropri-ate in most written work.

we lost
▶ When the server crashed unexpectedly, three hours of unsaved

data. ~~went down the tubes.~~
^
disgust you.
▶ The government's "filth" guidelines for food will ~~gross you out.~~
^

Regional expressions are common to a group in a geographic area. *Let's talk with the bark off* (for *Let's speak frankly*) is an expres-sion in the southern United States, for example. Regional expressions have the same limitations as slang and are therefore inappropriate in most writing.

▶ John was four blocks from the house before he remembered to
turn on
~~cut~~ the headlights. ~~on.~~
^   ^

▶ Seamus wasn't ~~for~~ sure, but he thought the whales might be

migrating during his visit to Oregon.

Standard English is the language used in all academic, business, and professional fields. Nonstandard English is spoken by people with a common regional or social heritage. Although nonstandard English may be appropriate when spoken within a close group, it is out of place in most formal and informal writing.

doesn't
▶ The governor said he ~~don't~~ know if he will approve the budget
^
without the clean air provision.

If you speak a nonstandard dialect, try to identify the ways in which your dialect differs from standard English. Look especially for the fol-lowing features of nonstandard English, which commonly cause prob-lems in writing.

Misusing verb forms such as *began* and *begun* (See G2-a.)

Leaving -*s* endings off verbs (See G2-c.)

Leaving -*ed* endings off verbs (See G2-d.)

Leaving out necessary verbs (See G2-e.)

Using double negatives (See G4-d.)

W4-d Choose an appropriate level of formality.

In deciding on a level of formality, consider both your subject and your audience. Does the subject demand a dignified treatment, or is a relaxed tone more suitable? Will readers be put off if you assume too close a relationship with them, or might you alienate them by seeming too distant?

For most college and professional writing, some degree of formality is appropriate. In a job application letter, for example, it is a mistake to sound too breezy and informal.

> **TOO INFORMAL**   I'd like to get that sales job you've got in the paper.
>
> **MORE FORMAL**   I would like to apply for the position of sales associate advertised in the *Peoria Journal Star*.

Informal writing is appropriate for private letters, personal e-mail and text messages, and business correspondence between close associates. In choosing a level of formality, above all be consistent. When a writer's voice shifts from one level of formality to another, readers receive mixed messages.

> ▶ Once a pitcher for the Blue Jays, Jorge shared with me the secrets
> of his trade. His lesson ~~commenced~~ *began* with his famous curveball,
> ~~implemented~~ *thrown* by tucking the little finger behind the ball. Next
> he ~~elucidated~~ *revealed* the mysteries of the sucker pitch, a slow ball
> coming behind a fast windup.

Commenced and *elucidated* are inappropriate for the subject, and they clash with informal terms such as *sucker pitch* and *fast windup*.

W4-e Avoid sexist language.

Sexist language is language that stereotypes, excludes, or demeans women or men. Using nonsexist language is a matter of courtesy — of respect for and sensitivity to the feelings of others.

Recognizing sexist language

Some sexist language is easy to recognize because it reflects genuine contempt for women: referring to a woman as a "chick," for example, or calling a lawyer a "lady lawyer."

Other forms of sexist language are less blatant. The following practices, while they may not result from conscious sexism, reflect stereotypical thinking: referring to members of one profession as exclusively male or exclusively female (teachers as women or computer engineers as men, for instance) or using different conventions when naming or identifying women and men.

STEREOTYPICAL LANGUAGE

After a nursing student graduates, *she* must face a difficult
state board examination. [Not all nursing students are women.]

Running for city council are Boris Stotsky, an attorney, and *Mrs.
Cynthia Jones*, a professor of English and *mother of three*. [The title
Mrs. and the description *mother of three* are irrelevant.]

Still other forms of sexist language result from outdated traditions. The pronouns *he*, *him*, and *his*, for instance, were traditionally used to refer generically to persons of either sex. Some writers now use *she*, *her*, and *hers* generically or substitute the female pronouns alternately with the male pronouns.

GENERIC PRONOUNS

A journalist is motivated by *his* deadline.

A good interior designer treats *her* clients' ideas respectfully.

But both forms are sexist—for excluding one sex entirely and for making assumptions about the members of particular professions.

Similarly, the nouns *man* and *men* were once used to refer generically to persons of either sex. Current usage demands gender-neutral terms for references to both men and women.

INAPPROPRIATE	APPROPRIATE
chairman	chairperson, moderator, chair, head
congressman	member of Congress, representative, legislator
fireman	firefighter
foreman	supervisor
mailman	mail carrier, postal worker, letter carrier
to man	to operate, to staff
mankind	people, humans
manpower	personnel, staff
policeman	police officer
weatherman	forecaster, meteorologist

Revising sexist language

When revising sexist language, you may be tempted to substitute *he or she* and *his or her*. These terms are inclusive but wordy; fine in small doses, they can become awkward when repeated throughout an essay. A better revision strategy is to write in the plural; yet another strategy is to recast the sentence so that the problem does not arise.

SEXIST

A journalist is motivated by *his* deadline.

A good interior designer treats *her* clients' ideas respectfully.

ACCEPTABLE BUT WORDY

A journalist is motivated by *his or her* deadline.

A good interior designer treats *his or her* clients' ideas respectfully.

BETTER: USING THE PLURAL

Journalists are motivated by *their* deadlines.

Good interior designers treat *their* clients' ideas respectfully.

BETTER: RECASTING THE SENTENCE

A journalist is motivated by *a* deadline.

A good interior designer treats clients' ideas respectfully.

For more examples of these revision strategies, see G3-a.

W4-f Revise language that may offend groups of people.

Obviously it is impolite to use offensive terms such as *Polack* and *red-neck*, but biased language can take more subtle forms. Because language evolves over time, names once thought acceptable may become offensive. When describing groups of people, choose names that the groups currently use to describe themselves.

► North Dakota takes its name from the ~~Indian~~ *Lakota* word meaning "friend" or "ally."

► Many ~~Oriental~~ *Asian* immigrants have recently settled in our town.

Negative stereotypes (such as "drives like a teenager" or "sour as a spinster") are of course offensive. But you should avoid stereotyping a person or a group even if you believe your generalization to be positive.

► It was no surprise that Greer, ~~a Chinese American,~~ *an excellent math and science student,* was selected for the honors chemistry program.

W5 Exact language

Two reference works will help you find words to express your meaning exactly: a good dictionary, such as *Merriam-Webster's Online Dictionary* or *The American Heritage Dictionary*, and a thesaurus, such as *Roget's International Thesaurus*. (See W6.)

TIP: Do not turn to a thesaurus in search of flowery or impressive language. Look instead for words that exactly express your meaning.

W5-a Select words with appropriate connotations.

In addition to their strict dictionary meanings (or *denotations*), words have *connotations*, emotional colorings that affect how readers respond to them. The word *steel* denotes "commercial iron that contains carbon," but it also calls up a cluster of images associated with steel. These associations give the word its connotations—cold, hard, smooth, unbending.

If the connotation of a word does not seem appropriate for your purpose, your audience, or your subject matter, you should change the word. When a more appropriate synonym does not come quickly to mind, consult a dictionary or a thesaurus. (See W6.)

▶ When American soldiers returned home after World War II, many
  left
  women a̶b̶a̶n̶d̶o̶n̶e̶d̶ their jobs in favor of marriage.
  ^
  The word *abandoned* is too negative for the context.

W5-b Prefer specific, concrete nouns.

Unlike general nouns, which refer to broad classes of things, specific nouns point to particular items. *Film*, for example, names a general class, *fantasy film* names a narrower class, and *The Golden Compass* is more specific still.

Unlike abstract nouns, which refer to qualities and ideas (*justice, beauty, realism, dignity*), concrete nouns point to immediate, often sensory experience and to physical objects (*steeple, asphalt, lilac, stone, garlic*).

Specific, concrete nouns express meaning more vividly than general or abstract ones. Although general and abstract language is sometimes necessary to convey your meaning, use specific, concrete words whenever possible.

▶ The senator spoke about the challenges of our state's future: *pollution, dwindling natural resources, and overcrowded prisons.* ~~the environment and crime.~~
      ^

Nouns such as *thing*, *area*, *aspect*, *factor*, and *individual* are especially dull and imprecise.

                                          motherhood, and memory.
▶ Toni Morrison's *Beloved* is about slavery, ~~among other things.~~
                                              ^
                                          experienced technician.
▶ Try pairing a new employee with an ~~individual with technical~~
                                        ^
~~experience.~~

W5-c Do not misuse words.

If a word is not in your active vocabulary, you may find yourself misusing it, sometimes with embarrassing consequences. When in doubt, check the dictionary.

                        climbing
▶ Fans who arrived late were ~~migrating~~ up the bleachers in search of
                              ^
seats.

Writing
with
sources

MLA-style
citation

                  argues
▶ Marie Winn ~~quarrels~~ that television viewing is bad for families
              ^
because it "serves to anesthetize parents into accepting their

family's diminished state" (357).

When you are introducing a quotation with a signal phrase, be sure to choose a verb that clearly reflects the source's intention. *Quarrel* suggests a heated or angry dispute; *argue* is a more neutral word. (See also MLA-3b on using signal phrases.)

Be especially alert for misused word forms — using a noun such as *absence*, *significance*, or *persistence*, for example, when your meaning requires the adjective *absent*, *significant*, or *persistent*.

                        persistent
▶ Most dieters are not ~~persistence~~ enough to make a permanent change
                        ^
in their eating habits.

W5-d Use standard idioms.

Idioms are speech forms that follow no easily specified rules. The English say "Bernadette went *to hospital*," an idiom strange to American ears, which are accustomed to hearing *to the hospital*. Native speakers of a language seldom have problems with idioms, but prepositions (such as *with*, *to*, *at*, and *of*) sometimes cause trouble, especially when they follow certain verbs and adjectives. When in doubt, consult a dictionary.

UNIDIOMATIC	IDIOMATIC
abide with (a decision)	abide by (a decision)
according with	according to
agree to (an idea)	agree with (an idea)
angry at (a person)	angry with (a person)
capable to	capable of
comply to	comply with
desirous to	desirous of
different than (a person or thing)	different from (a person or thing)
intend on doing	intend to do
off of	off
plan on doing	plan to do
preferable than	preferable to
prior than	prior to
similar than	similar to
superior than	superior to
sure and	sure to
think on	think of, about
try and	try to
type of a	type of

ESL   Because idioms follow no particular rules, you must learn them individually. You may find it helpful to keep a list of idioms that you frequently encounter in conversation and in reading. See M5.

W5-e Do not rely heavily on clichés.

The pioneer who first announced that he had "slept like a log" no doubt amused his companions with a fresh, unlikely comparison. Today, however, that comparison is a cliché, a saying that can no longer add emphasis or surprise.

PRACTICE   hackerhandbooks.com/writersref
  > Word choice > W5–7

To see just how dully predictable clichés are, put your hand over the right-hand column in the following list and then finish the phrases on the left.

cool as a	cucumber
beat around	the bush
blind as a	bat
busy as a	bee, beaver
crystal	clear
out of the frying pan and	into the fire
light as a	feather
like a bull	in a china shop
playing with	fire
nutty as a	fruitcake
selling like	hotcakes
starting out at the bottom	of the ladder
water under the	bridge
white as a	sheet, ghost
avoid clichés like the	plague

The solution for clichés is simple: Just delete them or rewrite them.

► When I received a full scholarship from my second-choice school,
    felt squeezed to settle for second best.
  I found myself between a rock and a hard place.
      ^

Sometimes you can write around a cliché by adding an element of surprise. One student, for example, who had written that she had butterflies in her stomach, revised her cliché like this:

> If all of the action in my stomach is caused by butterflies, there must be a horde of them, with horseshoes on.

The image of butterflies wearing horseshoes is fresh and unlikely, not predictable like the original cliché.

W5-f Use figures of speech with care.

A figure of speech is an expression that uses words imaginatively (rather than literally) to make abstract ideas concrete. Most often, figures of speech compare two seemingly unlike things to reveal surprising similarities.

In a *simile*, the writer makes the comparison explicitly, usually by introducing it with *like* or *as*: *By the time cotton had to be picked, Grandfather's neck was as red as the clay he plowed.* In a *metaphor*, the *like* or *as* is omitted, and the comparison is implied. For example, in the Old Testament Song of Solomon, a young woman compares the man she loves to a fruit tree: *With great delight I sat in his shadow, and his fruit was sweet to my taste.*

Although figures of speech are useful devices, writers sometimes use them without thinking through the images they evoke. The result is sometimes a *mixed metaphor*, the combination of two or more images that don't make sense together.

▶ Our manager decided to put all controversial issues ~~in a holding~~

~~pattern~~ on a back burner until after the annual meeting.

Here the writer is mixing airplanes (*holding pattern*) and stoves (*back burner*). Simply deleting one of the images corrects the problem.

W6 The dictionary and thesaurus

W6-a The dictionary

A good dictionary, whether print or online—such as *The American Heritage Dictionary of the English Language, The Random House College Dictionary,* or *Merriam-Webster's Collegiate Dictionary*—is an indispensable writer's aid.

A sample print dictionary entry, taken from *The American Heritage Dictionary,* appears on page 170. Labels show where various kinds of information about a word can be found in that dictionary.

A sample online dictionary entry, taken from *Merriam-Webster Online Dictionary,* appears on page 171.

Spelling, word division, and pronunciation

The main entry (*re•gard* in the sample entries) shows the correct spelling of the word. When there are two correct spellings of a word (as in *collectible, collectable,* for example), both are given, with the preferred spelling usually appearing first.

The main entry also shows how the word is divided into syllables. The dot between *re* and *gard* separates the two syllables and indicates where the word should be divided if it can't fit at the end of a line of type (see P7-h). When a word is compound, the main entry shows how to write it: as one word (*crossroad*), as a hyphenated word (*cross-stitch*), or as two words (*cross section*).

The word's pronunciation is given just after the main entry. The accents indicate which syllables are stressed; the other marks are explained in the dictionary's pronunciation key. In print dictionaries, this key usually appears at the bottom of every page or every other page. Many online entries include an audio link to a person's voice pronouncing the word. And most online dictionaries have an audio pronunciation guide.

PRINT DICTIONARY ENTRY

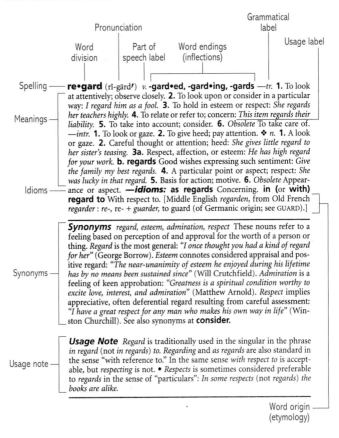

Pronunciation

Word division

Part of speech label

Word endings (inflections)

Grammatical label

Usage label

Spelling — **re•gard** (rĭ-gärd′) *v.* **-gard•ed, -gard•ing, -gards** —*tr.* **1.** To look at attentively; observe closely. **2.** To look upon or consider in a particular way: *I regard him as a fool.* **3.** To hold in esteem or respect: *She regards her teachers highly.* **4.** To relate or refer to; concern: *This item regards their liability.* **5.** To take into account; consider. **6.** *Obsolete* To take care of. —*intr.* **1.** To look or gaze. **2.** To give heed; pay attention. ❖ *n.* **1.** A look or gaze. **2.** Careful thought or attention; heed: *She gives little regard to her sister's teasing.* **3a.** Respect, affection, or esteem: *He has high regard for your work.* **b. regards** Good wishes expressing such sentiment: *Give the family my best regards.* **4.** A particular point or aspect; respect: *She was lucky in that regard.* **5.** Basis for action; motive. **6.** *Obsolete* Appearance or aspect. —*idioms:* **as regards** Concerning. **in** (or **with**) **regard to** With respect to. [Middle English *regarden*, from Old French *regarder* : *re-*, re- + *guarder*, to guard (of Germanic origin); see GUARD).]

Meanings

Idioms

Synonyms regard, esteem, admiration, respect These nouns refer to a feeling based on perception of and approval for the worth of a person or thing. *Regard* is the most general: *"I once thought you had a kind of regard for her"* (George Borrow). *Esteem* connotes considered appraisal and positive regard: *"The near-unanimity of esteem he enjoyed during his lifetime has by no means been sustained since"* (Will Crutchfield). *Admiration* is a feeling of keen approbation: *"Greatness is a spiritual condition worthy to excite love, interest, and admiration"* (Matthew Arnold). *Respect* implies appreciative, often deferential regard resulting from careful assessment: *"I have a great respect for any man who makes his own way in life"* (Winston Churchill). See also synonyms at **consider.**

Synonyms

Usage Note *Regard* is traditionally used in the singular in the phrase *in regard* (not *in regards*) *to. Regarding* and *as regards* are also standard in the sense "with reference to." In the same sense *with respect to* is acceptable, but *respecting* is not. • *Respects* is sometimes considered preferable to *regards* in the sense of "particulars": *In some respects* (not *regards*) *the books are alike.*

Usage note

Word origin (etymology)

Word endings and grammatical labels

When a word takes endings to indicate grammatical functions (called *inflections*), the endings are listed in boldface, as with *-garded*, *-garding*, and *-gards* in the sample print entry (p. 170).

Labels for the parts of speech and for other grammatical terms are sometimes abbreviated, as they are in the print entry. The most commonly used abbreviations are these:

n.	noun	adj.	adjective
pl.	plural	adv.	adverb
sing.	singular	pron.	pronoun
v.	verb	prep.	preposition
tr.	transitive verb	conj.	conjunction
intr.	intransitive verb	interj.	interjection

ONLINE DICTIONARY ENTRY

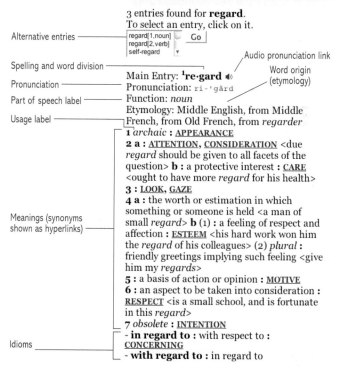

Meanings, word origin, synonyms, and antonyms

Each meaning for the word is given a number. Occasionally a word's use is illustrated in a quoted sentence. Sometimes a word can be used as more than one part of speech (*regard*, for instance, can be used as either a verb or a noun). In such a case, all the meanings for one part of speech are given before all the meanings for another, as in the sample entries. The entries also give idiomatic uses of the word.

The origin of the word, called its *etymology*, appears in brackets after all the meanings in the print version; in the online version, it appears before the meanings.

Synonyms, words similar in meaning to the main entry, are frequently listed. In the sample print entry (p. 170), the dictionary draws distinctions in meaning among the various synonyms. In the online entry (p. 171), synonyms appear as hyperlinks. Antonyms, which do not appear in the sample entries, are words having a meaning opposite from that of the main entry.

Usage

Usage labels indicate when, where, or under what conditions a particular meaning for a word is appropriately used. Common labels are *informal* (or *colloquial*), *slang*, *archaic*, *poetic*, *nonstandard*, *dialect*, *obsolete*, and *British*. In the sample print entry (p. 170), two meanings of *regard* are labeled *obsolete* because they are no longer in use. The sample online entry (p. 171) has meanings labeled both *archaic* and *obsolete*.

Dictionaries sometimes include usage notes as well. In the sample print entry, the dictionary offers advice on several uses of *regard* not specifically covered by the meanings. Such advice is based on the opinions of many experts and on actual usage in current magazines, newspapers, and books.

W6-b The thesaurus

When you are looking for just the right word, you may want to consult a collection of synonyms and antonyms such as *Roget's International Thesaurus*. Look up the adjective *still*, for example, and you will find synonyms such as *tranquil*, *quiet*, *quiescent*, *reposeful*, *calm*, *pacific*, *halcyon*, *placid*, and *unruffled*. The list will likely contain words you've never heard of or with which you are only vaguely familiar. Whenever you are tempted to use one of these words, first look it up in the dictionary to avoid misusing it.

Do not turn to a thesaurus in search of exotic, fancy words to embellish your essays. Look instead for words that express your meaning exactly and that are familiar to both you and your readers.

G1 Subject-verb agreement

In the present tense, verbs agree with their subjects in number (singular or plural) and in person (first, second, or third): *I sing, you sing, he sings, she sings, we sing, they sing.* Even if your ear recognizes the standard subject-verb combinations presented in G1-a, you will no doubt encounter tricky situations such as those described in G1-b to G1-k.

G1-a Consult this section for standard subject-verb combinations.

This section describes the basic guidelines for making present-tense verbs agree with their subjects. The present-tense ending *-s* (or *-es*) is used on a verb if its subject is third-person singular (*he, she, it,* and singular nouns); otherwise the verb takes no ending. Consider, for example, the present-tense forms of the verbs *love* and *try,* given at the beginning of the chart on the following page.

The verb *be* varies from this pattern; unlike any other verb, it has special forms in *both* the present and the past tense. These forms appear at the end of the chart on page 176.

If you aren't confident that you know the standard forms, use the charts on pages 176 and 177 as you proofread for subject-verb agreement. You may also want to look at G2-c on *-s* endings of regular and irregular verbs.

G1-b Make the verb agree with its subject, not with a word that comes between.

Word groups often come between the subject and the verb. Such word groups, usually modifying the subject, may contain a noun that at first appears to be the subject. By mentally stripping away such modifiers, you can isolate the noun that is in fact the subject.

The *samples* on the tray in the lab *need* testing.

▶ High levels of air pollution causes damage to the respiratory

tract.

The subject is *levels,* not *pollution.* Strip away the phrase *of air pollution* to hear the correct verb: *levels cause.*

Subject-verb agreement at a glance

Present-tense forms of *love* and *try* (typical verbs)

	SINGULAR		PLURAL	
FIRST PERSON	I	love	we	love
SECOND PERSON	you	love	you	love
THIRD PERSON	he/she/it*	loves	they**	love

	SINGULAR		PLURAL	
FIRST PERSON	I	try	we	try
SECOND PERSON	you	try	you	try
THIRD PERSON	he/she/it*	tries	they**	try

Present-tense forms of *have*

	SINGULAR		PLURAL	
FIRST PERSON	I	have	we	have
SECOND PERSON	you	have	you	have
THIRD PERSON	he/she/it*	has	they**	have

Present-tense forms of *do* (including negative forms)

	SINGULAR		PLURAL	
FIRST PERSON	I	do/don't	we	do/don't
SECOND PERSON	you	do/don't	you	do/don't
THIRD PERSON	he/she/it*	does/doesn't	they**	do/don't

Present-tense and past-tense forms of *be*

	SINGULAR		PLURAL	
FIRST PERSON	I	am/was	we	are/were
SECOND PERSON	you	are/were	you	are/were
THIRD PERSON	he/she/it*	is/was	they**	are/were

*And singular nouns (*child, Roger*)
**And plural nouns (*children, the Mannings*)

▶ The slaughter of pandas for their pelts ~~have~~ *has* caused the panda population to decline drastically.

The subject is *slaughter*, not *pandas* or *pelts*.

NOTE: Phrases beginning with the prepositions *as well as, in addition to, accompanied by, together with*, and *along with* do not make a singular subject plural.

When to use the -s (or -es) form of a present-tense verb

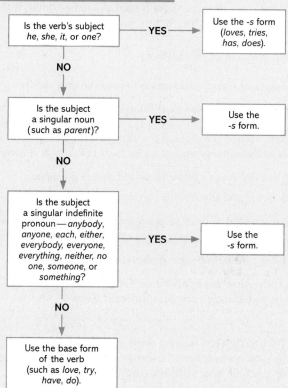

Is the verb's subject *he, she, it,* or *one*? —— **YES** ——▶ Use the *-s* form (*loves, tries, has, does*).

NO

Is the subject a singular noun (such as *parent*)? —— **YES** ——▶ Use the *-s* form.

NO

Is the subject a singular indefinite pronoun—*anybody, anyone, each, either, everybody, everyone, everything, neither, no one, someone,* or *something*? —— **YES** ——▶ Use the *-s* form.

NO

Use the base form of the verb (such as *love, try, have, do*).

EXCEPTION: Choosing the correct present-tense form of *be* (*am, is,* or *are*) is not always so simple. See the chart on the previous page for both present- and past-tense forms of *be*.

ESL TIP: Do not use the *-s* form of a verb if it follows a modal verb such as *can, must,* or *should* or another helping verb. (See M1-c.)

▶ The governor as well as his press secretary ~~were~~ on

was
⌃

the plane.

To emphasize that two people were on the plane, the writer could use *and* instead: *The governor and his press secretary were on the plane.*

G1-c Treat most subjects joined with *and* as plural.

A subject with two or more parts is said to be compound. If the parts are connected with *and*, the subject is nearly always plural.

Leon and Jan often *jog* together.

▶ The Supreme Court's willingness to hear the case and its
                                                    have
affirmation of the lower court's decision ~~has~~ set a new precedent.

EXCEPTIONS: When the parts of the subject form a single unit or when they refer to the same person or thing, treat the subject as singular.

Fish and chips was a last-minute addition to the menu.

Sue's friend and adviser was surprised by her decision.

When a compound subject is preceded by *each* or *every*, treat it as singular.

Each tree, shrub, and vine needs to be sprayed.

This exception does not apply when a compound subject is followed by *each: Alan and Marcia each have different ideas.*

G1-d With subjects joined with *or* or *nor* (or with *either . . . or* or *neither . . . nor*), make the verb agree with the part of the subject nearer to the verb.

A driver's *license* or credit *card is* required.

A driver's *license* or two credit *cards are* required.

                      is
▶ If an infant or a child ~~are~~ having difficulty breathing, seek

medical attention immediately.

▶ Neither the chief financial officer nor the marketing
                    were
managers ~~was~~ able to convince the client to reconsider.

The verb must be matched with the part of the subject closer to it: *child is* in the first sentence, *managers were* in the second.

NOTE: If one part of the subject is singular and the other is plural, put the plural one last to avoid awkwardness.

G1-e Treat most indefinite pronouns as singular.

Indefinite pronouns are pronouns that do not refer to specific persons or things. The following commonly used indefinite pronouns are singular.

anybody	each	everyone	nobody	somebody
anyone	either	everything	no one	someone
anything	everybody	neither	nothing	something

Many of these words appear to have plural meanings, and they are often treated as plural in casual speech. In formal written English, however, they are nearly always treated as singular.

Everyone on the team *supports* the coach.

> Each of the furrows ~~have~~ been seeded.
> *has*

> Nobody who participated in the clinical trials ~~were~~ given a placebo.
> *was*

The subjects of these sentences are *Each* and *Nobody*. These indefinite pronouns are third-person singular, so the verbs must be *has* and *was*.

A few indefinite pronouns (*all, any, none, some*) may be singular or plural depending on the noun or pronoun they refer to.

SINGULAR   *Some* of our *luggage was* lost.

None of his *advice makes* sense.

PLURAL   *Some* of the *rocks are* slippery.

None of the *eggs were* broken.

NOTE: When the meaning of *none* is emphatically "not one," *none* may be treated as singular: *None* [meaning "Not one"] *of the eggs was broken.* Using *not one* instead is sometimes clearer: *Not one of the eggs was broken.*

G1-f Treat collective nouns as singular unless the meaning is clearly plural.

Collective nouns such as *jury, committee, audience, crowd, troop, family,* and *couple* name a class or a group. In American English, collective nouns are nearly always treated as singular: They emphasize the group as a unit. Occasionally, when there is some reason to draw attention to the individual members of the group, a collective noun may be treated as plural. (See also p. 198.)

SINGULAR　The *class respects* the teacher.

PLURAL　The *class are* debating among themselves.

To emphasize the notion of individuality in the second sentence, many writers would add a clearly plural noun.

PLURAL　The class *members are* debating among themselves.

▶ The board of trustees ~~meet~~ *meets* in Denver twice a year.

The board as a whole meets; there is no reason to draw attention to its individual members.

▶ A young couple ~~was~~ *were* arguing about politics while holding hands.

The meaning is clearly plural. Only separate individuals can argue and hold hands.

NOTE: The phrase *the number* is treated as singular, *a number* as plural.

SINGULAR　*The number* of school-age children *is* declining.

PLURAL　A *number* of children *are* attending the wedding.

NOTE: In general, when fractions or units of measurement are used with a singular noun, treat them as singular; when they are used with a plural noun, treat them as plural.

SINGULAR　*Three-fourths* of the salad *has* been eaten.

Twenty *inches* of wallboard *was* covered with mud.

PLURAL　*One-fourth* of the drivers *were* texting.

Two *pounds* of blueberries *were* used to make the pie.

G1-g Make the verb agree with its subject even when the subject follows the verb.

Verbs ordinarily follow subjects. When the normal order is reversed, it is easy to be confused. Sentences beginning with *there is* or *there are* (or *there was, there were*) are inverted; the subject follows the verb.

There *are* surprisingly few *honeybees* left in southern China.

were
▶ There ~~was~~ a social worker and a neighbor at the scene of the crash.
   ^

The subject, *worker and neighbor*, is plural, so the verb must be *were*.

Occasionally you may invert a sentence for variety or effect. If you do, check to make sure that your subject and verb agree.

are
▶ Of particular concern ~~is~~ penicillin and tetracycline, antibiotics
   ^

used to make animals more resistant to disease.

The subject, *penicillin and tetracycline*, is plural, so the verb must be *are*.

G1-h Make the verb agree with its subject, not with a subject complement.

One basic sentence pattern in English consists of a subject, a linking verb, and a subject complement: *Jack is a lawyer.* Because the subject complement (*lawyer*) names or describes the subject (*Jack*), it is sometimes mistaken for the subject. (See B2-b on subject complements.)

is
▶ A major force in today's economy ~~are~~ children—as consumers,
   ^

decision makers, and trend spotters.

Force is the subject, not *children*. If the corrected version seems too awkward, make *children* the subject: *Children are a major force in today's economy—as consumers, decision makers, and trend spotters.*

are
▶ A tent and a sleeping bag ~~is~~ the required equipment for all campers.
   ^

Tent and bag is the subject, not *equipment*.

G1-i *Who, which,* and *that* take verbs that agree with their antecedents.

Like most pronouns, the relative pronouns *who, which,* and *that* have antecedents, nouns or pronouns to which they refer. Relative pronouns used as subjects of subordinate clauses take verbs that agree with their antecedents.

ANT   PN   V
Take a *course that prepares* you for classroom management.

One of the

Constructions such as *one of the students who* [or *one of the things that*] may cause problems for writers. Do not assume that the antecedent must be *one*. Instead, consider the logic of the sentence.

▶ Our ability to use language is one of the things that set̸s us

apart from animals.

The antecedent of *that* is *things*, not *one*. Several things set us apart from animals.

Only one of the

When the word *only* comes before *one*, you are safe in assuming that *one* is the antecedent of the relative pronoun.

▶ Veronica was the only one of the first-year Spanish students who
was
~~were~~ fluent enough to apply for the exchange program.
^
The antecedent of *who* is *one*, not *students*. Only one student was fluent enough.

G1-j Words such as *athletics, economics, mathematics, physics, politics, statistics, measles,* and *news* are usually singular, despite their plural form.

is
▶ Politics ~~are~~ among my mother's favorite pastimes.
^

EXCEPTION: Occasionally some of these words, especially *economics, mathematics, politics,* and *statistics,* have plural meanings:

Office politics often sway decisions about hiring and promotion.

The economics of the building plan are prohibitive.

G1-k Titles of works, company names, words mentioned as words, and gerund phrases are singular.

describes
▶ *Lost Cities* ~~describe~~ the discoveries of fifty ancient civilizations.
^
specializes
▶ Delmonico Brothers ~~specialize~~ in organic produce and
^
additive-free meats.

who, which, that • words like *politics* • titles, *-ing* phrases •
standard verb forms • irregular verbs (*go, went, gone*, etc.)

G2-a   183

▶ *Controlled substances* ~~are~~ a euphemism for illegal drugs.
                                is
                                ^

A gerund phrase consists of an *-ing* verb form followed by any objects, complements, or modifiers (see B3-b). Treat gerund phrases as singular.

▶ Encountering long hold times ~~make~~ customers impatient with
                                makes
                                ^
telephone tech support.

G2 Verb forms, tenses, and moods

Section G-1 deals with subject-verb agreement, and section W3 offers advice on active and passive verbs. This section describes other potential challenges with verbs:

  a. irregular verb forms (such as *drive, drove, driven*)
  b. *lie* and *lay*
  c. *-s* (or *-es*) endings on verbs
  d. *-ed* endings on verbs
  e. omitted verbs
  f. tense
  g. subjunctive mood

> **ESL** If English is not your native language, see also M1 for more help with verbs.

G2-a Choose standard English forms of irregular verbs.

Except for the verb *be*, all verbs in English have five forms. The following list shows the five forms and provides a sample sentence in which each might appear.

BASE FORM	Usually I (*walk, ride*).
PAST TENSE	Yesterday I (*walked, rode*).
PAST PARTICIPLE	I have (*walked, ridden*) many times before.
PRESENT PARTICIPLE	I am (*walking, riding*) right now.
-S FORM	He/she/it (*walks, rides*) regularly.

The verb *be* has eight forms instead of the usual five: *be, am, is, are, was, were, being, been.*

For all regular verbs, the past-tense and past-participle forms are the same (ending in *-ed* or *-d*), so there is no danger of confusion. This is not true, however, for irregular verbs, such as the following.

BASE FORM	PAST TENSE	PAST PARTICIPLE
go	went	gone
break	broke	broken
fly	flew	flown
sing	sang	sung

The past-tense form always occurs alone, without a helping verb. It expresses action that occurred entirely in the past: *I rode to work yesterday. I walked to work last Tuesday.* The past participle is used with a helping verb. It forms the perfect tenses with *has, have,* or *had;* it forms the passive voice with *be, am, is, are, was, were, being,* or *been.* (See B1-c for a complete list of helping verbs and G2-f for a survey of tenses.)

PAST TENSE	Last July, we *went* to Paris.
HELPING VERB + PAST PARTICIPLE	We *have gone* to Paris twice.

The list of common irregular verbs beginning at the bottom of this page will help you distinguish between the past tense and the past participle. Choose the past-participle form if the verb in your sentence requires a helping verb; choose the past-tense form if the verb does not require a helping verb. (See verb tenses in G2-f.)

▶ Yesterday we ~~seen~~ *saw* a documentary about Isabel Allende.

The past-tense *saw* is required because there is no helping verb.

▶ The truck was apparently ~~stole~~ *stolen* while the driver ate lunch.

▶ By Friday, the stock market had ~~fell~~ *fallen* two hundred points.

Because of the helping verbs *was* and *had,* the past-participle forms are required: *was stolen, had fallen.*

Common irregular verbs

BASE FORM	PAST TENSE	PAST PARTICIPLE
arise	arose	arisen
awake	awoke, awaked	awaked, awoke, awoken
be	was, were	been

BASE FORM	PAST TENSE	PAST PARTICIPLE
beat	beat	beaten, beat
become	became	become
begin	began	begun
bend	bent	bent
bite	bit	bitten, bit
blow	blew	blown
break	broke	broken
bring	brought	brought
build	built	built
burst	burst	burst
buy	bought	bought
catch	caught	caught
choose	chose	chosen
cling	clung	clung
come	came	come
cost	cost	cost
deal	dealt	dealt
dig	dug	dug
dive	dived, dove	dived
do	did	done
drag	dragged	dragged
draw	drew	drawn
dream	dreamed, dreamt	dreamed, dreamt
drink	drank	drunk
drive	drove	driven
eat	ate	eaten
fall	fell	fallen
fight	fought	fought
find	found	found
fly	flew	flown
forget	forgot	forgotten, forgot
freeze	froze	frozen
get	got	gotten, got
give	gave	given
go	went	gone
grow	grew	grown
hang (execute)	hanged	hanged
hang (suspend)	hung	hung
have	had	had
hear	heard	heard
hide	hid	hidden
hurt	hurt	hurt
keep	kept	kept
know	knew	known
lay (put)	laid	laid
lead	led	led
lend	lent	lent
let (allow)	let	let

BASE FORM	PAST TENSE	PAST PARTICIPLE
lie (recline)	lay	lain
lose	lost	lost
make	made	made
prove	proved	proved, proven
read	read	read
ride	rode	ridden
ring	rang	rung
rise (get up)	rose	risen
run	ran	run
say	said	said
see	saw	seen
send	sent	sent
set (place)	set	set
shake	shook	shaken
shoot	shot	shot
shrink	shrank	shrunk
sing	sang	sung
sink	sank	sunk
sit (be seated)	sat	sat
slay	slew	slain
sleep	slept	slept
speak	spoke	spoken
spin	spun	spun
spring	sprang	sprung
stand	stood	stood
steal	stole	stolen
sting	stung	stung
strike	struck	struck, stricken
swear	swore	sworn
swim	swam	swum
swing	swung	swung
take	took	taken
teach	taught	taught
throw	threw	thrown
wake	woke, waked	waked, woken
wear	wore	worn
wring	wrung	wrung
write	wrote	written

G2-b Distinguish among the forms of *lie* and *lay*.

Writers and speakers frequently confuse the various forms of *lie* (meaning "to recline or rest on a surface") and *lay* (meaning "to put or place something"). *Lie* is an intransitive verb; it does not take a direct object: *The tax forms lie on the table.* The verb *lay* is transitive; it takes a direct object: *Please lay the tax forms on the table.* (See B2-b.)

In addition to confusing the meaning of *lie* and *lay*, writers and speakers are often unfamiliar with the standard English forms of these verbs.

BASE FORM	PAST TENSE	PAST PARTICIPLE	PRESENT PARTICIPLE
lie ("recline")	lay	lain	lying
lay ("put")	laid	laid	laying

▶ Sue was so exhausted that she ~~laid~~ down for a nap.
                                    ^lay

The past-tense form of *lie* ("to recline") is *lay*.

▶ The patient had ~~laid~~ in an uncomfortable position all night.
                   ^lain

The past-participle form of *lie* ("to recline") is *lain*. If the correct English seems too stilted, recast the sentence: *The patient had been lying in an uncomfortable position all night.*

▶ The prosecutor ~~lay~~ the pistol on a table close to the jurors.
                  ^laid

The past-tense form of *lay* ("to place") is *laid*.

▶ Letters dating from the Civil War were ~~laying~~ in the corner of the
                                          ^lying
chest.

The present participle of *lie* ("to rest on a surface") is *lying*.

G2-c Use *-s* (or *-es*) endings on present-tense verbs that have third-person singular subjects.

All singular nouns (*child*, *tree*) and the pronouns *he*, *she*, and *it* are third-person singular; indefinite pronouns such as *everyone* and *neither* are also third-person singular. When the subject of a sentence is third-person singular, its verb takes an *-s* or *-es* ending in the present tense. (See also G1.)

	SINGULAR		PLURAL	
FIRST PERSON	I	know	we	know
SECOND PERSON	you	know	you	know
THIRD PERSON	he/she/it	knows	they	know
	child	knows	parents	know
	everyone	knows		

▶ My neighbor ~~drive~~ *drives* to Marco Island every weekend.

▶ Sulfur dioxide ~~turn~~ *turns* leaves yellow, ~~dissolve~~ *dissolves* marble, and ~~eat~~ *eats* away iron and steel.

> The subjects *neighbor* and *sulfur dioxide* are third-person singular, so the verbs must end in -*s*.

TIP: Do not add the -*s* ending to the verb if the subject is not third-person singular. The writers of the following sentences, knowing they sometimes dropped -*s* endings from verbs, overcorrected by adding the endings where they don't belong.

▶ I prepares program specifications and logic diagrams.

> The writer mistakenly concluded that the -*s* ending belongs on present-tense verbs used with *all* singular subjects, not just *third-person* singular subjects. The pronoun *I* is first-person singular, so its verb does not require the -*s*.

▶ The dirt floors requires continual sweeping.

> The writer mistakenly thought that the verb needed an -*s* ending because of the plural subject. But the -*s* ending is used only on present-tense verbs with third-person *singular* subjects.

In nonstandard speech, the -*s* verb form *has, does,* or *doesn't* is sometimes replaced with *have, do,* or *don't.* In standard English, use *has, does,* or *doesn't* with a third-person singular subject. (See also G1-a.)

▶ This respected musician always ~~have~~ *has* a message in his work.

▶ ~~Do~~ *Does* she know the correct procedure for the experiment?

▶ My uncle ~~don't~~ *doesn't* want to change jobs right now.

G2-d Do not omit -*ed* endings on verbs.

Speakers who do not fully pronounce -*ed* endings sometimes omit them unintentionally in writing. Leaving off -*ed* endings is common in many dialects and in informal speech even in standard English. In the following frequently used words and phrases, for example, the -*ed* ending is not always fully pronounced.

advised	developed	prejudiced	supposed to
asked	fixed	pronounced	used to
concerned	frightened	stereotyped	

When a verb is regular, both the past tense and the past participle are formed by adding -ed (or -d) to the base form of the verb.

Past tense

Use the ending -ed or -d to express the past tense of regular verbs. The past tense is used when the action occurred entirely in the past.

▶ Over the weekend, Ed ~~fix~~ his brother's skateboard and tuned up
                  fixed ^

   his mother's 1991 Fiat.

▶ Last summer, my counselor ~~advise~~ me to ask my chemistry
                  advised ^

   instructor for help.

Past participles

Past participles are used in three ways: (1) following *have, has,* or *had* to form one of the perfect tenses; (2) following *be, am, is, are, was, were, being,* or *been* to form the passive voice; and (3) as adjectives modifying nouns or pronouns. The perfect tenses are listed on page 191, and the passive voice is discussed in W3. For a discussion of participles as adjectives, see B3-b.

▶ Robin has ~~ask~~ for more housing staff for next year.
           asked ^

   Has asked is present perfect tense (*have* or *has* followed by a past participle).

▶ Though it is not a new phenomenon, domestic violence is now
   publicized
   ~~publicize~~ more than ever.
   ^

   Is publicized is a verb in the passive voice (a form of *be* followed by a past participle).

▶ All kickboxing classes end in a cool-down period to stretch
   tightened
   ~~tighten~~ muscles.
   ^

   The past participle *tightened* functions as an adjective modifying the noun *muscles.*

G2-e Do not omit needed verbs.

Although standard English allows some linking verbs and helping verbs to be contracted in informal contexts, it does not allow them to be omitted.

Linking verbs, used to link subjects to subject complements, are frequently a form of *be*: *be, am, is, are, was, were, being, been*. (See B2-b.) Some of these forms may be contracted (*I'm, she's, we're, you're, they're*), but they should not be omitted altogether.

> When we quiet in the evening, we can hear crickets in the woods.

        are

Helping verbs, used with main verbs, include forms of *be, do,* and *have* and the modal verbs *can, will, shall, could, would, should, may, might,* and *must*. (See B1-c.) Some helping verbs may be contracted (*he's leaving, we'll celebrate, they've been told*), but they should not be omitted altogether.

> We been in Chicago since last Thursday.

        have

ESL   Some languages do not require a linking verb between a subject and its complement. English, however, requires a verb in every sentence. See M3-a.

> Every night, I read a short book to my daughter. When I
>
>   *am*
>
> too busy, my husband reads to her.

G2-f Choose the appropriate verb tense.

Tenses indicate the time of an action in relation to the time of the speaking or writing about that action.

The most common problem with tenses—shifting confusingly from one tense to another—is discussed in section S4. Other problems with tenses are detailed in this section, after the following survey of tenses.

Survey of tenses

Tenses are classified as present, past, and future, with simple, perfect, and progressive forms for each.

missing verbs • linking verbs (*is, were*) • tenses •
simple (*walk*) • perfect (*had walked*) • progressive (*am walking*)

G2-f   191

SIMPLE TENSES   The simple tenses indicate relatively simple time relations. The *simple present* tense is used primarily for actions occurring at the same time they are being discussed or for actions occurring regularly. The *simple past* tense is used for actions completed in the past. The *simple future* tense is used for actions that will occur in the future. In the following table, the simple tenses are given for the regular verb *walk*, the irregular verb *ride*, and the highly irregular verb *be*.

SIMPLE PRESENT

SINGULAR		PLURAL	
I	walk, ride, am	we	walk, ride, are
you	walk, ride, are	you	walk, ride, are
he/she/it	walks, rides, is	they	walk, ride, are

SIMPLE PAST

SINGULAR		PLURAL	
I	walked, rode, was	we	walked, rode, were
you	walked, rode, were	you	walked, rode, were
he/she/it	walked, rode, was	they	walked, rode, were

SIMPLE FUTURE

I, you, he/she/it, we, they	will walk, ride, be

PERFECT TENSES   More complex time relations are indicated by the perfect tenses. A verb in one of the perfect tenses (a form of *have* plus the past participle) expresses an action that was or will be completed at the time of another action.

PRESENT PERFECT

I, you, we, they	have walked, ridden, been
he/she/it	has walked, ridden, been

PAST PERFECT

I, you, he/she/it, we, they	had walked, ridden, been

FUTURE PERFECT

I, you, he/she/it, we, they	will have walked, ridden, been

PROGRESSIVE FORMS   The simple and perfect tenses have progressive forms that describe actions in progress. A progressive verb consists of a form of *be* followed by a present participle. The progressive forms are not normally used with certain verbs, such as *believe, know, hear, seem,* and *think*.

PRESENT PROGRESSIVE

I	am walking, riding, being
he/she/it	is walking, riding, being
you, we, they	are walking, riding, being

PAST PROGRESSIVE

I, he/she/it	was walking, riding, being
you, we, they	were walking, riding, being

FUTURE PROGRESSIVE

I, you, he/she/it, we, they	will be walking, riding, being

PRESENT PERFECT PROGRESSIVE

I, you, we, they	have been walking, riding, being
he/she/it	has been walking, riding, being

PAST PERFECT PROGRESSIVE

I, you, he/she/it, we, they	had been walking, riding, being

FUTURE PERFECT PROGRESSIVE

I, you, he/she/it, we, they	will have been walking, riding, being

ESL   See M1-a for more specific examples of verb tenses that can be challenging for multilingual writers.

Special uses of the present tense

Use the present tense when expressing general truths, when writing about literature, and when quoting, summarizing, or paraphrasing an author's views.

General truths or scientific principles should appear in the present tense unless such principles have been disproved.

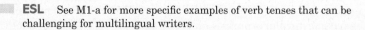

▶ Galileo taught that the earth ~~revolved~~ around the sun.

Because Galileo's teaching has not been discredited, the verb should be in the present tense. The following sentence, however, is acceptable: *Ptolemy taught that the sun revolved around the earth.*

When writing about a work of literature, you may be tempted to use the past tense. The convention, however, is to describe fictional events in the present tense.

>   *reaches*
> ▶ In Masuji Ibuse's *Black Rain,* a child ~~reached~~ for a pomegranate
>   ^   *is*
> in his mother's garden, and a moment later he ~~was~~ dead, killed
>   ^
> by the blast of the atomic bomb.

When you are quoting, summarizing, or paraphrasing the author of a nonliterary work, use present-tense verbs such as *writes*, *reports*, *asserts*, and so on to introduce the source. This convention is usually followed even when the author is dead (unless a date or the context specifies the time of writing).

>   *argues*
> ▶ Dr. Jerome Groopman ~~argued~~ that doctors are "susceptible
>   ^
> to the subtle and not so subtle efforts of the pharmaceutical
>
> industry to sculpt our thinking" (9).

*Writing
with
sources*

MLA-style
citation

In MLA style, signal phrases are written in the present tense, not the past tense. (See also MLA-3b.)

APA NOTE: When you are documenting a paper with the APA (American Psychological Association) style of in-text citations, use past tense verbs such as *reported* or *demonstrated* or present perfect verbs such as *has reported* or *has demonstrated* to introduce the source.

> E. Wilson (1994) reported that positive reinforcement alone was a less effective teaching technique than a mixture of positive reinforcement and constructive criticism.

The past perfect tense

The past perfect tense consists of a past participle preceded by *had* (*had worked*, *had forgotten*). This tense is used for an action already completed by the time of another past action or for an action already completed at some specific past time.

> Everyone *had spoken* by the time I arrived.
>
> I pleaded my case, but Paula *had made up* her mind.

Writers sometimes use the simple past tense when they should use the past perfect.

>
> ▶ We built our cabin high on a pine knoll, forty feet above an
>   *had been*
> abandoned quarry that ~~was~~ flooded in 1920 to create a lake.
>   ^

The building of the cabin and the flooding of the quarry both occurred in the past, but the flooding was completed before the time of building.

> *had*
> ▶ By the time dinner was served, the guest of honor ~~left~~.
>   ^

The past perfect tense is needed because the action of leaving was already completed at a specific past time (when dinner was served).

Some writers tend to overuse the past perfect tense. Do not use the past perfect if two past actions occurred at the same time.

> *wrote*
> ▶ When Ernest Hemingway lived in Cuba, he ~~had written~~ *For Whom*
>   ^
> *the Bell Tolls.*

Sequence of tenses with infinitives and participles

An infinitive is the base form of a verb preceded by *to*. (See B3-b.) Use the present infinitive to show action occurring at the same time as or later than the action of the verb in the sentence.

> *raise*
> ▶ The club had hoped to ~~have raised~~ fifteen thousand dollars by
>   ^
> April 1.

The action expressed in the infinitive (*to raise*) occurred later than the action of the sentence's verb (*had hoped*).

Use the perfect form of an infinitive (*to have* followed by the past participle) for an action occurring earlier than that of the verb in the sentence.

> *have joined*
> ▶ Dan would like to ~~join~~ the navy, but he did not pass the physical.
>   ^

The liking occurs in the present; the joining would have occurred in the past.

Like the tense of an infinitive, the tense of a participle is governed by the tense of the sentence's verb. Use the present participle (ending in *-ing*) for an action occurring at the same time as that of the sentence's verb.

> *Hiking* the Appalachian Trail in early spring, we spotted many wildflowers.

Use the past participle (such as *given* or *helped*) or the present perfect participle (*having* plus the past participle) for an action occurring before that of the verb.

Discovered off the coast of Florida, the Spanish galleon yielded many treasures.

Having worked her way through college, Lee graduated debt-free.

G2-g Use the subjunctive mood in the few contexts that require it.

There are three moods in English: the *indicative*, used for facts, opinions, and questions; the *imperative*, used for orders or advice; and the *subjunctive*, used in certain contexts to express wishes, requests, or conditions contrary to fact. For many writers, the subjunctive causes the most problems.

Forms of the subjunctive

In the subjunctive mood, present-tense verbs do not change form to indicate the number and person of the subject (see G1-a). Instead, the subjunctive uses the base form of the verb (*be, drive, employ*) with all subjects.

It is important that you *be* [not *are*] prepared for the interview.

We asked that she *drive* [not *drives*] more slowly.

Also, in the subjunctive mood, there is only one past-tense form of *be*: *were* (never *was*).

If I *were* [not *was*] you, I'd try a new strategy.

Uses of the subjunctive

The subjunctive mood appears in only a few contexts: in contrary-to-fact clauses beginning with *if* or expressing a wish; in *that* clauses following verbs such as *ask, insist, recommend, request,* and *suggest*; and in certain set expressions.

IN CONTRARY-TO-FACT CLAUSES BEGINNING WITH *IF* When a subordinate clause beginning with *if* expresses a condition contrary to fact, use the subjunctive *were* in place of *was*.

▶ The astronomers would be able to see the moons of Jupiter
tonight if the weather ~~was~~ *were* clearer.

The verb in the subordinate clause expresses a condition that does not exist: The weather is not clear.

▶ *were*
If I ~~was~~ a member of Congress, I would vote for that bill.
    ^

The writer is not a member of Congress, so the verb in the *if* clause must be *were*.

Do not use the subjunctive mood in *if* clauses expressing conditions that exist or may exist.

If Dana *wins* the contest, she will leave for Barcelona in June.

IN CONTRARY-TO-FACT CLAUSES EXPRESSING A WISH In formal English, use the subjunctive *were* in clauses expressing a wish or desire. While use of the indicative is common in informal speech, it is not appropriate in academic writing.

> INFORMAL   I wish that Dr. Vaughn *was* my professor.
>
> FORMAL   I wish that Dr. Vaughn *were* my professor.

IN *THAT* CLAUSES FOLLOWING VERBS SUCH AS *ASK*, *INSIST*, *REQUEST*, AND *SUGGEST* Because requests have not yet become reality, they are expressed in the subjunctive mood.

▶ *be*
Professor Moore insists that her students ~~are~~ on time.
                        ^

▶ *file*
We recommend that Lambert ~~files~~ form 1050 soon.
                    ^

IN CERTAIN SET EXPRESSIONS The subjunctive mood appears in certain expressions: *be that as it may*, *as it were*, *far be it from me*, and so on.

G3 Pronouns

Pronouns are words that substitute for nouns (see B1-b). Pronoun errors are typically related to the four topics discussed in this section:

    a.   pronoun-antecedent agreement (singular vs. plural)
    b.   pronoun reference (clarity)
    c.   pronoun case (personal pronouns such as *I* vs. *me*, *she* vs. *her*)
    d.   pronoun case (*who* vs. *whom*)

For more help with pronouns, consult the glossary of usage (W1).

G3-a Make pronouns and antecedents agree.

Many pronouns have antecedents, nouns or pronouns to which they refer. A pronoun and its antecedent agree when they are both singular or both plural.

SINGULAR   *Dr. Ava Berto* finished *her* rounds.

PLURAL   The hospital *interns* finished *their* rounds.

> **ESL**   The pronouns *he, his, she, her, it,* and *its* must agree in gender (masculine, feminine, or neuter) with their antecedents, not with the words they modify.
>
>   *Steve* visited *his* [not *her*] sister in Seattle.

Indefinite pronouns

Indefinite pronouns refer to nonspecific persons or things. Even though some of the following indefinite pronouns may seem to have plural meanings, treat them as singular in formal English.

anybody	each	everyone	nobody	somebody
anyone	either	everything	no one	someone
anything	everybody	neither	nothing	something

Everyone performs at *his or her* [not *their*] own fitness level.

When a plural pronoun refers mistakenly to a singular indefinite pronoun, you can usually choose one of three options for revision:

1.   Replace the plural pronoun with *he or she* (or *his or her*).
2.   Make the antecedent plural.
3.   Rewrite the sentence so that no agreement problem exists.

▶ When someone travels outside the United States for the first time,
   he or she needs
   ~~they need~~ to apply for a passport.
  ^

    people travel
▶ When ~~someone travels~~ outside the United States for the first time,
    ^
   they need to apply for a passport.

PRACTICE   hackerhandbooks.com/writersref
  > Grammatical sentences > G3–8 to G3–10

Anyone who
▶ ~~When someone~~ travels outside the United States for the first time,/
  ^
  needs
  ~~they need~~ to apply for a passport.
  ^

Because the *he or she* construction is wordy, often the second or third revision strategy is more effective. Using *he* (or *his*) to refer to persons of either sex, while less wordy, is considered sexist, as is using *she* (or *her*) for all persons. See W4-e for strategies that avoid sexist usage.

NOTE: If you change a pronoun from singular to plural (or vice versa), check to be sure that the verb agrees with the new pronoun (see G1-e).

Generic nouns

A generic noun represents a typical member of a group, such as *a typical student*, or any member of a group, such as *any lawyer*. Although generic nouns may seem to have plural meanings, they are singular.

> Every *runner* must train rigorously if *he or she wants* [not *they want*] to excel.

When a plural pronoun refers mistakenly to a generic noun, you will usually have the same revision options as on page 197.

                                      he or she wants
▶ A medical student must study hard if ~~they want~~ to succeed.
                                        ^

  Medical students
▶ ~~A medical student~~ must study hard if they want to succeed.
  ^

▶ A medical student must study hard ~~if they want~~ to succeed.

Collective nouns

Collective nouns such as *jury, committee, audience, crowd, class, troop, family, team,* and *couple* name a group. Ordinarily the group functions as a unit, so the noun should be treated as singular; if the members of the group function as individuals, however, the noun should be treated as plural. (See also G1-f.)

AS A UNIT   The *committee* granted *its* permission to build.

AS INDIVIDUALS   The *committee* put *their* signatures on the letter.

When treating a collective noun as plural, many writers prefer to add a clearly plural antecedent such as *members* to the sentence: *The members of the committee put their signatures on the letter.*

▶ Defense attorney Clarence Darrow urged the jury to find his client,

John Scopes, guilty so that he could appeal the case to a higher

its
court. The jury complied, returning ~~their~~ verdict in nine minutes.
                                      ^
There is no reason to draw attention to the individual members of the
jury, so *jury* should be treated as singular.

Compound antecedents

Treat most compound antecedents joined with *and* as plural.

In 1987, *Reagan and Gorbachev* held a summit where *they*
signed the Intermediate-Range Nuclear Forces Treaty.

With compound antecedents joined with *or* or *nor* (or with *either . . . or* or
neither . . . nor), make the pronoun agree with the nearer antecedent.

Either *Bruce* or *Tom* should receive first prize for *his* poem.

Neither the *mouse* nor the *rats* could find *their* way through the maze.

NOTE: If one of the antecedents is singular and the other plural, as
in the second example, put the plural one last to avoid awkwardness.

EXCEPTION: If one antecedent is male and the other female, do not
follow the traditional rule. The sentence *Either Bruce or Elizabeth
should receive first prize for her short story* makes no sense. A better
solution is to recast the sentence: *The prize for best short story should
go to either Bruce or Elizabeth.*

G3-b Make pronoun references clear.

In a sentence like *After Andrew intercepted the ball, he kicked it as
hard as he could,* the pronouns *he* and *it* substitute for the nouns
Andrew and *ball.* The word a pronoun refers to is called its *antecedent.*

Ambiguous reference

Ambiguous pronoun reference occurs when a pronoun could refer to
two possible antecedents.

PRACTICE hackerhandbooks.com/writersref
  > Grammatical sentences > G3–11 to G3–13

The pitcher broke when Gloria set it
▶ ~~When Gloria set the pitcher~~ on the glass-topped table~~/~~. ~~it broke.~~
  ^   ^

"You have
▶ Tom told James~~, that he had~~ won the lottery."
  ^   ^

What broke—the pitcher or the table? Who won the lottery—Tom or James? The revisions eliminate the ambiguity.

Implied reference

A pronoun should refer to a specific antecedent, not to a word that is implied but not present in the sentence.

                                                              the braids
▶ After braiding Ann's hair, Sue decorated ~~them~~ with colorful
                                              ^

silk ribbons.

The pronoun *them* referred to Ann's braids (implied by the term *braiding*), but the word *braids* did not appear in the sentence.

Modifiers, such as possessives, cannot serve as antecedents. A modifier may strongly imply the noun that a pronoun might logically refer to, but it is not itself that noun.

                              Jamaica Kincaid
Writing
with
sources
MLA-style
citation
▶ In ~~Jamaica Kincaid's~~ "Girl," ~~she~~ describes the advice a mother
                              ^

gives her daughter, including the mysterious warning not to be

"the kind of woman who the baker won't let near the bread" (454).

Using the possessive form of an author's name to introduce a source leads to a problem later in this sentence: The pronoun *she* cannot refer logically to a possessive modifier (*Jamaica Kincaid's*). The revision substitutes the noun *Jamaica Kincaid* for the pronoun *she*, thereby eliminating the problem.

Broad reference of this, that, which, *and* it

For clarity, the pronouns *this*, *that*, *which*, and *it* should ordinarily refer to specific antecedents rather than to whole ideas or sentences. When a pronoun's reference is needlessly broad, either replace the pronoun with a noun or supply an antecedent to which the pronoun clearly refers.

▶ By advertising on television, pharmaceutical companies gain

exposure for their prescription drugs. Patients respond
                                           the ads
to ~~this~~ by requesting drugs they might not need.
    ^

unclear, unstated antecedent • *this, that, which, it* •
they, it, you • *I* vs. *me, he* vs. *him, they* vs. *them,* etc.

G3-c   201

For clarity, the writer substituted the noun *ads* for the pronoun *this,* which referred broadly to the idea expressed in the preceding sentence.

▶ Romeo and Juliet were both too young to have acquired much
                    a fact
wisdom, ~~and~~ that accounts for their rash actions.
              ^

The writer added an antecedent (*fact*) that the pronoun *that* clearly refers to.

Indefinite use of *they, it, and* you

Do not use the pronoun *they* to refer indefinitely to persons who have not been specifically mentioned. *They* should always refer to a specific antecedent.

                  the board
▶ In June, ~~they~~ announced that parents would have to pay a fee
          ^
for their children to participate in sports and music programs

starting in September.

The word *it* should not be used indefinitely in constructions such as *It is said on television . . .* or *In the article, it says that. . . .*

      The
▶ ~~In the~~ encyclopedia ~~it~~ states that male moths can smell female
  ^
moths from several miles away.

The pronoun *you* is appropriate only when the writer is addressing the reader directly: *Once you have kneaded the dough, let it rise in a warm place.* Except in informal contexts, however, *you* should not be used to mean "anyone in general." Use a noun instead.

                                          a guest
▶ Ms. Pickersgill's *Guide to Etiquette* stipulates that ~~you~~
                                        ^
should not arrive at a party too early or leave too late.

G3-c Distinguish between pronouns such as *I* and *me.*

The personal pronouns in the following chart change what is known as *case form* according to their grammatical function in a sentence. Pronouns functioning as subjects or subject complements appear in the *subjective* case; those functioning as objects appear in the *objective* case; and those showing ownership appear in the *possessive* case.

PRACTICE   hackerhandbooks.com/writersref
> Grammatical sentences > G3–14 and G3–15
                        > G3–17 and G3–18 (pronoun review)

	SUBJECTIVE CASE	OBJECTIVE CASE	POSSESSIVE CASE
SINGULAR	I	me	my
	you	you	your
	he/she/it	him/her/it	his/her/its
PLURAL	we	us	our
	you	you	your
	they	them	their

Pronouns in the subjective and objective cases are frequently confused. Most of the rules in this section specify when to use one or the other of these cases (*I* or *me*, *he* or *him*, and so on). See page 205 for a special use of pronouns and nouns in the possessive case.

Subjective case (I, you, he, she, it, we, they)

When a pronoun functions as a subject or a subject complement, it must be in the subjective case.

SUBJECT   Sylvia and *he* shared the award.

SUBJECT   Greg announced that the winners were Sylvia
COMPLEMENT   and *he*.

Subject complements—words following linking verbs that complete the meaning of the subject—frequently cause problems for writers, since we rarely hear the correct form in casual speech. (See B2-b.)

▶ During the Lindbergh trial, Bruno Hauptmann repeatedly denied
  that the kidnapper was ~~him.~~ *he.*

If *kidnapper was he* seems too stilted, rewrite the sentence: *During the Lindbergh trial, Bruno Hauptmann repeatedly denied that he was the kidnapper.*

Objective case (me, you, him, her, it, us, them)

When a personal pronoun is used as a direct object, an indirect object, or the object of a preposition, it must be in the objective case.

DIRECT OBJECT   Bruce found Tony and brought *him* home.

INDIRECT   Alice gave *me* a surprise party.
OBJECT

OBJECT OF A   Jessica wondered if the call was for *her*.
PREPOSITION

I, you, he/she/it, we, they • subject pronouns • *me, you, him/her/it, us, them* • object pronouns • words that rename nouns • appositives

G3-c **203**

Compound word groups

When a subject or an object appears as part of a compound structure, you may occasionally become confused. To test for the correct pronoun, mentally strip away all of the compound word group except the pronoun in question.

▶ Joel ran away from home because his stepfather and ~~him~~ *he* had

quarreled.

His stepfather and he is the subject of the verb *had quarreled.* If we strip away the words *his stepfather and,* the correct pronoun becomes clear: *he had quarreled* (not *him had quarreled*).

▶ The most traumatic experience for her father and ~~I~~ *me* occurred long

after her operation.

Her father and me is the compound object of the preposition *for.* Strip away the words *her father and* to test for the correct pronoun: *for me* (not *for I*).

When in doubt about the correct pronoun, some writers try to avoid making the choice by using a reflexive pronoun such as *myself.* Using a reflexive pronoun in such situations is nonstandard.

▶ The Indian cab driver gave my cousin and ~~myself~~ *me* some good tips

on traveling in New Delhi.

My cousin and me is the indirect object of the verb *gave.* For correct uses of *myself,* see the glossary of usage (W1).

Appositives

Appositives are noun phrases that rename nouns or pronouns. A pronoun used as an appositive has the same function (usually subject or object) as the word(s) it renames.

▶ The chief strategists, Dr. Bell and ~~me,~~ *I,* could not agree on a plan.

The appositive *Dr. Bell and I* renames the subject, *strategists.* Test: *I could not agree* (not *me could not agree*).

▶ The newspaper reporter interviewed only two witnesses, the bicyclist

and ~~I.~~ *me.*

The appositive *the bicyclist and me* renames the direct object, *witnesses*. Test: *interviewed me* (not *interviewed I*).

We *or* us *before a noun*

When deciding whether *we* or *us* should precede a noun, choose the pronoun that would be appropriate if the noun were omitted.

> *We*
> ▶ ~~Us~~ tenants would rather fight than move.
>   ^

> ▶ Management is shortchanging ~~we~~ tenants.
>   *us* ^

No one would say *Us would rather fight than move* or *Management is shortchanging we.*

Comparisons with than *or* as

When a comparison begins with *than* or *as*, your choice of a pronoun will depend on your meaning. To test for the correct pronoun, mentally complete the sentence: *My roommate likes football more than I [do].*

> ▶ In our position paper supporting nationalized health care in the
>
> United States, we argued that Canadians are much better off
> *we.*
> than ~~us.~~
>   ^

We is the subject of the verb *are*, which is understood: *Canadians are much better off than we [are].* If the correct English seems too formal, you can always add the verb.

> ▶ We respected no other candidate for the city council as much
> *her.*
> as ~~she.~~
>   ^

This sentence means that we respected no other candidate as much as *we respected her. Her* is the direct object of the understood verb *respected*.

Subjects and objects of infinitives

An infinitive is the word *to* followed by the base form of a verb. (See B3-b.) Subjects of infinitives are an exception to the rule that subjects must be in the subjective case. Whenever an infinitive has a subject, it must be in the objective case. Objects of infinitives also are in the objective case.

> *me*   *her*
> ▶ Ms. Wilson asked John and ~~I~~ to drive the senator and ~~she~~ to the
>   ^   ^
> airport.

we or us with noun • with *than* or *as* • *me, you, him,* etc.
with infinitive (*to see*) • *my, your, their,* etc. with *-ing* form

G3-d   205

John and me is the subject of the infinitive *to drive*; *senator and her* is the direct object of the infinitive.

Possessive case to modify a gerund

A pronoun that modifies a gerund or a gerund phrase should be in the possessive case (*my, your, his, her, its, our, their*). A gerund is a verb form ending in *-ing* that functions as a noun. Gerunds frequently appear in phrases; when they do, the whole gerund phrase functions as a noun. (See B3-b.)

▶ The chances of ~~you~~ ^{your} being hit by lightning are about two million

to one.

Your modifies the gerund phrase *being hit by lightning*.

Nouns as well as pronouns may modify gerunds. To form the possessive case of a noun, use an apostrophe and an *-s* (*victim's*) or just an apostrophe (*victims'*). (See P4-a.)

▶ The old order in France paid a high price for the ~~aristocracy~~ ^{aristocracy's}

exploiting the lower classes.

The possessive noun *aristocracy's* modifies the gerund phrase *exploiting the lower classes*.

G3-d Distinguish between *who* and *whom*.

The choice between *who* and *whom* (or *whoever* and *whomever*) occurs primarily in subordinate clauses and in questions. *Who* and *whoever*, subjective-case pronouns, are used for subjects and subject complements. *Whom* and *whomever*, objective-case pronouns, are used for objects.

An exception to this general rule occurs when the pronoun functions as the subject of an infinitive (see p. 207).

In subordinate clauses

When *who* and *whom* (or *whoever* and *whomever*) introduce subordinate clauses, their case is determined by their function within the clause they introduce.

PRACTICE   hackerhandbooks.com/writersref
  > Grammatical sentences > G3–16
          > G3–17 and G3–18 (pronoun review)

In the following two examples, the pronouns *who* and *whoever* function as the subjects of the clauses they introduce.

▶ First prize goes to the runner ~~whom~~ earns the most points.

who

The subordinate clause is *who earns the most points*. The verb of the clause is *earns*, and its subject is *who*.

▶ Maya Angelou's *I Know Why the Caged Bird Sings* should be read by ~~whomever~~ is interested in the effects of racial prejudice on

whoever

children.

The writer selected the pronoun *whomever*, thinking that it was the object of the preposition *by*. However, the object of the preposition is the entire subordinate clause *whoever is interested in the effects of racial prejudice on children*. The verb of the clause is *is*, and the subject of the verb is *whoever*.

When functioning as an object in a subordinate clause, *whom* (or *whomever*) appears out of order, before the subject and verb. To choose the correct pronoun, you can mentally restructure the clause.

▶ You will work with our senior traders, ~~who~~ you will meet after

whom

your orientation.

The subordinate clause is *whom you will meet after your orientation*. The subject of the clause is *you*, and the verb is *will meet*. *Whom* is the direct object of the verb. The correct choice becomes clear if you mentally restructure the clause: *you will meet whom*.

When functioning as the object of a preposition in a subordinate clause, *whom* is often separated from its preposition.

▶ The tutor ~~who~~ I was assigned to was very supportive.

whom

Whom is the object of the preposition *to*. In this sentence, the writer might choose to drop *whom*: *The tutor I was assigned to was very supportive.*

NOTE: Inserted expressions such as *they know*, *I think*, and *she says* should be ignored in determining whether to use *who* or *whom*.

▶ The speech pathologist reported a particularly difficult session with a stroke patient ~~whom~~ she knew was suffering from aphasia.

who

Who is the subject of *was suffering*, not the object of *knew*.

In questions

The case of an interrogative pronoun is determined by its function within the question.

▶ ~~Whom~~ *Who* was responsible for creating that computer virus?

Who is the subject of the verb *was*.

When *whom* functions as the object in a question, it appears out of normal order. To choose the correct pronoun, you can mentally restructure the question.

▶ ~~Who~~ *Whom* did the Democratic Party nominate in 2004?

Whom is the direct object of the verb *did nominate*. This becomes clear if you restructure the question: *The Democratic Party did nominate whom in 2004?*

For subjects or objects of infinitives

An infinitive is the word *to* followed by the base form of a verb. (See B3-b.) Subjects of infinitives are an exception to the rule that subjects must be in the subjective case. The subject of an infinitive must be in the objective case. Objects of infinitives also are in the objective case. (See also p. 204.)

▶ When it comes to money, I know ~~who~~ *whom* to believe.

The infinitive phrase *whom to believe* is the direct object of the verb *know*, and *whom* is the subject of the infinitive *to believe*.

G4 Adjectives and adverbs

Adjectives modify nouns or pronouns. They usually come before the word they modify; occasionally they function as complements following the word they modify. Adverbs modify verbs, adjectives, or other adverbs. (See B1-d and B1-e.)

Many adverbs are formed by adding *-ly* to adjectives (*normal, normally; smooth, smoothly*). But don't assume that all words ending in *-ly* are adverbs or that all adverbs end in *-ly*. Some adjectives end in *-ly* (*lovely, friendly*), and some adverbs don't (*always, here, there*). When in doubt, consult a dictionary.

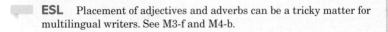

> **ESL** Placement of adjectives and adverbs can be a tricky matter for multilingual writers. See M3-f and M4-b.

G4-a Use adjectives to modify nouns.

Adjectives ordinarily precede the nouns they modify. But they can also function as subject complements or object complements, following the nouns they modify.

> **ESL** In English, adjectives are not pluralized to agree with the words they modify: *The red* [not *reds*] *roses were a surprise.*

Subject complements

A subject complement follows a linking verb and completes the meaning of the subject. (See B2-b.) When an adjective functions as a subject complement, it describes the subject.

Justice is *blind.*

Problems can arise with verbs such as *smell, taste, look,* and *feel,* which sometimes, but not always, function as linking verbs. If the word following one of these verbs describes the subject, use an adjective; if the word following the verb modifies the verb, use an adverb.

ADJECTIVE   The detective looked *cautious.*

ADVERB   The detective looked *cautiously* for fingerprints.

The adjective *cautious* describes the detective; the adverb *cautiously* modifies the verb *looked.*

Linking verbs suggest states of being, not actions. Notice, for example, the different meanings of *looked* in the preceding examples. To look cautious suggests the state of being cautious; to look cautiously is to perform an action in a cautious way.

▶ The lilacs in our backyard smell especially ~~sweetly~~ *sweet* this year.

The verb *smell* suggests a state of being, not an action. Therefore, it should be followed by an adjective, not an adverb.

▶ The drawings looked ~~well~~ *good* after the architect made a few changes.

The verb *looked* is a linking verb suggesting a state of being, not an action. The adjective *good* is appropriate following the linking verb to describe *drawings*. (See also the note on p. 210.)

When the verb *feel* refers to the state of a person's health or emotions, it is a linking verb and should be followed by an adjective (such as *bad*) instead of an adverb (such as *badly*).

>   *bad*
> ▶ We felt ~~badly~~ when we heard of your grandmother's death.
>   ^

Object complements

An object complement follows a direct object and completes its meaning. (See B2-b.) When an adjective functions as an object complement, it describes the direct object.

> Sorrow makes *us wise*.

Object complements occur with verbs such as *call, consider, create, find, keep,* and *make*. When a modifier follows the direct object of one of these verbs, use an adjective to describe the direct object; use an adverb to modify the verb.

ADJECTIVE	The referee called the plays *perfect*.
ADVERB	The referee called the plays *perfectly*.

The first sentence means that the referee considered the plays to be perfect; the second means that the referee did an excellent job of calling the plays.

G4-b Use adverbs to modify verbs, adjectives, and other adverbs.

When adverbs modify verbs (or verbals), they nearly always answer the question When? Where? How? Why? Under what conditions? How often? or To what degree? When adverbs modify adjectives or other adverbs, they usually qualify or intensify the meaning of the word they modify. (See B1-e.)

Adjectives are often used incorrectly in place of adverbs in casual or nonstandard speech.

>   *perfectly*
> ▶ The transportation arrangement worked out ~~perfect~~ for everyone.
>   ^
>   *smoothly*   *efficiently.*
> ▶ The manager must see that the office runs ~~smooth~~ and ~~efficient.~~
>   ^   ^

The adverb *perfectly* modifies the verb *worked out*; the adverbs *smoothly* and *efficiently* modify the verb *runs*.

▶ The chance of recovering any property lost in the fire looks
really
~~real~~ slim.
  ^

Only adverbs can modify adjectives or other adverbs. *Really* intensifies the meaning of the adjective *slim*.

NOTE: The incorrect use of the adjective *good* in place of the adverb *well* to modify a verb is especially common in casual and nonstandard speech. Use *well*, not *good*, to modify a verb in your writing.

                                     well
▶ We were glad that Sanya had done ~~good~~ on the CPA exam.
                                        ^

The adverb *well* should be used to modify the verb *had done*.

The word *well* is an adjective, however, when it means "healthy," "satisfactory," or "fortunate": *I feel very well today. All is well. It is just as well.*

For more help with *well* and *good*, consult the glossary of usage (W1).

ESL   The placement of adverbs varies from language to language. Unlike some languages, such as French and Spanish, English does not allow an adverb between a verb (*poured*) and its direct object (*the liquid*). See M3-f.

                                            slowly
▶ In the last stage of our experiment, we poured ~~slowly~~ the
                                             ^

  liquid into the container.

G4-c Use comparatives and superlatives with care.

Most adjectives and adverbs have three forms: the positive, the comparative, and the superlative.

POSITIVE	COMPARATIVE	SUPERLATIVE
soft	softer	softest
fast	faster	fastest
careful	more careful	most careful
bad	worse	worst
good	better	best

Comparative versus superlative

Use the comparative to compare two things, the superlative to compare three or more.

> *better?*
> ▶ Which of these two low-carb drinks is ~~best~~?
> ^

> *most*
> ▶ Though Shaw and Jackson are impressive, Hobbs is the ~~more~~
> ^
> qualified of the three candidates running for mayor.

Forming comparatives and superlatives

To form comparatives and superlatives of one-syllable adjectives, use the endings *-er* and *-est*: *smooth, smoother, smoothest; dark, darker, darkest*. For adjectives with three or more syllables, use *more* and *most* (or *less* and *least* for downward comparisons): *exciting, more exciting, most exciting; interesting, less interesting, least interesting.* Two-syllable adjectives form comparatives and superlatives in both ways: *lovely, lovelier, loveliest; helpful, more helpful, most helpful.*

Some one-syllable adverbs take the endings *-er* and *-est* (*fast, faster, fastest*), but longer adverbs and all of those ending in *-ly* form the comparative and superlative with *more* and *most* (or *less* and *least*).

The comparative and superlative forms of some adjectives and adverbs are irregular: *good, better, best; well, better, best; bad, worse, worst; badly, worse, worst.*

> *most talented*
> ▶ The Kirov is the ~~talentedest~~ ballet company we have seen.
> ^

> ▶ According to our projections, sales at local businesses will be
> *worse*
> ~~worser~~ than those at the chain stores this winter.
> ^

Double comparatives or superlatives

Do not use double comparatives or superlatives. When you have added *-er* or *-est* to an adjective or adverb, do not also use *more* or *most* (or *less* or *least*).

> ▶ Of all her family, Julia is the ~~most~~ happiest about the move.

> *likely*
> ▶ All the polls indicated that Gore was more ~~likelier~~ to win than
> ^
> Bush.

Absolute concepts

Avoid expressions such as *more straight, less perfect, very round,* and *most unique.* Either something is unique or it isn't. It is illogical to suggest that absolute concepts come in degrees.

>   *unusual*
> ▶ That is the most ~~unique~~ wedding gown I have ever seen.

>   *valuable*
> ▶ The painting would have been even more ~~priceless~~ had it been
>
> signed.

G4-d Avoid double negatives.

Standard English allows two negatives only if a positive meaning is intended: *The orchestra was not unhappy with its performance* (meaning that the orchestra was happy). Using a double negative to emphasize a negative meaning is nonstandard.

Negative modifiers such as *never, no,* and *not* should not be paired with other negative modifiers or with negative words such as *neither, none, no one, nobody,* and *nothing.*

>   *anything*
> ▶ Management is not doing ~~nothing~~ to see that the trash is picked up.
>
> The double negative *not . . . nothing* is nonstandard.

The modifiers *hardly, barely,* and *scarcely* are considered negatives in standard English, so they should not be used with negatives such as *not, no one,* or *never.*

>   *can*
> ▶ Maxine is so weak that she ~~can't~~ hardly climb stairs.

≣ G5 Sentence fragments

A sentence fragment is a word group that pretends to be a sentence. Sentence fragments are easy to recognize when they appear out of context, like these:

When the cat leaped onto the table.

Running for the bus.

And immediately popped their flares and life vests.

Test for fragments

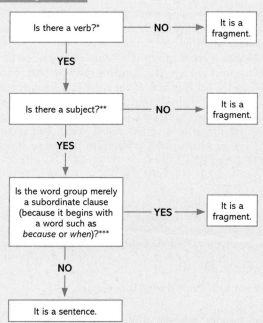

*Do not mistake verbals for verbs. A verbal is a verb form (such as *walking, to act*) that does not function as a verb of a clause. (See B3-b.)
**The subject of a sentence may be *you,* understood. (See B2-b.)
***A sentence may open with a subordinate clause, but the sentence must also include an independent clause. (See G5-a and B4-a.)

If you find any fragments, try one of these methods of revision (see G5-a to G5-c):

1. Attach the fragment to a nearby sentence.

2. Rewrite the fragment as a complete sentence.

When fragments appear next to related sentences, however, they are harder to spot.

We had just sat down to dinner. When the cat leaped onto the table.

I tripped and twisted my ankle. Running for the bus.

The pilots ejected from the burning plane, landing in the water not far from the ship. And immediately popped their flares and life vests.

Recognizing sentence fragments

To be a sentence, a word group must consist of at least one full independent clause. An independent clause includes a subject and a verb, and it either stands alone or could stand alone.

To test whether a word group is a complete sentence or a fragment, use the flowchart on page 213. By using the flowchart, you can see exactly why *When the cat leaped onto the table* is a fragment: It has a subject (*cat*) and a verb (*leaped*), but it begins with a subordinating word (*When*). *Running for the bus* is a fragment because it lacks a subject and a verb (*Running* is a verbal, not a verb). *And immediately popped their flares and life vests* is a fragment because it lacks a subject. (See also B3-b and B3-e.)

ESL Unlike some other languages, English requires a subject and a verb in every sentence (except in commands, where the subject *you* is understood but not present: *Sit down*). See M3-a and M3-b.

> *It is*
> ► ~~Is~~ often hot and humid during the summer.
>   ^

> *are*
> ► Students usually very busy at the end of the semester.
>   ^

Repairing sentence fragments

You can repair most fragments in one of two ways:

1. Pull the fragment into a nearby sentence.
2. Rewrite the fragment as a complete sentence.

> *when*
> ► We had just sat down to dinner / ~~When~~ the cat leaped onto the
>   ^
>
> table.

> *Running for the bus,*
> ► I tripped and twisted my ankle. ~~Running for the bus.~~
>   ^

> ► The pilots ejected from the burning plane, landing in the water
>
>   *They*
>   not far from the ship. ~~And~~ immediately popped their flares and
>   ^
>
>   life vests.

G5-a Attach fragmented subordinate clauses or turn them into sentences.

A subordinate clause is patterned like a sentence, with both a subject and a verb, but it begins with a word that marks it as subordinate. The following words commonly introduce subordinate clauses.

after	before	so that	until	while
although	even though	than	when	who
as	how	that	where	whom
as if	if	though	whether	whose
because	since	unless	which	why

Subordinate clauses function within sentences as adjectives, as adverbs, or as nouns. They cannot stand alone. (See B3-e.)

Most fragmented clauses beg to be pulled into a sentence nearby.

▶ Americans have come to fear the West Nile virus/ ~~Because~~ *because*

it is transmitted by the common mosquito.

Because introduces a subordinate clause, so it cannot stand alone. (For punctuation of subordinate clauses at the end of a sentence, see P2-f.)

If a fragmented clause cannot be attached to a nearby sentence or if you feel that attaching it would be awkward, try turning the clause into a sentence. The simplest way to do this is to delete the opening word or words that mark it as subordinate.

▶ Population increases and uncontrolled development are taking
a deadly toll on the environment. ~~So that across~~ *Across* the globe, fragile

ecosystems are collapsing.

G5-b Attach fragmented phrases or turn them into sentences.

Like subordinate clauses, phrases function within sentences as adjectives, as adverbs, or as nouns. They cannot stand alone. Fragmented phrases are often prepositional or verbal phrases; sometimes they are appositives, words or word groups that rename nouns or pronouns. (See B3-a, B3-b, and B3-c.)

Often a fragmented phrase may simply be pulled into a nearby sentence.

> *examining*
> ► The archaeologists worked slowly/, ~~Examining~~ and labeling
>   ^
>
> every pottery shard they uncovered.

The word group beginning with *Examining* is a verbal phrase.

>   *a*
> ► The patient displayed symptoms of ALS/, ~~A~~ neurodegenerative
>   ^
>
> disease.

A neurodegenerative disease is an appositive renaming the noun *ALS*. (For punctuation of appositives, see P1-e.)

If a fragmented phrase cannot be pulled into a nearby sentence effectively, turn the phrase into a sentence. You may need to add a subject, a verb, or both.

>   *She also taught us*
> ► Jamie explained how to access our new database. ~~Also~~ how to
>   ^
>
> submit expense reports and request vendor payments.

The revision turns the fragmented phrase into a sentence by adding a subject and a verb.

G5-c Attach other fragmented word groups or turn them into sentences.

Other word groups that are commonly fragmented include parts of compound predicates, lists, and examples introduced by *for example*, *in addition*, or similar expressions.

Parts of compound predicates

A predicate consists of a verb and its objects, complements, and modifiers (see B2-b). A compound predicate includes two or more predicates joined with a coordinating conjunction such as *and*, *but*, or *or*. Because the parts of a compound predicate have the same subject, they should appear in the same sentence.

> ► The woodpecker finch of the Galápagos Islands carefully selects a
> *and*
> twig of a certain size and shape/ ~~And~~ then uses this tool to pry out
>   ^
>
> grubs from trees.

The subject is *finch*, and the compound predicate is *selects . . . and . . . uses*. (For punctuation of compound predicates, see P2-a.)

incomplete sentences • fixing fragments • phrases as fragments •
compound verbs • lists • fragments with *for example* etc.

G5-c   **217**

Lists

To correct a fragmented list, often you can attach it to a nearby sentence with a colon or a dash. (See P3-d and P6-b.)

> It has been said that there are only three indigenous American
> *musical*
> art forms/: ~~Musical~~ comedy, jazz, and soap opera.
>   ^

Sometimes terms like *especially*, *like*, and *such as* introduce fragmented lists. Such fragments can usually be attached to the preceding sentence.

> In the twentieth century, the South produced some great American
> *such*
> writers/, ~~Such~~ as Flannery O'Connor, William Faulkner, Alice
>   ^
> Walker, and Tennessee Williams.

Examples introduced by for example, in addition, or similar expressions

Expressions that introduce examples or explanations can lead to fragments. Although a sentence may begin with a word or phrase like the following, the rest of the sentence must include a subject and a verb.

also	for example	mainly
and	for instance	or
but	in addition	that is

Often the easiest solution is to turn the fragment into a sentence.

> A streaming gauge is useful for measuring a river's height and
> *it provides*
> flow. In addition, ~~providing~~ residents with early flood warnings.
>   ^

The writer corrected this fragment by adding a subject—*it*—and substituting the verb *provides* for the verbal *providing*.

Writing
with
sources

MLA-style
citation

> Tannen claims that men and women have different ideas about
> *she explains*
> communication. For example, that a woman "expects her husband
>   ^
> to be a new and improved version of her best friend" (441).

A quotation must be part of a complete sentence. *That a woman "expects her husband to be a new and improved version of her best friend"* is a fragment—a subordinate clause. Adding a signal phrase that includes a subject and a verb (*she explains*) corrects the fragment.

G5-d **Exception: A fragment may be used for effect.**

Writers occasionally use sentence fragments for special purposes.

FOR EMPHASIS   Following the dramatic Americanization of their children, even my parents grew more publicly confident. *Especially my mother.*   —Richard Rodriguez

TO ANSWER   Are these new drug tests 100 percent
A QUESTION   reliable? *Not in the opinion of most experts.*

TRANSITIONS   *And now the opposing arguments.*

EXCLAMATIONS   *Not again!*

IN ADVERTISING   *Fewer carbs. Improved taste.*

Although fragments are sometimes effective, writers and readers do not always agree on when they are appropriate. That's why you will find it safer to write in complete sentences.

G6 Run-on sentences

Run-on sentences are independent clauses that have not been joined correctly. An independent clause is a word group that can stand alone as a sentence. (See B4-a.) When two independent clauses appear in one sentence, they must be joined in one of these ways:

- with a comma and a coordinating conjunction (*and, but, or, nor, for, so, yet*)
- with a semicolon (or occasionally with a colon or a dash)

Recognizing run-on sentences

There are two types of run-on sentences. When a writer puts no mark of punctuation and no coordinating conjunction between independent clauses, the result is called a *fused sentence.*

FUSED   ┌──────── INDEPENDENT CLAUSE ────────┐ ┌──────
Air pollution poses risks to all humans it can be

── INDEPENDENT CLAUSE ──┐
deadly for asthma sufferers.

A far more common type of run-on sentence is the *comma splice*—two or more independent clauses joined with a comma but without a coordinating conjunction. In some comma splices, the comma appears alone.

> **COMMA**   Air pollution poses risks to all humans, it can be
> **SPLICE**   deadly for asthma sufferers.

In other comma splices, the comma is accompanied by a joining word that is *not* a coordinating conjunction (*and, but, or, nor, for, so,* and *yet*).

> **COMMA**   Air pollution poses risks to all humans, however, it can
> **SPLICE**   be deadly for asthma sufferers.

However is a transitional expression and cannot be used with only a comma to join two independent clauses (see G6-b).

Revising run-on sentences

To revise a run-on sentence, you have four choices.

1. Use a comma and a coordinating conjunction (*and, but, or, nor, for, so, yet*).

   ▶ Air pollution poses risks to all humans, ^{but} it can be deadly for

   asthma sufferers.

2. Use a semicolon (or, if appropriate, a colon or a dash). A semicolon may be used alone or with a transitional expression.

   ▶ Air pollution poses risks to all humans/; it can be deadly for

   asthma sufferers.

   ▶ Air pollution poses risks to all humans/; ^{however,} it can be deadly for

   asthma sufferers.

3. Make the clauses into separate sentences.

   ▶ Air pollution poses risks to all humans/. ^{It} it can be deadly for

   asthma sufferers.

4. Restructure the sentence, perhaps by subordinating one of the clauses.

   ▶ ^{Although air} ~~Air~~ pollution poses risks to all humans, it can be deadly for

   asthma sufferers.

One of these revision techniques usually works better than the others for a particular sentence. The fourth technique, the one requiring the most extensive revision, is often the most effective.

G6-a Consider separating the clauses with a comma and a coordinating conjunction.

There are seven coordinating conjunctions in English: *and*, *but*, *or*, *nor*, *for*, *so*, and *yet*. When a coordinating conjunction joins independent clauses, it is usually preceded by a comma. (See P1-a.)

▶ Some lesson plans include exercises, *but* completing them should not

be the focus of all class periods.

G6-b Consider separating the clauses with a semicolon (or, if appropriate, with a colon or a dash).

When the independent clauses are closely related and their relation is clear without a coordinating conjunction, a semicolon is an acceptable method of revision. (See P3-a.)

▶ Tragedy depicts the individual confronted with the fact of death/;

comedy depicts the adaptability of human society.

A semicolon is required between independent clauses that have been linked with a transitional expression (such as *however*, *therefore*, *moreover*, *in fact*, or *for example*). For a longer list, see P3-a.

▶ In his film adaptation of the short story "Killings," director Todd

Field changed key details of the plot/; as a matter of fact, he

added whole scenes that do not appear in the story.

A colon or a dash may be more appropriate if the first independent clause introduces the second or if the second clause summarizes or explains the first. (See P3-d and P6-b.) In formal writing, the colon is usually preferred to the dash.

▶ Nuclear waste is hazardous: ~~this~~ *This* is an indisputable fact.

▶ The female black widow spider is often a widow of her own

making/ she has been known to eat her partner after mating.

Recognizing run-on sentences

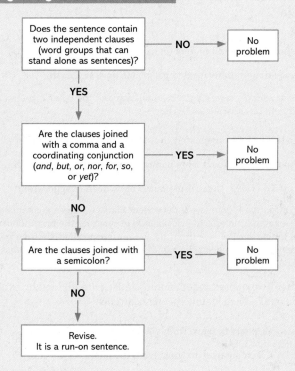

If you find an error, choose an effective method of revision. See G6-a to G6-d for revision strategies.

A colon is an appropriate method of revision if the first independent clause introduces a quoted sentence.

▶ Nobel Peace Prize winner Al Gore had this to say about climate

change/: "The truth is that our circumstances are not only
   ∧

new; they are completely different than they have ever been

in all of human history."

G6-c Consider making the clauses into separate sentences.

▶ Why should we spend money on expensive space exploration/?
 We
 ~~we~~ have enough underfunded programs here on Earth.

Since one independent clause is a question and the other is a statement, they should be separate sentences.

Writing
with
sources
APA-style
citation

▶ Some studies have suggested that the sexual relationships of
 A
 bonobos set them apart from common chimpanzees/. ~~a~~ccording
 to Stanford (1998), these differences have been exaggerated.

Using a comma to join two independent clauses creates a comma splice. In this example, an effective revision is to separate the first independent clause (*Some studies . . .*) from the second independent clause (*these differences . . .*) and to keep the signal phrase with the second clause. (See also APA-3.)

NOTE: When two quoted independent clauses are divided by explanatory words, make each clause its own sentence.

▶ "It's always smart to learn from your mistakes," quipped my
 "It's
 boss/. "~~it's~~ even smarter to learn from the mistakes of others."

G6-d Consider restructuring the sentence, perhaps by subordinating one of the clauses.

If one of the independent clauses is less important than the other, turn it into a subordinate clause or a phrase. (For more about subordination, see S6, especially the list on p. 130.)

▶ One of the most famous advertising slogans is Wheaties
 which
 cereal's "Breakfast of Champions," ~~it~~ was penned in 1933.

▶ Mary McLeod Bethune, ~~was~~ the seventeenth child of former slaves,
 ~~she~~ founded the National Council of Negro Women in 1935.

This section of *A Writer's Reference* is primarily for multilingual writers. You may find this section helpful if you learned English as a second language (ESL) or if you speak a language other than English with your friends and family.

M1 Verbs

Both native and nonnative speakers of English encounter challenges with verbs. Section M1 focuses on specific challenges that multilingual writers sometimes face. You can find more help with verbs in other sections in the book:

making subjects and verbs agree (G1)

using irregular verb forms (G2-a, G2-b)

leaving off verb endings (G2-c, G2-d)

choosing the correct verb tense (G2-f)

avoiding inappropriate uses of the passive voice (W3-a)

M1-a Use the appropriate verb form and tense.

This section offers a brief review of English verb forms and tenses. For additional help, see G2-f and B1-c.

Basic verb forms

Every main verb in English has five forms, which are used to create all of the verb tenses in standard English. The chart on page 226 shows these forms for the regular verb *help* and the irregular verbs *give* and *be*. See G2-a for the forms of other common irregular verbs.

Verb tenses

Section G2-f describes all the verb tenses in English, showing the forms of a regular verb, an irregular verb, and the verb *be* in each tense. The chart on pages 227–28 provides more details about the tenses commonly used in the active voice in writing; the chart on page 229 gives details about tenses commonly used in the passive voice.

PRACTICE AND MODELS   hackerhandbooks.com/writersref
> Multilingual/ESL > Charts and study help
> Sample student paper (draft and final)
> Exercises
> Links to online resources

Basic verb forms

	REGULAR VERB *HELP*	IRREGULAR VERB *GIVE*	IRREGULAR VERB *BE**
BASE FORM	help	give	be
PAST TENSE	helped	gave	was, were
PAST PARTICIPLE	helped	given	been
PRESENT PARTICIPLE	helping	giving	being
-S FORM	helps	gives	is

*Be also has the forms *am* and *are*, which are used in the present tense.

M1-b **To write a verb in the passive voice, use a form of *be* with the past participle.**

When a sentence is written in the passive voice, the subject receives the action instead of doing it. (See B2-b.)

> The solution *was measured* by the lab assistant.

> Melissa *was taken* to the hospital.

To form the passive voice, use a form of *be*—*am, is, are, was, were, being, be,* or *been*—followed by the past participle of the main verb: *was chosen, are remembered.* (Sometimes a form of *be* follows another helping verb: *will be stopped, could have been broken.*)

For details on forming the passive in various tenses, consult the chart on page 229. (For appropriate uses of the passive voice, see W3-a.)

> *written*
> ▶ *Dreaming in Cuban* was ~~writing~~ by Cristina García.
> ^
> In the passive voice, the past participle *written,* not the present participle *writing,* must follow *was* (the past tense of *be*).

> *be*
> ▶ Senator Dixon will defeated.
> ^
> The passive voice requires a form of *be* before the past participle.

> *teased.*
> ▶ The child was being ~~tease.~~
> ^
> The past participle *teased,* not the base form *tease,* must be used with *was being* to form the passive voice.

Verb tenses commonly used in the active voice

For descriptions and examples of all verb tenses, see G2-f. For verb tenses commonly used in the passive voice, see the chart on page 229.

Simple tenses
For general facts, states of being, habitual actions

Simple present	Base form or *-s* form
■ general facts	College students often *study* late at night.
■ states of being	Water *becomes* steam at 100° centigrade.
■ habitual, repetitive actions	We *donate* to a different charity each year.
■ scheduled future events	The train *arrives* tomorrow at 6:30 p.m.

NOTE: For advice about using the present tense in writing about literature, see page 192.

Simple past	Base form + *-ed* or *-d* or irregular form
■ completed actions at a specific time in the past	The storm *destroyed* their property. She *drove* to Montana three years ago.
■ facts or states of being in the past	When I *was* young, I usually *walked* to school with my sister.

Simple future	*will* + base form
■ future actions, promises, or predictions	I *will exercise* tomorrow. The snowfall *will begin* around midnight.

Simple progressive forms
For continuing actions

Present progressive	*am, is, are* + present participle
■ actions in progress at the present time, not continuing indefinitely	The students *are taking* an exam in Room 105. Jonathan *is parking* the car.
■ future actions (with *go, leave, come, move*, etc.)	I *am leaving* tomorrow morning.

Past progressive	*was, were* + present participle
■ actions in progress at a specific time in the past	They *were swimming* when the storm struck.
■ *was going to, were going to* for past plans that did not happen	We *were going to* drive to Florida for spring break, but the car broke down.

→

Verb tenses commonly used in the active voice (continued)

NOTE: Some verbs are not normally used in the progressive: *appear, believe, belong, contain, have, hear, know, like, need, see, seem, taste, understand,* and *want.*

    want
▶ I ~~am wanting~~ to see August Wilson's *Radio Golf.*
    ^

Perfect tenses
For actions that happened or will happen before another time

Present perfect	***has, have* + past participle**
• repetitive or constant actions that began in the past and continue to the present	I *have loved* cats since I was a child. Alicia *has worked* in Kenya for ten years.
• actions that happened at an unknown or unspecific time in the past	Stephen *has visited* Wales three times.

Past perfect	***had* + past participle**
• actions that began or occurred before another time in the past	She *had* just *crossed* the street when the runaway car crashed into the building.

NOTE: For more discussion of uses of the past perfect tense, see G2-f. For advice about using the past perfect in conditional sentences, see M1-e.

Perfect progressive forms
For continuous past actions before another time

Present perfect progressive	***has, have* + *been* + present participle**
• continuous actions that began in the past and continue to the present	Yolanda *has been trying* to get a job in Boston for five years.

Past perfect progressive	***had* + *been* + present participle**
• actions that began and continued in the past until some other past action	By the time I moved to Georgia, I *had been supporting* myself for five years.

tenses • active voice (*study, will perform*) •
passive voice (*are served, is being shown*) • perfect (*had been fought*)

M1-b   229

Verb tenses commonly used in the passive voice

For details about verb tenses in the active voice, see pages 227–28.

Simple tenses (passive voice)

Simple present — ***am*, *is*, *are* + past participle**

- general facts — Breakfast *is served* daily.
- habitual, repetitive actions — The receipts *are counted* every night.

Simple past — ***was*, *were* + past participle**

- completed past actions — He *was punished* for being late.

Simple future — ***will be* + past participle**

- future actions, promises, or predictions — The decision *will be made* by the committee next week.

Simple progressive forms (passive voice)

Present progressive — ***am*, *is*, *are* + *being* + past participle**

- actions in progress at the present time — The new stadium *is being built* with private money.
- future actions (with *go*, *leave*, *come*, *move*, etc.) — Jo *is being moved* to a new class next month.

Past progressive — ***was*, *were* + *being* + past participle**

- actions in progress at a specific time in the past — We thought we *were being followed*.

Perfect tenses (passive voice)

Present perfect — ***has*, *have* + *been* + past participle**

- actions that began in the past and continue to the present — The flight *has been delayed* because of violent storms in the Midwest.
- actions that happened at an unknown or unspecific time in the past — Wars *have been fought* throughout history.

Past perfect — ***had* + *been* + past participle**

- actions that began or occurred before another time in the past — He *had been given* all the hints he needed to complete the puzzle.

NOTE: The future progressive, future perfect, and perfect progressive forms are not used in the passive voice.

NOTE: Only transitive verbs, those that take direct objects, may be used in the passive voice. Intransitive verbs such as *occur, happen, sleep, die, become,* and *fall* are not used in the passive. (See B2-b.)

▶ The accident ~~was~~ happened suddenly.

fell
▶ Stock prices ~~were fallen~~ all week.
　　　　　^

M1-c Use the base form of the verb after a modal.

The modal verbs are *can, could, may, might, must, shall, should, will,* and *would.* (*Ought to* is also considered a modal verb.) The modals are used with the base form of a verb to show certainty, necessity, or possibility.

Modals and the verbs that follow them do not change form to indicate tense. For a summary of modals and their meanings, see the chart on pages 232–33. (See also G2-e.)

launch
▶ The art museum will ~~launches~~ its fundraising campaign next month.
　　　　　　　　　　^
The modal *will* must be followed by the base form *launch*, not the present tense *launches*.

speak
▶ The translator could ~~spoke~~ many languages, so the ambassador
　　　　　　　　　　　^
hired her for the European tour.

The modal *could* must be followed by the base form *speak*, not the past tense *spoke*.

TIP: Do not use *to* in front of a main verb that follows a modal.

▶ Gina can ~~to~~ drive us home if we miss the last train.

For the use of modals in conditional sentences, see M1-e.

M1-d To make negative verb forms, add *not* in the appropriate place.

If the verb is the simple present or past tense of *be* (*am, is, are, was, were*), add *not* after the verb.

Mario *is not* a member of the club.

verbs with objects • modals (*can, may*, etc.) • avoiding
double negative (*don't have no*) • *if, when* clauses • conditional

M1-e   231

For simple present-tense verbs other than *be*, use *do* or *does* plus *not* before the base form of the verb. (For the correct forms of *do* and *does*, see the chart in G1-a.)

>   *does not*
> ▶ Mariko ~~no~~ want more dessert.
>   ^

> ▶ Mariko does not wants̸ more dessert.

For simple past-tense verbs other than *be*, use *did* plus *not* before the base form of the verb.

>   *plant*
> ▶ They did not ~~planted~~ corn this year.
>   ^

In a verb phrase consisting of one or more helping verbs and a present or past participle (*is watching, were living, has played, could have been driven*), use the word *not* after the first helping verb.

>   *not*
> ▶ Inna should have ~~not~~ gone dancing last night.
>   ^

>   *not*
> ▶ Bonnie is ~~no~~ singing this weekend.
>   ^

NOTE: English allows only one negative in an independent clause to express a negative idea; using more than one is an error known as a *double negative* (see G4-d).

>   *any*
> ▶ We could not find ~~no~~ books about the history of our school in the
>   ^
>
> public library.

M1-e In a conditional sentence, choose verb tenses according to the type of condition expressed in the sentence.

Conditional sentences contain two clauses: a subordinate clause (usually starting with *if, when,* or *unless*) and an independent clause. The subordinate clause (sometimes called the *if* or *unless* clause) states the condition or cause; the independent clause states the result or effect. In each example in this section, the subordinate clause (*if* clause) is marked SUB, and the independent clause is marked IND. (See B3-e on clauses.)

PRACTICE hackerhandbooks.com/writersref
> Multilingual/ESL > M1–7

Modals and their meanings

can

- general ability
  (present)

  Ants *can survive* anywhere, even in space.
  Jorge *can run* a marathon faster than his
  brother.

- informal requests or
  permission

  Can you *tell* me where the light is? Sandy
  can borrow my calculator.

could

- general ability
  (past)

  Lea *could read* when she was only three
  years old.

- polite, informal
  requests or
  permission

  Could you *give* me that pen?

may

- formal requests or
  permission

  May I *see* the report? Students *may park*
  only in the yellow zone.

- possibility

  I *may try* to finish my homework tonight,
  or I *may wake up* early and *finish* it
  tomorrow.

might

- possibility

  Funding for the language lab *might
  double* by 2017.

NOTE: *Might* usually expresses a stronger possibility than *may*.

must

- necessity (present
  or future)

  To be effective, welfare-to-work programs
  must provide access to job training.

- strong probability

  Amy *must be* sick. [She is probably sick.]

- near certainty
  (present or past)

  I *must have left* my wallet at home.
  [I almost certainly left my wallet at home.]

should

- suggestions or advice

  Diabetics *should drink* plenty of water
  every day.

- obligations or duties

  The government *should protect*
  citizens' rights.

- expectations

  The books *should arrive* soon. [We expect
  the books to arrive soon.]

→

modals • *can, could, may, might, must, should, will, would* • *if* clauses •
when clauses • conditional • expressing facts • predicting

M1-e   233

will	
▪ certainty	If you don't leave now, you *will be* late.
▪ requests	*Will* you *help* me study for my test?
▪ promises and offers	Jonah *will arrange* the carpool.

would	
▪ polite requests	*Would* you *help* me carry these books? I *would like* some coffee. [*Would like* is more polite than *want*.]
▪ habitual or repeated actions (past)	Whenever Elena needed help with sewing, she *would call* her aunt.

Factual

Factual conditional sentences express relations based on fact. If the relationship is a scientific truth, use the present tense in both clauses.

━━━━━━━ SUB ━━━━━━━┐ ┌─ IND ─┐
If water *cools* to 32° Fahrenheit, it *freezes*.

If the sentence describes a condition that is or was habitually true, use the same tense in both clauses.

━━━━━ SUB ━━━━━┐ ┌━━━━ IND ━━━━┐
When Sue *jogs* along the canal, her dog *runs* ahead of her.

━━━━━━ SUB ━━━━━━┐ ┌━ IND ━┐
Whenever the coach *asked* for help, I *volunteered*.

Predictive

Predictive conditional sentences are used to predict the future or to express future plans or possibilities. To form a predictive sentence, use a present-tense verb in the subordinate clause; in the independent clause, use the modal *will, can, may, should,* or *might* plus the base form of the verb.

━━━ SUB ━━━┐ ┌━━━━━ IND ━━━━━┐
If you *practice* regularly, your tennis game *should improve*.

━━━━━ IND ━━━━━┐┌━ SUB ━┐
We *will lose* our remaining wetlands unless we *act* now.

TIP: In all types of conditional sentences (factual, predictive, and speculative), *if* or *unless* clauses do not use the modal verb *will*.

       passes
▶ If Jenna ~~will pass~~ her history test, she will graduate this year.
    ^

Speculative

Speculative conditional sentences express unlikely, contrary-to-fact, or impossible conditions. English uses the past or past perfect tense in the *if* clause, even for conditions in the present or the future.

UNLIKELY POSSIBILITIES   If the condition is possible but unlikely in the present or the future, use the past tense in the subordinate clause; in the independent clause, use *would*, *could*, or *might* plus the base form of the verb.

> ┌──── SUB ────┐ ┌──── IND ────┐
> If I *won* the lottery, I *would travel* to Egypt.

The writer does not expect to win the lottery. Because this is a possible but unlikely present or future situation, the subordinate clause uses the past tense.

CONDITIONS CONTRARY TO FACT   In conditions that are currently unreal or contrary to fact, use the past-tense verb *were* (not *was*) in the *if* clause for all subjects. (See also G2-g, on the subjunctive mood.)

> *were*
> ▶ If I ~~was~~ president, I would make children's issues a priority.
>   ^

The writer is not president, so *were* is correct in the *if* clause.

EVENTS THAT DID NOT HAPPEN   In a conditional sentence that speculates about an event that did not happen or was impossible in the past, use the past perfect tense in the *if* clause; in the independent clause, use *would have*, *could have*, or *might have* with the past participle. (See also past perfect tense, p. 228.)

> ┌──── SUB ────┐ ┌──── IND ────┐
> If I *had saved* more money, I *would have visited* Laos last year.

The writer did not save more money and did not travel to Laos. This sentence shows a possibility that did not happen.

> ┌──────── SUB ────────┐ ┌── IND ──┐
> If Aunt Grace *had been* alive for your graduation, she *would have*
> ┌────┐
> *been* very proud.

Aunt Grace was not alive at the time of the graduation. This sentence shows an impossible situation in the past.

M1-f Become familiar with verbs that may be followed by gerunds or infinitives.

A gerund is a verb form that ends in -*ing* and is used as a noun: *sleeping*, *dreaming*. (See B3-b.) An infinitive is the word *to* plus the base form of the verb: *to sleep, to dream*. (The word *to* is an infinitive marker, not a preposition, in this use.)

A few verbs may be followed by either a gerund or an infinitive; others may be followed by a gerund but not by an infinitive; still others may be followed by an infinitive but not by a gerund.

Verb + gerund or infinitive (no change in meaning)

The following commonly used verbs may be followed by a gerund or an infinitive, with little or no difference in meaning:

begin	hate	love
continue	like	start

I love *skiing*. I love *to ski*.

Verb + gerund or infinitive (change in meaning)

With a few verbs, the choice of a gerund or an infinitive changes the meaning dramatically:

forget	remember	stop	try

She stopped *speaking* to Lucia. [She no longer spoke to Lucia.]

She stopped *to speak* to Lucia. [She paused so that she could speak to Lucia.]

Verb + gerund

These verbs may be followed by a gerund but not by an infinitive:

admit	enjoy	postpone	resist
appreciate	escape	practice	risk
avoid	finish	put off	suggest
deny	imagine	quit	tolerate
discuss	miss	recall	

Bill enjoys *playing* [not *to play*] the piano.

Jamie quit *smoking*.

Verb + infinitive

These verbs may be followed by an infinitive but not by a gerund:

agree	expect	need	refuse
ask	help	offer	wait
beg	hope	plan	want
claim	manage	pretend	wish
decide	mean	promise	would like

Jill has offered *to water* [not *watering*] the plants while we are away.

Joe finally managed *to find* a parking space.

The man refused *to join* the rebellion.

A few of these verbs may be followed either by an infinitive directly or by a noun or pronoun plus an infinitive:

ask	help	promise	would like
expect	need	want	

We asked *to speak* to the congregation.

We asked *Rabbi Abrams to speak* to our congregation.

Alex expected *to get* the lead in the play.

Ira expected *Alex to get* the lead in the play.

Verb + noun or pronoun + infinitive

With certain verbs in the active voice, a noun or pronoun must come between the verb and the infinitive that follows it. The noun or pronoun usually names a person who is affected by the action of the verb.

advise	convince	order	tell
allow	encourage	persuade	urge
cause	have ("own")	remind	warn
command	instruct	require	

V   N   ⌐ INF ⌐
The class encouraged Luis to tell the story of his escape.

The counselor *advised Haley to take* four courses instead of the usual five.

Professor Howlett *instructed us to write* our names on the left side of the paper.

Verb + noun or pronoun + unmarked infinitive

An unmarked infinitive is an infinitive without *to*. A few verbs (often called *causative verbs*) may be followed by a noun or pronoun and an unmarked infinitive.

have ("cause")	let ("allow")
help	make ("force")

Jorge *had the valet park* his car.

▶ Please let me ~~to~~ pay for the tickets.

▶ Frank made me ~~to~~ carry his book for him.

NOTE: *Help* can be followed by a noun or pronoun and either an unmarked or a marked infinitive:

Emma *helped Brian wash* the dishes.

Emma *helped Brian to wash* the dishes.

M2 Articles

Articles (*a, an, the*) are part of a category of words known as *noun markers* or *determiners*.

M2-a Be familiar with articles and other noun markers.

Standard English uses noun markers to help identify the nouns that follow. In addition to articles (*a, an,* and *the*), noun markers include

- possessive nouns, such as *Elena's* (See P4-a.)
- possessive pronoun/adjectives: *my, your, his, her, its, our, their* (See B1-b.)
- demonstrative pronoun/adjectives: *this, that, these, those* (See B1-b.)
- quantifiers: *all, any, each, either, every, few, many, more, most, much, neither, several, some,* and so on (See M2-d.)
- numbers: *one, twenty-three,* and so on

Types of nouns

Common or proper

Common nouns

- name general persons, places, things, or ideas
- begin with lowercase

Examples

religion	beauty
knowledge	student
rain	country

Proper nouns

- name specific persons, places, things, or ideas
- begin with capital letter

Examples

Hinduism	President Adams
Philip	Washington Monument
Vietnam	Renaissance

Count or noncount (common nouns only)

Count nouns

- name persons, places, things, or ideas that can be counted
- have plural forms

Examples

girl, girls
city, cities
goose, geese
philosophy, philosophies

Noncount nouns

- name things or abstract ideas that cannot be counted
- cannot be made plural

Examples

dirt	patience
silver	knowledge
furniture	air

NOTE: See the chart on page 243 for commonly used noncount nouns.

Singular or plural (both common and proper)

**Singular nouns
(count and noncount)**

- represent one person, place, thing, or idea

Examples

backpack	rain
country	beauty
woman	Nile River
achievement	Block Island

**Plural nouns
(count only)**

- represent more than one person, place, thing, or idea
- must be count nouns

Examples

backpacks	Ural Mountains
countries	Falkland Islands
women	achievements

→

Specific (definite) or general (indefinite) (count and noncount)	
Specific nouns	**Examples**
▪ name persons, places, things, or ideas that can be identified within a group of the same type	*The students* in *Professor Martin's class* should study. *The airplane* carrying *the senator* was late. *The furniture* in *the truck* was damaged.
General nouns	**Examples**
▪ name categories of persons, places, things, or ideas (often plural)	*Students* should study. *Books* help *cultures* connect. *The airplane* has made commuting between *cities* easy.

Using articles and other noun markers

Articles and other noun markers always appear before nouns; sometimes other modifiers, such as adjectives, come between a noun marker and a noun.

      ART N
Felix is reading a book about mythology.

      ART ADJ N
We took an exciting trip to Alaska last summer.

NOUN
MARKER ADV ADJ N
That very delicious meal was expensive.

In most cases, do not use an article with another noun marker.

   My
▶ ~~The my~~ older brother lives in Wisconsin.
   ^

Expressions like *a few*, *the most*, and *all the* are exceptions: *a few potatoes*, *all the rain*. See also M2-d.

Types of articles and types of nouns

To choose an appropriate article for a noun, you must first determine whether the noun is *common* or *proper*, *count* or *noncount*, *singular* or *plural*, and *specific* or *general*. The chart on pages 238–39 describes the types of nouns.

Articles are classified as *indefinite* and *definite*. The indefinite articles, *a* and *an*, are used with general nouns. The definite article, *the*, is used with specific nouns. (The last section of the chart, on p. 239, explains general and specific nouns.)

A and *an* both mean "one" or "one among many." Use *a* before a consonant sound: *a banana, a tree, a picture, a happy child, a united family.* Use *an* before a vowel sound: *an eggplant, an occasion, an uncle, an honorable person.* (See also *a, an* in W1.)

The shows that a noun is specific; use *the* with one or more than one specific thing: *the newspaper, the soldiers.*

M2-b Use *the* with most specific common nouns.

The definite article, *the*, is used with most nouns—both count and noncount—that the reader can identify specifically. Usually the identity will be clear to the reader for one of the following reasons. (See also the chart on p. 242.)

1. The noun has been previously mentioned.

   ▶ A truck cut in front of our van. When ^*the* truck skidded a few seconds later, we almost crashed into it.

   The article *A* is used before *truck* when the noun is first mentioned. When the noun is mentioned again, it needs the article *the* because readers can now identify which truck skidded—the one that cut in front of the van.

2. A phrase or clause following the noun restricts its identity.

   ▶ Bryce warned me that ^*the* computer on his desk had just crashed.

   The phrase *on his desk* identifies the specific computer.

NOTE: Descriptive adjectives do not necessarily make a noun specific. A specific noun is one that readers can identify within a group of nouns of the same type.

   ▶ If I win the lottery, I will buy ~~the~~ ^*a* brand-new bright red sports car.

   The reader cannot identify which specific brand-new bright red sports car the writer will buy. Even though *car* has several adjectives in front of it, it is a general noun in this sentence.

3. A superlative adjective such as *best* or *most intelligent* makes the noun's identity specific. (See also G4-c on comparatives and superlatives.)

▶ Our petite daughter dated ^{the} tallest boy in her class.
    ^

The superlative *tallest* makes the noun *boy* specific. Although there might be several tall boys, only one boy can be the tallest.

4. The noun describes a unique person, place, or thing.

▶ During an eclipse, one should not look directly at ^{the} sun.
    ^

There is only one sun in our solar system, so its identity is clear.

5. The context or situation makes the noun's identity clear.

▶ Please don't slam ^{the} door when you leave.
    ^

Both the speaker and the listener know which door is meant.

6. The noun is singular and refers to a scientific class or category of items (most often animals, musical instruments, and inventions).

▶ ~~Tin~~ *The tin* whistle is common in traditional Irish music.
    ^

The writer is referring to the tin whistle as a class of musical instruments.

M2-c Use *a* (or *an*) with common singular count nouns that refer to "one" or "any."

If a count noun refers to one unspecific item (not a whole category), use the indefinite article, *a* or *an*. *A* and *an* usually mean "one among many" but can also mean "any one." (See the chart on p. 242.)

▶ My English professor asked me to bring ^a dictionary to class.
    ^

The noun *dictionary* refers to "one unspecific dictionary" or "any dictionary."

▶ We want to rent ^{an} apartment close to the lake.
    ^

The noun *apartment* refers to "any apartment close to the lake," not a specific apartment.

Choosing articles for common nouns

Use *the*

- if the reader has enough information to identify the noun specifically

COUNT: Please turn on *the lights*. We're going to *the beach* tomorrow.

NONCOUNT: *The food* throughout Italy is excellent.

Use *a* or *an*

- if the noun refers to one item

and

- if the item is singular but not specific

COUNT: Bring *a pencil* to class. Charles wrote *an essay* about his first job.

NOTE: Do not use *a* or *an* with plural or noncount nouns.

Use a quantifier (*enough, many, some,* etc.)

- if the noun represents an unspecified amount of something
- if the amount is more than one but not all items in a category

COUNT (PLURAL): Amir showed us *some photos* of his trip to India. *Many turtles* return to the same nesting site each year.

NONCOUNT: We didn't get *enough rain* this summer.

NOTE: Sometimes no article conveys an unspecified amount: *Amir showed us photos of his trip to India.*

Use no article

- if the noun represents all items in a category
- if the noun represents a category in general

COUNT (PLURAL): *Students* can attend the show for free. *Runners* must report to the officials' table at 7:00 a.m.

NONCOUNT: *Coal* is a natural resource.

NOTE: *The* is occasionally used when a singular count noun refers to all items in a class or a specific category: *The bald eagle is no longer endangered in the United States.*

Commonly used noncount nouns

Food and drink

beef, bread, butter, candy, cereal, cheese, cream, meat, milk, pasta, rice, salt, sugar, water, wine

Nonfood substances

air, cement, coal, dirt, gasoline, gold, paper, petroleum, plastic, rain, silver, snow, soap, steel, wood, wool

Abstract nouns

advice, anger, beauty, confidence, courage, employment, fun, happiness, health, honesty, information, intelligence, knowledge, love, poverty, satisfaction, wealth

Other

biology (and other areas of study), clothing, equipment, furniture, homework, jewelry, luggage, machinery, mail, money, news, poetry, pollution, research, scenery, traffic, transportation, violence, weather, work

NOTE: A few noncount nouns (such as *love*) can also be used as count nouns: *He had two loves: music and archery.*

M2-d Use a quantifier such as *some* or *more*, not *a* or *an*, with a noncount noun to express an approximate amount.

Do not use *a* or *an* with noncount nouns. Also do not use numbers or words such as *several* or *many* because they must be used with plural nouns, and noncount nouns do not have plural forms. (See the chart on this page for a list of commonly used noncount nouns.)

▶ Dr. Snyder gave us ~~an~~ information about the Peace Corps.

▶ Do you have ~~many~~ money with you?

You can use quantifiers such as *enough, less,* and *some* to suggest approximate amounts or nonspecific quantities of noncount nouns: *any homework, enough wood, less information, much pollution.*

▶ Vincent's mother told him that she had ~~a~~ news that would
surprise him.
some

M2-e Do not use articles with nouns that refer to all of something or something in general.

When a noncount noun refers to all of its type or to a concept in general, it is not marked with an article.

> *Kindness*
> ▶ ~~The kindness~~ is a virtue.
>   ^
>
> The noun represents kindness in general; it does not represent a specific type of kindness.

> ▶ In some parts of the world, ~~the~~ rice is preferred to all other grains.
>
> The noun *rice* represents rice in general, not a specific type or portion of rice.

In most cases, when you use a count noun to represent a general category, make the noun plural. Do not use unmarked singular count nouns to represent whole categories.

> *Fountains are*
> ▶ ~~Fountain is~~ an expensive element of landscape design.
>   ^
> *Fountains* is a count noun that represents fountains in general.

EXCEPTION: In some cases, *the* can be used with singular count nouns to represent a class or specific category: *The Chinese alligator is smaller than the American alligator*. See also number 6 in M2-b.

M2-f Do not use articles with most singular proper nouns. Use *the* with most plural proper nouns.

Since singular proper nouns are already specific, they typically do not need an article: *Prime Minister Cameron, Jamaica, Lake Huron, Mount Etna.*

There are, however, many exceptions. In most cases, if the proper noun consists of a common noun with modifiers (adjectives or an *of* phrase), use *the* with the proper noun.

> *the*
> ▶ We visited Great Wall of China last year.
>   ^

> *the*
> ▶ Rob wants to be a translator for Central Intelligence Agency.
>   ^

The is used with most plural proper nouns: *the McGregors, the Bahamas, the Finger Lakes, the United States.*

Using *the* with geographic nouns

When to omit *the*

streets, squares, parks	Ivy Street, Union Square, Denali National Park
cities, states, counties	Miami, New Mexico, Bee County
most countries, continents	Italy, Nigeria, China, South America, Africa
bays, single lakes	Tampa Bay, Lake Geneva
single mountains, islands	Mount Everest, Crete

When to use *the*

country names with *of* phrase	the United States (of America), the People's Republic of China
large regions, deserts	the East Coast, the Sahara
peninsulas	the Baja Peninsula, the Sinai Peninsula
oceans, seas, gulfs	the Pacific Ocean, the Dead Sea, the Persian Gulf
canals and rivers	the Panama Canal, the Amazon
mountain ranges	the Rocky Mountains, the Alps
groups of islands	the Solomon Islands

Geographic names create problems because there are so many exceptions to the rules. When in doubt about whether or not to use an article, consult the chart on this page, check a dictionary, or ask a native speaker.

M3 Sentence structure

Although their structure can vary widely, sentences in English generally flow from subject to verb to object or complement: *Bears eat fish*. This section focuses on the major challenges that multilingual students face when writing sentences in English. For more details on the parts of speech and the elements of sentences, consult sections B1–B4.

M3-a Use a linking verb between a subject and its complement.

Some languages, such as Russian and Turkish, do not use linking verbs (*is*, *are*, *was*, *were*) between subjects and complements (nouns or adjectives that rename or describe the subject). Every English sentence, however, must include a verb. For more on linking verbs, see G2-e.

▶ Jim *is* intelligent.
      ∧

▶ Many streets in San Francisco *are* very steep.
                                 ∧

M3-b Include a subject in every sentence.

Some languages, such as Spanish and Japanese, do not require a subject in every sentence. Every English sentence, however, must have a subject. Commands are an exception: The subject *you* is understood but not present ([*You*] *Give me the book*).

▶ Your aunt is very energetic. ~~Seems~~ *She seems* young for her age.
                               ∧

The word *it* is used as the subject of a sentence describing the weather or temperature, stating the time, indicating distance, or suggesting an environmental fact.

▶ *It is* ~~Is~~ raining in the valley and snowing in the mountains.
  ∧

▶ *It is* ~~Is~~ 9:15 a.m.
  ∧

▶ *It is* ~~Is~~ three hundred miles to Chicago.
  ∧

In most English sentences, the subject appears before the verb. Some sentences, however, are inverted: The subject comes after the verb. In these sentences, a placeholder called an *expletive* (*there* or *it*) often comes before the verb.

EXP V ┌── S ──┐   ┌── S ──┐ V
There are many people here today. (Many people are here today.)

▶ *There is* ~~Is~~ an apple in the refrigerator.
  ∧

▶ As you know, many religious sects in India. *there are*
                                              ∧

Notice that the verb agrees with the subject that follows it: *apple is, sects are.* (See G1-g.)

Sometimes an inverted sentence has an infinitive (*to work*) or a noun clause (*that she is intelligent*) as the subject. In such sentences, the placeholder *it* is needed before the verb. (Also see B3-b and B3-e.)

EXP V ┌─ S ─┐ ┌─ S ─┐ V
It is important to study daily. (To study daily is important.)

                  it
▶ Because the road is flooded, is necessary to change our route.
                        ^

The placeholder *it* is required before the verb *is* because the subject *to change our route* follows the verb.

TIP: The words *here* and *there* are not used as subjects. When they mean "in this place" (*here*) or "in that place" (*there*), they are adverbs, not nouns.

                                  It   *there.*
▶ I just returned from a vacation in Japan. ~~There~~ is very beautiful/
                                     ^   ^

This school   *that school*
▶ ~~Here~~ offers a master's degree; ~~there~~ has only a bachelor's program.
  ^   ^

M3-c Do not use both a noun and a pronoun to perform the same grammatical function in a sentence.

English does not allow a subject to be repeated in its own clause.

▶ The doctor ~~she~~ advised me to cut down on salt.

The pronoun *she* cannot repeat the subject, *doctor.*

Do not add a pronoun even when a word group comes between the subject and the verb.

▶ The watch that I bought on vacation ~~it~~ was not expensive.

The pronoun *it* cannot repeat the subject, *watch.*

Some languages allow "topic fronting," placing a word or phrase (a "topic") at the beginning of a sentence and following it with an independent clause that explains something about the topic. This form is not allowed in English because the sentence seems to start with one subject but then introduces a new subject in an independent clause.

              ┌─ TOPIC ─┐ ┌───── IND CLAUSE ─────┐
INCORRECT   The seeds I planted them last fall.

The sentence can be corrected by bringing the topic (*seeds*) into the independent clause.

the seeds
▶ ~~The seeds~~ I planted ~~them~~ last fall.
  ^

M3-d Do not repeat an object or an adverb in an adjective clause.

Adjective clauses begin with relative pronouns (*who, whom, whose, which, that*) or relative adverbs (*when, where*). Relative pronouns usually serve as subjects or objects in the clauses they introduce; another word in the clause cannot serve the same function. Relative adverbs should not be repeated by other adverbs later in the clause.

┌──────── ADJ CLAUSE ────────┐
The cat ran under the car that was parked on the street.

▶ The cat ran under the car that ~~it~~ was parked on the street.

The relative pronoun *that* is the subject of the adjective clause, so the pronoun *it* cannot be added as a subject.

▶ Myrna enjoyed the investment seminars that she attended ~~them~~ last week.

The relative pronoun *that* is the object of the verb *attended*. The pronoun *them* cannot also serve as an object.

Sometimes the relative pronoun is understood but not present in the sentence. In such cases, do not add another word with the same function as the understood pronoun.

▶ Myrna enjoyed the investment seminars she attended ~~them~~ last week.

The relative pronoun *that* is understood after *seminars* even though it is not present in the sentence.

If the clause begins with a relative adverb, do not use another adverb with the same meaning later in the clause.

▶ The office where I work ~~there~~ is one hour from the city.

The adverb *there* cannot repeat the relative adverb *where*.

M3-e Avoid mixed constructions beginning with *although* or *because*.

A word group that begins with *although* cannot be linked to a word group that begins with *but* or *however*. The result is an error called a *mixed construction* (see also S5-a). Similarly, a word group that begins with *because* cannot be linked to a word group that begins with *so* or *therefore*.

If you want to keep *although* or *because*, drop the other linking word.

▶ Although Nikki Giovanni is best known for her poetry for

adults, ~~but~~ she has written several books for children.

▶ Because German and Dutch are related languages, ~~therefore~~

tourists from Berlin can usually read a few signs in Amsterdam.

If you want to keep the other linking word, omit *although* or *because*.

▶ ~~Although~~ Nikki Giovanni is best known for her poetry for

adults, but she has written several books for children.

▶ ~~Because~~ German and Dutch are related languages/; therefore,
                                                    ^   ^
tourists from Berlin can usually read a few signs in Amsterdam.

For advice about using commas and semicolons with linking words, see P1-a, P1-b, and P3-a.

M3-f Do not place an adverb between a verb and its direct object.

Adverbs modifying verbs can appear in various positions: at the beginning or end of a sentence, before or after a verb, or between a helping verb and the main verb.

Slowly, we drove along the rain-slick road.

Mia handled the teapot *very carefully*.

Martin *always* wins our tennis matches.

Christina is *rarely* late for our lunch dates.

My daughter has *often* spoken of you.

The election results were being *closely* followed by analysts.

An adverb cannot appear between a verb and its direct object.

> ► Mother wrapped ~~carefully~~ the gift.
>   *carefully*
>   ^

The adverb *carefully* cannot appear between the verb, *wrapped*, and its direct object, *the gift*.

M4 Using adjectives

M4-a Distinguish between present participles and past participles used as adjectives.

Both present and past participles may be used as adjectives. The present participle always ends in *-ing*. Past participles usually end in *-ed*, *-d*, *-en*, *-n*, or *-t*. (See G2-a.)

PRESENT PARTICIPLES	confusing, speaking, boring
PAST PARTICIPLES	confused, spoken, bored

Like all other adjectives, participles can come before nouns; they also can follow linking verbs, in which case they describe the subject of the sentence. (See B2-b.)

Use a present participle to describe a person or thing *causing or stimulating an experience.*

> The printer came with *confusing instructions.* [The instructions caused confusion.]

Use a past participle to describe a person or thing *undergoing an experience.*

> *Rachel* was *confused* by the instructions. [Rachel experienced confusion.]

Participles that describe emotions or mental states often cause the most confusion.

annoying/annoyed   exhausting/exhausted
boring/bored   fascinating/fascinated
confusing/confused   frightening/frightened
depressing/depressed   satisfying/satisfied
exciting/excited   surprising/surprised

>   *exhausting.*
> Our hike was ~~exhausted.~~
>   ^

Exhausting suggests that the hike caused exhaustion.

>   *exhausted*
> The ~~exhausting~~ hikers reached the campground just before
>   ^
>
> sunset.

Exhausted describes how the hikers felt.

M4-b Place cumulative adjectives in an appropriate order.

Adjectives usually come before the nouns they modify and may also come after linking verbs. (See B1-d and B2-b.)

      ADJ N   V   ADJ
Janine wore new shoes. Janine's shoes were new.

Cumulative adjectives, which cannot be joined by the word *and* or separated by commas, must come in a particular order. If you use cumulative adjectives before a noun, the chart on page 252 can help you determine their order. The chart is only a guide; don't be surprised if you encounter exceptions. (See also P2-d.)

>   *smelly red plastic*
> My dorm room has only a small desk and a ~~plastic red smelly~~
>   ^
>
> chair.

>   *clear blue*
> Nice weather, ~~blue clear~~ water, and ancient monuments attract
>   ^
>
> many people to Italy.

Order of cumulative adjectives

FIRST   **ARTICLE OR OTHER NOUN MARKER**   a, an, the, her, this, my, Joe's, two, many, some

EVALUATIVE WORD   attractive, dedicated, delicious, ugly, disgusting

SIZE   large, enormous, small, little

LENGTH OR SHAPE   long, short, round, square

AGE   new, old, young, antique

COLOR   yellow, blue, crimson

NATIONALITY   French, Peruvian, Vietnamese

RELIGION   Catholic, Protestant, Jewish, Muslim

MATERIAL   silver, walnut, wool, marble

LAST   **NOUN/ADJECTIVE**   tree (as in *tree* house), kitchen (as in *kitchen* table)

THE NOUN MODIFIED   house, coat, bicycle, bread, woman, coin

My large blue wool coat is in the attic.

Joe's collection includes *two small antique silver* coins.

M5 Prepositions and idiomatic expressions

M5-a Become familiar with prepositions that show time and place.

The most frequently used prepositions in English are *at, by, for, from, in, of, on, to,* and *with.* Prepositions can be difficult to master because the differences among them are subtle and idiomatic. The chart on page 253 is limited to three troublesome prepositions that show time and place: *at, on,* and *in.*

Not every possible use is listed in the chart, so don't be surprised when you encounter exceptions and idiomatic uses that you must learn one at a time. For example, in English a person rides *in* a car but *on* a bus, plane, train, or subway.

PRACTICE   hackerhandbooks.com/writersref
> Multilingual/ESL > M5–2

At, on, and in to show time and place

Showing time

AT   *at* a specific time: *at* 7:20, *at* dawn, *at* dinner

ON   *on* a specific day or date: *on* Tuesday, *on* June 4

IN   *in* a part of a 24-hour period: *in* the afternoon, *in* the daytime [but *at* night]

        in a year or month: *in* 1999, *in* July

        in a period of time: finished *in* three hours

Showing place

AT   *at* a meeting place or location: *at* home, *at* the club

        at the edge of something: sitting *at* the desk

        at the corner of something: turning *at* the intersection

        at a target: throwing the snowball *at* Lucy

ON   *on* a surface: placed *on* the table, hanging *on* the wall

        on a street: the house *on* Spring Street

        on an electronic medium: *on* television, *on* the Internet

IN   *in* an enclosed space: *in* the garage, *in* an envelope

        in a geographic location: *in* San Diego, *in* Texas

        in a print medium: *in* a book, *in* a magazine

▶ My first class starts ~~on~~ *at* 8:00 a.m.

▶ The farmers go to market ~~in~~ *on* Wednesday.

▶ I want to work at one of the biggest companies ~~on~~ *in* the world.

M5-b Use nouns (including *-ing* forms) after prepositions.

In a prepositional phrase, use a noun (not a verb) after the preposition. Sometimes the noun will be a gerund, the *-ing* verb form that functions as a noun (see B3-b).

▶ Our student government is good at ~~save~~ *saving* money.

Distinguish between the preposition *to* and the infinitive marker *to*. If *to* is a preposition, it should be followed by a noun or a gerund.

> ▶ We are dedicated to ~~help~~ the poor.
>   *helping*

If *to* is an infinitive marker, it should be followed by the base form of the verb.

> ▶ We want to ~~helping~~ the poor.
>   *help*

To test whether *to* is a preposition or an infinitive marker, insert a word that you know is a noun after the word *to*. If the noun makes sense in that position, *to* is a preposition. If the noun does not make sense after *to*, then *to* is an infinitive marker.

Zoe is addicted *to* _____.

They are planning *to* _____.

In the first sentence, a noun (such as *magazines*) makes sense after *to*, so *to* is a preposition and should be followed by a noun or a gerund: Zoe is addicted *to magazines*. Zoe is addicted *to running*.

In the second sentence, a noun (such as *magazines*) does not make sense after *to*, so *to* is an infinitive marker and must be followed by the base form of the verb: They are planning *to build* a new school.

M5-c Become familiar with common adjective + preposition combinations.

Some adjectives appear only with certain prepositions. These expressions are idiomatic and may be different from the combinations used in your native language.

> ▶ Paula is married ~~with~~ Jon.
>   *to*

Check an ESL dictionary for combinations that are not listed in the chart on page 255.

M5-d Become familiar with common verb + preposition combinations.

Many verbs and prepositions appear together in idiomatic phrases. Pay special attention to the combinations that are different from the combinations used in your native language.

▶ Your success depends ~~of~~ *on* your effort.

Check an ESL dictionary for combinations that are not listed in the chart below.

Adjective + preposition combinations

accustomed to	connected to	guilty of	preferable to
addicted to	covered with	interested in	proud of
afraid of	dedicated to	involved in	responsible for
angry with	devoted to	involved with	satisfied with
ashamed of	different from	known as	scared of
aware of	engaged in	known for	similar to
committed to	engaged to	made of (*or*	tired of
concerned	excited about	made from)	worried about
about	familiar with	married to	
concerned with	full of	opposed to	

Verb + preposition combinations

agree with	compare with	forget about	speak to (*or*
apply to	concentrate on	happen to	speak with)
approve of	consist of	hope for	stare at
arrive at	count on	insist on	succeed at
arrive in	decide on	listen to	succeed in
ask for	depend on	participate in	take advantage of
believe in	differ from	rely on	take care of
belong to	disagree with	reply to	think about
care about	dream about	respond to	think of
care for	dream of	result in	wait for
compare to	feel like	search for	wait on

≡ P1 The comma

The comma was invented to help readers. Without it, sentence parts can collide into one another unexpectedly, causing misreadings.

CONFUSING　　If you cook Elmer will do the dishes.

CONFUSING　　While we were eating a rattlesnake approached our campsite.

Add commas in the logical places (after *cook* and *eating*), and suddenly all is clear. No longer is Elmer being cooked, the rattlesnake being eaten.

Various rules have evolved to prevent such misreadings and to speed readers along through complex grammatical structures. Those rules are detailed in this section. (P2 explains when not to use commas.)

P1-a Use a comma before a coordinating conjunction joining independent clauses.

When a coordinating conjunction connects two or more independent clauses — word groups that could stand alone as separate sentences — a comma must precede the conjunction. There are seven coordinating conjunctions in English: *and, but, or, nor, for, so,* and *yet.*

A comma tells readers that one independent clause has come to a close and that another is about to begin.

▶ The department sponsored a seminar on college survival skills,
　　　　　　　　　　　　　　　　　　　　　　　　　　　　　　　　^
　and it also hosted a barbecue for new students.

EXCEPTION:　If the two independent clauses are short and there is no danger of misreading, the comma may be omitted.

　The plane took off and we were on our way.

TIP:　As a rule, do *not* use a comma to separate compound elements that are not independent clauses. (See P2-a.)

▶ A good money manager controls expenses / and invests surplus

　dollars to meet future needs.

　The word group following *and* is not an independent clause; it is the second half of a compound predicate (*controls . . . and invests*).

P1-b Use a comma after an introductory phrase or clause.

The most common introductory word groups are phrases and clauses functioning as adverbs. Such word groups usually tell when, where, how, why, or under what conditions the main action of the sentence occurred. (See B3-a, B3-b, and B3-e.)

A comma tells readers that the introductory phrase or clause has come to a close and that the main part of the sentence is about to begin.

▶ **Near a small stream at the bottom of the canyon, the park**
                                                    ^
rangers discovered an abandoned mine.

The comma tells readers that the introductory prepositional phrase has come to a close.

▶ **When Irwin was ready to iron, his cat tripped on the extension**
                                ^
cord.

Without the comma, readers may have Irwin ironing his cat. The comma signals that *his cat* is the subject of a new clause, not part of the introductory one.

EXCEPTION: The comma may be omitted after a short adverb clause or phrase if there is no danger of misreading.

In no time we were at 2,800 feet.

Sentences also frequently begin with participial phrases describing the noun or pronoun immediately following them. The comma tells readers that they are about to learn the identity of the person or thing described; therefore, the comma is usually required even when the phrase is short. (See B3-b.)

▶ **Thinking his motorcade drive through Dallas was routine,**
                                                          ^
President Kennedy smiled and waved at the crowds.

▶ **Buried under layers of younger rocks, the earth's oldest rocks**
                                        ^
contain no fossils.

NOTE: Other introductory word groups include transitional expressions and absolute phrases (see P1-f).

P1-c Use a comma between all items in a series.

When three or more items are presented in a series, those items should be separated from one another with commas. Items in a series may be single words, phrases, or clauses.

▶ Bubbles of air, leaves, ferns, bits of wood, and insects are often
   ‸
found trapped in amber.

▶ Langston Hughes's poetry is concerned with racial pride,

social justice, and the diversity of the African American
         ‸
experience.

Although some writers view the comma between the last two items as optional, most experts advise using the comma because its omission can result in ambiguity or misreading.

▶ David willed his oldest niece all of his property, houses, and
                                                          ‸
warehouses.

Did Uncle David will his property *and* houses *and* warehouses—or simply his property, consisting of houses and warehouses? If the former meaning is intended, a comma is necessary to prevent ambiguity.

▶ The activities include touring the White House, visiting the Air and

Space Museum, attending a lecture about the Founding Fathers,
                                                             ‸
and kayaking on the Potomac River.

Without the comma, the activities might seem to include a lecture about kayaking, not participating in kayaking. The comma makes it clear that *kayaking on the Potomac River* is a separate item in the series.

P1-d Use a comma between coordinate adjectives not joined with *and*. Do not use a comma between cumulative adjectives.

When two or more adjectives each modify a noun separately, they are coordinate.

Roberto is a *warm, gentle, affectionate* father.

TEST: If the adjectives can be joined with *and*, the adjectives are coordinate, so you should use commas: *warm* and *gentle* and *affectionate* (*warm, gentle, affectionate*).

Adjectives that do not modify the noun separately are cumulative.

Three large gray shapes moved slowly toward us.

Beginning with the adjective closest to the noun *shapes*, these modifiers lean on one another, piggyback style, with each modifying a larger word group. *Gray* modifies *shapes*, *large* modifies *gray shapes*, and *three* modifies *large gray shapes*. Cumulative adjectives cannot be joined with *and* (not *three* and *large* and *gray shapes*).

COORDINATE ADJECTIVES

▶ Should patients with severe, irreversible brain damage

be put on life support systems?

CUMULATIVE ADJECTIVES

▶ Ira ordered a rich/ chocolate/ layer cake.

P1-e Use commas to set off nonrestrictive elements. Do not use commas to set off restrictive elements.

Certain word groups that modify nouns or pronouns can be restrictive or nonrestrictive — that is, essential or not essential to the meaning of a sentence. These word groups are usually adjective clauses, adjective phrases, or appositives.

Restrictive elements

A restrictive element defines or limits the meaning of the word it modifies; it is therefore essential to the meaning of the sentence and is not set off with commas. If you remove a restrictive modifier from a sentence, the meaning changes significantly, becoming more general than you intended.

RESTRICTIVE (NO COMMAS)

The campers need clothes *that are durable*.

Scientists *who study the earth's structure* are called geologists.

The first sentence does not mean that the campers need clothes in general. The intended meaning is more limited: The campers need durable clothes. The second sentence does not mean that scientists in general are called geologists; only those scientists who specifically study the earth's structure are called geologists. The italicized word groups are essential and are therefore not set off with commas.

Nonrestrictive elements

A nonrestrictive modifier describes a noun or pronoun whose meaning has already been clearly defined or limited. Because the modifier contains nonessential or parenthetical information, it is set off with commas. If you remove a nonrestrictive element from a sentence, the meaning does not change dramatically. Some meaning may be lost, but the defining characteristics of the person or thing described remain the same.

> **NONRESTRICTIVE (WITH COMMAS)**
>
> The campers need sturdy shoes, *which are expensive.*
>
> The scientists, *who represented eight different universities*, met to review applications for the prestigious O'Hara Award.

In the first sentence, the campers need sturdy shoes, and the shoes happen to be expensive. In the second sentence, the scientists met to review applications for the O'Hara Award; that they represented eight different universities is informative but not critical to the meaning of the sentence. The nonessential information in both sentences is set off with commas.

NOTE: Often it is difficult to tell whether a word group is restrictive or nonrestrictive without seeing it in context and considering the writer's meaning. Both of the following sentences are grammatically correct, but their meanings are slightly different.

> The dessert made with fresh raspberries was delicious.
>
> The dessert, made with fresh raspberries, was delicious.

In the first example, the phrase *made with fresh raspberries* tells readers which of two or more desserts the writer is referring to. In the example with commas, the phrase merely adds information about the dessert.

Adjective clauses

Adjective clauses are patterned like sentences, containing subjects and verbs, but they function within sentences as modifiers of nouns or pronouns. They always follow the word they modify, usually immediately. Adjective clauses begin with a relative pronoun (*who, whom, whose, which, that*) or with a relative adverb (*where, when*). (See B3-e.)

Nonrestrictive adjective clauses are set off with commas; restrictive adjective clauses are not.

NONRESTRICTIVE CLAUSE (WITH COMMAS)

▶ Ed's house, which is located on thirteen acres, was completely
  ^   ^
  furnished with bats in the rafters and mice in the kitchen.

The adjective clause *which is located on thirteen acres* does not restrict the meaning of *Ed's house*; the information is nonessential and is therefore enclosed in commas.

RESTRICTIVE CLAUSE (NO COMMAS)

▶ The giant panda/ that was born at the San Diego Zoo in 2003/ was

  sent to China in 2007.

Because the adjective clause *that was born at the San Diego Zoo in 2003* identifies one particular panda out of many, the information is essential and is therefore not enclosed in commas.

NOTE: Use *that* only with restrictive (essential) clauses. Many writers prefer to use *which* only with nonrestrictive (nonessential) clauses, but usage varies.

Adjective phrases

Prepositional or verbal phrases functioning as adjectives may be restrictive or nonrestrictive. (See B3-a and B3-b.) Nonrestrictive phrases are set off with commas; restrictive phrases are not.

NONRESTRICTIVE PHRASE (WITH COMMAS)

▶ The helicopter, with its million-candlepower spotlight
              ^
  illuminating the area, circled above.
                    ^

The *with* phrase is nonessential because its purpose is not to specify which of two or more helicopters is being discussed.

RESTRICTIVE PHRASE (NO COMMAS)

▶ One corner of the attic was filled with newspapers/ dating from

  the early 1900s.

Dating from the early 1900s restricts the meaning of *newspapers*, so the comma should be omitted.

▶ The bill/ proposed by the Illinois representative/ would lower

taxes and provide services for middle-income families.

Proposed by the Illinois representative identifies exactly which bill is meant.

Appositives

An appositive is a noun or noun phrase that renames a nearby noun. Nonrestrictive appositives are set off with commas; restrictive appositives are not.

NONRESTRICTIVE APPOSITIVE (WITH COMMAS)

▶ Darwin's most important book, *On the Origin of Species,* was the
  ^   ^
result of many years of research.

Most important restricts the meaning to one book, so the appositive *On the Origin of Species* is nonrestrictive and should be set off with commas.

RESTRICTIVE APPOSITIVE (NO COMMAS)

▶ The song/ "Viva la Vida/" was blasted out of huge amplifiers at the

concert.

Once they've read *song*, readers still don't know precisely which song the writer means. The appositive following *song* restricts its meaning, so the appositive should not be enclosed in commas.

P1-f Use commas to set off transitional and parenthetical expressions, absolute phrases, and word groups expressing contrast.

Transitional expressions

Transitional expressions serve as bridges between sentences or parts of sentences. They include conjunctive adverbs such as *however, therefore,* and *moreover* and transitional phrases such as *for example, as a matter of fact,* and *in other words.* (For complete lists of these expressions, see P3-a.)

When a transitional expression appears between independent clauses in a compound sentence, it is preceded by a semicolon and is usually followed by a comma. (See P3-a.)

▶ Minh did not understand our language; moreover, he was
   ˄
   unfamiliar with our customs.

When a transitional expression appears at the beginning of a sentence or in the middle of an independent clause, it is usually set off with commas.

▶ As a matter of fact, American football was established by fans
   ˄
   who wanted to play a more organized game of rugby.

▶ Natural foods are not always salt free; celery, for example,
   ˄   ˄
   contains more sodium than most people would imagine.

EXCEPTION: If a transitional expression blends smoothly with the rest of the sentence, calling for little or no pause in reading, it does not need to be set off with a comma. Expressions such as *also, at least, certainly, consequently, indeed, of course, moreover, no doubt, perhaps, then,* and *therefore* do not always call for a pause.

Alice's bicycle is broken; *therefore* you will need to borrow Sue's.

Parenthetical expressions

Expressions that are distinctly parenthetical, providing only supplemental information, should be set off with commas.

▶ Evolution, as far as we know, doesn't work this way.
   ˄   ˄

▶ The bass weighed about twelve pounds, give or take a few ounces.
                                         ˄

Absolute phrases

An absolute phrase, which modifies the whole sentence, usually consists of a noun followed by a participle or participial phrase. (See B3-d.) Absolute phrases may appear at the beginning or at the end of a sentence. Wherever they appear, they should be set off with commas.

```
┌──────────── ABSOLUTE PHRASE ────────────┐
│   N   PARTICIPLE                         │
```
The sun appearing for the first time in a week, we were at last able to begin the archaeological dig.

▶ Elvis Presley made music industry history in the 1950s, his
^
records having sold more than ten million copies.

NOTE: Do not insert a comma between the noun and the participle in
an absolute construction.

▶ The next contestant/ being five years old, the emcee adjusted the
height of the microphone.

Word groups expressing contrast

Sharp contrasts beginning with words such as *not*, *never*, and *unlike*
are set off with commas.

▶ The Epicurean philosophers sought mental, not bodily, pleasures.
^   ^

▶ Unlike Robert, Celia loved dance contests.
^

P1-g Use commas to set off words and phrases according to convention.

Direct address, yes and no

▶ Forgive me, Angela, for forgetting your birthday.
^   ^

▶ Yes, the loan will probably be approved.
^

Interrogative tags, mild interjections

▶ The film was faithful to the book, wasn't it?
^

▶ Well, cases like these are difficult to decide.
^

Direct quotations

▶ In his "Letter from Birmingham Jail," Martin Luther King Jr.
wrote, "We know through painful experience that freedom is never
^
voluntarily given by the oppressor; it must be demanded by the
oppressed" (225).

▶ "Happiness in marriage is entirely a matter of chance," says
 ^
Charlotte Lucas in *Pride and Prejudice*, a novel that ends with two

happy marriages (69; ch. 6).

See P5-a on the use of quotation marks and pages 397–98 on citing
literary sources in MLA style.

Dates

In dates, the year is set off from the rest of the sentence with a pair of
commas.

▶ On December 12, 1890, orders were sent out for the arrest of
 ^   ^
Sitting Bull.

EXCEPTIONS: Commas are not necessary if the date is inverted or if
only the month and year are given.

The security alert system went into effect on 15 April 2009.

January 2008 was an extremely cold month.

Addresses

The elements of an address or a place name are separated with commas. A zip code, however, is not preceded by a comma.

▶ John Lennon was born in Liverpool, England, in 1940.
 ^   ^

▶ Please send the package to Greg Tarvin at 708 Spring Street,
 ^
Washington, IL 61571.
 ^

Personal titles

If a title follows a name, separate the title from the rest of the sentence with a pair of commas.

▶ Sandra Belinsky, MD, has been appointed to the hospital board.
 ^   ^

Numbers

In numbers more than four digits long, use commas to separate the
numbers into groups of three, starting from the right. In numbers
four digits long, a comma is optional.

3,500 [*or* 3500]

100,000

5,000,000

EXCEPTIONS: Do not use commas in street numbers, zip codes, telephone numbers, or years with four or fewer digits.

P1-h Use a comma to prevent confusion.

In certain situations, a comma is necessary to prevent confusion. If
the writer has intentionally left out a word or phrase, for example, a
comma may be needed to signal the omission.

▶ To err is human; to forgive, divine.
                                   ^

If two words in a row echo each other, a comma may be needed
for ease of reading.

▶ All of the catastrophes that we had feared might happen,
                                                          ^
   happened.

Sometimes a comma is needed to prevent readers from grouping
words in ways that do not match the writer's intention.

▶ Patients who can, walk up and down the halls several times
                   ^
   a day.

P2 Unnecessary commas

Many common misuses of the comma result from misunderstanding
of the major comma rules presented in P1.

P2-a Do not use a comma between compound elements that are not independent clauses.

Though a comma should be used before a coordinating conjunction joining independent clauses (see P1-a), this rule should not be extended to
other compound word groups.

▶ Marie Curie discovered radium/ and later applied her work

on radioactivity to medicine.

And links two verbs in a compound predicate: *discovered* and *applied*.

▶ Jake told us that his illness is serious/ but that changes in

his lifestyle can improve his chances for survival.

The coordinating conjunction *but* links two subordinate clauses, each beginning with *that*: *that his illness is serious* and *that changes in his lifestyle....*

P2-b Do not use a comma to separate a verb from its subject or object.

A sentence should flow from subject to verb to object without unnecessary pauses. Commas may appear between these major sentence elements only when a specific rule calls for them.

▶ Zoos large enough to give the animals freedom to roam/ are

becoming more popular.

The comma should not separate the subject, *Zoos*, from the verb, *are becoming*.

▶ Maxine Hong Kingston writes/ that many Chinese

American families struggle "to figure out how the invisible

world the emigrants built around our childhoods fits in

solid America" (107).

Writing with sources

MLA-style citation

The comma should not separate the verb, *writes*, from its object, the subordinate clause beginning with *that*. A signal phrase ending in a word like *writes* or *says* is followed by a comma only when a direct quotation immediately follows: *Kingston writes, "Those of us in the first American generations have had to figure out how the invisible world ..." (107)*. (See also P5-e.)

P2-c Do not use a comma before the first or after the last item in a series.

Though commas are required between items in a series (P1-c), do not place them either before or after the whole series.

no comma to separate verb from subject or object • before or after
a series • between adjectives • with essential word groups

P2-e   271

▶ Other causes of asthmatic attacks are/ stress, change in

temperature, and cold air.

▶ Ironically, even novels that focus on horror, evil, and alienation/

often have themes of spiritual renewal and redemption.

P2-d Do not use a comma between cumulative adjectives, between an adjective and a noun, or between an adverb and an adjective.

Commas are required between coordinate adjectives (those that can be joined with *and*), but they do not belong between cumulative adjectives (those that cannot be joined with *and*). (For a full discussion, see P1-d.)

▶ In the corner of the closet, we found an old/ maroon hatbox.

A comma should never be used between an adjective and the noun that follows it.

▶ It was a senseless, dangerous/ mission.

Nor should a comma be used between an adverb and an adjective that follows it.

▶ The Hillside is a good home for severely/ disturbed youths.

P2-e Do not use commas to set off restrictive or mildly parenthetical elements.

Restrictive elements are modifiers or appositives that restrict the meaning of the nouns they follow. Because they are essential to the meaning of the sentence, they are not set off with commas. (For a full discussion of restrictive and nonrestrictive elements, see P1-e.)

▶ Drivers/ who think they own the road/ make cycling a dangerous

sport.

The modifier *who think they own the road* restricts the meaning of *Drivers* and is therefore essential to the meaning of the sentence. Putting commas around the *who* clause falsely suggests that all drivers think they own the road.

▶ Margaret Mead's book,/ *Coming of Age in Samoa,/* stirred up

considerable controversy when it was published in 1928.

Since Mead wrote more than one book, the appositive contains information essential to the meaning of the sentence.

Although commas should be used with distinctly parenthetical
expressions (see P1-f), do not use them to set off elements that are
only mildly parenthetical.

▶ Texting has,/ essentially,/ replaced e-mail for casual communication.

P2-f Do not use a comma to set off a concluding adverb clause that is essential to the meaning of the sentence.

When adverb clauses introduce a sentence, they are nearly always
followed by a comma (see P1-b). When they conclude a sentence, however, they are not set off by commas if their content is essential to the
meaning of the earlier part of the sentence. Adverb clauses beginning
with *after, as soon as, because, before, if, since, unless, until,* and *when*
are usually essential.

▶ Don't visit Paris at the height of the tourist season,/ unless you

have booked hotel reservations.

Without the *unless* clause, the meaning of the sentence might at first
seem broader than the writer intended.

When a concluding adverb clause is nonessential, it should be
preceded by a comma. Clauses beginning with *although, even though,
though,* and *whereas* are usually nonessential.

▶ The lecture seemed to last only a short time‸ although the clock
                                                ^
said it had gone on for more than an hour.

P2-g Do not use a comma after a phrase that begins an inverted sentence.

Though a comma belongs after most introductory phrases (see P1-b),
it does not belong after phrases that begin an inverted sentence. In
an inverted sentence, the subject follows the verb, and a phrase that
ordinarily would follow the verb is moved to the beginning.

▶ At the bottom of the hill/ sat the stubborn mule.

P2-h Avoid other common misuses of the comma.

Do not use a comma in the following situations.

AFTER A COORDINATING CONJUNCTION (*AND, BUT, OR, NOR, FOR, SO, YET*)

▶ Occasionally TV talk shows are performed live, but/ more
often they are taped.

AFTER *SUCH AS* OR *LIKE*

▶ Shade-loving plants such as/ begonias, impatiens, and
coleus can add color to a shady garden.

BEFORE *THAN*

▶ Touring Crete was more thrilling for us/ than visiting the
Greek islands frequented by the rich.

AFTER *ALTHOUGH*

▶ Although/ the air was balmy, the water was too cold for
swimming.

BEFORE A PARENTHESIS

▶ At InterComm, Sylvia began at the bottom/ (with only
three and a half walls and a swivel chair), but within three
years she had been promoted to supervisor.

TO SET OFF AN INDIRECT (REPORTED) QUOTATION

▶ Samuel Goldwyn once said/ that a verbal contract isn't
worth the paper it's written on.

WITH A QUESTION MARK OR AN EXCLAMATION POINT

▶ "Why don't you try it?/ " she coaxed. "You can't do any
worse than the rest of us."

P3 The semicolon and the colon

The semicolon is used to connect major sentence elements of equal grammatical rank (see P3-a and P3-b). The colon is used primarily to call attention to the words that follow it (see P3-d). In addition, the colon has some conventional uses (see P3-e).

P3-a Use a semicolon with independent clauses.

Between independent clauses with no coordinating conjunction

When two independent clauses appear in one sentence, they are usually linked with a comma and a coordinating conjunction (*and*, *but*, *or*, *nor*, *for*, *so*, *yet*). The coordinating conjunction signals the relation between the clauses. If the clauses are closely related and the relation is clear without a conjunction, they may be linked with a semicolon instead.

> In film, a low-angle shot makes the subject look powerful; a high-angle shot does just the opposite.

A semicolon must be used whenever a coordinating conjunction has been omitted between independent clauses. To use merely a comma creates a type of run-on sentence known as a *comma splice*. (See G6.)

▶ In 1800, a traveler needed six weeks to get from New York City

to Chicago/; in 1860, the trip by railroad took as little as two

days.

Between independent clauses with a transitional expression

Transitional expressions include conjunctive adverbs and transitional phrases.

CONJUNCTIVE ADVERBS

accordingly	furthermore	moreover	still
also	hence	nevertheless	subsequently
anyway	however	next	then
besides	incidentally	nonetheless	therefore
certainly	indeed	now	thus
consequently	instead	otherwise	
conversely	likewise	similarly	
finally	meanwhile	specifically	

TRANSITIONAL PHRASES

after all	even so	in fact
as a matter of fact	for example	in other words
as a result	for instance	in the first place
at any rate	in addition	on the contrary
at the same time	in conclusion	on the other hand

When a transitional expression appears between independent clauses, it is preceded by a semicolon and usually followed by a comma.

▶ Many corals grow very gradually/; in fact, the creation of a coral
          ^

reef can take centuries.

When a transitional expression appears in the middle or at the end of the second independent clause, the semicolon goes *between the clauses.*

▶ Biologists have observed laughter in primates other than humans/;
                                                                  ^

chimpanzees, however, sound more like they are panting than

laughing.

Transitional expressions should not be confused with the coordinating conjunctions *and, but, or, nor, for, so,* and *yet,* which are preceded by a comma when they link independent clauses. (See P1-a.)

P3-b Use a semicolon between items in a series containing internal punctuation.

▶ Classic science fiction sagas include *Star Trek*, with Captain Kirk,

Dr. McCoy, and Mr. Spock/; *Battlestar Galactica*, with its
                        ^

Cylons/; and *Star Wars*, with Han Solo, Luke Skywalker, and
       ^

Darth Vader.

Without the semicolons, the reader would have to sort out the major groupings, distinguishing between important and less important pauses according to the logic of the sentence. By inserting semicolons at the major breaks, the writer does this work for the reader.

P3-c Avoid common misuses of the semicolon.

Do not use a semicolon in the following situations.

BETWEEN A SUBORDINATE CLAUSE AND THE REST OF THE SENTENCE

▶ Although children's literature was added to the National Book Awards in 1969⁏, it has had its own award, the Newbery Medal, since 1922.

BETWEEN AN APPOSITIVE AND THE WORD IT REFERS TO

▶ The scientists were fascinated by the species *Argyroneta aquatica⁏,* a spider that lives underwater.

TO INTRODUCE A LIST

▶ Some of my favorite celebrities have their own blogs⁏: Lindsay Lohan, Rosie O'Donnell, and Zach Braff.

BETWEEN INDEPENDENT CLAUSES JOINED BY *AND, BUT, OR, NOR, FOR, SO,* OR *YET*

▶ Five of the applicants had worked with spreadsheets⁏, but only one was familiar with database management.

P3-d Use a colon after an independent clause to direct attention to a list, an appositive, a quotation, or a summary or an explanation.

A LIST
The daily routine should include at least the following: twenty knee bends, fifty sit-ups, fifteen leg lifts, and five minutes of running in place.

AN APPOSITIVE
My roommate is guilty of two of the seven deadly sins: gluttony and sloth.

A QUOTATION
Consider the words of Benjamin Franklin: "There never was a good war or a bad peace."

A SUMMARY OR AN EXPLANATION
Faith is like love: It cannot be forced.

The novel is clearly autobiographical: The author even gives his own name to the main character.

NOTE: For other ways of introducing quotations, see "Introducing quoted material" on pages 284–85. When an independent clause follows a colon, it may begin with a capital or a lowercase letter (see P8-e).

P3-e Use a colon according to convention.

SALUTATION IN A LETTER   Dear Sir or Madam:

HOURS AND MINUTES   5:30 p.m.

PROPORTIONS   The ratio of women to men was 2:1.

TITLE AND SUBTITLE   *The Glory of Hera: Greek Mythology and the Greek Family*

BIBLIOGRAPHIC ENTRIES   Boston: Bedford, 2011

NOTE: In biblical references, a colon is ordinarily used between chapter and verse (Luke 2:14). The Modern Language Association (MLA) recommends a period instead (Luke 2.14).

P3-f Avoid common misuses of the colon.

A colon must be preceded by a full independent clause. Therefore, avoid using it in the following situations.

BETWEEN A VERB AND ITS OBJECT OR COMPLEMENT

▶ Some important vitamins found in vegetables are:/ vitamin A, thiamine, niacin, and vitamin C.

BETWEEN A PREPOSITION AND ITS OBJECT

▶ The heart's two pumps each consist of:/ an upper chamber, or atrium, and a lower chamber, or ventricle.

AFTER *SUCH AS, INCLUDING,* OR *FOR EXAMPLE*

▶ The NCAA regulates college athletic teams, including:/ basketball, baseball, softball, and football.

P4 The apostrophe

P4-a **Use an apostrophe to indicate that a noun or an indefinite pronoun is possessive.**

The possessive form of a noun or an indefinite pronoun usually indicates ownership, as in *Tim's hat*, *the lawyer's desk*, or *someone's glove*. Frequently, however, ownership is only loosely implied: *the tree's roots*, *a day's work*. If you are not sure whether a word is possessive, try turning it into an *of* phrase: the roots *of the tree*, the work *of a day*.

When to add -'s to a noun

1. If the noun does not end in *-s*, add *-'s*.

   Luck often propels a rock musician's career.

   The Children's Defense Fund is a nonprofit organization that supports programs for poor and minority children.

2. If the noun is singular and ends in *-s* or an *s* sound, add *-'s*.

   Lois's sister spent last year in India.

   Her article presents an overview of Marx's teachings.

NOTE: To avoid potentially awkward pronunciation, some writers use only the apostrophe with a singular noun ending in *-s*: *Sophocles'*.

When to add only an apostrophe to a noun

If the noun is plural and ends in *-s*, add only an apostrophe.

   Both diplomats' briefcases were searched by guards.

Joint possession

To show joint possession, use *-'s* or *(-s')* with the last noun only; to show individual possession, make all nouns possessive.

   Have you seen Joyce and Greg's new camper?

   John's and Marie's expectations of marriage couldn't have been more different.

Joyce and Greg jointly own one camper. John and Marie individually have different expectations.

possessives • using -'s or -s' • compound nouns (*father-in-law's*) •
everyone's, somebody's, etc. • contractions (*isn't*) • no apostrophe

P4-c 279

Compound nouns

If a noun is compound, use -'s (or -s') with the last element.

> My father-in-law's memoir about his childhood in Sri Lanka was
> published in October.

Indefinite pronouns

Indefinite pronouns refer to no specific person or thing: *everyone, someone, no one, something.* (See B1-b.)

> Someone's raincoat has been left behind.

P4-b Use an apostrophe to mark omissions in contractions and numbers.

In a contraction, the apostrophe takes the place of one or more missing letters.

> It's a shame that Frank can't go on the tour.

It's stands for *it is, can't* for *cannot.*

The apostrophe is also used to mark the omission of the first two
digits of a year (*the class of '08*) or years (*the '60s generation*).

P4-c Do not use an apostrophe to form the plural of numbers, letters, abbreviations, and words mentioned as words.

An apostrophe typically is not used to pluralize numbers, letters, abbreviations, and words mentioned as words. Note the few exceptions and be
consistent throughout your paper.

Plural of numbers

Do not use an apostrophe in the plural of any numbers, including
decades.

> Oksana skated nearly perfect figure 8s.

> The 1920s are known as the Jazz Age.

Plural of letters

Italicize the letter and use roman (regular) font style for the -*s* ending.
Do not italicize academic grades.

Two large *J*s were painted on the door.

He received two Ds for the first time in his life.

EXCEPTIONS: To avoid misreading, use an apostrophe to form the plural of lowercase letters and the capital letters *A* and *I*: *p*'s, *A*'s.

Beginning readers often confuse *b*'s and *d*'s.

MLA NOTE: The Modern Language Association recommends using an apostrophe for the plural of both capital and lowercase letters: *J*'s, *p*'s.

Plural of abbreviations

Do not use an apostrophe to pluralize an abbreviation.

Harriet has thirty DVDs on her desk.

Marco earned two PhDs before his thirtieth birthday.

Plural of words mentioned as words

Generally, omit the apostrophe to form the plural of words mentioned as words. If the word is italicized, the *-s* ending appears in roman (regular) type.

We've heard enough *maybe*s.

Words mentioned as words may also appear in quotation marks. When you choose this option, use the apostrophe.

We've heard enough "maybe's."

P4-d Avoid common misuses of the apostrophe.

Do not use an apostrophe in the following situations.

WITH NOUNS THAT ARE NOT POSSESSIVE

outpatients
► Some ~~outpatient's~~ have special parking permits.
      ^

IN THE POSSESSIVE PRONOUNS *ITS, WHOSE, HIS, HERS, OURS, YOURS,* **AND** *THEIRS*

its
► Each area has ~~it's~~ own conference room.
      ^
It's means "it is." The possessive pronoun *its* contains no apostrophe despite the fact that it is possessive.

▶ *The House on Mango Street* was written by Sandra Cisneros,
   whose
   ~~who's~~ work focuses on the Latino community in the United
   ^
   States.

Who's means "who is." The possessive pronoun is *whose*.

P5 Quotation marks

Writers use quotation marks primarily to enclose direct quotations of
another person's spoken or written words. You will also find these other
uses and exceptions:

- for quotations within quotations (single quotation marks: P5-b)
- for titles of short works (P5-c)
- for words used as words (P5-d)
- with other marks of punctuation (P5-e)
- with brackets and ellipsis marks (P6-b, P6-c)
- no quotation marks for long quotations (P5-a)
- no quotation marks for indirect quotations, summaries, and
  paraphrases (P5-a, MLA-2c, APA-2c, CMS-2c)

P5-a Use quotation marks to enclose direct quotations.

Direct quotations of a person's words, whether spoken or written, must
be in quotation marks.

> "The contract negotiations are stalled," the airline executive told
> reporters, "but I am prepared to work night and day to bring both
> sides together."

In dialogue, begin a new paragraph to mark a change in speaker.

> "Mom, his name is Willie, not William. A thousand times I've told
> you, it's *Willie*."
> "Willie is a derivative of William, Lester. Surely his birth certifi-
> cate doesn't have Willie on it, and I like calling people by their
> proper names."
> "Yes, it does, ma'am. My mother named me Willie K. Mason."
> — Gloria Naylor

If a single speaker utters more than one paragraph, introduce each paragraph with a quotation mark, but do not use a closing quotation mark until the end of the speech.

Exception: indirect quotations

Do not use quotation marks around indirect quotations. An indirect quotation reports someone's ideas without using that person's exact words. In academic writing, indirect quotation is called *paraphrase* or *summary*. (See R3-c.)

> The airline executive told reporters that although contract negotiations were at a standstill, she was prepared to work hard with both labor and management to bring about a settlement.

Exception: long quotations

Long quotations of prose or poetry are generally set off from the text by indenting. Quotation marks are not used because the indented format tells readers that the quotation is taken word-for-word from the source.

> After making an exhaustive study of the historical record, James Horan evaluates Billy the Kid like this:
>
> > The portrait that emerges of [the Kid] from the thousands of pages of affidavits, reports, trial transcripts, his letters, and his testimony is neither the mythical Robin Hood nor the stereotyped adenoidal moron and pathological killer. Rather Billy appears as a disturbed, lonely young man, honest, loyal to his friends, dedicated to his beliefs, and betrayed by our institutions and the corrupt, ambitious, and compromising politicians in his time. (158)

The number in parentheses is a citation handled according to MLA style. (See MLA-4a.)

MLA, APA, and CMS (*Chicago*) have specific guidelines for what constitutes a long quotation and how it should be indented (see pp. 381, 485, and 506, respectively).

P5-b Use single quotation marks to enclose a quotation within a quotation.

> Megan Marshall notes that what Elizabeth Peabody "hoped to accomplish in her school was not merely 'teaching' but 'educating children morally and spiritually as well as intellectually from the first'" (107).

P5-c Use quotation marks around the titles of short works.

Short works include newspaper and magazine articles, poems, short stories, songs, episodes of television and radio programs, and chapters or subdivisions of books.

> James Baldwin's story "Sonny's Blues" tells the story of two brothers who come to understand each other's suffering.

NOTE: Titles of books, plays, Web sites, television and radio programs, films, magazines, and newspapers are put in italics. (See P10-a.)

P5-d Quotation marks may be used to set off words used as words.

Although words used as words are ordinarily italicized (see P10-b), quotation marks are also acceptable. Be consistent throughout your paper.

> The words "accept" and "except" are frequently confused.

> The words *accept* and *except* are frequently confused.

P5-e Use punctuation with quotation marks according to convention.

This section describes the conventions American publishers use in placing various marks of punctuation inside or outside quotation marks. It also explains how to punctuate when introducing quoted material.

Periods and commas

Place periods and commas inside quotation marks.

> "I'm here as part of my service-learning project," I told the classroom teacher. "I'm hoping to become a reading specialist."

This rule applies to single quotation marks as well as double quotation marks. (See P5-b.) It also applies to all uses of quotation marks: for quoted material, for titles of works, and for words used as words.

EXCEPTION: In the Modern Language Association's style of parenthetical in-text citations (see MLA-4a), the period follows the citation in parentheses. (See the example on p. 284.)

James M. McPherson comments, approvingly, that the Whigs "were not averse to extending the blessings of American liberty, even to Mexicans and Indians" (48).

Colons and semicolons

Put colons and semicolons outside quotation marks.

Harold wrote, "I regret that I am unable to attend the fundraiser for AIDS research"; his letter, however, came with a substantial contribution.

Question marks and exclamation points

Put question marks and exclamation points inside quotation marks unless they apply to the whole sentence.

Contrary to tradition, bedtime at my house is marked by "Mommy, can I tell you a story now?"

Have you heard the old proverb "Do not climb the hill until you reach it"?

In the first sentence, the question mark applies only to the quoted question. In the second sentence, the question mark applies to the whole sentence.

NOTE: In MLA style for a quotation that ends with a question mark or an exclamation point, the parenthetical citation and a period should follow the entire quotation.

Rosie Thomas asks, "Is nothing in life ever straight and clear, the way children see it?" (77).

Introducing quoted material

After a word group introducing a quotation, choose a colon, a comma, or no punctuation at all, whichever is appropriate in context.

FORMAL INTRODUCTION   If a quotation is formally introduced, a colon is appropriate. A formal introduction is a full independent clause, not just an expression such as *he said* or *she remarked*.

Thomas Friedman provides a challenging yet optimistic view of the future: "We need to get back to work on our country and on our planet. The hour is late, the stakes couldn't be higher, the project couldn't be harder, the payoff couldn't be greater" (25).

EXPRESSION SUCH AS *HE SAID*   If a quotation is introduced with an expression such as *he said* or *she remarked*—or if it is followed by such an expression—a comma is needed.

> About New England's weather, Mark Twain once declared, "In the spring I have counted one hundred and thirty-six different kinds of weather within four and twenty hours" (55).

> "Unless another war is prevented it is likely to bring destruction on a scale never before held possible and even now hardly conceived," Albert Einstein wrote in the aftermath of the atomic bomb (29).

BLENDED QUOTATION   When a quotation is blended into the writer's own sentence, either a comma or no punctuation is appropriate, depending on the way in which the quotation fits into the sentence structure.

> The future champion could, as he put it, "float like a butterfly and sting like a bee."

> Virginia Woolf wrote in 1928 that "a woman must have money and a room of her own if she is to write fiction" (4).

BEGINNING OF SENTENCE   If a quotation appears at the beginning of a sentence, use a comma after it unless the quotation ends with a question mark or an exclamation point.

> "I've always thought of myself as a reporter," claimed American poet Gwendolyn Brooks (162).

> "What is it?" she asked, bracing herself.

INTERRUPTED QUOTATION   If a quoted sentence is interrupted by explanatory words, use commas to set off the explanatory words.

> "With regard to air travel," Stephen Ambrose notes, "Jefferson was a full century ahead of the curve" (53).

If two successive quoted sentences from the same source are interrupted by explanatory words, use a comma before the explanatory words and a period after them.

> "Everyone agrees journalists must tell the truth," Bill Kovach and Tom Rosenstiel write. "Yet people are befuddled about what 'the truth' means" (37).

P5-f Avoid common misuses of quotation marks.

Do not use quotation marks to draw attention to familiar slang, to disown trite expressions, or to justify an attempt at humor.

▶ The economist estimated that single-family home prices would decline another 5 percent by the end of the year, emphasizing that this was only a ⸍ballpark figure.⸍

Do not use quotation marks around the title of your own essay.

P6 Other punctuation marks

P6-a End punctuation

The period

Use a period to end all sentences except direct questions or genuine exclamations. Also use periods in abbreviations according to convention.

TO END SENTENCES   Most sentences should end with a period. Problems sometimes arise when a writer must choose between a period and a question mark or between a period and an exclamation point.

If a sentence reports a question instead of asking it directly, it should end with a period, not a question mark.

▶ The professor asked whether talk therapy was more beneficial

than antidepressants~~?~~.
　　　　　　　　　　 ^

If a sentence is not a genuine exclamation, it should end with a period, not an exclamation point. (See also p. 287.)

▶ After years of working her way through school, Geeta finally

graduated with high honors~~!~~.
　　　　　　　　　　　 ^

IN ABBREVIATIONS   A period is conventionally used in abbreviations of titles and Latin words or phrases, including the time designations for morning and afternoon.

Mr.	i.e.	a.m. (or AM)
Ms.	e.g.	p.m. (or PM)
Dr.	etc.	

NOTE: If a sentence ends with a period marking an abbreviation, do not add a second period.

Do not use a period with US Postal Service abbreviations for states: MD, TX, CA.

Current usage is to omit the period in abbreviations of organization and country names, academic degrees, and designations for eras.

NATO	UNESCO	UCLA	BS	BC
IRS	AFL-CIO	NIH	PhD	BCE

The question mark

A direct question should be followed by a question mark.

What is the horsepower of a 777 engine?

If a polite request is written in the form of a question, it may be followed by a period.

Would you please send me your catalog of lilies.

TIP: Do not use a question mark after an indirect question, one that is reported rather than asked directly. Use a period instead.

▶ He asked me who was teaching the mythology course this year~~?~~.
                                                              ^

NOTE: Questions in a series may be followed by question marks even when they are not complete sentences.

We wondered where Calamity had hidden this time. Under the sink? Behind the furnace? On top of the bookcase?

The exclamation point

Use an exclamation point after a word group or sentence to express exceptional feeling or to provide special emphasis. The exclamation point is rarely appropriate in academic writing.

When Gloria entered the room, I switched on the lights, and we all yelled, "Surprise!"

TIP: Do not overuse the exclamation point.

▶ In the fisherman's memory, the fish lives on, increasing in length

and weight with each passing year, until at last it is big enough

to shade a fishing boat~~!~~.
                        ^
This sentence doesn't need to be pumped up with an exclamation point. It is emphatic enough without it.

▶ Whenever I see my favorite hitter, Derrek Lee, in the batter's box,

I dream of making it to the big leagues⟩. My team would win
                                        ^
every time!

The first exclamation point should be deleted so that the second one will
have more force.

P6-b The dash, parentheses, and brackets

The dash

When typing, use two hyphens to form a dash (--). Do not put spaces
before or after the dash. If your word processing program has what is
known as an "em-dash" (—), you may use it instead, with no space
before or after it.

A dash can be used to set off parenthetical material that deserves
emphasis.

> Everything that went wrong—from the peeping Tom at Theodora's
> window last night to my head-on collision today—we blamed on
> our move.

A pair of dashes is useful to enclose an appositive that contains
commas. An appositive is a noun or noun phrase that renames a nearby
noun. Ordinarily appositives are set off with commas (see P1-e), but
when the appositive itself contains commas, a pair of dashes helps
readers see the relative importance of all the pauses.

> In my hometown, the basic needs of people—food, clothing, and
> shelter—are less costly than in a big city like Los Angeles.

A dash is a dramatic, somewhat informal way to introduce a list, a
restatement, an amplification, or a striking shift in tone or thought.

> Along the wall are the bulk liquids—sesame seed oil, honey,
> safflower oil, and that half-liquid "peanuts only" peanut butter.

> In his last semester, Peter tried to pay more attention to his
> priorities—applying to graduate school, getting financial aid, and
> finding a roommate.

> Everywhere we looked there were little kids—a box of Cracker
> Jacks in one hand and Mommy or Daddy's sleeve in the other.

> Kiere took a few steps back, came running full speed, kicked a
> mighty kick—and missed the ball.

In the first two examples, the writer could also use a colon. (See P3-d.) The colon is more formal than the dash and not quite as dramatic.

TIP: Unless there is a specific reason for using the dash, avoid it. Unnecessary dashes create a choppy effect.

▶ Insisting that students use computers as instructional

tools ⫽ for information retrieval ⫽ makes good sense. Herding

them ⫽ sheeplike ⫽ into computer technology does not.

Parentheses

Use parentheses to enclose supplemental material, minor digressions, and afterthoughts.

> Nurses record patients' vital signs (temperature, pulse, and blood pressure) several times a day.

Use parentheses to enclose letters or numbers labeling items in a series.

> Regulations stipulated that only the following equipment could be used on the survival mission: (1) a knife, (2) thirty feet of parachute line, (3) a book of matches, (4) a poncho, (5) an E tool, and (6) a signal flare.

TIP: Do not overuse parentheses. Rough drafts are likely to contain more afterthoughts than necessary. As writers head into a sentence, they often think of additional details, occasionally working them in as best they can with parentheses. Usually such sentences should be revised so that the additional details no longer seem to be afterthoughts.

▶ Researchers have said that seventeen million ~~(estimates run~~
from
to ^
~~as high as~~ twenty-three million)^Americans have diabetes.
^

Brackets

Use brackets to enclose any words or phrases that you have inserted into an otherwise word-for-word quotation.

> *Audubon* reports that "if there are not enough young to balance deaths, the end of the species [California condor] is inevitable" (4).

The sentence quoted from the *Audubon* article did not contain the words *California condor* (since the context of the full article made clear what species was meant), so the writer needed to add the name in brackets.

The Latin word "sic" in brackets indicates that an error in a quoted sentence appears in the original source.

> According to the review, Nelly Furtado's performance was brilliant, "exceding [sic] the expectations of even her most loyal fans."

Do not overuse "sic," however, since calling attention to others' mistakes can appear snobbish. The preceding quotation, for example, might have been paraphrased instead: *According to the review, even Nelly Furtado's most loyal fans were surprised by the brilliance of her performance.*

P6-c The ellipsis mark

The ellipsis mark consists of three spaced periods. Use an ellipsis mark to indicate that you have deleted words from an otherwise word-for-word quotation.

> Reuben reports that "when the amount of cholesterol circulating in the blood rises over . . . 300 milligrams per 100, the chances of a heart attack increase dramatically."

If you delete a full sentence or more in the middle of a quoted passage, use a period before the three ellipsis dots.

> "Most of our efforts," writes Dave Erikson, "are directed toward saving the bald eagle's wintering habitat along the Mississippi River. . . . It's important that the wintering birds have a place to roost, where they can get out of the cold wind."

TIP: Ordinarily, do not use the ellipsis mark at the beginning or at the end of a quotation. Readers will understand that the quoted material is taken from a longer passage. If you have cut some words from the end of the final quoted sentence, however, MLA requires an ellipsis mark, as in the first example on page 381.

In quoted poetry, use a full line of ellipsis dots to indicate that you have dropped a line or more from the poem, as in this example from "To His Coy Mistress" by Andrew Marvell:

> Had we but world enough, and time,
> This coyness, lady, were no crime.
> . . . .
> But at my back I always hear
> Time's wingèd chariot hurrying near; (1-2, 21-22)

The ellipsis mark may also be used to indicate a hesitation or an interruption in speech or to suggest unfinished thoughts.

> "The apartment building next door . . . it's going up in flames!" yelled Marcia.

> Before falling into a coma, the victim whispered, "It was a man with a tattoo on his . . . "

P6-d The slash

Use the slash to separate two or three lines of poetry that have been run into your text. Add a space both before and after the slash.

> In the opening lines of "Jordan," George Herbert pokes gentle fun at popular poems of his time: "Who says that fictions only and false hair / Become a verse? Is there in truth no beauty?" (1-2).

More than three lines of poetry should be handled as an indented quotation. (See p. 282.)

The slash may occasionally be used to separate paired terms such as *pass/fail* and *producer/director*. Do not use a space before or after the slash. Be sparing in this use of the slash. In particular, avoid the use of *and/or*, *he/she*, and *his/her*. Instead of using *he/she* and *his/her* to solve sexist language problems, you can usually find more graceful alternatives. (See W4-e and G3-a.)

P7 Spelling and hyphenation

You learned to spell from repeated experience with words in both reading and writing, but especially writing. Words have a look, a sound, and even a feel to them as the hand moves across the page. As you proofread, you can probably tell if a word doesn't look quite right. In such cases, the solution is obvious: Look up the word in the dictionary. (See W6-a.)

P7-a Become familiar with the major spelling rules.

i *before* e *except after* c

Use *i* before *e* except after *c* or when sounded like *ay*, as in *neighbor* and *weigh*.

I BEFORE *E*	relieve, believe, sieve, niece, fierce, frieze
E BEFORE *I*	receive, deceive, sleigh, freight, eight
EXCEPTIONS	seize, either, weird, height, foreign, leisure

Suffixes

FINAL SILENT -*E*   Generally, drop a final silent -*e* when adding a suffix that begins with a vowel. Keep the final -*e* if the suffix begins with a consonant.

combine, combination	achieve, achievement
desire, desiring	care, careful
prude, prudish	entire, entirety
remove, removable	gentle, gentleness

Words such as *changeable, acknowledgment, judgment, argument,* and *truly* are exceptions.

FINAL -*Y*   When adding -*s* or -*d* to words ending in -*y*, ordinarily change -*y* to -*ie* when the -*y* is preceded by a consonant but not when it is preceded by a vowel.

comedy, comedies	monkey, monkeys
dry, dried	play, played

With proper names ending in -*y*, however, do not change the -*y* to -*ie* even if it is preceded by a consonant: *the Dougherty family, the Doughertys.*

FINAL CONSONANTS   If a final consonant is preceded by a single vowel *and* the consonant ends a one-syllable word or a stressed syllable, double the consonant when adding a suffix beginning with a vowel.

bet, betting	occur, occurrence
commit, committed	

Plurals

-*S* OR -*ES*   Add -*s* to form the plural of most nouns; add -*es* to singular nouns ending in -*s*, -*sh*, -*ch*, and -*x*.

table, tables	church, churches
paper, papers	dish, dishes

Ordinarily add -*s* to nouns ending in -*o* when the -*o* is preceded by a vowel. Add -*es* when it is preceded by a consonant.

radio, radios	hero, heroes
video, videos	tomato, tomatoes

OTHER PLURALS   To form the plural of a hyphenated compound word, add -*s* to the chief word even if it does not appear at the end.

mother-in-law, mothers-in-law

English words derived from other languages such as Latin, Greek,
or French sometimes form the plural as they would in their original
language.

medium, media   chateau, chateaux
criterion, criteria

ESL   Spelling varies slightly among English-speaking countries.
This can be particularly confusing for multilingual students in the
United States, who may have learned British English. Following is a
list of some common words spelled differently in American and
British English. Consult a dictionary for others.

AMERICAN	BRITISH
canceled, traveled	cancelled, travelled
color, humor	colour, humour
judgment	judgement
check	cheque
realize, apologize	realise, apologise
defense	defence
anemia, anesthetic	anaemia, anaesthetic
theater, center	theatre, centre
fetus	foetus
mold, smolder	mould, smoulder
civilization	civilisation
connection, inflection	connexion, inflexion
licorice	liquorice

P7-b **Discriminate between words that sound alike but
have different meanings.**

Words that sound alike or nearly alike but have different meanings and
spellings are called *homophones*. The following sets of words are so commonly confused that a good writer will double-check their every use.

affect (verb: to exert an influence)
effect (verb: to accomplish; noun: result)

its (possessive pronoun: of or belonging to it)
it's (contraction for *it is* or *it has*)

loose (adjective: free, not securely attached)
lose (verb: to fail to keep, to be deprived of)

principal (adjective: most important; noun: head of a school)
principle (noun: a fundamental guideline or truth)

their (possessive pronoun: belonging to them)
they're (contraction for *they are*)
there (adverb: that place or position)

who's (contraction for *who is* or *who has*)
whose (possessive form of *who*)

your (possessive pronoun: belonging to you)
you're (contraction for *you are*)

To check for correct use of these and other commonly confused words, consult the glossary of usage (W1).

P7-c Consult the dictionary to determine whether to hyphenate a compound word.

The dictionary will tell you whether to treat a compound word as a hyphenated compound (*water-repellent*), one word (*waterproof*), or two words (*water table*). If the compound word is not in the dictionary, treat it as two words.

▶ The prosecutor chose not to cross-examine any witnesses.

▶ All students are expected to record their data in a small

note book.

▶ Alice walked through the looking/glass into a backward world.

P7-d Hyphenate two or more words used together as an adjective before a noun.

▶ Mrs. Douglas gave Toshiko a seashell and some newspaper-wrapped

fish to take home to her mother.

▶ Richa Gupta is not yet a well-known candidate.

Newspaper-wrapped and *well-known* are adjectives used before the nouns *fish* and *candidate*.

Generally, do not use a hyphen when such compounds follow the noun.

▶ After our television campaign, Richa Gupta will be well/known.

Do not use a hyphen to connect *-ly* adverbs to the words they modify.

▶ A slowly/moving truck tied up traffic.

NOTE: When two or more hyphenated adjectives in a row modify the same noun, you can suspend the hyphens.

Do you prefer first-, second-, or third-class tickets?

P7-e Hyphenate fractions and certain numbers when they are spelled out.

For numbers written in words, use a hyphen in all fractions and in compound numbers from twenty-one to ninety-nine.

▶ One-fourth of my income pays for child care, and one-third
pays the rent.

P7-f Use a hyphen with the prefixes *all-*, *ex-* (meaning "former"), and *self-* and with the suffix *-elect*.

▶ The private foundation is funneling more money into self-help
projects.
▶ The Student Senate bylaws require the president-elect to attend
all senate meetings between the election and the official transfer
of office.

P7-g Use a hyphen in certain words to avoid ambiguity or to separate awkward double or triple letters.

Without the hyphen, there would be no way to distinguish between words such as *re-creation* and *recreation*.

Bicycling in the city is my favorite form of recreation.

The film was praised for its astonishing re-creation of nineteenth-century London.

Hyphens are sometimes used to separate awkward double or triple letters in compound words (*anti-intellectual*, *cross-stitch*). Always check a dictionary for the standard form of the word.

P7-h Check for correct hyphenation at the ends of lines.

Some word processing programs and other computer applications automatically generate word breaks at the ends of lines. When you're writing an academic paper, it's best to set your computer application not to hyphenate automatically. This setting will ensure that only words already containing a hyphen (such as *long-distance*, *pre-Roman*) will be hyphenated at the ends of lines. (See also C6.)

E-mail addresses, URLs, and other electronic addresses need special attention when they occur at the end of a line of text or in bibliographic citations. You can't rely on your computer application to divide these terms correctly, so you must make a decision in each case. Do not insert a hyphen to divide electronic addresses. Instead, break an e-mail address after the @ symbol or before a period. Break a URL after a slash or a double slash or before any other punctuation mark.

> I repeatedly e-mailed Janine at janine.r.rose@dunbaracademy.org before I gave up and called her cell phone.

> To find a zip code quickly, I always use the United States Postal Service Web site at http://zip4.usps.com/zip4/welcome.jsp.

For breaks in URLs in MLA, APA, and CMS (*Chicago*) documentation styles, see MLA-5a, APA-5a, and CMS-5a, respectively.

P8 Capitalization

In addition to the rules in this section, a good dictionary can tell you when to use capital letters.

P8-a Capitalize proper nouns and words derived from them; do not capitalize common nouns.

Proper nouns are the names of specific persons, places, and things. All other nouns are common nouns. The following types of words are usually capitalized: names of deities, religions, religious followers, sacred books; words of family relationship used as names; particular places;

nationalities and their languages, races, tribes; educational institutions, departments, degrees, particular courses; government departments, organizations, political parties; historical movements, periods, events, documents; specific electronic sources; and trade names.

PROPER NOUNS	COMMON NOUNS
God (used as a name)	a god
Book of Common Prayer	a sacred book
Uncle Pedro	my uncle
Father (used as a name)	my father
Lake Superior	a picturesque lake
the Capital Center	a center for advanced studies
the South	a southern state
Wrigley Field	a baseball stadium
University of Wisconsin	a state university
Geology 101	geology
Environmental Protection Agency	a federal agency
Phi Kappa Psi	a fraternity
a Democrat	an independent
the Enlightenment	the eighteenth century
the Treaty of Versailles	a treaty
the World Wide Web, the Web	a home page
the Internet, the Net	a computer network
Advil	a painkiller

Months, holidays, and days of the week are treated as proper nouns; the seasons and numbers of the days of the month are not.

> Our academic year begins on a Tuesday in early September, right after Labor Day.

> Graduation is in early summer, on the second of June.

EXCEPTION: Capitalize Fourth of July (or July Fourth) when referring to the holiday.

Names of school subjects are capitalized only if they are names of languages. Names of particular courses are capitalized.

> This semester Austin is taking math, geography, geology, French, and English.

> Professor Obembe offers Modern American Fiction 501 to graduate students.

CAUTION: Do not capitalize common nouns to make them seem important: *Our company is currently hiring computer programmers* (not *Company, Computer Programmers*).

P8-b **Capitalize titles of persons when used as part of a proper name but usually not when used alone.**

> Professor Margaret Barnes; Dr. Sinyee Sein; John Scott Williams Jr.
>
> District Attorney Marshall was reprimanded for badgering the witness.
>
> The district attorney was elected for a two-year term.

Usage varies when the title of an important public figure is used alone: *The president* [or *President*] *vetoed the bill.*

P8-c **Capitalize the first, last, and all major words in titles and subtitles of works.**

In both titles and subtitles of works (books, articles, songs, artwork, and online documents) major words—nouns, pronouns, verbs, adjectives, and adverbs—should be capitalized. Minor words—articles, prepositions, and coordinating conjunctions—are not capitalized unless they are the first or last word of a title or subtitle.

Capitalize the second part of a hyphenated term in a title if it is a major word but not if it is a minor word. Capitalize chapter titles and the titles of other major divisions of a work following the same guidelines used for titles of complete works.

> *Seizing the Enigma: The Race to Break the German U-Boat Codes*
> *A River Runs through It*
> "I Want to Hold Your Hand"
> *The Canadian Green Page*

To learn why some of the titles in the list are italicized and some are put in quotation marks, see P10-a and P5-c.

P8-d **Capitalize the first word of a sentence.**

The first word of a sentence should be capitalized. When a sentence appears within parentheses, capitalize its first word unless the parentheses appear within another sentence.

> Early detection of breast cancer significantly increases survival rates. (See table 2.)
>
> Early detection of breast cancer significantly increases survival rates (see table 2).

Capitalize the first word of a quoted sentence but not a quoted phrase.

> Robert Hughes writes, "There are only about sixty Watteau paintings on whose authenticity all experts agree" (102).

> Russell Baker has written that in this country, sports are "the opiate of the masses" (46).

If a quoted sentence is interrupted by explanatory words, do not capitalize the first word after the interruption. (See P5-e.)

> "If you want to go out," he said, "tell me now."

When quoting poetry, copy the poet's capitalization exactly. Many poets capitalize the first word of every line of poetry; a few contemporary poets dismiss capitalization altogether.

> it was the week   that
> i felt the city's narrow breezes rush about
> me   —Don L. Lee

P8-e Capitalize the first word after a colon if it begins an independent clause.

If a word group following a colon could stand on its own as a complete sentence, capitalize the first word.

> Clinical trials called into question the safety profile of the drug: A high percentage of participants reported hypertension and kidney problems.

Preferences vary among academic disciplines. See MLA-5a, APA-5a, and CMS-5a for MLA, APA, and CMS (*Chicago*) style, respectively.

Always use lowercase for a list or an appositive that follows a colon.

> Students were divided into two groups: residents and commuters.

P8-f Capitalize abbreviations according to convention.

Abbreviations for government agencies, companies, and other organizations as well as call numbers for radio and television stations are capitalized.

> EPA, FBI, DKNY, IBM, WCRB, KNBC-TV

P9 Abbreviations and numbers

P9-a Use standard abbreviations for titles immediately before and after proper names.

TITLES BEFORE PROPER NAMES	TITLES AFTER PROPER NAMES
Mr. Rafael Zabala	William Albert Sr.
Ms. Nancy Linehan	Thomas Hines Jr.
Mrs. Edward Horn	Anita Lor, PhD
Dr. Margaret Simmons	Robert Simkowski, MD
Rev. John Stone	Margaret Chin, LLD
Prof. James Russo	Polly Stein, DDS

Abbreviate a title only if it is used with a proper name.

> *professor*
> ▶ My history ~~prof.~~ is an expert on twentieth-century race relations in
> ^
> South Africa.

Avoid redundant titles such as *Dr. Amy Day, MD.* Choose one title or the other: *Dr. Amy Day* or *Amy Day, MD.*

P9-b Use abbreviations only when you are sure your readers will understand them.

Familiar abbreviations, written without periods, are acceptable.

CIA	FBI	MD	NAACP
NBA	NEA	PhD	CD-ROM
YMCA	CBS	USA	ESL

Talk show host Conan O'Brien is a Harvard graduate with a BA in history.

The YMCA has opened a new gym close to my office.

NOTE: When using an unfamiliar abbreviation (such as NASW for National Association of Social Workers) throughout a paper, write the full name followed by the abbreviation in parentheses at the first mention of the name. Then use just the abbreviation throughout the rest of the paper.

abbreviations • titles with names (*Dr.*, *Prof.*) • familiar terms •
dates • times of day • money • Latin (*e.g.*, *et al.*)

P9-d   301

P9-c **Use *BC*, *AD*, *a.m.*, *p.m.*, *No.*, and *$* only with specific dates, times, numbers, and amounts.**

The abbreviation *BC* ("before Christ") follows a date, and *AD* ("*anno Domini*") precedes a date. Acceptable alternatives are *BCE* ("before the common era") and *CE* ("common era"), both of which follow a date.

40 BC (or 40 BCE)	4:00 a.m. (or AM)	No. 12 (or no. 12)
AD 44 (or 44 CE)	6:00 p.m. (or PM)	$150

Avoid using *a.m.*, *p.m.*, *No.*, or *$* when not accompanied by a specific figure.

▶ The governor argued that the new sales tax would raise
                money
much-needed $ for the state.
       ^

P9-d **Be sparing in your use of Latin abbreviations.**

Latin abbreviations are acceptable in footnotes and bibliographies and in informal writing for comments in parentheses.

cf. (Latin *confer*, "compare")

e.g. (Latin *exempli gratia*, "for example")

et al. (Latin *et alia*, "and others")

etc. (Latin *et cetera*, "and so forth")

i.e. (Latin *id est*, "that is")

N.B. (Latin *nota bene*, "note well")

The text for our sociology class is Harold Simms et al., *Introduction to Social Systems*.

Alfred Hitchcock directed many classic thrillers (e.g., *Psycho*, *Rear Window*, and *Vertigo*).

In formal writing, use the appropriate English phrases.

                                      for example,
▶ Many obsolete laws remain on the books; ~~e.g.,~~ a law in Vermont
                                        ^
forbids an unmarried man and woman to sit closer than six inches

apart on a park bench.

P9-e Avoid inappropriate abbreviations.

In formal writing, abbreviations for the following are not commonly accepted.

PERSONAL NAMES   Charles (not Chas.)

UNITS OF MEASUREMENT   feet (not ft.)

DAYS OF THE WEEK   Monday (not Mon.)

HOLIDAYS   Christmas (not Xmas)

MONTHS   January, February, March (not Jan., Feb., Mar.)

COURSES OF STUDY   political science (not poli. sci.)

DIVISIONS OF WRITTEN WORKS   chapter, page (not ch., p.)

STATES AND COUNTRIES   Massachusetts (not MA or Mass.)

PARTS OF A BUSINESS NAME   Adams Lighting Company (not Adams Lighting Co.); Kim and Brothers (not Kim and Bros.)

▶ The American Red Cross requires that blood donors be at least
seventeen ~~yrs.~~ old, weigh at least 110 ~~lb.,~~ and not have given blood
in the past eight ~~wks.~~

years *pounds,* *weeks.*

EXCEPTION: Abbreviate states and provinces in complete addresses, and always abbreviate DC when used with Washington.

P9-f Follow the conventions in your discipline for spelling out or using numerals to express numbers.

In the humanities, which generally follow either Modern Language Association (MLA) style or CMS (*Chicago*) style, use numerals only for specific numbers above one hundred: *353; 1,020.* Spell out numbers one hundred and below and large round numbers: *eleven, thirty-five, sixty, fifteen million.*

The social sciences and sciences, which follow the style guidelines of the American Psychological Association (APA) or the Council of Science Editors (CSE), use numerals for all but the numbers one through nine.

In all fields, treat related numbers in a passage consistently: *The survey found that 89 of 157 respondents had not taken any courses related to alcohol use.*

when not to abbreviate • numbers • when to spell out • when to use
numbers • dates • addresses • fractions • other everyday uses

P9-g   303

When one number immediately follows another, spelling out one number and using numerals for the other is usually effective: *three 100-meter events, 25 four-poster beds*.

▶ It's been ~~8~~ *eight* years since I visited Peru.

▶ Enrollment in the charter school in its first year will be limited to ~~three hundred forty~~ *340* students.

If a sentence begins with a number, spell out the number or rewrite the sentence.

▶ ~~150~~ *One hundred fifty* children in our program need expensive dental treatment.

Rewriting the sentence will also correct the error and may be less awkward if the number is long: *In our program, 150 children need expensive dental treatment.*

P9-g Use numerals according to convention in dates, addresses, and so on.

DATES   July 4, 1776; 56 BC

ADDRESSES   77 Latches Lane, 519 West 42nd Street

PERCENTAGES   55 percent (or 55%)

FRACTIONS, DECIMALS   ½, 0.047

SCORES   7 to 3, 21–18

STATISTICS   average age 37, average weight 180

SURVEYS   4 out of 5

EXACT AMOUNTS OF MONEY $105.37, $106,000

DIVISIONS OF BOOKS   volume 3, chapter 4, page 189

DIVISIONS OF PLAYS   act 3, scene 3 (or act III, scene iii)

IDENTIFICATION NUMBERS   serial number 10988675

TIME OF DAY   4:00 p.m., 1:30 a.m.

▶ The foundation raised ~~four hundred thirty thousand dollars~~ *$430,000* for cancer research.

NOTE: When not using *a.m.* or *p.m.*, write out the time in words (*two o'clock in the afternoon, twelve noon, seven in the morning*).

P10 Italics

This section describes conventional uses for italics. While italics is recommended by all three style guides covered in this book (MLA, APA, and CMS), some instructors may prefer underlining in student papers. If that is the case in your course, simply substitute underlining for italics in the examples in this section.

Some computer and online applications do not allow for italics. To indicate words that should be italicized, you can use underscore marks or asterisks before and after the italic words.

I am planning to write my senior thesis on _Memoirs of a Geisha_.

NOTE: Excessive use of italics to emphasize words or ideas, especially in academic writing, is distracting and should be avoided.

P10-a Italicize the titles of works according to convention.

Titles of the following types of works, including electronic works, should be italicized.

TITLES OF BOOKS   *The Known World, Middlesex, Encarta*

MAGAZINES   *Time, Scientific American, Salon.com*

NEWSPAPERS   the *Baltimore Sun*, the *Orlando Sentinel Online*

PAMPHLETS   *Common Sense, Facts about Marijuana*

LONG POEMS   *The Waste Land, Beowulf*

PLAYS   *'Night Mother, Wicked*

FILMS   *Casablanca, The Hurt Locker*

TELEVISION PROGRAMS   *American Idol, Frontline*

RADIO PROGRAMS   *All Things Considered*

MUSICAL COMPOSITIONS   *Porgy and Bess*

CHOREOGRAPHIC WORKS   *Brief Fling*

WORKS OF VISUAL ART   *American Gothic*

ELECTRONIC DATABASES   *ProQuest*

WEB SITES   *ZDNet, Google*

ELECTRONIC GAMES   *Everquest, Call of Duty*

The titles of other works, such as short stories, essays, episodes of radio and television programs, songs, and short poems, are enclosed in quotation marks. (See P5-c.)

NOTE: Do not use italics when referring to the Bible, titles of books in the Bible (Genesis, not *Genesis*), or titles of legal documents (the Constitution, not the *Constitution*). Do not italicize the titles of computer software (Keynote, Photoshop). Do not italicize the title of your own paper.

P10-b Italicize other terms according to convention.

SPACECRAFT, SHIPS, AIRCRAFT
Challenger, *Queen Mary 2*, *Spirit of St. Louis*

The success of the Soviets' *Sputnik* energized the US space program.

FOREIGN WORDS
Shakespeare's Falstaff is a comic character known for both his excessive drinking and his general *joie de vivre*.

EXCEPTION: Do not italicize foreign words that have become a standard part of the English language—"laissez-faire," "fait accompli," "modus operandi," and "per diem," for example.

WORDS, LETTERS, NUMBERS AS THEMSELVES
Tomás assured us that the chemicals could probably be safely mixed, but his *probably* stuck in our minds.

Some toddlers have trouble pronouncing the letter *s*.

A big *3* was painted on the stage door.

NOTE: Quotation marks may be used instead of italics to set off words mentioned as words. (See P5-d.)

nouns • persons, places, things, ideas •
pronouns (*we, their, who, anyone,* etc.)

B1-b   309

B1 Parts of speech

Traditional grammar recognizes eight parts of speech: noun, pronoun, verb, adjective, adverb, preposition, conjunction, and interjection. Many words can function as more than one part of speech. For example, depending on its use in a sentence, the word *paint* can be a noun (*The paint is wet*) or a verb (*Please paint the ceiling next*).

B1-a Nouns

A noun is the name of a person, place, thing, or concept.

>   N   N   N
> The *lion* in the *cage* growled at the *zookeeper*.

Nouns sometimes function as adjectives modifying other nouns. Because of their dual roles, nouns used in this manner may be called *noun/adjectives*.

>   N/ADJ   N/ADJ
> The *leather* notebook was tucked in the *student's* backpack.

Nouns are classified in a variety of ways. *Proper* nouns are capitalized, but *common* nouns are not (see P8-a). For clarity, writers choose between *concrete* and *abstract* nouns (see W5-b). The distinction between *count* nouns and *noncount* nouns can be especially helpful to multilingual writers (see M2-a). Most nouns have singular and plural forms; *collective* nouns may be either singular or plural, depending on how they are used (see G1-f and G3-a). *Possessive* nouns require an apostrophe (see P4-a).

B1-b Pronouns

A pronoun is a word used in place of a noun. Usually the pronoun substitutes for a specific noun, known as its *antecedent*.

> When the *battery* wears down, we recharge *it*.

Although most pronouns function as substitutes for nouns, some can function as adjectives modifying nouns. Because they have the form of a pronoun and the function of an adjective, such pronouns may be called *pronoun/adjectives*.

PN/ADJ
This bird was at the same window yesterday morning.

Pronouns are classified as personal, possessive, intensive and reflexive, relative, interrogative, demonstrative, indefinite, and reciprocal.

PERSONAL PRONOUNS   Personal pronouns refer to specific persons or things. They always function as noun equivalents.

Singular: I, me, you, she, her, he, him, it

Plural: we, us, you, they, them

POSSESSIVE PRONOUNS   Possessive pronouns indicate ownership.

Singular: my, mine, your, yours, her, hers, his, its

Plural: our, ours, your, yours, their, theirs

Some of these possessive pronouns function as adjectives modifying nouns: *my, your, her, his, its, our, their*.

INTENSIVE AND REFLEXIVE PRONOUNS   Intensive pronouns emphasize a noun or another pronoun (The senator *herself* met us at the door). Reflexive pronouns, which have the same form as intensive pronouns, name a receiver of an action identical with the doer of the action (Paula cut *herself*).

Singular: myself, yourself, himself, herself, itself

Plural: ourselves, yourselves, themselves

RELATIVE PRONOUNS   Relative pronouns introduce subordinate clauses functioning as adjectives (The writer *who won the award* refused to accept it). In addition to introducing the clause, the relative pronoun (in this case *who*) points back to a noun or pronoun that the clause modifies (*writer*). (See B3-e.)

who, whom, whose, which, that

INTERROGATIVE PRONOUNS   Interrogative pronouns introduce questions (*Who* is expected to win the election?).

who, whom, whose, which, what

DEMONSTRATIVE PRONOUNS Demonstrative pronouns identify or point to nouns. Frequently they function as adjectives (*This* chair is my favorite), but they may also function as noun equivalents (*This* is my favorite chair).

> this, that, these, those

INDEFINITE PRONOUNS Indefinite pronouns refer to nonspecific persons or things. Most are always singular (*everyone, each*); some are always plural (*both, many*); a few may be singular or plural (see G1-e). Most indefinite pronouns function as noun equivalents (*Something* is burning), but some can also function as adjectives (*All* campers must check in at the lodge).

all	anything	everyone	nobody	several
another	both	everything	none	some
any	each	few	no one	somebody
anybody	either	many	nothing	someone
anyone	everybody	neither	one	something

RECIPROCAL PRONOUNS Reciprocal pronouns refer to individual parts of a plural antecedent (By turns, the penguins fed *one another*).

> each other, one another

NOTE: Using pronouns correctly can be challenging. See pronoun-antecedent agreement (G3-a), pronoun reference (G3-b), distinguishing between pronouns such as *I* and *me* (G3-c), and distinguishing between *who* and *whom* (G3-d).

B1-c Verbs

The verb of a sentence usually expresses action (*jump, think*) or being (*is, become*). It is composed of a main verb possibly preceded by one or more helping verbs.

> MV
> The horses *exercise* every day.

> HV   MV
> The task force report *was* not *completed* on schedule.

Notice that words, usually adverbs, can intervene between the helping verb and the main verb (was *not* completed). (See B1-e.)

PRACTICE hackerhandbooks.com/writersref
> Basic grammar > B1–9 and B1–10

Helping verbs

There are twenty-three helping verbs in English: forms of *have*, *do*, and *be*, which may also function as main verbs; and nine modals, which function only as helping verbs. *Have*, *do*, and *be* change form to indicate tense; the nine modals do not.

> **FORMS OF *HAVE*, *DO*, AND *BE***
>
> have, has, had
>
> do, does, did
>
> be, am, is, are, was, were, being, been
>
> **MODALS**
>
> can, could, may, might, must, shall, should, will, would

The verb phrase *ought to* is often classified as a modal as well.

Main verbs

The main verb of a sentence is always the kind of word that would change form if put into these test sentences:

> **BASE FORM**   Usually I (*walk*, *ride*).
>
> **PAST TENSE**   Yesterday I (*walked*, *rode*).
>
> **PAST PARTICIPLE**   I have (*walked*, *ridden*) many times before.
>
> **PRESENT PARTICIPLE**   I am (*walking*, *riding*) right now.
>
> ***-S* FORM**   Usually he/she/it (*walks*, *rides*).

If a word doesn't change form when slipped into the test sentences, you can be certain that it is not a main verb. For example, the noun *revolution*, though it may seem to suggest an action, can never function as a main verb. Just try to make it behave like one (*Today I revolution . . . Yesterday I revolutioned . . .*) and you'll see why.

When both the past-tense and the past-participle forms of a verb end in *-ed*, the verb is regular (*walked*, *walked*). Otherwise, the verb is irregular (*rode*, *ridden*). (See G2-a.)

The verb *be* is highly irregular, having eight forms instead of the usual five: the base form *be*; the present-tense forms *am*, *is*, and *are*; the past-tense forms *was* and *were*; the present participle *being*; and the past participle *been*.

Helping verbs combine with the various forms of main verbs to create tenses. For a survey of tenses, see G2-f.

NOTE: Some verbs are followed by words that look like prepositions but are so closely associated with the verb that they are a part of its meaning. These words are known as *particles*. Common verb-particle combinations include *bring up*, *call off*, *drop off*, *give in*, *look up*, *run into*, and *take off*.

> Sharon *packed up* her broken laptop and *sent* it *off* to the repair shop.

TIP: You can find more information about using verbs in other sections of the handbook: active verbs (W3), subject-verb agreement (G1), standard English verb forms (G2-a to G2-d), verb tense and mood (G2-f and G2-g), and multilingual/ESL challenges with verbs (M1).

B1-d Adjectives

An adjective is a word used to modify, or describe, a noun or pronoun. An adjective usually answers one of these questions: Which one? What kind of? How many?

> ADJ
> the *frisky* horse [Which horse?]

> ADJ ADJ
> *cracked old* plates [What kind of plates?]

> ADJ
> *nine* months [How many months?]

Adjectives usually precede the words they modify. They may also follow linking verbs, in which case they describe the subject. (See B2-b.)

> ADJ
> The decision was *unpopular*.

The definite article *the* and the indefinite articles *a* and *an* are also classified as adjectives.

> ART ART ART
> *A* defendant should be judged on *the* evidence provided to *the* jury, not on hearsay.

Some possessive, demonstrative, and indefinite pronouns can function as adjectives: *their*, *its*, *this*, *all*, and so on (see B1-b). And nouns can function as adjectives when they modify other nouns: *apple pie* (the noun *apple* modifies the noun *pie*; see B1-a).

TIP: You can find more details about using adjectives in G4. If you are a multilingual writer, you may also find help with articles and specific uses of adjectives in M2 and M4.

PRACTICE hackerhandbooks.com/writersref
> Basic grammar > B1–11 to B1–14
> B1–15 and B1–16 (all parts of speech)

B1-e Adverbs

An adverb is a word used to modify, or qualify, a verb (or verbal), an adjective, or another adverb. It usually answers one of these questions: When? Where? How? Why? Under what conditions? To what degree?

> Pull *firmly* on the emergency handle. [Pull how?]

> Read the text *first* and *then* work the exercises. [Read when? Work when?]

Adverbs modifying adjectives or other adverbs usually intensify or limit the intensity of the word they modify.

>   ADV   ADV
> Be *extremely* kind, and you will *probably* have many friends.

The words *not* and *never* are classified as adverbs.

B1-f Prepositions

A preposition is a word placed before a noun or pronoun to form a phrase modifying another word in the sentence. The prepositional phrase nearly always functions as an adjective or as an adverb.

>   P   P   P
> The road *to* the summit travels *past* craters *from* an extinct volcano.

To the summit functions as an adjective modifying the noun *road*; *past craters* functions as an adverb modifying the verb *travels*; *from an extinct volcano* functions as an adjective modifying the noun *craters*. (For more on prepositional phrases, see B3-a.)

English has a limited number of prepositions. The most common are included in the following list.

about	beside	from	outside	toward
above	besides	in	over	under
across	between	inside	past	underneath
after	beyond	into	plus	unlike
against	but	like	regarding	until
along	by	near	respecting	unto
among	concerning	next	round	up
around	considering	of	since	upon
as	despite	off	than	with
at	down	on	through	within
before	during	onto	throughout	without
behind	except	opposite	till	
below	for	out	to	

adverbs • prepositions (*in*, *at*, *from*, etc.) •
conjunctions (*and*, *but*, *after*, *because*, etc.) • *however* etc.

B1-g   315

Some prepositions are more than one word long. *Along with*, *as well as*, *in addition to*, *next to*, and *rather than* are common examples.

TIP: Prepositions are used in idioms such as *capable of* and *dig up* (see W5-d). For a discussion of specific issues for multilingual writers, see M5.

B1-g Conjunctions

Conjunctions join words, phrases, or clauses, and they indicate the relation between the elements they join.

COORDINATING CONJUNCTIONS A coordinating conjunction is used to connect grammatically equal elements. (See S1-b and S6.) The coordinating conjunctions are *and*, *but*, *or*, *nor*, *for*, *so*, and *yet*.

CORRELATIVE CONJUNCTIONS Correlative conjunctions come in pairs. Like coordinating conjunctions, they connect grammatically equal elements. (See S1-b.)

either . . . or   whether . . . or
neither . . . nor   both . . . and
not only . . . but also

SUBORDINATING CONJUNCTIONS A subordinating conjunction introduces a subordinate clause and indicates the relation of the clause to the rest of the sentence. (See B3-e.) The most common subordinating conjunctions are *after*, *although*, *as*, *as if*, *because*, *before*, *if*, *in order that*, *once*, *since*, *so that*, *than*, *that*, *though*, *unless*, *until*, *when*, *where*, *whether*, and *while*. (For a complete list, see p. 325.)

CONJUNCTIVE ADVERBS Conjunctive adverbs connect independent clauses and indicate the relation between the clauses. The most common conjunctive adverbs are *finally*, *furthermore*, *however*, *moreover*, *nevertheless*, *similarly*, *then*, *therefore*, and *thus*. (See P3-a for a complete list.)

TIP: The ability to distinguish between conjunctive adverbs and coordinating conjunctions will help you avoid run-on sentences and make punctuation decisions (see G6, P1-a, and P1-b). The ability to recognize subordinating conjunctions will help you avoid sentence fragments (see G5).

B1-h Interjections

An interjection is a word used to express surprise or emotion (*Oh! Hey! Wow!*).

B2 Parts of sentences

Most English sentences flow from subject to verb to any objects or complements. The part of the sentence containing the verb plus its objects, complements, and modifiers is called the *predicate*.

B2-a Subjects

The subject of a sentence names who or what the sentence is about. The simple subject is always a noun or a pronoun; the complete subject consists of the simple subject and any words or word groups modifying the simple subject.

The complete subject

To find the complete subject, ask Who? or What?, insert the verb, and finish the question. The answer is the complete subject.

┌─────── COMPLETE SUBJECT ───────┐
The devastating effects of famine can last for many years.

Who or what lasts for many years? *The devastating effects of famine.*

┌──────────── COMPLETE SUBJECT ────────────┐
Adventure novels that contain multiple subplots are often made into successful movies.

Who or what are made into movies? *Adventure novels that contain multiple subplots.*

COMPLETE
┌─── SUBJECT ───┐
In our program, student teachers work full-time for ten months.

What or who works full-time for ten months? *Student teachers.* Notice that *In our program, student teachers* is not a sensible answer to the question. (It is not safe to assume that the subject must always appear first in a sentence.)

PRACTICE   hackerhandbooks.com/writersref
  > Basic grammar > B2–4 and B2–5

The simple subject

To find the simple subject, strip away all modifiers in the complete subject. This includes single-word modifiers such as *the* and *devastating*, phrases such as *of famine*, and subordinate clauses such as *that contain multiple subplots*.

┌ SS ┐
The devastating effects of famine can last for many years.

A sentence may have a compound subject containing two or more simple subjects joined with a coordinating conjunction such as *and*, *but*, or *or*.

┌──── SS ────┐   ┌SS┐
Great commitment and a little luck make a successful actor.

Understood subjects

In imperative sentences, which give advice or issue commands, the subject is understood to be *you*.

[*You*] Put your clothes in the hamper.

Subject after the verb

Although the subject ordinarily comes before the verb (*The planes took off*), occasionally it does not. When a sentence begins with *There is* or *There are* (or *There was* or *There were*), the subject follows the verb. In such inverted constructions, the word *There* is an expletive, an empty word serving merely to get the sentence started.

┌ SS ┐
There are *eight planes waiting to take off.*

Occasionally a writer will invert a sentence for effect.

┌ SS ┐
Joyful is *the child whose school closes for snow.*

In questions, the subject frequently appears between the helping verb and the main verb.

HV   ┌──── SS ────┐   MV
Do *Kenyan marathoners* train year-round?

TIP: The ability to recognize the subject of a sentence will help you edit for a variety of problems: sentence fragments (G5), subject-verb agreement (G1), choice of pronouns such as *I* and *me* (G3-c), missing subjects (M3-b), and repeated subjects (M3-c).

B2-b Verbs, objects, and complements

Section B1-c explains how to find the verb of a sentence. A sentence's verb is classified as linking, transitive, or intransitive, depending on the kinds of objects or complements the verb can (or cannot) take.

Linking verbs and subject complements

Linking verbs connect the subject to a subject complement, a word or word group that completes the meaning of the subject by renaming or describing it.

If the subject complement renames the subject, it is a noun or noun equivalent (sometimes called a *predicate noun*).

    ┌──────── S ────────┐ ┌ V ┐┌ SC ┐
An e-mail requesting personal information may be a scam.

If the subject complement describes the subject, it is an adjective or adjective equivalent (sometimes called a *predicate adjective*).

    ┌──── S ────┐┌ V ┐ SC
Last month's temperatures were mild.

Whenever they appear as main verbs (rather than helping verbs), the forms of *be*—*be, am, is, are, was, were, being, been*—usually function as linking verbs. In the preceding examples, for instance, the main verbs are *be* and *were*.

Verbs such as *appear, become, feel, grow, look, make, seem, smell, sound,* and *taste* are linking when they are followed by a word group that renames or describes the subject.

    ┌ S ┐┌ V ┐   SC
As it thickens, the sauce will look unappealing.

Transitive verbs and direct objects

A transitive verb takes a direct object, a word or word group that names a receiver of the action.

    ┌── S ──┐ V ┌──── DO ────┐
The hungry cat clawed the bag of dry food.

The simple direct object is always a noun or pronoun, in this case *bag*. To find it, simply strip away all modifiers.

Transitive verbs usually appear in the active voice, with the subject doing the action and a direct object receiving the action. Active-voice sentences can be transformed into the passive voice, with the subject receiving the action instead. (See also W3-a.)

ACTIVE VOICE   Volunteers distributed food and clothing.

PASSIVE VOICE   Food and clothing were distributed by volunteers.

Transitive verbs, indirect objects, and direct objects

The direct object of a transitive verb is sometimes preceded by an indirect object, a noun or pronoun telling to whom or for whom the action of the sentence is done.

$$S \quad V \quad IO \quad \ulcorner\!\!-\, DO\, -\!\!\urcorner \qquad S \quad \ulcorner\!-\, V\, -\!\urcorner \quad IO \quad \ulcorner\, DO\, \urcorner$$
You give her some yarn, and she will knit you a scarf.

Transitive verbs, direct objects, and object complements

The direct object of a transitive verb is sometimes followed by an object complement, a word or word group that renames or describes the object.

$$S \qquad\qquad V \qquad DO \quad \ulcorner\!\!-\!\!-\, OC\, -\!\!-\!\!\urcorner$$
People often consider chivalry a thing of the past.

$$\ulcorner\!-\, S\, -\!\urcorner \quad V \quad DO \quad \ulcorner\!-\, OC\, -\!\urcorner$$
The kiln makes clay firm and strong.

When the object complement renames the direct object, it is a noun or pronoun (such as *thing*). When it describes the direct object, it is an adjective (such as *firm* and *strong*).

Intransitive verbs

Intransitive verbs take no objects or complements.

$$\ulcorner\!\!-\!\!-\, S\, -\!\!-\!\!\urcorner \quad V$$
The audience laughed.

$$\ulcorner\!-\, S\, -\!\urcorner \quad V$$
The driver accelerated in the straightaway.

Nothing receives the actions of laughing and accelerating in these sentences, so the verbs are intransitive. Notice that such verbs may or may not be followed by adverbial modifiers. In the second sentence, *in the straightaway* is an adverbial prepositional phrase modifying *accelerated*.

NOTE: The dictionary will tell you whether a verb is transitive or intransitive. Some verbs have both transitive and intransitive functions.

TRANSITIVE   Sandra *flew* her small plane over the canyon.

INTRANSITIVE   A flock of geese *flew* overhead.

In the first example, *flew* has a direct object that receives the action: *her small plane*. In the second example, the verb is followed by an adverb (*overhead*), not by a direct object.

B3 Subordinate word groups

Subordinate word groups include phrases and clauses. Phrases are subordinate because they lack a subject and a verb; they are classified as prepositional, verbal, appositive, and absolute (see B3-a to B3-d). Subordinate clauses have a subject and a verb, but they begin with a word (such as *although*, *that*, or *when*) that marks them as subordinate (see B3-e; see also B4-a).

B3-a Prepositional phrases

A prepositional phrase begins with a preposition such as *at*, *by*, *for*, *from*, *in*, *of*, *on*, *to*, or *with* (see B1-f) and usually ends with a noun or noun equivalent: *on the table*, *for him*, *by sleeping late*. The noun or noun equivalent is known as the *object of the preposition*.

Prepositional phrases function either as adjectives or as adverbs. When functioning as an adjective, a prepositional phrase nearly always appears immediately following the noun or pronoun it modifies.

The hut had *walls of mud*.

Adjective phrases usually answer one or both of the questions Which one? and What kind of? If we ask Which walls? or What kind of walls? we get a sensible answer: *walls of mud*.

Adverbial prepositional phrases usually modify the verb, but they can also modify adjectives or other adverbs. When a prepositional phrase modifies the verb, it can appear nearly anywhere in a sentence.

James *walked* his dog *on a leash*.

PRACTICE hackerhandbooks.com/writersref
 > Basic grammar > B3–4 to B3–6

Sabrina *will in time adjust* to life in Ecuador.

During a mudslide, the terrain *can change* drastically.

Adverbial word groups usually answer one of these questions:
When? Where? How? Why? Under what conditions? To what degree?

James walked his dog *how*? *On a leash.*

Sabrina will adjust to life in Ecuador *when*? *In time.*

The terrain can change drastically *under what conditions*? *During a mudslide.*

B3-b Verbal phrases

A verbal is a verb form that does not function as the verb of a clause.
Verbals include infinitives (the word *to* plus the base form of the verb),
present participles (the *-ing* form of the verb), and past participles
(the verb form usually ending in *-d, -ed, -n, -en,* or *-t*). (See G2-a.)
Instead of functioning as the verb of a clause, a verbal functions as an
adjective, a noun, or an adverb.

ADJECTIVE	*Broken* promises cannot be fixed.
NOUN	Constant *complaining* becomes wearisome.
ADVERB	Can you wait *to celebrate*?

Verbals with objects, complements, or modifiers form verbal
phrases. Like verbals, verbal phrases function as adjectives, nouns, or
adverbs. Verbal phrases are ordinarily classified as participial, gerund,
and infinitive.

Participial phrases

Participial phrases always function as adjectives. Their verbals are
either present participles (such as *dreaming, asking*) or past participles
(such as *stolen, reached*).

Participial phrases frequently appear immediately following the
noun or pronoun they modify.

Congress shall make no *law abridging the freedom of speech*

or of the press.

Unlike other word groups that function as adjectives (prepositional phrases, infinitive phrases, adjective clauses), which must always follow the noun or pronoun they modify, participial phrases are often movable. They can precede the word they modify.

Being a weight-bearing joint, the *knee* is among the most often injured.

They may also appear at some distance from the word they modify.

Last night we saw a *play* that affected us deeply, *written with profound insight into the lives of immigrants*.

Gerund phrases

Gerund phrases are built around present participles (verb forms that end in *-ing*), and they always function as nouns: usually as subjects, subject complements, direct objects, or objects of a preposition.

DO

Lizards usually enjoy sunning themselves.

Infinitive phrases

Infinitive phrases, usually constructed around *to* plus the base form of the verb (*to call, to drink*), can function as nouns, as adjectives, or as adverbs. When functioning as a noun, an infinitive phrase may appear in almost any noun slot in a sentence, usually as a subject, subject complement, or direct object.

S

To live without health insurance is risky.

Infinitive phrases functioning as adjectives usually appear immediately following the noun or pronoun they modify.

The Twentieth Amendment gave women the *right to vote*.

Adverbial infinitive phrases usually qualify the meaning of the verb, telling when, where, how, why, under what conditions, or to what degree an action occurred.

phrases • gerund (*eating well*) • *-ing* verb form • infinitive
(*to watch birds*) • appositive • absolute • clauses with *who, that,* etc.

B3-e   323

Volunteers *rolled up* their pants *to wade through the flood waters.*

NOTE: In some constructions, the infinitive is unmarked; in other words, the *to* does not appear. (See also M1-f.)

Graphs and charts can help researchers [*to*] *present complex data.*

B3-c Appositive phrases

Appositive phrases describe nouns or pronouns. Instead of modifying nouns or pronouns, however, appositive phrases rename them. In form they are nouns or noun equivalents.

Bloggers, *conversationalists at heart*, are the online equivalent of radio talk show hosts.

B3-d Absolute phrases

An absolute phrase modifies a whole clause or sentence, not just one word. It consists of a noun or noun equivalent usually followed by a participial phrase.

Her words reverberating in the hushed arena, the senator urged the crowd to support her former opponent.

B3-e Subordinate clauses

Subordinate clauses are patterned like sentences, having subjects and verbs and sometimes objects or complements. But they function within sentences as adjectives, adverbs, or nouns. They cannot stand alone as complete sentences.

Adjective clauses

Adjective clauses modify nouns or pronouns, usually answering the question Which one? or What kind of ? They begin with a relative pronoun (*who, whom, whose, which,* or *that*) or occasionally with a relative adverb (usually *when, where,* or *why*). (See p. 325.)

The coach chose *players who would benefit from intense drills.*

In addition to introducing the clause, the relative pronoun points back to the noun that the clause modifies.

A *book that goes unread* is a writer's worst nightmare.

Relative pronouns are sometimes "understood."

The things [*that*] *we cherish most* are the things [*that*] *we might lose*.

The parts of an adjective clause are often arranged as in sentences (subject/verb/object or complement).

S   V   DO

Sometimes it is our closest friends who disappoint us.

Frequently, however, the object or complement appears first.

DO S   V

They can be the very friends whom we disappoint.

TIP: For punctuation of adjective clauses, see P1-e and P2-e. For advice about avoiding repeated words in adjective clauses, see M3-d.

Adverb clauses

Adverb clauses modify verbs, adjectives, or other adverbs, usually answering one of these questions: When? Where? Why? How? Under what conditions? To what degree? They always begin with a subordinating conjunction (such as *after, although, because, that, though, unless,* or *when*). (For a complete list, see p. 325.)

When the sun went down, the hikers *prepared* their camp.

Kate *would have made* the team *if she hadn't broken her ankle*.

Noun clauses

A noun clause functions just like a single-word noun, usually as a subject, a subject complement, a direct object, or an object of a preposition. It usually begins with one of the following words: *how, if, that, what, whatever, when, where, whether, which, who, whoever, whom, whomever, whose, why*. (For a complete list, see p. 325.)

clauses with *who*, *that*, etc. • clauses with *if*, *when*, etc. • clauses with *that*, *which*, etc. • sentence types

B4   325

Words that introduce subordinate clauses

Words introducing adverb clauses

Subordinating conjunctions: after, although, as, as if, because, before, even though, if, in order that, since, so that, than, that, though, unless, until, when, where, whether, while

Words introducing adjective clauses

Relative pronouns: that, which, who, whom, whose

Relative adverbs: when, where, why

Words introducing noun clauses

Relative pronouns: that, which, who, whom, whose

Other pronouns: what, whatever, whichever, whoever, whomever

Other subordinating words: how, if, when, whenever, where, wherever, whether, why

---

┌──────── S ────────┐
Whoever leaves the house last must double-lock the door.

┌──────────────── DO ────────────────┐
Copernicus argued that the sun is the center of the universe.

The subordinating word introducing the clause may not play a significant role in the clause. In the preceding example sentences, *Whoever* is the subject of its clause, but *that* does not perform a function in its clause.

As with adjective clauses, the parts of a noun clause may appear in normal order (subject/verb/object or complement) or out of normal order.

　　　　　　　　　S　　V ┌── DO ──┐
Loyalty is what keeps a friendship strong.

　　　　　　　DO　S　V
New Mexico is where we live.

B4 Sentence types

Sentences are classified in two ways: according to their structure (simple, compound, complex, and compound-complex) and according to their purpose (declarative, imperative, interrogative, and exclamatory).

B4-a Sentence structures

Depending on the number and types of clauses they contain, sentences are classified as simple, compound, complex, or compound-complex.

Clauses come in two varieties: independent and subordinate. An independent clause contains a subject and a predicate, and it either stands alone or could stand alone as a sentence. A subordinate clause also contains a subject and a predicate, but it functions within a sentence as an adjective, an adverb, or a noun; it cannot stand alone. (See B3-e.)

Simple sentences

A simple sentence is one independent clause with no subordinate clauses.

> ─────────────── INDEPENDENT CLAUSE ───────────────
> Without a passport, Eva could not visit her parents in Lima.

A simple sentence may contain compound elements—a compound subject, verb, or object, for example—but it does not contain more than one full sentence pattern. The following sentence is simple because its two verbs (*comes in* and *goes out*) share a subject (*Spring*).

> ─────────────── INDEPENDENT CLAUSE ───────────────
> Spring comes in like a lion and goes out like a lamb.

Compound sentences

A compound sentence is composed of two or more independent clauses with no subordinate clauses. The independent clauses are usually joined with a comma and a coordinating conjunction (*and*, *but*, *or*, *nor*, *for*, *so*, *yet*) or with a semicolon. (See P1-a and P3-a.)

> INDEPENDENT   INDEPENDENT
> ── CLAUSE ──   ── CLAUSE ──
> The car broke down, but a rescue van arrived within minutes.

> ─── INDEPENDENT CLAUSE ─── ── INDEPENDENT CLAUSE ──
> A shark was spotted near shore; people left immediately.

sentence structures • simple • compound • complex • compound-
complex • independent + subordinate clauses • sentence purpose

B4-b   327

Complex sentences

A complex sentence is composed of one independent clause with one or more subordinate clauses. (See B3-e.)

> SUBORDINATE
> ┌──── CLAUSE ────┐
> If you leave late, take a cab home.

> SUBORDINATE
> ┌──────── CLAUSE ────────┐
> What matters most to us is a quick commute.

Compound-complex sentences

A compound-complex sentence contains at least two independent clauses and at least one subordinate clause. The following sentence contains two independent clauses, each of which contains a subordinate clause.

> ┌──── INDEPENDENT CLAUSE ────┐   ┌──── INDEPENDENT CLAUSE ────
> ┌── SUB CL ──┐   ┌── SUB CL ──
> Tell the doctor how you feel, and she will decide whether you
>
> ─────────────┐
> ─────────────┐
> can go home.

B4-b Sentence purposes

Writers use declarative sentences to make statements, imperative sentences to issue requests or commands, interrogative sentences to ask questions, and exclamatory sentences to make exclamations.

DECLARATIVE	The echo sounded in our ears.
IMPERATIVE	Love your neighbor.
INTERROGATIVE	Did the better team win tonight?
EXCLAMATORY	We're here to save you!

College research assignments ask you to pose a question worth exploring, to read widely in search of possible answers, to interpret what you read, to draw reasoned conclusions, and to support those conclusions with valid and well-documented evidence. The process takes time—for researching and for drafting, revising, and documenting the paper in the style recommended by your instructor (see the tabbed dividers marked MLA and APA/CMS). Before beginning a research project, set a realistic schedule of deadlines.

One student created a calendar to map out her tasks for a paper assigned on October 3 and due October 31, keeping in mind that some tasks might overlap or need to be repeated.

RESEARCH TIP: Think of research as a process. As your topic evolves, you may find new questions arising that require you to create a new

SAMPLE CALENDAR FOR A RESEARCH ASSIGNMENT

2	3	4	5	6	7	8
	Receive and analyze the assignment.	Pose questions you might explore. ⟶	Talk with a reference librarian; plan a ⟶ search strategy.		Settle on a topic; narrow the focus.	Revise research questions. Locate ⟶ sources.
9	**10**	**11**	**12**	**13**	**14**	**15**
Read, take notes, and ⟶ compile a working bibliography.			⟶	Draft a working thesis and an outline.	Draft the paper. ⟶	
16	**17**	**18**	**19**	**20**	**21**	**22**
⟶ Draft the paper. ⟶			Visit the writing center for feedback.	Do additional research if needed. ⟶		
23	**24**	**25**	**26**	**27**	**28**	**29**
Ask peers for feedback. Revise the paper; ⟶ if necessary, revise the thesis.				Prepare a list of ⟶ works cited.		Proofread the final draft. ⟶
30	**31**					
Proofread the final draft.	**Submit the final draft.**					

search strategy, find additional sources, and challenge your initial assumptions. Keep an open mind throughout the process, be curious, and enjoy the detective work.

R1 Conducting research

Throughout this tabbed section, you will encounter examples related to three sample research papers:

- A paper on Internet surveillance in the workplace, written by a student in an English composition class (see pp. 436–40). The student, Anna Orlov, uses the MLA (Modern Language Association) style of documentation. (See highlights of Orlov's research process on pp. 432–35.)

- A paper on the limitations of medications to treat childhood obesity, written by a student in a psychology class (see pp. 488–96). The student, Luisa Mirano, uses the APA (American Psychological Association) style of documentation.

- A paper on the extent to which Civil War general Nathan Bedford Forrest can be held responsible for the Fort Pillow massacre, written by a student in a history class (see pp. 532–37). The student, Ned Bishop, uses the CMS (*Chicago Manual of Style*) documentation system.

R1-a Pose questions worth exploring.

Working within the guidelines of your assignment, pose a few questions that seem worth researching—questions that you want to explore, that you feel would interest your audience, and about which there is a substantial debate. Here, for example, are some preliminary questions jotted down by students enrolled in a variety of courses in different disciplines.

- Should the FCC broaden its definition of indecency to include violence?

- Which geological formations are the safest repositories for nuclear waste?

- What was Marcus Garvey's contribution to the fight for racial equality?

- How can governments and zoos help preserve Asia's endangered snow leopard?

- Why was amateur archaeologist Heinrich Schliemann such a controversial figure in his own time?

Approaching your topic with a series of worthwhile questions can help you focus your research and guide you toward developing an answer. As you think about possible questions, make sure that they are appropriate lines of inquiry for a research paper. Choose questions that are narrow (not too broad), challenging (not too bland), and grounded (not too speculative).

Choosing a narrow question

If your initial question is too broad, given the length of the paper you plan to write, look for ways to restrict your focus. Here, for example, is how two students narrowed their initial questions.

TOO BROAD	NARROWER
What are the hazards of fad diets?	Why are low-carbohydrate diets hazardous?
What are the benefits of stricter auto emissions standards?	How will stricter auto emissions standards create new, more competitive auto industry jobs?

Choosing a challenging question

Your research paper will be more interesting to both you and your audience if you base it on an intellectually challenging line of inquiry. Draft questions that provoke thought or engage readers in a debate.

TOO BLAND	CHALLENGING
What is obsessive-compulsive disorder?	Why is obsessive-compulsive disorder so difficult to treat?
How does DNA testing work?	How reliable is DNA testing?

You may need to address a bland question in the course of answering a more challenging one. For example, if you were writing about promising treatments for obsessive-compulsive disorder, you would no doubt answer the question "What is obsessive-compulsive disorder?" at some point in your paper. It would be a mistake, however, to use the bland question as the focus for the whole paper.

Choosing a grounded question

Finally, you will want to make sure that your research question is grounded, not too speculative. Although speculative questions—such as those that address morality or beliefs—are worth asking and may receive some attention in a research paper, they are inappropriate central questions. For most college courses, the central argument of a research paper should be grounded in facts.

TOO SPECULATIVE	GROUNDED
Is it wrong to share pornographic personal photos by cell phone?	What role should the US government play in regulating mobile content?
Do medical scientists have the right to experiment on animals?	How have technology breakthroughs made medical experiments on animals increasingly unnecessary?

R1-b Map out a search strategy.

A search strategy is a systematic plan for tracking down sources. To create a search strategy appropriate for your research question, consult a reference librarian and take a look at your library's Web site, which will give you an overview of available resources.

Including the library in your plan

Reference librarians are information specialists who can save you time by steering you toward relevant and reliable sources. With the help of an expert, you can make the best use of electronic databases, Web search engines, your library's catalog, and other reference tools.

Before you ask a reference librarian for help, be sure you have thought through the following questions:

- What is your assignment?
- In which academic discipline are you writing?
- What is your tentative research question?
- How long will the paper be?
- How much time can you spend on the project?

It's a good idea to bring a copy of the assignment with you.

In addition to speaking with a reference librarian, take some time to explore your library's Web site. You will typically find links to the library's catalog and to a variety of databases and electronic sources. You may also find resources listed by subject, research guides, information about interlibrary loans, and links to Web sites selected by librarians for their quality. Many libraries also offer online reference assistance to help you locate information and refine your search strategy.

NOTE FOR ONLINE STUDENTS: Even if you are unable to visit the library, as an enrolled student you can still use its resources. Most libraries offer chat reference services and remote access to online databases, though you may have to follow special procedures to use them. Check your library's Web site for information for distance learners.

Starting with your library's databases

You may be tempted to go straight to the Internet and ignore your library's resources, but using them early and often in the research process can save you time in the end. Libraries make a wide range of quality materials readily available, and they weed out questionable sources.

While a general Internet search might seem quick and convenient, it is often more time-consuming and can be less reliable than a search in a library's databases. Initial Internet searches may generate thousands of results. Figuring out which of these are credible, relevant, and worth further investigation can require many additional steps:

- Refining search terms (See the chart on refining keyword searches on p. 338.)
- Narrowing the domain name to include only .org, .gov, or .edu sites
- Weeding out any advertisements associated with results
- Scanning titles and sometimes content for relevant results
- Combing through sites to determine their currency and relevance as well as the credibility of their authors

Starting with your library's collection of databases can save time and effort. Because you can limit library database searches to only academic databases, you can count on finding reliable sources. Not all of the results will be worth examining in detail, but many library searches automatically sort them into subject categories that allow you to view narrowed results with just one click.

Choosing an appropriate search strategy

No single search strategy works for every topic. For some topics, it may be appropriate to search for information in newspapers, magazines, and Web sites. For others, the best sources might be found in scholarly journals and books and specialized reference works. Still other topics might be enhanced by field research—interviews, surveys, or direct observation.

With the help of a reference librarian, each of the students mentioned on page 332 constructed a search strategy appropriate for his or her research question.

ANNA ORLOV   Anna Orlov's topic, Internet surveillance in the workplace, was current and influenced by technological changes, so she
relied heavily on recent sources, especially those online. To find information on her topic, Orlov decided to

- search her library's general database for articles in magazines,
  newspapers, and journals
- check the library's catalog for recently published books
- use Web search engines, such as *Google*, to locate articles and government publications that might not show up in a database search

LUISA MIRANO   Luisa Mirano's topic, the limitations of medications
for childhood obesity, is the subject of psychological studies as well as
articles in newspapers and magazines aimed at the general public.
Thinking that both scholarly and popular works would be appropriate, Mirano decided to

- locate books through the library's online catalog
- check a specialized encyclopedia, *Encyclopedia of Psychology*
- search a specialized database, *PsycINFO*, for scholarly articles
- search her library's general database for popular articles

NED BISHOP   Ned Bishop's topic, Nathan Bedford Forrest's role in the
Fort Pillow massacre, has been investigated and debated by professional historians. Given the nature of his historical topic, Ned Bishop
decided to

- locate books through the library's online catalog
- locate scholarly articles by searching a specialized database,
  America: History and Life
- locate newspaper articles from 1864 by searching the historical
  archive at the *New York Times* Web site
- search the Web for other historical primary sources (See p. 353.)

R1-c To locate articles, search a database or consult a print index.

Libraries subscribe to a variety of electronic databases (sometimes
called *periodical* or *article databases*) that give students access to
articles and other materials without charge. Because many databases
are limited to relatively recent works, you may need to consult a print
index as well.

What databases offer

Your library has access to databases that can lead you to articles in periodicals such as newspapers, magazines, and scholarly or technical journals. General databases cover several subject areas; subject-specific databases cover one subject area in depth.

Many databases, especially general databases, include the full text of at least some articles; others list only citations or citations with short summaries called *abstracts* (see also p. 352). When the full text is not available, a citation usually will give you enough information to track down an article. Your library's Web site will help you determine which articles are available in your library, either in print or in electronic form.

Your library might subscribe to some of the following databases.

GENERAL DATABASES

The information in general databases is not restricted to a specific discipline or subject area. You may find searching a general database helpful in the early stages of your research process.

Academic Search Premier. An interdisciplinary database that indexes thousands of popular and scholarly journals on all subjects.

Expanded Academic ASAP. An interdisciplinary database that indexes the contents of magazines, newspapers, and scholarly journals in all subject areas.

JSTOR. A full-text archive of scholarly journals from many disciplines; unlike most databases, it includes articles published decades ago but does not include articles from the most recent issues of publications.

LexisNexis. A database that is particularly strong in coverage of news, business, legal, and political topics.

ProQuest. A database of periodical articles. Through *ProQuest*, your library may subscribe to databases in subjects such as nursing, biology, and psychology.

SUBJECT-SPECIFIC DATABASES

Libraries have access to dozens of specialized databases, each of which covers a specific area of research. To find out what's available, consult your library's Web site or ask your reference librarian. The following are examples of subject-specific databases.

ERIC. A database offering education-related documents and abstracts of articles published in education journals.

Refining keyword searches in databases and search engines

Although command terms and characters vary in electronic databases and Web search engines, some common functions are listed here.

- Use quotation marks around words that are part of a phrase: "gateway drug".
- Use AND to connect words that must appear in a document: hyperactivity AND children. In some search engines—*Google*, for example—AND is assumed, so typing it is unnecessary. Other search engines require a plus sign instead: hyperactivity + children.
- Use NOT in front of words that must not appear in a document: Persian Gulf NOT war. Some search engines require a minus sign (hyphen) instead: Persian Gulf -war.
- Use OR if only one of the terms must appear in a document: "mountain lion" OR cougar.
- Use an asterisk as a substitute for letters that might vary: "marine biolog*" (to find *marine biology* or *marine biologist*, for example).
- Use parentheses to group a search expression and combine it with another: (standard OR student OR test*) AND reform.

NOTE: Many search engines and databases offer an advanced search option for refining your search with filters for exact phrases that must appear, specific words that should not appear, date restrictions, and so on.

MLA Bibliography. A database of literary criticism, with citations to help researchers find articles, books, and dissertations.

PsycINFO. A comprehensive database of psychology research, including abstracts of articles in journals and books.

Public Affairs Information Service (PAIS). A database that indexes books, journals, government documents, statistical directories, and research reports in the social sciences.

PubMed. A database offering millions of abstracts of medical research studies.

How to search a database

To find articles on your topic in a database, start by searching with keywords, terms that describe the information you need. If the first keyword you try results in too few or no matches, experiment with synonyms or ask a librarian for suggestions. For example, if you're searching for sources on a topic related to education, you might also want to try the terms *teaching*, *learning*, and *curriculum*. If your keyword search results in too many matches, narrow it by using one of the strategies in the chart on page 338.

For her paper on Internet surveillance in the workplace, Anna Orlov conducted a keyword search in a general database. She typed in *"internet use"* and *employee* and *surveillance* (see the database screen on this page). This search brought up twenty possible articles, some of which looked promising. (See p. 433 for Orlov's annotated list of search results.) Orlov e-mailed several full-text articles to herself and printed citations to other sources so that she could locate them in the library.

> **Making the most of your handbook**
>
> Freewriting, listing, and clustering can help you come up with additional search terms.
>
> ▶ Ways to explore your subject: **C1-b**

When to use a print index

A print index to periodical articles is a useful tool when you are researching a historical topic, especially from the early to mid-twentieth century. *The Readers' Guide to Periodical Literature* and *Poole's Index to Periodical Literature* index magazine articles beginning around

DATABASE SCREEN: KEYWORD SEARCH

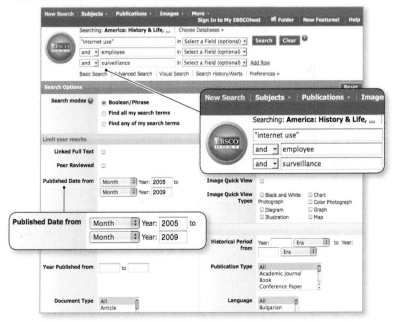

1900, many of which are too old to appear in electronic databases. You can usually access the print articles themselves in your library's shelves or on microfilm.

R1-d To locate books, consult the library's catalog.

The books your library owns are listed along with other resources in its catalog. You can search the catalog by author, title, or subject.

If your first search calls up too few results, try different keywords or search for books on broader topics. If your search gives you too many results, use the strategies in the chart on page 338 or try an advanced search tool to combine concepts and limit your results. If those strategies don't work, ask a librarian for suggestions.

When Luisa Mirano, whose topic was childhood obesity, entered the term *obesity* into the library's catalog, she was faced with an unmanageable number of hits. She narrowed her search by adding two more specific terms to *obesity*: *child** (to include the terms *child, children*, and *childhood*) and *treatment*. When she still got too many results, she limited the first two terms to subject searches to find books that had obesity in children as their primary subject (see screen 1). Screen 2 shows the complete record for one of the books she found. The call number, listed beside *Availability*, is the book's address on the shelf. When you're retrieving a book from the shelf, take time to scan other books in the area since they are likely to be on the same topic.

RESEARCH TIP: The catalog record for a book lists related subject headings. These headings are a good way to locate other books on your

LIBRARY CATALOG SCREEN 1:
ADVANCED SEARCH

LIBRARY CATALOG SCREEN 2: COMPLETE RECORD FOR A BOOK

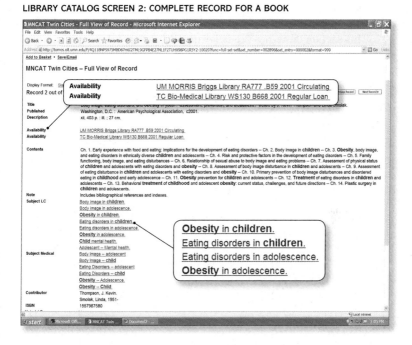

subject. For example, the record in screen 2 lists the terms *obesity in children* and *obesity in adolescence* as related subject headings. By clicking on these new terms, Mirano found more books on her subject. Subject headings can be useful terms for a database search as well.

R1-e To locate other sources, use a variety of online tools.

You can find a variety of reliable sources by using online tools beyond those offered by your library. For example, most government agencies post information on their Web sites, and federal and state governments use Web sites to communicate with citizens. The sites of many private organizations, such as Doctors without Borders and the Sierra Club, contain useful information about current issues. Museums and libraries often post digital versions of primary sources, such as photographs, political speeches, and classic literary texts.

Although the Internet at large can be a rich source of information, some of which can't be found anywhere else, it lacks quality control. The material on many sites has not necessarily been reviewed by experts. So when you're not working with your library's tools to locate online sources, carefully evaluate what you find (see R2).

This section describes the following Web resources: search engines, directories, digital archives, government and news sites, blogs, and wikis.

Search engines

When using a search engine, such as *Google* or *Yahoo!*, focus your search as narrowly as possible. You can refine your search by using many of the tips in the chart on page 338 or by using the search engine's advanced search form. For her paper on Internet surveillance in the workplace, Anna Orlov had difficulty restricting the number of hits. When she typed the words *Internet*, *surveillance*, *workplace*, and *privacy* into a search engine, she received more than 80,000 matches. After examining the first page of her results and viewing some that looked promising, Orlov grouped her search terms into the phrases *"Internet surveillance"* and *"workplace privacy"* and added the term *employee* to narrow the focus. The result was 422 matches. To refine her search further, Orlov clicked on Advanced Search and restricted her search to sites with URLs ending in *.org* and to those updated in the last three months. (See the results screen on p. 343.)

Directories

If you want to find good resources on topics too broad for a search engine, try a directory. Unlike search engines, directories are put together by information specialists who choose reputable sites and arrange them by topic: education, health, politics, and so on.

Try the following directories for scholarly research.

Internet Scout Project: http://scout.wisc.edu/Archives

Librarian's Internet Index: http://www.lii.org

Open Directory Project: http://www.dmoz.org

WWW Virtual Library: http://www.vlib.org

Digital archives

Archives are a good place to find primary sources: the texts of poems, books, speeches, and historically significant documents; photographs; and political cartoons. (See p. 353.)

The materials in these sites are usually limited to official documents and older works because of copyright laws.

SEARCH ENGINE SCREEN: RESULTS OF AN ADVANCED SEARCH

We b Results 1 - 5 of about 9 over the past 3 months for "Internet surveillance" employee "workplace privacy"

We b Results 1 - 5 of about 9 over the past 3 months for "Internet surveillance" employee "workplace privacy" site: .org(0.44 seconds)

Tip: Try removing quotes from your search to get more results.

EPIC/PI - Privacy & Human Rights 2000
Now the supervision of **employee**'s performance, behavior and... [89] Information and
Privacy Commissioner/Ontario, **Workplace Privacy**. The Need for a..
www.privacyinternational.org/survey/phr2000/threats.html - 131k Cached - Similar pages

Privacy and Human Rights 2003: Threats to Privacy
Other issues that raise **workplace privacy** concerns are employer requirements that
employees complete medical tests, questionnaires, and polygraph tests..
www.privacyinternational.org/survey/phr2003/threats.htm - 279k Cached - Similar pages
[More results from www.privacyinternational.org]

[PDF] Monitoring **Employee** E-Mail And Internet Usage: Avoiding The..
File Format: PDF/Adobe Acrobat - View as HTML
Internet surveillance by employers in the American workplace. At present, US **employees**
in the private workplace have no constitutional, common law or statu
lsr.nellco.org/cgi/viewcontent.cgi?article=1006&context=suffolk/ip - Similar pages

Previous EPIC Top News
The agencies plan to use RFID to track **employees**' movements and in ID cards... For more
information on **workplace privacy**, see the EPIC **Workplace Privacy** ...
www.epic.org/news/2005.html - 163k Cached - Similar pages

American Memory: http://memory.loc.gov

Avalon Project: http://www.yale.edu/lawweb/avalon/avalon.htm

Eurodocs: http://eudocs.lib.byu.edu

Google Books: http://books.google.com

Google Scholar: http://scholar.google.com

The Making of America: http://quod.lib.umich.edu/m/moagrp

The New York Public Library Digital Collections: http://www
.nypl.org/digital

Online Books Page: http://digital.library.upenn.edu/books

Government and news sites

For current topics, both government and news sites can prove useful.
Many government agencies at every level provide online information.
Government-maintained sites include resources such as legal texts,

facts and statistics, government reports, and searchable reference databases. Here are just a few government sites:

Fedstats: http://www.fedstats.gov

GPO Access: http://www.gpoaccess.gov

United Nations: http://www.un.org

University of Michigan Documents Center: http://www.lib.umich .edu/m/moagrp

US Census Bureau: http://www.census.gov

Many news organizations offer up-to-date information on the Web. Some require registration and may charge fees for some articles. (Find out if your library subscribes to news sites so that you can access them at no charge.) The following news sites offer many free resources.

BBC: http://www.bbc.co.uk

Google News: http://news.google.com

Kidon Media-Link: http://www.kidon.com/media-link

New York Times: http://nytimes.com

Reuters: http://www.reuters.com

Blogs

A blog (short for *Weblog*) is a site that contains text or multimedia entries usually written and maintained by one person, with comments contributed by readers. Though some blogs are personal diaries and others are devoted to partisan politics, many journalists and academics maintain blogs that cover topics of interest to researchers. Some blogs feature short essays that provide useful insights or analysis; others point to new developments in a particular area of interest. The following Web sites can lead you to a wide range of blogs.

Academic Blog Portal: http://academicblogs.org

Google Blog Search: http://www.google.com/blogsearch

Science Blogs: http://scienceblogs.com

Technorati: http://technorati.com

Wikis

A wiki is a collaborative Web site with many contributions and with content that may change frequently. *Wikipedia*, the collaborative online encyclopedia, is one of the most frequently consulted wikis.

In general, *Wikipedia* may be helpful if you're checking for something that is common knowledge (facts available in multiple sources, such as dates and well-known historical events) or looking for current information about a topic in contemporary culture that isn't covered elsewhere. However, many scholars do not consider *Wikipedia* and wikis in general to be appropriate sources for college research. Authorship is not limited to experts; articles may be written by amateurs who are not well informed. And because the articles can be changed by anyone, controversial texts are often altered to reflect a particular perspective and are susceptible to bias. When possible, locate and cite another, more reliable source for any useful information you find in a wiki.

R1-f Use other search tools.

In addition to articles, books, and online sources, you may want to consult references such as encyclopedias and almanacs. Citations in scholarly works can also lead you to additional sources.

Reference works

The reference section of the library holds both general and specialized encyclopedias, dictionaries, almanacs, atlases, and biographical references, some available in electronic form through the library's Web site. Such works often provide a good overview of your subject and include references to the most significant works on a topic. Check with a reference librarian to see which works are most appropriate for your project.

GENERAL REFERENCE WORKS   General reference works are good places to check facts and get basic information. Here are a few frequently used general references:

American National Biography

National Geographic Atlas of the World

The New Encyclopaedia Britannica

The Oxford English Dictionary

Statistical Abstract of the United States

Although general encyclopedias are often a good place to find background for your topic, you should rarely use them in your final paper. Most instructors expect you to rely on more specialized sources.

SPECIALIZED REFERENCE WORKS   Specialized reference works often explore a topic in depth, usually in the form of articles written by leading authorities. They offer a quick way to gain an expert's overview of a complex topic. Many specialized works are available, including these:

Contemporary Authors

Encyclopedia of Bioethics

Encyclopedia of Crime and Justice

Encyclopedia of Psychology

Encyclopedia of World Environmental History

International Encyclopedia of Communication

New Encyclopedia of Africa

Bibliographies and scholarly citations as shortcuts

Scholarly books and articles list the works the author has cited, usually at the end. These lists can be useful shortcuts to additional reliable sources on your topic. For example, most of the scholarly articles Luisa Mirano consulted contained citations to related research studies; through these citations, she quickly located other sources related to her topic, treatments for childhood obesity.

R1-g Conduct field research, if appropriate.

Your own field research can enhance or be the focus of a writing project. For a composition class, for example, you might want to interview a local politician about a current issue, such as the use of alternative energy sources. For a sociology class, you might decide to conduct a survey regarding campus trends in community service. At work, you might need to learn how food industry executives have responded to reports that their products are contributing to health problems.

NOTE: Colleges and universities often require researchers to submit projects to an institutional review board (IRB) if the research involves human subjects outside of a classroom setting. Before administering a survey or conducting other fieldwork, check with your instructor to see if IRB approval is required.

R2 Evaluating sources

You can often locate dozens or even hundreds of potential sources for your topic—far more than you will have time to read. Your challenge will be to determine what kinds of sources you need and to zero in on a

bibliographies • field research • interviews • surveys • how sources
work in a paper • selecting sources • scanning search results

R2-b

347

reasonable number of quality sources, those truly worthy of your time and attention.

Later, once you have decided on some sources worth consulting, your challenge will be to read them with an open mind and a critical eye.

R2-a Think about how sources might contribute to your writing.

How you plan to use sources will affect how you evaluate them. Not every source must directly support your thesis; sources can have other functions in a paper. They can

- provide background information or context for your topic
- explain terms or concepts that your readers might not understand
- provide evidence for your argument
- lend authority to your argument
- offer alternative interpretations and counterevidence to your argument

For examples of how student writers use sources for a variety of purposes, see MLA-1c, APA-1c, and CMS-1c.

R2-b Select sources worth your time and attention.

Sections R1-c through R1-e show how to refine your searches in databases, in the library's catalog, and in search engines. This section explains how to scan through the results for the most promising sources and how to preview them to see whether they are likely to live up to your expectations and meet your needs.

Scanning search results

As you scan through a list of search results, watch for clues indicating whether a source might be useful for your purposes or is not worth pursuing. (For an annotated list of one student's search results, see p. 433.) You will need to use somewhat different strategies when scanning search results from a database, a library catalog, and a Web search engine.

Making the most of your handbook

Annotating bibliography entries can help you evaluate sources.

▶ Maintain a working bibliography: R3-a

▶ Summarize sources: A1-c

▶ Analyze sources: A1-d

▶ Consider how sources inform your argument: MLA-1c, APA-1c, CMS-1c

DATABASES   Most databases (see p. 337) list at least the following information, which can help you decide if a source is relevant, current, scholarly enough (see the chart on p. 352), and a suitable length for your purposes.

> Title and brief description (How relevant?)
>
> Date (How current?)
>
> Name of periodical (How scholarly?)
>
> Length (How extensive in coverage?)

At the bottom of this page are just a few of the hits Ned Bishop came up with when he consulted a general database for articles on the Fort Pillow massacre, using the search term *Fort Pillow*.

Many databases allow you to sort your list of results by relevance or date; sorting may help you scan the information more efficiently. By scanning the titles in his search results, Bishop saw that only one contained the words *Fort Pillow*. The name of the periodical in which it appeared, *Journal of American History*, suggested that the source was scholarly. The 1989 publication date was not a problem, since currency is not necessarily a criterion for historical sources. The article's length (eight pages) is given in parentheses at the end of the citation. While the article may seem short, the topic—a statistical note—is narrow enough to ensure adequate depth of coverage. Bishop decided that the article was worth consulting. Because the other sources were irrelevant or too broad, he decided not to consult them.

LIBRARY CATALOGS   A library's catalog usually lists enough basic information about books, periodicals, DVDs, and other material to give you a first impression. A book's title and date of publication, for example, will often be your first clues as to whether the book is worth consulting. If a title looks interesting, you can click on it for further information about

---

EVALUATING SEARCH RESULTS: LIBRARY DATABASE

Popular magazine. Not relevant.

☐ Black, blue and gray: the other Civil War; African-American soldiers, sailors and spies were the unsung heroes. *Ebony* Feb 1991 v46 n4 p96(6)
Mark   View text and retrieval choices

Movie review. Not relevant.

☐ The Civil War. (movie reviews) Lewis Cole. *The Nation* Dec 3, 1990 v251 n19 p694(5)
Mark   View text and retrieval choices

Subject too broad.

☐ The hard fight was getting into the fight at all. (black soldiers in the Civil War) Jack Fincher.
Mark   *Smithsonian* Oct 1990 v21 n7 p46(13)
View text and retrieval choices

Brief scholarly article. Matches the student's topic. Promising.

☑ The Fort Pillow massacre: a statistical note. John Cimprich, Robert C. Mainfort Jr.. *Journal of America*
Mark   *History* Dec 1989 v76 n3 p830(8)
View extended citation and retrieval choices

EVALUATING SEARCH RESULTS: INTERNET SEARCH ENGINE

American **Obesity** Association - **Childhood Obesity** **Childhood Obesity. Obesity** in **children** ... Note: The term "**childhood obesity**" may refer to both **children** and adolescents. In general, we ... www.**obesity**.org/subs/**childhood**/ - 17k - Jan 8, 2005 - Cached - Similar pages	Content from a research- based organization. Promising.
Childhood Obesity KS Logo, **Childhood Obesity**. advertisement. Source. ERIC Clearinghouse on Teaching and Teacher Education. Contents. ... Back to the Top Causes of **Childhood Obesity**. ... www.kidsource.com/kidsource/content2/**obesity**.html - 18k - Cached - Similar pages	Popular rather than scholarly source. Not relevant.
Childhood Obesity, June 2002 Word on Health - National Institutes ... **Childhood Obesity** on the Rise, an article in the June 2002 edition of The NIH Word on Health - Consumer Information Based on Research from the National ... www.nih.gov/news/WordonHealth/ jun2002/**childhoodobesity**.htm - 22k - Cached - Similar pages	Content too general. Not relevant.
MayoClinic.com - **Childhood obesity**: Parenting advice ... **Childhood obesity**: Parenting advice By Mayo Clinic staff. ... Here are some other tips to help your **obese child** — and yourself: Be a positive role model. ... www.mayoclinic.com/invoke.cfm?id=FL00058 - 42k - Jan 8, 2005 - Cached - Similar pages	Popular and too general. Not relevant.

the book's subject matter and its length. The table of contents may also be available, offering a glimpse of what's inside. (See also p. 341.)

WEB SEARCH ENGINES   Because anyone can publish a Web site, legitimate sources and unreliable sources live side-by-side online. As you scan through search results, look for the following clues about the probable relevance, currency, and reliability of a site—but be aware that the clues are by no means foolproof.

The title, keywords, and lead-in text (How relevant?)

A date (How current?)

An indication of the site's sponsor or purpose (How reliable?)

The URL, especially the domain name extension: for example, .com, .edu, .gov, or .org (How relevant? How reliable?)

At the top of this page are a few of the results that Luisa Mirano retrieved after typing the keywords *childhood obesity* into a search engine; she limited her search to works with those words in the title.

Mirano found the first site, sponsored by a research-based organization, promising enough to explore for her paper. The second and fourth sites held less promise because they seemed to offer popular rather than scholarly information. In addition, the second site was full of distracting commercial advertisements. Mirano rejected the third source not because she doubted its reliability—in fact, research from the National Institutes of Health was what she hoped to find—but because a skim of its contents revealed that the information was too general for her purposes.

COMMON FEATURES OF A SCHOLARLY SOURCE

1 Formal presentation includes abstract and research methods.
2 Includes review of previous research studies.
3 Reports original research.
4 Includes references.
5 Often has multiple authors who are academics.

Cyberbullying: Using Virtual Scenarios to Educate and Raise Awareness

Vivian H. Wright, Joy J. Burnham, Christopher T. Inman, and Heather N. Ogorchock

Abstract ❶

This study examined cyberbullying in three distinct phases to facilitate a multifaceted understanding of cyberbullying. The phases included (a) a quantitative survey, (b) a qualitative focus group, and (c) development of educational scenarios/simulations (within the Second Life virtual environment). Phase III was based on adolescent feedback about cyberbullying from Phases I and II of this study. In all three phases, adolescent reactions to cyberbullying were examined and reported to raise awareness and to

❷ Research suggests that cyberbullying has distinct gender and age differences. According to the literature, girls are more likely to be online and to cyberbully (Beale & Hall, 2007; Kowalski & Limber, 2007; Li, 2006, 2007). This finding is "opposite of what happens off-line," where boys are more likely to bully than girls (Beale & Hall, p. 8). Age also appears to be a factor in cyberbullying. Cyberbullying increases in the elementary years, peaks during the middle school years, and declines in the high school years (Beale & Hall). Based on the literature, cyberbullying is a growing concern among middle school-aged children (Beale & Hall; Hinduja & Patchin, 2008; Kowalski & Limber, 2007; Li, 2007; Pellegrini & Bartini, 2000; Smith, Mahdavi, Carvalho, & Tippett, 2006; Williams & Guerra, 2007). Of the middle school grades, 6th grade students are usually the

❸ **Table 2: Percentage of Students Who Experienced Cyberbullying through Various Methods**

	E-mail	Facebook	MySpace	Cell Phone	Online Video	Chat Rooms
Victim	35.3%	11.8%	52.9%	50%	14.7%	11.8%
Bully	17.6%	0%				

❹ **References**

Bainbridge, W. S. (2007, July). The scientific research potential of virtual worlds. *Science, 317,* 472–476.

07, September/October). Cyberbullying: nd parents) can do. *The Clearing House,*

ns of bullying and associated trauma dur- *chool Counseling, 11*(3), 179–187.

, C., & Gowen, K. (2001). Middle school

❺ *Vivian H. Wright is an associate professor of instructional technology at the University of Alabama. In addition to teaching in the graduate program, Dr. Wright works with teacher educators on innovative ways to infuse technology in the curriculum to enhance teaching and learning. She has helped initiate and develop projects such as the Master Technology Teacher and Technology on Wheels. Dr. Wright's scholarship includes publications and presentations in the research areas of K–12 technology integration, emerging technologies, and asynchronous education.*

Wright, Vivian H., et al. "Cyberbullying: Using Virtual Scenarios to Educate and Raise Awareness." *Journal of Computing in Teacher Education* 26.1 (2009): 35-42.

COMMON FEATURES OF A POPULAR SOURCE

1 Often has a provocative title.

2 Author is typically a staff reporter, not an expert.

3 The bulk of the article presents anecdotes about the topic.

4 Presents a summary of research but no original research.

5 No consistent citation of sources.

McKenna, Phil. "The Cyber-Bullies Are Always with You...." *New Scientist* July 2007: 26-27.

Determining if a source is scholarly

For many college assignments, you will be asked to use scholarly sources. These are written by experts for a knowledgeable audience and usually go into more depth than books and articles written for a general audience. (Scholarly sources are sometimes called *refereed* or *peer-reviewed* because the work is evaluated by experts in the field before publication.) To determine if a source is scholarly, look for the following:

- Formal language and presentation
- Authors with academic or scientific credentials
- Footnotes or a bibliography documenting the works cited by the author in the source
- Original research and interpretation (rather than a summary of other people's work)
- Quotations from and analysis of primary sources (in humanities disciplines such as literature, history, and philosophy)
- A description of research methods or a review of related research (in the sciences and social sciences)

See pages 350–51 for a sample scholarly source and popular source.

NOTE: In some databases, searches can be limited to refereed or peer-reviewed journals.

Selecting appropriate versions of electronic sources

An online source may appear as an abstract, an excerpt, or a full-text article or book. It is important to distinguish among these versions of sources and to use a complete version of a source for your research.

Abstracts and excerpts are shortened versions of complete works. An abstract—a summary of a work's contents—might appear in a database record for a periodical article. An excerpt is the first few sentences or paragraphs of a newspaper or magazine article; it sometimes appears in a list of hits in an online search. Abstracts and excerpts often provide enough information for you to determine whether the complete article would be useful for your paper. Both are brief (usually fewer than five hundred words) and generally do not contain enough information to function alone as sources in a research paper. Reading the complete article is the best way to understand the author's argument before referring to it in your own writing. A full-text work may appear online as a PDF (portable document format) file or as an HTML file (sometimes called a *text file*). If your source is available in both formats, choose the PDF file for your research because it will include page numbers for your citations.

R2-c Read with an open mind and a critical eye.

As you begin reading the sources you have chosen, keep an open mind. Do not let your personal beliefs prevent you from listening to new ideas and opposing viewpoints. Your research question — not a snap judgment about the question — should guide your reading.

When you read critically, you are not necessarily judging an author's work harshly; you are simply examining its assumptions, assessing its evidence, and weighing its conclusions. (For one student's careful reading of a source text, see p. 434.)

> **Academic English** When you research on the Web, it is easy to ignore views different from your own. Web pages that appeal to you will often link to other pages that support the same viewpoint. If your sources all seem to agree with you — and with one another — seek out opposing views and evaluate them with an open mind.

Distinguishing between primary and secondary sources

As you begin assessing evidence in a source, determine whether you are reading a primary or a secondary source. Primary sources are original documents such as letters, diaries, photographs, legislative bills, laboratory studies, field research reports, and eyewitness accounts. Secondary sources are commentaries on primary sources — another writer's opinions about or interpretation of a primary source. A primary source for Ned Bishop was Nathan Bedford Forrest's official report on the battle at Fort Pillow. Bishop also consulted a number of secondary sources, some of which relied heavily on primary sources such as letters.

Although a primary source is not necessarily more reliable than a secondary source, it has the advantage of being a firsthand account. Naturally, you can better evaluate what a secondary source says if you have first read any primary sources it discusses.

Being alert for signs of bias

Some sources are more objective than others. Even publications that are considered reputable can be editorially biased. For example, *USA Today*, *National Review*, and the *Economist* are all credible sources, but they are also likely to interpret events quite differently from one another. If you are uncertain about a periodical's special interests, consult *Magazines for Libraries*. To check for bias in a book, see what book reviewers have written about it. A reference librarian can help you locate reviews and assess the credibility of both the book and the reviewers.

Evaluating all sources

Checking for signs of bias

- Does the author or publisher endorse political or religious views that could affect objectivity?
- Is the author or publisher associated with a special-interest group, such as Greenpeace or the National Rifle Association, that might present only one side of an issue?
- Are alternative views presented and addressed? How fairly does the author treat opposing views? (See A3-c.)
- Does the author's language show signs of bias?

Assessing an argument

- What is the author's central claim or thesis?
- How does the author support this claim—with relevant and sufficient evidence or with just a few anecdotes or emotional examples?
- Are statistics consistent with those you encounter in other sources? Have they been used fairly? (It is possible to "lie" with statistics by using them selectively or by omitting details.) Does the author explain where the statistics come from?
- Are any of the author's assumptions questionable?
- Does the author consider opposing arguments and refute them persuasively? (See A3-c.)
- Does the author fall prey to any logical fallacies? (See A3-a.)

Like publishers, some authors are more objective than others. If you have reason to believe that a writer is particularly biased, you will want to assess his or her arguments with special care. For questions to ask about a source's possible bias, see the chart on this page.

Assessing the author's argument

In nearly all academic writing, there is some element of argument, so don't be surprised to encounter experts who disagree. When you find areas of disagreement, you will want to read each source's arguments with special care, testing them with your own critical intelligence. The questions in the chart on this page can help you weigh the strengths and weaknesses of each author's argument.

Making the most of your handbook

Good college writers read critically.

▶ Judging whether a source is reasonable: A3-a

▶ Judging whether a source is fair: A3-c

Evaluating Web sources

Authorship

- Does the Web site or document have an author? You may need to do some clicking and scrolling to find the author's name. If you have landed directly on an internal page of a site, for example, you may need to navigate to the home page or find an "about this site" link to learn the name of the author.
- If there is an author, can you tell whether he or she is knowledgeable and credible? When the author's qualifications aren't listed on the site itself, look for links to the author's home page, which may provide evidence of his or her interests and expertise.

Sponsorship

- Who, if anyone, sponsors the site? The sponsor of a site is often named and described on the home page and is sometimes listed alongside the copyright date: © 2009 Plymouth State College.
- What does the URL tell you? The domain name extension often indicates the type of group hosting the site: commercial (.com), educational (.edu), nonprofit (.org), governmental (.gov), military (.mil), or network (.net). URLs may also indicate a country of origin: .uk (United Kingdom) or .jp (Japan), for instance.

Purpose and audience

- Why was the site created: To argue a position? To sell a product? To inform readers?
- Who is the site's intended audience?

Currency

- How current is the site? Check for the date of publication or the latest update, often located at the bottom of the home page or at the beginning or end of an internal page.
- How current are the site's links? If many of the links no longer work, the site may be too dated for your purposes.

R2-d Assess Web sources with special care.

Web sources can provide valuable information, but verifying their credibility may take time. Before using a Web source in your paper, make sure you know who created the material and for what purpose.

Many sophisticated-looking sites contain questionable informa-tion. Even a well-designed hate site may at first appear unbiased and

EVALUATING A WEB SITE: CHECKING RELIABILITY

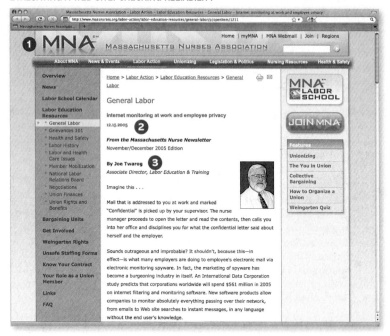

1   This article on Internet monitoring is on a site sponsored by the Massachusetts Nurses Association, a professional health care association and union whose staff and members advocate for nurses in the workplace. The URL ending .org marks this sponsor as a nonprofit organization.

2   Clear dates of publication show currency.

3   The author is a credible expert whose credentials can be verified.

---

informative. Sites with reliable information, however, can stand up to careful scrutiny. For a checklist on evaluating Web sources, see the chart on page 355.

In researching Internet surveillance and workplace privacy, Anna Orlov encountered sites that raised her suspicions. In particular, some sites were authored by surveillance software companies, which have an obvious interest in emphasizing the benefits of such software to company management. When you know something about the creator of a site and have a sense of the site's purpose, you can quickly determine whether a source is reliable, credible, and worth a closer look. Consider, for example, the two sites pictured on this page and on page 357. Anna Orlov decided that the first Web site would be more useful for her project than sites like the second.

EVALUATING A WEB SITE: CHECKING PURPOSE

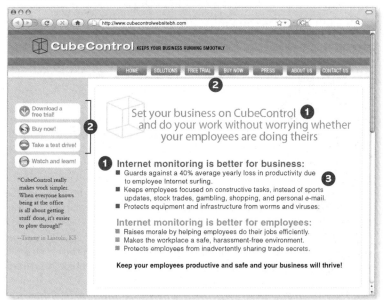

1   The site is sponsored by a company that specializes in employee monitoring software.

2   Repeated links for trial downloads and purchase suggest the site's intended audience: consumers seeking to purchase software (probably not researchers seeking detailed information about employees' use of the Internet in the workplace).

3   The site appears to provide information and even shows statistics from studies, but ultimately the purpose of the site is to sell a product.

R3 Managing information; avoiding plagiarism

An effective researcher is a good record keeper. Whether you decide to keep records on paper or on your computer—or both—your challenge as a researcher will be to find systematic ways of managing information. More specifically, you will need methods for maintaining a working bibliography, keeping track of source materials, and taking notes without plagiarizing your sources. (For more on avoiding plagiarism, see MLA-2, APA-2, or CMS-2.)

R3-a Maintain a working bibliography.

Keep a record of any sources you decide to consult. You will need this record, called a *working bibliography*, when you compile the list of sources that will appear at the end of your paper. The format of this list depends on the documentation style you are using. (For MLA style, see MLA-4b; for APA style, see APA-4b; for CMS style, see CMS-4c.) Using the proper style in your working bibliography will ensure that you have all the information you need to correctly cite any sources you use. Your working bibliography will probably contain more sources than you will actually include in your list of works cited in your final paper.

Most researchers print or save bibliographic information from the library's online catalog, its periodical databases, and the Web. The information you need to collect is given in the chart on page 360. If you download a visual, you must gather the same information as for a print source.

For Web sources, some bibliographic information may not be available, but spend time looking for it before assuming that it doesn't exist. When information isn't available on the home page, you may have to drill into the site, following links to interior pages. Look especially for the author's name, the date of publication (or latest update), and the name of any sponsoring organization. Do not omit such information unless it is genuinely unavailable.

Once you have created a working bibliography, you can annotate it. Writing several brief sentences summarizing key points of a source will help you identify how it relates to your argument and to your other sources. You should evaluate the source in your own words and use quotations sparingly. Clarifying the source's ideas at this stage will help you separate them from your own and avoid plagiarizing them later.

SAMPLE ANNOTATED BIBLIOGRAPHY ENTRY (MLA STYLE)

Gonsalves, Chris. "Wasting Away on the Web." *eWeek.com*. Ziff Davis Enterprise Holdings, 8 Aug. 2005. Web. 16 Feb. 2009.

Summarize the source.

Annotations should be three to seven sentences long.

In this editorial, Gonsalves considers the implications of several surveys, including one in which 61% of respondents said that their companies have the right to spy on them. The author agrees with this majority, claiming that it's fine if his company chooses to monitor him as long as the company discloses its monitoring practices. He argues that "the days of Internet freedom at work are

Use quotations sparingly. Put quotation marks around any words from the source.

MODELS hackerhandbooks.com/writersref
> Model papers > MLA annotated bibliography: Orlov
> APA annotated bibliography: Haddad

keeping records • building a bibliography • annotated bibliography •
keeping copies of sources • taking notes • avoiding plagiarism

R3-c 359

justifiably finished," adding that he would prefer not to

Interpret the relationship between this source and others in the bibliography. know the extent of the surveillance. Gonsalves writes for *eWeek.com*, a publication focused on technology products. He presents himself as an employee who is comfortable with being monitored, but his job may be a source of bias. This **Evaluate the source for bias and relevance.** editorial contradicts some of my other sources, which claim that employees want to know and should know all the details of their company's monitoring procedures.

R3-b Keep track of source materials.

The best way to keep track of source materials is to save a copy of each one. Many database subscription services will allow you to e-mail, save, or print citations or full texts of articles, and you can easily download, copy, or take screen shots of information from the Web.

Working with photocopies, printouts, and electronic files—as opposed to relying on memory or hastily written notes—has several benefits. You can highlight key passages, perhaps even color-coding them to reflect topics in your outline. You can annotate the source in the margins by hand or with your word processing program's comment feature and get a head start on note taking (for an example, see the annotated article on p. 434). Finally, you reduce the chances of unintentional plagiarism, since you will be able to compare your use of a source in your paper with the actual source, not just with your notes (see R3-c).

NOTE: It's especially important to keep print or electronic copies of Web sources, which may change or even become inaccessible over time. Make sure that your copy includes the site's URL and your date of access.

TIP: Your school may provide citation software, which allows researchers to download references directly from online sources. Similarly, many databases format citations with a mouse click, and Web sites offer fill-in-the-blank forms for generating formatted citations. You must proofread such citations carefully, however, because the programs sometimes provide incorrect results.

R3-c As you take notes, avoid unintentional plagiarism.

When you take notes and jot down ideas, be very careful not to use language from your sources unless you clearly identify borrowed words and phrases as quotations. Even if you half-copy the author's

Information for a working bibliography

For an entire book

- All authors; any editors or translators
- Title and subtitle
- Edition (if not the first)
- Publication information: city, publisher, and date

For a periodical article

- All authors of the article
- Title and subtitle of the article
- Title of the magazine, journal, or newspaper
- Date; volume, issue, and page numbers

For a periodical article retrieved from a database (in addition to preceding information)

- Name of the database and an item number, if available
- Name of the subscription service
- URL of the subscription service (for an online database)
- Accession number or other number assigned by the database
- Digital object identifier (DOI), if there is one
- Date you retrieved the source

NOTE: Use particular care when printing or saving articles in PDF format. These files may not include some of the elements you need to properly cite the source. You may need to record additional information from the database or Web site where you retrieved the file.

For a Web source (including visuals)

- All authors, editors, or creators of the source
- Editor or compiler of the Web site, if there is one
- Title and subtitle of the source
- Title of the site
- Publication information for the source, if available
- Page or paragraph numbers, if any
- Date of online publication (or latest update)
- Sponsor of the site
- Date you accessed the source
- The site's URL

NOTE: For the exact bibliographic format to use in your working bibliography and in the final paper, see MLA-4b, APA-4b, or CMS-4c.

sentences—either by mixing the author's phrases with your own without using quotation marks or by plugging your synonyms into the author's sentence structure—you are committing plagiarism, a serious academic offense. (For examples of this kind of plagiarism, see MLA-2, APA-2, and CMS-2.)

To prevent unintentional borrowing, resist the temptation to look at the source as you take notes—except when you are quoting. Keep the source close by so you can check for accuracy, but don't try to put ideas in your own words with the source's sentences in front of you. When you need to quote the exact words of a source, make sure you copy the words precisely and put quotation marks around them.

TIP: Be especially careful when using copy and paste functions in electronic files. Some researchers have unintentionally plagiarized their sources because they lost track of which words came from sources and which were their own. To prevent unintentional plagiarism, put quotation marks around any exact language you save from your sources.

> **Academic English**   Even in the early stages of note taking, it is
> important to keep in mind that, in the United States, written texts
> are considered an author's property. (This "property" isn't a physical
> object, so it is often referred to as *intellectual property*.) The author
> (or publisher) owns the language as well as any original ideas
> contained in the writing, whether the source is published in print
> or electronic form. When you use another author's property in your
> own writing, you need to follow certain conventions for citing the
> material; if you don't, you risk committing *plagiarism*.

Summarizing, paraphrasing, and quoting are three ways of taking notes. Be sure to include exact page references for all three types of notes, since you will need the page numbers later if you use the information in your paper.

Summarizing without plagiarizing

A summary condenses information, perhaps reducing a chapter to a short paragraph or a paragraph to a single sentence. A summary should be written in your own words; if you use phrases from the source, put them in quotation marks.

On page 362 is a passage from a source about mountain lions. Following the passage is the student's summary. (The bibliographic information is recorded in MLA style.)

ORIGINAL SOURCE

In some respects, the increasing frequency of mountain lion encounters in California has as much to do with a growing *human* population as it does with rising mountain lion numbers. The scenic solitude of the western ranges is prime cougar habitat, and it is falling swiftly to the developer's spade. Meanwhile, with their ideal habitat already at its carrying capacity, mountain lions are forcing younger cats into less suitable terrain, including residential areas. Add that cougars have generally grown bolder under a lengthy ban on their being hunted, and an unsettling scenario begins to emerge.
— Rychnovsky, Ray. "Clawing into Controversy."
Outdoor Life Jan. 1995: 38–42. Print. [p. 40]

SUMMARY

Source: Rychnovsky, Ray. "Clawing into Controversy." *Outdoor Life* Jan. 1995:
38–42. Print. [p. 40]

Encounters between mountain lions and humans are on the rise in California because increasing numbers of lions are competing for a shrinking habitat. As the lions' wild habitat shrinks, older lions force younger lions into residential areas. These lions have lost some of their fear of humans because of a ban on hunting (Rychnovsky 40).

Paraphrasing without plagiarizing

Like a summary, a paraphrase is written in your own words; but whereas a summary reports significant information in fewer words than the source, a paraphrase retells the information in roughly the same number of words. If you retain occasional choice phrases from the source, use quotation marks so that later you will know which phrases are not your own.

As you read the following paraphrase of the original source at the top of this page, notice that the language is significantly different from that in the original.

PARAPHRASE

Source: Rychnovsky, Ray. "Clawing into Controversy." *Outdoor Life* Jan. 1995:
38–42. Print. [p. 40]

Californians are encountering mountain lions more frequently because increasing numbers of humans and a rising population of lions are competing for the same territory. Humans have moved into mountainous regions once dominated by the lions, and the wild habitat that is left cannot sustain the current lion population.

Therefore, the older lions are forcing younger lions into residential areas. And because of a ban on hunting, these younger lions have become bolder—less fearful of encounters with humans (Rychnovsky 40).

Using quotation marks to avoid plagiarizing

A quotation consists of the exact words from a source. In your notes, put all quoted material in quotation marks; do not assume that you will remember later which words, phrases, and passages you have quoted and which are your own. When you quote, be sure to copy the words of your source exactly, including punctuation and capitalization.

QUOTATION

Source: Rychnovsky, Ray. "Clawing into Controversy." *Outdoor Life* Jan. 1995: 38–42. Print. [p. 40]

Rychnovsky explains that as humans expand residential areas into mountain ranges, the cougar's natural habitat "is falling swiftly to the developer's spade" (40).

Avoiding Internet plagiarism

UNDERSTAND WHAT PLAGIARISM IS. When you use another author's intellectual property—language, visuals, or ideas—in your own writing without giving proper credit, you commit a kind of academic theft called *plagiarism*.

TREAT WEB SOURCES IN THE SAME WAY YOU TREAT PRINT SOURCES. Any language that you find on the Internet must be carefully cited, even if the material is in the public domain or is publicly accessible on free sites. When you use material from Web sites sponsored by federal, state, or municipal governments (.gov sites) or by nonprofit organizations (.org sites), you must acknowledge that material, too, as intellectual property owned by those agencies.

KEEP TRACK OF WHICH WORDS COME FROM SOURCES AND WHICH ARE YOUR OWN. To prevent unintentional plagiarism when you copy and paste passages from Web sources to an electronic file, put quotation marks around any text that you have inserted into your own notes or paper. In addition, during note taking and drafting, you might use highlighting or a different color font to draw attention to text taken from sources—so that material from articles, Web sites, and other sources stands out unmistakably as someone else's words.

Integrating and citing sources to avoid plagiarism

Source text

Our language is constantly changing. Like the Mississippi, it keeps forging new channels and abandoning old ones, picking up debris, depositing unwanted silt, and frequently bursting its banks. In every generation there are people who deplore changes in the language and many who wish to stop its flow. But if our language stopped changing it would mean that American society had ceased to be dynamic, innovative, pulsing with life—that the great river had frozen up.

> —Robert MacNeil and William Cran,
> *Do You Speak American?*, p. 1

NOTE: The examples in this chart follow MLA style (see MLA-4). For information on APA and CMS (*Chicago*) styles, see APA-4 and CMS-4, respectively.

If you are using an exact sentence from a source, with no changes . . .	→	. . . put quotation marks around the sentence. Use a signal phrase and include a page number in parentheses.
		MacNeil and Cran write, "Our language is constantly changing" (1).
If you are using a few exact words from the source but not an entire sentence . . .	→	. . . put quotation marks around the exact words that you have used from the source. Use a signal phrase and include a page number in parentheses.
		The English language, according to MacNeil and Cran, is "like the Mississippi" (1).
If you are using near-exact words from the source but changing some word forms (*I* to *she*, *walk* to *walked*) or adding words to clarify and make the quotation flow with your own text . . .	→	. . . put quotation marks around the quoted words, and put brackets around the changes you have introduced. Include a signal phrase and follow the quotation with the page number in parentheses.
		MacNeil and Cran compare the English language to the Mississippi River, which "forg[es] new channels and abandon[s] old ones" (1).

→

MacNeil and Cran write, "In every generation there are people who deplore changes in the [English] language and many who wish to stop its flow" (1).

If you are paraphrasing or summarizing the source, using the author's ideas but not any of the author's exact words . . .	→	. . . introduce the ideas with a signal phrase and put the page number at the end of your sentence. Do not use quotation marks. (See MLA-2, APA-2, and CMS-2.)

MacNeil and Cran argue that changes in the English language are natural and that they represent cultural progress (1).

If you have used the source's sentence structure but substituted a few synonyms for the author's words . . .	→	STOP! This is a form of plagiarism even if you use a signal phrase and a page number. Change your sentence by using one of the techniques given in this chart or in MLA-3, APA-3, or CMS-3.

PLAGIARIZED

MacNeil and Cran claim that, like a river, English creates new waterways and discards old ones.

INTEGRATED AND CITED CORRECTLY

MacNeil and Cran claim, "Like the Mississippi, [English] keeps forging new channels and abandoning old ones" (1).

AVOID WEB SITES THAT BILL THEMSELVES AS "RESEARCH SERVICES" AND SELL ESSAYS. When you use Web search engines to research a topic, you will often see links to sites that appear to offer legitimate writing support but that actually sell college essays. Of course, submitting a paper that you have purchased is cheating, but even using material from such a paper is considered plagiarism.

For more on avoiding plagiarism while working with sources, see MLA-2, APA-2, or CMS-2.

R4 Choosing a documentation style

The various academic disciplines use their own style for citing sources and for listing the works that are cited in a paper. *A Writer's Reference* describes three commonly used styles: MLA (Modern Language Association), APA (American Psychological Association), and CMS (*Chicago Manual of Style*). See the appropriate tabbed section for details about each style.

NOTE: For a list of style manuals in a variety of disciplines, visit *Research and Documentation Online* at hackerhandbooks.com/resdoc.

R4-a Select a style appropriate for your discipline.

In researched writing, sources are cited for several reasons. First, it is important to acknowledge the contributions of others. If you fail to credit sources properly, you commit plagiarism, a serious academic offense. Second, by choosing appropriate sources, you will add credibility to your work; in a sense, you are calling on authorities to serve as expert witnesses. The more care you have taken in choosing reliable sources, the stronger your argument will be. Finally — and most importantly — you are engaging in a scholarly conversation: when you cite your sources, you show readers where they can pursue your topic in greater depth.

All of the academic disciplines cite sources for these same reasons. However, the different styles for citing sources are based on the values and intellectual goals of scholars in different disciplines.

MLA and APA in-text citations

MLA style and APA style both use citations in the text of a paper that refer to a list of works at the end of the paper. The systems work somewhat differently, however, because MLA style was created for scholars in English composition and literature and APA style was created for researchers in the social sciences.

MLA IN-TEXT CITATION

Brandon Conran argues that the story is written from "a bifocal point of view" (111).

APA IN-TEXT CITATION

As researchers Yanovski and Yanovski (2002) have explained, obesity was once considered "either a moral failing or evidence of underlying psychopathology" (p. 592).

While MLA and APA styles work in a similar way, some basic disciplinary differences show up in these key elements:

- author's name
- date of publication
- page numbers
- verb tense in signal phrases

MLA style gives the author's full name when it is first mentioned. This approach emphasizes authorship and interpretation. APA style, which uses only the last names of authors, gives a date after the author's name. This approach reflects the social scientist's concern with the currency of research. MLA style places the date in the works cited list but omits it in the text. While currency is important, what someone had to say a century ago may be as significant as the latest contribution to the field.

Both styles include page numbers for quotations. MLA style requires page numbers for summaries and paraphrases as well; with a page number, readers can easily find the original passage that has been summarized or paraphrased. While APA does not require page numbers for summaries and paraphrases, it recommends that writers use a page number if doing so would help readers find the passage in a longer work.

Finally, MLA style uses the present tense (such as *argues*) to introduce cited material, whereas APA style uses the past or present perfect tense (such as *argued* or *have argued*) in signal phrases. The present tense evokes the timelessness of a literary text; the past or present perfect tense emphasizes that research or experimentation occurred in the past.

CMS footnotes or endnotes

Most historians and many scholars in the humanities use the style of footnotes or endnotes recommended by *The Chicago Manual of Style* (CMS). Historians base their work on a wide variety of primary and secondary sources, all of which must be cited. The CMS note system has the virtue of being relatively unobtrusive; even when a paper or an article is thick with citations, readers will not be overwhelmed. In the text of the paper, only a raised number appears. Readers who are interested can consult the accompanying numbered note, which is given either at the foot of the page or at the end of the paper.

TEXT

Historian Albert Castel quotes several eyewitnesses on both the Union and the Confederate sides as saying that Forrest ordered his men to stop firing.[7]

NOTE

7. Albert Castel, "The Fort Pillow Massacre: A Fresh Examination of the Evidence," *Civil War History* 4, no. 1 (1958): 44-45.

The CMS system gives as much information as the MLA or APA system, but less of that information appears in the text of the paper.

MLA Papers

Most English instructors and some humanities instructors will ask you to document your sources with the Modern Language Association (MLA) system of citations described in MLA-4. When writing an MLA paper that is based on sources, you face three main challenges: (1) supporting a thesis, (2) citing your sources and avoiding plagiarism, and (3) integrating quotations and other source material.

Examples in this tabbed section are drawn from a student's research about online monitoring of employees' computer use. Anna Orlov's research paper, in which she argues that electronic surveillance in the workplace threatens employees' privacy, appears on pages 436–40. (See highlights of Anna Orlov's research process on pp. 432–35.)

MLA-1 Supporting a thesis

Most research assignments ask you to form a thesis, or main idea, and to support that thesis with well-organized evidence.

MLA-1a Form a working thesis.

Once you have read a variety of sources and considered your issue from different perspectives, you are ready to form a working thesis: a one-sentence (or occasionally a two-sentence) statement of your central idea (see also C2-a). Because it is a working, or tentative, thesis, you can remain flexible and revise it as your ideas develop. In a research paper, your thesis will answer the central research question you pose (see R1-a). Here, for example, are Anna Orlov's research question and working thesis.

RESEARCH QUESTION

Should employers monitor their employees' online activities in the workplace?

WORKING THESIS

Employers should not monitor their employees' online activities because electronic surveillance can compromise workers' privacy.

After you have written a rough draft and perhaps done more reading, you may decide to revise your thesis, as Orlov did.

REVISED THESIS

Although companies often have legitimate concerns that lead them to monitor employees' Internet usage—from expensive security breaches to reduced productivity—the benefits of electronic surveillance are outweighed by its costs to employees' privacy and autonomy.

The thesis usually appears at the end of the introductory paragraph. To read Anna Orlov's thesis in the context of her introduction, see page 436.

MLA-1b Organize ideas with a rough outline.

The body of your paper will consist of evidence in support of your thesis. Instead of getting tangled up in a formal outline early in the process, sketch an informal plan that organizes your ideas in bold strokes. Anna Orlov, for example, used this simple plan to outline the structure of her argument:

- Compared with older types of surveillance, electronic surveillance allows employers to monitor workers more efficiently.
- Some experts argue that companies have important financial and legal reasons to monitor employees' Internet usage.
- But monitoring employees' Internet usage may lower worker productivity when the threat to privacy creates distrust.
- Current laws do little to protect employees' privacy rights, so employees and employers have to negotiate the potential risks and benefits of electronic surveillance.

> **Making the most of your handbook**
>
> It's helpful to start off with a working thesis and a rough outline — especially when writing from sources.
>
> ▶ Drafting a working thesis: C1-c
>
> ▶ Sketching a plan: C1-d

After you have written a rough draft, a more formal outline can be a useful way to shape the complexities of your argument. See C1-d for an example.

MLA-1c Use sources to inform and support your argument.

Used thoughtfully, the source materials you have gathered will make your argument more complex and convincing for readers. Sources can play several different roles as you develop your points.

Providing background information or context

You can use facts and statistics to support generalizations or to emphasize the importance of your topic, as student writer Anna Orlov does in her introduction.

> As the Internet has become an integral tool of businesses, company policies on Internet usage have become as common as policies regarding vacation days or sexual harassment. A 2005 study by the American Management Association and ePolicy Institute found that 76% of companies monitor employees' use of the Web,

and the number of companies that block employees' access to certain Web sites has increased 27% since 2001 (1).

Explaining terms or concepts

If readers are unlikely to be familiar with words or ideas important to your topic, you must explain them. Quoting or paraphrasing a source can help you define terms and concepts in accessible language.

> One popular monitoring method is keystroke logging, which is done by means of an undetectable program on employees' computers. . . . As Lane explains, these programs record every key entered into the computer in hidden directories that can later be accessed or uploaded by supervisors; the programs can even scan for keywords tailored to individual companies (128-29).

Supporting your claims

As you draft your argument, make sure to back up your assertions with facts, examples, and other evidence from your research. (See also A2-e.) Orlov, for example, uses an anecdote from one of her sources to support her claim that limiting computer access causes resentment among a company's staff.

> Monitoring online activities can have the unintended effect of making employees resentful. . . . Kesan warns that "prohibiting personal use can seem extremely arbitrary and can seriously harm morale. . . . Imagine a concerned parent who is prohibited from checking on a sick child by a draconian company policy" (315-16). As this analysis indicates, employees can become disgruntled when Internet usage policies are enforced to their full extent.

Lending authority to your argument

Expert opinion can give weight to your argument. (See also A2-e.) But don't rely on experts to make your argument for you. Construct your argument in your own words and, when appropriate, cite the judgment of an authority in the field to support your position.

> Additionally, many experts disagree with employers' assumption that online monitoring can increase productivity. Employment law attorney Joseph Schmitt argues that, particularly for employees who are paid a salary rather than an hourly wage, "a company shouldn't care whether employees spend one or 10 hours on the Internet as long as they are getting their jobs done—and provided that they are not accessing inappropriate sites" (qtd. in Verespej).

Anticipating and countering objections

Do not ignore sources that seem contrary to your position or that offer arguments different from your own. Instead, use them to give voice to opposing points of view and to state potential objections to your argument before you counter them (see A-2f). Anna Orlov, for example, cites conflicting evidence to acknowledge that some readers may feel that unlimited Internet access in the workplace hinders productivity. In doing so, she creates an opportunity to counter that objection and persuade those readers.

> On the one hand, computers and Internet access give employees powerful tools to carry out their jobs; on the other hand, the same technology offers constant temptations to avoid work. As a 2005 study by *Salary.com* and *America Online* indicates, the Internet ranked as the top choice among employees for ways of wasting time on the job; it beat talking with co-workers—the second most popular method—by a margin of nearly two to one (Frauenheim).

MLA-2 Citing sources; avoiding plagiarism

Your research paper is a collaboration between you and your sources. To be fair and ethical, you must acknowledge your debt to the writers of those sources. If you don't, you commit plagiarism, a serious academic offense.

In general, these three acts are considered plagiarism: (1) failing to cite quotations and borrowed ideas, (2) failing to enclose borrowed language in quotation marks, and (3) failing to put summaries and paraphrases in your own words. Definitions of plagiarism may vary; it's a good idea to find out how your school defines academic dishonesty.

MLA-2a Cite quotations and borrowed ideas.

Sources are cited for two reasons:

1. to tell readers where your information comes from—so that they can assess its reliability and, if interested, find and read the original source

2. to give credit to the writers from whom you have borrowed words and ideas

Making the most of your handbook

When you use exact language from a source, you need to show that it is a quotation.

▶ Quotation marks for direct quotations: **P5-a**

You must cite anything you borrow from a source, including direct quotations; statistics and other specific facts; visuals such as cartoons, graphs, and diagrams; and any ideas you present in a summary or paraphrase.

The only exception is common knowledge—information your readers could easily find in any number of general sources. For example, most encyclopedias will tell readers that Alfred Hitchcock directed *Notorious* in 1946 and that Emily Dickinson published only a handful of her many poems during her lifetime.

As a rule, when you have seen information repeatedly in your reading, you don't need to cite it. However, when information has appeared in only one or two sources, when it is highly specific (as with statistics), or when it is controversial, you should cite the source. If a topic is new to you and you are not sure what is considered common knowledge or what is controversial, ask your instructor or someone else with expertise. When in doubt, cite the source.

The Modern Language Association recommends a system of in-text citations. Here, briefly, is how the MLA citation system usually works:

1. The source is introduced by a signal phrase that names its author.
2. The material being cited is followed by a page number in parentheses.
3. At the end of the paper, a list of works cited (arranged alphabetically by authors' last names) gives complete publication information about the source.

IN-TEXT CITATION

Legal scholar Jay Kesan points out that the law holds employers liable for employees' actions such as violations of copyright laws, the distribution of offensive or graphic sexual material, and illegal disclosure of confidential information (312).

ENTRY IN THE LIST OF WORKS CITED

Kesan, Jay P. "Cyber-Working or Cyber-Shirking? A First Principles Examination of Electronic Privacy in the Workplace." *Florida Law Review* 54.2 (2002): 289-332. Print.

This basic MLA format varies for different types of sources. For a detailed discussion of other models, see MLA-4.

MLA-2b Enclose borrowed language in quotation marks.

To indicate that you are using a source's exact phrases or sentences, you must enclose them in quotation marks unless they have been set off from the text by indenting (see the bottom of p. 381). To omit the quotation marks is to claim—falsely—that the language is your own. Such an omission is plagiarism even if you have cited the source.

ORIGINAL SOURCE

Without adequate discipline, the World Wide Web can be a tremendous time sink; no other medium comes close to matching the Internet's depth of materials, interactivity, and sheer distractive potential.

—Frederick Lane, *The Naked Employee*, p. 142

PLAGIARISM

Frederick Lane points out that if people do not have adequate discipline, the World Wide Web can be a tremendous time sink; no other medium comes close to matching the Internet's depth of materials, interactivity, and sheer distractive potential (142).

BORROWED LANGUAGE IN QUOTATION MARKS

Frederick Lane points out that for those not exercising self-control, "the World Wide Web can be a tremendous time sink; no other medium comes close to matching the Internet's depth of materials, interactivity, and sheer distractive potential" (142).

MLA-2c Put summaries and paraphrases in your own words.

A summary condenses information from a source; a paraphrase conveys the information using roughly the same number of words as the original source. When you summarize or paraphrase, it is not enough to name the source; you must restate the source's meaning using your own language. (See also R3-c.) You commit plagiarism if you half-copy the author's sentences—either by mixing the author's phrases with your own without using quotation marks or by plugging your synonyms into the author's sentence structure.

The first paraphrase of the following source is plagiarized—even though the source is cited—because too much of its language is borrowed from the original. The underlined strings of words have been copied exactly (without quotation marks). In addition, the writer has closely echoed the sentence structure of the source, merely substituting some synonyms (*restricted* for *limited*, *modern era* for *computer age*, *monitoring* for *surveillance*, and *inexpensive* for *cheap*).

ORIGINAL SOURCE

In earlier times, surveillance was limited to the information that a supervisor could observe and record firsthand and to primitive count- ing devices. In the computer age surveillance can be instantaneous, unblinking, cheap, and, maybe most importantly, easy.

> —Carl Botan and Mihaela Vorvoreanu, "What Do Employees Think about Electronic Surveillance at Work?" p. 126

PLAGIARISM: UNACCEPTABLE BORROWING

Scholars Carl Botan and Mihaela Vorvoreanu argue that in earlier times monitoring of employees was restricted to the information that a supervisor could observe and record firsthand. In the modern era, monitoring can be instantaneous, inexpensive, and, most importantly, easy (126).

To avoid plagiarizing an author's language, resist the temptation to look at the source while you are summarizing or paraphrasing. After you have read the original passage, set the source aside. Ask yourself, "What is the author's meaning?" In your own words, state the author's basic point. Return to the source and check that you haven't used the author's language or sentence structure or misrepre- sented the author's ideas. When you fully understand another writer's meaning, you can more easily and accurately present those ideas in your own words.

ACCEPTABLE PARAPHRASE

Scholars Carl Botan and Mihaela Vorvoreanu claim that the nature of workplace surveillance has changed over time. Before the arrival of computers, managers could collect only small amounts of information about their employees based on what they saw or heard. Now, because computers are standard workplace technology, employers can monitor employees efficiently (126).

MLA-3 Integrating sources

Quotations, summaries, paraphrases, and facts will help you develop your argument, but they cannot speak for you. You can use several strategies to integrate information from research sources into your paper while maintaining your own voice.

MLA-3a Use quotations appropriately.

Limiting your use of quotations

Although it is tempting to insert many quotations in your paper and to use your own words only for connecting passages, do not quote excessively. In your academic writing, keep the emphasis on your ideas; use your own words to summarize and to paraphrase your sources and to explain your points. Sometimes, however, quotations can be the most effective way to integrate a source's ideas.

WHEN TO USE QUOTATIONS

- When language is especially vivid or expressive
- When exact wording is needed for technical accuracy
- When it is important to let the debaters of an issue explain their positions in their own words
- When the words of an authority lend weight to an argument
- When the language of a source is the topic of your discussion (as in an analysis or interpretation)

It is not always necessary to quote full sentences from a source. To reduce your reliance on the words of others, you can often integrate language from a source into your own sentence structure. (For the use of signal phrases in integrating quotations, see MLA-3b.)

> Kizza and Ssanyu observe that technology in the workplace has been accompanied by "an array of problems that needed quick answers" such as electronic monitoring to prevent security breaches (4).

Using the ellipsis mark and brackets

Two useful marks of punctuation, the ellipsis mark and brackets, allow you to keep quoted material to a minimum and to integrate it smoothly into your text.

The ellipsis mark To condense a quoted passage, you can use the ellipsis mark (three periods, with spaces between) to indicate that you have left words out. What remains must be grammatically complete.

> Lane acknowledges the legitimate reasons that many companies have for monitoring their employees' online activities, particularly management's concern about preventing "the theft of information that can be downloaded to a . . . disk, e-mailed to oneself . . . , or even posted to a Web page for the entire world to see" (12).

The writer has omitted from the source the words *floppy or Zip* before *disk* and *or a confederate* after *oneself.*

On the rare occasions when you want to leave out one or more full sentences, use a period before the three ellipsis dots.

> Charles Lewis, director of the Center for Public Integrity, points out that "by 1987, employers were administering nearly 2,000,000 polygraph tests a year to job applicants and employees. . . . Millions of workers were required to produce urine samples under observation for drug testing . . ." (22).

Ordinarily, do not use an ellipsis mark at the beginning or at the end of a quotation. Your readers will understand that the quoted material is taken from a longer passage, so such marks are not necessary. The only exception occurs when you have dropped words at the end of the final quoted sentence. In such cases, put three ellipsis dots before the closing quotation mark and parenthetical reference, as in the previous example.

Make sure omissions and ellipsis marks do not distort the meaning of your source.

Brackets   Brackets allow you to insert your own words into quoted material. You can insert words in brackets to clarify a confusing reference or to keep a sentence grammatical in your context. You also use brackets to indicate that you are changing a letter from capital to lowercase (or vice versa) to fit into your sentence.

> Legal scholar Jay Kesan notes that "[a] decade ago, losses [from employees' computer crimes] were already mounting to five billion dollars annually" (311).

This quotation began *A decade ago . . .* in the source, so the writer indicated the change to lowercase with brackets and inserted words in brackets to clarify the meaning of *losses.*

To indicate an error such as a misspelling in a quotation, insert [sic], including the brackets, right after the error.

> Johnson argues that "while online monitoring is often imagined as harmles [sic], the practice may well threaten employees' rights to privacy" (14).

Setting off long quotations

When you quote more than four typed lines of prose or more than three lines of poetry, set off the quotation by indenting it one inch from the left margin.

Long quotations should be introduced by an informative sentence, usually followed by a colon. Quotation marks are unnecessary because the indented format tells readers that the passage is taken word-for-word from the source.

> Botan and Vorvoreanu examine the role of gender in company practices of
> electronic surveillance:
>
> > There has never been accurate documentation of the extent of
> > gender differences in surveillance, but by the middle 1990s,
> > estimates of the proportion of surveilled employees that were
> > women ranged from 75% to 85%. . . . Ironically, this gender
> > imbalance in workplace surveillance may be evening out today
> > because advances in surveillance technology are making surveillance
> > of traditionally male dominated fields, such as long-distance truck
> > driving, cheap, easy, and frequently unobtrusive. (127)

Notice that at the end of an indented quotation the parenthetical citation goes outside the final mark of punctuation. (When a quotation is run into your text, the opposite is true. See the sample citations on p. 380.)

MLA-3b Use signal phrases to integrate sources.

Whenever you include a paraphrase, summary, or direct quotation of another writer in your paper, prepare your readers for it with a *signal phrase*. A signal phrase usually names the author of the source and often provides some context. It commonly appears before the source material. To vary your sentence structure, you may decide to interrupt source material with a signal phrase or place the signal phrase after your paraphrase, summary, or direct quotation.

When you write a signal phrase, choose a verb that is appropriate for the way you are using the source (see MLA-1c). Are you providing background, explaining a concept, supporting a claim, lending authority, or refuting a belief? See the chart on page 383 for a list of verbs commonly used in signal phrases. Note that MLA style calls for verbs in the present or present perfect tense (*argues* or *has argued*) to introduce source material unless you include a date that specifies the time of the original author's writing.

Marking boundaries

Readers need to move from your words to the words of a source without feeling a jolt. Avoid dropping quotations into the text without warning. Instead, provide clear signal phrases, including at least the author's name, to indicate the boundary between your words and the source's words. (The signal phrase is highlighted in the second example.)

Using signal phrases in MLA papers

To avoid monotony, try to vary both the language and the placement of your signal phrases.

Model signal phrases

In the words of researchers Greenfield and Davis, ". . ."

As legal scholar Jay Kesan has noted, ". . ."

The ePolicy Institute, an organization that advises companies about reducing risks from technology, reports that ". . ."

". . .," writes Daniel Tynan, ". . ."

". . .," attorney Schmitt claims.

Kizza and Ssanyu offer a persuasive counterargument: ". . ."

Verbs in signal phrases

acknowledges	comments	endorses	reasons
adds	compares	grants	refutes
admits	confirms	illustrates	rejects
agrees	contends	implies	reports
argues	declares	insists	responds
asserts	denies	notes	suggests
believes	disputes	observes	thinks
claims	emphasizes	points out	writes

DROPPED QUOTATION

Some experts have argued that a range of legitimate concerns justifies employer monitoring of employee Internet usage. "Employees could accidentally (or deliberately) spill confidential corporate information . . . or allow worms to spread throughout a corporate network" (Tynan).

QUOTATION WITH SIGNAL PHRASE

Some experts have argued that a range of legitimate concerns justifies employer monitoring of employee Internet usage. As *PC World* columnist Daniel Tynan points out, "Employees could accidentally (or deliberately) spill confidential corporate information . . . or allow worms to spread throughout a corporate network."

Establishing authority

Good research writing uses evidence from reliable sources. The first time you mention a source, include in the signal phrase the author's title, credentials, or experience—anything that would help your readers recognize the source's authority. (Signal phrases are highlighted in the next two examples.)

SOURCE WITH NO CREDENTIALS

Jay Kesan points out that the law holds employers liable for employees' actions such as violations of copyright laws, the distribution of offensive or graphic sexual material, and illegal disclosure of confidential information (312).

SOURCE WITH CREDENTIALS

Legal scholar Jay Kesan points out that the law holds employers liable for employees' actions such as violations of copyright laws, the distribution of offensive or graphic sexual material, and illegal disclosure of confidential information (312).

When you establish your source's authority, as with the phrase *Legal scholar* in the previous example, you also signal to readers your own credibility as a responsible researcher who has located trustworthy sources.

Introducing summaries and paraphrases

Introduce most summaries and paraphrases with a signal phrase that names the author and places the material in the context of your argument. Readers will then understand that everything between the signal phrase and the parenthetical citation summarizes or paraphrases the cited source.

Without the signal phrase (highlighted) in the following example, readers might think that only the quotation at the end is being cited, when in fact the whole paragraph is based on the source.

Frederick Lane believes that the personal computer has posed new challenges for employers worried about workplace productivity. Whereas early desktop computers were primitive enough to prevent employees from using them to waste time, the machines have become so sophisticated that they now make non-work-related computer activities easy and inviting. Many employees spend considerable company time customizing features and playing games on their computers. But perhaps most problematic from the employer's point of view, Lane asserts, is giving employees access to the Internet, "roughly the equivalent of installing a gazillion-channel television set for each employee" (15-16).

There are times when a summary or a paraphrase does not require a signal phrase naming the author. When the context makes clear where the cited material begins, you may omit the signal phrase and include the author's last name in parentheses.

Integrating statistics and other facts

When you are citing a statistic or another specific fact, a signal phrase is often not necessary. In most cases, readers will understand that the citation refers to the statistic or fact (not the whole paragraph).

> Roughly 60% of responding companies reported disciplining employees who had used the Internet in ways the companies deemed inappropriate; 30% had fired their employees for those transgressions (Greenfield and Davis 347).

There is nothing wrong, however, with using a signal phrase to introduce a statistic or another fact.

Putting source material in context

Readers should not have to guess why source material appears in your paper. A signal phrase can help you connect your own ideas and those of another writer by clarifying how the source will contribute to your paper (see R2-a).

If you use another writer's words, you must explain how they relate to your point. In other words, you must put the source in context. It's a good idea to embed a quotation between sentences of your own. In addition to introducing it with a signal phrase, follow it with interpretive comments that link the quotation to your paper's argument (see also MLA-3c).

QUOTATION WITH EFFECTIVE CONTEXT

The difference, Lane argues, between old methods of data gathering and electronic surveillance involves quantity:

> Technology makes it possible for employers to gather enormous amounts of data about employees, often far beyond what is necessary to satisfy safety or productivity concerns. And the trends that drive technology—faster, smaller, cheaper—make it possible for larger and larger numbers of employers to gather ever-greater amounts of personal data. (3-4)

In an age when employers can collect data whenever employees use their computers—when they send e-mail, surf the Web, or even arrive at or depart from their workstations—the challenge for both employers and employees is to determine how much is too much.

MLA-3c Synthesize sources.

When you synthesize multiple sources in a research paper, you create a conversation about your research topic. You show readers that your argument is based on your active analysis and integration of ideas, not just a list of quotations and paraphrases. Your synthesis will show how your sources relate to one another; one source may support, extend, or counter the ideas of another. Readers should be able to see how each source functions in your argument (see R2-a).

Considering how sources relate to your argument

Before you integrate sources and show readers how they relate to one another, consider how each one might contribute to your own argument. As student writer Anna Orlov became more informed about Internet surveillance in the workplace, she asked herself these questions: *What do I think about monitoring employees online? Which sources might extend or illustrate the points I want to make? Which sources voice opposing points of view that I need to address?* With these questions in mind, Orlov read and annotated sources, including an argument in favor of workplace surveillance. (See the example on p. 434.)

Placing sources in conversation

When you synthesize sources, you show readers how the ideas of one source relate to those of another by connecting and analyzing the ideas in the context of your argument. Keep the emphasis on your own writing. After all, you've done the research and thought through the issues, so you should control the conversation. The thread of your argument should be easy to identify and to understand, with or without your sources.

SAMPLE SYNTHESIS (DRAFT)

Student writer Anna Orlov begins with a claim that needs support.	• Productivity is not easily measured in the wired workplace. As a result, employers find it difficult to determine how much freedom to allow their employees. On the one hand, computers and Internet access give employees powerful tools to carry out their jobs; on the	Student writer
Signal phrases indicate how sources contribute to Orlov's paper and show that the ideas that follow are not her own.	other hand, the same technology offers constant temptations to avoid work. As a 2005 study by *Salary.com* and *America Online* indicates, the Internet ranked as the top choice among employees for ways of wasting time on the job (Frauenheim). Chris Gonsalves, an editor for	Source 1

eWeek.com, argues that technology has changed the terms | Source 2
between employers and employees: "While bosses can
easily detect and interrupt water-cooler chatter," he
writes, "the employee who is shopping at Lands' End or
IMing with fellow fantasy baseball managers may actually
appear to be working." The gap between observable
behaviors and actual online activities has motivated some | Student writer
employers to invest in surveillance programs.

Orlov presents a counterposition to extend her argument. → Many experts, however, disagree with employers'
assumption that online monitoring can increase productivity.
Employment law attorney Joseph Schmitt argues that, par- | Source 3
ticularly for salaried employees, "a company shouldn't care
whether employees spend one or 10 hours on the Internet
as long as they are getting their jobs done—and provided
that they are not accessing inappropriate sites" (qtd. in
Verespej). Other experts even argue that time spent on | Student writer
personal Internet browsing can actually be productive

Orlov builds her case—each quoted passage offers a more detailed claim or example in support of her larger claim. → for companies. According to Bill Coleman, an executive at
Salary.com, "Personal Internet use and casual office conver- | Source 4
sations often turn into new business ideas or suggestions
for gaining operating efficiencies" (qtd. in Frauenheim).
Employers, in other words, may benefit from showing more | Student writer
faith in their employees' ability to exercise their autonomy.

In this draft, Orlov uses her own analyses to shape the conversation among her sources. She does not simply string quotations together or allow her sources to overwhelm her writing. The final sentence, written in her own voice, gives her an opportunity to explain to readers how the various sources support her argument.

When synthesizing sources, ask yourself the following questions:

- Which sources inform, support, or extend your argument?
- Have you varied the function of sources—to provide background, to explain concepts, to lend authority, and to anticipate counterarguments? Do you use signal phrases to indicate these functions?
- Do you explain how your sources support your argument?
- Do you connect and analyze sources in your own voice?
- Is your own argument easy to identify and to understand, with or without your sources?

Use of quotations

- Is quoted material enclosed in quotation marks (unless it has been set off from the text)? (See MLA-2b.)
- Is quoted language word-for-word accurate? If not, do brackets or ellipsis marks indicate the changes or omissions? (See pp. 380–81.)
- Does a clear signal phrase (usually naming the author) prepare readers for each quotation and for the purpose the quotation serves? (See MLA-3b.)
- Does a parenthetical citation follow each quotation? (See MLA-4a.)
- Is each quotation put in context? (See MLA-3c.)

Use of summaries and paraphrases

- Are summaries and paraphrases free of plagiarized wording—not copied or half-copied from the source? (See MLA-2c.)
- Are summaries and paraphrases documented with parenthetical citations? (See MLA-4a.)
- Do readers know where the cited material begins? In other words, does a signal phrase mark the boundary between your words and the summary or paraphrase? Or does the context alone make clear exactly what you are citing? (See MLA-3b.)
- Does a signal phrase prepare readers for the purpose the summary or paraphrase has in your argument?

Use of statistics and other facts

- Are statistics and facts (other than common knowledge) documented with parenthetical citations? (See MLA-2a.)
- If there is no signal phrase, will readers understand exactly which facts are being cited? (See MLA-3b.)

MLA-4 Documenting sources

In English and other humanities classes, you may be asked to use the MLA (Modern Language Association) system for documenting sources, which is set forth in the *MLA Handbook for Writers of Research Papers,* 7th ed. (New York: MLA, 2009).

MLA recommends in-text citations that refer readers to a list of works cited. A typical in-text citation names the author of the source, often in a signal phrase, and gives a page number in parentheses. At the end of the paper, a list of works cited provides publication information about the source; the list is alphabetized by authors' last names (or by titles for works without authors). There is a direct connection between the in-text citation and the alphabetized listing. In the following example, that connection is highlighted in orange.

IN-TEXT CITATION

Jay Kesan notes that even though many companies now routinely monitor employees through electronic means, "there may exist less intrusive safeguards for employers" (293).

ENTRY IN THE LIST OF WORKS CITED

Kesan, Jay P. "Cyber-Working or Cyber-Shirking? A First Principles Examination of Electronic Privacy in the Workplace." *Florida Law Review* 54.2 (2002): 289-332. Print.

For a list of works cited that includes this entry, see page 440.

MLA-4a MLA in-text citations

MLA in-text citations are made with a combination of signal phrases and parenthetical references. A signal phrase introduces information taken from a source (a quotation, summary, paraphrase, or fact); usually the signal phrase includes the author's name. The parenthetical reference comes after the cited material, often at the end of the sentence. It includes at least a page number (except for unpaginated sources, such as those found online). In the models in MLA-4a, the elements of the in-text citation are highlighted in orange.

IN-TEXT CITATION

Kwon points out that the Fourth Amendment does not give employees any protections from employers' "unreasonable searches and seizures" (6).

Readers can look up the author's last name in the alphabetized list of works cited, where they will learn the work's title and other publication information. If readers decide to consult the source, the page number will take them straight to the passage that has been cited.

For a directory to the in-text citation models in this section, see page 371, immediately following the tabbed divider.

Basic rules for print and online sources

The MLA system of in-text citations, which depends heavily on authors' names and page numbers, was created with print sources in mind. Although many online sources have unclear authorship and lack page numbers, the basic rules are the same for both print and online sources.

The models in this section (items 1–5) show how the MLA system usually works and explain what to do if your source has no author or page numbers.

1. Author named in a signal phrase Ordinarily, introduce the material being cited with a signal phrase that includes the author's name. In addition to preparing readers for the source, the signal phrase allows you to keep the parenthetical citation brief.

> Frederick Lane reports that employers do not necessarily have to use software
> to monitor how their employees use the Web: employers can "use a hidden
> video camera pointed at an employee's monitor" and even position a camera
> "so that a number of monitors [can] be viewed at the same time" (147).

The signal phrase—*Frederick Lane reports*—names the author; the parenthetical citation gives the page number of the book in which the quoted words may be found.

Notice that the period follows the parenthetical citation. When a quotation ends with a question mark or an exclamation point, leave the end punctuation inside the quotation mark and add a period at the end of your sentence. (See also the note on p. 284.)

> O'Connor asks a critical question: "When does Internet surveillance cross the
> line between corporate responsibility and invasion of privacy?" (16).

2. Author named in parentheses If a signal phrase does not name the author, put the author's last name in parentheses along with the page number. Use no punctuation between the name and the page number.

> Companies can monitor employees' every keystroke without legal penalty, but
> they may have to combat low morale as a result (Lane 129).

3. Author unknown Either use the complete title in a signal phrase or use a short form of the title in parentheses. Titles of books are italicized; titles of articles are put in quotation marks.

> A popular keystroke logging program operates invisibly on workers' computers
> yet provides supervisors with details of the workers' online activities
> ("Automatically").

TIP: Before assuming that a Web source has no author, do some detective work. Often the author's name is available but is not easy to find. For example, it may appear at the end of the page, in tiny print. Or it may appear on another page of the site, such as the home page.

NOTE: If a source has no author and is sponsored by a corporation or government agency, name the corporation or agency as the author (see items 8 and 17 on pp. 392 and 395, respectively).

4. Page number unknown Do not include the page number if a work lacks page numbers, as is the case with many Web sources. Even if a printout from a Web site shows page numbers, treat the source as unpaginated in the in-text citation because not all printouts give the same page numbers. (When the pages of a Web source are stable, as in PDF files, supply a page number in your in-text citation.)

> As a 2005 study by *Salary.com* and *America Online* indicates, the Internet
> ranked as the top choice among employees for ways of wasting time on the
> job; it beat talking with co-workers—the second most popular method—by
> a margin of nearly two to one (Frauenheim).

If a source has numbered paragraphs or sections, use "par." (or "pars.") or "sec." (or "secs.") in the parentheses: (Smith, par. 4). Notice that a comma follows the author's name.

5. One-page source If the source is one page long, MLA allows (but does not require) you to omit the page number. Even so, it's a good idea to supply the page number because without it readers may not know where your citation ends or, worse, may not realize that you have provided a citation at all.

NO PAGE NUMBER IN CITATION

> Anush Yegyazarian reports that in 2000 the National Labor Relations Board's
> Office of the General Counsel helped win restitution for two workers who had
> been dismissed because their employers were displeased by the employees'
> e-mails about work-related issues. The case points to the ongoing struggle to
> define what constitutes protected speech in the workplace.

PAGE NUMBER IN CITATION

> Anush Yegyazarian reports that in 2000 the National Labor Relations Board's
> Office of the General Counsel helped win restitution for two workers who had
> been dismissed because their employers were displeased by the employees'
> e-mails about work-related issues (62). The case points to the ongoing
> struggle to define what constitutes protected speech in the workplace.

Variations on the basic rules

This section describes the MLA guidelines for handling a variety of situations not covered by the basic rules in items 1–5. These rules for in-text citations are the same for both print and online sources.

6. Two or three authors Name the authors in a signal phrase, as in the following example, or include their last names in the parenthetical reference: (Kizza and Ssanyu 2).

> Kizza and Ssanyu note that "employee monitoring is a dependable, capable, and very affordable process of electronically or otherwise recording all employee activities at work" and elsewhere (2).

When three authors are named in the parentheses, separate the names with commas: (Alton, Davies, and Rice 56).

7. Four or more authors Name all of the authors or include only the first author's name followed by "et al." (Latin for "and others"). The format you use should match the format in your works cited entry (see item 3 on p. 399).

> The study was extended for two years, and only after results were reviewed by an independent panel did the researchers publish their findings (Blaine et al. 35).

8. Organization as author When the author is a corporation or an organization, name that author either in the signal phrase or in the parentheses. (For a government agency as author, see item 17 on p. 395.)

> According to a 2001 survey of human resources managers by the American Management Association, more than three-quarters of the responding companies reported disciplining employees for "misuse or personal use of office telecommunications equipment" (2).

In the list of works cited, the American Management Association is treated as the author and alphabetized under *A*. When you give the organization name in parentheses, abbreviate common words in the name: "Assn.," "Dept.," "Natl.," "Soc.," and so on.

> In a 2001 survey of human resources managers, more than three-quarters of the responding companies reported disciplining employees for "misuse or personal use of office telecommunications equipment" (Amer. Management Assn. 2).

9. Authors with the same last name   If your list of works cited includes works by two or more authors with the same last name, include the author's first name in the signal phrase or first initial in the parentheses.

> Estimates of the frequency with which employers monitor employees' use of the Internet each day vary widely (A. Jones 15).

10. Two or more works by the same author   Mention the title of the work in the signal phrase or include a short version of the title in the parentheses.

> The American Management Association and ePolicy Institute have tracked employers' practices in monitoring employees' e-mail use. The groups' 2003 survey found that one-third of companies had a policy of keeping and reviewing employees' e-mail messages ("2003 E-mail" 2); in 2005, more than 55% of companies engaged in e-mail monitoring ("2005 Electronic" 1).

Titles of articles and other short works are placed in quotation marks; titles of books are italicized.

In the rare case when both the author's name and a short title must be given in parentheses, separate them with a comma.

> A 2004 survey found that 20% of employers responding had employees' e-mail "subpoenaed in the course of a lawsuit or regulatory investigation," up 7% from the previous year (Amer. Management Assn. and ePolicy Inst., "2004 Workplace" 1).

11. Two or more works in one citation   To cite more than one source in the parentheses, give the citations in alphabetical order and separate them with a semicolon.

> Several researchers have analyzed the reasons that companies monitor employees' use of the Internet at work (Botan and Vorvoreanu 128-29; Kesan 317-19; Kizza and Ssanyu 3-7).

Multiple citations can be distracting, so you should not overuse the technique. If you want to point to several sources that discuss a particular topic, consider using an information note instead (see MLA-4c).

12. Repeated citations from the same source   When your paper is about a single work of fiction or nonfiction (such as an essay), you do not need to include the author's name each time you quote from or paraphrase the work. After you mention the author's name at the beginning of your paper, you may include just the page numbers in your parenthetical citations.

> In Susan Glaspell's short story "A Jury of Her Peers," two women accompany their husbands and a county attorney to an isolated house where a farmer named John Wright has been choked to death in his bed with a rope. The chief suspect is Wright's wife, Minnie, who is in jail awaiting trial. The sheriff's wife, Mrs. Peters, has come along to gather some personal items for Minnie, and Mrs. Hale has joined her. Early in the story, Mrs. Hale sympathizes with Minnie and objects to the way the male investigators are "snoopin' round and criticizin'" her kitchen (191). In contrast, Mrs. Peters shows respect for the law, saying that the men are doing "no more than their duty" (191).

In a paper with multiple sources, if you are citing a source more than once in a paragraph, you may omit the author's name after the first mention in the paragraph as long as it is clear that you are still referring to the same source.

13. Encyclopedia or dictionary entry   Unless an entry in an encyclopedia or a dictionary has an author, the source will be alphabetized in the list of works cited under the word or entry that you consulted (see item 27 on p. 409). Either in your text or in your parenthetical citation, mention the word or entry. No page number is required, since readers can easily look up the word or entry.

> The word *crocodile* has a surprisingly complex etymology ("Crocodile").

14. Multivolume work   If your paper cites more than one volume of a multivolume work, indicate in the parentheses the volume you are referring to, followed by a colon and the page number.

> In his studies of gifted children, Terman describes a pattern of accelerated language acquisition (2: 279).

If you cite only one volume of a multivolume work throughout your paper, you will include the volume number in the list of works cited and will not need to include it in the parentheses. (See the second example in item 26, at the top of p. 409.)

15. Entire work   Use the author's name in a signal phrase or a parenthetical citation. There is no need to use a page number.

> Lane explores the evolution of surveillance in the workplace.

16. Selection in an anthology Put the name of the author of the selection (not the editor of the anthology) in the signal phrase or the parentheses.

> In "Love Is a Fallacy," the narrator's logical teachings disintegrate when Polly declares that she should date Petey because "[h]e's got a raccoon coat" (Shulman 379).

In the list of works cited, the work is alphabetized by the author's last name, not by the name of the editor of the anthology. (See item 24 on pp. 407–08.)

> Shulman, Max. "Love Is a Fallacy." *Current Issues and Enduring Questions.* Ed. Sylvan Barnet and Hugo Bedau. 8th ed. Boston: Bedford, 2008. 371-79. Print.

17. Government document When a government agency is the author, you will alphabetize it in the list of works cited under the name of the government, such as *United States* or *Great Britain* (see item 73 on p. 424). For this reason, you must name the government as well as the agency in your in-text citation.

> Online monitoring by the United States Department of the Interior over a one-week period found that employees' use of "sexually explicit and gambling websites . . . accounted for over 24 hours of Internet use" and that "computer users spent over 2,004 hours accessing game and auction sites" during the same period (3).

18. Historical document For a historical document, such as the United States Constitution or the Canadian Charter of Rights and Freedoms, provide the document title, neither italicized nor in quotation marks, along with relevant article and section numbers. In parenthetical citations, use common abbreviations such as "art." and "sec." and abbreviations of well-known titles (US Const., art. 1, sec. 2).

> While the United States Constitution provides for the formation of new states (art. 4, sec. 3), it does not explicitly allow or prohibit the secession of states.

For other historical documents, cite as you would any other work, by the first element in the works cited entry (see item 74 on p. 425).

19. Legal source For legislative acts (laws) and court cases, name the act or case either in a signal phrase or in parentheses. Italicize the names of cases but not the names of acts.

> The Jones Act of 1917 granted US citizenship to Puerto Ricans.

> In 1857, Chief Justice Roger B. Taney declared in *Dred Scott v. Sandford* that
> blacks, whether enslaved or free, could not be citizens of the United States.

20. Visual such as a photograph, map, or chart To cite a visual that has a figure number in the source, use the abbreviation "fig." and the number in place of a page number in your parenthetical citation: (Manning, fig. 4). Spell out the word "figure" if you refer to it in your text.

To cite a visual that does not have a figure number in a print source, use the visual's title or a general description in your text and cite the author and page number as for any other source.

For a visual that is not contained in a source such as a book or periodical, identify the visual in your text and then cite it using the first element in the works cited entry: the photographer's or artist's name or the title of the work. (See items 69 and 72 on pp. 423 and 424.)

> Photographs such as *Woman Aircraft Worker* (Bransby) and *Women Welders*
> (Parks) demonstrate the US government's attempt to document the
> contributions of women on the home front during World War II.

21. E-mail, letter, or personal interview Cite e-mail messages, personal letters, and personal interviews by the name listed in the works cited entry, as you would for any other source. Identify the type of source in your text if you feel it is necessary. (See item 53 on p. 419 and items 83 and 84 on p. 427.)

22. Web site or other electronic source Your in-text citation for an electronic source should follow the same guidelines as for other sources. If the source lacks page numbers but has numbered paragraphs, sections, or divisions, use those numbers with the appropriate abbreviation in your in-text citation: "par.," "sec.," "ch.," "pt.," and so on. Do not add such numbers if the source itself does not use them; simply give the author or title in your in-text citation.

> Julian Hawthorne points out profound differences between his father and Ralph
> Waldo Emerson but concludes that, in their lives and their writing, "together
> they met the needs of nearly all that is worthy in human nature" (ch. 4).

23. Indirect source (source quoted in another source) When a writer's or a speaker's quoted words appear in a source written by someone else, begin the parenthetical citation with the abbreviation "qtd. in."

> According to Bill Coleman, an executive at *Salary.com*, "Personal Internet use
> and casual office conversations often turn into new business ideas or suggestions
> for gaining operating efficiencies" (qtd. in Frauenheim).

Literary works and sacred texts

Literary works and sacred texts are usually available in a variety of
editions. Your list of works cited will specify which edition you are
using, and your in-text citation will usually consist of a page number
from the edition you consulted (see item 24). When possible, give enough
information—such as book parts, play divisions, or line numbers—
so that readers can locate the cited passage in any edition of the work
(see items 25–27).

24. Literary work without parts or line numbers   Many literary works,
such as most short stories and many novels and plays, do not have parts
or line numbers. In such cases, simply cite the page number.

> At the end of Kate Chopin's "The Story of an Hour," Mrs. Mallard drops dead
> upon learning that her husband is alive. In the final irony of the story, doctors
> report that she has died of a "joy that kills" (25).

25. Verse play or poem   For verse plays, give act, scene, and line
numbers that can be located in any edition of the work. Use arabic
numerals and separate the numbers with periods.

> In Shakespeare's *King Lear,* Gloucester, blinded for suspected treason, learns a
> profound lesson from his tragic experience: "A man may see how this world
> goes / with no eyes" (4.2.148-49).

For a poem, cite the part, stanza, and line numbers, if it has
them, separated by periods.

> The Green Knight claims to approach King Arthur's court "because the praise of
> you, prince, is puffed so high, / And your manor and your men are considered
> so magnificent" (1.12.258-59).

For poems that are not divided into numbered parts or stanzas, use
line numbers. For a first reference, use the word "lines": (lines 5-8).
Thereafter use just the numbers: (12-13).

26. Novel with numbered divisions   When a novel has numbered
divisions, put the page number first, followed by a semicolon and the
book, part, or chapter in which the passage may be found. Use abbreviations such as "bk.," "pt.," and "ch."

> One of Kingsolver's narrators, teenager Rachel, pushes her vocabulary beyond its
> limits. For example, Rachel complains that being forced to live in the Congo with
> her missionary family is "a sheer tapestry of justice" because her chances of
> finding a boyfriend are "dull and void" (117; bk. 2, ch. 10).

27. Sacred text When citing a sacred text such as the Bible or the Qur'an, name the edition you are using in your works cited entry (see item 28 on p. 409). In your parenthetical citation, give the book, chapter, and verse (or their equivalent), separated with periods. Common abbreviations for books of the Bible are acceptable.

> Consider the words of Solomon: "If your enemy is hungry, give him bread to eat; and if he is thirsty, give him water to drink" (*Oxford Annotated Bible,* Prov. 25.21).

The title of a sacred work is italicized when it refers to a specific edition of the work, as in the preceding example. If you refer to the book in a general sense in your text, neither italicize it nor put it in quotation marks. (See also the note in P10-a, p. 305.)

> The Bible and the Qur'an provide allegories that help readers understand how to lead a moral life.

MLA-4b MLA list of works cited

An alphabetized list of works cited, which appears at the end of your research paper, gives publication information for each of the sources you have cited in the paper. Include only sources that you have quoted, summarized, or paraphrased. (For information about preparing the list, see p. 431; for a sample list of works cited, see p. 440.)

For a directory to the works cited models in this section, see pages 371–72, immediately following the tabbed divider.

General guidelines for works cited in MLA style

In an MLA works cited entry, invert the first author's name (last name first, followed by a comma and the first name); put all other names in normal order. In titles of works, capitalize all words except articles (*a, an, the*), prepositions (*into, between,* and so on), coordinating conjunctions (*and, but, or, nor, for, so, yet*), and the *to* in infinitives—unless they are the first or last word of the title or subtitle. Use quotation marks for titles of articles and other short works, such as brief documents from Web sites; italicize titles of books and other long works, such as entire Web sites.

Give the city of publication without a state name. Shorten publishers' names, usually to the first principal word ("Wiley" for "John Wiley and Sons," for instance); abbreviate "University" and "Press" in the names of university publishers: UP of Florida. For the date of publication, use the date on the title page or the most recent date on the copyright page.

For all works cited entries, include the medium in which a work was published, produced, or delivered. Usually put the medium at the end of the entry, capitalized but neither italicized nor in quotation marks. Typical designations for the medium are "Print," "Web," "Radio," "Television," "CD," "Film," "Videocassette," "DVD," "Photograph," "Performance," "Lecture," "MP3 file," and "PDF file." (See specific items throughout MLA-4b.)

Listing authors (print and online)

Alphabetize entries in the list of works cited by authors' last names (or by title if a work has no author). The author's name is important because citations in the text of the paper refer to it and readers will look for it at the beginning of an entry in the alphabetized list.

NAME CITED IN TEXT

According to Nancy Flynn, . . .

BEGINNING OF WORKS CITED ENTRY

Flynn, Nancy.

1. Single author

author: last name first | title (book) | city of publication | publisher | date | medium

Wood, James. *How Fiction Works*. New York: Farrar, 2008. Print.

2. Two or three authors

first author: last name first | second author: in normal order | title (book) | city of publication | publisher

Gourevitch, Philip, and Errol Morris. *Standard Operating Procedure*. New York: Penguin,

date | medium

2008. Print.

first author: last name first | other authors: in normal order | title (newspaper article)

Farmer, John, John Azzarello, and Miles Kara. "Real Heroes, Fake Stories."

newspaper title | date of publication | page(s) | medium

New York Times 14 Sept. 2008: WK10. Print.

3. Four or more authors

first author: last name first | other authors: in normal order | title (book) | edition number

Harris, Shon, Allen Harper, Chris Eagle, and Jonathan Ness. *Gray Hat Hacking*. 2nd ed.

city of publication | publisher | date | medium

New York: McGraw, 2007. Print.

Name all the authors or name the first author followed by "et al." (Latin for "and others"). In an in-text citation, use the same form for the authors' names as you use in the works cited entry. See item 7 on page 392.

4. Organization as author

author: organization name, not abbreviated — title (book)

National Wildlife Federation. *Rain Check: Conservation Groups Monitor Mercury Levels in Milwaukee's Rain.* Ann Arbor: Natl. Wildlife Federation, 2001. Print.

city of publication — publisher, with common abbreviations — date — medium

For a publication by a government agency, see item 73. Your in-text citation should also treat the organization as the author (see item 8 on p. 392).

5. Unknown author

Article or other short work

title (newspaper article) — label — newspaper title — date of publication — page(s) — medium

"Poverty, by Outdated Numbers." Editorial. *Boston Globe* 20 Sept. 2008: A16. Print.

title (TV episode) — title (TV program) — producer — network — station — city of broadcast — date of broadcast — medium

"Heat." *Frontline.* Prod. Martin Smith. PBS. KTWU, Topeka. 21 Oct. 2008. Television.

For other examples of an article with no author and of a television program, see items 13 and 65, respectively.

Book, entire Web site, or other long work

title (book) — city of publication — publisher — date — medium

New Concise World Atlas. New York: Oxford UP, 2007. Print.

title (Web site)

Women of Protest: Photographs from the Records of the National Woman's Party.

sponsor of site — no date — medium — access date

Lib. of Cong., n.d. Web. 29 Sept. 2008.

Before concluding that the author of an online source is unknown, check carefully (see the tip at the top of p. 391). Also remember that an organization or a government may be the author (see items 4 and 73).

6. Two or more works by the same author   If your list of works cited includes two or more works by the same author, first alphabetize the works by title (ignoring the article *A, An,* or *The* at the beginning of a title). Use the author's name for the first entry only; for subsequent entries, use three hyphens followed by a period. The three hyphens must stand for exactly the same name or names as in the first entry.

Knopp, Lisa. *Field of Vision.* Iowa City: U of Iowa P, 1996. Print.

---. *The Nature of Home: A Lexicon and Essays.* Lincoln: U of Nebraska P, 2002. Print.

Articles in periodicals (print)

This section shows how to prepare works cited entries for articles in print magazines, journals, and newspapers. See "General guidelines" and "Listing authors" on pages 398 and 399 for how to handle basic parts of the entries. See also "Online sources" beginning on page 412 for articles from Web sites and articles accessed through a library's database.

For articles appearing on consecutive pages, provide the range of pages (see items 7 and 8). When an article does not appear on consecutive pages, give the first page number followed by a plus sign: 32+. For dates requiring a month, abbreviate all but May, June, and July. For an illustrated citation of an article in a periodical, see pages 402–03.

7.   Article in a journal (paginated by volume or by issue)

author: last
name first   article title   journal title

Blackburn, Robin. "Economic Democracy: Meaningful, Desirable, Feasible?" *Daedalus*

volume,
issue   year   page(s) medium
136.3   (2007): 36-45. Print.

8.   Article in a monthly magazine

author: last
name first   article title   magazine title   date: month + year   page(s)

Lanting, Frans. "Life: A Journey through Time." *Audubon* Nov.-Dec. 2006: 48-52.

medium
Print.

Citation at a glance: Article in a periodical (MLA)

To cite an article in a print periodical in MLA style, include the following elements:

1 Author of article
2 Title and subtitle of article
3 Title of periodical

4 Volume and issue number (for journal)
5 Date or year of publication
6 Page number(s) of article
7 Medium

TITLE PAGE

FIRST PAGE OF ARTICLE

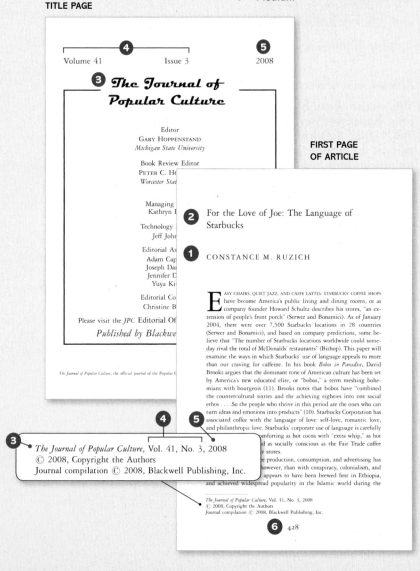

Volume 41   Issue 3   2008

The Journal of Popular Culture

Editor
GARY HOPPENSTAND
Michigan State University

Book Review Editor
PETER C. H...
Worcester Stat...

Managing
Kathryn ...

Technology
Jeff John...

Editorial As...
Adam Cap...
Joseph Dar...
Jennifer D...
Yuya Ki...

Editorial Co...
Christine B...

Please visit the *JPC* Editorial Of...

Published by Blackwe...

The Journal of Popular Culture, the official journal of the Popular C...

2 For the Love of Joe: The Language of Starbucks

1 CONSTANCE M. RUZICH

EASY CHAIRS, QUIET JAZZ, AND CAFFE LATTES: STARBUCKS' COFFEE SHOPS have become America's public living and dining rooms, or as company founder Howard Schultz describes his stores, "an extension of people's front porch" (Serwer and Bonamici). As of January 2004, there were over 7,500 Starbucks locations in 28 countries (Serwer and Bonamici), and based on company predictions, some believe that "The number of Starbucks locations worldwide could someday rival the total of McDonalds' restaurants" (Bishop). This paper will examine the ways in which Starbucks' use of language appeals to more than our craving for caffeine. In his book *Bobos in Paradise,* David Brooks argues that the dominant tone of American culture has been set by America's new educated elite, or "bobos," a term meshing bohemians with bourgeois (11). Brooks notes that bobos have "combined the countercultural sixties and the achieving eighties into one social ethos . . . .So the people who thrive in this period are the ones who can turn ideas and emotions into products" (10). Starbucks Corporation has associated coffee with the language of love: self-love, romantic love, and philanthropic love. Starbucks' corporate use of language is carefully ...omforting as hot cocoa with "extra whip," as hot ...d as socially conscious as the Fair Trade coffee ...r stores.

...e production, consumption, and advertising has ...however, than with conspiracy, colonialism, and ... appears to have been brewed first in Ethiopia, and achieved widespread popularity in the Islamic world during the

3 *The Journal of Popular Culture,* Vol. 41, No. 3, 2008
© 2008, Copyright the Authors
Journal compilation © 2008, Blackwell Publishing, Inc.

The Journal of Popular Culture, Vol. 41, No. 3, 2008
© 2008, Copyright the Authors
Journal compilation © 2008, Blackwell Publishing, Inc.

6 428

WORKS CITED ENTRY FOR AN ARTICLE IN A PRINT PERIODICAL

Ruzich, Constance M. "For the Love of Joe: The Language of Starbucks." *Journal of*

Popular Culture 41.3 (2008): 428-42. Print.

For more on citing print periodical articles in MLA style, see pages 401–04.

9. Article in a weekly magazine

von Drehle, David. "The Ghosts of Memphis." *Time* 7 Apr. 2008: 34-37. Print.

10. Article in a daily newspaper   Give the page range of the article. If the article does not appear on consecutive pages, use a plus sign (+) after the first page number. If the city of publication is not obvious from the title of the newspaper, include the city in brackets after the name of the newspaper.

If sections are identified by letter, include the section letter as part of the page number. If sections are numbered, include the section number between the date and the page number, using the abbreviation "sec."

Page number with section letter

McKenna, Phil. "It Takes Just One Village." *New York Times* 23 Sept. 2008, New England ed.: D1. Print.

Page number with section number

Knox, David Blake. "Lord Archer, Storyteller." *Sunday Independent* [Dublin] 14 Sept. 2008, sec. 2: 9. Print.

11. Abstract of a journal article   Include the word "Abstract" after the title of the article.

Walker, Joyce. "Narratives in the Database: Memorializing September 11th Online."

Abstract. *Computers and Composition* 24.2 (2007): 121. Print.

12. Article with a title in its title Use single quotation marks around a title of a short work or a quoted term that appears in an article title. Italicize a title or term normally italicized. (See also P5-c.)

Shen, Min. "'Quite a Moon!' The Archetypal Feminine in *Our Town*." *American Drama* 16.2

(2007): 1-14. Print.

13. Editorial or other unsigned article Begin with the article title and alphabetize the entry by the title in the list of works cited.

"Getting the Message: Communicating Electronically with Doctors Can Spur Honesty from

Young Patients." Editorial. *Columbus* [OH] *Dispatch* 19 June 2008: 10A. Print.

14. Letter to the editor

Morris, David. "Fiercely Proud." Letter. *Progressive* Feb. 2008: 6. Print.

15. Review For a review of a book, a film, or another type of work, begin with the name of the reviewer and the title of the review, if it has one. Add the words "Rev. of" and the title of the work reviewed, followed by the author, director, or other significant contributor. Give the publication information for the periodical in which the review appears. If the review has no author and no title, begin with "Rev. of" and alphabetize the entry by the first principal word in the title of the work reviewed.

Dodge, Chris. Rev. of *The Radical Jack London: Writings on War and Revolution,* ed. Jonah

Raskni. *Utne Reader* Sept.-Oct. 2008: 35. Print.

Lane, Anthony. "Dream On." Rev. of *The Science of Sleep* and *Renaissance,* dir. Michel

Gondry. *New Yorker* 25 Sept. 2006: 155-57. Print.

Books (print)

Items 16–33 apply to print books. For online books, see items 41 and 42. For an illustrated citation of a print book, see page 406.

16. Basic format for a book

author: last name first — book title — city of publication — publisher — date

Sacks, Oliver. *Musicophilia: Tales of Music and the Brain.* New York: Knopf, 2007.

medium

Print.

Take the information about the book from its title page and copyright page. Use a short form of the publisher's name; omit terms such as "Press," "Inc.," and "Co." except when naming university presses ("Howard UP," for example). If the copyright page lists more than one date, use the most recent one.

17. Book with an author and an editor

author: last
name first   book title   editor: city of
                                                             in normal order publication

Plath, Sylvia. *The Unabridged Journals of Sylvia Plath*. Ed. Karen V. Kukil. New York:

imprint-publisher   date medium

Anchor-Doubleday, 2000. Print.

The abbreviation "Ed." means "Edited by," so it is the same for one or multiple editors.

18. Book with an author and a translator   "Trans." means "Translated by," so it is the same for one or multiple translators.

Scirocco, Alfonso. *Garibaldi: Citizen of the World*. Trans. Allan Cameron. Princeton:

Princeton UP, 2007. Print.

19. Book with an editor   Begin with the editor's name. For one editor, use "ed." (for "editor") after the name; for multiple editors, use "eds." (for "editors").

Lago, Mary, Linda K. Hughes, and Elizabeth MacLeod Walls, eds. *The BBC Talks of*

E. M. Forster, 1929-1960. Columbia: U of Missouri P, 2008. Print.

20. Graphic narrative or illustrated book   For a book that combines text and illustrations, begin your citation with the person you wish to emphasize (writer, illustrator, artist) and list any other contributors after the title of the book. Use the abbreviation "illus." and other common labels to identify contributors. If the writer and illustrator are the same person, cite the work as you would a book, with no labels.

Weaver, Dustin, illus. *The Tenth Circle*. By Jodi Picoult. New York: Washington Square,

2006. Print.

Moore, Alan. *V for Vendetta*. Illus. David Lloyd. New York: Vertigo-DC Comics, 2008.

Print.

Thompson, Craig. *Blankets*. Marietta: Top Shelf, 2005.

Citation at a glance: Book (MLA)

To cite a print book in MLA style, include the following elements:

1 Author
2 Title and subtitle
3 City of publication
4 Publisher
5 Date of publication
6 Medium

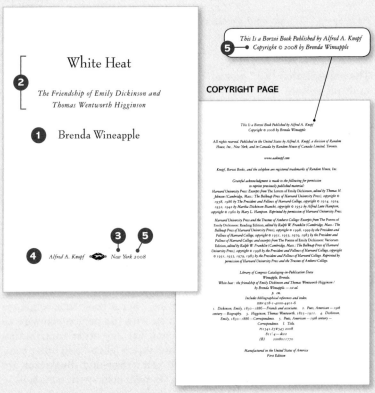

TITLE PAGE

White Heat

The Friendship of Emily Dickinson and
Thomas Wentworth Higginson

Brenda Wineapple

Alfred A. Knopf ━━ New York 2008

This Is a Borzoi Book Published by Alfred A. Knopf
Copyright © 2008 by Brenda Wineapple

COPYRIGHT PAGE

This Is a Borzoi Book Published by Alfred A. Knopf
Copyright © 2008 by Brenda Wineapple

All rights reserved. Published in the United States by Alfred A. Knopf, a division of Random
House, Inc., New York, and in Canada by Random House of Canada Limited, Toronto.

www.aaknopf.com

Knopf, Borzoi Books, and the colophon are registered trademarks of Random House, Inc.

WORKS CITED ENTRY FOR A PRINT BOOK

Wineapple, Brenda. *White Heat: The Friendship of Emily Dickinson and Thomas Wentworth Higginson.* New York: Knopf, 2008. Print.

For more on citing print books in MLA style, see pages 404–11.

21. Book with an author using a pseudonym Give the author's name as it appears on the title page (the pseudonym), and follow it with the author's real name in brackets.

Dinesen, Isak [Karen Blixen]. *Winter's Tales.* 1942. New York: Vintage, 1993. Print.

22. Book in a language other than English If your readers are not familiar with the language of the book, include a translation of the title, italicized and in brackets. Capitalize the title according to the conventions of the book's language, and give the original publication information.

Nemtsov, Boris, and Vladimir Milov. *Putin. Itogi. Nezavisimyi Ekspertnyi Doklad*

[*Putin. The Results: An Independent Expert Report*]. Moscow: Novaya Gazeta,

2008. Print.

23. Entire anthology An anthology is a collection of works on a common theme, often with different authors for the selections and usually with an editor for the entire volume. (For an anthology with one editor, use the abbreviation "ed." after the editor's name. For more than one editor, use "eds.")

Dumanis, Michael, and Cate Marvin, eds. *Legitimate Dangers: American Poets of the New*

Century. Louisville: Sarabande, 2006. Print.

24. One or more selections from an anthology

One selection from anthology

author of selection: title of
last name first   selection   title of anthology

Brouwer, Joel. "The Spots." *Legitimate Dangers: American Poets of the New Century.*

              editor(s) of anthology: city of   page(s) of
              name(s) in normal order   publication   publisher   date   selection

    Ed. Michael Dumanis and Cate Marvin. Louisville: Sarabande, 2006. 51-52.

medium

Print.

The abbreviation "Ed." means "Edited by," so it is the same for one or multiple editors. For an illustrated citation of a selection from an anthology, see pages 410–11.

Two or more selections, with separate anthology entry

If you use two or more works from the same anthology in your paper, provide an entry for the entire anthology (see item 23) and give a shortened entry for each selection. Use the medium only in the entry for the complete anthology. For an illustrated citation of a selection from an anthology, see pages 410–11.

author of   title of   editor(s) of anthology: pages(s)
selection   selection   last name(s) only   of selection

Brouwer, Joel. "The Spots." Dumanis and Marvin 51-52.

editor(s) of anthology   title of anthology

Dumanis, Michael, and Cate Marvin, eds. *Legitimate Dangers: American Poets of the*

city of
publication   publisher   date   medium

New Century. Louisville: Sarabande, 2006. Print.

author of   title of   editor(s) of anthology: page(s) of
selection   selection   last name(s) only   selection

Keith, Sally. "Orphean Song." Dumanis and Marvin 195-96.

25. Edition other than the first Include the number of the edition (1st, 2nd, 3rd, and so on). If the book has a translator or an editor in addition to the author, give the name of the translator or editor before the edition number, using the abbreviation "Trans." for "Translated by" (see item 18) or "Ed." for "Edited by" (see item 17).

Auletta, Ken. *The Underclass.* 2nd ed. Woodstock: Overlook, 2000. Print.

26. Multivolume work Include the total number of volumes before the city and publisher, using the abbreviation "vols." If the volumes were published over several years, give the inclusive dates of publication. The abbreviation "Ed." means "Edited by," so it is the same for one or multiple editors.

author: last   editor   total   city of   inclusive
name first   title   in normal order   volumes publication   publisher   dates

Stark, Freya. *Letters.* Ed. Lucy Moorehead. 8 vols. Salisbury: Compton, 1974-82.

medium

Print.

If you cite only one of the volumes in your paper, include the volume number before the city and publisher and give the date of publication for that volume. After the date, give the medium of publication followed by the total number of volumes.

author: last name first / title / editor: in normal order / volume cited / city of publication / publisher / date of volume / medium

Stark, Freya. *Letters*. Ed. Lucy Moorehead. Vol. 5. Salisbury: Compton, 1978. Print.

total volumes

8 vols.

27. Encyclopedia or dictionary entry List the author of the entry (if there is one), the title of the entry, the title of the reference work, the edition number (if any), the date of the edition, and the medium. Volume and page numbers are not necessary because the entries in the source are arranged alphabetically and are therefore easy to locate.

Posner, Rebecca. "Romance Languages." *The Encyclopaedia Britannica: Macropaedia*.

15th ed. 1987. Print.

"Sonata." *The American Heritage Dictionary of the English Language*. 4th ed. 2000. Print.

28. Sacred text Give the title of the sacred text (taken from the title page), italicized; the editor's or translator's name (if any); publication information; and the medium. Add the name of the version, if there is one.

The Oxford Annotated Bible with the Apocrypha. Ed. Herbert G. May and Bruce M.

Metzger. New York: Oxford UP, 1965. Print. Rev. Standard Vers.

The Qur'an: Translation. Trans. Abdullah Yusuf Ali. Elmhurst: Tahrike, 2000. Print.

29. Foreword, introduction, preface, or afterword

author of foreword: last name first / book part / book title

Bennett, Hal Zina. Foreword. *Shimmering Images: A Handy Little Guide to Writing*

author of book: in normal order / city of publication / imprint-publisher / date / page(s) of foreword

Memoir. By Lisa Dale Norton. New York: Griffin-St. Martin's, 2008. xiii-xvi.

medium

Print.

If the book part has a title, include it in quotation marks immediately after the author's name and before the label for the book part. If the author of the book part is also the author or editor of the complete work, give only the last name of the author the second time it is used.

Ozick, Cynthia. "Portrait of the Essay as a Warm Body." Introduction. *The Best American*

Essays 1998. Ed. Ozick. Boston: Houghton, 1998. xv-xxi. Print.

Citation at a glance: Selection from an anthology (MLA)

To cite a selection from a print anthology in MLA style, include the following elements:

1   Author of selection
2   Title of selection
3   Title and subtitle of anthology
4   Editor(s) of anthology

5   City of publication
6   Publisher
7   Date of publication
8   Page number(s) of selection
9   Medium

TITLE PAGE

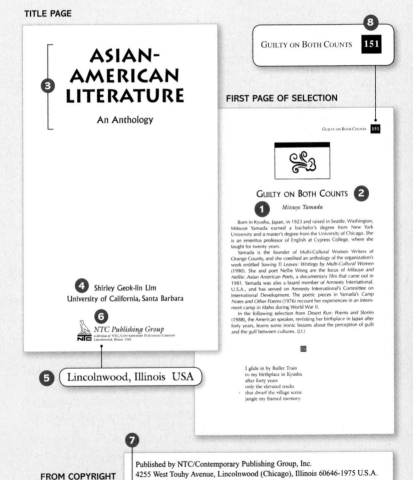

8
GUILTY ON BOTH COUNTS   **151**

ASIAN-AMERICAN LITERATURE

An Anthology

3

FIRST PAGE OF SELECTION

GUILTY ON BOTH COUNTS   151

GUILTY ON BOTH COUNTS   **2**

1   *Mitsuye Yamada*

Born in Kyushu, Japan, in 1923 and raised in Seattle, Washington, Mitsuye Yamada earned a bachelor's degree from New York University and a master's degree from the University of Chicago. She is an emeritus professor of English at Cypress College, where she taught for twenty years.

Yamada is the founder of Multi-Cultural Women Writers of Orange County, and she coedited an anthology of the organization's work entitled *Sowing Ti Leaves: Writings by Multi-Cultural Women* (1990). She and poet Nellie Wong are the focus of *Mitsuye and Nellie: Asian American Poets*, a documentary film that came out in 1981. Yamada was also a board member of Amnesty International, U.S.A., and has served on Amnesty International's Committee on International Development. The poetic pieces in Yamada's *Camp Notes and Other Poems* (1976) recount her experiences in an internment camp in Idaho during World War II.

In the following selection from *Desert Run: Poems and Stories* (1988), the American speaker, revisiting her birthplace in Japan after forty years, learns some ironic lessons about the perception of guilt and the gulf between cultures. (J.I.)

I glide in by Bullet Train
to my birthplace in Kyushu
after forty years
only the elevated tracks
that dwarf the village scene
jangle my framed memory.

4   Shirley Geok-lin Lim
University of California, Santa Barbara

6
NTC Publishing Group
a division of NTC/CONTEMPORARY PUBLISHING COMPANY
Lincolnwood, Illinois USA

5   Lincolnwood, Illinois USA

7

FROM COPYRIGHT PAGE

Published by NTC/Contemporary Publishing Group, Inc.
4255 West Touhy Avenue, Lincolnwood (Chicago), Illinois 60646-1975 U.S.A.
©2000 NTC/Contemporary Publishing Group, Inc.

WORKS CITED ENTRY FOR A SELECTION FROM AN ANTHOLOGY

```
       ┌──── 1 ────┐ ┌──── 2 ────────┐ ┌──────────── 3 ────────────┐
```
Yamada, Mitsuye. "Guilty on Both Counts." *Asian-American Literature: An Anthology.*

```
    ┌──────── 4 ────────┐ ┌──── 5 ───┐ ┌6┐┌7┐ ┌─8─┐ ┌─9─┐
```
Ed. Shirley Geok-lin Lim. Lincolnwood: NTC, 2000. 151-54. Print.

For more on citing selections from anthologies in MLA style, see pages 407–08.

30. Book with a title in its title If the book title contains a title normally italicized, neither italicize the internal title nor place it in quotation marks.

Woodson, Jon. *A Study of Joseph Heller's* Catch-22: *Going Around Twice*. New York: Lang,
   2001. Print.

If the title within the title is normally put in quotation marks, retain the quotation marks and italicize the entire book title.

Millás, Juan José. *"Personality Disorders" and Other Stories*. Trans. Gregory B. Kaplan.
   New York: MLA, 2007. Print. MLA Texts and Trans.

31. Book in a series After the publication information, give the medium of publication and then the series name as it appears on the title page, followed by the series number, if any.

Douglas, Dan. *Assessing Languages for Specific Purposes*. Cambridge: Cambridge UP,
   2000. Print. Cambridge Applied Linguistics Ser.

32. Republished book After the title of the book, give the original publication date, followed by the current publication information. If the republished book contains new material, such as an introduction or afterword, include information about the new material after the original date.

Trilling, Lionel. *The Liberal Imagination*. 1950. Introd. Louis Menand. New York: New
   York Review of Books, 2008. Print.

33. Publisher's imprint If a book was published by a division (an imprint) of a publishing company, give the name of the imprint, a hyphen, and the name of the publisher.

Ackroyd, Peter. *The Fall of Troy*. New York: Talese-Doubleday, 2007. Print.

Online sources

MLA guidelines assume that readers can locate most online sources by entering the author, title, or other identifying information in a search engine or a database. Consequently, the *MLA Handbook* does not require a Web address (URL) in citations for online sources. If your instructor requires one, see the note at the end of item 34.

MLA style calls for a sponsor or a publisher in works cited entries for most online sources. If a source has no sponsor or publisher, use the abbreviation "N.p." (for "No publisher") in the sponsor position. If there is no date of publication or update, use "n.d." (for "no date") after the sponsor. For an article in an online journal or an article from a database, give page numbers if they are available; if they are not, use the abbreviation "n. pag." (See item 37.)

34. Entire Web site

Web site with author

author: last name first | title of Web site | sponsor of site (personal page) | update | medium

Peterson, Susan Lynn. *The Life of Martin Luther.* Susan Lynn Peterson, 2005. Web.

date of access: day + month + year

24 Jan. 2009.

Web site with organization (group) as author

organization name: not abbreviated | title of Web site | sponsor: abbreviated | update | medium

American Library Association. *American Library Association.* ALA, 2008. Web.

date of access: day + month + year

14 Jan. 2009.

Web site with no author

title of Web site | sponsor of site | update | medium

Margaret Sanger Papers Project. History Dept., New York U, 18 Oct. 2000. Web.

date of access: day + month + year

6 Jan. 2009.

Web site with editor

See item 19 (p. 405) for listing the name(s) of editor(s).

Halsall, Paul, ed. *Internet Modern History Sourcebook.* Fordham U, 22 Sept. 2001. Web.

19 Jan. 2009.

Web site with no title

Use the label "Home page" or another appropriate description in place
of a title.

Yoon, Mina. Home page. Oak Ridge Natl. Laboratory, 28 Dec. 2006. Web. 12 Jan. 2009.

NOTE: If your instructor requires a URL for Web sources, include the
URL, enclosed in angle brackets, at the end of the entry. When a URL in
a works cited entry must be divided at the end of a line, break it after a
slash. Do not insert a hyphen.

Peterson, Susan Lynn. *The Life of Martin Luther.* Susan Lynn Peterson, 2005. Web. 24 Jan.

2009. <http://www.susanlynnpeterson.com/index_files/luther.htm>.

35. Short work from a Web site   Short works include articles, poems,
and other documents that are not book length or that appear as internal pages on a Web site. For an illustrated citation of a short work from
a Web site, see pages 414–15.

Short work with author

author: last name first	title of short work	title of Web site	sponsor	no update date	medium

Shiva, Vandana. "Bioethics: A Third World Issue." *NativeWeb.* NativeWeb, n.d. Web.

date of access: day + month + year

22 Jan. 2010.

Short work with no author

title of short work	title of Web site	sponsor of site	update	medium	date of access: day + month + year

"Sister Aimee." *American Experience.* PBS Online, 2 Apr. 2007. Web. 30 Oct. 2010.

36. Web site with an author using a pseudonym   Begin the entry
with the pseudonym and add the author's or creator's real name, if
known, in brackets. Follow with the information required for a Web
site or a short work from a Web site (see item 34 or 35).

Grammar Girl [Mignon Fogarty]. "What Is the Plural of 'Mouse'?" *Grammar Girl: Quick and*

Dirty Tips for Better Writing. Holtzbrinck, 16 Sept. 2008. Web. 10 Nov. 2010.

37. Article in an online journal

author: last name first	article title

Mason, John Edwin. "'Mannenberg': Notes on the Making of an Icon and Anthem."

journal title	volume, issue	year	not paginated	medium	date of access: day + month + year

African Studies Quarterly 9.4 (2007): n. pag. Web. 23 Feb. 2010.

Citation at a glance: Short work from a Web site (MLA)

To cite a short work from a Web site in MLA style, include the following elements:

1 Author of short work (if any)
2 Title of short work
3 Title of Web site
4 Sponsor of Web site ("N.p." if none)

5 Update date ("n.d." if none)
6 Medium
7 Date you accessed the source

INTERNAL PAGE OF WEB SITE

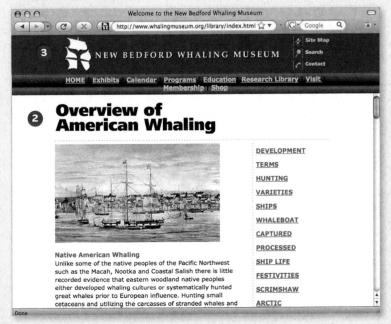

Welcome to the New Bedford Whaling Museum

http://www.whalingmuseum.org/library/index.html

3 NEW BEDFORD WHALING MUSEUM

Site Map
Search
Contact

HOME Exhibits Calendar Programs Education Research Library Visit
Membership Shop

2 **Overview of American Whaling**

DEVELOPMENT
TERMS
HUNTING
VARIETIES
SHIPS
WHALEBOAT
CAPTURED
PROCESSED
SHIP LIFE
FESTIVITIES
SCRIMSHAW
ARCTIC

Native American Whaling
Unlike some of the native peoples of the Pacific Northwest such as the Macah, Nootka and Coastal Salish there is little recorded evidence that eastern woodland native peoples either developed whaling cultures or systematically hunted great whales prior to European influence. Hunting small cetaceans and utilizing the carcasses of stranded whales and

FOOTER ON HOME PAGE

the local area. It houses the most extensive collection of art, artifacts, and manuscripts pertaining to American whaling in the age of sail - late eighteenth century to the early twentieth, when sailing ships dominated merchant trade and whaling.

18 Johnny Cake Hill | New Bedford, MA | 02740-6398 | Tel. (508) 997-0046
Fax: (508) 997-0018 | Library Fax: (508) 207-1064

5 ©Copyright 2009 Old Dartmouth Historical Society / New Bedford Whaling Museum **4**

WORKS CITED ENTRY FOR A SHORT WORK FROM A WEB SITE

┌─────────── 2 ───────────┐ ┌─────────── 3 ───────────┐ ┌────── 4 ──────┐
"Overview of American Whaling." *New Bedford Whaling Museum.* Old Dartmouth Hist.

┌─────── 5 ─┐ ┌─ 6 ─┐ ┌── 7 ──┐
Soc./New Bedford Whaling Museum, 2009. Web. 27 Oct. 2009.

For more on citing sources from Web sites in MLA style, see pages 412–13.

38. Article in an online magazine Give the author; the title of the
article, in quotation marks; the title of the magazine, italicized;
the sponsor or publisher of the site (use "N.p." if there is none); the date of
publication; the medium; and your date of access.

Burton, Robert. "The Certainty Epidemic." *Salon.com.* Salon Media Group, 29 Feb. 2008.

Web. 18 Jan. 2010.

39. Article in an online newspaper Give the author; the title of the
article, in quotation marks; the title of the newspaper, italicized;
the sponsor or publisher of the site (use "N.p." if there is none); the date of
publication; the medium; and your date of access.

Smith, Andrew D. "Poll: More than 70% of US Workers Use Internet on the Job."

Dallasnews.com. Dallas Morning News, 25 Sept. 2008. Web. 29 Sept. 2008.

40. Work from a database For a source retrieved from a library's
subscription database, first list the publication information for the
source (see items 7–15) and then provide information about the database. For an illustrated citation of an article from a database, see
page 416.

author of source: title of   volume,
last name first   article   journal title   issue   year   page(s)
┌───────────┐ ┌───────┐ ┌──────────────┐ ┌───┐ ┌────┐ ┌──────┐
Heyen, William. "Sunlight." *American Poetry Review* 36.2 (2007): 55-56. *Expanded*

date of access:
database name   medium day + month + year
┌───────────┐ ┌───┐ ┌──────────────┐
Academic ASAP. Web. 24 Mar. 2010.

Barrera, Rebeca María. "A Case for Bilingual Education." *Scholastic Parent and Child*

Nov.-Dec. 2004: 72-73. *Academic Search Premier.* Web. 1 Feb. 2009.

Williams, Jeffrey J. "Why Today's Publishing World Is Reprising the Past." *Chronicle*

of Higher Education 13 June 2008: n. pag. *LexisNexis Academic.* Web.

29 Sept. 2009.

Citation at a glance: Article from a database (MLA)

To cite an article from a database in MLA style, include the following elements:

1 Author of article
2 Title of article
3 Title of periodical
4 Volume and issue numbers (for journal)
5 Date or year of publication

6 Page number(s) of article ("n. pag." if none)
7 Name of database
8 Medium
9 Date you accessed the source

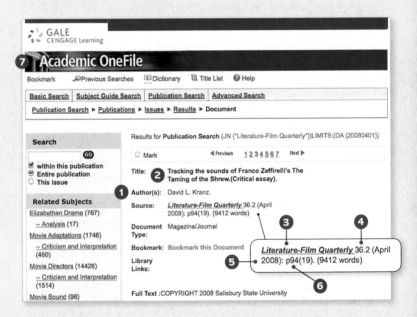

WORKS CITED ENTRY FOR AN ARTICLE FROM A DATABASE

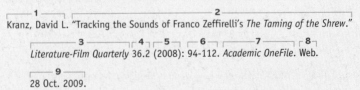

Kranz, David L. "Tracking the Sounds of Franco Zeffirelli's *The Taming of the Shrew*."

Literature-Film Quarterly 36.2 (2008): 94-112. *Academic OneFile*. Web.

28 Oct. 2009.

For more on citing articles from a database in MLA style, see item 40.

41. Online book-length work   Cite an online book or an online book-length work, such as a play or a long poem, as you would a short work from a Web site (see item 35), but italicize the title of the work.

author: last
name first   title of long poem   title of Web site   sponsor of site   update medium

Milton, John. *Paradise Lost: Book I. Poetryfoundation.org.* Poetry Foundation, 2008. Web.

    date of access:
    day + month + year

    14 Dec. 2009.

Give the print publication information for the work, if available (see items 16–33), followed by the title of the Web site, the medium, and your date of access.

author: last
name first   book title   editor of original book

Jacobs, Harriet A. *Incidents in the Life of a Slave Girl: Written by Herself.* Ed. L. Maria Child.

   city of
   publication   year   title of Web site   medium   date of access:
   day + month + year

    Boston, 1861. *Documenting the American South.* Web. 3 Feb. 2010.

42. Part of an online book   Begin as for a part of a print book (see item 29 on p. 409). If the online book part has no page numbers, use "N. pag." following the publication information. End with the Web site on which the work is found, the medium, and your date of access.

Adams, Henry. "Diplomacy." *The Education of Henry Adams.* Boston: Houghton, 1918.

    N. pag. *Bartleby.com: Great Books Online.* Web. 8 Jan. 2010.

43. Digital archives   Digital archives are online collections of documents or records—books, letters, photographs, data—that have been converted to digital form. Cite publication information for the original document, if it is available, using the models throughout section MLA-4b. Then give the location of the document, if any, neither italicized nor in quotation marks; the name of the archive, italicized; the medium ("Web"); and your date of access.

Fiore, Mark. *Shockwaves.* 18 Oct. 2001. *September 11 Digital Archive.* Web. 3 Apr. 2009.

Oblinger, Maggie. Letter to Charlie Thomas. 31 Mar. 1895. Nebraska State Hist. Soc.

    Prairie Settlement: Nebraska Photographs and Family Letters, 1862-1912. Web.

    3 Nov. 2009.

WPA Household Census for 1047 W. 50th Street, Los Angeles County. 1939. USC Lib. Spec.

    Collections. *USC Libraries Digital Archive.* Web. 12 Mar. 2010.

44. Entry in an online reference work Give the author of the entry, if there is one. Otherwise begin with the title of the entry, in quotation marks. Then give the title of the site; the sponsor and the update date (use "n.d." if there is none); the medium; and your date of access.

"Native American Church." *Britannica*. Encyclopaedia Britannica, 2008. Web. 29 Jan.

2010.

45. Online poem Cite as you would a short work from a Web site (item 35) or part of an online book (item 42).

Bell, Acton [Anne Brontë]. "Mementos." *Poems by Currer, Ellis, and Acton Bell*.

London, 1846. N. pag. *A Celebration of Women Writers*. Web. 18 Sept. 2009.

46. Entire blog (Weblog) Cite a blog as you would an entire Web site (see item 34).

Gristmill. Grist Magazine, 2008. Web. 19 Jan. 2009.

47. Entry or comment in a blog (Weblog) Cite an entry or a comment (a response to an entry) in a blog as you would a short work from a Web site (see item 35). If the comment or entry has no title, use the label "Weblog entry" or "Weblog comment." Follow with the remaining information as for an entire blog in item 46.

"Social Media: Facebook and MySpace as University Curricula." *Open Education*. Open

Education.net, n.d. Web. 19 Sept. 2008.

Cynthia. Weblog comment. *Open Education*. Open Education.net, 8 Jan. 2010. Web.

14 Feb. 2010.

48. Academic course or department home page Cite as a short work from a Web site (see item 35). For a course home page, begin with the name of the instructor and the title of the course or title of the page (use "Course home page" if there is no other title). For a department home page, begin with the name of the department and the label "Dept. home page."

Marrone, Carole. "355:301: College Writing and Research." *Rutgers School of Arts and*

Sciences. Writing Program, Rutgers U, 2010. Web. 19 Mar. 2010.

Comparative Media Studies. Dept. home page. *Massachusetts Institute of Technology*.

MIT, 2010. Web. 6 Feb. 2010.

online sources • dictionary, encyclopedia • poem • blog • course
home page • video clip • abstract • editorial • review • e-mail

MLA-4b   **419**

49. Online video clip   Cite as you would a short work from a Web site (see item 35).

author: last
name first   video title   title of Web site   sponsor   update   medium

Murphy, Beth. "Tips for a Good Profile Piece." *YouTube*. YouTube, 7 Sept. 2008. Web.

date of access:
day + month + year

19 Apr. 2010.

50. Online abstract   Cite as you would an abstract of a journal article (see item 11), giving whatever print information is available, followed by the medium and your date of access. If you found the abstract in an online periodical database, include the name of the database after the print publication information (see item 40).

Turner, Fred. "Romantic Automatism: Art, Technology, and Collaborative Labor in

Cold War America." Abstract. *Journal of Visual Culture* 7.1 (2008): 5. Web.

25 Oct. 2009.

51. Online editorial or letter to the editor   Cite as you would an editorial or a letter to the editor in a print publication (see item 13 or 14), followed by information for a short work from a Web site (see item 35).

"Compromise Is Key with Religion at Work." Editorial. *StarTribune.com*. Star Tribune,

18 June 2008. Web. 25 June 2008.

52. Online review   Begin the entry as you would for a review in a magazine or newspaper (see item 15). If the review is published in print as well as online, first give publication information as for an article in a periodical (see items 7–10). Then add the Web site on which the review appears, the medium ("Web"), and your date of access. If the review is published only on the Web, give the information required for a short work from a Web site (see item 35). If you found the review in a database, cite as in item 40.

Greer, W. R. "Who's the Fairest One of All?" Rev. of *Mirror, Mirror*, by Gregory Maguire.

Reviewsofbooks.com. Reviewsofbooks.com, 2003. Web. 26 Oct. 2009.

53. E-mail message   Begin with the writer's name and the subject line. Then write "Message to" followed by the name of the recipient. End with the date of the message and the medium ("E-mail").

Lowe, Walter. "Review Questions." Message to the author. 15 Mar. 2010. E-mail.

54. Posting to an online discussion list When possible, cite archived versions of postings. If you cannot locate an archived version, keep a copy of the posting for your records. Begin with the author's name, followed by the title or subject line, in quotation marks (use the label "Online posting" if the posting has no title). Then proceed as for a short work from a Web site (see item 35).

Fainton, Peter. "Re: Backlash against New Labour." *Media Lens Message Board*. Media

Lens, 7 May 2008. Web. 2 June 2008.

55. Entry in a wiki A wiki is an online reference that is openly edited by its users. Treat an entry in a wiki as you would a short work from a Web site (see item 35). Because wiki content is, by definition, collectively edited and can be updated frequently, do not include an author. Give the title of the entry; the name of the wiki, italicized; the sponsor or publisher of the wiki (use "N.p." if there is none); the date of the last update; the medium; and your date of access.

"Hip Hop Music." *Wikipedia*. Wikimedia Foundation, 2 Mar. 2010. Web. 18 Mar. 2010.

"Negation in Languages." *UniLang Wiki*. UniLang, 12 Jan. 2009. Web. 9 Mar. 2010.

Audio and visual sources (including online versions)

56. Digital file A digital file is any document or image that exists in digital form, independent of a Web site. To cite a digital file, begin with information required for the source (such as a photograph, a report, a sound recording, or a radio program), following the guidelines throughout MLA-4b. Then for the medium, indicate the type of file: "JPEG file," "PDF file," "MP3 file," and so on.

photographer	photograph title	date of composition	location of photograph

Hine, Lewis W. *Girl in Cherryville Mill*. 1908. Prints and Photographs Div., Lib. of Cong.

medium: file type

JPEG file.

"Scenes from a Recession." *This American Life*. Narr. Ira Glass. NPR, 30 Mar. 2009.

MP3 file.

National Institute of Mental Health. *What Rescue Workers Can Do*. Washington: US Dept.

of Health and Human Services, 2006. PDF file.

57. Podcast If you view or listen to a podcast online, cite it as you would a short work from a Web site (see item 35). If you download the podcast and view or listen to it on a computer or portable player, cite it as a digital file (see item 56).

Podcast online

"Calculating the Demand for Charter Schools." Narr. David Guenthner. *Texas PolicyCast*.

Texas Public Policy Foundation, 28 Aug. 2008. Web. 10 Jan. 2009.

Podcast downloaded as digital file

"Calculating the Demand for Charter Schools." Narr. David Guenthner. *Texas PolicyCast*.

Texas Public Policy Foundation, 28 Aug. 2008. MP3 file.

58. Musical score For print and online, begin with the composer's name; the title of the work, italicized (unless it is named by form, number, and key); and the date of composition. For a print source, give the place, publisher, date of publication, and medium. For an online source, give the title of the Web site; the publisher or sponsor; the date of Web publication; the medium; and your date of access.

Handel, G. F. *Messiah: An Oratorio*. N.d. *CCARH Publications: Scores and Parts*. Center for

Computer Assisted Research in the Humanities, 2003. Web. 5 Jan. 2009.

59. Sound recording Begin with the name of the person you want to emphasize: the composer, conductor ("Cond."), or performer ("Perf."). For a long work, give the title, italicized (unless it is named by form, number, and key); the names of pertinent artists (such as performers, readers, or musicians); and the orchestra and conductor, if relevant. End with the manufacturer, the date, and the medium.

Bizet, Georges. *Carmen*. Perf. Jennifer Laramore, Thomas Moser, Angela Gheorghiu,

and Samuel Ramey. Bavarian State Orch. and Chorus. Cond. Giuseppe Sinopoli.

Warner, 1996. CD.

For a song, put the title in quotation marks. If you include the name of the album or CD, italicize it.

Blige, Mary J. "Be without You." *The Breakthrough*. Geffen, 2005. CD.

60. Film Typically, begin with the title, italicized, followed by the director and lead actors ("Perf.") or narrator ("Narr."); the distributor; the year of the film's release; and the medium ("Film," "Videocassette").

If your paper emphasizes a person involved with the film, you may begin with that person, as in the first example in item 61.

movie title   director   major performers

Frozen River. Dir. Courtney Hunt. Perf. Melissa Leo, Charlie McDermott, and Misty Upham.

             release
distributor date medium

Sony, 2008. Film.

61. DVD   For a film on DVD, cite as you would a film, giving "DVD" as the medium. If you are citing the film as a whole, use the model in item 60. If your paper emphasizes a particular person, begin with that person's name and title, as shown here.

Forster, Marc, dir. *Finding Neverland*. Perf. Johnny Depp, Kate Winslet, Julie Christie,

Radha Mitchell, and Dustin Hoffman. Miramax, 2004. DVD.

For any other work on DVD, such as an educational work or a game, cite as you would a film, giving whatever information is available about the author, director, distributor, and so on.

Across the Drafts: Students and Teachers Talk about Feedback. Harvard Expository Writing

Program, 2005. DVD.

62. Special feature on a DVD   Begin with the title of the feature, in quotation marks, and the names of any important contributors, as for films or DVDs (item 60 or 61). End with information about the DVD, as in item 61, including the disc number, if any.

"Sweeney's London." Prod. Eric Young. *Sweeney Todd: The Demon Barber of Fleet Street*.

Dir. Tim Burton. DreamWorks, 2007. DVD. Disc 2.

63. CD-ROM   At the end, add the medium ("CD-ROM").

"Pimpernel." *The American Heritage Dictionary of the English Language*. 4th ed. Boston:

Houghton, 2000. CD-ROM.

64. Computer software or video game   List the developer or author of the software (if any); the title, italicized; the distributor and date of publication; and the platform or medium.

Firaxis Games. *Sid Meier's Civilization Revolution*. Take-Two Interactive, 2008. Xbox 360.

65. Radio or television program   Begin with the title of the radio segment or television episode (if there is one), in quotation marks. Then give the title of the program or series, italicized; relevant information about the program, such as the writer ("By"), director ("Dir."), performers ("Perf."), or narrator ("Narr."); the network; the local station (if any) and location; the date of broadcast; and the medium ("Television," "Radio"). For a program you accessed online, after the information about the program give the network, the original broadcast date, the title of the Web site, the medium ("Web"), and your date of access.

"Machines of the Gods." *Ancient Discoveries*. History Channel. 14 Oct. 2008. Television.

"Elif Shafak: Writing under a Watchful Eye." *Fresh Air*. Narr. Terry Gross. Natl. Public

Radio, 6 Feb. 2007. *NPR.org*. Web. 22 Feb. 2009.

66. Radio or television interview   Begin with the name of the person who was interviewed, followed by the word "Interview" and the interviewer's name, if relevant. End with information about the program as in item 65.

De Niro, Robert, Barry Levinson, and Art Linson. Interview by Charlie Rose. *Charlie Rose*.

PBS. WGBH, Boston, 13 Oct. 2008. Television.

67. Live performance   For a live performance of a concert, a play, a ballet, or an opera, begin with the title of the work performed, italicized. Then give the author or composer of the work ("By"); relevant information such as the director ("Dir."), the choreographer ("Chor."), the conductor ("Cond."), or the major performers ("Perf."); the orchestra or the theater, ballet, or opera company, if any; the theater and location; the date of the performance; and the label "Performance."

The Brothers Size. By Tarell Alvin McCraney. Dir. Bijan Sheibani. Young Vic Theatre,

London. 15 Oct. 2008. Performance.

Symphony no. 4 in G. By Gustav Mahler. Cond. Mark Wigglesworth. Perf. Juliane Banse

and Boston Symphony Orch. Symphony Hall, Boston. 17 Apr. 2009. Performance.

68. Lecture or public address   Begin with the speaker's name, followed by the title of the lecture (if any), in quotation marks; the organization sponsoring the lecture; the location; the date; and a label such as "Lecture" or "Address."

Wellbery, David E. "On a Sentence of Franz Kafka." Franke Inst. for the Humanities.

Gleacher Center, Chicago. 1 Feb. 2006. Lecture.

69. Work of art   Cite the artist's name; the title of the artwork, italicized; the date of composition; the medium of composition (for instance, "Lithograph on paper," "Photograph," "Charcoal on paper"); and the institution and city in which the artwork is located. For artworks found online, omit the medium of composition and include the title of the Web site, the medium ("Web"), and your date of access.

Constable, John. *Dedham Vale*. 1802. Oil on canvas. Victoria and Albert Museum,
London.

Hessing, Valjean. *Caddo Myth*. 1976. Joslyn Art Museum, Omaha. *Joslyn Art Museum*.
Web. 19 Apr. 2009.

70. Cartoon Give the cartoonist's name; the title of the cartoon, if it has one, in quotation marks; the label "Cartoon" or "Comic strip"; publication information; and the medium. To cite an online cartoon, instead of publication information give the title of the Web site, the sponsor or publisher, the medium, and your date of access.

Keefe, Mike. "Veterans Affairs Overruns." Cartoon. *Denverpost.com*. Denver Post, 11 Oct.
2009. Web. 12 Dec. 2009.

71. Advertisement Name the product or company being advertised, followed by the word "Advertisement." Give publication information for the source in which the advertisement appears.

Truth by Calvin Klein. Advertisement. *Vogue* Dec. 2000: 95-98. Print.

Arbella Insurance. Advertisement. *Boston.com*. NY Times, n.d. Web. 3 Sept. 2009.

72. Map or chart Cite a map or a chart as you would a book or a short work within a longer work. Use the word "Map" or "Chart" following the title. Add the medium and, for an online source, the sponsor or publisher and the date of access.

Joseph, Lori, and Bob Laird. "Driving While Phoning Is Dangerous." Chart. *USA Today*
16 Feb. 2001: 1A. Print.

"Serbia." Map. *Syrena Maps*. Syrena, 2 Feb. 2001. Web. 17 Mar. 2009.

Other sources (including online versions)

This section includes a variety of sources not covered elsewhere. For online sources, consult the appropriate model in this section and also see items 34–55.

73. Government document Treat the government agency as the author, giving the name of the government followed by the name of the department and the agency, if any. For print sources, add the medium at the end of the entry. For online sources, follow the model for an entire Web site (item 34) or a short work from a Web site (item 35).

government   department   agency

United States. Dept. of the Interior. Office of Inspector General. "Excessive

document title

Indulgences: Personal Use of the Internet at the Department of the Interior."

                                              publication
Web site title   publisher/sponsor   date   medium

Office of Inspector General. Dept. of the Interior, Sept. 1999. Web.

date of access:
day + month + year

20 May 2010.

Canada. Minister of Indian Affairs and Northern Dev. *Gathering Strength: Canada's*
    Aboriginal Action Plan. Ottawa: Minister of Public Works and Govt. Services Can.,
    2000. Print.

74. Historical document   To cite a historical document, such as the US Constitution or the Canadian Charter of Rights and Freedoms, begin with the document author, if it has one, and then give the document title, neither italicized nor in quotation marks, and the document date. For a print version, continue as for a selection in an anthology (see item 24) or for a book (with the title not italicized). For an online version, cite as a short work from a Web site (see item 35).

Jefferson, Thomas. First Inaugural Address. 1801. *The American Reader*. Ed. Diane
    Ravitch. New York: Harper, 1990. 42-44. Print.

The Virginia Declaration of Rights. 1776. *A Chronology of US Historical Documents*.
    U of Oklahoma Coll. of Law, 2008. Web. 23 Feb. 2009.

75. Legal source

Legislative act (law)

Begin with the name of the act, neither italicized nor in quotation marks. Then provide the act's Public Law number; its Statutes at Large volume and page numbers; its date of enactment; and the medium of publication.

Electronic Freedom of Information Act Amendments of 1996. Pub. L. 104-231. 110 Stat.
    3048. 2 Oct. 1996. Print.

Court case

Name the first plaintiff and the first defendant. Then give the volume, name, and page numbers of the law report; the court name; the year of the decision; and publication information. Do not italicize the name of the case. (In the text of the paper, the name of the case is italicized; see item 19 on p. 395.)

Utah v. Evans. 536 US 452. Supreme Court of the US. 2002. *Supreme Court Collection.*
    Legal Information Inst., Cornell U Law School, n.d. Web. 30 Apr. 2008.

76. Pamphlet or brochure   Cite as you would a book (see items 16–33).

Commonwealth of Massachusetts. Dept. of Jury Commissioner. *A Few Facts about Jury
    Duty.* Boston: Commonwealth of Massachusetts, 2004. Print.

77. Unpublished dissertation   Begin with the author's name, followed by the dissertation title in quotation marks; the abbreviation "Diss."; the name of the institution; the year the dissertation was accepted; and the medium of the dissertation.

Jackson, Shelley. "Writing Whiteness: Contemporary Southern Literature in Black and
    White." Diss. U of Maryland, 2000. Print.

78. Published dissertation   For dissertations that have been published in book form, italicize the title. After the title and before the book's publication information, give the abbreviation "Diss.," the name of the institution, and the year the dissertation was accepted. Add the medium of publication at the end.

Damberg, Cheryl L. *Healthcare Reform: Distributional Consequences of an Employer
    Mandate for Workers in Small Firms.* Diss. Rand Graduate School, 1995. Santa
    Monica: Rand, 1996. Print.

79. Abstract of a dissertation   Cite an abstract as you would an unpublished dissertation. After the dissertation date, give the abbreviation *DA* or *DAI* (for *Dissertation Abstracts* or *Dissertation Abstracts International*), followed by the volume and issue numbers; the year of publication; inclusive page numbers or, if the abstract is not numbered, the item number; and the medium of publication. For an abstract accessed in an online database, give the item number in place of the page number, followed by the name of the database, the medium, and your date of access.

Chen, Shu-Ling. "Mothers and Daughters in Morrison, Tan, Marshall, and Kincaid." Diss.
    U of Washington, 2000. *DAI* 61.6 (2000): AAT9975963. *ProQuest Dissertations and
    Theses.* Web. 22 Feb. 2009.

80. Published proceedings of a conference   Cite as you would a book, adding the name, date, and location of the conference after the title.

Urgo, Joseph R., and Ann J. Abadie, eds. *Faulkner and Material Culture*. Proc. of Faulkner
and Yoknapatawpha Conf., 25-29 July 2004, U of Mississippi. Jackson: UP of
Mississippi, 2007. Print.

81. Paper in conference proceedings   Cite as you would a selection in an anthology (see item 24), giving information about the conference after the title and editors of the conference proceedings (see item 80).

Henninger, Katherine R. "Faulkner, Photography, and a Regional Ethics of Form."
Faulkner and Material Culture. Ed. Joseph R. Urgo and Ann J. Abadie. Proc. of
Faulkner and Yoknapatawpha Conf., 25-29 July 2004, U of Mississippi. Jackson:
UP of Mississippi, 2007. 121-38. Print.

82. Published interview   Name the person interviewed, followed by the title of the interview (if there is one). If the interview does not have a title, include the word "Interview" after the interviewee's name. Give publication information for the work in which the interview was published.

Simon, David. "Beyond the Choir: An Interview with David Simon." *Film Quarterly* 62.2
(2008/2009): 44-49. Print.

If you wish to include the name of the interviewer, put it after the title of the interview (or after the name of the interviewee if there is no title).

Florida, Richard. "The Great Reset." Interview by Conor Clarke. *Atlantic*. Atlantic Monthly
Group, Feb. 2009. Web. 28 Feb. 2010.

83. Personal interview   To cite an interview that you conducted, begin with the name of the person interviewed. Then write "Personal interview" or "Telephone interview," followed by the date of the interview.

Akufo, Dautey. Personal interview. 11 Apr. 2010.

84. Personal letter   To cite a letter that you received, begin with the writer's name and add the phrase "Letter to the author," followed by the date. Add the medium ("MS" for "manuscript," or a handwritten letter; "TS" for "typescript," or a typed letter).

Primak, Shoshana. Letter to the author. 6 May 2010. TS.

85. Published letter Begin with the writer of the letter, the words "Letter to" and the recipient, and the date of the letter (use "N.d." if the letter is undated). Then add the title of the collection and proceed as for a selection in an anthology (see item 24).

Wharton, Edith. Letter to Henry James. 28 Feb. 1915. *Henry James and Edith Wharton:*

   Letters, 1900-1915. Ed. Lyall H. Powers. New York: Scribner's, 1990. 323-26.

   Print.

86. Manuscript Give the author, a title or a description of the manuscript, and the date of composition, followed by the abbreviation "MS" for "manuscript" (handwritten) or "TS" for "typescript." Add the name and location of the institution housing the material. For a manuscript found online, give the preceding information but omit "MS" or "TS." Then list the title of the Web site, the medium ("Web"), and your date of access.

Arendt, Hannah. *Between Past and Present.* N.d. 1st draft. Hannah Arendt Papers.

   MS Div., Lib. of Cong. *Manuscript Division, Library of Congress.* Web. 24 Apr. 2009.

MLA-4c MLA information notes (optional)

Researchers who use the MLA system of parenthetical documentation may also use information notes for one of two purposes:

1. to provide additional material that is important but might interrupt the flow of the paper
2. to refer to several sources that support a single point or to provide comments on sources

Information notes may be either footnotes or endnotes. Footnotes appear at the foot of the page; endnotes appear on a separate page at the end of the paper, just before the list of works cited. For either style, the notes are numbered consecutively throughout the paper. The text of the paper contains a raised arabic numeral that corresponds to the number of the note.

TEXT

In the past several years, employees have filed a number of lawsuits against

employers because of online monitoring practices.[1]

NOTE

   1. For a discussion of federal law applicable to electronic surveillance in the

workplace, see Kesan 293.

MLA-5 MLA manuscript format; student research process and sample paper

The following guidelines are consistent with advice given in the *MLA Handbook for Writers of Research Papers*, 7th ed. (New York: MLA, 2009), and with typical requirements for student papers. For a sample MLA paper, see pages 436–40.

MLA-5a MLA manuscript format

Formatting the paper

Papers written in MLA style should be formatted as follows.

Materials and font   Use good-quality 8½″ × 11″ white paper. If your instructor does not require a specific font, choose one that is standard and easy to read (such as Times New Roman).

Title and identification   MLA does not require a title page. On the first page of your paper, place your name, your instructor's name, the course title, and the date on separate lines against the left margin. Then center your title. (See p. 436 for a sample first page.)

If your instructor requires a title page, ask for formatting guidelines. A format similar to the one on page 532 may be acceptable.

Pagination   Put the page number preceded by your last name in the upper right corner of each page, one-half inch below the top edge. Use arabic numerals (1, 2, 3, and so on).

Margins, line spacing, and paragraph indents   Leave margins of one inch on all sides of the page. Left-align the text.

Double-space throughout the paper. Do not add extra space above or below the title of the paper or between paragraphs.

Indent the first line of each paragraph one-half inch from the left margin.

Capitalization and italics   In titles of works, capitalize all words except articles (*a, an, the*), prepositions (*to, from, between,* and so on), coordinating conjunctions (*and, but, or, nor, for, so, yet*), and the *to* in infinitives — unless they are the first or last word of the title or subtitle. Follow these guidelines in your paper even if the title appears in all capital or all lowercase letters in the source.

In the text of an MLA paper, when a complete sentence follows a colon, lowercase the first word following the colon unless the sentence is a direct quotation or a well-known expression or principle. (See the examples in item 1 on p. 390.)

Italicize the titles of books, periodicals, and other long works, such as Web sites. Use quotation marks around the titles of periodical articles, short stories, poems, and other short works. (If your instructor prefers underlining, use it consistently in place of italics.)

Long quotations   When a quotation is longer than four typed lines of prose or three lines of verse, set it off from the text by indenting the entire quotation one inch from the left margin. Double-space the indented quotation, and do not add extra space above or below it.

Quotation marks are not needed when a quotation has been set off from the text by indenting. See page 436 for an example.

URLs (Web addresses)   When you need to break a URL at the end of a line in the text of your paper, break it only after a slash and do not insert a hyphen. For MLA rules on dividing URLs in your list of works cited, see page 431.

Headings   MLA neither encourages nor discourages the use of headings and provides no guidelines for their use. If you would like to insert headings in a long essay or research paper, check first with your instructor.

Visuals   MLA classifies visuals as tables and figures (figures include graphs, charts, maps, photographs, and drawings). Label each table with an arabic numeral ("Table 1," "Table 2," and so on) and provide a clear caption that identifies the subject. Capitalize the caption as you would a title (see P8-c); do not italicize the label and caption or place them in quotation marks. The label and caption should appear on separate lines above the table, flush with the left margin.

For a table that you have borrowed or adapted, give the source below the table in a note like the following:

Source: David N. Greenfield and Richard A. Davis; "Lost in Cyberspace: The Web @ Work"; *CyberPsychology and Behavior* 5.4 (2002): 349; print.

For each figure, place the figure number (using the abbreviation "Fig.") and a caption below the figure, flush left. Capitalize the caption as you would a sentence; include source information following the caption. (When referring to the figure in your paper, use the abbreviation "fig." in parenthetical citations; otherwise spell out the word.) See page 439 for an example of a figure in a paper.

Place visuals in the text, as close as possible to the sentences that relate to them, unless your instructor prefers that visuals appear in an appendix.

Preparing the list of works cited

Begin the list of works cited on a new page at the end of the paper. Center the title "Works Cited" about one inch from the top of the page. Double-space throughout. See page 440 for a sample list of works cited.

Alphabetizing the list   Alphabetize the list by the last names of the authors (or editors); if a work has no author or editor, alphabetize by the first word of the title other than *A, An,* or *The.*

If your list includes two or more works by the same author, use the author's name for the first entry only. For subsequent entries, use three hyphens followed by a period. List the titles in alphabetical order. (See item 6 on p. 401.)

Indenting   Do not indent the first line of each works cited entry, but indent any additional lines one-half inch. This technique highlights the beginning of each entry, making it easy for readers to scan the alphabetized list. See page 440.

URLs (Web addresses)   If you need to include a URL in a works cited entry and it must be divided across lines, break the URL only after a slash. Do not insert a hyphen at the end of the line. Insert angle brackets around the URL. (See the note following item 34 on p. 413.) If your word processing program automatically turns URLs into links (by underlining them and changing the color), turn off this feature.

MLA-5b Highlights of one student's research process

The following pages describe key steps in student writer Anna Orlov's research process, from selecting a research question to documenting sources. At each step, cross-references in the margins point to more discussion and examples elsewhere in the handbook. Samples from Orlov's process illustrate strategies and skills she used to create an accurate and effective essay. See pages 436–40 for Orlov's final paper.

Making the most of your handbook
Highlights of one student's research process (MLA style)

Anna Orlov, a student in a composition class, was assigned a research essay related to technology and the American workplace. The assignment called for her to use a variety of print and electronic sources and to follow MLA style. She developed some questions and strategies to guide her research and writing.

"How do I begin a research paper?"

Before getting started, Orlov worked with a writing tutor to break her research plan into several stages. (Section numbers in blue refer to relevant discussions throughout the book.)

- Ask worthwhile questions about my topic.   C1-b, R1-a
- Talk with a reference librarian about useful types of sources and where to find them.   R1-b
- Consider how each source can contribute to my paper.   R2-a
- Decide which search results are worth a closer look.   R2-b
- Evaluate the sources.   R2-c, R2-d
- Take notes and keep track of the sources.   R3
- Write a working thesis.   C1-c, MLA-1a
- Write a draft and integrate sources.   C2, MLA-3, MLA-4a
- Document sources.   MLA-4

R1-a: Posing questions for a research paper

Orlov began by jotting down her research question: *Is Internet surveillance in the workplace fair or unfair to employees?* She thought the practice might be unfair but wanted to consider all sides of the issue. Orlov knew she would have to be open-minded and flexible and revisit her main ideas as she examined the information and arguments in her sources.

"What sources do I need, and where should I look for them?"

R2-a: Roles sources can play in a paper

Orlov worked with a reference librarian to develop a search strategy. She looked for sources that would provide that background, evidence, and counterevidence.

R1-b: Working with reference librarians

Library databases Because her topic was current, Orlov turned to her library's subscription databases for trustworthy, scholarly, up-to-date articles with concrete examples of workplace Internet surveillance.

R1-c to R1-e: Searching databases, library catalogs, and the Web

Library catalogs Orlov looked for recently published books that could offer in-depth context, including the history of online monitoring and the laws governing workplace surveillance. One book on the topic had the subject heading "electronic monitoring in the workplace." Using that heading as a search term, Orlov found a more focused list of books.

The Web Using a general search engine, Orlov found Web sites, articles, and government publications that would explain the software used by employers and various opinions held by those who use the Internet and e-mail in the workplace.

"What search terms should I use?"

Orlov asked a librarian to help her conduct a narrower search with her library's general periodical database. She could count on the database for fewer, more reliable results than an Internet search could provide.

Orlov's search terms	Date restrictions
employee	Past five years
internet use	**Number of results**
surveillance	20

R1-c and p. 338: Refining key-word searches, selecting search terms

"How do I select sources from my search results?"

Orlov used several criteria to decide which results from her general periodical database search were worth a closer look. Would a source

- be relevant to her topic?
- provide authoritative support?
- provide background information?
- offer a range of views or evidence that Orlov could address when forming her argument?

R2: Evaluating sources

DATABASE SCREEN: SEARCH RESULTS

This article's focus on surveillance cameras was not relevant.
> "A New Look at Big Brother"
> *Business Week Online*, December 20, 2007, Technology, 959 words, Peter Burrows

Orlov would want to respond to this survey if she argued that Internet surveillance is unfair.
> "Wasting Away on the Web; More Employers Taking Workers' Web Use Seriously"
> *eWeek*, August 8, 2005, 692 words, Chris Gonsalves

The *Wall Street Journal* is widely respected and might offer background for Orlov's topic.
> "Snooping E-Mail by Software Is Now a Workplace Norm"
> *The Wall Street Journal Online*, March 9, 2005, Pui-Wing Tam et al.

Orlov wondered if the *Progressive* had a political slant. She made a note to check for bias.
> "Snooping Bosses; Electronic Surveillance Program"
> *The Progressive*, February 1, 2006: 14, Barbara Ehrenreich

Reviewed by legal experts, a law review article could provide legal context and lend credibility.
> "Cyber-Working or Cyber-Shirking? A First Principles Examination of Electronic Privacy in the Workplace"
> *Florida Law Review* 54.2 (2002): 289-332, Jay P. Kesan

"How do I evaluate my sources?"

After Orlov had conducted several searches and narrowed her list of results, she downloaded her sources and began evaluating them. She wanted to see what evidence and claims she would need to address to strengthen her argument.

R2-b to R2-d: Assessing print and online sources

She looked carefully at an article in *eWeek*, an online business computing magazine. To keep track of her thoughts about the author's text, she made notes in the margins as she read. Taking good notes would help her to begin forming her own lines of argument and avoid plagiarism.

R3: Managing your information

ORLOV'S NOTES ON AN ARTICLE

Wasting Away on the Web
Opinion: More employers are taking workers' Web use seriously.

Writer is sympathetic to employers?

By Chris Gonsalves
2005-08-08

SECTION: OPINION; Pg. 26

Consider statistics. Is spending work time on personal Internet use so bad?

The issue of IT surveillance was driven home last month when Salary.com and America Online released a survey of 10,000 American workers, many of whom admitted that goofing off on the Internet was their primary method of frittering away the workday. In a sign of the times, it beat out socializing with co-workers, 45 percent to 23 percent.

Strong case for surveillance, but I'm not convinced. Counter with useful workplace Web surfing?

While bosses can easily detect and interrupt water-cooler chatter, the employee who is shopping at Lands' End or IMing with fellow fantasy baseball managers may actually appear to be working. Thwarting the activity is a technology challenge, and it's one that more and more enterprises are taking seriously, despite resistance from privacy advocates and some employees themselves.

Common examples—readers can relate.

Does the AMA side with employers? Survey results—good for background and counter-argument.

According to the American Management Association, 78 percent of large U.S. employers are regularly checking workers' e-mail messages, Internet use, computer files and phone calls. Nearly half of such employers store employee e-mail messages for review. The AMA also found that 65 percent of enterprises had disciplined employees for misuse of e-mail or the Internet at work, and 27 percent had actually fired someone over such offenses.

According to a recent poll of workers in technology-related fields published by the executive recruiting company FPC, 61 percent said they felt their bosses had the right to cyber-spy on them, but only with consent. Just 28 percent felt IT had the right to monitor their activity without consent, and only 1 percent said an employer never has the right to monitor Internet use.

Employees want employers to be up front about monitoring.

"It's not surprising that companies want to assure that their employees' time is predominantly spent on work-related computer usage," said FPC President Ron Herzog. "The majority of employees ... would like to be informed, so it is always in the company's best interest to have an Internet usage policy clearly outlining the company's expectations, which all employees sign upon hiring."

When is workplace surveillance unfair and when not?

As the stakes grow beyond a few wasted man-hours and some misappropriated bandwidth, it grows increasingly important for IT to let everyone in the company know they might be watched.

Executive Editor/News Chris Gonsalves can be contacted at chris_gonsalves@ziffdavis.com.
LOAD-DATE: August 8, 2005
LANGUAGE: English

Copyright 2005 Ziff Davis Media Inc. All Rights Reserved

evaluating sources • reading critically • integrating sources • taking
notes • keeping records • documenting sources • sample paper

MLA-5c **435**

"How do I integrate sources into my paper?"

C1-c and
MLA-1a: Writing
a working thesis

C1–C2: Planning
and drafting

After reading and evaluating a number of sources, Orlov wrote
her working thesis: *Though companies may have legitimate reasons to monitor employees' Internet usage, electronic surveillance
is more unfair than beneficial to employees since it threatens their
privacy.* She then sketched an informal plan to organize her ideas
and began writing a rough draft. As she wrote and revised, she
integrated sources from her research.

R3-c and
MLA-2: Quoting,
summarizing, and
paraphrasing

For example, Orlov had selected a book on electronic surveillance in the workplace, written by Frederick Lane III. She
looked through the table of contents and selected a few chapters
that seemed relevant to her working thesis. She read the chapters for ideas and information that she could paraphrase, summarize, or quote to provide background, support her argument,
and help her counter the kind of pro-surveillance position that
Chris Gonsalves takes in his *eWeek* article.

"How do I keep track of and document my sources?"

R3-b: Keeping
track of source
materials

Because Orlov took careful notes about publication information and
page numbers for source material throughout her research process,
she didn't need to hunt down information as she cited her sources.

MLA-4:
Documenting
sources

She followed the MLA (Modern Language Association) system to document her sources.

ENTRY IN WORKS CITED LIST

      author   title and subtitle

Lane, Frederick S., III. *The Naked Employee: How Technology Is*

                                      city of
                               publication   publisher

Compromising Workplace Privacy. New York: Amer. Management Assn.,

publication
  date   medium
2003. Print.

MLA-5c Sample research paper: MLA style

On the following pages is a research paper on the topic of electronic
surveillance in the workplace, written by Anna Orlov, a student in a
composition class. Orlov's paper is documented with in-text citations
and a list of works cited in MLA style. Annotations in the margins of
the paper draw your attention to Orlov's use of MLA style and her
effective writing.

MODELS **hackerhandbooks.com/writersref**
> Model papers > MLA research papers: Orlov; Daly; Levi
> MLA annotated bibliography: Orlov

Orlov 1

Anna Orlov

Professor Willis

English 101

17 March 2009

Title is centered.

Online Monitoring:

A Threat to Employee Privacy in the Wired Workplace

Opening sentences provide background for the thesis.

As the Internet has become an integral tool of businesses, company policies on Internet usage have become as common as policies regarding vacation days or sexual harassment. A 2005 study by the American Management Association and ePolicy Institute found that 76% of companies monitor employees' use of the Web, and the number of companies that block employees' access to certain Web sites has increased 27% since 2001 (1). Unlike other company rules, however, Internet usage policies often include language authorizing companies to secretly monitor their employees, a practice that raises questions about rights in the

Thesis asserts Orlov's main point.

workplace. Although companies often have legitimate concerns that lead them to monitor employees' Internet usage—from expensive security breaches to reduced productivity—the benefits of electronic surveillance are outweighed by its costs to employees' privacy and autonomy.

While surveillance of employees is not a new phenomenon, electronic surveillance allows employers to monitor workers with unprecedented

Summary and long quotation are each introduced with a signal phrase naming the author.

efficiency. In his book *The Naked Employee*, Frederick Lane describes offline ways in which employers have been permitted to intrude on employees' privacy for decades, such as drug testing, background checks, psychological exams, lie detector tests, and in-store video surveillance. The difference, Lane argues, between these old methods of data gathering and electronic surveillance involves quantity:

Long quotation is set off from the text; quotation marks are omitted.

> Technology makes it possible for employers to gather enormous amounts of data about employees, often far beyond what is necessary to satisfy safety or productivity concerns. And the trends that drive technology—faster, smaller, cheaper—make it possible for larger and larger numbers of employers to gather

Page number is given in parentheses after the final period.

ever-greater amounts of personal data. (3-4)

In an age when employers can collect data whenever employees use their

Marginal annotations indicate MLA-style formatting and effective writing.

Orlov 2

computers—when they send e-mail, surf the Web, or even arrive at or depart from their workstations—the challenge for both employers and employees is to determine how much is too much.

Another key difference between traditional surveillance and electronic surveillance is that employers can monitor workers' computer use secretly. One popular monitoring method is keystroke logging, which is done by means of an undetectable program on employees' computers. The Web site of a vendor for Spector Pro, a popular keystroke logging program, explains that the software can be installed to operate in "Stealth" mode so that it "does not show up as an icon, does not appear in the Windows system tray, . . . [and] cannot be uninstalled without the Spector Pro password which YOU specify" ("Automatically"). As Lane explains, these programs record every key entered into the computer in hidden directories that can later be accessed or uploaded by supervisors; the programs can even scan for keywords tailored to individual companies (128-29).

Some experts have argued that a range of legitimate concerns justifies employer monitoring of employee Internet usage. As *PC World* columnist Daniel Tynan points out, companies that don't monitor network traffic can be penalized for their ignorance: "Employees could accidentally (or deliberately) spill confidential information . . . or allow worms to spread throughout a corporate network." The ePolicy Institute, an organization that advises companies about reducing risks from technology, reported that breaches in computer security cost institutions $100 million in 1999 alone (Flynn). Companies also are held legally accountable for many of the transactions conducted on their networks and with their technology. Legal scholar Jay Kesan points out that the law holds employers liable for employees' actions such as violations of copyright laws, the distribution of offensive or graphic sexual material, and illegal disclosure of confidential information (312).

These kinds of concerns should give employers, in certain instances, the right to monitor employee behavior. But employers rushing to adopt surveillance programs might not be adequately weighing the effect such programs can have on employee morale. Employers must consider the possibility that employees will perceive surveillance as a breach of trust that can make them feel like disobedient children, not responsible

Clear topic sentences, like this one, are used throughout the paper.

Source with an unknown author is cited by a shortened title.

Orlov anticipates objections and provides sources for opposing views.

Transition helps readers move from one paragraph to the next.

Orlov 3

adults who wish to perform their jobs professionally and autonomously.

Orlov treats both sides fairly; she provides a transition to her own argument.

Yet determining how much autonomy workers should be given is complicated by the ambiguous nature of productivity in the wired workplace. On the one hand, computers and Internet access give employees powerful tools to carry out their jobs; on the other hand, the same technology offers constant temptations to avoid work. As a 2005 study by *Salary.com* and *America Online* indicates, the Internet ranked as the top choice among employees for ways of wasting time on the job; it beat talking with co-workers—the second most popular method—by a margin of nearly two to one (Frauenheim). Chris Gonsalves, an editor for *eWeek.com*, argues that the technology has changed the terms between employers and employees: "While bosses can easily detect and interrupt water-cooler chatter," he writes, "the employee who is shopping at Lands' End or IMing with fellow fantasy baseball managers may actually appear to be working." The gap between behaviors that are observable to managers and the employee's actual activities when sitting behind a computer has created additional motivations for employers to invest in surveillance programs. "Dilbert," a popular cartoon that spoofs office culture, aptly captures how rampant recreational Internet use has become in the workplace (see fig. 1).

No page number is available for this Web source.

Orlov counters opposing views and provides support for her argument.

But monitoring online activities can have the unintended effect of making employees resentful. As many workers would be quick to point out, Web surfing and other personal uses of the Internet can provide needed outlets in the stressful work environment; many scholars have argued that limiting and policing these outlets can exacerbate tensions between employees and managers. Kesan warns that "prohibiting personal use can seem extremely arbitrary and can seriously harm morale. . . . Imagine a concerned parent who is prohibited from checking on a sick child by a draconian company policy" (315-16). As this analysis indicates, employees can become disgruntled when Internet usage policies are enforced to their full extent.

Orlov uses a brief signal phrase to move from her argument to the words of a source.

Additionally, many experts disagree with employers' assumption that online monitoring can increase productivity. Employment law attorney Joseph Schmitt argues that, particularly for employees who are paid a salary rather than an hourly wage, "a company shouldn't care whether employees spend one or 10 hours on the Internet as long as they are

Orlov 4

Fig. 1. This "Dilbert" comic strip suggests that personal Internet usage is widespread in the workplace (Adams 106).

Illustration has figure number, caption, and source information.

getting their jobs done—and provided that they are not accessing inappropriate sites" (qtd. in Verespej). Other experts even argue that time spent on personal Internet browsing can actually be productive for companies. According to Bill Coleman, an executive at *Salary.com*, "Personal Internet use and casual office conversations often turn into new business ideas or suggestions for gaining operating efficiencies" (qtd. in Frauenheim). Employers, in other words, may benefit from showing more faith in their employees' ability to exercise their autonomy.

Orlov cites an indirect source: words quoted in another source.

Employees' right to privacy and autonomy in the workplace, however, remains a murky area of the law. Although evaluating where to draw the line between employee rights and employer powers is often a duty that falls to the judicial system, the courts have shown little willingness to intrude on employers' exercise of control over their computer networks. Federal law provides few guidelines related to online monitoring of employees, and only Connecticut and Delaware require companies to disclose this type of surveillance to employees (Tam et al.). "It is unlikely that we will see a legally guaranteed zone of privacy in the American workplace," predicts Kesan (293). This reality leaves employees and employers to sort the potential risks and benefits of technology in contract agreements and terms of employment. With continuing advances in technology, protecting both employers and employees will require greater awareness of these programs, better disclosure to employees, and a more public discussion about what types of protections are necessary to guard individual freedoms in the wired workplace.

Orlov sums up her argument and suggests a course of action.

Heading is centered.

Works Cited

Adams, Scott. *Dilbert and the Way of the Weasel*. New York: Harper, 2002.
Print.

List is alphabetized
by authors' last
names (or by title
when a work has no
author).

American Management Association and ePolicy Institute. "2005 Electronic
Monitoring and Surveillance Survey." *American Management
Association*. Amer. Management Assn., 2005. Web. 15 Feb. 2009.

"Automatically Record Everything They Do Online! Spector Pro 5.0
FAQ's." *Netbus.org*. Netbus.Org, n.d. Web. 17 Feb. 2009.

Abbreviation "n.d."
indicates that the
online source has no
update date.

Flynn, Nancy. "Internet Policies." *ePolicy Institute*. ePolicy Inst., n.d.
Web. 15 Feb. 2009.

Frauenheim, Ed. "Stop Reading This Headline and Get Back to Work."
CNET News.com. CNET Networks, 11 July 2005. Web. 17 Feb.
2009.

First line of each
entry is at the left
margin; extra lines
are indented ¹/₂".

Gonsalves, Chris. "Wasting Away on the Web." *eWeek.com*. Ziff Davis
Enterprise Holdings, 8 Aug. 2005. Web. 16 Feb. 2009.

Kesan, Jay P. "Cyber-Working or Cyber-Shirking? A First Principles
Examination of Electronic Privacy in the Workplace." *Florida
Law Review* 54.2 (2002): 289-332. Print.

Double-spacing is
used throughout.

Lane, Frederick S., III. *The Naked Employee: How Technology Is
Compromising Workplace Privacy*. New York: Amer. Management
Assn., 2003. Print.

A work with four
authors is listed by
the first author's
name and the
abbreviation "et al."
(for "and others").

Tam, Pui-Wing, et al. "Snooping E-Mail by Software Is Now a Workplace
Norm." *Wall Street Journal* 9 Mar. 2005: B1+. Print.

Tynan, Daniel. "Your Boss Is Watching." *PC World*. PC World
Communications, 6 Oct. 2004. Web. 17 Sept. 2009.

Verespej, Michael A. "Inappropriate Internet Surfing." *Industry Week*.
Penton Media, 7 Feb. 2000. Web. 16 Feb. 2009.

*Directory to **CMS-style note and bibliography models** is on page 498.*

444   APA   APA papers

Directory to APA reference list models (continued)

ONLINE SOURCES (continued)

39. Report or long document from a Web site, 475
40. Section in a Web document, 476
41. Short work from a Web site, 476
42. Document from a university or government agency Web site, 476
43. Article in an online newsletter, 476
44. Podcast, 476
45. Blog (Weblog) post, 477
46. Online audio or video file, 477
47. Entry in a wiki, 477
48. Data set or graphic representation, 477
49. Conference hearing, 480
50. E-mail, 480
51. Online posting, 480

OTHER SOURCES (INCLUDING ONLINE VERSIONS)

52. Dissertation from a database, 480
53. Unpublished dissertation, 480

54. Government document, 480
55. Report from a private organization, 481
56. Legal source, 481
57. Conference proceedings, 481
58. Paper presented at a meeting or symposium (unpublished), 481
59. Poster session at a conference, 481
60. Map or chart, 481
61. Advertisement, 481
62. Published interview, 482
63. Lecture, speech, or address, 482
64. Work of art or photograph, 482
65. Brochure, pamphlet, or fact sheet, 482
66. Presentation slides, 482
67. Film or video (motion picture), 482
68. Television program, 483
69. Sound recording, 483
70. Computer software or video game, 483

This tabbed section shows how to document sources in APA style for the social sciences and fields like nursing and business, and in CMS (*Chicago*) style for history and some humanities classes. It also includes discipline-specific advice on three important topics: supporting a thesis, citing sources and avoiding plagiarism, and integrating sources.

NOTE: For advice on finding and evaluating sources and on managing information in courses across the disciplines, see the tabbed section R, Researching.

APA Papers

Many writing assignments in the social sciences are either reports of original research or reviews of the literature (previously published research) on a particular topic. Often an original research report contains a "review of the literature" section that places the writer's project in the context of previous research.

Most social science instructors will ask you to document your sources with the American Psychological Association (APA) system of in-text citations and references described in APA-4. You face three main challenges when writing a social science paper that draws on sources: (1) supporting a thesis, (2) citing your sources and avoiding plagiarism, and (3) integrating quotations and other source material.

Examples in this section appear in APA style and are drawn from one student's research for a review of the literature on treatments for childhood obesity. Luisa Mirano's complete paper appears on pages 488–96.

APA-1 Supporting a thesis

Most assignments ask you to form a thesis, or main idea, and to support that thesis with well-organized evidence. In a paper reviewing the literature on a topic, this thesis analyzes the often competing conclusions drawn by a variety of researchers.

APA-1a Form a working thesis.

Once you have read a variety of sources and considered your issue from different perspectives, you are ready to form a working thesis: a one-sentence (or occasionally a two-sentence) statement of your central idea. (See also C1-c.) Because it is a working, or tentative, thesis, you can remain flexible and revise it as your ideas develop. Ultimately, your thesis will express not just your opinion but your informed, reasoned answer to your research question (see R1-a). Here, for example, is a research question posed by Luisa Mirano, a student in a psychology class, followed by her thesis in answer to that question.

RESEARCH QUESTION

Is medication the right treatment for the escalating problem of childhood obesity?

WORKING THESIS

Treating cases of childhood obesity with medication alone is too narrow an approach for this growing problem.

Notice that the thesis expresses a view on a debatable issue—an issue about which intelligent, well-meaning people might disagree. The writer's job is to persuade such readers that this view is worth taking seriously.

APA-1b Organize your ideas.

The American Psychological Association encourages the use of headings to help readers follow the organization of a paper. For an original research report, the major headings often follow a standard model: Method, Results, Discussion. The introduction is not given a heading; it consists of the material between the title of the paper and the first heading.

For a literature review, headings will vary. The student who wrote about treatments for childhood obesity used four questions to focus her research; the questions then became headings in her paper (see pp. 488–96).

> **Making the most of your handbook**
>
> A working thesis and rough outline can help writers get started.
>
> ▶ Drafting a working thesis: C1-c
>
> ▶ Sketching a plan: C1-d

APA-1c Use sources to inform and support your argument.

Used thoughtfully, your source materials will make your argument more complex and convincing for readers. Sources can play several different roles as you develop your points.

Providing background information or context

You can use facts and statistics to support generalizations or to establish the importance of your topic, as student writer Luisa Mirano does in her introduction.

> In March 2004, U.S. Surgeon General Richard Carmona called attention to a health problem in the United States that, until recently, has been overlooked: childhood obesity. Carmona said that the "astounding" 15% child obesity rate constitutes an "epidemic." Since the early 1980s, that rate has "doubled in children and tripled in adolescents." Now more than 9 million children are classified as obese.

Explaining terms or concepts

If readers are unlikely to be familiar with a word, a phrase, or an idea important to your topic, you must explain it for them. Quoting or paraphrasing a source can help you define terms and concepts in accessible

organizing ideas • headings • how sources work
in a paper • supporting arguments • counterargument
APA-1c   **447**

language. Luisa Mirano uses a scholarly source to explain how one of the major obesity drugs functions.

> Sibutramine suppresses appetite by blocking the reuptake of the
> neurotransmitters serotonin and norepinephrine in the brain (Yanovski &
> Yanovski, 2002, p. 594).

Supporting your claims

As you draft your argument, make sure to back up your assertions with facts, examples, and other evidence from your research (see also A2-e). Luisa Mirano, for example, uses one source's findings to support her central idea that the medical treatment of childhood obesity has limitations.

> As journalist Greg Critser (2003) noted in his book *Fat Land*, use of weight-loss
> drugs is unlikely to have an effect without the proper "support system"—one that
> includes doctors, facilities, time, and money (p. 3).

Lending authority to your argument

Expert opinion can add credibility to your argument (see also A2-e). But don't rely on experts to make your argument for you. Construct your argument in your own words and, when appropriate, cite the judgment of an authority in the field for support.

> Both medical experts and policymakers recognize that solutions might come not
> only from a laboratory but also from policy, education, and advocacy. A handbook
> designed to educate doctors on obesity called for "major changes in some aspects
> of western culture" (Hoppin & Taveras, 2004, Conclusion section, para. 1).

Anticipating and countering alternative interpretations

Do not ignore sources that seem contrary to your position or that offer interpretations different from your own. Instead, use them to give voice to opposing points of view and alternative interpretations before you counter them (see A2-f). Readers often have objections in mind already, whether or not they agree with you. Mirano uses a source to acknowledge value in her opponents' position that medication alone can successfully treat childhood obesity.

> As researchers Yanovski and Yanovski (2002) have explained, obesity was once
> considered "either a moral failing or evidence of underlying psychopathology"
> (p. 592). But this view has shifted: Many medical professionals now consider
> obesity a biomedical rather than a moral condition, influenced by both genetic

and environmental factors. Yanovski and Yanovski have further noted that the development of weight-loss medications in the early 1990s showed that "obesity should be treated in the same manner as any other chronic disease . . . through the long-term use of medication" (p. 592).

☰ APA-2 Citing sources; avoiding plagiarism

Your research paper is a collaboration between you and your sources. To be fair and ethical, you must acknowledge your debt to the writers of those sources. Failure to do so is a form of academic dishonesty known as *plagiarism*.

Three different acts are considered plagiarism: (1) failing to cite quotations and borrowed ideas, (2) failing to enclose borrowed language in quotation marks, and (3) failing to put summaries and paraphrases in your own words. It's a good idea to find out how your school defines and addresses academic dishonesty. (See also R3-c.)

APA-2a Cite quotations and borrowed ideas.

Sources are cited for two reasons:

- to tell readers where your information comes from — so that they can assess its reliability and, if interested, find and read the original source
- to give credit to the writers from whom you have borrowed words and ideas

You must cite anything you borrow from a source, including direct quotations; statistics and other specific facts; visuals such as tables, graphs, and diagrams; and any ideas you present in a summary or paraphrase.

The only exception is common knowledge — information that your readers may know or could easily locate in any number of reference sources. For example, most general encyclopedias will tell readers that Sigmund Freud wrote *The Interpretation of Dreams* and that chimpanzees can learn American Sign Language.

As a rule, when you have seen certain information repeatedly in your reading, you don't need to cite it. However, when information has appeared in only a few sources, when it is highly specific (as with statistics), or when it is controversial, you should cite the source.

The American Psychological Association recommends an author-date system of citations. The following is a brief description of how the author-date system often works.

1. The source is introduced by a signal phrase that includes the last name of the author followed by the date of publication in parentheses.
2. The material being cited is followed by a page number in parentheses.
3. At the end of the paper, an alphabetized list of references gives complete publication information for the source.

IN-TEXT CITATION

As researchers Yanovski and Yanovski (2002) have explained, obesity was once considered "either a moral failing or evidence of underlying psychopathology" (p. 592).

ENTRY IN THE LIST OF REFERENCES

Yanovski, S. Z., & Yanovski, J. A. (2002). Drug therapy: Obesity. *The New England Journal of Medicine, 346,* 591-602.

This basic APA format varies for different types of sources. For a detailed discussion and other models, see APA-4.

APA-2b Enclose borrowed language in quotation marks.

To indicate that you are using a source's exact phrases or sentences, you must enclose them in quotation marks unless they have been set off from the text by indenting (see p. 453). To omit the quotation marks is to claim—falsely—that the language is your own. Such an omission is plagiarism even if you have cited the source.

ORIGINAL SOURCE

In an effort to seek the causes of this disturbing trend, experts have pointed to a range of important potential contributors to the rise in childhood obesity that are unrelated to media: a reduction in physical education classes and after-school athletic programs, an increase in the availability of sodas and snacks in public schools, the growth in the number of fast-food outlets across the country, the trend toward "super-sizing" food portions in restaurants, and the increasing number of highly processed high-calorie and high-fat grocery products.

> —Henry J. Kaiser Family Foundation, "The Role of Media in Childhood Obesity" (2004), p. 1

PLAGIARISM

According to the Henry J. Kaiser Family Foundation (2004), experts have pointed
to a range of important potential contributors to the rise in childhood obesity that
are unrelated to media (p. 1).

BORROWED LANGUAGE IN QUOTATION MARKS

According to the Henry J. Kaiser Family Foundation (2004), "experts have pointed
to a range of important potential contributors to the rise in childhood obesity that
are unrelated to media" (p. 1).

NOTE: When quoted sentences are set off from the text by indenting,
quotation marks are not needed (see p. 453).

APA-2c Put summaries and paraphrases in your own words.

Summaries and paraphrases are written in your own words. A summary condenses information; a paraphrase conveys the information
using roughly the same number of words as in the original source. When
you summarize or paraphrase, it is not enough to name the source; you
must restate the source's meaning using your own language. (See also
R3-c.) You commit plagiarism if you half-copy the author's sentences—
either by mixing the author's phrases with your own without using quotation marks or by plugging your own synonyms into the author's
sentence structure. The following paraphrases are plagiarized—even
though the source is cited—because their language and sentence structure are too close to those of the source.

ORIGINAL SOURCE

In an effort to seek the causes of this disturbing trend, experts have
pointed to a range of important potential contributors to the rise in
childhood obesity that are unrelated to media.
— Henry J. Kaiser Family Foundation, "The Role
of Media in Childhood Obesity" (2004), p. 1

UNACCEPTABLE BORROWING OF PHRASES

According to the Henry J. Kaiser Family Foundation (2004), experts have indicated a
range of significant potential contributors to the rise in childhood obesity that are
not linked to media (p. 1).

UNACCEPTABLE BORROWING OF STRUCTURE

According to the Henry J. Kaiser Family Foundation (2004), experts have identified
a variety of key factors causing a rise in childhood obesity, factors that are not
tied to media (p. 1).

To avoid plagiarizing an author's language, resist the temptation to look at the source while you are summarizing or paraphrasing. After you have read the passage you want to paraphrase, set the source aside. Ask yourself, "What is the author's meaning?" In your own words, state your understanding of the author's basic point. Return to the source and check that you haven't used the author's language or sentence structure or misrepresented the author's ideas. When you fully understand another writer's meaning, you can more easily and accurately present those ideas in your own words.

ACCEPTABLE PARAPHRASE

A report by the Henry J. Kaiser Family Foundation (2004) described causes other than media for the childhood obesity crisis (p. 1).

APA-3 Integrating sources

Quotations, summaries, paraphrases, and facts will help you develop your argument, but they cannot speak for you. You can use several strategies to integrate information from sources into your paper while maintaining your own voice.

APA-3a Use quotations appropriately.

In your academic writing, keep the emphasis on your ideas; use your own words to summarize and to paraphrase your sources and to explain your points. Sometimes, however, quotations can be the most effective way to integrate a source.

WHEN TO USE QUOTATIONS

- When language is especially vivid or expressive
- When exact wording is needed for technical accuracy
- When it is important to let the debaters of an issue explain their positions in their own words
- When the words of an authority lend weight to an argument
- When the language of a source is the topic of your discussion

Limiting your use of quotations Although it is tempting to insert many quotations in your paper and to use your own words only for connecting passages, do not quote excessively. It is almost impossible to integrate numerous long quotations smoothly into your own text.

It is not always necessary to quote full sentences from a source. To reduce your reliance on the words of others, you can often integrate language from a source into your own sentence structure.

> Carmona (2004) advised the subcommittee that the situation constitutes an "epidemic" and that the skyrocketing statistics are "astounding."

> As researchers continue to face a number of unknowns about obesity, it may be helpful to envision treating the disorder, as Yanovski and Yanovski (2002) suggested, "in the same manner as any other chronic disease" (p. 592).

Using the ellipsis mark To condense a quoted passage, you can use the ellipsis mark (three periods, with spaces between) to indicate that you have omitted words. What remains must be grammatically complete.

> Roman (2003) reported that "social factors are nearly as significant as individual metabolism in the formation of . . . dietary habits of adolescents" (p. 345).

The writer has omitted the words *both healthy and unhealthy* from the source.

When you want to leave out one or more full sentences, use a period before the three ellipsis dots.

> According to Sothern and Gordon (2003), "Environmental factors may contribute as much as 80% to the causes of childhood obesity. . . . Research suggests that obese children demonstrate decreased levels of physical activity and increased psychosocial problems" (p. 104).

Ordinarily, do not use an ellipsis mark at the beginning or at the end of a quotation. Readers will understand that you have taken the quoted material from a longer passage, so such marks are not necessary. The only exception occurs when you have dropped words at the end of the final quoted sentence. In such cases, put three ellipsis dots before the closing quotation mark. Make sure that omissions and ellipsis marks do not distort the meaning of your source.

Using brackets Brackets allow you to insert your own words into quoted material. You can insert words in brackets to clarify a confusing reference or to keep a sentence grammatical in your context.

> The cost of treating obesity currently totals $117 billion per year—a price, according to the surgeon general, "second only to the cost of [treating] tobacco use" (Carmona, 2004).

To indicate an error such as a misspelling in a quotation, insert [*sic*], italicized and with brackets around it, right after the error. (See P6-b.)

Setting off long quotations   When you quote forty or more words from a source, set off the quotation by indenting it one-half inch from the left margin. Use the normal right margin and do not single-space the quotation.

Long quotations should be introduced by an informative sentence, usually followed by a colon. Quotation marks are unnecessary because the indented format tells readers that the passage is taken word-for-word from the source.

> Yanovski and Yanovski (2002) have described earlier treatments of obesity that focused on behavior modification:
>
> > With the advent of behavioral treatments for obesity in the 1960s, hope arose that modification of maladaptive eating and exercise habits would lead to sustained weight loss, and that time-limited programs would produce permanent changes in weight. Medications for the treatment of obesity were proposed as short-term adjuncts for patients, who would presumably then acquire the skills necessary to continue to lose weight, reach "ideal body weight," and maintain a reduced weight indefinitely. (p. 592)

Notice that at the end of an indented quotation the parenthetical citation goes outside the final mark of punctuation. (When a quotation is run into your text, the opposite is true. See the sample citations on p. 452.)

APA-3b Use signal phrases to integrate sources.

Whenever you include a paraphrase, summary, or direct quotation of another writer's work in your paper, prepare your readers for it with a signal phrase. A signal phrase usually names the author of the source, gives the publication year in parentheses, and often provides some context. It commonly appears before the source material. To vary your sentence structure, you may decide to interrupt source material with a signal phrase or place the signal phrase after your paraphrase, summary, or direct quotation. It is generally acceptable in the social sciences to call authors by their last name only, even on a first mention. If your paper refers to two authors with same last name, use initials as well.

Using signal phrases in APA papers

To avoid monotony, try to vary both the language and the placement of your signal phrases.

Model signal phrases

In the words of Carmona (2004), ". . ."

As Yanovski and Yanovski (2002) have noted, ". . ."

Hoppin and Taveras (2004), medical researchers, pointed out that ". . ."

". . .," claimed Critser (2003).

". . .," wrote Duenwald (2004), ". . ."

Researchers McDuffie et al. (2003) have offered a compelling argument for this view: ". . ."

Hilts (2002) answered objections with the following analysis: ". . ."

Verbs in signal phrases

admitted	contended	reasoned
agreed	declared	refuted
argued	denied	rejected
asserted	emphasized	reported
believed	insisted	responded
claimed	noted	suggested
compared	observed	thought
confirmed	pointed out	wrote

When you write a signal phrase, choose a verb that is appropriate for the way you are using the source (see APA-1c). Are you providing background, explaining a concept, supporting a claim, lending authority, or refuting an argument? See the chart on this page for a list of verbs commonly used in signal phrases. Note that APA requires using verbs in the past tense or present perfect tense (*explained* or *has explained*) to introduce source material. Use the present tense only for discussing the results of an experiment (*the results show*) or knowledge that has been clearly established (*researchers agree*).

Marking boundaries

Readers need to move from your words to the words of a source without feeling a jolt. Avoid dropping direct quotations into your text without warning. Instead, provide clear signal phrases, including at least the author's name and the year of publication. Signal phrases mark the boundaries between source material and your

own words; they can also tell readers why a source is worth quoting.
(The signal phrase is highlighted in the second example.)

DROPPED QUOTATION

Obesity was once considered in a very different light. "For many years, obesity
was approached as it if were either a moral failing or evidence of underlying
psychopathology" (Yanovski & Yanovski, 2002, p. 592).

QUOTATION WITH SIGNAL PHRASE

Obesity was once considered in a very different light. As researchers Yanovski and
Yanovski (2002) have explained, obesity was widely thought of as "either a moral
failing or evidence of underlying psychopathology" (p. 592).

Using signal phrases with summaries and paraphrases

As with quotations, you should introduce most summaries and paraphrases with a signal phrase that mentions the author and the year
and places the material in the context of your argument. Readers will
then understand where the summary or paraphrase begins.

Without the signal phrase (highlighted) in the following example,
readers might think that only the last sentence is being cited, when
in fact the whole paragraph is based on the source.

Carmona (2004) advised a Senate subcommittee that the problem of childhood
obesity is dire and that the skyrocketing statistics—which put the child
obesity rate at 15%—are cause for alarm. More than 9 million children,
double the number in the early 1980s, are classified as obese. Carmona
warned that obesity can cause myriad physical problems that only worsen
as children grow older.

There are times, however, when a summary or a paraphrase does
not require a signal phrase naming the author. When the context makes
clear where the cited material begins, you may omit the signal phrase
and include the author's name and the year in parentheses. Unless the
work is short, also include the page number in the parentheses.

Integrating statistics and other facts

When you are citing a statistic or another specific fact, a signal phrase
is often not necessary. In most cases, readers will understand that the
citation refers to the statistic or fact (not the whole paragraph).

In purely financial terms, the drugs cost more than $3 a day on average
(Duenwald, 2004).

There is nothing wrong, however, with using a signal phrase to introduce a statistic or another fact.

> Duenwald (2004) reported that the drugs cost more than $3 a day on average.

Putting source material in context

Readers should not have to guess why source material appears in your paper. If you use another writer's words, you must explain how they relate to your point. In other words, you must put the source in context. It's a good idea to embed a quotation between sentences of your own, introducing it with a signal phrase and following it up with interpretive comments that link the quotation to your paper's argument. (See also APA-3c.)

> **QUOTATION WITH EFFECTIVE CONTEXT**
>
> A report by the Henry J. Kaiser Family Foundation (2004) outlined trends that may have contributed to the childhood obesity crisis, including food advertising for children as well as
>
>> a reduction in physical education classes . . . , an increase in the availability of sodas and snacks in public schools, the growth in the number of fast-food outlets . . . , and the increasing number of highly processed high-calorie and high-fat grocery products. (p. 1)
>
> Addressing each of these areas requires more than a doctor armed with a prescription pad; it requires a broad mobilization not just of doctors and concerned parents but of educators, food industry executives, advertisers, and media representatives.

APA-3c Synthesize sources.

When you synthesize multiple sources in a research paper, you create a conversation about your research topic. You show readers that your argument is based on your active analysis and integration of ideas, not just a list of quotations and paraphrases. Your synthesis will show how your sources relate to one another; one source may support, extend, or counter the ideas of another. Readers should be able to see how each one functions in your argument (see R2-a).

Considering how sources relate to your argument

Before you integrate sources and show readers how they relate to one another, consider how each one might contribute to your own argument. As student writer Luisa Mirano became more informed through her research about treatments for childhood obesity, she asked herself these questions: *What do I think about the various treatments for childhood obesity? Which sources might support my ideas? Which sources might help extend or illustrate the points I want to make? What common counterarguments do I need to address to strengthen my position?* Mirano kept these questions in mind as she read and annotated sources.

Placing sources in conversation

When you synthesize sources, you show readers how the ideas of one source relate to those of another by connecting and analyzing the ideas in the context of your argument. Keep the emphasis on your own writing. After all, you've done the research and thought through the issues, so you should control the conversation. The thread of your argument should be easy to identify and to understand, with or without your sources.

SAMPLE SYNTHESIS (DRAFT)

Student writer Luisa Mirano begins with a claim that needs support.

Medical treatments have clear costs for individual patients, including unpleasant side effects, little information about long-term use, and uncertainty that they will yield significant weight loss. The financial burden is heavy as well; the drugs cost more than $3 a day on average (Duenwald, 2004). In each of the clinical trials, use of medication was accompanied by expensive behavioral therapies, including counseling, nutrition education, fitness advising, and monitoring. As Critser (2003) noted in his book *Fat Land*, use of weight-loss drugs is unlikely to have an effect without the proper "support system"—one that includes doctors, facilities, time, and money (p. 3). For many families, this level of care is prohibitively expensive.

Signal phrases indicate how sources contribute to Mirano's paper and show that the ideas that follow are not her own.

Student writer

Source 1

Student writer

Source 2

Student writer

Mirano interprets and connects sources. Each paragraph ends with her own thoughts.

Both medical experts and policymakers recognize that solutions might come not only from a laboratory but also from policy, education, and advocacy. A handbook designed to educate doctors on obesity called for "major changes in some aspects of western culture" (Hoppin & Taveras, 2004, Conclusion section, para. 1). Solving the childhood obesity problem will require broad mobilization of doctors and concerned parents and also of educators, food industry executives, advertisers, and media representatives.

Source 3

Student writer

In this draft, Mirano uses her own analyses to shape the conversation among her sources. She does not simply string quotations and statistics together or allow her sources to overwhelm her writing. The final sentence, written in her own voice, gives her an opportunity to explain to readers how her sources support and extend her argument.

When synthesizing sources, ask yourself these questions:

- Which sources inform, support, or extend your argument?
- Have you varied the functions of sources—to provide background, explain concepts, lend authority, and anticipate counterarguments? Do your signal phrases indicate these functions?
- Do you explain how your sources support your argument?
- Do you connect and analyze sources in your own voice?
- Is your own argument easy to identify and to understand, with or without your sources?

APA-4 Documenting sources

In most social science classes, you will be asked to use the APA system for documenting sources, which is set forth in the *Publication Manual of the American Psychological Association,* 6th ed. (Washington: APA, 2010). APA recommends in-text citations that refer readers to a list of references.

An in-text citation usually gives the author of the source (often in a signal phrase), the year of publication, and at times a page number in parentheses. At the end of the paper, a list of references provides publication information about the source (see p. 496 for a sample list). The direct link between the in-text citation and the entry in the reference list is highlighted in green in the following example.

IN-TEXT CITATION

Yanovski and Yanovski (2002) reported that "the current state of the treatment for obesity is similar to the state of the treatment of hypertension several decades ago" (p. 600).

ENTRY IN THE LIST OF REFERENCES

Yanovski, S. Z., & Yanovski, J. A. (2002). Drug therapy: Obesity. *The New England Journal of Medicine, 346,* 591-602.

For a reference list that includes this entry, see page 496.

synthesis • working with two or more sources • citing sources •
quotation • summary • paraphrase • in-text citations   **APA-4a**   **459**

APA-4a APA in-text citations

APA's in-text citations provide at least the author's last name and the year of publication. For direct quotations and some paraphrases, a page number is given as well.

For a directory to the in-text citation models in this section, see page 443, immediately following the tabbed divider.

NOTE: APA style requires the use of the past tense or the present perfect tense in signal phrases introducing cited material: *Smith (2005) reported . . . , Smith (2005) has argued. . . .*

1. Basic format for a quotation Ordinarily, introduce the quotation with a signal phrase that includes the author's last name followed by the year of publication in parentheses. Put the page number preceded by "p." (or "pp." for more than one page) in parentheses after the quotation.

> Critser (2003) noted that despite growing numbers of overweight Americans, many health care providers still "remain either in ignorance or outright denial about the health danger to the poor and the young" (p. 5).

If the author is not named in the signal phrase, place the author's name, the year, and the page number in parentheses after the quotation: (Critser, 2003, p. 5).

NOTE: APA style requires the year of publication in an in-text citation. Do not include a month, even if the entry in the reference list includes the month.

2. Basic format for a summary or a paraphrase Include the author's last name and the year either in a signal phrase introducing the material or in parentheses following it. Give a page number to help readers find the passage you are citing. (For the use of paragraph numbers and headings in online sources, see "No page numbers" on pp. 462–63.)

> Yanovski and Yanovski (2002) explained that sibutramine suppresses appetite by blocking the reuptake of the neurotransmitters serotonin and norepinephrine in the brain (p. 594).

> Sibutramine suppresses appetite by blocking the reuptake of the neurotransmitters serotonin and norepinephrine in the brain (Yanovski & Yanovski, 2002, p. 594).

PRACTICE hackerhandbooks.com/writersref
> APA > APA 4–1 to APA 4–3

3. Work with two authors Give the names of both authors in the signal phrase or the parentheses each time you cite the work. In the parentheses, use "&" between the authors' names; in the signal phrase, use "and."

> According to Sothern and Gordon (2003), "Environmental factors may contribute as much as 80% to the causes of childhood obesity" (p. 104).

> Obese children often engage in limited physical activity (Sothern & Gordon, 2003, p. 104).

4. Work with three to five authors Identify all authors in the signal phrase or the parentheses the first time you cite the source.

> In 2003, Berkowitz, Wadden, Tershakovec, and Cronquist concluded, "Sibutramine . . . must be carefully monitored in adolescents, as in adults, to control increases in [blood pressure] and pulse rate" (p. 1811).

In subsequent citations, use the first author's name followed by "et al." in either the signal phrase or the parentheses.

> As Berkowitz et al. (2003) advised, "Until more extensive safety and efficacy data are available, . . . weight-loss medications should be used only on an experimental basis for adolescents" (p. 1811).

5. Work with six or more authors Use the first author's name followed by "et al." in the signal phrase or the parentheses.

> McDuffie et al. (2002) tested 20 adolescents, aged 12-16, over a three-month period and found that orlistat, combined with behavioral therapy, produced an average weight loss of 4.4 kg, or 9.7 pounds (p. 646).

6. Work with unknown author If the author is unknown, mention the work's title in the signal phrase or give the first word or two of the title in the parenthetical citation. Titles of short works such as articles and chapters are put in quotation marks; titles of long works such as books and reports are italicized. (For online sources with no author, see item 12 on p. 462.)

> Children struggling to control their weight must also struggle with the pressures of television advertising that, on the one hand, encourages the consumption of junk food and, on the other, celebrates thin celebrities ("Television," 2002).

NOTE: In the rare case when "Anonymous" is specified as the author, treat it as if it were a real name: (Anonymous, 2001). In the list of references, also use the name Anonymous as author.

7.   Organization as author   If the author is a government agency or another organization, name the organization in the signal phrase or in the parenthetical citation the first time you cite the source.

> Obesity puts children at risk for a number of medical complications, including
> Type 2 diabetes, hypertension, sleep apnea, and orthopedic problems (Henry J.
> Kaiser Family Foundation, 2004, p. 1).

If the organization has a familiar abbreviation, you may include it in brackets the first time you cite the source and use the abbreviation alone in later citations.

> **FIRST CITATION**   (Centers for Disease Control and Prevention [CDC], 2009)
>
> **LATER CITATIONS**   (CDC, 2009)

8.   Authors with the same last name   To avoid confusion, use initials with the last names if your reference list includes two or more authors with the same last name.

> Research by E. Smith (1989) revealed that. . . .

9.   Two or more works by the same author in the same year   When your list of references includes more than one work by the same author in the same year, use lowercase letters ("a," "b," and so on) with the year to order the entries in the reference list. (See item 6 on p. 465.) Use those same letters with the year in the in-text citation.

> Research by Durgin (2003b) has yielded new findings about the role of
> counseling in treating childhood obesity.

10. Two or more works in the same parentheses   When your parenthetical citation names two or more works, put them in the same order that they appear in the reference list, separated with semicolons.

> Researchers have indicated that studies of pharmacological treatments for
> childhood obesity are inconclusive (Berkowitz et al., 2003; McDuffie et al.,
> 2002).

11. Personal communication Personal interviews, memos, letters, e-mail, and similar unpublished communications should be cited in the text only, not in the reference list. (Use the first initial with the last name in parentheses.)

> One of Atkinson's colleagues, who has studied the effect of the media on children's eating habits, has contended that advertisers for snack foods will need to design ads responsibly for their younger viewers (F. Johnson, personal communication, October 20, 2009).

12. Electronic source When possible, cite electronic sources, including online sources, as you would any other source, giving the author and the year.

> Atkinson (2001) found that children who spent at least four hours a day watching TV were less likely to engage in adequate physical activity during the week.

Electronic sources sometimes lack authors' names, dates, or page numbers.

Unknown author

If no author is named in the source, mention the title of the source in the signal phrase or give the first word or two of the title in the parentheses (see also item 6). (If an organization serves as the author, see item 7.)

> The body's basal metabolic rate, or BMR, is a measure of its at-rest energy requirement ("Exercise," 2003).

Unknown date

When the date is unknown, use the abbreviation "n.d." (for "no date").

> Attempts to establish a definitive link between television programming and children's eating habits have been problematic (Magnus, n.d.).

No page numbers

APA requires page numbers for quotations, summaries, and paraphrases. When an electronic source lacks stable numbered pages, include paragraph numbers or headings, if the source has them, to help readers locate the particular passage you are citing.

If the source has numbered paragraphs, use the paragraph number preceded by the abbreviation "para.": (Hall, 2008, para. 5). If the source contains headings, cite the appropriate heading in parentheses; you may also indicate the paragraph under the heading that you are referring to, even if the paragraphs are not numbered.

Hoppin and Taveras (2004) pointed out that several other medications were
classified by the Drug Enforcement Administration as having the "potential for
abuse" (Weight-Loss Drugs section, para. 6).

NOTE: Electronic files in portable document format (PDF) often have
stable page numbers. For such sources, give the page number in the
parenthetical citation.

13. Indirect source If you use a source that was cited in another
source (a secondary source), name the original source in your signal
phrase. List the secondary source in your reference list and include it in
your parenthetical citation, preceded by the words "as cited in." In the
following example, Satcher is the original source, and Critser is the secondary source, given in the reference list.

Former surgeon general Dr. David Satcher described "a nation of young people
seriously at risk of starting out obese and dooming themselves to the difficult
task of overcoming a tough illness" (as cited in Critser, 2003, p. 4).

14. Sacred or classical text Identify the text, the version or edition
you used, and the relevant part (chapter, verse, line). It is not necessary
to include the source in the reference list.

Peace activists have long cited the biblical prophet's vision of a world without
war: "And they shall beat their swords into plowshares, and their spears into
pruning hooks; nation shall not lift up sword against nation, neither shall they
learn war any more" (Isaiah 2:4, Revised Standard Version).

APA-4b APA list of references

In APA style, the alphabetical list of works cited, which appears at the
end of the paper, is titled "References." For advice on preparing the list,
see pages 486–87. For a sample reference list, see page 496.

For a directory to the reference list models in this section, see
pages 443–44, immediately following the tabbed divider.

Alphabetize entries in the list of references by authors' last names;
if a work has no author, alphabetize it by its title. The first element
of each entry is important because citations in the text of the paper
refer to it and readers will be looking for it in the alphabetized list.
The date of publication appears immediately after the first element of
the citation.

In APA style, titles of books are italicized; titles of articles are
neither italicized nor put in quotation marks. (For rules on capitalization of titles, see p. 485.)

General guidelines for listing authors (print and online)

In APA style, all authors' names are inverted (the last name comes first), and initials are used for all first and middle names.

NAME AND DATE CITED IN TEXT

Duncan (2008) has reported that. . . .

BEGINNING OF ENTRY IN THE LIST OF REFERENCES

Duncan, B. (2008).

1. Single author

author: last name
+ initial(s)   year   title (book)

Egeland, J. (2008). *A billion lives: An eyewitness report from the frontlines of humanity.*

                place of
            publication   publisher

New York, NY: Simon & Schuster.

2. Multiple authors

List up to seven authors by last names followed by initials. Use an ampersand (&) before the name of the last author. If there are more than seven authors, list the first six followed by three ellipsis dots and the last author's name. (See p. 460 for citing works with multiple authors in the text of your paper.)

Two to seven authors

            all authors: place of
    last name + initial(s)   year   title (book)   publication

Musick, M. A., & Wilson, J. (2007). *Volunteers: A social profile.* Bloomington: Indiana

          publisher

University Press.

                    all authors:
                 last name + initial(s)   year

Diessner, R., Solom, R. C., Frost, N. K., Parsons, L., & Davidson, J. (2008). Engagement

                          title (article)

with beauty: Appreciating natural, artistic, and moral beauty. *The Journal*

     journal title   volume   page(s)

of Psychology, 142, 303-329.

Eight or more authors

Mulvaney, S. A., Mudasiru, E., Schlundt, D. G., Baughman, C. L., Fleming, M., VanderWoude,

      A., . . . Rothman, R. (2008). Self-management in Type 2 diabetes: The adolescent

      perspective. *The Diabetes Educator, 34,* 118-127.

3. Organization as author

author:
organization name   year   title (book)

American Psychiatric Association. (1994). *Diagnostic and statistical manual of mental*

edition   place   organization as author
number   of publication   and publisher

disorders (4th ed.). Washington, DC: Author.

If the publisher is not the same as the author, give the publisher's name at the end as you would for any other source.

4. Unknown author   Begin the entry with the work's title.

place of
title (book)   year   publication   publisher

New concise world atlas. (2007). New York, NY: Oxford University Press.

year + month + day   volume,
title (article)   (for weekly publication)   journal title   issue   page(s)

Order in the jungle. (2008, March 15). *The Economist, 386*(8571), 83-85.

5. Two or more works by the same author   Use the author's name for all entries. List the entries by year, the earliest first.

Barry, P. (2007, December 8). Putting tumors on pause. *Science News, 172,* 365.

Barry, P. (2008, August 2). Finding the golden genes. *Science News, 174,* 16-21.

6. Two or more works by the same author in the same year   List the works alphabetically by title. In the parentheses, following the year add "a," "b," and so on. Use these same letters when giving the year in the in-text citation. (See also p. 486.)

Elkind, D. (2008a, Spring). Can we play? *Greater Good, 4*(4), 14-17.

Elkind, D. (2008b, June 27). The price of hurrying children [Web log post]. Retrieved
    from http://blogs.psychologytoday.com/blog/digital-children

Articles in periodicals (print)

Periodicals include journals, magazines, and newspapers. For a journal or a magazine, give only the volume number if the publication is paginated continuously throughout each volume; give the volume and issue numbers if each issue of the volume begins on page 1. Italicize the volume number and put the issue number, not italicized, in parentheses.

For all periodicals, when an article appears on consecutive pages, provide the range of pages. When an article does not appear on consecutive pages, give all page numbers: A1, A17. (See also "Online sources" beginning on p. 472 for online articles and articles accessed through a library's database.) For an illustrated citation of an article in a print journal or magazine, see page 467.

7. Article in a journal

Zhang, L.-F. (2008). Teachers' styles of thinking: An exploratory study. *The Journal of Psychology, 142,* 37-55.

8. Article in a magazine
Cite as you would a journal article, but give the year and the month for monthly magazines; add the day for weekly magazines.

McKibben, B. (2007, October). Carbon's new math. *National Geographic, 212*(4), 32-37.

9. Article in a newspaper

Svoboda, E. (2008, October 21). Deep in the rain forest, stalking the next pandemic. *The New York Times,* p. D5.

Give the year, month, and day for daily and weekly newspapers. Use "p." or "pp." before page numbers.

10. Article with three to seven authors

Ungar, M., Brown, M., Liebenberg, L., Othman, R., Kwong, W. M., Armstrong, M., & Gilgun, J. (2007). Unique pathways to resilience across cultures. *Adolescence, 42,* 287-310.

11. Article with eight or more authors
List the first six authors followed by three ellipsis dots and the last author.

Krippner, G., Granovetter, M., Block, F., Biggart, N., Beamish, T., Hsing, Y., . . . O'Riain, S. (2004). Polanyi Symposium: A conversation on embeddedness. *Socio-Economic Review, 2,* 109-135.

12. Abstract of a journal article

Lahm, K. (2008). Inmate-on-inmate assault: A multilevel examination of prison violence [Abstract]. *Criminal Justice and Behavior, 35*(1), 120-137.

Citation at a glance: Article in a journal or magazine (APA)

To cite an article in a print journal or magazine in APA style, include the following elements:

1 Author
2 Year of publication for journal; complete date for magazine
3 Title of article
4 Name of journal or magazine
5 Volume number; issue number, if required (see p. 466)
6 Page number(s) of article

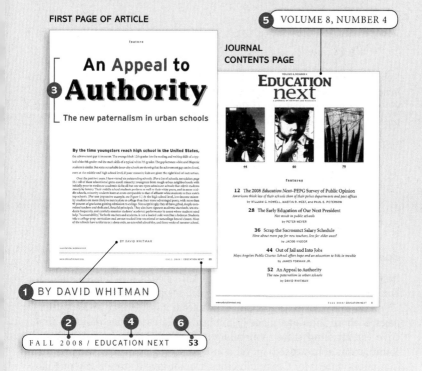

REFERENCE LIST ENTRY FOR AN ARTICLE IN A PRINT JOURNAL OR MAGAZINE

Whitman, D. (2008). An appeal to authority: The new paternalism in urban schools. *Education Next, 8*(4), 53-58.

For variations on citing articles in print journals or magazines in APA style, see pages 466–68.

13. Letter to the editor Follow the appropriate model for a journal, magazine, or newspaper (see items 7–9) and insert the words "Letter to the editor" in brackets after the title of the letter. If the letter has no title, use the bracketed words as the title.

Park, T. (2008, August). Defining the line [Letter to the editor]. *Scientific American, 299*(2), 10.

14. Editorial or other unsigned article

The global justice movement [Editorial]. (2005). *Multinational Monitor, 26*(7/8), 6.

15. Newsletter article

Setting the stage for remembering. (2006, September). *Mind, Mood, and Memory, 2*(9), 4-5.

16. Review Give the author and title of the review (if any) and, in brackets, the type of work, the title, and the author for a book or the year for a motion picture. If the review has no author or title, use the material in brackets as the title.

Applebaum, A. (2008, February 14). A movie that matters [Review of the motion picture *Katyn*, 2007]. *The New York Review of Books, 55*(2), 13-15.

Agents of change. (2008, February 2). [Review of the book *The power of unreasonable people: How social entrepreneurs create markets that change the world,* by J. Elkington & P. Hartigan]. *The Economist, 386*(8565), 94.

Books (print)

Items 17–29 apply to print books. For online books, see items 36 and 37. For an illustrated citation of a print book, see page 470.

Take the information about a book from its title page and copyright page. If more than one place of publication is listed, use only the first. Give the city and state (abbreviated) for all US cities or the city and country (not abbreviated) for all non-US cities; also include the province (not abbreviated) for Canadian cities. Do not give a state if the publisher's name includes it (as in many university presses, for example).

17. Basic format for a book

author: last   year of
name + initial(s)   publication   book title

McKenzie, F. R. (2008). *Theory and practice with adolescents: An applied approach.*

place of
publication   publisher

Chicago, IL: Lyceum Books.

18. Book with an editor

all editors:
last name + initial(s)   year of
                              publication   book title   edition

Aronson, J., & Aronson, E. (Eds.). (2008). *Readings about the social animal* (10th ed.).

place of
publication   publisher

New York, NY: Worth.

The abbreviation "Eds." is for multiple editors. If the book has one editor, use "Ed."

19. Book with an author and an editor

author: last name   year of
 + initial(s)   publication   book title   name(s) of editor(s):
                                                                                in normal order

McLuhan, M. (2003). *Understanding me: Lectures and interviews* (S. McLuhan & D. Staine,

place of publication
(city, province, country)   publisher

Eds.). Toronto, Ontario, Canada: McClelland & Stewart.

The abbreviation "Eds." is for multiple editors. If the book has one editor, use "Ed."

20. Book with an author and a translator
After the title, name the
translator, followed by "Trans.," in parentheses. Add the original date
of publication at the end of the entry.

Steinberg, M. D. (2003). *Voices of revolution, 1917* (M. Schwartz, Trans.). New Haven,

CT: Yale University Press. (Original work published 2001)

21. Edition other than the first

O'Brien, J. A. (Ed.). (2006). *The production of reality: Essays and readings on social
interaction* (4th ed.). Thousand Oaks, CA: Pine Forge Press.

If the entry also requires volume numbers (see item 23), put the volume
numbers after the edition number: (3rd ed., Vols. 1-3).

22. Article or chapter in an edited book or an anthology

author of chapter:
last name + initial(s)   year of
                         publication   title of chapter

Denton, N. A. (2006). Segregation and discrimination in housing. In R. G. Bratt,

book editor(s):
in normal order   book title

M. E. Stone, & C. Hartman (Eds.), *A right to housing: Foundation of a new*

page(s)
for chapter   place of
                  publication   publisher

social agenda (pp. 61-81). Philadelphia, PA: Temple University Press.

Citation at a glance: Book (APA)

To cite a print book in APA style, include the following elements:

1 Author
2 Year of publication
3 Title and subtitle

4 Place of publication
5 Publisher

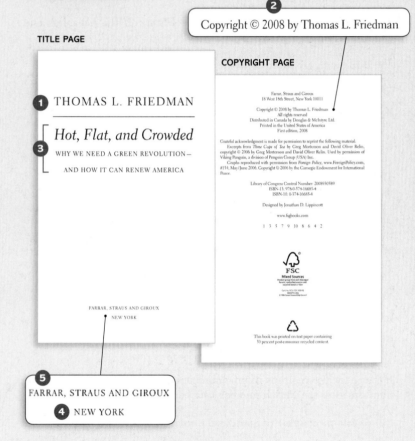

② Copyright © 2008 by Thomas L. Friedman

TITLE PAGE

① THOMAS L. FRIEDMAN

③ *Hot, Flat, and Crowded*
WHY WE NEED A GREEN REVOLUTION—
AND HOW IT CAN RENEW AMERICA

FARRAR, STRAUS AND GIROUX
NEW YORK

COPYRIGHT PAGE

Farrar, Straus and Giroux
18 West 18th Street, New York 10011

Copyright © 2008 by Thomas L. Friedman
All rights reserved
Distributed in Canada by Douglas & McIntyre Ltd.
Printed in the United States of America
First edition, 2008

Grateful acknowledgment is made for permission to reprint the following material:
Excerpts from *Three Cups of Tea* by Greg Mortenson and David Oliver Relin,
copyright © 2006 by Greg Mortenson and David Oliver Relin. Used by permission of
Viking Penguin, a division of Penguin Group (USA) Inc.
Graphs reproduced with permission from *Foreign Policy*, www.ForeignPolicy.com,
#154, May/June 2006. Copyright © 2006 by the Carnegie Endowment for International
Peace.

Library of Congress Control Number: 2008930589
ISBN-13: 978-0-374-16685-4
ISBN-10: 0-374-16685-4

Designed by Jonathan D. Lippincott

www.fsgbooks.com

1 3 5 7 9 10 8 6 4 2

FSC
Mixed Sources

This book was printed on text paper containing
30 percent post-consumer recycled content.

⑤ FARRAR, STRAUS AND GIROUX
④ NEW YORK

REFERENCE LIST ENTRY FOR A PRINT BOOK

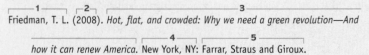

━━1━━ ━━2━━ ━━━━━━━━━━3━━━━━━━━━━
Friedman, T. L. (2008). *Hot, flat, and crowded: Why we need a green revolution—And*

━━━━━━━━━━ ━━4━━ ━━5━━
how it can renew America. New York, NY: Farrar, Straus and Giroux.

For more on citing print books in APA style, see pages 468–71.

The abbreviation "Eds." is for multiple editors. If the book has one editor, use "Ed."

23. Multivolume work   Give the number of volumes after the title.

Luo, J. (Ed.). (2005). *China today: An encyclopedia of life in the People's Republic* (Vols. 1-2). Westport, CT: Greenwood Press.

If the work is published in an edition other than the first (see item 21), put the edition number before the volume numbers: (3rd ed., Vols. 1-3).

24. Introduction, preface, foreword, or afterword

Gore, A. (2000). Foreword. In B. Katz (Ed.), *Reflections on regionalism* (pp. ix-x). Washington, DC: Brookings Institution Press.

25. Dictionary or other reference work

Leong, F. T. L. (Ed.). (2008). *Encyclopedia of counseling* (Vols. 1-4). Thousand Oaks, CA: Sage.

26. Article in a reference work

Konijn, E. A. (2008). Affects and media exposure. In W. Donsbach (Ed.), *The international encyclopedia of communication* (Vol. 1, pp. 123-129). Malden, MA: Blackwell.

27. Republished book

Mailer, N. (2008). *Miami and the siege of Chicago: An informal history of the Republican and Democratic conventions of 1968.* New York, NY: New York Review Books. (Original work published 1968)

28. Book with a title in its title   If the book title contains another book title or an article title, neither italicize the internal title nor place it in quotation marks.

Marcus, L. (Ed.). (1999). *Sigmund Freud's* The interpretation of dreams: *New interdisciplinary essays.* Manchester, England: Manchester University Press.

29. Sacred or classical text   It is not necessary to list sacred works such as the Bible or the Qur'an or classical Greek and Roman works in your reference list. See item 14 on page 463 for how to cite these sources in the text of your paper.

Online sources

When citing an online article, include publication information as for a print periodical (see items 7–16) and add information about the online version (see items 30–35).

Online articles and books sometimes include a DOI (digital object identifier). APA uses the DOI, when available, in place of a URL in reference list entries.

Use a retrieval date for an online source only if the content is likely to change. Most of the examples in this section do not show a retrieval date because the content of the sources is stable; if you are unsure about whether to use a retrieval date, consult your instructor.

If you must break a DOI or a URL at the end of a line, break it after a double slash or before any other mark of punctuation; do not add a hyphen. Do not put a period at the end of the entry.

30. Article in an online journal

author: last name + initial(s) | year of publication | article title | journal title | volume

Whitmeyer, J. M. (2000). Power through appointment. *Social Science Research, 29,*

page(s) | DOI

535-555. doi:10.1006/ssre.2000.0680

If there is no DOI, include the URL for the journal's home page.

Ashe, D. D., & McCutcheon, L. E. (2001). Shyness, loneliness, and attitude toward
celebrities. *Current Research in Social Psychology, 6,* 124-133. Retrieved from
http://www.uiowa.edu/~grpproc/crisp/crisp.html

31. Article in an online magazine Give the author, date, article title, and magazine title. Follow with the volume, issue, and page numbers, if they are available. End with the URL for the magazine's home page.

Shelburne, E. C. (2008, September). The great disruption. *The Atlantic, 302*(2). Retrieved
from http://www.theatlantic.com/

Rupley, S. (2010, February 26). The myth of the benign monopoly. *Salon.* Retrieved from
http://www.salon.com/

32. Article in an online newspaper Give the author, date, article title, and newspaper title. Follow with the page numbers, if they are available. End with the URL for the newspaper's home page.

Watson, P. (2008, October 19). Biofuel boom endangers orangutan habitat. *Los Angeles
Times.* Retrieved from http://www.latimes.com/

33. Supplemental material published only online   If a journal, magazine, or newspaper contains extra material (an article or a chart, for example) only in its online version, give whatever publication information is available in the source and add the description "Supplemental material" in brackets after the title.

Samuel, T. (2009, March 27). Mind the wage gap [Supplemental material]. *The American Prospect.* Retrieved from http://www.prospect.org/

34. Article from a database   Start with the publication information for the source (see items 7–16). If the database entry includes a DOI for the article, use the DOI number at the end. For an illustrated citation of a work from a database, see page 474.

all authors:
last name + initial(s)   year   article title
Eskritt, M., & McLeod, K. (2008). Children's note taking as a mnemonic tool.

                 journal title   volume page(s)   DOI
Journal of Experimental Child Psychology, 101, 52-74. doi:10.1016

/jecp.2008.05.007

If there is no DOI, include the URL for the home page of the journal. If the URL is not included in the database entry, you can search for it on the Web.

Howard, K. R. (2007). Childhood overweight: Parental perceptions and readiness for change. *The Journal of School Nursing, 23,* 73-79. Retrieved from http://jsn .sagepub.com/

35. Abstract for an online article

Brockerhoff, E. G., Jactel, H., Parrotta, J. A., Quine, C. P., & Sayer, J. (2008). Plantation forests and biodiversity: Oxymoron or opportunity? [Abstract]. *Biodiversity and Conservation, 17,* 925-951. doi:10.1007/s10531-008-9380-x

36. Online book

Adams, B. (2004). *The theory of social revolutions.* Retrieved from http://www .gutenberg.org/catalog/world/readfile?fk_files=44092 (Original work published 1913)

37. Chapter in an online book

Clinton, S. J. (1999). What can be done to prevent childhood obesity? In *Understanding childhood obesity* (pp. 81-98). Retrieved from http://www.questia.com/

Citation at a glance: Article from a database (APA)

To cite an article from a database in APA style, include the following elements:

1 Author(s)
2 Date of publication
3 Title of article
4 Name of periodical
5 Volume number; issue number, if required (see p. 465)

6 Page number(s)
7 DOI (digital object identifier)
8 URL for journal's home page (if there is no DOI)

ON-SCREEN VIEW OF DATABASE RECORD

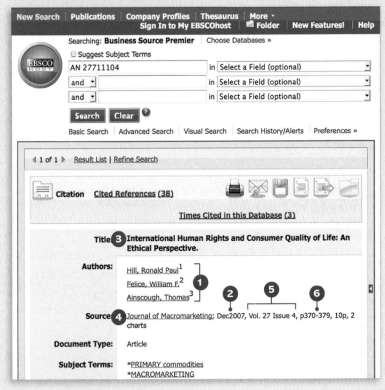

END OF
DATABASE
RECORD

ISSN: 0276-1467

DOI: 10.1177/027614670307128

REFERENCE LIST ENTRY FOR AN ARTICLE FROM A DATABASE

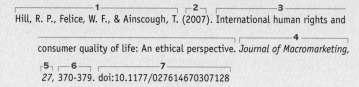

Hill, R. P., Felice, W. F., & Ainscough, T. (2007). International human rights and

consumer quality of life: An ethical perspective. *Journal of Macromarketing,*

27, 370-379. doi:10.1177/027614670307128

For more on citing articles from a database in APA style, see item 34.

38. Online reference work

Swain, C. M. (2004). Sociology of affirmative action. In N. J. Smelser & P. B. Baltes

(Eds.), *International encyclopedia of the social and behavioral sciences.* Retrieved

from http://www.sciencedirect.com/science/referenceworks/9780080430768

Include a retrieval date only if the content of the work is likely to change.

39. Report or long document from a Web site   List the author's name, publication date (or "n.d." if there is no date), document title (in italics), and URL for the document. Give a retrieval date only if the content of the source is likely to change. If a source has no author, begin with the title and follow it with the date in parentheses (see item 4 on p. 465).

Source with date

all authors: online
last name + initial(s)   publication date   document title

Cain, A., & Burris, M. (1999, April). *Investigation of the use of mobile phones while driving.*

URL

Retrieved from http://www.cutr.usf.edu/pdf/mobile_phone.PDF

Source with no date

Archer, D. (n.d.). *Exploring nonverbal communication.* Retrieved from http://nonverbal
.ucsc.edu

40. Section in a Web document

author (organization)   year   title of section
National Institute on Media and the Family. (2009). Mobile networking. In

      title of Web document
    Guide to social networking: Risks. Retrieved from http://www.mediafamily.org

           URL
    /network_pdf/MediaWise_Guide_to_Social_Networking_Risks_09.pdf

For an illustrated citation of a section in a Web document, see page 478.

41. Short work from a Web site

NATO statement endangers patients in Afghanistan. (2010, March 11). *Médecins*

    sans frontières/Doctors without borders. Retrieved from http://www

    .doctorswithoutborders.org/

42. Document from a university or government agency Web site

Cosmides, L., & Tooby, J. (1997). *Evolutionary psychology: A primer.* Retrieved from

    University of California, Santa Barbara, Center for Evolutionary Psychology

    website: http://www.psych.ucsb.edu/research/cep/primer.html

43. Article in an online newsletter   Cite as an online article (see items 30–32), giving the title of the newsletter and whatever other information is available, including volume and issue numbers.

In the face of extinction. (2008, May). *NSF Current.* Retrieved from http://www.nsf.gov

    /news/newsletter/may_08/index.jsp

44. Podcast

organization as producer   date of posting
National Academies (Producer). (2007, June 6). Progress in preventing childhood

        podcast title   descriptive label   series title
    obesity: How do we measure up? [Audio podcast]. *The sounds of science podcast.*

           URL
    Retrieved from http://media.nap.edu/podcasts/

  writer/
  presenter   date of posting   podcast title
Chesney, M. (2007, September 13). Gender differences in the use of complementary

                  podcast number   descriptive label
    and alternative medicine (No. 12827) [Audio podcast]. Retrieved from University

      Web site hosting podcast   URL
    of California Television website: http://www.uctv.tv/ondemand

45. Blog (Weblog) post   Give the writer's name, the date of the post, the subject, the label "Web log post" in brackets, and the URL. For a response to a post, use the label "Web log comment."

Kellermann, M. (2007, May 23). Disclosing clinical trials [Web log post]. Retrieved from
http://www.iq.harvard.edu/blog/sss/archives/2007/05

46. Online audio or video file   Give the medium or a description of the source file in brackets following the title.

writer/ presenter	no date	title	descriptive label	URL

Chomsky, N. (n.d.). The new imperialism [Audio file]. Retrieved from http://www

.rhapsody.com/noamchomsky

Zakaria, F. (Host), & McCullough, C. (Writer). (2007, March 6). In focus: American
teens, Rwandan truths [Video file]. Retrieved from http://www.pulitzercenter
.org/showproject.cfm?id=26

47. Entry in a wiki   Begin with the title of the entry and the date of posting, if there is one (use "n.d." for "no date" if there is not). Then add your retrieval date and the URL for the wiki entry. Include the date of retrieval because the content of a wiki can change frequently. If an author or an editor is identified, include that name at the beginning of the entry.

Ethnomethodology. (n.d.). Retrieved June 18, 2010, from http://stswiki.org/index
.php?title=Ethnomethodology

48. Data set or graphic representation   Give information about the type of source in brackets following the title. If there is no title, give a brief description of the content of the source in brackets in place of the title.

U.S. Department of Agriculture, Economic Research Service. (2009). *Eating and health
module (ATUS): 2007 data* [Data set]. Retrieved from http://www.ers.usda.gov
/Data/ATUS/Data/2007/2007data.htm

Gallup. (2008, October 23). *No increase in proportion of first-time voters* [Graphs].
Retrieved from http://www.gallup.com/poll/111331/No-Increase-Proportion
-First-Time-Voters.aspx

Citation at a glance: Section in a Web document (APA)

To cite a section from a Web document in APA style, include the following elements:

1 Author
2 Date of publication or most recent update
3 Title of section
4 Title of document
5 URL of section or of document

BROWSER PRINTOUT OF WEB SITE

2008 Minnesota Health Statistics Annual Summary – Minnesota Dept. of Health

 Minnesota Department of Health
Protecting, maintaining and improving the health of all Minnesotans   MDH

4 2008 Minnesota Health Statistics Annual Summary

The Minnesota "Annual Summary" or "Minnesota Health Statistics" is a report published yearly. The most recent version of this report is **2008 Minnesota Health Statistics**, published January 2010. This report provides statistical data on the following subjects for the state of Minnesota.

 published January 2010.

To view the PDF files, you will need Adobe Acrobat Re___ site).

- Introduction, Technical Notes, Definitions (PDF: 42KB/7 pages)
- Overview of 2008 Annual Summary (PDF: 66KB/11 pages)
- Live Births (PDF: 196KB/21 pages)
- Fertility (PDF: 26KB/2 pages)  3
- Infant Mortality and Fetal Deaths (PDF: 188KB/15 pages)
- General Mortality (PDF: 333KB/40 pages)
- Marriage/Dissolution of Marriage Divorce (PDF: 25KB/2 pages)
- Population (PDF: 73KB/12 pages)

Note: Induced abortion statistics previously reported in this publication are now published separately.
See Report to the Legislature: Induced Abortions in Minnesota

See also Minnesota Health Statistics Annual Summary Main Page

For further information about the Annual Summary, please contact:

**Center for Health Statistics
Minnesota Department of Health
Golden Rule Building, 3rd Floor
85 East Seventh Place**

http://www.health.state.mn.us/divs/chs/annsum/08annsum/index.html   Page 1 of 2

5 http://www.health.state.mn.us/divs/chs/annsum/08annsum/Fertility08.pdf

ON-SCREEN VIEW OF DOCUMENT

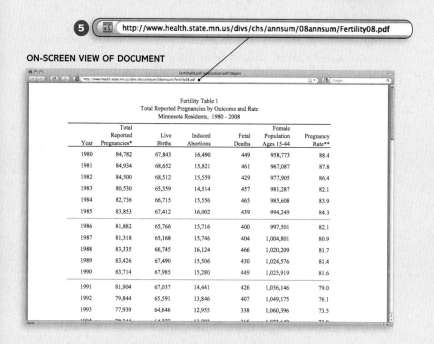

Fertility Table 1
Total Reported Pregnancies by Outcome and Rate
Minnesota Residents, 1980 - 2008

Year	Total Reported Pregnancies*	Live Births	Induced Abortions	Fetal Deaths	Female Population Ages 15-44	Pregnancy Rate**
1980	84,782	67,843	16,490	449	958,773	88.4
1981	84,934	68,652	15,821	461	967,087	87.8
1982	84,500	68,512	15,559	429	977,905	86.4
1983	80,530	65,559	14,514	457	981,287	82.1
1984	82,736	66,715	15,556	465	985,608	83.9
1985	83,853	67,412	16,002	439	994,249	84.3
1986	81,882	65,766	15,716	400	997,501	82.1
1987	81,318	65,168	15,746	404	1,004,801	80.9
1988	83,335	66,745	16,124	466	1,020,209	81.7
1989	83,426	67,490	15,506	430	1,024,576	81.4
1990	83,714	67,985	15,280	449	1,025,919	81.6
1991	81,904	67,037	14,441	426	1,036,146	79.0
1992	79,844	65,591	13,846	407	1,049,175	76.1
1993	77,939	64,646	12,955	338	1,060,396	73.5

REFERENCE LIST ENTRY FOR A SECTION IN A WEB DOCUMENT

—————1————— ————2———— —3— ————4————

Minnesota Department of Health. (2010, January). Fertility. In *2008 Minnesota health*

————————————————— ——————5——————

statistics annual summary. Retrieved from http://www.health.state.mn.us/divs

—————————————

/chs/annsum/08annsum/Fertility08.pdf

For more on citing documents from Web sites in APA style, see pages 475–80.

49. Conference hearing

Carmona, R. H. (2004, March 2). *The growing epidemic of childhood obesity.* Testimony before the Subcommittee on Competition, Foreign Commerce, and Infrastructure of the U.S. Senate Committee on Commerce, Science, and Transportation. Retrieved from http://www.hhs.gov/asl/testify/t040302.html

50. E-mail   E-mail messages, letters, and other personal communications are not included in the list of references. (See item 11 on p. 462 for citing these sources in the text of your paper.)

51. Online posting   If an online posting is not archived, cite it as a personal communication in the text of your paper and do not include it in the list of references. If the posting is archived, give the URL and the name of the discussion list if it is not part of the URL.

McKinney, J. (2006, December 19). Adult education-healthcare partnerships [Electronic mailing list message]. Retrieved from http://www.nifl.gov/pipermail /healthliteracy/2006/000524.html

Other sources (including online versions)

52. Dissertation from a database

Hymel, K. M. (2009). *Essays in urban economics* (Doctoral dissertation). Available from ProQuest Dissertations and Theses database. (AAT 3355930)

53. Unpublished dissertation

Mitchell, R. D. (2007). *The Wesleyan Quadrilateral: Relocating the conversation* (Unpublished doctoral dissertation). Claremont School of Theology, Claremont, CA.

54. Government document

U.S. Census Bureau. (2006). *Statistical abstract of the United States.* Washington, DC: Government Printing Office.

U.S. Census Bureau, Bureau of Economic Analysis. (2008, August). *U.S. international trade in goods and services* (Report No. CB08-121, BEA08-37, FT-900). Retrieved from http://www.census.gov/foreign-trade/Press-Release/2008pr /06/ftdpress.pdf

55. Report from a private organization If the publisher is also the author, begin with the publisher's name in the author position. For a print source, use "Author" in the publisher position at the end of the entry (see item 3 on p. 465); for an online source, give the URL. If the report has a number, put it in parentheses following the title.

Ford Foundation. (n.d.). *Helping citizens to understand and influence state budgets.* Retrieved from http://www.fordfound.org/pdfs/impact/evaluations/state_fiscal _initiative.pdf

56. Legal source

Sweatt v. Painter, 339 U.S. 629 (1950). Retrieved from Cornell University Law School, Legal Information Institute website: http://www.law.cornell.edu/supct/html /historics/USSC_CR_0339_0629_ZS.html

57. Conference proceedings

Stahl, G. (Ed.). (2002). *Proceedings of CSCL '02: Computer support for collaborative learning.* Hillsdale, NJ: Erlbaum.

58. Paper presented at a meeting or symposium (unpublished)

Anderson, D. N. (2008, May). *Cab-hailing and the micropolitics of gesture.* Paper presented at the Arizona Linguistics and Anthropology Symposium, Tucson, AZ.

59. Poster session at a conference

Wang, Z., & Keogh, T. (2008, June). *A click away: Student response to clickers.* Poster session presented at the annual conference of the American Library Association, Anaheim, CA.

60. Map or chart

Ukraine [Map]. (2008). Retrieved from the University of Texas at Austin Perry-Castañeda Library Map Collection website: http://www.lib.utexas.edu /maps/cia08/ukraine_sm_2008.gif

61. Advertisement

Xbox 360 [Advertisement]. (2007, February). *Wired, 15*(2), 71.

62. Published interview

Murphy, C. (2007, June 22). As the Romans did [Interview by G. Hahn]. Retrieved from
http://www.theatlantic.com/

63. Lecture, speech, or address

Fox, V. (2008, March 5). *Economic growth, poverty, and democracy in Latin America:
A president's perspective.* Address at the Freeman Spogli Institute, Stanford
University, Stanford, CA.

64. Work of art or photograph

Weber, J. (1992). *Toward freedom* [Outdoor mural]. Sherman Oaks, CA.

Newkirk, K. (2006). *Gainer (part II).* Museum of Contemporary Art, Chicago, IL.

65. Brochure, pamphlet, or fact sheet

National Council of State Boards of Nursing. (n.d.). *Professional boundaries* [Brochure].
Retrieved from https://www.ncsbn.org/Professional_Boundaries_2007_Web.pdf

World Health Organization. (2007, October). *Health of indigenous peoples* (No. 326)
[Fact sheet]. Retrieved from http://www.who.int/mediacentre/factsheets/fs326
/en/index.html

66. Presentation slides

Boeninger, C. F. (2008, August). *Web 2.0 tools for reference and instructional services*
[Presentation slides]. Retrieved from http://libraryvoice.com/archives/2008
/08/04/opal-20-conference-presentation-slides/

67. Film or video (motion picture) Give the director, producer, and
other relevant contributors, followed by the year of the film's release, the
title, the description "Motion picture" in brackets, the country where the
film was made, and the studio. If you viewed the film on videocassette or
DVD, indicate that medium in brackets in place of "Motion picture." If
the original release date and the date of the DVD or videocassette are
different, add "Original release" and that date in parentheses at the end
of the entry. If the motion picture would be difficult for your readers to
find, include the name and address of its distributor instead of the country and studio.

Guggenheim, D. (Director), & Bender, L. (Producer). (2006). *An inconvenient truth*
[DVD]. United States: Paramount Home Entertainment.

Spurlock, M. (Director). (2004). *Super size me* [Motion picture]. Available from IDP
Films, 1133 Broadway, Suite 926, New York, NY 10010

68. Television program List the producer and the date of the program. Give the title, followed by "Television broadcast" in brackets, the city, and the television network or service.

Pratt, C. (Executive producer). (2008, October 5). *Face the nation* [Television broadcast].
Washington, DC: CBS News.

For a television series, use the year in which the series was produced, and follow the title with "Television series" in brackets. For an episode in a series, list the writer and director and the year. After the episode title, put "Television series episode" in brackets. Follow with information about the series.

Fanning, D. (Executive producer). (2008). *Frontline* [Television series]. Boston,
MA: WGBH.

Smith, M. (Writer/producer). (2008). Heat [Television series episode]. In D. Fanning
(Executive producer), *Frontline*. Boston, MA: WGBH.

69. Sound recording

Thomas, G. (1996). Breath. On *Didgeridoo: Ancient sound of the future* [CD]. Oxnard, CA:
Aquarius International Music.

70. Computer software or video game Add the words "Computer software" in brackets after the title of the program.

Sims 2 [Computer software]. (2005). New York, NY: Maxis.

APA-5 Manuscript format; sample paper

The American Psychological Association makes a number of recommendations for formatting a paper and preparing a list of references. The following guidelines are consistent with advice given in the *Publication Manual of the American Psychological Association*, 6th ed. (Washington: APA, 2010).

APA-5a Manuscript format

The APA manual provides guidelines for papers prepared for publication in a scholarly journal; it does not provide separate guidelines for papers prepared for undergraduate classes. The formatting guidelines in this section and the sample paper on pages 488–96 can be used for either type of paper. (See p. 497 for alternative formatting.) If you are in doubt about the specific format preferred or required in your course, ask your instructor.

Formatting the paper

Many instructors in the social sciences require students to follow APA guidelines for formatting a paper.

Materials and font Use good-quality 8½"× 11" white paper. If your instructor does not require a specific font, choose one that is standard and easy to read (such as Times New Roman).

Title page Begin at the top left with the words "Running head," followed by a colon and the title of your paper (shortened to no more than fifty characters) in all capital letters. Put the page number 1 flush with the right margin.

About halfway down the page, center the full title of your paper (capitalizing all words of four letters or more), your name, and your school's name. At the bottom of the page, you may add the heading "Author Note," centered, followed by a brief paragraph that lists specific information about the course or department or provides acknowledgments or contact information. See page 488 for a sample title page.

Some instructors may instead require a title page like the one on page 497. If in doubt about the requirements in your course, check with your instructor.

Page numbers and running head Number all pages with arabic numerals (1, 2, and so on) in the upper right corner about one-half inch from the top of the page. The title page should be numbered 1.

On every page, in the upper left corner on the same line as the page number, place a running head. The running head consists of the title of the paper (shortened to no more than fifty characters) in all capital letters. (On the title page only, include the words "Running head" followed by a colon before the shortened title.) See pages 488–96. (See an alternative running head on p. 497.)

Margins, line spacing, and paragraph indents   Use margins of one inch on all sides of the page. Left-align the text.

Double-space throughout the paper. Indent the first line of each paragraph one-half inch.

Capitalization, italics, and quotation marks   Capitalize all words of four letters or more in titles of works and in headings that appear in the text of the paper. Capitalize the first word after a colon if the word begins a complete sentence.

Italicize the titles of books, periodicals, and other long works, such as Web sites. Use quotation marks around the titles of periodical articles, short stories, poems, and other short works.

NOTE: APA has different requirements for titles in the reference list. See page 487.

Long quotations and footnotes   When a quotation is longer than forty words, set it off from the text by indenting it one-half inch from the left margin. Double-space the quotation. Do not use quotation marks around it. See page 495 for an example.

If you insert a footnote number in the text of your paper, place the note at the bottom of the page on which the number appears. Insert an extra double-spaced line between the last line of text on the page and the footnote. Double-space the footnote and indent the first line one-half inch. Begin the note with the superscript arabic numeral that corresponds to the number in the text. See page 490 for an example.

Abstract   If your instructor requires an abstract, include it immediately after the title page. Center the word "Abstract" one inch from the top of the page; double-space the abstract.

An abstract is a 100-to-150-word paragraph that provides readers with a quick overview of your essay. It should express your main idea and your key points; it might also briefly suggest any implications or applications of the research you discuss in the paper. See page 489 for an example.

Headings   Although headings are not always necessary, their use is encouraged in the social sciences. For most undergraduate papers, one level of heading will usually be sufficient.

In APA style, major headings are centered and boldface. Capitalize the first word of the heading along with all words except articles, short prepositions, and coordinating conjunctions. See the sample paper on pages 488–96 for the use of headings.

Visuals   APA classifies visuals as tables and figures (figures include graphs, charts, drawings, and photographs). Keep visuals as simple as possible.

Label each table with an arabic numeral (Table 1, Table 2, and so on) and provide a clear title. The label and title should appear on separate lines above the table, flush left and double-spaced.

Below the table, give its source in a note. If any data in the table require an explanatory footnote, use a superscript lowercase letter in the body of the table and in a footnote following the source note. Double-space source notes and footnotes and do not indent the first line of each note. See page 493 for an example of a table in a student paper.

For each figure, place a label and a caption below the figure, flush left and double-spaced. The label and caption need not appear on separate lines.

In the text of your paper, discuss significant features of each visual. Place the visual as close as possible to the sentences that relate to it unless your instructor prefers that visuals appear in an appendix.

Preparing the list of references

Begin your list of references on a new page at the end of the paper. Center the title "References" one inch from the top of the page, and double-space throughout. For a sample reference list, see page 496.

Indenting entries   Use a hanging indent in the reference list: Type the first line of each entry flush left and indent any additional lines one-half inch, as shown on page 496.

Alphabetizing the list   Alphabetize the reference list by the last names of the authors (or editors); when a work has no author (or editor), alphabetize by the first word of the title other than *A, An,* or *The.*

If your list includes two or more works by the same author, arrange the entries by year, the earliest first. If your list includes two or more works by the same author in the same year, arrange the works alphabetically by title. Add the letters "a," "b," and so on within the parentheses after the year. Use only the year and the letter for articles in journals: (2002a). Use the full date and the letter for articles in magazines and newspapers in the reference list: (2005a, July 7). Use only the year and the letter in the in-text citation.

Authors' names   Invert all authors' names and use initials instead of first names. Separate the names with commas. With two to seven authors, use an ampersand (&) before the last author's name. If there are eight or more authors, give the first six authors, three ellipsis dots, and the last author (see p. 464).

Titles of books and articles   Italicize the titles and subtitles of books. Do not italicize or use quotation marks around the titles of articles. Capitalize only the first word of the title and subtitle (and all proper nouns) of books and articles. Capitalize names of periodicals as you would capitalize them normally (see P8-c).

Abbreviations for page numbers   Abbreviations for "page" and "pages" ("p." and "pp.") are used before page numbers of newspaper articles and articles in edited books (see item 9 on p. 466 and item 22 on p. 469) but not before page numbers of articles in magazines and scholarly journals (see items 7 and 8 on p. 466).

Breaking a URL or DOI   When a URL or a DOI (digital object identifier) must be divided, break it after a double slash or before any other mark of punctuation. Do not insert a hyphen, and do not add a period at the end.

For information about the exact format of each entry in your list, consult the models on pages 464–83.

APA-5b Sample research paper: APA style

On pages 488–96 is a research paper on the effectiveness of treatments for childhood obesity, written by Luisa Mirano, a student in a psychology class. Mirano's assignment was to write a review of the literature and document it with APA-style citations and references. (See p. 497 for a sample of alternative formatting.)

MODELS   hackerhandbooks.com/writersref
> Model papers > APA papers: Mirano; Charat; Gibson; Riss
> APA annotated bibliography: Haddad

A running head, which will be used in the printed journal article, consists of a title (shortened to no more than fifty characters) in all capital letters. On the title page, it is preceded by the label "Running head." Page numbers appear in the upper right corner.

Running head: CAN MEDICATION CURE OBESITY IN CHILDREN?   1

Full title, writer's name, and school name are centered halfway down the page.

Can Medication Cure Obesity in Children?

A Review of the Literature

Luisa Mirano

Northwest-Shoals Community College

An author's note lists specific information about the course or department and can provide acknowledgments and contact information.

Author Note

This paper was prepared for Psychology 108, Section B, taught by Professor Kang.

Marginal annotations indicate APA-style formatting and effective writing.

CAN MEDICATION CURE OBESITY IN CHILDREN?   2

Abstract

In recent years, policymakers and medical experts have expressed alarm about the growing problem of childhood obesity in the United States. While most agree that the issue deserves attention, consensus dissolves around how to respond to the problem. This literature review examines one approach to treating childhood obesity: medication. The paper compares the effectiveness for adolescents of the only two drugs approved by the Food and Drug Administration (FDA) for long-term treatment of obesity, sibutramine and orlistat. This examination of pharmacological treatments for obesity points out the limitations of medication and suggests the need for a comprehensive solution that combines medical, social, behavioral, and political approaches to this complex problem.

Abstract appears on a separate page.

CAN MEDICATION CURE OBESITY IN CHILDREN?   3

Full title, centered.   Can Medication Cure Obesity in Children?

A Review of the Literature

In March 2004, U.S. Surgeon General Richard Carmona called attention to a health problem in the United States that, until recently, has been overlooked: childhood obesity. Carmona said that the "astounding" 15% child obesity rate constitutes an "epidemic." Since the early 1980s, that rate has "doubled in children and tripled in adolescents." Now more than 9 million children are classified as obese.[1] While the traditional response to a medical epidemic is to hunt for a vaccine or a cure-all pill, childhood obesity is more elusive. The lack of success of recent initiatives suggests that medication might not be the answer for the escalating problem. This literature review considers whether the use of medication is a promising approach for solving the childhood obesity problem by responding to the following questions:

Mirano sets up her organization by posing four questions.

1. What are the implications of childhood obesity?

2. Is medication effective at treating childhood obesity?

3. Is medication safe for children?

4. Is medication the best solution?

Mirano states her thesis.

Understanding the limitations of medical treatments for children highlights the complexity of the childhood obesity problem in the United States and underscores the need for physicians, advocacy groups, and policymakers to search for other solutions.

Headings, centered, help readers follow the organization.

What Are the Implications of Childhood Obesity?

Obesity can be a devastating problem from both an individual and a societal perspective. Obesity puts children at risk for a number of medical complications, including Type 2 diabetes, hypertension, sleep apnea, and orthopedic problems (Henry J. Kaiser Family Foundation, 2004, p. 1).

In a signal phrase, the word "and" links the names of two authors; the date is given in parentheses.

Researchers Hoppin and Taveras (2004) have noted that obesity is often associated with psychological issues such as depression, anxiety, and binge eating (Table 4).

Obesity also poses serious problems for a society struggling to cope with rising health care costs. The cost of treating obesity currently totals

Mirano uses a footnote to define an essential term that would be cumbersome to define within the text.

[1]Obesity is measured in terms of body-mass index (BMI): weight in kilograms divided by square of height in meters. A child or an adolescent with a BMI in the 95th percentile for his or her age and gender is considered obese.

CAN MEDICATION CURE OBESITY IN CHILDREN? 4

$117 billion per year—a price, according to the surgeon general, "second only to the cost of [treating] tobacco use" (Carmona, 2004). And as the number of children who suffer from obesity grows, long-term costs will only increase.

Because the author (Carmona) is not named in the signal phrase, his name and the date appear in parentheses.

Is Medication Effective at Treating Childhood Obesity?

The widening scope of the obesity problem has prompted medical professionals to rethink old conceptions of the disorder and its causes. As researchers Yanovski and Yanovski (2002) have explained, obesity was once considered "either a moral failing or evidence of underlying psychopathology" (p. 592). But this view has shifted: Many medical professionals now consider obesity a biomedical rather than a moral condition, influenced by both genetic and environmental factors. Yanovski and Yanovski have further noted that the development of weight-loss medications in the early 1990s showed that "obesity should be treated in the same manner as any other chronic disease . . . through the long-term use of medication" (p. 592).

Ellipsis mark indicates omitted words.

The search for the right long-term medication has been complicated. Many of the drugs authorized by the Food and Drug Administration (FDA) in the early 1990s proved to be a disappointment. Two of the medications— fenfluramine and dexfenfluramine—were withdrawn from the market because of severe side effects (Yanovski & Yanovski, 2002, p. 592), and several others were classified by the Drug Enforcement Administration as having the "potential for abuse" (Hoppin & Taveras, 2004, Weight-Loss Drugs section, para. 6). Currently only two medications have been approved by the FDA for long-term treatment of obesity: sibutramine (marketed as Meridia) and orlistat (marketed as Xenical). This section compares studies on the effectiveness of each.

In a parenthetical citation, an ampersand links the names of two authors.

Sibutramine suppresses appetite by blocking the reuptake of the neurotransmitters serotonin and norepinephrine in the brain (Yanovski & Yanovski, 2002, p. 594). Though the drug won FDA approval in 1998, experiments to test its effectiveness for younger patients came considerably later. In 2003, University of Pennsylvania researchers Berkowitz, Wadden, Tershakovec, and Cronquist released the first double-blind placebo study testing the effect of sibutramine on adolescents, aged 13-17, over a 12-month period. Their findings are summarized in Table 1.

Mirano draws attention to an important article.

After 6 months, the group receiving medication had lost 4.6 kg

CAN MEDICATION CURE OBESITY IN CHILDREN?   5

(about 10 pounds) more than the control group. But during the second half of the study, when both groups received sibutramine, the results were more ambiguous. In months 6-12, the group that continued to take sibutramine gained an average of 0.8 kg, or roughly 2 pounds; the control group, which switched from placebo to sibutramine, lost 1.3 kg, or roughly 3 pounds (p. 1808). Both groups received behavioral therapy covering diet, exercise, and mental health.

These results paint a murky picture of the effectiveness of the medication: While initial data seemed promising, the results after one year raised questions about whether medication-induced weight loss could be sustained over time. As Berkowitz et al. (2003) advised, "Until more extensive safety and efficacy data are available, . . . weight-loss medications should be used only on an experimental basis for adolescents" (p. 1811).

A study testing the effectiveness of orlistat in adolescents showed similarly ambiguous results. The FDA approved orlistat in 1999 but did not authorize it for adolescents until December 2003. Roche Laboratories (2003), maker of orlistat, released results of a one-year study testing the drug on 539 obese adolescents, aged 12-16. The drug, which promotes weight loss by blocking fat absorption in the large intestine, showed some effectiveness in adolescents: an average loss of 1.3 kg, or roughly 3 pounds, for subjects taking orlistat for one year, as opposed to an average gain of 0.67 kg, or 1.5 pounds, for the control group (pp. 8-9). See Table 1.

Short-term studies of orlistat have shown slightly more dramatic results. Researchers at the National Institute of Child Health and Human Development tested 20 adolescents, aged 12-16, over a three-month period and found that orlistat, combined with behavioral therapy, produced an average weight loss of 4.4 kg, or 9.7 pounds (McDuffie et al., 2002, p. 646). The study was not controlled against a placebo group; therefore, the relative effectiveness of orlistat in this case remains unclear.

Is Medication Safe for Children?

While modest weight loss has been documented for both medications, each carries risks of certain side effects. Sibutramine has been observed to increase blood pressure and pulse rate. In 2002, a

For a source with six or more authors, the first author's surname followed by "et al." is used for the first and subsequent references.

CAN MEDICATION CURE OBESITY IN CHILDREN?   6

Table 1

Effectiveness of Sibutramine and Orlistat in Adolescents

Mirano uses a table to summarize the findings presented in two sources.

Medication	Subjects	Treatment[a]	Side effects	Average weight loss/gain
Sibutramine	Control	0-6 mos.: placebo 6-12 mos.: sibutramine	Mos. 6-12: increased blood pressure; increased pulse rate	After 6 mos.: loss of 3.2 kg (7 lb) After 12 mos.: loss of 4.5 kg (9.9 lb)
	Medicated	0-12 mos.: sibutramine	Increased blood pressure; increased pulse rate	After 6 mos.: loss of 7.8 kg (17.2 lb) After 12 mos.: loss of 7.0 kg (15.4 lb)
Orlistat	Control	0-12 mos.: placebo	None	Gain of 0.67 kg (1.5 lb)
	Medicated	0-12 mos.: orlistat	Oily spotting; flatulence; abdominal discomfort	Loss of 1.3 kg (2.9 lb)

Note. The data on sibutramine are adapted from "Behavior Therapy and Sibutramine for the Treatment of Adolescent Obesity," by R. I. Berkowitz, T. A. Wadden, A. M. Tershakovec, & J. L. Cronquist, 2003, *Journal of the American Medical Association, 289*, pp. 1807-1809. The data on orlistat are adapted from *Xenical (Orlistat) Capsules: Complete Product Information*, by Roche Laboratories, December 2003, retrieved from http://www.rocheusa.com/products/xenical/pi.pdf

A note gives the source of the data.

[a]The medication and/or placebo were combined with behavioral therapy in all groups over all time periods.

A content note explains data common to all subjects.

consumer group claimed that the medication was related to the deaths of 19 people and filed a petition with the Department of Health and Human Services to ban the medication (Hilts, 2002). The sibutramine study by Berkowitz et al. (2003) noted elevated blood pressure as a side effect, and dosages had to be reduced or the medication discontinued in 19 of the 43 subjects in the first six months (p. 1809).

The main side effects associated with orlistat were abdominal discomfort, oily spotting, fecal incontinence, and nausea (Roche Laboratories, 2003, p. 13). More serious for long-term health is the concern that orlistat, being a fat-blocker, would affect absorption of fat-soluble vitamins, such as vitamin D. However, the study found that this side effect can be minimized or eliminated if patients take vitamin supplements two hours before or after administration of orlistat (p. 10). With close monitoring of patients taking the medication, many of the risks can be reduced.

Is Medication the Best Solution?

The data on the safety and efficacy of pharmacological treatments of childhood obesity raise the question of whether medication is the best solution for the problem. The treatments have clear costs for individual patients, including unpleasant side effects, little information about long-term use, and uncertainty that they will yield significant weight loss.

In purely financial terms, the drugs cost more than $3 a day on average (Duenwald, 2004). In each of the clinical trials, use of medication was accompanied by an expensive regime of behavioral therapies, including counseling, nutritional education, fitness advising, and monitoring. As journalist Greg Critser (2003) noted in his book *Fat Land,* use of weight-loss drugs is unlikely to have an effect without the proper "support system"—one that includes doctors, facilities, time, and money (p. 3). For some, this level of care is prohibitively expensive.

A third complication is that the studies focused on adolescents aged 12-16, but obesity can begin at a much younger age. Few data exist to establish the safety or efficacy of medication for treating very young children.

While the scientific data on the concrete effects of these medications in children remain somewhat unclear, medication is not the only avenue for addressing the crisis. Both medical experts and

---

When this article was first cited, all four authors were named. In subsequent citations of a work with three to five authors, "et al." is used after the first author's name.

Mirano develops the paper's thesis.

CAN MEDICATION CURE OBESITY IN CHILDREN? 8

policymakers recognize that solutions might come not only from a laboratory but also from policy, education, and advocacy. A handbook designed to educate doctors on obesity called for "major changes in some aspects of western culture" (Hoppin & Taveras, 2004, Conclusion section, para. 1). Cultural change may not be the typical realm of medical professionals, but the handbook urged doctors to be proactive and "focus [their] energy on public policies and interventions" (Conclusion section, para. 1).

> Brackets indicate a word not in the original source.

The solutions proposed by a number of advocacy groups underscore this interest in political and cultural change. A report by the Henry J. Kaiser Family Foundation (2004) outlined trends that may have contributed to the childhood obesity crisis, including food advertising for children as well as

> a reduction in physical education classes and after-school athletic programs, an increase in the availability of sodas and snacks in public schools, the growth in the number of fast-food outlets . . . , and the increasing number of highly processed high-calorie and high-fat grocery products. (p. 1)

> A quotation longer than forty words is indented without quotation marks.

Addressing each of these areas requires more than a doctor armed with a prescription pad; it requires a broad mobilization not just of doctors and concerned parents but of educators, food industry executives, advertisers, and media representatives.

> Mirano interprets the evidence; she doesn't just report it.

The barrage of possible approaches to combating childhood obesity—from scientific research to political lobbying—indicates both the severity and the complexity of the problem. While none of the medications currently available is a miracle drug for curing the nation's 9 million obese children, research has illuminated some of the underlying factors that affect obesity and has shown the need for a comprehensive approach to the problem that includes behavioral, medical, social, and political change.

> The tone of the conclusion is objective.

List of references
begins on a new
page. Heading is
centered.

References

Berkowitz, R. I., Wadden, T. A., Tershakovec, A. M., & Cronquist, J. L.
(2003). Behavior therapy and sibutramine for the treatment of
adolescent obesity. *Journal of the American Medical Association,
289,* 1805-1812.

List is alphabetized
by authors' last
names. All authors'
names are inverted.

Carmona, R. H. (2004, March 2). *The growing epidemic of childhood
obesity.* Testimony before the Subcommittee on Competition,
Foreign Commerce, and Infrastructure of the U.S. Senate
Committee on Commerce, Science, and Transportation. Retrieved
from http://www.hhs.gov/asl/testify/t040302.html

Critser, G. (2003). *Fat land.* Boston, MA: Houghton Mifflin.

The first line of an
entry is at the left
margin; subsequent
lines indent ½˝.

Duenwald, M. (2004, January 6). Slim pickings: Looking beyond ephedra.
The New York Times, p. F1. Retrieved from http://nytimes.com/

Henry J. Kaiser Family Foundation. (2004, February). *The role of media
in childhood obesity.* Retrieved from http://www.kff.org
/entmedia/7030.cfm

Hilts, P. J. (2002, March 20). Petition asks for removal of diet drug
from market. *The New York Times,* p. A26. Retrieved from http://
nytimes.com/

Double-spacing is
used throughout.

Hoppin, A. G., & Taveras, E. M. (2004, June 25). Assessment and
management of childhood and adolescent obesity. *Clinical Update.*
Retrieved from http://www.medscape.com/viewarticle/481633

McDuffie, J. R., Calis, K. A., Uwaifo, G. I., Sebring, N. G., Fallon, E. M.,
Hubbard, V. S., & Yanovski, J. A. (2002). Three-month tolerability
of orlistat in adolescents with obesity-related comorbid conditions.
Obesity Research, 10, 642-650.

Roche Laboratories. (2003, December). *Xenical (orlistat) capsules: Complete
product information.* Retrieved from http://www.rocheusa
.com/products/xenical/pi.pdf

Yanovski, S. Z., & Yanovski, J. A. (2002). Drug therapy: Obesity. *The New
England Journal of Medicine, 346,* 591-602.

ALTERNATIVE APA TITLE PAGE

Obesity in Children 1   Short title and page
number in the upper
right corner on all
pages.

Can Medication Cure Obesity in Children?   Full title, centered.
A Review of the Literature

Luisa Mirano   Writer's name,
Psychology 108, Sector B   course, instructor's
name, and date, all
Professor Kang   centered at the
October 31, 2004   bottom of the page.

ALTERNATIVE APA RUNNING HEAD

Obesity in Children 5

were classified by the Drug Enforcement Administration as having the
"potential for abuse" (Hoppin & Taveras, 2004, Weight-Loss Drugs
section, para. 6). Currently only two medications have been approved
by the FDA for long-term treatment of obesity: sibutramine (marketed

Marginal annotations indicate APA-style formatting.

Directory to CMS-style note and bibliography models

CMS (*Chicago*) Papers

Most assignments in history and other humanities classes are based to some extent on reading. At times you will be asked to respond to one or two readings, such as essays or historical documents. At other times you may be asked to write a research paper that draws on a wide variety of sources.

Many history instructors and some humanities instructors require you to document sources with footnotes or endnotes based on *The Chicago Manual of Style*, 16th ed. (Chicago: U of Chicago P, 2010). (See CMS-4.) When you write a paper using sources, you face three main challenges: (1) supporting a thesis, (2) citing your sources and avoiding plagiarism, and (3) integrating quotations and other source material.

Examples in this section appear in CMS style and are drawn from one student's research on the Fort Pillow massacre. Sample pages from Ned Bishop's paper appear on pages 532–37.

CMS-1 Supporting a thesis

Most research assignments ask you to form a thesis, or main idea, and to support that thesis with well-organized evidence.

CMS-1a Form a working thesis.

Once you have read a variety of sources and considered your issue from different perspectives, you are ready to form a working thesis: a one-sentence (or occasionally a two-sentence) statement of your central idea. (See also C1-c.) In a research paper, your thesis will answer the central research question that you pose. Here, for example, are student writer Ned Bishop's research question and working thesis statement.

RESEARCH QUESTION

To what extent was Confederate Major General Nathan Bedford Forrest responsible for the massacre of Union troops at Fort Pillow?

WORKING THESIS

By encouraging racism among his troops, Nathan Bedford Forrest was directly responsible for the massacre of Union troops at Fort Pillow.

Notice that the thesis expresses a view on a debatable issue—an issue about which intelligent, well-meaning people might disagree. The writer's job is to persuade such readers that this view is worth taking seriously. To read Ned Bishop's thesis in the context of his introduction, see page 533.

PRACTICE hackerhandbooks.com/writersref
> CMS (*Chicago*) > CMS 1–1

CMS-1b Organize your ideas.

The body of your paper will consist of evidence in support of your thesis. Instead of getting tangled up in a formal outline early in the process, sketch an informal plan that organizes your ideas in bold strokes. Ned Bishop, for example, used a simple outline to structure his ideas. In the paper itself, these points became headings that help readers follow his line of argument.

> What happened at Fort Pillow?
>
> Did Forrest order the massacre?
>
> Can Forrest be held responsible for the massacre?

CMS-1c Use sources to inform and support your argument.

Used thoughtfully, your source materials will make your argument more complex and convincing for readers. Sources can play several different roles as you develop your points.

Providing background information or context

You can use facts and statistics to support generalizations or to establish the importance of your topic, as student writer Ned Bishop does early in his paper.

> Fort Pillow, Tennessee, which sat on a bluff overlooking the Mississippi River, had been held by the Union for two years. It was garrisoned by 580 men, 292 of them from United States Colored Heavy and Light Artillery regiments, 285 from the white Thirteenth Tennessee Cavalry. Nathan Bedford Forrest commanded about 1,500 troops.[1]

Explaining terms or concepts

If readers are unlikely to be familiar with a word, a phrase, or an idea important to your topic, you must explain it for them. Quoting or paraphrasing a source can help you define terms and concepts clearly and concisely.

> The Civil War practice of giving no quarter to an enemy—in other words, "denying [an enemy] the right of survival"—defied Lincoln's mandate for humane and merciful treatment of prisoners.[9]

Supporting your claims

As you draft your argument, make sure to back up your assertions with
facts, examples, and other evidence from your research (see also A2-e).
Ned Bishop, for example, uses an eyewitness report of the racially
motivated violence perpetrated by Nathan Bedford Forrest's troops.

> The slaughter at Fort Pillow was no doubt driven in large part by racial hatred. . . .
> A Southern reporter traveling with Forrest makes clear that the discrimination was
> deliberate: "Our troops maddened by the excitement, shot down the ret[r]eating
> Yankees, and not until they had attained t[h]e water's edge and turned to beg for
> mercy, did any prisoners fall in [t]o our hands—Thus the whites received quarter,
> but the negroes were shown no mercy."[19]

Lending authority to your argument

Expert opinion can give weight to your argument (see also A2-e). But
don't rely on experts to make your argument for you. Construct your
argument in your own words and, when appropriate, cite the judgment of an authority in the field for support.

> Fort Pillow is not the only instance of a massacre or threatened massacre of black
> soldiers by troops under Forrest's command. Biographer Brian Steel Wills points out
> that at Brice's Cross Roads in June 1864, "black soldiers suffered inordinately" as
> Forrest looked the other way and Confederate soldiers deliberately sought out
> those they termed "the damned negroes."[21]

Anticipating and countering alternative interpretations

Do not ignore sources that seem contrary to your position or that offer
interpretations different from your own. Instead, use them to give
voice to opposing points of view and alternative interpretations before
you counter them (see A2-f). Readers often have objections in mind
already, whether or not they agree with you. Ned Bishop, for example,
presents conflicting evidence to acknowledge that some readers may
credit Nathan Bedford Forrest with stopping the massacre. In doing
so, Bishop creates an opportunity to counter that objection and persuade those readers that Forrest can be held accountable.

> Hurst suggests that the temperamental Forrest "may have ragingly ordered a massacre
> and even intended to carry it out—until he rode inside the fort and viewed the
> horrifying result" and ordered it stopped.[15] While this is an intriguing interpretation
> of events, even Hurst would probably admit that it is merely speculation.

CMS-2 Citing sources; avoiding plagiarism

Your research paper is a collaboration between you and your sources. To be fair and ethical, you must acknowledge your debt to the writers of those sources. Failure to do so is a form of academic dishonesty known as *plagiarism*.

Three different acts are generally considered plagiarism: (1) failing to cite quotations and borrowed ideas, (2) failing to enclose borrowed language in quotation marks, and (3) failing to put summaries and paraphrases in your own words. Definitions of plagiarism may vary; it's a good idea to find out how your school defines and addresses academic dishonesty. (See also R3-c.)

CMS-2a Cite quotations and borrowed ideas.

You must cite anything you borrow from a source, including direct quotations; statistics and other facts; visuals such as tables, maps, and photographs; and any ideas you present in a summary or paraphrase.

The only exception is common knowledge—information your readers could easily find in any number of general sources. For example, most encyclopedias will tell readers that the Korean War ended in 1953 and that President Theodore Roosevelt was the first American to receive a Nobel Prize. As a rule, when you have seen certain information repeatedly in your reading, you don't need to cite it. However, when information has appeared in only a few sources, when it is highly specific (as with statistics), or when it is controversial, you should cite the source.

CMS citations consist of superscript numbers in the text of the paper that refer readers to notes with corresponding numbers either at the foot of the page (footnotes) or at the end of the paper (endnotes).

TEXT

Governor John Andrew was not allowed to recruit black soldiers from out of state. "Ostensibly," writes Peter Burchard, "no recruiting was done outside Massachusetts but it was an open secret that Andrew's agents were working far and wide."[1]

NOTE

1. Peter Burchard, *One Gallant Rush: Robert Gould Shaw and His Brave Black Regiment* (New York: St. Martin's, 1965), 85.

This basic CMS format varies for different types of sources. For a detailed discussion and other models, see CMS-4. When you use footnotes or endnotes, you will usually need to provide a bibliography as well (see CMS-4b).

CMS-2b Enclose borrowed language in quotation marks.

To indicate that you are using a source's exact phrases or sentences, you must enclose them in quotation marks unless they have been set off from the text by indenting (see the bottom of p. 506). To omit the quotation marks is to claim—falsely—that the language is your own. Such an omission is plagiarism even if you have cited the source.

ORIGINAL SOURCE

For many Southerners it was psychologically impossible to see a black man bearing arms as anything but an incipient slave uprising complete with arson, murder, pillage, and rapine.
— Dudley Taylor Cornish, *The Sable Arm*, p. 158

PLAGIARISM

According to Civil War historian Dudley Taylor Cornish, for many Southerners it was psychologically impossible to see a black man bearing arms as anything but an incipient slave uprising complete with arson, murder, pillage, and rapine.[2]

BORROWED LANGUAGE IN QUOTATION MARKS

According to Civil War historian Dudley Taylor Cornish, "For many Southerners it was psychologically impossible to see a black man bearing arms as anything but an incipient slave uprising complete with arson, murder, pillage, and rapine."[2]

NOTE: Long quotations are set off from the text by indenting and do not need quotation marks (see the example on p. 507).

CMS-2c Put summaries and paraphrases in your own words.

Summaries and paraphrases are written in your own words. A summary condenses information; a paraphrase conveys the information using roughly the same number of words as in the original source. When you summarize or paraphrase, it is not enough to name the source; you must restate the source's meaning using your own language. (See also R3-c.) You commit plagiarism if you half-copy the author's sentences—either by mixing the author's phrases with your own without using quotation marks or by plugging your own synonyms into the author's sentence structure.

The first paraphrase of the following source is plagiarized—even though the source is cited—because too much of its language is borrowed from the original. The underlined strings of words have been copied exactly (without quotation marks). In addition, the writer has closely followed the sentence structure of the original source, merely making a few substitutions (such as *Fifty percent* for *Half* and *angered and perhaps frightened* for *enraged and perhaps terrified*).

ORIGINAL SOURCE

Half of the force holding Fort Pillow were Negroes, former slaves now enrolled in the Union Army. Toward them Forrest's troops had the fierce, bitter animosity of men who had been educated to regard the colored race as inferior and who for the first time had encountered that race armed and fighting against white men. The sight enraged and perhaps terrified many of the Confederates and aroused in them the ugly spirit of a lynching mob.

—Albert Castel, "The Fort Pillow Massacre," pp. 46–47

PLAGIARISM: UNACCEPTABLE BORROWING

Albert Castel suggests that much of the brutality at Fort Pillow can be traced to racial attitudes. Fifty percent of the troops holding Fort Pillow were Negroes, former slaves who had joined the Union Army. Toward them Forrest's soldiers displayed the savage hatred of men who had been taught the inferiority of blacks and who for the first time had confronted them armed and fighting against white men. The vision angered and perhaps frightened the Confederates and aroused in them the ugly spirit of a lynching mob.[3]

To avoid plagiarizing an author's language, resist the temptation to look at the source while you are summarizing or paraphrasing. After you have read the passage you want to paraphrase, set the source aside. Ask yourself, "What is the author's meaning?" In your own words, state your understanding of the author's basic point. Return to the source and check that you haven't used the author's language or sentence structure or misrepresented the author's ideas. When you fully understand another writer's meaning, you can more easily and accurately present those ideas in your own words.

ACCEPTABLE PARAPHRASE

Albert Castel suggests that much of the brutality at Fort Pillow can be traced to racial attitudes. Nearly half of the Union troops were blacks, men whom the Confederates had been raised to consider their inferiors. The shock and perhaps fear of facing armed ex-slaves in battle for the first time may well have unleashed the fury that led to the massacre.[3]

CMS-3 Integrating sources

Quotations, summaries, paraphrases, and facts will help you develop your argument, but they cannot speak for you. You can use several strategies to integrate information from sources into your paper while maintaining your own voice.

CMS-3a Use quotations appropriately.

In your academic writing, keep the emphasis on your ideas; use your own words to summarize and to paraphrase your sources and to explain your points. Sometimes, however, quotations can be the most effective way to integrate a source.

WHEN TO USE QUOTATIONS

- When language is especially vivid or expressive
- When exact wording is needed for technical accuracy
- When it is important to let the debaters of an issue explain their positions in their own words
- When the words of an authority lend weight to an argument
- When the language of a source is the topic of your discussion

Limiting your use of quotations   Although it is tempting to insert many quotations in your paper and to use your own words only for connecting passages, do not quote excessively. It is almost impossible to integrate numerous long quotations smoothly into your own text.

It is not always necessary to quote full sentences from a source. To reduce your reliance on the words of others, you can often integrate language from a source into your own sentence structure.

> As Hurst has pointed out, until "an outcry erupted in the Northern press," even the Confederates did not deny that there had been a massacre at Fort Pillow.[4]

> Union surgeon Dr. Charles Fitch testified that after he was in custody, he "saw" Confederate soldiers "kill every negro that made his appearance dressed in Federal uniform."[20]

Two useful marks of punctuation, the ellipsis mark and brackets, allow you to keep quoted material to a minimum and to integrate it smoothly into your text.

PRACTICE hackerhandbooks.com/writersref
  > CMS (Chicago) > CMS 3–1 to CMS 3–4

Using the ellipsis mark To condense a quoted passage, you can use the ellipsis mark (three periods, with spaces between) to indicate that you have omitted words. What remains must be grammatically complete.

> Union surgeon Fitch's testimony that all women and children had been evacuated from Fort Pillow before the attack conflicts with Forrest's report: "We captured . . . about 40 negro women and children."[6]

The writer has omitted several words not relevant to the issue at hand: *164 Federals, 75 negro troops, and.*

When you want to leave out one or more full sentences, use a period before the three ellipsis dots. For an example, see the long quotation on page 507.

Ordinarily, do not use an ellipsis mark at the beginning or at the end of a quotation. Readers will understand that you have taken the quoted material from a longer passage, so such marks are not necessary. The only exception occurs when you have dropped words at the end of the final quoted sentence. In such cases, put three ellipsis dots before the closing quotation mark.

Using brackets Brackets allow you to insert your own words into quoted material, perhaps to explain a confusing reference or to keep a sentence grammatical in your context.

> According to Albert Castel, "It can be reasonably argued that he [Forrest] was justified in believing that the approaching steamships intended to aid the garrison [at Fort Pillow]."[7]

NOTE: To indicate an error such as a misspelling in a quotation, insert the word [*sic*], italicized and with brackets around it, right after the error. (See the example on p. 507 and in P6-b for more information.)

Setting off long quotations CMS style allows you some flexibility in deciding whether to set off a long quotation or run it into your text. For emphasis, you may want to set off a quotation of more than four or five typed lines of text; almost certainly you should set off quotations of ten or more lines. To set off a quotation, indent it one-half inch from the left margin and use the normal right margin. Double-space the indented quotation.

Long quotations should be introduced by an informative sentence, often followed by a colon. Quotation marks are unnecessary because the indented format tells readers that the passage is taken word-for-word from the source.

In a letter home, Confederate officer Achilles V. Clark recounted what happened at Fort Pillow:

> Words cannot describe the scene. The poor deluded negroes would run up to our men fall upon their knees and with uplifted hands scream for mercy but they were ordered to their feet and then shot down. The whitte [*sic*] men fared but little better. . . . I with several others tried to stop the butchery and at one time had partially succeeded, but Gen. Forrest ordered them shot down like dogs, and the carnage continued.[8]

CMS-3b Use signal phrases to integrate sources.

Whenever you include a paraphrase, summary, or direct quotation of another writer's work in your paper, prepare your readers for it with a *signal phrase*. A signal phrase usually names the author of the source and often provides some context. It commonly appears before the source material. To vary your sentence structure, you may decide to interrupt source material with a signal phrase or place the signal phrase after your paraphrase, summary, or direct quotation.

When the signal phrase includes a verb, choose one that is appropriate for the way you are using the source (see CMS-1c). Are you providing background, explaining a concept, supporting a claim, lending authority, or refuting an argument? See the chart on page 508 for a list of verbs commonly used in signal phrases.

Note that CMS style calls for verbs in the present tense or present perfect tense (*points out* or *has pointed out*) to introduce source material unless you include a date that specifies the time of the original author's writing.

The first time you mention an author, use the full name: *Shelby Foote argues. . . .* When you refer to the author again, you may use the last name only: *Foote raises an important question.*

Marking boundaries

Readers need to move from your words to the words of a source without feeling a jolt. Avoid dropping quotations into your text without warning. Instead, provide clear signal phrases, usually including the author's name, to indicate the boundary between your words and the source's words. (The signal phrase is highlighted in the second example on page 508.)

Using signal phrases in CMS papers

To avoid monotony, try to vary both the language and the placement of your signal phrases.

Model signal phrases

In the words of historian James M. McPherson, ". . ."[1]

As Dudley Taylor Cornish has argued, ". . ."[2]

In a letter to his wife, a Confederate soldier who witnessed the massacre wrote that ". . ."[3]

". . .," claims Benjamin Quarles.[4]

". . .," writes Albert Castel, ". . ."[5]

Shelby Foote offers an intriguing interpretation: ". . ."[6]

Verbs in signal phrases

admits	compares	insists	rejects
agrees	confirms	notes	reports
argues	contends	observes	responds
asserts	declares	points out	suggests
believes	denies	reasons	thinks
claims	emphasizes	refutes	writes

DROPPED QUOTATION

Not surprisingly, those testifying on the Union and Confederate sides recalled events at Fort Pillow quite differently. Unionists claimed that their troops had abandoned their arms and were in full retreat. "The Confederates, however, all agreed that the Union troops retreated to the river with arms in their hands."[9]

QUOTATION WITH SIGNAL PHRASE

Not surprisingly, those testifying on the Union and Confederate sides recalled events at Fort Pillow quite differently. Unionists claimed that their troops had abandoned their arms and were in full retreat. "The Confederates, however," writes historian Albert Castel, "all agreed that the Union troops retreated to the river with arms in their hands."[9]

Using signal phrases with summaries and paraphrases

As with quotations, you should introduce most summaries and para-phrases with a signal phrase that mentions the author and places the

material in the context of your argument. Readers will then understand where the summary or paraphrase begins.

Without the signal phrase (highlighted) in the following example,
readers might think that only the last sentence is being cited, when
in fact the whole paragraph is based on the source.

> According to Jack Hurst, official Confederate policy was that black soldiers were to
> be treated as runaway slaves; in addition, the Confederate Congress decreed that
> white Union officers commanding black troops be killed. Confederate Lieutenant
> General Kirby Smith went one step further, declaring that he would kill all captured
> black troops. Smith's policy never met with strong opposition from the Richmond
> government.[10]

Integrating statistics and other facts

When you are citing a statistic or another specific fact, a signal phrase
is often not necessary. In most cases, readers will understand that
the citation refers to the statistic or another fact (not the whole
paragraph).

> Of 295 white troops garrisoned at Fort Pillow, 168 were taken prisoner. Black
> troops fared worse, with only 58 of 262 captured and most of the rest presumably
> killed or wounded.[12]

There is nothing wrong, however, with using a signal phrase to introduce a statistic or fact.

> Shelby Foote notes that of 295 white troops garrisoned at Fort Pillow, 168 were
> taken prisoner but that black troops fared worse, with only 58 of 262 captured and
> most of the rest presumably killed or wounded.[12]

Putting source material in context

Readers should not have to guess why source material appears in your
paper. If you use another writer's words, you must explain how they
relate to your point. In other words, you must put the source in context.
It's a good idea to embed a quotation between sentences of your own,
introducing it with a signal phrase and following it up with interpretive
comments that link the quotation to your paper's argument.

QUOTATION WITH EFFECTIVE CONTEXT

> In a respected biography of Nathan Bedford Forrest, Hurst suggests that the
> temperamental Forrest "may have ragingly ordered a massacre and even intended

to carry it out—until he rode inside the fort and viewed the horrifying result" and ordered it stopped.[11] While this is an intriguing interpretation of events, even Hurst would probably admit that it is merely speculation.

NOTE: When you bring other sources into a conversation about your research topic, you are synthesizing. For more on synthesis, see MLA-3c.

≡ CMS-4 Documenting sources

In history and some humanities courses, you may be asked to use the documentation system set forth in *The Chicago Manual of Style*, 16th ed. (Chicago: U of Chicago P, 2010). In *Chicago* (CMS) style, superscript numbers in the text of the paper refer readers to notes with corresponding numbers either at the foot of the page (footnotes) or at the end of the paper (endnotes). A bibliography is often required as well; it appears at the end of the paper and gives publication information for all the works cited in the notes.

TEXT

A Union soldier, Jacob Thompson, claimed to have seen Forrest order the killing, but when asked to describe the six-foot-two general, he called him "a little bit of a man."[12]

FOOTNOTE OR ENDNOTE

12. Brian Steel Wills, *A Battle from the Start: The Life of Nathan Bedford Forrest* (New York: HarperCollins, 1992), 187.

BIBLIOGRAPHY ENTRY

Wills, Brian Steel. *A Battle from the Start: The Life of Nathan Bedford Forrest.* New York: HarperCollins, 1992.

CMS-4a First and subsequent notes for a source

The first time you cite a source, the note should include publication information for that work as well as the page number on which the passage being cited may be found.

1. Peter Burchard, *One Gallant Rush: Robert Gould Shaw and His Brave Black Regiment* (New York: St. Martin's, 1965), 85.

For subsequent references to a source you have already cited, you may simply give the author's last name, a short form of the title, and the page or pages cited. A short form of the title of a book is italicized; a short form of the title of an article is put in quotation marks.

4. Burchard, *One Gallant Rush,* 31.

When you have two consecutive notes from the same source, you may use "Ibid." (meaning "in the same place") and the page number for the second note. Use "Ibid." alone if the page number is the same.

5. Jack Hurst, *Nathan Bedford Forrest: A Biography* (New York: Knopf, 1993), 8.

6. Ibid., 174.

CMS-4b CMS-style bibliography

A bibliography, which appears at the end of your paper, lists every work you have cited in your notes; in addition, it may include works that you consulted but did not cite. For advice on constructing the list, see page 531. A sample bibliography appears on page 537.

NOTE: If you include a bibliography, *The Chicago Manual of Style* suggests that you shorten all notes, including the first reference to a source, as described at the top of this page. Check with your instructor, however, to see whether using an abbreviated note for a first reference to a source is acceptable.

CMS-4c Model notes and bibliography entries

The following models are consistent with guidelines in *The Chicago Manual of Style*, 16th ed. For each type of source, a model note appears first, followed by a model bibliography entry. The note shows the format you should use when citing a source for the first time. For subsequent citations of a source, use shortened notes (see CMS-4a). For a directory to models in this section, see page 498.

Some online sources, typically periodical articles, use a permanent locator called a digital object identifier (DOI). Use the DOI, when it is available, in place of a URL in your citations of online sources.

When a URL (Web address) or a DOI must break across lines, do not insert a hyphen or break at a hyphen if the URL or DOI contains one. Instead, break after a colon or a double slash or before any other mark of punctuation.

Books (print and online)

1. Basic format for a print book

1. Mary N. Woods, *Beyond the Architect's Eye: Photographs and the American Built Environment* (Philadelphia: University of Pennsylvania Press, 2009).

Woods, Mary N. *Beyond the Architect's Eye: Photographs and the American Built Environment.* Philadelphia: University of Pennsylvania Press, 2009.

For an illustrated citation of a print book, see pages 514–15.

2. Basic format for an online book

2. John Dewey, *Democracy and Education* (1916; ILT Digital Classics, 1994), chap. 4, http://www.ilt.columbia.edu/publications/dewey.html.

Dewey, John. *Democracy and Education.* 1916. ILT Digital Classics, 1994. http://www.ilt.columbia.edu/publications/dewey.html.

3. Basic format for an e-book (electronic book)

3. Leo Tolstoy, *War and Peace*, trans. Richard Pevear and Larissa Volokhonsky (New York: Knopf, 2007), Kindle edition, vol. 1, pt. 1, chap. 3.

Tolstoy, Leo. *War and Peace.* Translated by Richard Pevear and Larissa Volokhonsky. New York: Knopf, 2007. Kindle edition.

4. Two or more authors

For a work with two or three authors, give all authors' names in both the note and the bibliography entry. For a work with four or more authors, in the note give the first author's name followed by "et al." (for "and others"); in the bibliography entry, list all authors' names.

4. Chris Stringer and Peter Andrews, *The Complete World of Human Evolution* (London: Thames and Hudson, 2005), 45.

Stringer, Chris, and Peter Andrews. *The Complete World of Human Evolution.* London: Thames and Hudson, 2005.

4. Lynn Hunt et al., *The Making of the West: Peoples and Cultures,* 3rd ed. (Boston: Bedford/St. Martin's, 2009), 541.

Hunt, Lynn, Thomas R. Martin, Barbara H. Rosenwein, R. Po-chia Hsia, and Bonnie G. Smith. *The Making of the West: Peoples and Cultures.* 3rd ed. Boston: Bedford/St. Martin's, 2009.

5.   Organization as author

5. Dormont Historical Society, *Images of America: Dormont* (Charleston, SC: Arcadia Publishing, 2008), 24.

Dormont Historical Society. *Images of America: Dormont.* Charleston, SC: Arcadia
    Publishing, 2008.

6.   Unknown author

6. *The Men's League Handbook on Women's Suffrage* (London, 1912), 23.

The Men's League Handbook on Women's Suffrage. London, 1912.

7.   Multiple works by the same author   In the bibliography, use six hyphens in place of the author's name in the second and subsequent entries. Arrange the entries alphabetically by title.

Harper, Raymond L. *A History of Chesapeake, Virginia.* Charleston, SC: History Press, 2008.

------. *South Norfolk, Virginia, 1661-2005.* Charleston, SC: History Press, 2005.

8.   Edited work without an author

8. Jack Beatty, ed., *Colossus: How the Corporation Changed America* (New York: Broadway Books, 2001), 127.

Beatty, Jack, ed. *Colossus: How the Corporation Changed America.* New York: Broadway
    Books, 2001.

9.   Edited work with an author

9. Ted Poston, *A First Draft of History,* ed. Kathleen A. Hauke (Athens: University of Georgia Press, 2000), 46.

Poston, Ted. *A First Draft of History.* Edited by Kathleen A. Hauke. Athens: University of
    Georgia Press, 2000.

10. Translated work

10. Tonino Guerra, *Abandoned Places,* trans. Adria Bernardi (Barcelona: Guernica, 1999), 71.

Guerra, Tonino. *Abandoned Places.* Translated by Adria Bernardi. Barcelona: Guernica, 1999.

11. Edition other than the first

11. Arnoldo DeLeon, *Mexican Americans in Texas: A Brief History*, 3rd ed. (Wheeling, IL: Harlan Davidson, 2009), 34.

DeLeon, Arnoldo. *Mexican Americans in Texas: A Brief History.* 3rd ed. Wheeling,
    IL: Harlan Davidson, 2009.

Citation at a glance: Book (CMS)

To cite a print book in CMS (*Chicago*) style, include the following elements:

1 Author
2 Title and subtitle
3 City of publication

4 Publisher
5 Year of publication
6 Page number(s) cited (for notes)

TITLE PAGE

A MIDWIFE'S TALE

2 *The Life of Martha Ballard,
Based on Her Diary,
1785–1812*

1 *Laurel Thatcher Ulrich*

Vintage Books **4**
A Division of Random House, Inc.
3 *New York*

5 JUNE 1991

COPYRIGHT PAGE

FIRST VINTAGE BOOKS EDITION, JUNE 1991

Copyright © 1990 by Laurel Thatcher Ulrich
Maps copyright © 1990 by Karen Hansen

reserved under International and Pan-American Copyright
Published in the United States by Vintage Books, a division of
se, Inc., New York, and simultaneously in Canada by Random
a Limited, Toronto. Originally published in hardcover by Alfred
A. Knopf, Inc., New York, in 1990.

brary of Congress Cataloging-in-Publication Data
Ulrich, Laurel.
: the life of Martha Ballard, based on her diary, 1785-1812 / Laurel
Thatcher Ulrich.—1st Vintage Books ed.
p. cm.
cludes bibliographical references (p.   ) and index.
ISBN 0-679-73376-0
tha, 1735-1812.   2. Hallowell (Me.)—Biography.   3. Augusta
(Me.)—Biography.   4. Kennebec River Valley (Me.)—Social life and customs.
5. Midwives—Maine—Hallowell—Biography.   6. Midwives—Maine—
Augusta—Biography.   I. Title.
[F29.H15U47 1991]
974.1'6—dc20
[B]   90-55674
CIP

Design by Dorothy Schmiderer Baker
Manufactured in the United States of America
79D8

NOTE

1. Laurel Thatcher Ulrich, *A Midwife's Tale: The Life of Martha Ballard, Based on Her Diary, 1785-1812* (New York: Vintage, 1991), 174.

BIBLIOGRAPHY

Ulrich, Laurel Thatcher. *A Midwife's Tale: The Life of Martha Ballard, Based on Her Diary, 1785-1812*. New York: Vintage, 1991.

For more on citing books in CMS (*Chicago*) style, see pages 512–17.

12. Volume in a multivolume work

12. Charles Reagan Wilson, ed., *Myth, Manner, and Memory*, vol. 4 of *The New Encyclopedia of Southern Culture* (Chapel Hill: University of North Carolina Press, 2006), 198.

Wilson, Charles Reagan, ed. *Myth, Manner, and Memory*. Vol. 4 of *The New Encyclopedia of Southern Culture*. Chapel Hill: University of North Carolina Press, 2006.

13. Work in an anthology

13. Zora Neale Hurston, "From *Dust Tracks on a Road*," in *The Norton Book of American Autobiography*, ed. Jay Parini (New York: Norton, 1999), 336.

Hurston, Zora Neale. "From *Dust Tracks on a Road*." In *The Norton Book of American Autobiography*, edited by Jay Parini, 333-43. New York: Norton, 1999.

14. Introduction, preface, foreword, or afterword

14. Nelson DeMille, foreword to *Flag: An American Biography*, by Marc Leepson (New York: Thomas Dunne, 2005), xii.

DeMille, Nelson. Foreword to *Flag: An American Biography*, by Marc Leepson, xi-xiv. New York: Thomas Dunne, 2005.

15. Republished book

15. Garry Wills, *Inventing America: Jefferson's Declaration of Independence* (1978; repr., Boston: Houghton Mifflin, 2002), 86.

Wills, Garry. *Inventing America: Jefferson's Declaration of Independence*. 1978. Reprint, Boston: Houghton Mifflin, 2002.

16. Work with a title in its title   Use quotation marks around any title within an italicized title.

16. Gary Schmidgall, ed., *Conserving Walt Whitman's Fame: Selections from Horace Traubel's "Conservator," 1890-1919* (Iowa City: University of Iowa Press, 2006), 165.

Schmidgall, Gary, ed. *Conserving Walt Whitman's Fame: Selections from Horace Traubel's "Conservator," 1890-1919.* Iowa City: University of Iowa Press, 2006.

17. Letter in a published collection   Use the day-month-year form for the date of the letter. If the letter writer's name is part of the book title, begin the note with only the writer's last name but begin the bibliography entry with the full name.

17. Mitford to Esmond Romilly, 29 July 1940, in *Decca: The Letters of Jessica Mitford*, ed. Peter Y. Sussman (New York: Knopf, 2006), 55-56.

Mitford, Jessica. *Decca: The Letters of Jessica Mitford.* Edited by Peter Y. Sussman. New York: Knopf, 2006.

For an illustrated citation of a letter in a published collection, see pages 518–19.

18. Work in a series

18. R. Keith Schoppa, *The Columbia Guide to Modern Chinese History,* Columbia Guides to Asian History (New York: Columbia University Press, 2000), 256-58.

Schoppa, R. Keith. *The Columbia Guide to Modern Chinese History.* Columbia Guides to Asian History. New York: Columbia University Press, 2000.

19. Encyclopedia or dictionary entry

19. *Encyclopaedia Britannica,* 15th ed., s.v. "Monroe Doctrine."

19. Bryan A. Garner, *Garner's Modern American Usage* (Oxford: Oxford University Press, 2003), s.v. "brideprice."

Garner, Bryan A. *Garner's Modern American Usage.* Oxford: Oxford University Press, 2003.

The abbreviation "s.v." is for the Latin *sub verbo* ("under the word").

Well-known reference works such as encyclopedias do not require publication information and are usually not included in the bibliography.

20. Sacred text

20. Matt. 20:4-9 (Revised Standard Version).

20. Qur'an 18:1-3.

Sacred texts are usually not included in the bibliography.

21. Source quoted in another source

21. Ron Grossman and Charles Leroux, "A Local Outpost of Democracy," *Chicago Tribune,* March 5, 1996, quoted in William Julius Wilson and Richard P. Taub, *There Goes the Neighborhood: Racial, Ethnic, and Class Tensions in Four Chicago Neighborhoods and Their Meaning for America* (New York: Knopf, 2006), 18.

Grossman, Ron, and Charles Leroux. "A Local Outpost of Democracy." *Chicago Tribune,* March 5, 1996. Quoted in William Julius Wilson and Richard P. Taub, *There Goes the Neighborhood: Racial, Ethnic, and Class Tensions in Four Chicago Neighborhoods and Their Meaning for America* (New York: Knopf, 2006), 18.

Articles in periodicals (print and online)

22. Article in a print journal Include the volume and issue numbers and the date; end the bibliography entry with the page range of the article.

For an illustrated citation of an article in a journal, see pages 520–21.

22. T. H. Breen, "Will American Consumers Buy a Second American Revolution?," *Journal of American History* 93, no. 2 (2006): 405.

Breen, T. H. "Will American Consumers Buy a Second American Revolution?" *Journal of American History* 93, no. 2 (2006): 404-8.

23. Article in an online journal Give the DOI if the article has one; if there is no DOI, give the URL for the article. For an unpaginated online article, in your note you may include locators, such as numbered paragraphs (if the article has them), or headings from the article.

23. Brian Lennon, "New Media Critical Homologies," *Postmodern Culture* 19, no. 2 (2009), http://pmc.iath.virginia.edu/text-only/issue.109/19.2lennon.txt.

Lennon, Brian. "New Media Critical Homologies." *Postmodern Culture* 19, no. 2 (2009). http://pmc.iath.virginia.edu/text-only/issue.109/19.2lennon.txt.

24. Journal article from a database Give whatever identifying information is available in the database listing: a DOI for the article; the name of the database and the number assigned by the database; or a "stable" or "persistent" URL for the article.

For an illustrated citation of an article from a database, see pages 522–23.

24. Constant Leung, "Language and Content in Bilingual Education," *Linguistics and Education* 16, no. 2 (2005): 239, doi:10.1016/j.linged.2006.01.004.

Leung, Constant. "Language and Content in Bilingual Education." *Linguistics and Education* 16, no. 2 (2005): 238-52. doi:10.1016/j.linged.2006.01.004.

Citation at a glance: Letter in a published collection (CMS)

To cite a letter in a published collection in CMS (*Chicago*) style, include the following elements:

1. Author of letter
2. Recipient of letter
3. Date of letter
4. Title of collection
5. Editor of collection
6. City of publication
7. Publisher
8. Year of publication
9. Page number(s) cited (for notes); page range of letter (for bibliography)

TITLE PAGE

8 Copyright © 1991

COPYRIGHT PAGE

AVON BOOKS
A division of
The Hearst Corporation
1350 Avenue of the Americas
New York, New York 10019

Copyright © 1991 by Jack McLaughlin
Cover painting by Giraudon/Art Resource, New York
Published by arrangement with W.W. Norton & Com
Library of Congress Catalog Card Number: 90-27824
ISBN: 0-380-71964-9

All rights reserved, which includes the right to repro
of in any form whatsoever except as provided by the
mation address W.W. Norton & Company, Inc., 500
York 10110.

The W.W. Norton & Company, Inc. edition cont
Congress Cataloging in Publication Data:
McLaughlin, Jack.
   To his excellency Thomas Jefferson : Letters to a
Jack McLaughlin.
      p. cm.
Includes bibliographical references and index. 1. Je
Correspondence. 2. Working class—United S
Presidents—United States—Correspondence. I. Jeff
Title.
E332.86 1991
973.4'6' 092—dc20   90-27824

First Avon Trade Books Printing: July 1993

AVON TRADEMARK REG. U.S. PAT. OFF. AND IN OTHER COUNTRIES. MARCA REGISTRADA,
HECHO EN U.S.A.

Printed in the U.S.A.

TO HIS EXCELLENCY THOMAS JEFFERSON **4**

········ *Letters to a President* ········

JACK McLAUGHLIN **5**

AVON BOOKS ▲ NEW YORK

AVON BOOKS ▲ NEW YORK
7   **6**

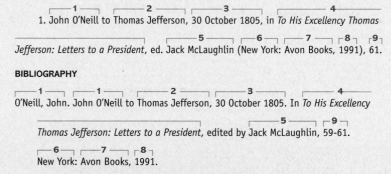

Washington 30th. Oct 1805 **3**

His Excellency Ths. Jefferson **2**

SIR,

    I have not the honor to be personally known to your Excellency therefore you will no doubt think it strange to receive this letter from a person of whom you have not the smallest knowledge. But in order to state to your Excellency in as few words as possible the purport of this address, I am a young man, a Roman Catholic who had been born and partly educated in Ireland but finding like many others who had been compelled to Migrate from that Kingdom in con-

Patronage   *6 1* **9**

your Excellency this very prolix letter which should it please your Excellency to give me some little Office or appointment in that extensive Country of Louisiana It should be my constant endeavour to merit the same by fidelity and an indefatigable attention to whatever business I should be assigned. May I have the satisfaction in whatsoever Country or situation [I] may be in to hear of your Excellencies long continuence of your Natural powers unempaired to conduct the Helm of this Extensive Country which are the sincere wishes of your Excellencies Mo. Obt. Hum. Servt.

1 JOHN O'NEILL

NOTE

  ┌———1———┐ ┌———2———┐ ┌———3———┐ ┌————4————┐

1. John O'Neill to Thomas Jefferson, 30 October 1805, in *To His Excellency Thomas*

                                ┌———5———┐ ┌—6—┐ ┌——7——┐ ┌8┐ ┌9┐

Jefferson: Letters to a President, ed. Jack McLaughlin (New York: Avon Books, 1991), 61.

BIBLIOGRAPHY

  ┌——1——┐ ┌——1——┐ ┌———2———┐ ┌———3———┐ ┌————4————┐

O'Neill, John. John O'Neill to Thomas Jefferson, 30 October 1805. In *To His Excellency*

                                      ┌———5———┐ ┌—9—┐

Thomas Jefferson: Letters to a President, edited by Jack McLaughlin, 59-61.

  ┌—6—┐ ┌—7—┐ ┌8┐

New York: Avon Books, 1991.

For another citation of a letter in CMS (*Chicago*) style, see item 17.

Citation at a glance: Article in a scholarly journal (CMS)

To cite a print article in a scholarly journal in CMS (*Chicago*) style, include the following elements:

1 Author
2 Title of article
3 Title of journal
4 Volume and issue numbers
5 Year of publication
6 Page number(s) cited (for notes); page range of article (for bibliography)

TITLE PAGE OF JOURNAL

VOLUME 113 · NUMBER 2 · APRIL 2008

VOLUME 113 · NUMBER 2 · APRIL 2008

The American Historical Review ③

AMERICAN HISTORICAL ASSOCIATION

FIRST PAGE OF ARTICLE

Editor: ROBERT A.
Associate Editor: S
Reviews Editor: MOU
Articles Editor: J
Production Manager:
Office Manager: MARY

Editorial Assistants: ELIZABE
KEVIN P. COLEMAN, ANDREW M. K
JENNIFER SOVDE, M. BENJAMIN

Advertising Manager: C
University of Chic

Board of E

TOBY L. DITZ
Johns Hopkins University

JANET J. EW
Duke Unive

GARY GERSTLE
Vanderbilt University

LLOYD S. KR
University of
Carolina, Chap

BENJAMIN NATHANS
University of Pennsylvania

MRINALINI S
Pennsylvania
Universit

WILLIAM B. TAYLOR
University of
California, Berkeley

JEFFREY N. WASS
University
California, I

② An Age of Imperial Revolutions

① JEREMY ADELMAN

WHEN THE VENEZUELAN CREOLE FRANCISCO DE MIRANDA led an expeditionary force to the shores of his native land to liberate it from Spanish rule in the summer of 1806, he brought with him a new weapon for making revolutions: a printing press. He hoped that his band of white, black, and mulatto patriots would start a revolt to free a continent with an alliance of swords and ideas. After dawdling for ten days, Miranda learned that royal troops (also white, black, and mulatto) were marching from Caracas. He withdrew before the two multiracial forces could clash. Consider Miranda's reasons for retreat: The nation he sought to free from its chains was not, in his opinion, a nation at all. While Venezuelans yearned for "Civil Liberty," they did not know how to grasp and protect it. They needed a liberation that would tutor them in the ways of liberty and fraternity, to create a nation of virtuous citizens out of a colony of subjects. This was why Miranda treated the printing press, a portable factory of words about liberty and sovereignty, as part of the arsenal of change: he wanted to create public opinion where there was none. But faced with the prospect of a violent clash and a scourge of "opposition and internal divisions," of a war waged mainly with swords, he preferred to pull out and bide his time.[1]

Miranda's dilemma—whether or not to move forward knowing how revolutions worked in imperial settings when their protagonists did not presume that their cause was self-evidently bound to triumph—evokes questions about the embedded politics of what we might now call, with a wince, "regime change." As empires gave way to successor systems in their colonies, those regimes began to call themselves nations not in order to cause imperial crises, but as the result of such crises. The study of imperial crises and the study of the origins of nationalism in colonial societies should inform each other more than they do. Bringing these two separate fields of scholarship together, and questioning the tacit and not-so-tacit beliefs upon which they rest, can help us reframe the complex passages from empires to successor states, free

I want to extend my thanks to Howard Adelman, Steve Aron, Tom Bender, Graham Burnett, Jorge Cañizares-Esguerra, Josep Fradera, Roy Hora, Dina Khapaeva, and Rafe Blaufarb for their suggestions on this article, and to the *AHR*'s thoughtful reviewers and editors. Versions of this essay were presented as papers at the Universidad San Andrés in Buenos Aires, Smolny College in St. Petersburg, Russia, and the University of Texas at Austin.

[1] Archivo General de Indias (Seville) [hereafter AGI], Gobierno, Caracas, Legajo 458, September 13, 1806, Manuel de Guevara Vasconcelos to Príncipe de la Paz; September 5, 1806, Francisco Cavallero Sarmiento to Príncipe de la Plaz; Estado/Caracas, 71/9, November 8, 1808, "Informe de Secretaría á S.M. sobre el asunto de Miranda"; Francisco de Miranda, "Todo pende de nuestra voluntad," in Miranda, *América espera* (Caracas, 1982), 356; Karen Racine, *Francisco de Miranda: A Transatlantic Life in the Age of Revolution* (Wilmington, Del., 2003).

⑥ 319

319

NOTE

┌────1────┐ ┌──────2──────┐ ┌──────3──────┐
1. Jeremy Adelman, "An Age of Imperial Revolutions," *American Historical Review*

┌───4───┐ ┌─5─┐ ┌6┐
113, no. 2 (2008): 321.

BIBLIOGRAPHY

┌────1────┐ ┌──────2──────┐ ┌──────3──────┐ ┌─4─
Adelman, Jeremy. "An Age of Imperial Revolutions," *American Historical Review* 113,

┌─5─┐ ┌─6─┐
no. 2 (2008): 319-40.

For more on citing articles from scholarly journals in CMS (*Chicago*) style, see page 517.

25. Article in a print magazine

25. Tom Bissell, "Improvised, Explosive, and Divisive," *Harper's,* January 2006, 42.

Bissell, Tom. "Improvised, Explosive, and Divisive." *Harper's,* January 2006, 41-54.

26. Article in an online magazine   Include the URL for the article.

26. Katharine Mieszkowski, "A Deluge Waiting to Happen," *Salon,* July 3, 2008, http://www.salon.com/news/feature/2008/07/03/floods/index.html.

Mieszkowski, Katharine. "A Deluge Waiting to Happen." *Salon,* July 3, 2008. http://www .salon.com/news/feature/2008/07/03/floods/index.html.

27. Magazine article from a database   Give whatever identifying information is available in the database listing: a DOI for the article; the name of the database and the number assigned by the database; or a "stable" or "persistent" URL for the article.

27. "Facing Facts in Afghanistan," *National Review*, November 2, 2009, 14, Expanded Academic ASAP (A209905060).

"Facing Facts in Afghanistan." *National Review*, November 2, 2009, 14. Expanded Academic ASAP (A209905060).

28. Article in a print newspaper   Page numbers are not necessary; a section letter or number, if available, is sufficient.

28. Randal C. Archibold, "These Neighbors Are Good Ones without a New Fence," *New York Times,* October 22, 2008, sec. A.

Archibold, Randal C. "These Neighbors Are Good Ones without a New Fence." *New York Times,* October 22, 2008, sec. A.

Citation at a glance: Journal article from a database (CMS)

To cite a journal article from a database in CMS (*Chicago*) style, include the following elements:

1 Author
2 Title of article
3 Title of journal
4 Volume and issue numbers
5 Year of publication

6 Page number(s) cited (for notes); page range of article (for bibliography)

7 DOI; database name and article number; *or* "stable" or "persistent" URL for article

ON-SCREEN VIEW OF DATABASE RECORD

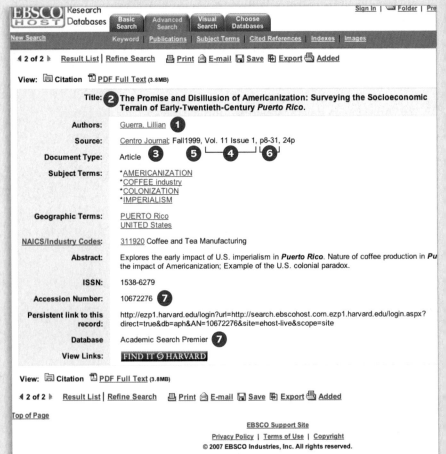

NOTE

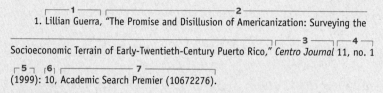

1. Lillian Guerra, "The Promise and Disillusion of Americanization: Surveying the Socioeconomic Terrain of Early-Twentieth-Century Puerto Rico," *Centro Journal* 11, no. 1 (1999): 10, Academic Search Premier (10672276).

BIBLIOGRAPHY

Guerra, Lillian. "The Promise and Disillusion of Americanization: Surveying the Socioeconomic Terrain of Early-Twentieth-Century Puerto Rico." *Centro Journal* 11, no. 1 (1999): 8-31. Academic Search Premier (10672276).

For more on citing journal, magazine, and newspaper articles from databases in CMS (*Chicago*) style, see pages 517, 521, and 523.

29. Article in an online newspaper   Include the URL for the article; if the URL is very long, use the URL for the newspaper's home page. Omit page numbers, even if the source provides them.

29. Doyle McManus, "The Candor War," *Chicago Tribune,* July 29, 2010, http://www.chicagotribune.com/.

McManus, Doyle. "The Candor War." *Chicago Tribune,* July 29, 2010. http://www.chicagotribune.com/.

30. Newspaper article from a database   Give whatever identifying information is available in the database listing: a DOI for the article; the name of the database and the number assigned by the database; or a "stable" or "persistent" URL for the article.

30. Clifford J. Levy, "In Kyrgyzstan, Failure to Act Adds to Crisis," *New York Times,* June 18, 2010, General OneFile (A229196045).

Levy, Clifford J. "In Kyrgyzstan, Failure to Act Adds to Crisis." *New York Times,* June 18, 2010. General OneFile (A229196045).

31. Unsigned newspaper article

31. "Renewable Energy Rules," *Boston Globe,* August 11, 2003, sec. A.

Boston Globe. "Renewable Energy Rules." August 11, 2003, sec. A.

32. Book review

32. Benjamin Wittes, "Remember the Titan," review of *Louis D. Brandeis: A Life*, by Melvin T. Urofsky, *Wilson Quarterly* 33, no. 4 (2009): 100.

Wittes, Benjamin. "Remember the Titan." Review of *Louis D. Brandeis: A Life*, by Melvin T. Urofsky. *Wilson Quarterly* 33, no. 4 (2009): 100-101.

33. Letter to the editor   Do not use the letter's title, even if the publication gives one.

33. David Harlan, letter to the editor, *New York Review of Books*, October 9, 2008.

Harlan, David. Letter to the editor. *New York Review of Books*, October 9, 2008.

Online sources

For most Web sites, include an author if a site has one, the title of the site, the sponsor, the date of publication or modified date (date of most recent update), and the site's URL. Do not italicize a Web site title unless the site is an online book or periodical. Use quotation marks for the titles of sections or pages in a Web site. If a site does not have a date of publication or modified date, give the date you accessed the site ("accessed January 3, 2010").

34. Web site

34. Chesapeake and Ohio Canal National Historical Park, National Park Service, last modified April 9, 2010, http://www.nps.gov/choh/index.htm.

Chesapeake and Ohio Canal National Historical Park. National Park Service. Last modified April 9, 2010. http://www.nps.gov/choh/index.htm.

35. Short work from a Web site   Place the title of the short work in quotation marks.

For an illustrated citation of a primary source from a Web site, see pages 526–27.

35. George P. Landow, "Victorian and Victorianism," Victorian Web, last modified August 2, 2009, http://victorianweb.org/vn/victor4.html.

Landow, George P. "Victorian and Victorianism." Victorian Web. Last modified August 2, 2009. http://victorianweb.org/vn/victor4.html.

36. Online posting or e-mail   If an online posting has been archived, include a URL. E-mails that are not part of an online discussion are treated as personal communications (see item 42). Online postings and e-mails are not included in the bibliography.

36. Susanna J. Sturgis to Copyediting-L discussion list, July 17, 2010, http://listserv.indiana.edu/archives/copyediting-l.html.

37. Blog (Weblog) post Treat as a short document from a Web site (see item 35). Put the title of the posting in quotation marks, and italicize the name of the blog. Insert "blog" in parentheses after the name if the word *blog* is not part of the name.

37. Miland Brown, "The Flawed Montevideo Convention of 1933," *World History Blog*, May 31, 2008, http://www.worldhistoryblog.com/2008/05/flawed-montevideo-convention-of-1933.html.

Brown, Miland. "The Flawed Montevideo Convention of 1933." *World History Blog*. May 31, 2008. http://www.worldhistoryblog.com/2008/05/flawed-montevideo-convention-of-1933.html.

38. Podcast Treat as a short work from a Web site (see item 35), including the following, if available: the author's (or speaker's) name; the title of the podcast, in quotation marks; an identifying number, if any; the title of the site on which the podcast appears; the sponsor of the site; and the URL. Before the URL, identify the type of podcast or file format and the date of posting or your date of access.

38. Paul Tiyambe Zeleza, "Africa's Global Past," Episode 40, Africa Past and Present, African Online Digital Library, podcast audio, April 29, 2010, http://afripod.aodl.org/.

Zeleza, Paul Tiyambe. "Africa's Global Past." Episode 40. Africa Past and Present. African Online Digital Library. Podcast audio. April 29, 2010. http://afripod.aodl.org/.

39. Online audio or video Cite as a short work from a Web site (see item 35). If the source is a downloadable file, identify the file format or medium before the URL.

39. Richard B. Freeman, "Global Capitalism, Labor Markets, and Inequality," Institute of International Studies, University of California at Berkeley, October 31, 2007, http://www.youtube.com/watch?v=cgNCFsXGUa0.

Freeman, Richard B. "Global Capitalism, Labor Markets, and Inequality." Institute of International Studies, University of California at Berkeley. October 31, 2007. http://www.youtube.com/watch?v=cgNCFsXGUa0.

Other sources (including online versions)

40. Government document

40. U.S. Department of State, *Foreign Relations of the United States: Diplomatic Papers, 1943* (Washington, DC: GPO, 1965), 562.

U.S. Department of State. *Foreign Relations of the United States: Diplomatic Papers, 1943*. Washington, DC: GPO, 1965.

Citation at a glance: Primary source from a Web site (CMS)

To cite a primary source (or any other document) from a Web site in CMS (*Chicago*) style, include as many of the following elements as are available:

1 Author

2 Title of document

3 Title of site

4 Sponsor of site

5 Publication date or modified date; date of access if none

6 URL

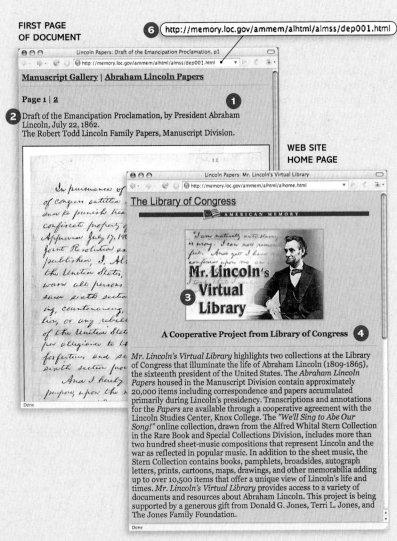

FIRST PAGE
OF DOCUMENT

6 http://memory.loc.gov/ammem/alhtml/almss/dep001.html

Lincoln Papers: Draft of the Emancipation Proclamation, p1

http://memory.loc.gov/ammem/alhtml/almss/dep001.html

Manuscript Gallery | Abraham Lincoln Papers

Page 1 | 2

1

2 Draft of the Emancipation Proclamation, by President Abraham Lincoln, July 22, 1862.
The Robert Todd Lincoln Family Papers, Manuscript Division.

WEB SITE
HOME PAGE

Lincoln Papers: Mr. Lincoln's Virtual Library

http://memory.loc.gov/ammem/alhtml/aihome.html

The Library of Congress

AMERICAN MEMORY

Mr. Lincoln's
3 Virtual
Library

A Cooperative Project from Library of Congress **4**

Mr. Lincoln's Virtual Library highlights two collections at the Library of Congress that illuminate the life of Abraham Lincoln (1809–1865), the sixteenth president of the United States. The *Abraham Lincoln Papers* housed in the Manuscript Division contain approximately 20,000 items including correspondence and papers accumulated primarily during Lincoln's presidency. Transcriptions and annotations for the *Papers* are available through a cooperative agreement with the Lincoln Studies Center, Knox College. The *"We'll Sing to Abe Our Song!"* online collection, drawn from the Alfred Whital Stern Collection in the Rare Book and Special Collections Division, includes more than two hundred sheet-music compositions that represent Lincoln and the war as reflected in popular music. In addition to the sheet music, the Stern Collection contains books, pamphlets, broadsides, autograph letters, prints, cartoons, maps, drawings, and other memorabilia adding up to over 10,500 items that offer a unique view of Lincoln's life and times. *Mr. Lincoln's Virtual Library* provides access to a variety of documents and resources about Abraham Lincoln. This project is being supported by a generous gift from Donald G. Jones, Terri L. Jones, and The Jones Family Foundation.

NOTE

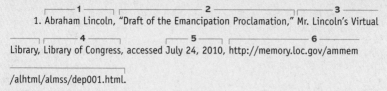

1. Abraham Lincoln, "Draft of the Emancipation Proclamation," Mr. Lincoln's Virtual Library, Library of Congress, accessed July 24, 2010, http://memory.loc.gov/ammem /alhtml/almss/dep001.html.

BIBLIOGRAPHY

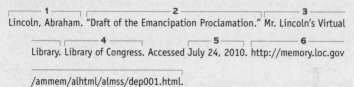

Lincoln, Abraham. "Draft of the Emancipation Proclamation." Mr. Lincoln's Virtual Library. Library of Congress. Accessed July 24, 2010. http://memory.loc.gov /ammem/alhtml/almss/dep001.html.

For more on citing documents from Web sites in CMS (*Chicago*) style, see pages 524–25.

41. Unpublished dissertation

41. Stephanie Lynn Budin, "The Origins of Aphrodite" (PhD diss., University of Pennsylvania, 2000), 301-2, ProQuest (AAT 9976404).

Budin, Stephanie Lynn. "The Origins of Aphrodite." PhD diss., University of Pennsylvania, 2000. ProQuest (AAT 9976404).

42. Personal communication

42. Sara Lehman, e-mail message to author, August 13, 2010.

Personal communications are not included in the bibliography.

43. Published or broadcast interview

43. Robert Downey Jr., interview by Graham Norton, *The Graham Norton Show*, BBC America, December 14, 2009.

Downey, Robert, Jr. Interview by Graham Norton. *The Graham Norton Show*. BBC America, December 14, 2009.

44. Published proceedings of a conference

44. Julie Kimber, Peter Love, and Phillip Deery, eds., *Labour Traditions: Proceedings of the Tenth National Labour History Conference,* University of Melbourne, Carlton, Victoria, Australia, July 4-6, 2007 (Melbourne: Australian Society for the Study of Labour History, 2007), 5.

Kimber, Julie, Peter Love, and Phillip Deery, eds. *Labour Traditions: Proceedings of the Tenth National Labour History Conference.* University of Melbourne, Carlton, Victoria, Australia, July 4-6, 2007. Melbourne: Australian Society for the Study of Labour History, 2007.

45. Video or DVD

45. *The Secret of Roan Inish,* directed by John Sayles (1993; Culver City, CA: Columbia TriStar Home Video, 2000), DVD.

The Secret of Roan Inish. Directed by John Sayles. 1993; Culver City, CA: Columbia TriStar Home Video, 2000. DVD.

46. Sound recording

46. Gustav Holst, *The Planets,* Royal Philharmonic Orchestra, conducted by André Previn, Telarc 80133, compact disc.

Holst, Gustav. *The Planets.* Royal Philharmonic Orchestra. Conducted by André Previn. Telarc 80133, compact disc.

47. Musical score or composition

47. Antonio Vivaldi, *L'Estro armonico,* op. 3, ed. Eleanor Selfridge-Field (Mineola, NY: Dover, 1999).

Vivaldi, Antonio. *L'Estro armonico,* op. 3. Edited by Eleanor Selfridge-Field. Mineola, NY: Dover, 1999.

48. Work of art

48. Aaron Siskind, *Untitled (The Most Crowded Block),* gelatin silver print, 1939, Kemper Museum of Contemporary Art, Kansas City, MO.

Siskind, Aaron. *Untitled (The Most Crowded Block).* Gelatin silver print, 1939. Kemper Museum of Contemporary Art, Kansas City, MO.

49. Performance

49. Robert Schenkkan, *The Kentucky Cycle,* directed by Richard Elliott, Willows Theatre, Concord, CA, August 31, 2007.

Schenkkan, Robert. *The Kentucky Cycle.* Directed by Richard Elliott. Willows Theatre, Concord, CA, August 31, 2007.

CMS-5 Manuscript format; sample pages

The following guidelines for formatting a CMS-style paper and preparing its endnotes and bibliography are based on *The Chicago Manual of Style,* 16th ed. (Chicago: U of Chicago P, 2010). For pages from a sample paper, see CMS-5b.

video • DVD • sound recording • musical score • artwork •
performance • paper format • title page • margins • long quotations

CMS-5a   **529**

CMS-5a Manuscript format

Formatting the paper

CMS manuscript guidelines are fairly generic because they were not created with a specific type of writing in mind.

Materials and font   Use good-quality 8½″ × 11″ white paper. If your instructor does not require a specific font, choose one that is standard and easy to read (such as Times New Roman).

Title page   Include the full title of your paper, your name, the course title, the instructor's name, and the date. See page 532 for a sample title page.

Pagination   Using arabic numerals, number the pages in the upper right corner. Do not number the title page but count it in the numbering; that is, the first page of the text will be numbered 2. Depending on your instructor's preference, you may also use a short title or your last name before the page numbers to help identify pages.

Margins and line spacing   Leave margins of at least one inch at the top, bottom, and sides of the page. Double-space the body of the paper, including long quotations that have been set off from the text. (For line spacing in notes and the bibliography, see p. 531.) Left-align the text.

Long quotations   You can choose to set off a long quotation of five to ten typed lines by indenting the entire quotation one-half inch from the left margin. (You should always set off quotations of ten or more lines.) Double-space the quotation; do not use quotation marks. (See p. 533 for a long quotation in the text of a paper; see also pp. 506–07.)

Capitalization and italics   In titles of works, capitalize all words except articles (*a, an, the*), prepositions (*at, from, between,* and so on), coordinating conjunctions (*and, but, or, nor, for, so, yet*), and *to* and *as*—unless one of these words is first or last in the title or subtitle. Follow these guidelines in your paper even if the title is styled differently in the source.

Lowercase the first word following a colon even if the word begins a complete sentence. When the colon introduces a series of sentences or questions, capitalize all sentences in the series, including the first.

Italicize the titles of books, periodicals, and other long works. Use quotation marks around the titles of periodical articles, short stories, poems, and other short works.

Visuals CMS classifies visuals as tables and illustrations (illustrations, or figures, include drawings, photographs, maps, and charts). Keep visuals as simple as possible.

Label each table with an arabic numeral ("Table 1," "Table 2," and so on) and provide a clear title that identifies the table's subject. The label and the title should appear on separate lines above the table, flush left. Below the table, give its source in a note like this one:

> *Source:* Edna Bonacich and Richard P. Appelbaum, *Behind the Label* (Berkeley: University of California Press, 2000), 145.

For each figure, place a label and a caption below the figure, flush left. The label and caption need not appear on separate lines. The word "Figure" may be abbreviated "Fig."

In the text of your paper, discuss significant features of each visual. Place visuals as close as possible to the sentences that relate to them unless your instructor prefers that visuals appear in an appendix.

URLs (Web addresses) When a URL must break across lines, do not insert a hyphen or break at a hyphen if the URL contains one. Instead, break the URL after a colon or a double slash or before any other mark of punctuation. If your word processing program automatically turns URLs into links (by underlining them and changing the color), turn off this feature.

Headings CMS does not provide guidelines for the use of headings in student papers. If you would like to insert headings in a long essay or research paper, check first with your instructor. See the sample pages of a CMS-style paper on pages 532–37 for typical placement and formatting of headings.

Preparing the endnotes

Begin the endnotes on a new page at the end of the paper. Center the title "Notes" about one inch from the top of the page, and number the pages consecutively with the rest of the manuscript. See page 536 for an example.

Indenting and numbering Indent the first line of each note one-half inch from the left margin; do not indent additional lines in the note. Begin the note with the arabic numeral that corresponds to the number in the text. Put a period after the number.

Line spacing Single-space each note and double-space between notes (unless your instructor prefers double-spacing throughout).

Preparing the bibliography

Typically, the notes in CMS-style papers are followed by a bibliography, an alphabetically arranged list of all the works cited or consulted. Center the title "Bibliography" about one inch from the top of the page. Number bibliography pages consecutively with the rest of the paper. See page 537 for a sample bibliography.

Alphabetizing the list Alphabetize the bibliography by the last names of the authors (or editors); when a work has no author or editor, alphabetize it by the first word of the title other than *A, An,* or *The.*

If your list includes two or more works by the same author, use six hyphens instead of the author's name in all entries after the first. Arrange the entries alphabetically by title.

Indenting and line spacing Begin each entry at the left margin, and indent any additional lines one-half inch. Single-space each entry and double-space between entries (unless your instructor prefers double-spacing throughout).

CMS-5b Sample pages from a research paper: CMS style

Following are pages from a research paper by Ned Bishop, a student in a history class. The assignment required CMS-style endnotes and bibliography. Bishop followed CMS guidelines in preparing his manuscript as well.

Title of paper.

The Massacre at Fort Pillow:

Holding Nathan Bedford Forrest Accountable

Writer's name.

Ned Bishop

Title of course,
instructor's name,
and date.

History 214

Professor Citro

March 22, 2008

Marginal annotations indicate CMS-style formatting and effective writing.

Bishop 2

Although Northern newspapers of the time no doubt exaggerated some of the Confederate atrocities at Fort Pillow, most modern sources agree that a massacre of Union troops took place there on April 12, 1864. It seems clear that Union soldiers, particularly black soldiers, were killed after they had stopped fighting or had surrendered or were being held prisoner. Less clear is the role played by Major General Nathan Bedford Forrest in leading his troops. Although we will never know whether Forrest directly ordered the massacre, evidence suggests that he was responsible for it.

What happened at Fort Pillow?

Fort Pillow, Tennessee, which sat on a bluff overlooking the Mississippi River, had been held by the Union for two years. It was garrisoned by 580 men, 292 of them from United States Colored Heavy and Light Artillery regiments, 285 from the white Thirteenth Tennessee Cavalry. Nathan Bedford Forrest commanded about 1,500 troops.[1]

The Confederates attacked Fort Pillow on April 12, 1864, and had virtually surrounded the fort by the time Forrest arrived on the battlefield. At 3:30 p.m., Forrest demanded the surrender of the Union forces, sending in a message of the sort he had used before: "The conduct of the officers and men garrisoning Fort Pillow has been such as to entitle them to being treated as prisoners of war. . . . Should my demand be refused, I cannot be responsible for the fate of your command."[2] Union Major William Bradford, who had replaced Major Booth, killed earlier by sharpshooters, asked for an hour to consider the demand. Forrest, worried that vessels in the river were bringing in more troops, "shortened the time to twenty minutes."[3] Bradford refused to surrender, and Forrest quickly ordered the attack.

The Confederates charged to the fort, scaled the parapet, and fired on the forces within. Victory came quickly, with the Union forces running toward the river or surrendering. Shelby Foote describes the scene like this:

> Some kept going, right on into the river, where a number drowned and the swimmers became targets for marksmen on the bluff. Others, dropping their guns in terror, ran back toward the Confederates with their hands up, and of these some were spared as prisoners, while others were shot down in the act of surrender.[4]

In his own official report, Forrest makes no mention of the massacre. He does make much of the fact that the Union flag was not lowered by the

Union forces, saying that if his own men had not taken down the flag, "few, if any, would have survived unhurt another volley."[5] However, as Jack Hurst points out and Forrest must have known, in this twenty-minute battle, "Federals running for their lives had little time to concern themselves with a flag."[6]

Quotation is introduced with a signal phrase.

The federal congressional report on Fort Pillow, which charged the Confederates with appalling atrocities, was strongly criticized by Southerners. Respected writer Shelby Foote, while agreeing that the report was "largely" fabrication, points out that the "casualty figures . . . indicated strongly that unnecessary killing had occurred."[7] In an important article, John Cimprich and Robert C. Mainfort Jr. argue that the most trustworthy evidence is that written within about ten days of the battle, before word of the congressional hearings circulated and Southerners realized the extent of Northern outrage. The article reprints a group of letters and newspaper sources written before April 22 and thus "untainted by the political overtones the controversy later assumed."[8] Cimprich and Mainfort conclude that these sources "support the case for the occurrence of a massacre" but that Forrest's role "remains clouded" because of inconsistencies in testimony.[9]

Bishop draws attention to an article that reprints primary sources.

Did Forrest order the massacre?

We will never really know whether Forrest directly ordered the massacre, but it seems unlikely. True, Confederate soldier Achilles Clark, who had no reason to lie, wrote to his sisters that "I with several others tried to stop the butchery . . . but Gen. Forrest ordered them [Negro and white Union troops] shot down like dogs, and the carnage continued."[10] But it is not clear whether Clark heard Forrest giving the orders or was just reporting hearsay. Many Confederates had been shouting "No quarter! No quarter!" and, as Shelby Foote points out, these shouts were "thought by some to be at Forrest's command."[11] A Union soldier, Jacob Thompson, claimed to have seen Forrest order the killing, but when asked to describe the six-foot-two general, he called him "a little bit of a man."[12]

Topic sentence states the main idea for this section.

Bishop presents a balanced view of the evidence.

Perhaps the most convincing evidence that Forrest did not order the massacre is that he tried to stop it once it had begun. Historian Albert Castel quotes several eyewitnesses on both the Union and Confederate sides as saying that Forrest ordered his men to stop firing.[13] In a letter to his wife three days after the battle, Confederate soldier Samuel Caldwell

Bishop 4

wrote that "if General Forrest had not run between our men & the Yanks with his pistol and sabre drawn not a man would have been spared."[14]

In a respected biography of Nathan Bedford Forrest, Hurst suggests that the temperamental Forrest "may have ragingly ordered a massacre and even intended to carry it out—until he rode inside the fort and viewed the horrifying result" and ordered it stopped.[15] While this is an intriguing interpretation of events, even Hurst would probably admit that it is merely speculation.

Can Forrest be held responsible for the massacre?

Even assuming that Forrest did not order the massacre, he can still be held accountable for it. That is because he created an atmosphere ripe for the possibility of atrocities and did nothing to ensure that it wouldn't happen. Throughout his career Forrest repeatedly threatened "no quarter," particularly with respect to black soldiers, so Confederate troops had good reason to think that in massacring the enemy they were carrying out his orders. As Hurst writes, "About all he had to do to produce a massacre was issue no order against one."[16] Dudley Taylor Cornish agrees:

> It has been asserted again and again that Forrest did not order a massacre. He did not need to. He had sought to terrify the Fort Pillow garrison by a threat of no quarter, as he had done at Union City and at Paducah in the days just before he turned on Pillow. If his men did enter the fort shouting "Give them no quarter; kill them; kill them; it is General Forrest's orders," he should not have been surprised.[17]

The slaughter at Fort Pillow was no doubt driven in large part by racial hatred. Numbers alone suggest this: of 295 white troops, 168 were taken prisoner, but of 262 black troops, only 58 were taken into custody, with the rest either dead or too badly wounded to walk.[18] A Southern reporter traveling with Forrest makes clear that the discrimination was deliberate: "Our troops maddened by the excitement, shot down the ret[r]eating Yankees, and not until they had attained t[h]e water's edge and turned to beg for mercy, did any prisoners fall in [t]o our hands—Thus the whites received quarter, but the negroes were shown no mercy."[19] Union surgeon Dr. Charles Fitch, who was taken prisoner by Forrest, testified that after he was in custody he "saw" Confederate soldiers "kill every negro that made his appearance dressed in Federal uniform."[20]

Topic sentence for this section reinforces the thesis.

Notes begin on a
new page.

First line of each
note is indented ½".

Note number is
not raised and is
followed by a period.

Authors' names are
not inverted.

Last name and title
refer to an earlier
note by the same
author.

Notes are single-
spaced, with double-
spacing between
notes. (Some
instructors may
prefer double-
spacing throughout.)

Notes

1. John Cimprich and Robert C. Mainfort Jr., eds., "Fort Pillow Revisited: New Evidence about an Old Controversy," *Civil War History* 28, no. 4 (1982): 293-94.

2. Quoted in Brian Steel Wills, *A Battle from the Start: The Life of Nathan Bedford Forrest* (New York: HarperCollins, 1992), 182.

3. Ibid., 183.

4. Shelby Foote, *The Civil War, a Narrative: Red River to Appomattox* (New York: Vintage, 1986), 110.

5. Nathan Bedford Forrest, "Report of Maj. Gen. Nathan B. Forrest, C. S. Army, Commanding Cavalry, of the Capture of Fort Pillow," Shotgun's Home of the American Civil War, accessed March 6, 2008, http://www .civilwarhome.com/forrest.htm.

6. Jack Hurst, *Nathan Bedford Forrest: A Biography* (New York: Knopf, 1993), 174.

7. Foote, *Civil War,* 111.

8. Cimprich and Mainfort, "Fort Pillow," 295.

9. Ibid., 305.

10. Ibid., 299.

11. Foote, *Civil War,* 110.

12. Quoted in Wills, *Battle from the Start,* 187.

13. Albert Castel, "The Fort Pillow Massacre: A Fresh Examination of the Evidence," *Civil War History* 4, no. 1 (1958): 44-45.

14. Cimprich and Mainfort, "Fort Pillow," 300.

15. Hurst, *Nathan Bedford Forrest,* 177.

16. Ibid.

17. Dudley Taylor Cornish, *The Sable Arm: Black Troops in the Union Army, 1861-1865* (Lawrence: University Press of Kansas, 1987), 175.

18. Foote, *Civil War,* 111.

19. Cimprich and Mainfort, "Fort Pillow," 304.

20. Quoted in Wills, *Battle from the Start,* 189.

21. Ibid., 215.

22. Quoted in Hurst, *Nathan Bedford Forrest,* 177.

23. Quoted in James M. McPherson, *Battle Cry of Freedom: The Civil War Era* (New York: Oxford University Press, 1988), 402.

Bishop 8

Bibliography

Castel, Albert. "The Fort Pillow Massacre: A Fresh Examination of the Evidence." *Civil War History* 4, no. 1 (1958): 37-50.

Cimprich, John, and Robert C. Mainfort Jr., eds. "Fort Pillow Revisited: New Evidence about an Old Controversy." *Civil War History* 28, no. 4 (1982): 293-306.

Cornish, Dudley Taylor. *The Sable Arm: Black Troops in the Union Army, 1861-1865*. Lawrence: University Press of Kansas, 1987.

Foote, Shelby. *The Civil War, a Narrative: Red River to Appomattox*. New York: Vintage, 1986.

Forrest, Nathan Bedford. "Report of Maj. Gen. Nathan B. Forrest, C. S. Army, Commanding Cavalry, of the Capture of Fort Pillow." Shotgun's Home of the American Civil War. Accessed March 6, 2008. http://www.civilwarhome.com/forrest.htm.

Hurst, Jack. *Nathan Bedford Forrest: A Biography*. New York: Knopf, 1993.

McPherson, James M. *Battle Cry of Freedom: The Civil War Era*. New York: Oxford University Press, 1988.

Wills, Brian Steel. *A Battle from the Start: The Life of Nathan Bedford Forrest*. New York: HarperCollins, 1992.

Bibliography begins on a new page.

Entries are alphabetized by authors' last names.

First line of entry is at left margin; additional lines are indented ½˝.

Entries are single-spaced, with double-spacing between entries. (Some instructors may prefer double-spacing throughout.)

Acknowledgments

Scott Adams, "Dilbert and the Way of the Weasel" comic from a student paper. DILBERT: © Scott Adams/Dist. by United Feature Syndicate, Inc. Reprinted with permission.

American Heritage Dictionary, definition for "regard" from *The American Heritage Dictionary of the English Language, Fourth Edition.* Copyright © 2009 by Houghton Mifflin Harcourt Publishing Company. Reproduced by permission of Houghton Mifflin Harcourt Publishing Company.

EBSCO Information Services, various screen shots of database search results. Copyright © 2010 by EBSCO Publishing, Inc. All rights reserved. Reprinted with permission.

Equal Exchange, annotated advertisement. Copyright © 2007 by Equal Exchange. Reprinted with permission.

Gale, screen shot from ACADEMIC ONEFILE. Copyright © Gale, a part of Cengage Learning, Inc. Reproduced by permission. www.cengage.com/permission.

Chris Gonsalves, excerpt from "Wasting Away on the Web" from *eWeek*, August 8, 2005. Copyright © 2005 Ziff Davis Media Inc. All rights reserved. Reprinted with permission of Ziff Davis Media Inc.

Massachusetts Nurses Association, screen shot of labor relations Web page from www.massnurses.org. Copyright © Massachusetts Nurses Association. Reprinted with permission.

Merriam-Webster Online, screen shot of online dictionary entry for "regard" from *Merriam-Webster's Collegiate ® Dictionary, 11th Edition.* Copyright © 2010 by Merriam-Webster, Incorporated (www.Merriam-Webster.com). Reprinted with permission.

New Bedford Whaling Museum, screen shot of "Overview of American Whaling" Web page. Courtesy of the New Bedford Whaling Museum. Reprinted by permission.

The New York Times, "Callings: Proportion of respondents who attribute 'very great prestige' to the following professions" chart. Copyright © 2008 The New York Times. Reprinted by permission.

The New York Times, screen shot of the article page "Sales Reflect End of Car Rebate Plan" by Jack Healy. Copyright © 2009 The New York Times. Reprinted by permission.

Screen shots of various pages from *The American Historical Review*, 113.2 (April 2008). Copyright © 2008. Reprinted by permission of University of Chicago Press.

Screen shots of the Table of Contents Page and the first page of "An Appeal to Authority" by David Whitman, from *Education Next* 8 (4) 2008 issue. Copyright © Education Next. All rights reserved. Reprinted by permission.

Screen shots of the Copyright Page and Title Page from *Asian American Literature: An Anthology* by Shirley Geok-lin Lim. Copyright © 1999 by McGraw-Hill Companies. Reprinted by permission of McGraw-Hill Companies.

Screen shots of the article page "For the Love of Joe: The Language of Starbucks" by Constance M. Ruzich and the Title Page of *The Journal of Popular Culture.* Copyright © 2008 by Blackwell Publishers, Ltd. Reprinted with the permission of Blackwell Publishers, Ltd.

Modal verbs (*can, might, should,*
etc.), **G**: 190, **M**: 230, 232–33,
B: 312. *See also* Helping verbs
Modern Language Association.
See MLA papers
Modifiers
adjectives as, **G**: 207–12,
B: 313
adverbs as, **G**: 207–12, **B**: 314
commas with, **P**: 261–62
dangling, **S**: 120–23
essential and nonessential,
P: 262–65
of gerunds, **G**: 205
limiting, **S**: 117–18
misplaced, **S**: 117–19
redundant, **W**: 153
split infinitives: **S**: 120
squinting, **S**: 118–19
Money, abbreviations for, **P**: 301
Mood of verbs, **G**: 195–96. *See
also* Conditional sentences
shifts in, avoiding, **S**: 124–25
more, most (comparative,
superlative), **G**: 210–12
moreover
comma with, **P**: 265–66
semicolon with, **P**: 274–75
most, **W**: 148
Motive. *See* Purpose in writing;
Writing situation
Multilingual writers, **M**: 223–55
adjectives, **M**: 250–52
adjectives and adverbs,
placement of, **M**: 251–52
articles (*a, an, the*), **M**: 237–45
idioms (common expressions),
M: 252–55
omitted subjects or expletives,
M: 246–47
omitted verbs, **M**: 246
nouns, types of, **M**: 238–40
participles, present vs. past,
M: 250–51
prepositions
with adjectives, **M**: 254–55
with nouns and *-ing*
forms, **M**: 253–54

to show time and place
(*at, in, on,* etc.),
M: 252–53
with verbs, **M**: 255
repeated objects or adverbs,
S: 131, **M**: 248
repeated subjects, **S**: 127,
M: 247–48
sentence structure, **M**: 245–50
verbs
active voice, **M**: 227–28
conditional, **M**: 231–34
forms of, **M**: 225–30
with gerunds or
infinitives, **M**: 235–37
modals (*can, might,
should,* etc.), **M**: 230,
232–33
negative forms, **M**: 230–31
passive voice, **M**: 226,
229–30
tenses, **M**: 225, 227–29
must, as modal verb, **M**: 230,
232, **B**: 312
must of. See *may of, might of,*
W: 148
myself, **W**: 148, **G**: 203

N

namely, and sentence fragments,
G: 217
Narration, as pattern of
organization, **C**: 35
Narrowing a subject, **C**: 6,
R: 333–34, **MLA**: 432
N.B., **P**: 301
nearly, placement of, **S**: 117–18
Needed words, **S**: 114–17
articles (*a, an, the*), **S**: 117,
M: 237–45
in comparisons, **S**: 115–16
in compound structures,
S: 114–15
it, **M**: 246–47
in parallel structures, **S**: 113–14
subjects, **M**: 246–47
that, **S**: 115

Words used as words
  italics for, **P**: 305
  plural of, **P**: 280
  quotation marks for, **P**: 283
  treated as singular, **G**: 182–83
Work in an anthology. *See*
  Anthology, selection in
Working bibliography, **R**: 358–59,
  360
Working thesis. *See* Thesis,
  drafting
Works cited list (MLA)
  directory to models for,
    MLA: 371–72
  formatting, **MLA**: 431
  models for, **MLA**: 398–428
  sample, **MLA**: 440
World Wide Web. *See* Electronic
  sources; Internet
Worn-out expressions. *See* Clichés
would, as modal verb, **M**: 230,
  233, **B**: 312
would of (nonstandard), **W**: 152
Writing in the disciplines. *See
  also* Academic writing
  asking questions, **A**: 100–02
  assignments
    business proposal, **A**: 106
    lab report, **A**: 107
    nursing practice paper,
      A: 108
    psychology literature
      review, **A**: 105
    understanding, **C**: 5,
      A: 104–08

choosing a citation style,
  A: 103, **R**: 366–68
general advice, **A**: 101
language conventions, **A**: 102
using evidence, **A**: 102, 103
Writing process. *See also*
  Research process,
  highlights of
  for academic writing, **A**: 101
  drafting, **C**: 14–20
  planning, **C**: 3–14
  revising, **C**: 20–28
Writing situation, **C**: 3–4, 6
Writing tutors, working with. *See*
  Revising with comments

Y

yes, no, commas with, **P**: 267
yet
  comma before, **P**: 259
  as coordinating conjunction,
    B: 315
you
  appropriate use of, **S**: 123,
    G: 201
  inappropriate use of, **W**: 152,
    G: 201
  vs. *I* or *they*, **S**: 123–24
  and shifts in point of view,
    avoiding, **S**: 123
  understood, **M**: 246, **B**: 317
your, you're, **W**: 152
YouTube. See Video clip

Directory to model papers and other sample documents

Visit **hackerhandbooks.com/writersref** for more than thirty model documents in five citation styles.

Multilingual/ESL Menu

A complete section for multilingual writers:

ESL and Academic English notes in other sections:

MM

Understanding and Composing Multimodal Projects

A Hacker Handbooks Supplement

Dànielle Nicole DeVoss
Michigan State University

BEDFORD / ST. MARTIN'S   BOSTON ◆ NEW YORK

Manufactured in the United States of America.

7   6   5   4
f   e   d

For information, write: Bedford/St. Martin's, 75 Arlington Street, Boston, MA 02116   (617-399-4000)

ISBN 978-1-4576-1779-9

ACKNOWLEDGMENTS

Acknowledgments and copyrights can be found at the back of the book on pages MM-105 to MM-106, which constitute an extension of the copyright page. It is a violation of the law to reproduce these selections by any means whatsoever without the written permission of the copyright holder.

MM

Understanding and Composing Multimodal Projects

Understanding and Composing Multimodal Projects

MM1 Introduction

In many of your college courses, you will be asked to read, analyze, and compose texts. The way you interact with texts can determine your success in college. The good news is that you have been reading, analyzing, and composing for years. Think of a magazine you read often, a job ad you once replied to, a Web site you've frequently visited, a book you discussed with friends, or a Facebook comment you recently made. Your college courses may give you the opportunity to analyze and compose *multimodal* texts as well, texts that rely on a combination of modes, such as images, words, and sounds, to communicate an idea. A common example is a print advertisement, a text that communicates meaning with both words and an image.

Understanding and Composing Multimodal Projects will help you take a broader look at yourself as a reader and as a writer.

MM1-a What does it mean to "read" a text?

This book asks you to take a new look at the act of reading. You know that a person can read an article, but can he "read" a painting? Someone can read a book, of course, but can she "read" a podcast? Your immediate answer might be "No, of course not!" but if you can rethink what it means to read—and consider that reading can mean taking a closer look or listening critically—your answer might be "Well, maybe!" This book also asks you to reconsider what is meant by the word text. Most people would call an essay or a poem a text. Can a movie soundtrack or a cartoon be called a text?

To dig into these terms, compare John Keats's drawing in Figure 1–1 (p. MM-6), an ancient urn, with his 1819 poem "Ode on a Grecian Urn." What are the characteristics that might lead us to call the drawing a text? What are the characteristics that might lead us to call the poem a text? How would we "read" the image of the urn? How do we "read" the poem?

Here is an excerpt from Keats's "Ode on a Grecian Urn":

> O Attic shape! Fair attitude! with brede
> Of marble men and maidens overwrought,
> With forest branches and the trodden weed;
> Thou, silent form, dost tease us out of thought
> As doth eternity: Cold Pastoral!
> When old age shall this generation waste,
> Thou shalt remain, in midst of other woe
> Than ours, a friend to man, to whom thou say'st,
> "Beauty is truth, truth beauty,"—that is all
> Ye know on earth, and all ye need to know.

If reading means discovering what a text is saying, it's helpful to consider how the text is presenting its meaning. In the poem, meaning is presented through written words. The drawing shows details from the actual urn, including images that communicate meaning. Both "texts" tell a story for a purpose and to an audience.

Reading may also require careful attention to the historical and cultural context in which a text is created. A text always emerges out of a time and a place and a social situation. To read Keats's poem effectively may require knowing something about the English Romantic literary movement. To read the image of the urn effectively may require a familiarity with the uses of urns and other pottery in ancient Greece.

FIGURE 1–1 JOHN KEATS'S DRAWING OF AN ANCIENT URN.

Almost anything can be read—that is, carefully approached and analyzed for *what* it does and *how* it does what it does. Almost anything can be a text—that is, something that conveys meaning. Reading carefully and critically often means asking questions about a text. When and by whom was the text created? What purpose was it intended to serve? What assumptions does the creator or composer make about the audience? Reading for a college course requires active, thoughtful investigation.

MM1-b What is multimodal composing?

This book refers to texts that include more than one way of presenting an idea as *multimodal*. Multimodal texts are those that draw on multiple (multi) modes of conveying information, including words, numbers, images, graphics, animations, transitions, sounds (voice and music), and more.

> WORDS   = MONOMODAL TEXT
> WORDS + [_____]   = MULTIMODAL TEXT

When ancient orators, or public speakers, tried to persuade audiences, they did so orally with the words they spoke and their tone of voice—but they also did so with another mode, their physical gestures.

Speakers throughout history have communicated their meaning by combining modes, or ways of presenting their message. The best, most convincing speakers know that a gesture combined with a word can be powerful—and when the word is spoken in a particular tone, it can be even more so. Clasped, raised hands can convey pleading or imploring, for instance, while a clenched fist often conveys might and strength.

SPEECH + GESTURES = MULTIMODAL TEXT

This is multimodal composing.

Think back to a high school earth science class, where you may have been studying earthquakes and plate tectonics. You may have had to compose a project that called for diagrams to represent the different types of plate movements within the earth's crust; a report on the specific physical features of a recent earthquake—Indonesia (2007), Chile (2010), Haiti (2010), or Japan (2011); and a brief slide show presentation of cause-and-effect findings to the class.

WORDS + IMAGES + SPEECH = MULTIMODAL TEXT

This is multimodal composing.

Using multiple modes causes us to rethink terminology. You may be accustomed to referring to those who compose texts as *authors* or *writers*. You may also use the term *writing* to describe most acts of communicating ideas. This book will describe communicating ideas as *composing*, which literally means "to produce something by putting together." And this book will refer to those who compose multimodal texts as *composers*.

Composers of texts may combine modes, and in some ways this makes their work more complicated. Composers have more options for sending a message, sharing an idea, posing an argument, teaching other people how to do something, and so forth. In other ways, combining modes makes composers' work more exciting and effective. They can send, share, teach, and explain in ways that include words *and* other elements.

MM1-c Composing *hasn't* changed

In some ways, composing has not changed all that much. It has always been crucial to how meaning is made and shared—how we communicate ideas from person to person, community to community, and generation to generation. Composing has always served to capture, save, and deliver ideas, messages, and meanings. Ancient cultures, for example, composed petroglyphs, rock carvings on cave walls and the sides of mountains, to share their ideas in a lasting way (Figure 1–2).

FIGURE 1-2 ANCIENT PETROGLYPHS ON CAVE WALLS.

(*Source:* US National Park Service; Pgiam)

FIGURE 1-3 MEDIEVAL ILLUMINATED MANUSCRIPT.

(*Source:* Duncan Walker)

Further, composing has often, to some extent, been multimodal. As far back as the fifth century CE, for example, monks created illuminated manuscripts—richly decorated books that combined illustrations and words. (Figure 1–3).

Though today's printed brochures aren't handwritten or decorated with gold leaf, they are a similarly effective combination of modes (words and images). Think about a catalog that includes full-color, glossy pages and perhaps a QR (quick response) code you can scan with your cell phone for more information (Figure 1–4). Or think about an e-book, which might include the typical contents of a printed book—a table of contents, numbered pages, lots of text, and so on—but which can also contain embedded video clips and animations.

FIGURE 1–4 QR (QUICK RESPONSE) CODE. (*Source:* Denso Wave Incorporated)

MM1-d Composing *has* changed

Composing has, in some ways, changed significantly in recent years. Today's composers blog, podcast, craft digital stories, prepare slide show presentations, design Web pages, write short blurbs to post as status updates and news, and much more. The ways in which composing has changed result primarily from a few recent technological innovations:

- The speed with which we can share and distribute documents. No longer do we have to take the time to print a document and mail it to others; instead, we can zip it along to others via e-mail or social media spaces.

- The ease with which we can draw on multiple media in one document. Word processing applications, for instance, allow writers to incorporate images. Web page creation spaces encourage composers to embed links to video-sharing sites like YouTube.

- Access to a range of media and materials. When writers wanted to compose a multimodal document before computer software made it easy to do so, they would have to physically cut and paste—with scissors and glue—to embed images in a textual document. Today, electronic copy-and-paste functions allow writers to almost seamlessly pull media from different online spaces and move those media across applications.

Together, these changes provide a broader context for composing *and* for sharing texts. Both the composers of centuries-old manuscripts and the composers of days-old YouTube videos thought about their purposes for communicating, the audiences they were trying to reach, the technology available to them at the time, and which modes were most useful in communicating their ideas.

MM1-e Composing in college

Most academic work involves producing traditional written pages that demonstrate certain elements of good writing: attention to your purpose and your audience; clear thesis statements; strong, well-formed paragraphs; evidence that might include citations and examples; bibliographies or works cited pages; and so on. Across academic disciplines, you'll be expected to approach, understand, and analyze different types of multimodal texts as well.

1. $-5y + 3 = 2(4y + 12)$

2. $\frac{4}{x^2 - 2x} - \frac{2}{x - 2} = -\frac{1}{2}$

3. $x\sqrt{x} = -x$

4. $|x - a| = a^2 - x^2$

5. $4x^2 + 1 - 2x^2 + 2 = 8$

6. $\log_2(2x - 1) + x = \log_4(144)$

7. $\begin{cases} x^2 + y^2 = 17 + 2x \\ (x - 1)^2 + (y - 8)^2 = 34 \end{cases}$

FIGURE 1–5 A MULTI-MODAL TEXT FROM A MATH COURSE.
(*Source:* umsolver.com)

For instance, in math courses, you will encounter equations that include not only numbers but also a range of shapes and figures with particular meaning (Figure 1–5). In a geology or physics course, you might study images that show various movements of the earth's crust (Figure 1–6). In an art history course, you might encounter collages by famous artists and be expected to interrogate them, analyze their meaning, and talk about your response to them (Figure 1–7).

In a variety of college courses, you'll also be expected to plan, outline, and create different types of multimodal texts.

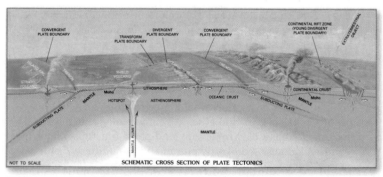

FIGURE 1–6 A MULTIMODAL TEXT FROM A GEOLOGY COURSE. (*Source:* US Geological Survey)

FIGURE 1–7 **A MULTIMODAL TEXT FROM AN ART HISTORY COURSE.**
(*Source:* Gilbert Mayer)

In an introduction to economics course, you might be asked to work in a group to prepare and present a slide show analyzing financial trends.

For an English class, you might be asked to write weekly blog posts in response to assigned readings.

In a biology class, you might be assigned to photograph a particular area over time to construct a visual record of the changes in foliage.

Constructing each of these multimodal texts—a slide show, a blog, a visual record—will require you to think critically and carefully about the different elements you might include (sound, video, charts, photographs, data, words) and how to compose with audience, purpose, organization, clarity, and responsibility in mind.

MM1-f Composing beyond college

College isn't the only place where you might have to analyze and produce multimodal texts. You may, for example, encounter public service ads like the one in Figure 1–8, which combines words and an image

FIGURE 1–8 A MULTIMODAL PUBLIC SERVICE AD. (*Source:* Sonda Dawes)

to prompt you to think about making an emergency plan for yourself and your family. Or you may be part of a community group hosting a fundraising event, for which you'll have to create eye-catching, compelling flyers to attract both sponsors and participants.

Knowing how to produce multimodal texts will be an asset as you start to look for a job. In a 2009 document called "Workplace Writing Skills," educator Christine Polk pointed out that although businesses and organizations rely on efficient and effective communication to profit and thrive, many people struggle to write effectively in the workplace. Job ads—seeking everything from engineering architects to park rangers to grocery store managers—often emphasize the ways in which companies and organizations value candidates who can effectively communicate in multimodal ways. Job candidates today may be expected to produce projects like these:

technical reports that include data or diagrams

planning documents that communicate the rationale for and placement of products in a retail environment

announcements to the public that include text and maps or illustrations

training videos for customers or new employees

Web site content to draw in clients or customers

Analyzing and composing multimodal texts in college can give you the practice you need to communicate effectively in civic, personal, or professional situations in the future.

MM1-g What this book offers

This book is anchored by the concepts discussed in the previous sections: that is, how composing has and hasn't changed, an expanded notion of what composing is, and the importance of composing in and outside of the classroom.

This book offers the following:

a process for analyzing multimodal texts

a vocabulary for analyzing multimodal texts

a process for producing multimodal texts

a close look at two students' multimodal composing processes

a way of thinking about the relation between analyzing and producing multimodal texts

Sections MM1 through MM6 will help you hone your skills of analysis as you explore different types of modes and texts. Sections MM7 through MM15 will help you think about the best processes, practices, and tools for conveying your own ideas in a multimodal composition.

Keep in mind that effective compositions transcend specific software programs and digital spaces. If you can adopt the habits of carefully analyzing and crafting different types of texts, you will become a flexible, smart communicator who knows how to select the best tool for the job and the best techniques for the composing task at hand.

MM1-h A toolkit for analyzing and composing multimodal texts

As a first step in looking at multimodal texts, you need to learn to identify the different modes a composer is using and to examine them separately. Sections MM2 through MM6 ask you to read and analyze written words, sounds, static images, moving images, and multimodal texts. The book includes a toolkit that helps you evaluate individual modes and multimodal compositions. You will learn to think in terms of What? How? Who? and Why? as you answer questions like these in sections MM2 through MM6:

Genre. What kind of text is it? A slide show? An audio essay? An advertisement?

Features. How would you describe the elements of the text? What styles and treatments has the composer used to create emphasis, maintain clarity, or inspire feeling?

Purpose and audience. What is the text doing? For what reason was the text created? Who is the intended reader/viewer/listener?

Meaning. What is your interpretation of the text? (Keep in mind that your interpretation—your take on the meaning—may differ from the composer's intended message.)

Sections MM2 through MM6 include specific advice about how to apply these tools to different types of texts—those composed of written words, sounds, static (or still) images, or moving images—and to compositions that combine these modes.

MM2 Analyzing written words

When written words appear alone in a document, it's clear that they have a message to convey. In much academic writing, the design of the document seems "invisible," whether the message is simple or complex. In other words, academic writers often avoid decorative or unusual fonts (such as Comic Sans) or font treatments (such as color)

Analyzing written words

Genre

In what kind of document do the words appear? A brochure? A letter? An essay?

Features

Is the text in a single font or a variety of fonts? How would you describe the font(s)? Are there different colors and sizes? Do you notice bold, italic, or highlighted words? Are any words animated—do they move or change in shape, color, or size?

Purpose and audience

What is the purpose of the text? Is it meant to teach, guide, warn, entertain, or provoke the reader?

Who is the intended audience for the written words? Readers who will take time to read them? Or readers who will need to grasp the message quickly? Are they consumers, children, workers, fans, protesters, commuters, or a mixed group?

Meaning

How do genre, features, purpose, and audience work together to convey a message? How do you interpret the use of the written words? (Keep in mind that your interpretation—your take on the meaning—may differ from the composer's intended message.)

that might distract readers or discourage them from taking the message seriously.

When used thoughtfully, however, different fonts and features can add meaning to written words and can be especially appropriate in multimodal compositions. Whether created for academic, professional, or creative purposes, multimodal compositions may use a variety of treatments and even animations to boost or otherwise alter the meaning of written words. When you're analyzing how written words function in a composition, consider the questions in the chart on page MM-14.

MM2-a Genre: In what kind of document do the written words appear?

Often you'll form ideas about the content of a document as soon as you look at it, before you read a single word. Determining what type of document you're dealing with is a key step in analyzing the words within the document.

Take a look at the document thumbnails in Figure 2–1. Although you can't read all of the words, thinking about where the words appear and how the overall document is formatted will give you a sense of what kind of information the words might convey.

Look closely at image (a) on page MM-16. How much space appears between the lines of text? What do you think is the function of the words in the upper left corner? What likely appears centered after those words? Answers to these questions tell us that these words are probably part of a traditional essay, with space devoted to the author's name, course, and date in the top left and the title centered on the line below.

Now consider image (d). How are the words arranged? The way the words are chunked together and placed in columns reveals at a glance that they are words in a menu. The arrangement of words in the document tells us what kind of information to expect—a list of foods organized by course: appetizers, entrees, and desserts. Imagine trying to read a menu without categories or labels, in which all the content is lumped together without being organized or easily identifiable.

MM2-b Features: What do the words look like?

We're so used to gathering meaning from written words simply by reading them that it may seem strange at first to analyze what the words look like. Words can, however, appear in a variety of sizes, shapes, colors, styles, and static or animated configurations. One of the first things

(a)

(b) (*Source:* FEMA)

(c)

(d)

FIGURE 2–1 EVERYDAY TEXTS.

to note is the font (or *typeface*) in which the words appear. Graphic designers often talk about fonts as the "voice" of the page.

When considering the effect that font choice has on a text, think about what adjectives you might associate with a particular font. For instance, you might describe Comic Sans as *fun*, *childish*, and *handwritten*. Even if you have never seen Comic Sans before, the scrawled feeling of the irregular shapes and angles of the letters will call such adjectives to mind. Understanding the visual aspects of written texts requires that we pay attention to the shape and the feel of the typeface itself.

What adjectives would you associate with the following typefaces?

Bauhaus 93

Broadway

COPPERPLATE GOTHIC

Kunstler Script

Forte

Times New Roman

As you consider the font, think about any treatment or formatting applied to it. For example, how has capitalization been applied? Are the words in *sentence case* (standard capitalization for a sentence) or some other case?

> Sentence case appears with an initial capital letter and a period at the end.
>
> all lowercase is written in all lowercase letters.
>
> ALL CAPS IS WRITTEN IN ALL CAPITAL LETTERS.
>
> mIxED cAsE iS a mIxTuRe oF cApItAL aNd LoweRCaSe leTterS.

What do you associate with each of these capitalization styles? In academic writing, sentences are usually presented in sentence case, and all caps is usually used only for headings or subheadings. In informal, creative, or multimodal texts, all caps might be used for emphasis or to signify "yelling" or some other strong emotion.

When considering the features of words, check for typographic elements, such as text set in bold, italics, quotation marks, color, or different sizes or text set with strikethrough or highlighting. Each of these elements shapes the way readers interact with the text. Words that convey a warning, for example, might be set in red, a color associated with fire and stop signs. If different font sizes are used in a text, readers will assume that larger words are more important than smaller ones.

MM2-c Purpose and audience: What is the purpose of the written words? Who is the intended reader?

Take a look at the text on the next page, a letter by Gerald Gainley, the CEO of Canyon Cove Chemicals. The company wants to expand its facilities; however, the local government has blocked that expansion because of concern over environmental damage and unchecked

LETTER WRITTEN TO A SPECIFIC AUDIENCE

Dear Springfield and All of the Supporters of Canyon Cove Chemicals:

I write to you to convey my dismay and disappointment with the city council, our elected governing body.

Earlier today, as you may know, the city council, under the leadership of Stanley Burris, decided to block the development of a new Canyon Cove Chemicals refining facility on Oak Wood Road, just ten miles north of our city center and north of the city offices in which this decision was made.

This decision was prefaced by a self-serving, self-promotional, unnecessarily accusatory statement made by Council Chair Burris, who attacked Canyon Cove Chemicals.

Canyon Cove Chemicals has been devoted to and supportive of our local community for more than seventy-five years. We have sponsored the little league teams on which our children have played. We have donated funds to build the playgrounds and skate park at which our youngsters enjoy outdoor activities. We have allocated a part of our annual revenue to supporting our high schoolers in continuing their education at our two area community colleges.

For Council Chair Burris to accuse the company of greed and overdevelopment is not only a travesty but also a threat to our fine community.

Better facilities for Canyon Cove Chemicals will mean more revenue and will provide our company with the ability to participate even more in supporting our community.

"I PERSONALLY GUARANTEE THAT CANYON COVE CHEMICALS, IF OUR FACILITIES EXPANSION MOVES FOR-WARD, WILL DONATE TWICE AS MUCH IN THE COMING YEAR AS WE DONATED LAST YEAR."

I will stake my reputation and the reputation of the company I so proudly run on this claim.

Gerald Gainley
CEO, Canyon Cove Chemicals

industrial growth in the area. In response, Gainley distributed this letter to the local media and posted it on the company's Web site.

Why do you think Gainley wrote this letter? What was his purpose in writing it? The CEO addresses the letter to the entire city ("Dear Springfield") and "All of the Supporters of Canyon Cove Chemicals," indicating that he hopes to maintain support for the company despite the fact that it suffered a bad outcome in a city council vote. To be successful, his message needs to appeal to the general public and especially to readers who work for the company, support the company, or are active in local government (as representatives and voters, for example). The letter has to ease their concerns and draw attention to the benefits the company brings to the city. Think about the choices Gainley makes as he tries to accomplish those goals. Consider his words as well as their typographical treatment.

In the letter, Gainley uses two different fonts. Comic Sans looks handwritten and is rarely used in professional communication. Times New Roman is a more standard font, often used in newspapers, books, and other publications. What message does each font convey to the reader? Comic Sans might not be an effective choice for someone who wants to be taken seriously, but a handwritten font does underscore the personal feel of Gainley's communication—he is speaking on behalf of the company, but he's also speaking as someone who has a personal stake in the company and the community. Think about how the effect of the text would be different if all of the words were set in Times New Roman.

Note Gainley's capitalization choices as well. Some statements are in sentence case, and others are in all caps (see p. MM-17). How do you think the CEO wants readers to feel about the all caps statement in quotation marks near the end of his letter? Formatting the statement in all caps adds emphasis and might be intended to convey Gainley's commitment to the words. Perhaps the quotation marks are meant to show that his promise is a quotable statement—one he expects community members to hold him to.

Consider also what the letter is *not*. It's not a television or radio spot. Why do you think Gainley chose a letter to the city to convey his message? Why do you think he sent the letter to local television and radio stations and posted the letter on the company Web site? Gainley could have paid to run television and radio ads to convey this message. Perhaps he felt that a written statement would have a more personal, sincere feel; the letter format allows him to address all residents of Springfield and the surrounding area directly—including those who work for the company or have family members who have benefited from the company's local donations and support. Why do you think he chose not to include any images? He may have felt that a picture would draw attention away from his words or that a picture of himself or the proposed new facility might make it harder for readers to think of him as their peer. His repeated use of the phrase *our community* makes it clear that he counts himself a citizen, not just the head of a company.

MM2-d Meaning: What effect do the words have on the reader?

Given what you know about Gainley's written statement regarding the city council's vote against Canyon Cove Chemicals' plan for expansion, what do you think of Gainley's chosen mode of expression—written words—and his decisions about how to present those words? Do you think his letter had the desired effect?

In an essay for his communications class, student—and Springfield resident—John Nikolakakis wrote the following analysis of Gainley's letter:

> In his letter to the city of Springfield, Gerald Gainley, the CEO of Canyon Cove Chemicals, expresses his "dismay" and, at times, disgust at a recent city council decision, in which the members voted against allowing the company to expand its facilities in north Springfield. He characterizes the city council members as shortsighted and essentially accuses them of putting the city in peril; that is, he doesn't say it directly, but he does imply that the company could move to another city, and then Springfield would lose the support and economic donations of the company. Gainley also makes an interesting promise to the city of Springfield.
>
> Gainley makes two textual choices that are worth attention: his use of fonts and his use of all capital letters (ALL CAPS). Gainley has formatted his letter almost entirely in Comic Sans. The font looks handwritten and may be perceived as bubbly and childish. Some of Gainley's critics have charged that the use of Comic Sans in this situation is inappropriate. If he were writing more formally, that criticism would be totally on the mark, but he wants the letter to be personal and to make him seem like a friend to its readers. The average Springfield citizen, Gainley's audience, will likely feel that the font is approachable and appropriate for a personal appeal.
>
> Interestingly, one sentence in the letter is not in Comic Sans. When Gainley pledges that Canyon Cove Chemicals "WILL DONATE TWICE AS MUCH IN THE COMING YEAR AS WE DONATED LAST YEAR" if the company is allowed to expand its facilities, the promise is set in Times New Roman and ALL CAPS. Both of these formatting choices show that Gainley wants the statement to stand out from the

rest of his letter and carry an official weight; he regards these words as a solemn oath to his readers.

When you analyze written words, it's important to consider the composer's choices of document type, font, and formatting. These choices may enhance or work against the composer's intended message. As you develop your own interpretation of the overall meaning of the text, think about how genre, features, purpose, and intended audience affect the reader's experience.

ACTIVITY MM2–1: Your understanding

Find a campaign banner or bumper sticker from a campus, local, or national election. Write a paragraph in which you analyze the features of the text you've selected. What font is used? What meaning does the font convey? What methods of emphasis are used with the text (for example, boldface or underline)? Think about the intended purpose and audience for the campaign piece and determine what message the text and the piece as a whole convey about the political candidate.

MM3 Analyzing sound

Sound is everywhere. Birds chirp, cars honk, music plays. Sometimes it's just in the background, but sometimes it's used for deliberate effect. Think about how sound functions in gambling casinos. Until recently, slot machines dispensed coins to winners. The noise of coins dropping from the winning machine was deliberately magnified so that other gamblers would notice and be encouraged to continue gambling. Most casinos have shifted to a receipt-based system—the machine generates a receipt that a gambler can turn in for cash. Because the sound of coins dropping out of a machine is so effective, however, machines still make that sound, even though no coins are involved. Sound can convey meaning on its own or enhance meaning when combined with other modes. When analyzing sound, consider the questions in the chart on page MM-22.

MM3-a Genre: What kind of sound is it?

Although we're surrounded by sound, we don't give it much thought most of the time. Even the music we listen to is often just background for other activities, unless we're studying music. But sound influences those who can hear it, even if they're not fully aware of the effect.

Analyzing sound

Genre

What kind of sound is it? Is it speech, music, or a noise associated with a particular object, for example?

Features

How would you describe the sound? Is it loud or quiet? Does it have a high or a low pitch? Is its pacing fast or slow? Is it in the background or in the foreground? Are certain sounds louder or quieter than others?

Purpose and audience

What is the purpose of the sound? Does it provide atmosphere? Is it accompanying something else, such as an image? Or is it the main or only mode of communication?

Who is the intended audience for the sound? A single listener with headphones? A room full of people? Children or adults? Experts or nonexperts? Sympathizers or opponents?

Meaning

How do genre, features, purpose, and audience work together to convey a message? How do you interpret the use of sound? (Keep in mind that your interpretation—your take on the meaning—may differ from the composer's intended message.)

Consider the music in a movie, which usually consists of the score (original music composed for the movie) and licensed music (clips from songs or orchestral works, for example). After you watch a movie, a few catchy tunes or notes might stick in your head, but for the most part you won't be able to describe what the music was like throughout the movie. And yet successful music will affect the way you perceive the entire film. A trumpet solo might make a scene or character seem more heroic, for example. Soft music might encourage viewers to feel thoughtful in a somber moment. Loud, fast-paced music might accompany a chase scene to enhance the sense of speed or urgency.

Music is just one type of sound that can be part of a movie soundtrack. To think about how sound as a whole functions in a composition such as a movie, you first need to identify what kinds of sounds are involved. A soundtrack can include dialogue—one or more people talking. It can also include sound effects—sounds associated with particular animals or objects, such as birdsong to signal morning or cars honking to provide a busy urban atmosphere. And the music might be a scene-setting background melody or part of a performance happening on the screen. You can use these categories to identify types of sounds in audio-only or multimodal compositions and to examine what purposes individual sound elements serve in a larger composition.

In movies, sound often provides a supporting role. Unless it's dialogue, sound is usually in the background, enhancing the action on-screen. What about sound in compositions that are strictly audio? A podcast, for example, can be an audio-only file designed to be downloaded from the Internet and listened to on a computer or portable music player.

In one composition class, students were asked to create a podcast on a compelling local issue. Before they wrote or recorded anything of their own, they analyzed podcasts created by other students. First-year student Talia Souza chose to analyze a podcast titled "Hustlers, Street Vendors, and Farmers," in which the author, King Anyi Howell, visited a Los Angeles farmers' market geared toward black customers. Souza knew she wanted to do something related to food and farming, and she was interested in Howell's focus on selling food in one community. Howell's podcast offered a rich mix of spoken text and background sounds for Souza to analyze.

Souza listened several times, first for content, then a second time to take careful notes on the content. The third time through, she listened for the various background sounds and made some notes on the podcast as a whole:

Narration by Molly Adams (welcome and intro)

Then upbeat, jazzy music (horns and drums?) plays under Molly's voice

Music fades out as Molly introduces the piece

King Anyi Howell's piece starts with the sound of two men talking, outside—can hear what sounds like car traffic and people walking by; can hear the rustling of one of the men putting something in a bag; can hear the men talking about the cost of what's being bagged

Howell's voice comes in over the two men talking, explaining that he's at a farmers' market

Howell describes the busy intersection (can hear street sounds in the background)

Howell introduces a young woman, a shopper who describes the market

ONLINE   hackerhandbooks.com/multimodal
     > Multimodal resources > Podcast
                   > King Anyi Howell, "Hustlers, Street
                       Vendors, and Farmers"

Howell describes a group of vendors, with men talking in the background

Sounds in piece: narration (by writers); clips of people talking; music; street noises

Whether you're analyzing sound in conjunction with other modes (when it's used in a movie, for example) or on its own (as in an audio podcast), it's a good idea to listen to the soundtrack or audio track several times. So that you can focus on the sound, do not take notes until the second or third time you listen. If there are layers of sound (talking in the foreground and street noise in the background, for example), first examine those elements separately and then think about how they work together.

MM3-b Features: Examine the pitch, pace, and volume of the sound

When analyzing sound, you'll also want to consider qualities like pitch, pace, and volume. *Pitch* is a measure of the highness or low-ness of sound. A child's voice, for example, is often high-pitched, whereas a lion's roar is low-pitched. In speech, pitch provides inflection, which affects how listeners interpret the words being spoken. A statement that pitches upward at the end usually sounds like a question. If you've seen the movie *Ferris Bueller's Day Off*, you probably remember the scene in which a teacher (played by Ben Stein) takes attendance. The teacher's monotonous delivery of the students' names reflects his overall persona in the classroom: flat and boring. The camera pans to show his students falling asleep before class has even begun. This serves as a humorous justification for Ferris's skipping class.

Pitch can offer valuable clues about what's happening in a segment or piece. When people become frightened or stressed, the pitch of their voice tends to go higher. Higher pitch in movie music can emphasize anxiety and fright on-screen and inspire those feelings in the audience.

In addition to pitch, think about pace and volume when analyzing sound. Does the sound seem to be fast or slow (*pace*)? Is one sound louder or softer than another (*volume*)? Does the pace or volume of a particular sound change? What is the effect of any changes on the listener? In the movie *Jaws*, pace and volume work together to create suspense. A simple set of tones plays when the shark is near. These tones get faster and louder as the shark gets closer to an unsuspecting swimmer, encouraging a sense of panic in the audience.

MM3-c Purpose and audience: What is sound being used for? Who is the intended listener?

When people use sound to convey a message, they usually make deliberate choices based on their intended message and the listeners they're trying to reach. When you analyze sound, it's important to think about the composer's choices. Consider King Anyi Howell's podcast, described on page MM-23. Why did Howell choose to create a podcast rather than make a movie to be watched or write a story to be read? Perhaps Howell imagined that a single listener, surrounded by the sounds of the podcast, would be more absorbed in the story than a viewer distracted by images on-screen or a reader with only words on paper to consider. A listener has to imagine the images; the background sounds Howell provides along with the spoken story makes those images vivid and absorbing.

MM3-d Meaning: What effect does sound have on the listener?

When you analyze sound, it's important to consider the composer's choice of sounds and the pitch, pace, and volume of those sounds. These choices may enhance or work against the composer's intended message. The following is an excerpt from Talia Souza's analysis of sound in King Anyi Howell's podcast, which Souza wrote in preparation for creating her own podcast.

> This podcast is hosted by Molly Adams, who provides a brief introduction with upbeat, jazzy music playing in the background. When the introduction is over, the main podcast begins. In it, King Anyi Howell uses three types of sounds. The first is human voice. Howell narrates the podcast, explaining the scene to listeners and interacting with the people he recorded for the podcast. He also includes segments of people talking, interacting with each other, and responding to his questions.
>
> The second type of sound is background noises, which include street sounds that help set the scene: car engine revving, cars whooshing by, plastic grocery bags crinkling, and change jingling. The third type of sound is music playing. Rather than using recorded studio music, Howell includes the sounds of live music being played at the farmers' market, so listeners can hear not only the music but also other noise, such as people talking. This makes the music feel more authentic and shows how the music is part of the market scene. At the end of the podcast,

Adams provides a conclusion, and the lively, jazzy music plays underneath her voice again.

What I took from this podcast that I want to apply in my podcast is to interview people and include other people's voices. It's one thing for me to say that people believe a particular thing or hold a certain opinion, but it's more compelling to include other people's voices saying what they believe. This worked really well in Howell's podcast. Also, music and sounds can enhance a podcast and help listeners better imagine a place. Right now, my plan is to do a podcast about the dining options in the student union and how healthy they are (or aren't). If I record in the student union and interview people there, it will help my listeners imagine the space. Another aspect I liked was that Howell included a clear introduction and conclusion. I don't want someone else to do my intro and conclusion, as Adams did in Howell's podcast, but I like the idea of setting up the main part of the podcast and then concluding it at the end.

Although a composer's choices about the type of sound and its qualities are usually deliberate, they don't necessarily convey the same meaning to all listeners in all contexts. They may not work the way the composer intended, or they may carry additional meanings the composer didn't anticipate. As you develop an interpretation about the meaning of sound on its own or as part of a multimodal piece, be sure to consider genre, features, purpose, and audience together.

ACTIVITY MM3-1: Your understanding

Online movie trailers, used to advertise and preview movies, are approximately three to four minutes long. Television ads for movies are typically much shorter and limited in terms of how they grab viewers' attention and condense the story line. In your Web browser, conduct a search for "movie trailer." Scan the results and select a movie trailer to watch. Choose a full-length trailer so that you'll have more audio material to work with for this activity.

Close your eyes and listen to the trailer; do not watch it. Closing your eyes will allow you to focus on just the sounds. As you listen, identify the different sounds you're hearing and think about what function they serve, what feelings they evoke in you, how they are sequenced together, and so on. Then watch the trailer. You'll hear the sounds, see the sequences of images, and perhaps begin to note how they fit together. As you play the trailer a third time, create a list—somewhat like Souza's list on page MM-23—of the different sounds you hear. Once you have a list, identify each sound by genre and think about how the sound helps convey meaning in the trailer. Create a chart like the one on page MM-27 to record your notes. Consider adapting the chart and using it to document sounds in the different types of texts you study.

STUDENT NOTES ON A *SHREK* MOVIE TRAILER

Time	Sound	Purpose
:02-:10	man singing with symphony-like music	establishes context; creates opening for trailer
:11-:20	prince talking to big mirror hanging on the wall, mirror talking back; crowd of knights gasp	helps to set plot; prince's voice is kind of pompous-sounding; sound of gasps creates sense of disbelief
:21-:22	knight smashes small mirror	shows that prince is malicious! sound of mirror shattering contrasts with the opening singing/music
:23-:24	knight turns back to talk to big mirror	establishes a threat!
:25-:33	different symphony-like music with voice-over explaining plot of movie	continues to explain plot of movie; narrator's voice-over rhymes and feels storytelling-like

MM4 Analyzing static images

On any given day, you'll encounter images on billboards, road signs, maps, posters, flyers, brochures, product packaging, logos, advertisements, and so on. Images are all around us. Whether they're selling a product, conveying a message, sending a warning, or informing us about a law, they all have something to say. Although often we don't consider them carefully or critically, most images are designed to plant ideas or influence our decisions. When you want to analyze an image—to pick apart its message and how it works—think about the questions in the chart on page MM-30.

MM4-a Genre: What kind of image is it?

One of the first things you'll want to do when analyzing a static (or still) image is to determine what kind of image it is. Certain types of images do certain work and should be used for specific purposes. Consider the images in the chart on pages MM-28 and MM-29. The genre of each example is given along with a common use for each type of image.

Think about an image you see every day—perhaps a billboard or subway map you see on your way to work or class. What type of image is it? What does it mean to you? How might it work differently—or not work at all—if it were a different type of image?

Genre: What kind of image is it?

Photograph

Photographs can be used to represent specific places, people, or things.

Sketch

Sketches provide an artistic rendering of places, people, or things.

Map

Maps show specific locations or routes to locations.

Clip art

Clip art can provide generic representations of a places, people, or things.

Sources (top to bottom): Straga; Danussa; Jami Garrison; Sapik.

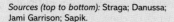

Chart

Charts provide data in a format that is easy to read at a glance.

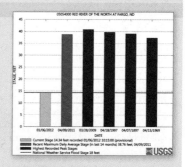

Diagram

Diagrams can be used to represent parts or functions of an object or process that are not usually visible.

Source (for both images): US Geological Survey.

Take a look at Figure 4–1, an image included in a set of instructions for applying women's hair dye. The image is a sketch, meant to represent any woman who might use the hair dye. If a photograph of a particular woman were used instead, viewers who look nothing like her might not be able to relate to her. But by using a sketch with generic features, the manufacturers are inviting all prospective users to imagine themselves following the instructions and using the hair dye carefully.

FIGURE 4–1 IMAGE ACCOMPANYING A SET OF INSTRUCTIONS. (*Source:* RetroClipArt)

Analyzing static images

Genre

What kind of image is it? Is it a photograph, cartoon, painting, map, chart, or diagram, for example?

Features

Is the image in color or black and white? In what context does the image appear? For example, is it large format (perhaps a poster) or small format (such as food packaging)? If the image has depth, what elements are in the foreground and the background? What is the perspective of the image (is it a close-up or an aerial view, for example)?

Purpose and audience

What is the purpose of the image? Is it accompanied by other modes, such as sound or written words? Or does it convey meaning on its own? Is it meant to teach, guide, warn, entertain, or provoke the viewer?

Who is the intended audience for the image? Someone zooming by in a car with only seconds to process the message? Someone who will spend time examining the image? Children or adults? Experts or nonexperts?

Meaning

How do genre, features, purpose, and audience work together to convey a message? How do you interpret the use of the image? (Keep in mind that your interpretation—your take on the meaning—may differ from the composer's intended message.)

MM4-b Features: Examine the context, perspective, and elements of the image

As you analyze an image, think about the context in which it appears. In other words, what surrounds the image? Is it an illustration in a book, a photo in a magazine, a warning in a building or vehicle, a painting in a gallery? How is the image presented? Do you have time to look at it, or do you need to absorb its meaning quickly? Does it need to be interesting, or straightforward? Should it make you want to buy something, find out more about something, or avoid something?

Think about images in product instructions. Because consumers usually want the assembly or use of a product to be as simple as possible, instructions typically use basic or generic images to illustrate steps, tips, or cautions. It can be difficult, however, to convey a clear message with a simple illustration.

In a technical writing course, students were asked to select a set of product instructions and choose one image from the instructions to analyze. Working with a one-page instruction sheet that came with an electric blanket he had recently purchased, Arman Chavva focused on the image of a dog's head with a circle and slash drawn over it.

The image I chose to analyze in this set of instructions appeared in a list titled "Instructions for Use." The image was next to item #17, "Do not use with pets."

I chose this image because it is ineffective. The image shows a specific breed of dog, so a literal translation might be "no German shepherds." "No German shepherds" does not mean the same thing as "Do not use with pets."

The technical writer who created the

Source: Boffi.

instructions was right in using the circle and slash, which in most cultures means "NO" or "DO NOT." However, the writer should probably have used a more general image to send the message of "pets." A photograph of a specific breed of dog doesn't send a general message. Instead, the author could have used simple shapes or clip art of a bird, a cat, and a dog, with the circle and slash over the shapes. The simple shapes would make users think of animals in general rather than one particular animal or one particular breed of animal.

FIGURE 4–2 **PHOTOGRAPH SHOWING AN UNUSUAL PERSPECTIVE.** (*Source:* Dleonis)

In addition to thinking about the context of an image, you'll want to consider its perspective. All images present a point of view.

The extreme low-angle shot of a dandelion in Figure 4–2 challenges our notions of this summertime weed. The photographer has shot the dandelion from underneath—from the point of view of the grass or the earth—and has made it look majestic rather than mundane.

It's often helpful to think about perspective and elements of an image together. These are often referred to collectively as the *composition* of the image. If the image you're analyzing is a photograph of a man, you should ask yourself whether the man appears close up or far away. Is his whole body in view, or is only part of him visible? Are you viewing him head-on, from the side, from above, or from below? What about other elements in the photo? Is the man in front of, behind, or surrounded by anything? How do the perspective and the elements affect your impression of the man in the picture? For example, if the perspective makes it seem as though you're viewing him from above and perhaps through a door frame, he may appear powerless or even trapped.

Consider, for example, the well-known photograph *Migrant Mother*, taken by Dorothea Lange in 1936 (Figure 4–3). The woman looks slightly to the side of the camera; her eyes don't meet the viewer's gaze. Her expression might be troubled, but she doesn't look to the viewer (or the photographer) for help. She is surrounded by her children, whose faces are turned from the camera and buried in her arms. It is also worth noting what's *not* in the photo. We don't see a father or any other adults. These absences lead us to believe that this woman cares for these children alone.

FIGURE 4–3
MIGRANT MOTHER BY
DOROTHEA LANGE,
1936. (*Source:* Library of Congress/Farm Security Administration)

MM4-c Purpose and audience: What is the image meant to convey? Who is the intended viewer?

Think about the perspective and the elements of the *Migrant Mother* photograph. Why do you think the photographer took this photo? What is the photographer's purpose? What is your overall impression of the scene? Many viewers will conclude that the woman in the photograph represents strength in the face of hardship and despair.

Part of analyzing an image involves asking *Why did the artist create this image*? Sometimes responses to this question are left to interpretation; at other times, however, determining purpose can mean doing research. A bit of research would reveal that Lange was one of a number of photographers commissioned by the US government to travel throughout the United States and document the lives of Americans during the Dust Bowl in the 1930s. Her photographs, which captured the poverty and despair of people uprooted from their homes, were intended to inspire and educate. But inspire and educate whom? It could be said that her audience, or intended viewers, were both contemporary Americans not directly affected by the ecological disaster and future generations. Asking *why* and *for whom* can be helpful in determining the message and the meaning of an image.

MM4-d Meaning: What effect does the image have on the viewer?

As you develop an interpretation about the meaning of an image on its own or as part of a multimodal piece, be sure to consider genre, features, purpose, and audience together. Although a composer's choices about the type of image and its features are usually deliberate, they don't necessarily convey the same meaning to all viewers in all contexts. They may not work the way the composer intended, or they may carry additional meanings the composer didn't anticipate.

Consider student writer Ian Washburn's analysis of two news photos showing the toppling of a Saddam Hussein statue in 2003, during the United States' war with Iraq.

> The two photos tell two different stories about what happened in Firdos Square in Baghdad in April 2003. At the time the event occurred, I was stationed nearby in Baghdad. Major media outlets, including BBC, CNN, Fox News, and others, ran photos like the top image in fig.1 [see next page]—showing a cheering, chanting, supportive crowd. The US government itself shared some photos from a similar perspective.
>
> Later, however, other photos from the day emerged on the Web, like the bottom image in fig. 1, which some bloggers and commentators used as proof in claiming that

Fig. 1. Two views of the toppling of a Saddam Hussein statue, Baghdad, 2003 (UPI/Newscom; Nickelsberg).

the toppling of the statue was a staged "media event." What is clear in these pictures is that US tanks were stationed at each exit into and out of the area and that the crowd was pushed close to the statue and photos were shot primarily from behind the crowd, to create an illusion of a very big gathering (estimates indicate that about a hundred Iraqi citizens were there for the toppling of the statue).

The event did happen, and the event was important in the war against terror. However, the ways that the photographs were taken and presented tell a different story about *how* the events happened that day.

In his analysis, Washburn interprets the differences in the images by studying both the perspective and the point of view of each. He also hints at the purpose of the image in his discussion of the initially released photo. Examining static images in this way helps the viewer think carefully about a composer's message and consider possible meanings.

ACTIVITY MM4–1: Your understanding

This image of Barack Obama originally appeared on posters during the 2008 presidential campaign. Consider the context of the image. How was this image used? How was it distributed? In what larger cultural and historical context was it important? Who was the intended audience?

Next think about how the image was transformed by various artists in other contexts. Consider the following examples. (You may find additional examples online by conducting an image search with terms like *obama* and *hope* and *poster* and *remix*.)

What effect does each image have on the viewer? Who do you think is the intended audience for each image? Why do you think the artists chose to invoke the Obama campaign poster when creating each of these images? What can you find out about the cultural and historical context in which these images were created?

Source: Shepard Fairey

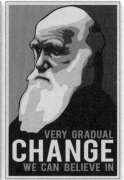

Sources (left to right): Michael Ian Weinfeld; Timothy P. Doyle; Mike Rosulek

MM5 Analyzing moving images

Today almost anyone can make a video and post it to YouTube. The opportunity is fairly new, however; before the Web and digital cameras, much of the video seen in an everyday context was "professional grade"—television shows, television ads, and movies, for instance. Today's composing tools allow users to craft moving images that can range from animated GIFs to moving type to digital video; the technology for making video has changed, and the term *moviemaker* is broader than it used to be.

The images in Figure 5–1 were created in 1887 by Eadweard Muybridge. To create the sequence of images, Muybridge placed a series of cameras in a row, with strings attached to the shutters. As the horse's legs hit the strings, a photo was snapped. In sequence, the photos show the physical movement of a galloping horse. This example is not necessarily a "moving image" as we think of it today, but it is the first photographic representation of a sequence of movement. What started out as a bet between friends—*Does a galloping horse ever have all four hooves off the ground at the same time?*—led to the birth of a new technology.

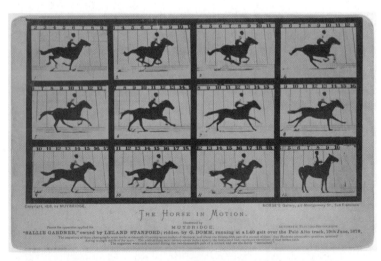

FIGURE 5–1 A SEQUENCE OF STILL IMAGES THAT REPRESENTS MOVEMENT. (*Source:* Library of Congress Prints and Photographs Division)

Analyzing moving images

Genre

What kind of moving image is it? Is it a feature-length film, a brief home-shot video clip, an animated sequence in a video game?

Features

What is the viewer's perspective? How are the elements of the images arranged? Do the images change quickly or slowly? Are any special effects used? How are the moving images combined with sound or words?

Purpose and audience

What is the purpose of the moving image? What did the composer hope to achieve with it?

Who is the intended audience? A viewer watching alone on a computer monitor? A large audience in a theater? Consumers? Students?

Meaning

How do genre, features, purpose, and audience work together to convey a message? How do you interpret the use of elements in the moving image? (Keep in mind that your interpretation—your take on the meaning—may differ from the composer's intended message.)

Today moving images entertain us, inform us, teach us, and encourage us to spend money. When you start to look critically at moving images, consider the questions in the chart above.

MM5-a Genre: What kind of moving image is it?

When it comes to moving images, the term *genre* can be used to describe thematic differences among feature films, such as "adventure" or "romantic comedy" or "documentary." Using terminology like this provides a convenient way to classify movies.

Because your examination of moving images may go beyond feature films, however, this section uses the term *genre* to discuss format rather than theme. Moving images can range from simple animated sequences to complex full-length movies. The chart on page MM-38 defines common genres.

Common genres (types) of moving images

GENRE	DESCRIPTION
Flip book	A physical animation created by drawing the same figure with slight changes on multiple pages and then flipping the pages to create an illusion of motion.
Simple animation	A computer-based animation using a series of still images and applying software techniques to make the images appear to be moving.
Stop-motion animation	An animated video effect created by moving an object a small amount at a time, photographing it each time, and then sequencing the images together to create a sense of movement.
Photo-realistic animation	Animation created through complex drawing, drafting, and computer rendering. The movies *Toy Story* and *Shrek* are examples of this kind of animation.
Playable animation	Animation sequences created by software designers and programmers for the specific purpose of interaction by viewers or players. These can be as simple as banner ads that change when viewers hover a cursor over the ad or sequences in longer video games.
Video clip	A short video that is typically created with a cell phone camera or a digital camera and posted, often unedited, to a site such as YouTube. Some video clips are edited before posting, especially those used for instructional or news purposes.
Film	Usually a feature-length motion picture, or movie. Perhaps the most common genre of moving image, film is used to bring fiction and nonfiction to life for entertainment and education.

MM5-b Features: Perspective, composition, and editing

As you analyze moving images, think about features such as perspective, composition, and editing. As a viewer of the moving image, you occupy a certain perspective. When viewing an instructional video, you are often the novice or student watching a teacher or trainer who walks viewers through a series of steps or a process for doing something. When you play a video game, you are often one of the characters in the game. Typically when you watch a movie, you are an observer, completely outside the action of the moving images. Perspective influences how viewers perceive what's happening on-screen.

For an assignment that required students to choose a movie and analyze one production aspect or element, Ellen Yin chose *Cloverfield*, a moving image that offers viewers an unusual perspective. The following is an excerpt from her essay.

> For most movies, the audience is supposed to be unaware of the camera. Viewers are supposed to have an experience of watching the movie and forgetting the existence of a camera filming and a stage, set, crew, and director. When we watch the Harry Potter movies, it's as if we're there observing the changes in the characters. When we watch *Transformers: Dark of the Moon*, it's as if we're there witnessing the battles between the Autobots and the Decepticons. The 2008 movie *Cloverfield*, however, was shot in a way that differs from most major movies; *Cloverfield* was shot primarily from a first-person perspective. The premise of the movie is that viewers are watching footage captured on a digital video camera found abandoned in New York City after the recorded action. This choice has a huge impact on viewers. Rather than being something we can overlook, the camera becomes a key element in the experience of watching the movie. The viewer feels as if she or he is holding the camera. By offering this first-person, handheld, low-quality perspective, *Cloverfield* forces viewers to join the main characters in their fight for survival.

Cloverfield is an example of a movie shot from a first-person perspective—making viewers feel as if they are there, experiencing the action themselves; the camera functions as the viewers' eyes (see Figure 5–2). This technique is sometimes called a *point of view perspective* or *subjective viewpoint*.

Another type of perspective is called *third-person view*. Video games often use this perspective: The "camera" is above and behind the player character, providing a bird's-eye view rather than the character's point of view.

Another quality of moving images to consider is the composition, or the artist's arrangement of the elements of the image—the

FIGURE 5–2 POINT-OF-VIEW PERSPECTIVE FROM THE MOVIE *CLOVERFIELD*.
(*Source:* Moviestore Collection)

people, props, products, and landscape. As a viewer, you might think critically about whether the people in the video seem close to or far away from the camera or close to or far away from other people. Or perhaps there are no people at all. Besides the frame of the movie, TV, or computer screen, can you find other "frames" as well—a window, perhaps, or an archway? Which on-screen elements seem to be emphasized in some way? Also consider what's *not* on-screen. Thinking carefully about what the composer may have left out of a scene could prompt an interesting analysis.

Professional film and TV producers use editing—choosing and sequencing shots—to craft a story and elicit a certain response from viewers. Some amateur video is edited (video-editing software can be inexpensive and easy to learn), and some isn't—usually depending on the composer's purpose and access to technology. When analyzing moving images, consider how editing affects the pace of the action and the narrative. Does the action proceed quickly from one shot to the next, as in a chase scene in an adventure movie? Or is the action more continuous? Does it proceed more slowly, as in a scene in which a character is shown deep in thought and gazing out a train window?

MM5-c Purpose and audience: What are the moving images being used for? Who is the intended viewer?

Creators of moving images make deliberate choices based on their purpose, or reason for creating the work, and on the viewers they're trying to reach. Thinking carefully about a composer's choices can help you understand the work and also help you prepare for making your own choices as a composer of similar works. It's important to ask both *why* the composer decided to convey a message with a moving image and *what* message a composer is trying to convey.

Think about a national news broadcast, for example, which usually involves some combination of desk reporting, field reporting, and presentation of feature reports that were filmed and edited before the broadcast. Why are the various stories handled differently? Why do the producers decide to use moving images to present certain topics? Perhaps previously filmed material is needed because reporters can't get access to the subject at the time of the live broadcast. Maybe the story requires clips from a variety of sources for support, and those can't be pieced together on the spot. Or showing action is more likely to elicit an emotional response than showing a still image while a reporter narrates an event.

Filming and editing ahead of time also allows composers to shape the story for their target audience. Anything that might bore or offend the audience can be removed, and anything that's particularly effective can be emphasized. Next time you watch an edited news feature, think about who the intended audience is and how the feature has been shaped to reach that audience. Take a filmed, edited story about rising gas prices, for example. Many such features include at-the-pump interviews. What do you see in the moving image? How would you describe the people being interviewed — their gender, race, clothing, age? What kinds of cars are they driving: sports cars, minivans, cars in good or poor repair? Do they appear to be driving to work or taking a road-trip vacation? Are they smiling or frowning? Are they holding anything in their hands? Try to describe the feature's target audience — viewers most likely to identify with the people being interviewed. Would the audience identify as closely if only still images of drivers and gas pumps were used to support the story? Asking *why* and *for whom* a moving image has been created can be helpful in determining its message and meaning.

MM5-d Meaning: What effect do the moving images have on the viewer?

Although a composer's choices about the type of moving image and its features are usually deliberate, they don't necessarily convey the same meaning to all viewers in all contexts. They may not work the way the composer intended, or they may carry additional meanings the composer didn't anticipate.

Read an excerpt from student writer LeShawn Carter's analysis of a theme in *American Beauty*, a full-length film he viewed in an introduction to film study course. Carter is careful to consider the director's technical choices and composition in his analysis of the scene.

> Sam Mendes's *American Beauty* has no shortage of scenes in which the camera work and mise-en-scène suggest that the characters are trapped. Lenny Burnham is shown, for example, encased in window and door frames and is tightly framed by the camera. One scene in which the eye seems to get a break is the plastic bag scene, which we're supposed to see as beauty and perhaps freedom as we watch a plastic bag dance around in the breeze. The bag seems to move freely, but in fact the bag is not free at all. Mendes shoots the scene so that the bag is still constrained by the wind and the wall. It tries to escape but is pulled back into the shot again and again—reinforcing the theme.

As you develop an interpretation about the meaning of a video, an animation, or a film, be sure to ask questions about the genre or type of moving image, its features, and the purpose and audience for which the text was composed.

ACTIVITY MM5–1: Your understanding

Public service announcements (PSAs) are advertisements meant not to sell a product but to encourage or discourage particular behaviors or to call an audience to action (to contribute to a political campaign or to recycle, for example).

Search online for the original 1980s "brain on drugs" PSA, sometimes called the "fried egg" PSA. This PSA was shot from a first-person perspective. In the PSA, we are looking down as an egg is broken into a pan and begins to fry, while a voiceover says, "This is your brain on drugs."

Source: Partnership for a Drug-Free America

Next search for an updated version of the PSA released in the 1990s, starring then-popular actor Rachel Leigh Cook. In this ad, Cook is the narrator. Rather than a first-person perspective, this version is shot more typically—viewers watch Cook smash the egg and then destroy the kitchen in which she appears.

Why do you think each of these techniques was chosen? Which do you think works better? Would the impact or effect of the older PSA be different if it had been shot with an actor and as a scene? How so? Would the impact or effect of the newer PSA be different if it had been shot from a first-person perspective, as if the viewer were the person smashing the egg and destroying the kitchen?

What other advertisements—either public service advertisements or ads for products—have you seen shot from a first-person perspective? Were they effective? Why or why not?

ACTIVITY MM5–2: Your understanding

Most moving images we see are not interactive. That is, we watch them or somewhat passively receive the content. Some artists and advertisements, however, have thought a bit more creatively and innovatively about inspiring interaction with moving images.

The following still images are from a Skittles online ad campaign. In each of the ads, the viewer is invited to place his or her finger on the screen, at the spot indicated by the candy. The moving image that then plays is interactive with the viewer's finger. Do a Web search to find other ads from this campaign. What difference does the interactivity make? How does the ad feel different, or how do you respond differently to it, because of its interactive nature?

Source: BBDO Toronto; Wm. Wrigley Jr. Company

MM6 Analyzing multimodal texts

Though the discussions in sections MM2 through MM5 each focused on a single mode, many of the examples in those sections were actually multimodal texts—texts that communicate with some combination of written words, static images, moving images, and sound. Look back at the brochure (image b) on page MM-16. The discussion in the text focuses on how words are arranged in different types of documents, but the brochure includes images as well. This section addresses analyzing different modes *together* in a multimodal composition, a task that is not as daunting as it may seem. On some level, you think about multimodal texts every day, simply because most texts *are* multimodal. Recipes and food packaging often include words

Analyzing multimodal texts

Genre

What kind of multimodal composition is it? An article with words and images, for example? A short film with sound and moving images?

Features

What modes (written words, sound, static images, moving images) are present in the composition? How does each mode work individually? How do the modes work together?

Purpose and audience

What is the purpose of the multimodal composition? Is it intended to provide information or argue a case, for example?

Who is the intended audience? The general public? Teenagers? Retirees? Professionals in a particular field?

Meaning

How do genre, features, purpose, and audience work together to convey a message in the multimodal composition? How do you interpret the combined effect of the modes used in the composition? (Keep in mind that your interpretation—your take on the meaning—may differ from the composer's intended message.)

and images. Television commercials usually include words, sound, and moving images. Even children's books, with words and illustrations, are multimodal.

When you start to look critically at multimodal texts, consider the questions in the chart at the top of the page.

MM6-a Genre: What kind of multimodal text is it?

Not only do people encounter multimodal texts every day, but they also create them every day. Personal photo albums with captions, slide shows with images and audio voice-over, social media posts with images and words—these are just a few common genres of multimodal composition. Different genres afford a composer different opportunities for sharing and shaping a message. For example, someone who wants to provide categories and subcategories of information might build an informational Web site, especially if the

Common genres of multimodal compositions

GENRE	DESCRIPTION
Informative Web site	Informative Web sites usually present statistics, research data, definitions, or other factual information. The Web site format allows composers to provide a large amount of information in manageable categories. A public transit Web site might, for example, have separate pages for timetables, maps, and policies.
Artistic video	Composers use artistic videos to present ideas on personal, political, environmental, and other themes. The video format allows composers to control the sequence of ideas.
Instructional video	Instructional videos often demonstrate steps for learning, creating, or installing something. A furniture manufacturer may, for example, provide an informational video to demonstrate the step-by-step assembly of a chair.
Slide presentation	Composers typically use slide presentations to present ideas and information in small chunks and in a particular sequence. A presenter might use slides to show how a proposed business plan could lead to corporate growth, for example.
Print advertisement	Print advertisements often occupy all or part of a page in a magazine, journal, or newspaper and can be used to promote products, services, or events. Because their space is limited and most readers won't spend more than a few seconds looking at them, print advertisements need to present key information at a glance.
Television commercial	In general, television commercials promote products, services, or events. Usually less than a minute long, commercials often rely on jingles and slogans to engage the viewer and convey their message in a quick, memorable way.

material doesn't need to be viewed in a particular sequence. If the order of information is essential, the composer might choose instead to create an informational video, to ensure that no one views the material out of order. When you're analyzing multimodal compositions, identify the genre and ask yourself why the composer chose that genre. The chart on page MM-45 shows common genres of multimodal compositions.

MM6-b Features: Which modes are represented? How do they work on their own and with each other?

When you analyze a multimodal composition, thinking about each mode on its own can be a helpful first step to interpreting the composition as a whole. Ask yourself what modes are present. Written words and static images? Audio and moving images? Then consider the role of each mode within the composition. What work does each mode do? For example, do written words convey information or make a plea? Does audio evoke an emotional response? Do moving or static images illustrate a concept or provide background?

Remember to consider the features of each mode as well. Are written words large or small? Bold or fine? Where do they appear? What size are the images, and how are they arranged? How are moving images sequenced? How loud or quiet is the audio? If you consider the modes separately, you'll be better equipped to think about how they work together.

Take a look at Figure 6–1, a public service message commissioned by the World Wildlife Fund, a group devoted to protecting nature. The composition uses two modes: written words and a static image. Which mode grabs your attention first? For most viewers, the cheetahs immediately draw the eye. But why? Think about the surrounding space. The background focus is so soft that no other distinct objects appear, only a dark blur. The cheetahs, however, are in sharp focus in the foreground. Their striking spots stand out against the muted background. It would be easy for a viewer to glance quickly at the public service message and see nothing but an adorable photo of cheetahs, except for one thing: the tags on their backs. Marked with "S" and "XL," these are unmistakably clothing tags. What at first appears to be a touching scene of mother and cub becomes more sinister with the recognition of these tags. These animals are going to be used for clothing.

Fashion claims more victims than you think.

FIGURE 6–1 A PUBLIC SERVICE MESSAGE. (*Source:* World Wildlife Fund)

Student writer Wayne Anderson made the following argument about the ad:

The makers of the ad could have inspired outrage by showing a violent image of cheetahs that had been killed for their furs. They probably recognized, however, that many viewers would instinctively look away and try to forget the image rather than absorb the message. By emphasizing the image of the two cheetahs, the mother guiding her cub in their natural habitat, the ad designers draw in their audience and elicit a sentimental response. Some viewers will feel sympathy and want the cheetahs to survive.

The image alone, however, does not convey the whole message. It delivers a troubling truth and makes viewers feel sympathetic and sad, but it might not have a lasting influence. The text in the upper right corner adds a subtle punch: "Fashion claims more victims than you think." The statement plays on the familiar concept of fashion victims, people whose clothing choices make them look ridiculous. Here the term *victim* is being applied to the cheetahs that may be killed to gratify someone's fashion sense. If the image showed two adult cheetahs or an entire group, the image probably would not be as effective. It's easier for

most people to think of cubs especially as needing protection from harm.
Maybe the term *victim* is supposed to make viewers feel protective and not
just sympathetic. Playing on this familiar phrase also helps make the
message memorable.

MM6-c Purpose and audience: What is the composition doing? Whom is it intended to reach?

When you think about the purpose of a multimodal composition, you might ask, *What is this composition meant to accomplish? Convey information? Inspire action or feeling? Make an argument?*

Thinking about audience, you might ask, *Whom is this meant to appeal to? Whom is this designed or written for? What assumptions is the composer making about the audience's beliefs and values?*

Consider again the two cheetahs. Why do you think the composers of that message decided to use the pronoun *you* in "Fashion claims more victims than you think"? Most public service messages aim to encourage or discourage specific behaviors. If the statement read "Fashion claims more victims than people think," it might be easier for the audience to dismiss the issue as someone else's fault or problem. Perhaps the composers hoped that addressing the statement to "you" would empower their audience to act—to refuse to buy furs or to spread the message. If the words are essential for reaching the audience, why do you think they're so small? Would the effect be different if they spanned the top or bottom of the image? Perhaps some viewers would feel alienated if they encountered the direct address (*you*) and the word *victim* before developing a sympathetic feeling toward the cheetah mother and cub.

Or take the example of restaurant menus. What is the purpose of a menu? The straightforward answer might be "to provide food options." But a menu might have other purposes as well: to differentiate a particular restaurant from its competitors, to show that the restaurant specializes in a particular type of food (for example, using the colors of the Italian flag or photos of pasta to show that the food is Italian), or to explicitly call attention to healthier menu options or options for people who have food allergies.

Who is the audience for a menu? The simple answer might be "hungry customers." But imagining how customers might encounter the menu reveals more about the intended audience. Although some customers viewing the menu might already be seated in the restaurant, others might be considering the menu online, trying to decide where to eat dinner. In making their decision, they might be comparing the menu side-by-side with another restaurant's menu. They might be considering different factors related to their dining decision, such as how much money they want to spend on their dinner. Higher prices might indicate that the restaurant aims to attract an older crowd. Unusual font choices might mean that the restaurant seeks an eclectic audience.

For multimodal compositions, the actual audience might be much broader than the intended audience, so it's important to consider how and where the composition has been published. Student composer Marisa Williamson created a video essay, "To the Children of America," for a class. Though her intended audience was fairly limited—her instructor and her peers—her actual audience grew when she published her school project on a video-sharing Web site. Williamson's project is featured in sections MM7 through MM15 of this book.

MM6-d Meaning: What effect does the multimodal composition have on the viewer?

Although a composer's choices about the modes integrated into a multimodal composition are usually deliberate, they don't necessarily convey the same meaning to all viewers in all contexts. They may not work the way the composer intended, or they may carry additional meanings the composer didn't anticipate.

In the following excerpt, student writer Marley Cole analyzes item collecting in role-playing video games. Her attention to sound, images, and other features of the games leads her to disagree with one of her sources. In her essay, she includes both text and screen captures from in-game play to support her points.

> *Gamasutra* writer Kris Graft suggests that the desire to collect items in a game
> world is similar to compulsive hoarding in the real world. The consequences of
> gathering items may not be as negative for the gamer, but gamers and hoarders,
> according to Graft, experience similar degrees of emotional investment and
> gratification when they acquire objects. Graft, however, does not account for the
> limits placed on acquisition in many game worlds and the penalties incurred
> when the gamer ignores those limits. Usually, a character cannot carry more
> than a certain amount. Sometimes that amount increases when the character
> gets stronger, but there is always a limit. When the character's pack is full, that

character can't pick up new items (see the image on right for an in-game inventory example). The character is forced to discard or sell old items to make room for new ones.

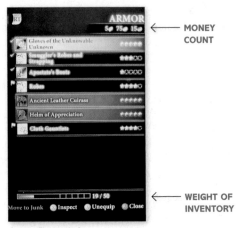

Source: Electronic Arts.

In some games, overburdened characters can't even move until they discard items. Rather than facilitating virtual hoarding, video games actually force gamers to be strategic about what they keep with them. In addition, the experience of parting with items is often positively reinforced. Selling an item can be accompanied by the sound of coins dropping into a pouch or the sight of a money count going up. A character who has lightened his pack might even be able to move faster.

Cole determines meaning by analyzing sounds and images in a multimodal text, a video game. As you develop an interpretation about the meaning of a multimodal piece, be sure to consider genre, features, purpose, and audience. Pulling together your individual impressions of the text's elements can help you look critically at the text as a whole.

ACTIVITY MM6–1: Your understanding

Many public service announcements (PSAs) are advertisements meant to encourage or discourage particular behaviors (such as voting or littering) or to call an audience to action (for example, contributing to a charitable organization).

Choose a nonprofit or community action or awareness organization. Find a campaign that the group has run or is running, and identify at least three different campaign components (such as a poster, a radio spot, a television PSA, a Web-based PSA, an interactive game). Analyze each of the three pieces, describing which modes are used, how the modes are layered together (or not), and how well you think each piece serves its purpose.

Some historical and contemporary campaigns you might look at include Rosie the Riveter, wildfire prevention, ready.gov, Make a Wish Foundation, and the Humane Society. You might also focus on the World Wildlife Fund campaign mentioned in MM6-b.

MM7 Starting your own multimodal project

Sections MM2 through MM6 focused on analyzing individual and multiple modes in the works of others. Sections MM7 through MM15 will help you think about your own multimodal composing. As you develop your own project, you'll want to keep genre, features, purpose, audience, and meaning in mind, just as you do when you analyze. Think about questions like these as you plan and compose:

Genre: What kind of composition do you plan to create? A video? A Web site? A poster with images and written words? (Depending on the genre, you may need to budget more time for the assignment, brush up on technical skills, or collaborate with others.)

Features: What kinds of images, colors, design elements, fonts, and type treatments are appropriate for your composition? What would make your composition most effective? Adding voiceover narration or including information in callout boxes, for example?

Purpose and audience: What does your composition need to do? Does it need to inform, instruct, argue, entertain, or persuade? Whom does it need to reach? Novices who need basic information? Experts who need to see detailed support? Children who would respond well to a colorful presentation? People who agree or disagree with you?

Meaning: What message do you want to convey? What is the goal of your project? How do your chosen genre and features help you achieve your purpose and reach your audience?

Keep in mind that you may not be able to answer all of these questions before you begin gathering information and drafting. The answers you come up with early on may change as you investigate your topic and begin to build your project. It's a good idea to revisit these questions throughout your composing process.

MM7-a Getting direction from the assignment

The composing process often begins with an assignment, which may provide answers to some of your questions about genre, features, purpose, audience, and meaning. Take a look at this assignment about binge drinking, for example:

Design a six-panel brochure that persuades college students not to binge drink. Your headings and body text—along with any graphs, diagrams, or photos—should work together to define the term and discuss the dangers of binge drinking.

The assignment provides the topic—binge drinking—and requires a specific multimodal genre—a brochure with images and written words. It also provides a general purpose—to persuade—and a target audience—college students. It's up to the student to determine the specific message. For example, *Binge drinking can lead to health problems that plague drinkers long after college* or *One night of binge drinking can be fatal and isn't worth the risk.* The student will need to think about what features will help make that message persuasive. What colors, typefaces, and images, for example, will be appropriate for the message?

MM7-b Considering the "So what?" question

If the assignment does not specify a topic, choose one that allows you to explore a genuine interest or address a real concern your audience may have.

Effective composers take stock of their own goals and the needs of their readers, asking *What, aside from a good grade, motivates me to compose?* Make sure you have a reason for composing—a reason that addresses the "So what?" question. A project that stems from genuine motivation will be more engaging to your audience. One student writer made a chart to help her decide how to respond to this prompt: *Persuade fellow students to take your side in a campus debate.*

SAMPLE STUDENT NOTES: DECIDING ON A TOPIC

Possible topic: Should the college convert two acres of campus green space to additional parking spaces for commuter students?	So what?	Hm. I'm not a commuter, so it's not that critical to me.
Possible topic: Should the college publish the school newspaper in an online format only and abandon a paper publication?	So what?	Seems like a no-brainer to me. We're all on our devices 24/7 anyway. And going online only is greener, right?
Possible topic: Should the college add a general education requirement that each full-time student must complete a minimum of 12 hours of community service by the end of the second year?	So what?	Volunteerism should absolutely NOT be required. I can convince fellow students that a requirement goes against the concept of volunteering—of giving back out of a sense of goodness. Plus, being a college student means making your OWN decisions.

The student chose this topic because she cared about it, felt her readers would care about it, and felt she could make compelling points to support her views.

You need to consider the "So what?" question even if your purpose is not to persuade or argue. If the assignment is to demonstrate a process for instruction purposes, think about what you can bring to that project that will make it especially clear or helpful. Your audience will see value in your work if you are invested in it.

MM7-c Understanding expectations and managing your time

Even if the assignment is detailed and clear, you'll probably have questions for your instructor as you get started. You'll want to consider questions like these, which are typical of almost any writing assignment:

- Do you need to run ideas by your instructor before you get started?
- Will you have time in class to work on the assignment?
- How can you break your project down into manageable steps?
- What sorts of research should you do? Should you conduct field research, such as interviews? Or should you focus on library sources, like books and journal articles?
- Are you working on your project alone? With a partner? Or with a group?
- How will the project be evaluated?

You'll also want to consider additional questions, however, that relate more to the multimodal aspects of the project, such as the following:

- Can you include images, videos, or sound clips in your composition?
- If you want to include links in your essay, how should you present those links?
- Where can you go for help if you've never created a multimodal composition before?
- What options do you have for sharing drafts and getting feedback if your project is a large file or in several pieces?
- If your final project is a large file, how should you submit it?
- How should you present a list of works cited for something like a video or a podcast?

Getting answers to questions like these before you begin your project can help clarify some of the details of your project and ensure that the project starts smoothly.

ACTIVITY MM7–1: Your understanding

Before moving further, take some time to view the two student projects discussed in sections MM7 through MM15. (Visit the URL at the bottom of this page.) One, an informative Web site, offers an overview of loose leaf tea. The other, a video essay, explores how YouTube helps young people experience events of the past. How are these compositions multimodal? Identify some of the successful features of each.

ACTIVITY MM7–2: Your project

Review a monomodal writing assignment you recently completed or a piece of writing you composed on your own (a traditional five-page academic essay, perhaps). Imagine if you had been asked to produce the composition as a multimodal piece instead. What genre would have been effective for your purpose, audience, and message? A slide show? A movie? A Web page? A collage? Consider some of the materials you might have drawn on to craft the piece as a multimodal composition: audio, video, animation or movement, still images, and so on. Write briefly about what you might have done and why.

MM8 Considering your purpose and audience

Purpose is the goal of your work—your aim or objective. Your purpose will inform many of the decisions you make as a composer. Your audience is made up of the people who will read, view, or listen to your work. When you're composing in college, it's easy to think that your audience is limited to "the teacher." Yes, your instructor is part of your audience, but usually your instructor is not your primary audience or the only audience you are writing to.

Often, the assignment will suggest or require both a purpose and an audience. In a composition course, for example, an instructor might ask each student to use photos and written words to argue a position in a current campus debate. In a marketing course, the assignment might call for a slide show presentation that analyzes consumer trends over time. In a natural sciences class, the assignment might ask students to write and direct a public service announcement that informs viewers about hurricane preparedness. These are all examples of academic projects, but the purposes are different for each. In these examples, the composition student's purpose is to *argue*, the marketing student's purpose is to *analyze*,

ONLINE   **hackerhandbooks.com/multimodal**
> Multimodal resources > Student multimodal projects
> D'Amato, "Loose Leaf Teas"
> Williamson, "To the Children of America"

and the natural sciences student's purpose is to *inform*. If, for example, the natural sciences student produced a short digital movie in which he made an argument that state agencies need more funding for hurricane preparedness, he would probably not be satisfying the assignment.

Audience considerations also influence the content and presentation of your project. Sometimes your instructor will give you guidance about who your audience is—other students on your campus, for example, or state legislators. Sometimes the assignment will direct you to address a particular audience, such as student athletes or readers of your campus newspaper. If your purpose is to persuade, your main audience will probably be those who disagree with you or are undecided. If your purpose is to instruct, your audience will probably be nonexperts, those who need basic or step-by-step information.

MM8-a Prewriting with your purpose in mind

Student composer Alyson D'Amato was assigned to create an informative text—that is, a text that teaches readers about a topic. D'Amato began thinking about what she needed to do by reviewing the assignment for the project.

> **ASSIGNMENT FOR AN INFORMATIVE PROJECT**
> Think about the ways in which information is provided in our culture. Your assignment is to take a subject that's familiar to you and to compose a multimodal project that informs or instructs your audience or explains something to them. You can create a slide show presentation, a Web site, a brief video, or something else. Engage your audience, make your purpose clear, deliver your information, and provide enough examples so that your audience comes away with a good grasp of the topic.

From the assignment, D'Amato knew she needed to create an informative, explanatory piece. She knew that she was expected to produce a multimodal project. Her instructor invited students to choose a topic they were interested in.

When D'Amato received the assignment, she analyzed her purpose. Her initial notes looked something like this:

- explain something, provide information
- include pictures and words
- teach people about something new or unknown
- start with what I know and care about

D'Amato's instructor provided the initial, formal purpose for the project: to create an informative piece. D'Amato decided that she had to do some additional prewriting to help her determine why the topic mattered to her.

> My purpose: Create something about brewing your own tea and teaching people how to do so. I love tea and make my own teas—I want to teach other people that making tea means more than dunking a tea bag in a mug!
>
> - explain something, provide information
>   - capture audience's attention
>   - teach them to do something that might be new to them
> - include pictures and words
>   - explain using text and use photos to illustrate the text
>   - use pictures to keep people's attention
>   - use pictures people can relate to (not too artistic or unrecognizable or anything)
> - teach people about something new or unknown
>   - use language people will understand—like the newspaper
>   - explain terms that might be unfamiliar
> - start with what *I know* and *care* about
>   - explain why it's important to me
>   - explain why it might be important to others—answer the "So what?" question!

It's fine to start out fairly broad, but before you begin drafting and creating, you'll want to have a strong sense of what you want and need to accomplish with your multimodal composition. D'Amato's notes provide a good model for how you might start thinking about your purpose.

MM8-b Identifying your audience's needs and perspectives

In the previous example, student composer Alyson D'Amato was asked in her assignment to "engage" her audience. To determine what the audience will find engaging, composers first need to *identify* an audience. Here are some questions you might ask as you think about who your audience is:

- Does the assignment provide any direction about who the audience is? What clues about audience has your instructor provided?

- Is there a particular audience you want to reach?
- Could you have more than one audience?
- What do you know about your audience's life experiences? Interests? Demographics (age, race, socioeconomic status, level of education, location)?
- What are the most effective ways to engage your audience members—attract their attention, get them interested, help them learn, and so forth?

Finding answers to these questions will allow you to see your topic from your audience's perspective.

Sometimes professionals in marketing or product development will create "profiles" of different types of people who make up their intended audience. These profiles help them to imagine specific details behind a general idea like "audience." For a project in a technical writing class, students were asked to write a proposal for a new, Web-based application to be used by their peers at the university on the school's Web site. To get a sense of the possible audience for their Web-based app, a group of students worked together to create user profiles. They interviewed other students and came up with two user profiles.

Group 1   One potential user group is made up of residential students who are online at least 7 hours a day and who primarily use Facebook to stay connected with friends. These users visit Web sites only to seek information not available through Facebook. They use the college Web site to look up their class schedules and check grades and sometimes to look for news about what's going on around campus. One student told us: "If there was a way to sync up the college Web site with Facebook, that'd be great!"

Group 2   Another potential user group is made up of commuter students, many of whom have transferred from a community college. They live off-campus and are not online as often as those in the first user group. Most work at least part-time and use the Internet primarily for work-related e-mail and projects. This group typically uses the college Web site only when enrolling for classes. One student told us: "I guess I'd need a reason to use the school site more."

You might create a similar profile for your audience. Or you might just do some brainstorming in answer to questions like these:

- Where are your readers/viewers/listeners from?
- When were they born?

- What groups or causes are they involved with?
- What experiences have they had with your topic?
- What are the best ways to reach them?
- How are they likely to receive your message?

NOTE: When creating profiles of your potential audience members, keep in mind that people are diverse. Creating audience profiles is helpful when it gives you a sense of the people you are trying to reach and what they are interested in and value. Your profiles should not turn into stereotypes that lead you to make faulty assumptions that homogenize or alienate your audience.

MM8-c Connecting with your audience

With your purpose in mind and your audience profile under way, you are ready to think about the best way to connect with your audience. The benefit of composing multimodally is that you have options for communicating your message. Consider the following scenarios and think about what decisions you would have to make to best connect to these audiences (highlighted).

- You are composing for a group of local second graders to teach them about air quality.
- You are composing for other college students to share advice on making sound financial decisions.
- You are composing for your school's administration to propose building a war memorial on campus.

How can you appeal to these audiences in these situations? The second graders, for instance, might need pictures to help explain the concept of air quality. The college students might be interested in hearing audio clips from other students who have faced specific financial challenges. You might reach the school administrators by knowing the school's mission statement and core values and presenting slides that connect those values to your proposal.

When student composer Marisa Williamson began working on her composition, she did some talking, reading, and exploring. Her assignment was to present an argument creatively on a topic of her choice and for an audience of her choice. She was familiar with writing argument essays; for this project, however, she decided to compose a video argument. Williamson wanted to explore historic events that had national attention in the United States and somehow tie them together. She wanted to connect to people her own age, so she began by thinking about events from her own childhood that made a lasting impression on her and had national significance. The event that stood out most clearly was the September 11, 2001, terrorist attack that destroyed the twin towers of the World Trade Center in New York City.

Williamson realized that what she was thinking about wasn't an argument yet. She started to think about other national events that were captured on film or video, what they have in common, and what it means to her generation to experience historic moving images recorded before their birth. To brainstorm ways of effectively reaching her audience, she also thought about arguments that she had encountered that had affected her thoughts or feelings on a subject. This process helped Williamson start shaping her argument and planning her project.

MM8-d Recognizing an unintended audience

Keep in mind that your composition will sometimes have a broader audience than your purpose or your assignment suggests or than you intended to reach. Because multimodal compositions often live online or in some portable electronic format, they typically can be publicly viewed or shared. Someone who runs a Web search on your name, for example, may find your project. Your project may also have a longer life span than you intend. If you take down a Web site you've created, pieces of it may have been downloaded and shared elsewhere by others. Even if you're creating your project for a specific group of people, make sure your work is something you'd be comfortable sharing with a broader audience that may include friends, family members, or future employers, for example.

ACTIVITY MM8–1: Your understanding

Look around campus for a poster that catches your eye. It could be hanging in the financial aid office, in the writing center, on an instructor's office door, or even in the kitchen of the dining hall. Take a picture of the poster or sketch it out on a notepad to refer to later. Identify the purpose or purposes of the poster. What clues help you identify the purpose?

ACTIVITY MM8–2: Your understanding

Take a look at just the home page of the following sites:

- the main Web site for your school
- the Web site of a professor at your school

- the Web site of a fast-food restaurant in your area
- the Web site of a small, locally owned restaurant in your area
- the Web site of the company that made the car you drive or that makes the car you'd like to drive
- the Web site for a branch or an agency of the US government (for example, the White House, the IRS, the FBI)
- the Web site for an individual who serves in the US government (such as a member of Congress)

As you look at each home page, generate a list of notes about who you think the primary audience is for each Web site. How do you know that this is the audience? What information—textual or visual—provides clues about who the audience is?

ACTIVITY MM8–3: Your project

With a current project in mind—in any class—consider your audience for composing. Take notes on the following questions.

- What sort of information do you need to gather about your audience? How will you go about gathering that information?
- Your audience members might have specific questions that are pertinent to their needs. Can you anticipate what those questions might be?
- Some members of your audience might be resistant to or skeptical about your topic; you might need to appeal to them using different types of evidence. What kinds of evidence might work best?

MM9 Planning your project

Composing a multimodal project requires planning, and planning takes time. You'll have to settle on a process that works for you or, if you're collaborating with one or more classmates, that works for all of you. You'll also have to identify a main idea and the best genre (an inspirational video or an informative Web site, for example) for expressing that main idea. If the genre is not your choice but has been assigned, it will take planning to figure out how to best communicate the main idea in a particular type of composition. Planning is hard work, but it's also full of opportunities to think and rethink, shape and reshape your project.

Sometimes you will start a project in one direction—perhaps thinking something like *I'll create a Web page that teaches people how to tie fly-fishing lures*—and find, as you do research and think about your audience and purpose, that a video might be a better way to instruct your audience. The good news is that you don't have to have everything planned before you start to compose.

MM9-a Understanding your own composing process

Have you ever put together, or watched someone else put together, a thousand-piece puzzle? Approaches for completing a puzzle vary. Some people start methodically with the border. Others start with a key image in the center of the puzzle and work outward. Still others work randomly, fitting together islands of puzzle pieces here and there and eventually joining them. There's no right way; it's just a matter of figuring out what method works for each puzzle and for the person putting it together.

Composers, too, have their own preferred ways of working, so it's important to think flexibly about the composing process. Sometimes you'll see the composing process presented in a fairly linear way, like this:

1. Brainstorm
2. Plan
3. Research
4. Compose
5. Revise

Those basic steps find their way into most projects, and the process usually begins with brainstorming and ends with revision, but composers usually take each step more than once and at several times throughout the process. Consider student composer Marisa Williamson's project: a video essay.

In talking with other people in her class and with friends, Williamson found that all of them had seen iconic footage and pictures from events in recent history, but few could remember key words spoken about the events or by those involved in the events. Based on what she knew about her audience, Williamson decided—with rough ideas about her purpose and how to proceed—to knit video clips, still images, audio files, and her own narration together to make an argument that would appeal to her peers. She used a video-editing application that allowed her to combine, sequence, and edit all the materials she had gathered and also to layer in text and titles.

A linear rendering of Williamson's composing process might look something like this:

1. Brainstorm about purpose and audience
2. Gather images and video
3. Choose songs
4. Write and record narration
5. Input images, audio, video, and narration
6. Add text
7. Produce video

Represented visually, Williamson's composing process might look something like Figure 9–1.

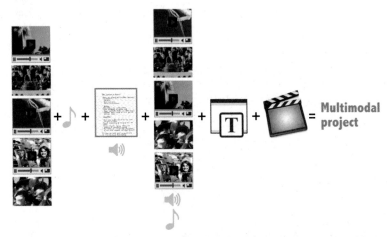

FIGURE 9–1 VISUALIZATION OF A LINEAR APPROACH TO THE COMPOSING PROCESS FOR A MULTIMODAL PROJECT.

This is a fairly neat and orderly way of visualizing the elements that are part of a composing process, and certainly these are important steps in the process. The way Williamson compiled, wrote, and thought through the different elements of her composition, however, might actually be better and more accurately represented visually as in Figure 9–2.

The student's composing process was not so much a linear path as it was a series of loops in which she revisited stages and elements of her composition. She began by gathering and watching different videos. She then selected some still images, collected some songs, and scripted her narration. Each of these pieces affected her thoughts about and presentation of the others. She went back to the video to edit it and to trim pieces, add to other pieces, and sequence

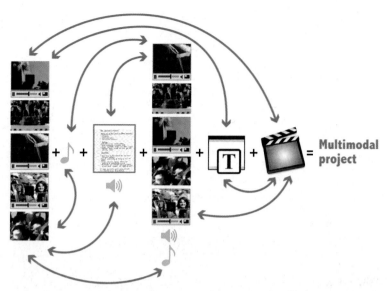

FIGURE 9–2 VISUALIZATION OF A REALISTIC APPROACH TO THE COMPOSING PROCESS FOR A MULTIMODAL PROJECT.

clips together. She worked with the music, trimming and editing and deciding how to layer it under her narration and on top of the video and images. She found different audio clips and replaced or changed the audio in the project. She did this over and over again, while she also continued to write and edit her script to reflect changes in the sequence of video pieces and images. What was essential for Williamson was budgeting enough time for the shaping and thinking and *re*shaping and *re*thinking.

MM9-b Collaborating effectively with others

Working in a pair or in a group can change your composing process — how you go about brainstorming, drafting, researching, and revising. The old saying is that "two heads are better than one," and composing with a group can be enriching. Collaborative work gives you an opportunity to explore ideas and practices that your peers bring to the project. It's also valuable practice for work you will do outside of school. Many professional projects are done in teams.

Collaborating effectively takes practice. It helps to pay attention to how you best work and how you best work with others. Here are a few important tips for working with a partner or a group:

Do the work together, and learn from each other. Sometimes students look at collaborative work as just a matter of divvying up tasks (for instance, one person does the research, another does the writing, and another does the designing and production). Managing a project in this way can result in a piece of work that looks somewhat like Frankenstein's monster—lots of pieces stitched together into a messy whole. Stronger, more coherent work is the result of people truly collaborating and working together on *every* aspect of a project. The process of doing so allows group members to learn from one another's strengths, and, in turn, everyone in the group becomes a stronger, more capable composer.

Organize yourselves, and stay on task. Functioning well as a group means checking in often and planning together. Three

Assessing your strengths as a collaborator

I am good at being a **team leader**.	yes	no	kind of
I am good at being a **team member**.	yes	no	kind of
I am good at **communication** (asking good questions and facilitating discussions).	yes	no	kind of
I am good at thinking about the **big picture** (staying focused on the main idea or goal of the project).	yes	no	kind of
I am good at thinking about **small details** (completing individual tasks and keeping track of smaller parts of the project).	yes	no	kind of
I am good at doing **research** (performing Web searches, gathering information from library databases, and conducting surveys or interviews with people).	yes	no	kind of
I am good at **design** work (working with or creating images, or thinking about layouts and color schemes).	yes	no	kind of
I am good at **writing** (brainstorming, drafting, and editing written materials).	yes	no	kind of
I have good **technology** skills (creating basic Web pages, making slide show presentations, and doing some work with digital video).	yes	no	kind of

ways to keep your group focused and make progress are to set up specific meeting times, to have someone take notes when you meet as a group, and to make sure everyone knows who's doing what for the project.

Know your own strengths, and be ready to admit your weaknesses. One way to start, especially if you're working with classmates you don't know, is to think about how you typically like to function in a team or a group. What do you do well? Individual members can assess their strengths by using a questionnaire (see the checklist on p. MM-64). The responses on the questionnaire can help you get to know each other and start a conversation about how to move forward.

MM9-c Deciding on a main idea

Just as well-planned essays begin with a working thesis statement, your multimodal project should have a main idea around which the entire composition is focused. And be sure that your main idea addresses the "So what?" question (see section MM7-b)—your main idea should be compelling and interesting and address a question or concern of interest to others. Having a main idea will help you select the best images, audio, and other elements to support that main idea. You may have to whittle away at a big, general idea to settle on a manageable main idea.

As you get started on a project, you'll likely have lots of ideas to explore. Sometimes it's tempting to stick with a broad subject. Most writers find, however, that doing so can actually be a problem, as there's too much material to cover and it's tricky to figure out how to approach the subject. "The World Wide Web," for instance, is a gigantic subject, but certainly a lot of academic writers get a lot of mileage out of projects about the Web. The trick is to ask questions about the subject in an attempt to narrow it to a topic and to find your particular angle, one that matters to you.

BROAD SUBJECT	The World Wide Web
QUESTION	*Great for shopping and communication, but what good is it doing in the world?*
NARROWER TOPIC	Using the Web during and after a disaster
QUESTION	*Where have we seen this? What has been the effect? Why is it important?*
MAIN IDEA	How Japanese citizens are using the Web as a tool for activism in the aftermath of the 2011 nuclear disaster and slow government response

Brainstorming ideas and then focusing and whittling down those ideas is a great way to get started. When student composer Alyson D'Amato started thinking about creating a project focused on tea (a broad subject), she came up with a list of possible angles:

organic tea	tea growing	history of tea
store-bought tea	tea brands or	tea flavors
black teas	companies	uses of tea
green teas	fair trade teas	bottled tea vs. brewed
tea and health	tea plants	tea
tea in different	tea popularity	serving tea (different
cultures	brewing tea yourself	rituals)

D'Amato knew that she couldn't address all of these possibilities in one project. Some of the issues—tea in different cultures, for example—seemed too complex for the scope of the assignment. Other ideas—store-bought tea, for example—seemed as though they might not be interesting for her or her audience.

She identified three possibilities from the big list she generated, and then she brainstormed what she might cover for each of those possibilities:

- black teas vs. green teas
  - focus on compare and contrast?
  - the differences in the plants
  - the differences in the flavors
  - the growing popularity of green tea
- serving tea
  - historical tools, like really old tea-serving pitchers
  - different cultural rituals (like "high tea" in England)
  - different types of ceremonies involving tea
  - from rituals and ceremonies to tea bags in a box bought at the grocery store
- brewing tea yourself
  - why do it when tea bags are so easy?
  - differences between tea bags and loose leaf tea
  - health benefits of tea
  - loose leaf tea recipes

Because she was so personally interested and invested in tea brewing herself, D'Amato decided to choose the third option, to compose a project that would teach people about brewing tea. She knew she would further develop and refine her main idea as she researched her topic, but now she had a focused starting point. (See your handbook for more on narrowing a subject to a topic and more on developing thesis statements.)

MM9-d Planning support for your main idea

A multimodal project often gives you new opportunities for presenting evidence in support of a main idea. You may think of evidence only as quotations from sources or perhaps as data from experiments. Multimodal projects allow you to think more broadly. You can support your idea with quoted written words—but also with quotations in the form of podcasts and other audio files. You can include data in the form of graphs and tables—but you can also present data in animations. Support in a multimodal composition can take the form of words, images, audio/sound, video, and so on.

Think about the visual rendering of student composer Marisa Williamson's writing process in Figure 9–1 (p. MM-62). As the visual shows, she chose to mix images, video, and audio (speech clips, music clips, and her own narration) in her video essay. Since she was planning to argue the thesis that online video-sharing sites such as YouTube bring together people of different generations by letting viewers experience events of the past, she knew that her best evidence was going to be YouTube videos. She made a list of possible events to include.

John F. Kennedy's inaugural address	Iranian hostage crisis
Martin Luther King Jr.'s "Dream" speech	Geraldine Ferraro's candidacy
Assassination of John F. Kennedy	Assassination attempt: Ronald Reagan
Assassination of Martin Luther King Jr.	Birth of MTV
Assassination of Robert F. Kennedy	Space shuttle *Challenger*
Landing on the moon	Million Man March
Woodstock	September 11
Apollo 13 crisis	Hurricane Katrina
1976 Bicentennial	

Marisa's list included patriotic events, political events, cultural events, tragic events, and natural disasters. When she reviewed her list, she decided that she wanted to focus on just one of these categories of events. The event that resonated most strongly for her was

MM-68 **MM9-e** Planning your project

the September 11 attacks. She remembered the strong sense of unity that followed throughout the country. So she decided to focus specifically on tragedies that have brought people together in the past and connect generations now through YouTube footage. Even after making that decision, she felt she needed to whittle the list down to one or two tragedies for each generation, so that her audience could easily connect with what other generations had felt.

Since Williamson wanted her audience to be able to experience what each generation saw and heard as these tragedies occurred, she chose to include as evidence excerpts from iconic speeches (of John F. Kennedy, Martin Luther King Jr., Ronald Reagan) to layer over the images and videos. She could have chosen to support her argument—that YouTube provides much more than a casual distraction—with clips of people talking about how video-sharing sites have revolutionized the way we experience and *re*experience events. But she thought primary sounds would be more powerful, more convincing support.

As you mine for and select evidence for your project, keep your purpose in mind. What are you trying to achieve—and why? What types of evidence will help you do so convincingly? Also keep your audience members in mind—their age, experiences, biases, and needs. What kind of evidence will be most effective?

Be sure to evaluate any potential evidence for relevance (to your purpose and audience), authority, currency, and accuracy. You'll need to question whether a photo, a podcast, a video, or anything else you choose will be compelling and credible to your audience. See your handbook's section on evaluating sources.

MM9-e Choosing a genre; deciding on a delivery method

Deciding how to deliver your ideas is an important part in planning your project. First, you'll need to think about your audience and purpose: Whom are you composing for—and why? When you're mulling over how to deliver your ideas, you'll also have to think about the support you plan to include in your composition.

When Alyson D'Amato began to plan her project, she thought about the ways in which people would want to learn about her topic. She felt that a slide show presentation about brewing tea wouldn't be too interesting and wouldn't really fit her purpose, especially since most slide show presentations are designed to be delivered by a speaker. She knew she wanted people to be able to easily access and use her information, and she knew they'd probably need to go through the information on their own.

She considered creating a video and was excited about the idea of actually recording herself talking about tea and making tea, but she wasn't sure how to include the recipes she wanted to share with her audience. To help organize herself as she considered different ways to convey the information, D'Amato created a table listing the pros and cons of different delivery methods (see p. MM-70).

D'Amato decided that a Web site would be the best way to share her ideas. With a Web site, she knew she could include written words and images, maybe embed video, and create an overall organization that would allow viewers to experience her site at their own pace.

Considering different formats, as D'Amato did, is an important part of your planning. For more on the technical aspects of delivering your project, see section MM15.

ACTIVITY MM9–1: Your understanding

Review a writing assignment you recently completed or a piece of writing you composed on your own. Imagine that it had been a collaborative, group project. How do you think your composing processes would have been different? What would you have learned or gained by collaborating? How might the project have turned out differently? What difficulties or opportunities might you have encountered if the project had been collaborative?

ACTIVITY MM9–2: Your understanding

Consider the broad subjects in the following list. Narrow each one by asking questions. Propose a manageable topic for a multimodal composition for at least two of the four subjects.

- The most recent presidential election
- Video games
- Social networking sites
- Environmental issues

ACTIVITY MM9–3: Your project

For a project you are currently planning, take some time to consider your own main idea. Is it narrow enough? Do you have a specific angle on the subject? Pair up with a classmate and share your idea. Pitch your plan for gathering support and seek feedback from your classmate. Are you planning the most convincing support for your main idea? Take notes from your conversation.

SAMPLE STUDENT NOTES: DECIDING ON A DELIVERY METHOD

Delivery method	Pros (+) and cons (-)
Slide show	+ Viewers can watch slides at their own pace and navigate back or skip ahead. + I can use images, written words, and links. + I can include any recipes I want to share. + I can use text animations to spice things up. - Slide show presentations often seem dry and not engaging. - The final file might be really large, and my audience would probably have to download it to view it. - To view my project, my audience might need to have the same slide show software I have.
Video	+ Video would seem cooler than a slide show. I could include a soundtrack with music and voiceover. + Actually watching someone make tea in a video might be more helpful than written instructions. + Video would allow me to control the sequence of information, but that's not really important to me for this project. - I'm not sure how I would include my recipes so that they could be saved and used. Maybe a download link at the end of my video? - I'd have to keep it short or risk boring my audience. - Video can be hard to edit. If I change any visuals, I might have to adjust the soundtrack.
Web site	+ A Web site would be easy to share. All I'd have to do is provide a URL. + Viewers would be able to control the order in which they see information and easily revisit things they find interesting. + I could include my recipes on the pages or as downloadable files. + I could include any image, audio, or video files I wanted to. + There are plenty of free Web site builders online that I can use.

MM10 Managing your project

A huge part of imagining, drafting, creating, revising, and publishing a multimodal project is managing the pieces of the project. When you write a typical academic essay, you often work with only one piece: your document filled with written words. When working on a multimodal project, you might be managing two, three, four, or dozens of pieces, most if not all of which are electronic files. Each of these files likely has a different name and is of a different type. It's easy to feel overwhelmed when negotiating .wmv, .mov, .bmp, .m4v, .pdf, .jpg, and other files.

This section offers a few good practices for managing files across a multimodal project:

- Saving all your files in one place
- Keeping track of where your sources came from
- Using clear, descriptive names when saving your files
- Keeping track of versions when sharing your files with others

MM10-a Saving all your files in one place

Before you really dig into a project, decide where you're going to work on it. If your project is digital and will include images, audio segments, or movie clips, for example, that workspace is probably a folder on your computer. With multimodal projects, often the different components need to sync with or "talk to" one another. If one file is saved on your computer's desktop and another file is saved in a "My Documents" folder, the applications you use to compile your project might not be able to find all the files. And you might not be able to find all the files either!

When Williamson began gathering clips and working on her video project, she created a "Writing Class Project" folder on her USB drive. This was a useful initial storage space for all her files. You can see in Figure 10–1 that she has sound files, video clips, and some word processing documents stored in the folder.

Fairly quickly, however, Williamson realized that she needed to be more organized—by the time she had twenty files in her "Writing Class Project" folder, she found it was getting harder and harder to sort through all the files and find specific pieces.

She created three separate folders within her "Writing Class Project" main folder—one for music, one for video clips, and another for audio clips (Figures 10–2 and 10–3). She left her word processing documents in the main folder because they dealt with the overall project, whereas the files in the subfolders were pieces of the larger project.

Williamson's file-saving strategy isn't the only way to save files for a major project, but she found that it worked well for her, and it's a good example of how you can create a file management system for a multimodal composing project.

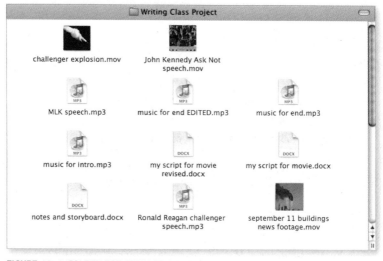

FIGURE 10–1 FOLDER FOR STORAGE OF MULTIMODAL FILES.

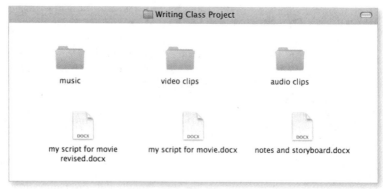

FIGURE 10–2 FOLDER FOR A MULTIMODAL PROJECT ORGANIZED WITH SUBFOLDERS FOR MUSIC, VIDEO CLIPS, AND AUDIO CLIPS.

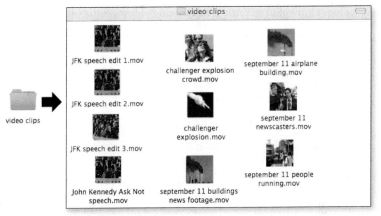

FIGURE 10-3 SUBFOLDER CONTAINING ALL THE VIDEO CLIPS FOR A MULTIMODAL PROJECT.

MM10-b Keeping track of all your files

As you brainstorm and research your project, gathering and selecting examples, resources, and other materials, you might think, "Oh, I'll remember where I found this!" But as you collect pieces from a variety of sources over a span of time, you will probably lose track of where you found at least a few things, and that can cause you problems further down the road. For example, if you use an audio quote in a draft of your project and later decide you'd like to include a few seconds more of what the speaker said, you'll have to find not only the original sound file but also the exact moment when the words you've quoted are spoken. Your job will be much easier if you've got the whole sound file in your project folder along with some notes about the speaker, where the file came from, when you downloaded the file, and the time stamp for the words you're interested in using. You may want to keep your notes in a list that provides key information about each of the files you're collecting.

Figure 10–4 shows part of a list Williamson kept in her "notes and storyboard" word processing document in her "Writing Class Project" folder.

Video assignment-sources.docx

<u>F</u>ile	<u>E</u>dit	<u>V</u>iew	<u>I</u>nsert	F<u>o</u>rmat	<u>T</u>ools	Ta<u>b</u>le	<u>W</u>indow

VIDEO SOURCES

John F. Kennedy. "Inaugural Speech."

http://www.youtube.com/watch?v=P1PbQlVMp98&feature=player_embedded

- found and viewed for the first time on January 27
- 4:32 long; recorded on Friday, January 20, 1961; posted to YouTube by evgondemand.com (site that offers pay-per-view access to famous speeches)
- visual focus is on Kennedy speaking at podium; audio is entirely Kennedy
- Kennedy's addressing people in attendance (vice pres, reps, citizens)
- good audio clips — maybe use in project?
  - o :53-:54 "the world is very different now" (talking about how we can abolish poverty, but that it's hard because there are still issues around the world)
  - o 1:36-2:21 "let the word go forth . . . we are committed today at home and around the world" (talking about defending human rights)

"Footage of JFK motorcade is discovered"

http://www.youtube.com/watch?v=d300ziN3wKA

- found and viewed for the first time on January 29
- 40 seconds long; posted to YouTube and tagged: "The silent, 8 mm color film is 'the clearest, best film of Jackie in the motorcade,' said Gary Mack, curator of the Sixth Floor Museum, which focuses on Kennedy's life and assassination."
- video sequence: people waving at the camera; broader street scene with motorcade coming down the street; motorcade passes by; shot of crowd again and then Texas School Book Depository; quick crowd shot (no audio)
- not sure how I might use this in my project; there are some pretty clear shots of Kennedy and Jackie in the car

"JFK Assassination Motorcade from Love Field to Dealey Plaza on to Parkland Hospital 22 Nov 1963"

http://www.youtube.com/watch?v=WnlL-pucCj0

- found and viewed for the first time on January 29
- 15 minutes long; posted to YouTube and tagged: "A chronological collection of original film footage, news reports and still photos, as John F Kennedy travels from Love Field in Dallas Texas through Dealey Plaza, and onto Parkland Hospital."
- voiceover: "the weather couldn't be better . . ." (a newscaster?); music in the background (part of the original video, or added by whoever compiled this?)
- voiceover describes what Kennedy and Jackie are doing — at the airport, shaking hands, heading to the limo to go downtown, limo pulling away; cut to clip showing motorcade
- 2:16 — audio changes to a different voice describing the motorcade and where it's going (recording doesn't sound as old); music is more ominous and heavy
- 3:46 — cool shot of the motorcade from behind (maybe use in project?)
- 5:08 — footage gets slower and choppy (effect created by whoever shot the video?)

FIGURE 10–4 SOURCES AND NOTES FOR A VIDEO ASSIGNMENT.

MM10-c Using clear, descriptive names when saving files

File names like "audio piece" or "draft 2" don't mean much when you're working with and compiling lots of files. One way to manage your files is to use a descriptive and consistent naming system. For instance, you might decide to include the word *audio* in the file name of all your audio clips: "audio_opening_music" and "audio_jayne_talking."

You might also consider date stamping your files when you save them. Your computer does this automatically, but it helps sometimes to see the date in the file name ("writing project May 5" or "writing project 05_08_12," for example). Doing so will help you make sure that when you resume working on your project, you're working with your most recent draft. Date stamping can also help you avoid writing over earlier drafts, which you might need later.

MM10-d Keeping track of versions when sharing files with others

Part of managing files, especially when you work collaboratively, is developing a system for sharing files. It's easy, and frustrating, to end up with multiple versions of a file that have to be merged. Say, for instance, that you are working on a project with two other students, John and Chelsea. You each have a copy of your project. John is making changes to it, and Chelsea is making changes to it. Suddenly, you have three different versions of your project: yours, John's, and Chelsea's. Figuring out who made what changes and getting all of those changes into a single draft is difficult and time-consuming.

Passing around one file and working on that one file individually is a good approach. If you're passing around a file, make sure that only one member of your group works on that file at a time. Or try uploading the file to a collaborative workspace, so that all members of your group make changes to a single version. Whatever strategy you adopt, maintaining good communication with your group members is essential.

ACTIVITY MM10-1: Your understanding

Online tools that help you create, manage, and save files can be especially helpful when you're working with files you need to share with others. Look online for three such tools (GoogleDocs, for example) and generate a list of pros and cons for each. As you create your list, think about what criteria are important to you. Here are a few questions to help you get started:

- Does the tool let you save multiple files in one place?
- How large can the files be?

- What types of files are allowed? Documents? Audio files? Image or movie files?
- Do files remain posted until you take them down? Or do they expire after a set time?
- Does the tool allow multiple people to edit a file at the same time?
- Does the tool record information about who makes saved changes?
- Can you easily download the file after all changes have been made and saved?

ACTIVITY MM10–2: Your project

Come up with a file-saving strategy for a project you're about to begin. If you're already working on something, describe your current file-saving strategy and think about what's working well and what you might improve. Think about how you want to handle different types of files, for example, and how you want to manage your series of drafts.

MM11 Outlining and drafting your project

In section MM9, on planning your project, you saw a visualization of Marisa Williamson's writing process—a visualization that was not neat and orderly (see Figure 9–2, p. MM-63). In the process of working on her project, Williamson moved back and forth across the pieces she was developing and working with, selecting an image here, identifying a video piece to use there, revising her narration before recording it. Although Williamson's *process* might have seemed a bit haphazard, her final *product* is sequenced, polished, and very well organized.

Your ideas might be expressed in written words, in audio, in moving images, in still images, or in some combination. Regardless of the media you're working with, organizing your ideas before and as you draft will help you meet your goals as a composer and will help you meet your audience's needs.

MM11-a Choosing the right organizing tool for your multimodal project

How you organize the information you're presenting depends on the type of document you will produce and what different modes you might use. A slide show presentation, for instance, is typically linear.

Most slide shows have a title slide, an introduction slide or two, body slides, a conclusion slide, and so forth (see Figure 11–1). If you're giving background information or presenting a problem that needs solving, you will want to do so early in your slide presentation. If

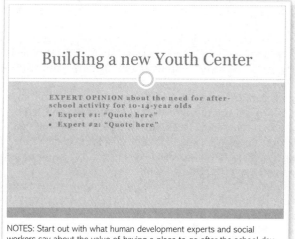

FIGURE 11–1 DRAFTING A SLIDE SHOW PRESENTATION WITH NOTES.

you are giving reasons for support, think about how to arrange those reasons: Strongest first? Strongest last? The notes feature in Power-Point and other presentation software can help you as you play with arrangement and build your script. What also helps is that you can move slides around fairly easily. Slide show templates can help you figure out what information should be placed where.

Unlike a slide presentation, Web sites don't function in a linear way. They can be arranged with hyperlinks across pages, so you may not want to create a specific path for readers; instead, you can give them different options for experiencing your ideas. What is most important in organizing Web site content is making sure your categories of information are clear.

After Alyson D'Amato had considered her purpose and audience, determined her genre (an informative site), and started planning her content (brewing tea), she considered the different ways she could present information on a Web site. Having one long page readers would scroll down to read didn't seem ideal—nor did it seem to her like a good way to effectively create a Web page.

D'Amato decided to create a wireframe, or mock-up, of her project before starting to build her Web site. At first, D'Amato was going to have only three main links: to her tea story, to brewing tea, and to tea types. "Making blends" was going to be a link within the brewing tea page, and black, green, and white tea information was going to be linked from the tea types page.

She decided, however, that she didn't want to bury all of that information and make users click to a page and then link deeper to get to information she thought was important, so she planned for six main links, shown in Figure 11–2.

How you organize the information you're presenting also depends on your purpose. If you are teaching your readers to do something new, you will probably need to provide straightforward, step-by-step,

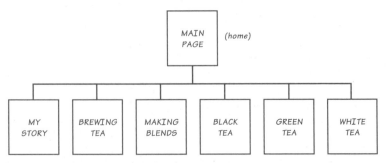

FIGURE 11–2 **REVISED WIREFRAME FOR A WEB SITE.**

numbered instructions. If you are composing a video essay that inspires people to reflect or to take action, you may have more flexibility in arranging your information for impact.

Once you have a strong sense of your topic and main idea and you've begun to assemble support, you'll want to think about organizing your ideas. Often for traditional essays, instructors focus on creating outlines, where you begin with a thesis statement and then develop the key ideas you will express in the body of your paper. Creating an outline is also an effective way to get started on a multimodal piece, because regardless of what you choose to include and how you choose to share information, it's crucial to have some guiding organization—a skeleton that you can flesh out in a draft.

Other tools can be useful for organizing your ideas. For instance, moviemakers often use a storyboard to think about how they will express ideas. A storyboard provides a space for a composer to describe the scene being set, any text that will appear on the screen, and the music or other sounds that will be in the scene. There's also room for the composer to add specific notes and a place for describing a transition (see Figure 11–3).

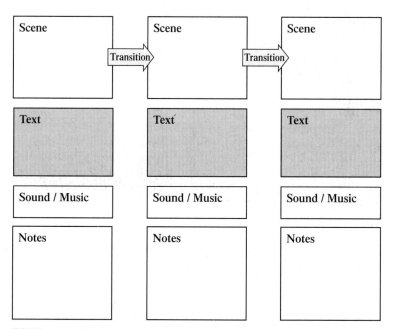

FIGURE 11–3 STORYBOARD FOR A MULTIMODAL PROJECT, WITH SPACE FOR THE SCENE, TEXT, SOUND OR MUSIC, AND NOTES.

MM11-b Drafting to support your main idea

Once you've settled on a main idea and sketched some sort of out-line (or wireframe or storyboard), you'll need to gather and select the content that will best support that main idea. This is a good time to take another look at the assignment. Reread the requirements and the prompt(s) to which you're responding.

There's nothing magical about drafting. It takes time, of course, and it helps to have notes about your main idea, your evidence, and your organization close by. Successful drafters ask, anticipate, and respond to questions as they work through a draft, whether they real-ize it or not. A writer who is composing an instructional booklet may ask, for example, *How do people learn something new?* or *How did I learn to do what I'm trying to describe?*

Think about creating a multimodal document that teaches peo-ple how to plant trees. Your main idea might be "A healthy tree starts with a proper planting." You know your audience will want to know what constitutes "a proper planting." You decide there are steps, but how many steps? What's the first step? Once you start fleshing out the steps—considering the climate, assessing how the roots are contained, digging the hole—you need to anticipate and respond to questions at each step: How big should the hole be? How deep? Why? How is the root ball set in? During your drafting, you might even ask which of the steps need illustrations or photos to complete the teach-ing or, in other words, to fulfill your purpose for your audience.

When you're composing a text that is less concrete—an inter-pretation or analysis, perhaps—you might find that questioning helps you get from a rough outline to full paragraphs. One student was assigned to write an interpretation of song lyrics or a poem of his choice. The assignment also included a requirement that students illustrate some part of the song or poem. The student chose the song "Pumped Up Kicks" by Foster the People, listened to the song and read through the lyrics numerous times, brainstormed some ideas that focused on the song's main character, and wrote a rough outline.

ROUGH OUTLINE

Interpretation of "Pumped Up Kicks"

Main idea: If the song is Robert's "story," is there any way he, who shoots and murders peers, can be seen as a sympathetic character? Close, but no.

- Robert is alone and lonely, and that's something the audience can understand and maybe relate to.
- Robert has a negative relationship with the "other" kids, and the audience can understand that fact as a powerful motivator.

- Robert makes devastating choices, so extreme that it's hard for the audience to relate.

The student was comfortable enough with his main idea and proceeded to draft an introduction focusing on what makes a character sympathetic. The following shows how he went about developing a paragraph from the first point in his rough outline.

Point in the rough outline	The composer's questions	Draft paragraph
Robert is alone and lonely, and that's something the audience can understand and maybe relate to.	*How can I tell Robert is alone? Where do I see this in the lyrics? Does alone = lonely?*	The lyrics show us a boy, a "kid," whose "Daddy works a long day" and who spends the day unsupervised. Robert is alone in his house and alone in his thoughts as he spends idle time digging in "his dad's closet" and trying his father's cigarettes. There's not really a hint of any kind of relationship (at least a positive relationship) in the story.
	Do I care? Does his loneliness make him sympathetic?	The father comes "home late," probably repeatedly, and Robert is left waiting "for a long time." There doesn't seem to be a mother figure or siblings. Even if we can't relate to Robert, maybe we can understand his actions as being the result of an unloving home environment. His being alone and lonely generates sympathy.

As the student moves from outline to draft, he successfully identifies evidence from the lyrics to support his point. He still needs to consider images that might help him communicate his analysis of the lyrics. After all, his assignment asks him to illustrate a part of the poem or lyrics. He's off to a good start, however.

When you proceed from your ideas and notes to full sentences and strings of ideas, keep in mind that a *draft* is flexible. The goal is to get something down on paper that makes some sense and can be played with and questioned later by you, a peer, or another reader. It helps to ask, anticipate, and respond to questions you have or your reader might have. And of course it helps to keep your purpose for writing and your audience in mind as you draft.

ACTIVITY MM11–1: Your understanding

To experiment with one type of organizing tool for a multimodal composition, try "reverse engineering" a brief video or a fairly simple Web site. Identify a video or Web site and strip it down to either an outline, a wireframe, or a storyboard.

ACTIVITY MM11–2: Your project

Take a current assignment and, as you work your way through your ideas for the assignment, try out at least one of the organizing tools discussed in this section. Write a brief reflective paragraph about whether the strategy was or was not helpful to you as you moved on to the drafting stage.

MM12 Emphasizing important information

When you look at a document, you'll notice that some information is emphasized, or treated more prominently, to catch the reader's attention or communicate a main idea. In print documents, emphasis is usually achieved by the placement of information on the page. Take a look at the sample documents, a résumé and a brochure, in Figures 12–1 and 12–2. What information jumps out at you? What information do you think is the most important in each one?

When you examine the résumé, think about the context and purpose of a résumé. The "work" a résumé does is to "sell" the author—to best portray his or her abilities, skills, and experiences. The author emphasizes his name with boldface type and centered placement. He presents categories that will be of interest to his reader in a consistent way. The second document, a brochure, would appear folded, with the panel on the right as the "cover." The emphasis is on a photograph of a puppy and a child. Why? The composer made choices to inspire the reader to act on behalf of the family pet.

Composers use different methods of emphasizing important information, depending on the type of composition they're producing. If you have written traditional essays, you may be used to creating emphasis with your words and sentence structure—using

FIGURE 12–1 A RÉSUMÉ.

FIGURE 12–2 A BROCHURE. (*Source:* FEMA)

phrases like "and most important" or "the strongest evidence yet." In traditional essays, information is expressed in written words, and it's up to your readers to be able to discern what information is critical without the aid of visual cues. When you compose multimodal essays, you'll have to first determine what information is most important to emphasize, given your purpose and audience, and then how you can best emphasize that information, given your genre and modes.

MM12-a Determining what needs emphasis

Before you can make decisions about how to emphasize certain information, you need to decide what information is most crucial to convey. This decision depends on your audience and your purpose.

If your purpose is to inform and your audience is peers (other college students) who are new to the topic, you'll want to think about overarching categories of information and what might motivate your audience to engage with the information. If your purpose is to persuade your audience to embrace your position in a debate, the most important information to emphasize might be the evidence you provide to support your key points.

Student composer Alyson D'Amato, who created an informative Web site about brewing tea, wanted to emphasize the benefits of brewing loose leaf tea and the pleasures of creating custom blends. She didn't want these ideas to get buried under other basic information such as different kinds of tea leaves. To start identifying information that needs emphasis in your own composition, think about the following questions:

- What is your reason for composing? What are you trying to accomplish, and why?
- Who are your audience members? What information is going to be most appealing to them? Most convincing?
- What's the main thing you want your readers to remember after they've experienced your composition?

MM12-b Choosing a strategy for creating emphasis

In a text-only document with minimal design, the words themselves carry importance; that is, how you format words and sentences and where you place them help provide emphasis. You would probably express an important idea in a topic sentence at the start of a paragraph, for example, rather than bury it in the middle of a long paragraph. In a text-only document with design features, important ideas can be emphasized with font choice and by styling words with boldface, underline, italics, and type size. Look at the documents in Figure 12–3. From a glance, what would you assume to be the most important information in each one?

The large boldface text in the first and third examples is likely the most important information. The first example also includes a "pull quote," which draws readers' eyes to the right side of the page. The second example includes some boldface text and a bulleted list, which help key information stand out from the rest of the text. In the third example, readers might assume that the text block at the bottom of the page is less important than the spaced-out, right-aligned text at the top of the page.

Consider the front page of Alyson D'Amato's Web site (Figure 12–4). Perhaps the most important information on the front page is the list of links at the top of the page, which allows readers to see the different topics addressed on the Web site and to go to the different pages of the site. This navigation bar stays at the top of each page, so readers can easily move around on the site from whichever page they land on. D'Amato has also emphasized the photo of tea leaves—with her audience (tea novices) in mind.

FIGURE 12-3 DOCUMENTS, SHOWING DIFFERENT WAYS TO CREATE EMPHASIS.

On the Web site home page, the body text appears in somewhat standard-size text, organized into paragraphs. The front page text is important, but perhaps not as important as the navigation bar.

If you listen to student composer Marisa Williamson's video, which argues that tragedies—even those experienced only on You-Tube—knit us together, you'll notice that she repeats some audio clips throughout the video. This repetition of information makes it stand out as particularly important.

She repeats three key audio clips across her work:

- "The world is very different now." (John F. Kennedy)
- "Now is the time." (Martin Luther King Jr.)
- "We cannot turn back." (Martin Luther King Jr.)

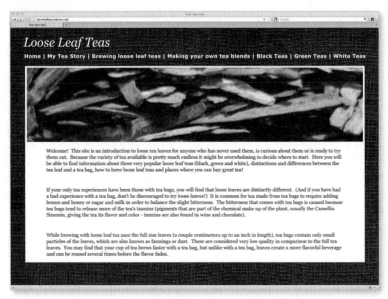

FIGURE 12–4 FIRST PAGE OF A WEB SITE, SHOWING LINKS, AN IMAGE, AND TEXT.

These clips contribute to her main idea that online video is now one of the primary ways that we experience formative events. She deliberately chose *not* to repeat a phrase that John F. Kennedy is perhaps most famous for: "Ask not what your country can do for you—ask what you can do for your country." Because this famous line is heard only once in Williamson's composition, it stands out as being particularly meaningful.

Another way that the student creates dramatic emphasis is by beginning and ending with audio clips of Ronald Reagan, US president in 1986 when the space shuttle *Challenger* disaster occurred.

You have a number of strategies for emphasizing important information at your disposal as you craft a multimodal piece. In a PowerPoint slide, you might style headings so that they communicate your key ideas prominently, and you might use bullet points to emphasize steps or points in your presentation. In an advertisement, you might add white space around a product shot to call attention to it. In a podcast, you might pause and use silence for emphasis. In a video, you might use subtitles to reinforce a message. Considering your purpose for composing, determining your audience, and understanding the genre in which you are composing are important steps in figuring out how to make an impact.

ACTIVITY MM12–1: Your understanding

In section MM8, you looked at the home pages of a few Web sites to identify the primary audience of each (see p. MM-59). Take a look again at the following sites, with emphasis in mind:

- the main Web site of your school
- the Web site of a professor at your school
- the Web site of a fast-food restaurant in your area
- the Web site of a small, locally owned restaurant in your area
- the Web site of the company that made the car you drive or that makes the car you'd like to drive
- the Web site for a branch or an agency of the US government (for example, the White House, the IRS, the FBI)
- the Web site for an individual who serves in the US government (such as a member of Congress)

As you look at each multimodal text, identify what information the composer seems to be emphasizing. How do you know it's important? What are some of the techniques used to highlight the most important information? Write brief notes for each piece, and be prepared to discuss them in class.

ACTIVITY MM12–2: Your project

For a project you are currently working on, make notes about the information you want to emphasize and some strategies you can use to do so. Take into consideration your purpose, your audience, and the genre you are working in. What textual formatting options might you use to draw attention to your key points? What visuals might you embed to support those points? Are there audio clips (dialogue, music, sound effects) or video clips that might help articulate the main points in your project?

MM13 Revising and editing your multimodal project

Very few writers sit down, write a first draft of a paper, and submit it for a successful grade. More typically, writers work on a draft in chunks, circling back occasionally to reread and rewrite. You may find that your instructors build time into an assignment for feedback, revising, and editing. Even if they don't, it's useful to set aside some time so that you can move comfortably from a first or second draft to a final piece. Revising and editing a multimodal composition may take substantially more time than revising and editing a traditional essay.

Your handbook includes advice about revising and editing. For the purposes of this brief discussion, keep in mind the following distinctions:

In general, **revising** involves

- rethinking your point or purpose
- reshaping your approach to fit your audience's needs
- reorganizing or strengthening evidence to help you achieve your purpose
- rearranging whole parts of your composition
- revisiting your message

In general, **editing** involves

- checking to see if sentences and paragraphs progress logically
- adding transitions where necessary to improve coherence
- changing wordy phrases
- deleting sentences that are off-topic
- making sure that word choice is precise and tailored to the purpose and audience

When revising and editing a traditional, words-only document, a writer might move around, add, or delete whole passages or sentences in a word processing program. The writer might print out a draft to mark corrections, changes, or points that need more clarification. The processes of revising a multimodal project, however, might be quite different, depending on the modes used. The overall point of revising and editing, whether your composition is multimodal or monomodal, is to make your work stronger, clearer, better organized, and on target for your purpose and audience.

MM13-a Seeking and using feedback

Before you revise and edit, it may help to seek feedback from classmates, your instructor, a tutor, or a friend. Tell each reviewer whether you want feedback about larger, more global issues (organization, main point, use of audio/visual/textual evidence, overall message) or surface-level issues (clear sentences, precise words, sentence logic). In other words, tell reviewers whether you are approaching a revising stage or an editing stage. Before you share a draft with a reviewer, think about three key questions you might want your reviewer to answer, and share those questions with him or her.

After student composer Alyson D'Amato had made initial decisions based on her purpose, audience, and content and after she had outlined and drafted her project, an informative Web site about tea, she met with a tutor at her school's writing center to get feedback on her site. Figure 13–1 shows a page from her draft site. She asked the tutor the following questions:

1. The assignment says that we have to have a good navigation, or a clear introduction and way for the reader/viewer to move through the composition. Is the navigation clear? How can I improve it?

2. I'm not sure about the pictures I've included, but I don't know what I would replace them with. Can you comment on the visuals?

3. Do you think that the text is well written and flows well? Can you point out areas that could be stronger?

D'Amato and her tutor spent some time looking at her site, and the tutor had D'Amato read parts of it out loud. They also looked at

FIGURE 13–1 DRAFT STUDENT PROJECT: AN INFORMATIVE WEB SITE.

a few other informative Web sites for ideas and inspiration. D'Amato left with a set of priorities for revising her work. The following are her revision goals.

ALYSON D'AMATO'S REVISION GOALS

- There's too much to read on each page. Streamline. We looked at another Web site with similar navigation but more manageable content. We came up with a way to break up the text.

- The tea photos are cool, but they don't really make sense, especially since one has a tea bag in it and my site is about brewing loose leaf teas. Maybe replace with images of loose leaf tea.

- The tutor also asked why I chose the font for "LOOSE LEAF TEA," and I just thought it looked cool. We looked at some other tea sites, and they all used a more elegant type of font that might be easier to read and more appealing to people interested in tea. Choose new font.

- The site will need more of an introduction—the tutor said I just jumped right into it here. There are also chunks of info that don't really fit or flow well. I marked those and need to revise them. NOTE TO SELF!!! Do this before reworking the text on different pages!

- The tutor also asked why I took up so much room on the left side with my name and class info. He suggested that because my audience is potential tea fans generally, I might want to cut the class-specific info, because it really makes this look like a student project, which some people might not take seriously.

Creating a list of goals is a good way to make the transition between feedback and revising. Keep in mind that you don't have to make every change a reviewer suggests. Look at the reviewer's suggestions through the lens of your own purpose, audience, and assignment. Not every suggestion is going to be right for your project. If you seek feedback from three reviewers, however, and all three say that your project seems a little hard to follow, you know that organization is going to be one area in which you'll want to focus your revision efforts.

MM13-b Revising and remixing a multimodal composition

Writers typically revise a draft by moving sentences or paragraphs around their paper. Word processing software makes it easy for writers to cut and paste chunks of text in a words-only draft. When a writer, for example, reads the final paragraph in a draft and realizes—either on his or her own or with a reader's help—that the main point is buried in the concluding paragraph, it's easy enough to move a sentence or group of sentences from one place to another and rewrite as needed.

When revising a multimodal piece, you might have to ask different kinds of revision questions depending on the mode(s) you've chosen to communicate your main idea.

- In revising a speech, you might ask, *Where is it important to pause and perhaps seek audience interaction? How can my speech be stronger with the use of props or visual aids?*

- In revising a slide show presentation, you might ask, *Is the balance of text and visuals right? Do I need this whole table as evidence, or can I use just a detail from it? Are the slides progressing at the right pace for my audience, mainly senior citizens?*

- In revising a video, you might ask, *Would narration help to provide "glue" between the testimony of my interviewees? Is the background music too distracting?*

Thinking about revision as *remix* can be helpful in approaching a multimodal project. *Remix* is a term typically used to describe the process of taking an original audio track and adding other elements. Perhaps one of the most infamous remixes in recent times was Danger Mouse's 2004 release of *The Grey Album*. To produce the album, Danger Mouse took Jay-Z's *Black Album* (2003) and remixed it with the Beatles' *White Album* (1968). Together, the lyrics and music from both albums—mixed and merged together—took on an entirely different tone and meaning.

A useful way to think about revision with a multimodal composition is that you are "remixing" your own work—taking an original piece or set of pieces and rearranging them, resequencing them, and perhaps adding elements. This remixing might result in a composition with more impact, better focus, or more awareness of the audience.

Student composer Marisa Williamson found that to revise her video essay, she had to keep circling back and remixing the elements of her draft. She had a lot of what she needed in her first draft; for her, revising meant rearranging in response to feedback from her classmates.

For example, when Williamson initially drafted her video piece, she sequenced the images and video chronologically—she included the images and video of John F. Kennedy's assassination first (1963), followed by footage related to Martin Luther King Jr.'s assassination (1968) and the space shuttle *Challenger* disaster (1986), and ended with video of the September 11 terrorist attacks in New York City (2001).

Fellow students who saw the draft suggested that she didn't need to tell the story chronologically to make her point. She resequenced the clips and even tried looping, or repeating, some of the clips for emphasis. Also, Williamson wasn't sure how she wanted to include her own words in her video. In her first draft, she included her words by scrolling them along the bottom of the movie. Her classmates, however, suggested that this was distracting and that it might be interesting to record and layer her own voice over the music. She tried that at the revising stage.

MM13-c Editing a multimodal composition

Editing is a stage in which a composer takes a closer look at the composition and asks, *Is it clear? Does it make sense?* Editing a words-only composition means looking at words and sentences and the transitions between sentences and paragraphs. Editing a multimodal composition can be a bit more complicated, in part because multimodal projects require composers to work across different modes and sometimes across different software. As you edit your project, you might find the questions in the following chart helpful.

Editing multimodal compositions

Editing words

- Have you chosen the clearest, most appropriate words for your purpose and audience?
- Are your sentences and paragraphs in logical order?
- Have you included transitions between sentences and paragraphs to improve the flow of your ideas?
- Could your ideas be expressed in more concise language?
- Do grammar or spelling errors distract from your message?

Editing sounds

- Is the volume appropriate? Do any sounds drown out other elements?
- Is the pace of the narration right? Not too slow or too fast?
- Do you need more sound or more silence?
- Is your sound synched properly to any static or moving images that go with it?

Editing static images

- Have you chosen the clearest, most appropriate images for your purpose and audience?
- Do you need more visual evidence? Do you have the right kind of visuals? Would a graph, for example, be better than a photograph for your composition?
- Have you used captions as needed for the images? Some visuals can't speak for themselves.
- Are the images you've chosen presented at an appropriate size?

Editing moving images

- If you're using video clips, is the length appropriate?
- Is the purpose of the moving images clear in your composition?
- Are the moving images emphasizing the right content?

Editing for consistency and clarity

- If you've made changes in one mode (edited words in the narration, for instance), do you need to make changes in another (edit words that appear on-screen)?
- If you've produced slides, do they have a consistent design?
- Are you using colors, font sizes, and headings purposefully and consistently?
- If you have navigation elements in your project, is it clear to your users/viewers how to get from one place to another?

Crediting and citing

- Have you cited the works you're quoting from, paraphrasing, or summarizing?
- Have you credited the artists whose music you've used?
- Have you credited the creators or photographers of the images you've used?
- Have you credited the composers of the video clips you've used?

ACTIVITY MM13–1: Your understanding

Popular examples of remixes are multimodal compositions in which composers rearrange the events in movie trailers to create a different, alternative tone or meaning. If you search the Web for "remixed" or "recut" movie trailers, you may find one that positions *The Hunger Games* as a comedy and *Twilight* as a creepy stalker film. Find two or three different remixed movie trailers. Identify what elements are probably "original" to the trailer, and then identify what elements have been remixed, added, or changed. What effect does the remix have? Why?

ACTIVITY MM13–2: Your project

Think about a project you're currently working on. Make a plan to seek feedback from a teacher, tutor, classmate, or friend. Make a list of three or four questions you want to ask this person. What sort of advice or feedback do you hope to get? After you meet with this person, compose a brief list of revision goals.

MM14 Integrating and documenting sources

Most composers at some point depend on source material—words, data, audio, or images that come from elsewhere. Writers in medicine depend on clinical studies; caseworkers in the social sciences depend on interviews; filmmakers depend on scripts. Responsible composers integrate and document their sources according to the conventions of their field. These conventions don't always translate well from field to field. Imagine watching a movie and having citations to reference material appear on the screen throughout the movie. Likewise, imagine reading an academic article that makes claims but offers no support and no citations. When you are composing, you will want to pay attention to the expectations for crediting your sources in the type of composition you are creating.

MM14-a Understanding why documenting sources is important

Giving formal credit to sources is necessary for a few key reasons. Documenting sources allows you to

- make evident to an audience that you have done your homework, researched the topic thoroughly, and are aware of larger conversations, discussions, and research related to the topic
- direct an audience to the original material that you gathered and used to conduct research and write up your findings
- give credit where credit is due, acknowledging your use of someone else's ideas—whether they're expressed in written words, static or moving images, sound, or multiple modes.

You may be familiar with instructors' expectations about different documentation styles (MLA, APA, *Chicago*, CSE). Your handbook covers how to cite sources in your written work using one of these styles.

MM14-b Knowing when a citation is needed

Sources don't always have to be formal academic articles or books. One of the trickiest aspects of citing your sources and documenting your work is recognizing what should be cited, regardless of the type of composition you are crafting.

You should generally cite a source in these cases:

- when you use or refer to somebody else's words or ideas from a magazine, book, newspaper, song, TV program, movie, Web page, computer program, letter, advertisement, or any other medium
- when you use information obtained through interviewing another person
- when you use data from experiments that you did not conduct
- when you use diagrams, illustrations, charts, or photos that you did not create
- when you use audio or video clips that you did not create

Typically, you do not need to document a source in these cases:

- when you are writing from your own experiences, your own observations, your own insights, your own thoughts, or your own conclusions about a subject
- when you are using "common knowledge"—folklore, common-sense observations, or shared information within your field of study or cultural group
- when you are compiling generally accepted facts
- when you are writing up your own experimental result

MM14-c Determining how to integrate sources in a multimodal composition

The Internet makes it easy to find images, photographs, articles, songs, sounds, and other material with a few clicks. With a fast Internet connection, downloading such materials is convenient. Most computer programs, from spreadsheet applications to presentation software to word processing tools, allow users to include images, sounds, and the like in their documents. Video production applications allow composers to include audio tracks and text on-screen.

Much of what you find on the Web, however, is owned by others—in other words, it is the copyright-protected property of other individuals. This doesn't mean that students can't use the materials for class projects, but being a college writer means knowing how to integrate and acknowledge sources responsibly and correctly.

When you integrate words (a quotation from, a paraphrase of, or a summary of source material) into a words-only document, you will typically do so with a signal phrase and a parenthetical reference.

> Many parents worry that youth and teens are meeting strangers online and that these relationships pose dangers. According to research funded by the MacArthur Foundation, however, youth and teens use digital media mainly to "extend" relationships they already have (Ito et al.). The danger comes when these existing relationships turn bad.

- The student's point.
- The student's signal phrase.
- Material from the source, followed by a parenthetical citation.
- The student's comment on the source.

In multimodal projects, however, using a signal phrase and a parenthetical reference may be disruptive. Slide show composers who include images on slides usually do so with design in mind, placing images near key words or ideas for emphasis. During a talk, the presenter might refer to a particular image: *As you can see from this table, the number of people in America who identify themselves as biracial has tripled in the past fifteen years.* The speaker may give the source of the information in the talk, include a source line in smaller type under the image, or include a bibliography in a final slide.

You may have a great deal of flexibility when *integrating* sources in a multimodal project. College instructors will expect you to *document* your sources; in doing so, you will have a little less flexibility. Be sure to ask your instructor for guidelines.

MM14-d Figuring out how to document sources in a multimodal composition

Composers can cite sources in different ways, for different modes. Student Marisa Williamson provides a separate works cited page for her video essay "To the Children of America," because that is what the assignment requires. She credits the owners of the music she used, the audio clips she used, and the images and video she used. Her works cited list provides enough information for her audience to find the complete, original files that she edited for her project. If she creates a video essay for another course, she might follow a convention typical of movies and include a credits section at the end of her video.

Another example of how sources are cited differently in different types of compositions is shown on the works cited page of Alyson D'Amato's Web site. D'Amato was, for much of the content, the expert. That is, she didn't need to do a lot of research because she knew a great deal about selecting and brewing tea. She was interested in learning more about tea rituals and tea history, so she cited the works she consulted as she worked on her site, and she also created a list of links to Web sites she mentioned on her own site (see Figure 14–1).

Identifying what citation conventions are typical of the delivery mode you plan to use and following those conventions is part of multimodal composing. See the chart on pages MM-98 and MM-99.

The list of genres in the chart is not exhaustive, but it gives some sense of the ways in which composers of multimodal works can document the use of materials and information they did not create. Depending on the course for which you are composing, you may be asked to consult a particular academic citation style, such as MLA, APA, or *Chicago*. See your handbook for more on documenting sources in these styles.

FIGURE 14–1 WEB PAGE SHOWING WORKS CITED, INCLUDING LINKS TO RELATED WEB SITES.

Documentation conventions for different genres

Genre	Documentation convention	Reason
Essay, article, or scientific report	Typically in a works cited or reference list at the end of the essay	For an author to show that she or he has done research and thoroughly explored the topic For others to access this original work that the author consulted
Slide show presentation	At the very end, embedded in a separate slide typically called "sources" or "works cited"	For an author to show that she or he has done research and thoroughly explored the topic For others to access this original work that the author consulted To give credit and provide information for video clips, music, and other material produced by someone other than the presentation's composer
Song lyrics	Usually in the liner notes, where the artist gives formal credit or points toward permission to use copyrighted lyrics	To give credit to the original author of the lyrics or text being set to music
Music	Usually in the liner notes, where the artist gives formal credit or points toward permission to use copyrighted music	To give credit to the original artist or composer

Genre	Documentation convention	Reason
Full-length movie	At the very end, embedded within what are typically called the "closing credits"	To list cast and crew To provide location information and acknowledge the help of a community To include complete names and artists for songs used in the movie For major motion pictures, there are strict standards regarding who gets credited and in what order.
Short video	At the very end, embedded within what are typically called the "credits"	For an author to show that she or he has done research and thoroughly explored the topic For others to access this original work that the author consulted To give credit and provide information for video clips, music, and other material produced by someone other than the video's composer
News broadcast	Usually mentioned by the reporter orally within the story itself Can be a mention of a story from another news source Can be credit given to an ordinary citizen	For the station or reporter to give credit to the original person who broke the story or provided the information To include more perspectives and viewpoints in a story

ACTIVITY MM14–1: Your understanding

Review a writing assignment you recently completed that required you to produce an essay or some other traditional document. How did you integrate and document your sources for the assignment? Imagine re-creating the composition in another format—perhaps as a video or a slide show presentation. How would your handling of the sources change?

ACTIVITY MM14–2: Your project

It's important to keep a working bibliography whenever you work with sources. Consult your handbook's guidelines for compiling and maintaining a working bibliography, and create a working bibliography for your current project.

MM15 Presenting or publishing your project

When you produce a typical essay, you usually turn in a printed, paper copy of that essay to your instructor, or perhaps you turn it in by uploading the word-processed document to a course management system like Blackboard or CompClass. Submitting the work is easy because most students have access to printers and because most essays—even those with a few images—are small electronic files.

Files that include multimodal projects, however, can be extremely large. Or you may have produced a multi*file* project. Submitting and sharing the project sometimes cannot be done by e-mail or on paper.

It's important to consider where and how you will publish your multimodal project. Will you post a video on a video-sharing site like YouTube? Will you create a Web site that your school can host? Will you upload a slide show to your course page? Your instructor may give guidelines about sharing your work with your intended audience. This section includes some tips for thinking through this final stage of the project.

MM15-a Knowing your options for presenting and publishing multimodal works

The first step in deciding how to present or publish your project is knowing the different spaces available to you.

Your instructor may recommend specific presentation or publication spaces for your project. For instance, some schools have their own intranet where students can store projects. Your instructor may prefer that you upload your work to a course management site or system.

There are many other options to consider. You may need to poke around online or consult with peers about the following:

Video-hosting sites: Web sites that allow you to upload video and that will generate a stable URL for your video. (One example: YouTube)

Web-creation sites: Web sites where you can compile and create your own Web site. These often allow you to copy and paste text, add images, and create links. (One example: Weebly)

Web-hosting sites: Web sites where you can upload your Web files and create your own Web site with a unique URL. These sites often have built-in Web-creation options, too. (One example: GoDaddy)

Slide show creation and hosting sites: Web sites that allow you to build a slide show presentation and store it for others to view. (One example: Prezi)

MM15-b Considering the pros and cons of the spaces available for presenting and publishing multimodal work

If you have a choice about how and where to share your work, you may want to consider the pros and cons of different spaces. See the chart on pages MM-102 and MM-103.

Once you've chosen a specific type of space for creating or hosting your project and then chosen a specific site, you'll need to familiarize yourself with the options that site provides. Your instructor may be able to help. You will probably need answers to at least a few of the following questions:

- Do you need an account to work in the space? If so, do you have to pay for the account?
- Will your readers/viewers need a password to access your work?
- Will your readers/viewers have to set up an account to access your work?
- Will your readers/viewers have to download or install any special software to view your work?
- How long will your work be available on the site?
- Will ads appear in or near your work when it is on the site?

Presentation spaces for multimodal projects

Presentation space	Pros	Cons
Your campus course management space	Password-protected, so only your instructor and perhaps other students in your class can access your work	Typically does not offer building and creation tools—just offers storage space Usually limited in terms of file size for student projects (so a 10 MB slide show might be fine, but a 100 MB video project might be too big)
Video-hosting sites	Allow you to upload and store big files Allow you to create videos that aren't software dependent (i.e., users/viewers don't have to have a specific type of software to see the video) Usually allow users to post comments and share feedback	Are often advertisement-based, so ads may appear around or even on top of your video Sometimes generate long and hard-to-remember URLs
Web-creation sites	Can make Web site creation and design easy	Are sometimes subscription- or fee-based (you have to pay to use them) Some are less intuitive than others
Web-hosting sites	Allow you to purchase your own URL Usually provide storage space for many different file types and sizes	Are sometimes subscription- or fee-based (you have to pay to use them) Can have complicated interfaces, making uploading your content difficult

Presentation space	Pros	Cons
Slide show creation and hosting sites	Allow you to create slide show presentations that aren't software dependent (i.e., users/viewers don't have to have a specific type of software to see the presentation)	Are sometimes subscription- or fee-based (you have to pay to use them)
	Can make slide show creation and design easy	Some are less intuitive than others

MM15-c Making your project accessible and usable

In earlier sections, you read about taking into consideration the needs of your audience. Often you need to think about whether your project will be accessible and usable to your audience. If it's not, you won't be able to communicate your message. *Accessibility* typically refers to someone's physical ability to access something. For instance, a building that has only steps at its entry is not physically accessible for people using wheelchairs. In terms of multimodal projects, accessibility refers to someone's ability to hear, see, or generally put to use a text. Multimodal texts that are not accessible have a more limited audience. For example, a person with hearing deficits might be unable to use a video lecture online because she can't hear the speaker and no transcript is provided.

Usability typically refers to ease of use—how easy it is to navigate a Web site or learn to use a product, for example. In terms of multimodal projects, usability has to do with how easy or difficult it is for the audience to find, experience, and understand the composer's ideas. For example, if a multimodal text needs to be downloaded for viewing, the composer can improve usability by reducing the file size to accommodate slower Internet connections.

Not everyone has a fast Internet connection or access to a computer. Not all of the audience for your multimodal work can see or hear, or can see or hear well. You can't plan for every possible audience need, but you can compose multimodal pieces that allow you to reach the widest possible audience. Here are some guidelines to keep in mind.

Consider what format works best for your audience. For many projects, your instructor is your main audience. If your instructor doesn't tell you the format in which you should submit your project, ask. It's better to know up front than to wrestle later with converting a complete project from one interface or delivery system to another. For other projects, you might have different audiences—the campus community, for instance, or YouTube users in general. To best create for your audience, you have to know their technical expectations and also the technical specifications of your delivery choice. For instance, if your instructor has asked you to upload your project to your course management system, that system might have a maximum upload file size, so you'll have to compress your file in order to share it. YouTube and other video-sharing spaces often have time restrictions; YouTube restricts general users to ten-minute clips.

Build in accessibility features. If, for instance, you suspect that your audience might include people who don't hear well or at all, you might add captions to your project. The captions might describe the sounds in your video ([MUSIC] or [LOUD FOOTSTEPS]) and might also offer written text for what's being heard or said in your piece. If you suspect that your audience might include people with vision difficulties, you might provide a text-only transcript of your piece. Most people with visual impairment use a program called a "screen reader," a kind of software that reads text to them. Screen readers, however, cannot easily translate text saved in a slide show presentation or in a movie. Including a transcript of your piece for a screen reader helps make your work accessible to those with vision problems. Providing captions and transcripts can also help reach members of your audience who experience technical difficulties and cannot get clear audio or a clear visual display.

ACTIVITY MM15–1: Your understanding

Find one additional example site for each of the types included in the list in MM15-a. Once you've chosen your example sites, read through their "about" pages and also look through the help areas of their sites. Think about your own degree of technical expertise and your experience with each kind of site. How easily could you become proficient in using each site?

ACTIVITY MM15–2: Your project

For a project you're currently planning or drafting, write a brief page of notes about what you may need to consider so that your audience will find your composition usable and accessible.

Acknowledgments

Figure 1–1: Grecian urn. Illustration by John Keats from Public Domain.

Figure 1–2: Geoglyph photograph. Courtesy of the U.S. National Park Service/U.S. Department of the Interior. Petroglyph photograph. Copyright © Pgiam/istockphoto.com.

Figure 1–3: Illuminated manuscript. Copyright © Duncan Walker/ istockphoto.com.

Figure 1–4: Quick Response Code. QR Code is a registered trademark of DENSO WAVE Incorporated. http://www.qrcode.com/faqpatent-e.html.

Figure 1–5: Numbered math equations. Courtesy of http://umsolver.com. "UMS software's free Algebraic Equation Solver will solve and explain any algebraic equation or system of equations."

Figure 1–6: Tectonic plates. Illustration courtesy of the U.S. Geological Survey. Simkin and others, 2006.

Figure 1–7: Music collage. Copyright © Gilbert Mayer/Superstock.

Figure 1–8: "Where is your family?" billlboard image. Copyright © Sonda Dawes/The Image Works.

Figure 2–1c: Pets brochure. Courtesy of FEMA/www.ready.gov.

Page MM-28: River photograph. Copyright © straga/shutterstock.com.

Page MM-28: Sketch of bridge. Copyright © Danussa/shutterstock.com.

Page MM-28: Map of Michigan. Copyright © Jami Garrison/istockphoto.com.

Page MM-28: River clip art. Copyright © Sapik/shutterstock.com.

Page MM-29: Flood tracking bar graph. Illustration courtesy of the U.S. Geological Survey.

Page MM-29: Elwha River diagram. Illustration courtesy of the U.S. Geological Survey. Duda, J. J., Warrick, J. A., and Magirl, C. S., 2011, Elwha River dam removal—Rebirth of a river: U.S. Geological Survey Fact Sheet 2011-3097, 4 p. Illustrator: Jonathan A. Warrick.

Figure 4–1: Woman washing hair illustration. Copyright © RetroClipArt/ shutterstock.com.

Page MM-31: German shepherd photograph. Copyright © gualtiero boffi/ shutterstock.com.

Figure 4–2: Dandelion photograph. Copyright © Dleonis/Dreamstime.com.

Figure 4–3: Migrant Mother by Dorothea Lange, 1936. Library of Congress/ Farm Security Administration, Office of War Information Photograph.

Page MM-34: CNN frame grab of Saddam Hussein statue falling. Uniphotos/ Newscom. Saddam Hussein statue toppling photograph. Copyright © Robert Nickelsberg/Getty Images.

Page MM-35: Obama HOPE poster. Courtesy of SHEPARD FAIREY/ OBEYGIANT.COM.

Page MM-35: POPE illustration. Courtesy of © Michael Ian Weinfeld.

Page MM-35: CHANGE INTO A TRUCK poster. Copyright © Timothy P. Doyle, 2009, www.mrdoyle.com.

Page MM-35: VERY GRADUAL CHANGE poster. Copyright © Mike Rosulek, 2009.

Figure 5–1: Illustration with photographs, by Eadweard Muybridge, 1878, Courtesy of the Library of Congress Prints and Photographs Division Washington, D.C. 20540 USA.

Figure 5–2: Flip still from *Cloverfield*. Moviestore Collection Ltd./Alamy.

Page MM-42: "Fried egg"/"brain on drugs" PSA image. The Partnership for a Drug-Free America, Inc.

Page MM-43: "Touch the Rainbow" Skittles advertisement. Images used with permission from Wm. Wrigley Jr. Company. Copyright © 2011. All rights reserved. SKITTLES, the S Device, and all affiliated designs are trademarks of Wm. Wrigley Jr. Company or its affiliates. Title: Touch Skittles on YouTube; Client: Wrigley Canada; Product/Service: Skittles; Agency: BBDO Toronto; Writer: Chris Joakim; Art Director: Mike Donaghey; Creative Directors: Carlos Moreno, Peter Ignazi; Account Management: Chitty Krishnappa, Bhreagh Rathbun; Producer: Ann Caverly; Planner: Zach Klein; Marketing Management: Dan Alvo, Laura Amantea, Thomas Tse; Directors: Woods & Low; Production house: OPC/FamilyStyle; Executive Producers: Harland Weiss, Donovan Boden; Producer: Dwight Phipps; Director of Photography: Vinit Borrison; Editorial: Griff Henderson, Posterboy Edit; Visual FX: AXYZ; Color Transfer: Notch; Audio: Eggplant; Online producer: Amy Miranda—Lunch; Online programming/FX: Pixel Pushers; Media: OMD; Seeding: Denizen.

Page MM-43: Man eating Skittles advertisement. Images used with permission from Wm. Wrigley Jr. Company. Copyright © 2011. All rights reserved. SKITTLES, the S Device, and all affiliated designs are trademarks of Wm. Wrigley Jr. Company or its affiliates. Title: Touch Skittles on YouTube; Client: Wrigley Canada; Product/Service: Skittles; Agency: BBDO Toronto; Writer: Chris Joakim; Art Director: Mike Donaghey; Creative Directors: Carlos Moreno, Peter Ignazi; Account Management: Chitty Krishnappa, Bhreagh Rathbun; Producer: Ann Caverly; Planner: Zach Klein; Marketing Management: Dan Alvo, Laura Amantea, Thomas Tse; Directors: Woods & Low; Production house: OPC/FamilyStyle; Executive Producers: Harland Weiss, Donovan Boden; Producer: Dwight Phipps; Director of Photography: Vinit Borrison; Editorial: Griff Henderson, Posterboy Edit; Visual FX: AXYZ; Color Transfer: Notch; Audio: Eggplant; Online producer: Amy Miranda—Lunch; Online programming/FX: Pixel Pushers; Media: OMD; Seeding: Denizen.

Figure 6–1: Cheetah PSA advertisement. Used with permission © World Wildlife Fund/wwf.org.

Page MM-50: Dragon Age II video game inventory screen. Dragon Age II image used with permission of Electronic Arts Inc.

Alyson D'Amato, "Loose Leaf Teas" Web site. Used with permission.

King Anyi Howell podcast. This story was produced by Youth Radio, a Peabody Award–winning media production company.

Marisa Williamson, "To the Children of America" video essay. Used with permission.

Index

D

Writing in the Disciplines

Advice and Models

A Hacker Handbooks Supplement

Jonathan S. Cullick
Northern Kentucky University

Terry Myers Zawacki
George Mason University

BEDFORD/ST. MARTIN'S   BOSTON ◆ NEW YORK

DISCIPLINE SPECIALISTS

For their assistance and advice as discipline specialists, we thank the following: Diana Belland, Northern Kentucky University (music); Jules Benjamin, Ithaca College (history); Dorinda J. Carter, Michigan State University (education); Jennifer DeForest, University of Virginia (education); Susan Durham, George Mason University (nursing); C. Dale Elifrits, Northern Kentucky University (geology/engineering); Aimee Frame, University of Cincinnati (engineering); Devon Johnson, George Mason University (criminal justice); Victoria McMillan, Colgate University (biology); James Morris, Harvard University (biology); Kirsten Olson, Wheaton College (education); Shannon Portillo, George Mason University (criminal justice); Sherry Robertson, Arizona State University (business); and Beth Schneider, George Mason University (business).

Manufactured in the United States of America.

6   5   4
f   e

For information, write: Bedford/St. Martin's, 75 Arlington Street, Boston, MA 02116   (617-399-4000)

ISBN-10: 0-312-65683-1
ISBN-13: 978-0-312-65683-6

ACKNOWLEDGMENTS

Jules Benjamin, "Wage Slavery or True Independence? Women Workers in the Lowell, Massachusetts, Textile Mills, 1820–1850," excerpt from *A Student's Guide to History*, Eleventh Edition. Copyright © 2010 by Bedford/St. Martin's. Reprinted with permission. "Regulations for the Boarding Houses of the Middlesex Company." Reprinted by permission of the American Textile History Museum, Lowell, MA.

Valerie Charat, "Always Out of Their Seats (and Fighting): Why Are Boys Diagnosed with ADHD More Often Than Girls?" (December 15, 2006). Reprinted with permission.

Onnalee L. Gibson, "A Reflection on Service Learning: Working with Eric" (April 25, 2006). Reprinted with permission.

Tom Houston, "Concert Review" (February 27, 2008). Reprinted with permission.

Marin Johnson and Laura Arnold, "Distribution Pattern of Dandelion (*Taraxacum officinale*) on an Abandoned Golf Course" (September 13, 2005). Reprinted with permission.

Victoria McMillan, excerpt from *Writing Papers in the Biological Sciences*, Fourth Edition. Copyright © 2006 by Bedford/St. Martin's. Reprinted with permission.

Alice O'Bryan, "Site Stabilization Plan for Erosion Control" (May 5, 2008). Reprinted with permission.

Kelly Ratajczak, "Proposal to Add a Wellness Program" (April 21, 2006). Reprinted with permission.

Julie Riss, "Acute Lymphoblastic Leukemia and Hypertension in One Client: A Nursing Practice Paper" (May 18, 2006). Reprinted with permission.

Brian Spencer, "Positively Affecting Employee Motivation" (March 9, 2006). Reprinted with permission.

Chris Thompson, "Crime in Leesburg, Virginia." Reprinted with permission.

D

Writing in the Disciplines

Advice and Models

D Writing in the Disciplines

D1 Introduction: Writing in different disciplines

Succeeding in college requires performing well in different kinds of courses and on various kinds of assignments. As you probably know, you will be assigned writing in your college writing courses. It may surprise you to know, however, that other college courses require writing—courses you might not expect, like nursing and psychology. The strategies you develop in your first-year composition course will help you write well in other academic courses.

The academic community is divided into broad subject areas called *disciplines*. The disciplines are generally grouped into five major fields of study, which are further broken down into more specific subjects. The five disciplines and a few representative subjects are social sciences (psychology, sociology, criminology); natural sciences (biology and chemistry); mathematics and engineering; humanities and the arts (history, literature, music); and professions and applied sciences (business, education, nursing).

Each discipline has its own set of expectations and conventions for both reading and writing. Some of the expectations and conventions—writing with a clear main idea, for instance—are common across disciplines; those are covered in your handbook. Other expectations and conventions are unique to each discipline. These include the following:

- purpose for writing
- audience
- questions asked by scholars and practitioners
- types of evidence used
- language and writing conventions
- citation style

When you are asked to write in a specific discipline, start by becoming familiar with the distinctive features of writing in that discipline. For example, if you are asked to write a lab report for a biology class, your purpose might be to present results of an experiment. Your evidence would be the data you collected while conducting your experiment, and you would use scientific terms in your report. You would also use the CSE (Council of Science Editors) guidelines for citation of your sources. If you are asked to write a case study for an education class, your purpose might be to analyze student-teacher interactions in a single classroom. Your evidence might be data on a combination of personal observations and interviews. You would use terms from the field in your case study and cite your sources using the guidelines of the American Psychological Association (APA).

The following sections provide guidelines for writing in nine disciplines: biology, business, criminal justice/criminology, education, engineering, history, music, nursing, and psychology. Each section begins with advice about the expectations for writing in that discipline and closes with a model or two of student writing.

D2 Writing in the biological sciences

Biologists use writing in many ways. They write reports analyzing the data they collect from their experiments as well as reviews of other scientists' research or proposed research. They write proposals to convince funding agencies to award grants for their research. If they teach, biologists also write lectures. Some biologists may communicate with a general audience by writing newspaper and magazine articles. In addition, they may lend their expertise to public-policy decision making by government officials, weighing in on, say, the issue of global warming or stem cell research.

When you write in biology courses, your goal will generally be to convince readers of the validity of the conclusions you draw from observations, from experimental data, or from your evaluations of previously published or proposed research. For most assignments, you will need to use a scientific style of writing, conveying your information to readers as succinctly and accurately as possible.

D2-a Determine your audience and their needs in the biological sciences.

When you write in biology, your audience may consist of researchers, professors, other students, and sometimes members of the government or business communities and the general public. Researchers or teachers may read to find out the results of an experiment, an analysis of new data, or information supporting or critiquing a theory. They may need this information to guide their own research projects or improve their assignments and classroom materials. Students read to learn about major concepts and discoveries as well as methods for conducting laboratory experiments. Researchers, teachers, and students expect detailed, specific presentation of data and findings in words and in graphic form, such as diagrams and graphs. Members of the general public want to understand how concepts affect personal decisions they must make about issues such as medical care or nutritional choices. People working in government or business may have to make decisions about funding for research proposals. For more general audiences, you may not need to provide the same level of detail. For example, the public or businesspeople may not need species names to be written in Latin. In all cases, however, your readers expect you to be completely objective and to present information as clearly as possible.

D2-b Recognize the forms of writing in the biological sciences.

When you take courses in biology, you may be asked to write any of the following:

- laboratory notebooks
- research papers
- laboratory reports
- literature reviews
- research proposals
- poster presentations

Laboratory notebooks

If you are required to complete laboratory exercises, you will need to carefully record your experiments in a notebook. A laboratory notebook should be detailed and accurate so that anyone who wishes to repeat your experiment can do so. The laboratory notebook also provides crucial material for any report or article you may write later about your experiment. Researchers take notebooks seriously, never removing a page or erasing entries. That practice keeps them from misrepresenting results.

Your notebook will typically have the following components:

- table of contents
- date of each experiment
- title
- purpose (the objective of the experiment)
- materials (a list of equipment, specimens, and chemicals you used in the experiment)

- procedures (the method you planned to follow as well as any alterations you made to that procedure while conducting the experiment)
- results (the data gathered from the experiment)
- data analysis (calculations based on your data)
- discussion (your assessment of whether the experiment was successful, your interpretation of your results, your accounting for any surprising results, and your conclusions about what you learned from the experiment)
- acknowledgments (those who helped you with the experiment)

Research papers and laboratory reports

When instructors refer to *research papers*, they may have different assignments in mind. One assignment might ask you to present your synthesis of many sources of information about, for instance, a genetic syndrome to demonstrate your understanding of the characteristics of the disorder and other researchers' investigations of the causes of the syndrome.

Another assignment might require you to report on the results of an experiment you conducted and to interpret your results; this document is typically called a *laboratory report*. Unlike the laboratory notebook, a lab report may relate your interpretations to what others in the field have concluded from their own experiments. Biologists publish research papers and reports in journals after the papers have undergone rigorous and impartial review by other biologists, called a *peer review*, to make sure that the scientific process used by the researchers is sound.

Whether published in a journal or written for a college course, research papers and reports based on original experiments follow a standard format and include the following sections:

- abstract (a 100-to-125-word summary of your report)
- introduction (the context for your experiment, such as what has been published on the topic in the field, as well as the purpose of the experiment)
- materials and methods (details of how you conducted the experiment so that other researchers can repeat the experiment to try to reproduce your results; your description of the methodology you used so that readers can determine if your interpretations are supported by the data)
- results (a presentation of what you observed in the experiment)
- figures and tables

- discussion (your interpretation of the results as well as a comparison of your interpretation and that of other researchers in the field)
- references (a list of the sources cited in your paper)

Literature reviews

Literature reviews can have different objectives, such as comparing or contrasting approaches to a problem or examining the literature in the field to propose an alternative theory. Another purpose is to inform biologists about the latest advances in the field. In a review, you will consider the findings of a number of research papers and evaluate those papers' conclusions and perhaps suggest a direction for future research. A critical review analyzes the methods and interpretations of data from one or more journal articles. You may be asked to write a literature review as an introduction to a larger piece of writing, such as a report of a study you conducted. In that case, the review will survey previously published findings relevant to the question that your study investigates.

A literature review assignment is an opportunity to learn about an area in the field and to see what old or new questions may benefit from research.

While the format of reviews varies with their purpose, reviews typically have an abstract, an introduction, a discussion of the research being reviewed, a conclusion, and a references section.

Research proposals

In a research proposal, the biologist poses a significant question and a hypothesis (or hypotheses) and suggests one or more experiments to test the hypothesis. The project can have specific practical applications; for example, one Arctic biologist submitted to the United States Geological Survey a proposal for an ecological monitoring program at a national park. Research proposals that seek funding for an experiment must include detailed budgets.

Whether written by scholars requesting support from an agency or by students in a course, research proposals are evaluated for how well they justify their project with a carefully conceived experiment design.

Poster presentations

At professional gatherings such as annual conventions in the field, biologists have the opportunity to present their work in the form of a poster rather than as a formal talk. Conference attendees approach presenters in an exhibit area to talk about their research, which the posters concisely summarize. A poster features a brief introduction to the presenter's research project, a description of the method, information about the experiment's subjects, the experiment's results, and the presenter's conclusions. Poster presentations also feature graphs and tables since it is important to convey information to attendees quickly and concisely as they walk through the exhibit area. An effective poster presentation will encourage the audience to ask questions and carry on an informal conversation with the presenter.

Your instructor may ask you to create a poster presentation about an experiment you or other researchers have conducted both to help you understand complex concepts and to practice your communication skills.

NOTE: Some presenters use presentation software to create a slide show that they can click through for a small audience or project on a screen for a larger group. Presenters generally include the same kinds of information in slide presentations as they do in poster presentations.

D2-c Know the questions biologists ask.

Biologists, like other scientists, ask questions about the natural world. Their questions are either *why* questions or *how* questions, such as the following:

- Why don't newborns see well?
- Why does body size of species skew to the right on a distribution curve? That is, why are there so many small animals?
- How does cellular senescence prevent cancer?
- How do island plants self-pollinate?

As they attempt to answer such questions, biologists first offer a tentative explanation, or hypothesis, for something they have observed. They perform an experiment to test their hypothesis. If the results from the experiment match the original predictions, then they consider the hypothesis supported, but not proved, since biologists cannot account for all conditions. Other biologists will continue to formulate new hypotheses and offer new findings.

D2-d Understand the kinds of evidence biologists use.

Biologists use many kinds of evidence:

- data from site studies or site surveys
- observations of specimens with the aid of special equipment, such as a microscope

- observations and measurements made in experimental settings
- data taken from reports that other biologists have published

Data in biology, which are either quantitative (that which can be counted) or qualitative (that which can be described without numbers), can take various forms, depending on the nature of the site, the type of experiment, or the specialized field in which the research is performed. Following are some examples:

- For a study of the mating choices of female swordfish, biologists might record and analyze responses from females placed in tanks with males.
- In forensic biology, researchers might interpret the data they collect from tests on criminal suspects' DNA samples.
- Plant biologists might analyze the rates of survival of native tree seedlings affected by chemicals released by invasive plant species.

Because evidence can have more than one plausible interpretation, biologists offer alternative explanations for the results obtained in experiments. For example, the authors of one article suggested that differences in the type and availability of prey could account for why Atlantic blue marlin larvae grew faster in one body of water than in another, but they also recognized that other possible causes related to differences in spawning populations.

D2-e Become familiar with writing conventions in the biological sciences.

Biologists agree on several conventions when they write:

- Scientific writing often uses the passive voice to describe how a researcher has performed an experiment (*Blue marlin larvae were collected*). The passive voice can be useful for drawing attention to the action itself, not to who has performed the action. But biologists use the active voice whenever possible to convey information clearly and efficiently (*Researchers collected blue marlin larvae*). With the use of the active voice, the first-person pronouns *I* and *we* are acceptable, even preferred, if the passive voice creates awkward-sounding sentences and adds unnecessary words.
- Direct quotation of sources is rare; instead, biologists paraphrase to demonstrate their understanding of the source material and to convey information economically.

- Biologists use the past tense to describe the materials and methods and the results of their own experiments.
- Biologists use the present tense to describe the published findings of other studies.
- Biologists often include specific scientific names for species (*Canis latrans* for the coyote, for instance).

D2-f Use the CSE system for citing sources.

Biologists typically use the style recommended by the Council of Science Editors (CSE) to format their paper, to cite sources in the text of the paper, and to list the sources at the end. The CSE describes three citation systems in *Scientific Style and Format: The CSE Manual for Authors, Editors, and Publishers*, 7th ed. (Reston: CSE, 2006). In the *name-year* system, the author's last name and the date of publication are cited in the text. In the *citation-sequence* system, each source is assigned a number the first time it is used in the text, and the same number identifies the source each time it appears. In the *citation-name* system, each source is assigned a number in the order in which it appears in the alphabetical list at the end of the paper. That number is used each time the source is cited in the text.

With all three systems, biologists place bibliographic information for each source at the end of the paper in a section called References or Cited References.

D2-g Sample student paper: Laboratory report

Conducting an experiment gives you practice in collecting and interpreting data. Writing a laboratory report allows you to describe an experiment and its results. The following laboratory report was written for a botany course. The writers used the style guidelines of the Council of Science Editors (CSE) for formatting their paper and citing and listing sources in the citation-sequence system.

Distribution Pattern of Dandelion

(*Taraxacum officinale*)

on an Abandoned Golf Course

Title page consists
of a descriptive title
and the writers'
names in the center
of the page and the
course, instructor,
and date centered at
the bottom of the
page.

Marin Johnson

Laura Arnold

Lab 4

Botany 100A

Professor Ketchum

September 13, 2005

Marginal annotations indicate CSE-style formatting and effective writing.

Distribution Pattern of Dandelion 2

An abstract summarizes the report in about 100–125 words. You may or may not be required to include an abstract with a brief lab report.

ABSTRACT

This paper reports our study of the distribution pattern of the common dandelion (*Taraxacum officinale*) at an abandoned golf course in Hilton, NY, on 10 July 2005. An area of 6 ha was sampled with 111 randomly placed 1×1 m^2 quadrats. The dandelion count from each quadrat was used to test observed frequencies against expected frequencies based on a hypothesized random distribution. We concluded that the distribution of dandelions was not random. We next calculated the coefficient of dispersion to test whether the distribution was aggregated (clumped) or uniform. The calculated value of this coefficient was greater than 1.0, suggesting that the distribution was aggregated. Such aggregated distributions are the most commonly observed types in natural populations.

Introduction states the purpose of the experiment.

INTRODUCTION

Theoretically, plants of a particular species may be aggregated (clumped), random, or uniformly distributed in space [1]. The distribution type may be determined by many factors, such as availability of nutrients, competition, distance of seed dispersal, and mode of reproduction [2].

Citations are numbered in the order in which they appear in the text (citation-sequence system).

The purpose of this study was to determine if the distribution pattern of the common dandelion (*Taraxacum officinale*) on an abandoned golf course was aggregated, random, or uniform.

METHODS

The study site was an abandoned golf course in Hilton, NY. The vegetation was predominantly grasses, along with dandelions, broad-leaf plantain (*Plantago major*), and bird's-eye speedwell (*Veronica chamaedrys*). We sampled an area of approximately 6 ha on 10 July 2005, approximately two weeks after the golf course had been mowed.

The writers use scientific names for plant species.

Detailed description of researchers' methods.

To ensure random sampling, we threw a tennis ball high in the air over the study area. At the spot where the tennis ball came to rest, we placed one corner of a 1×1 m^2 metal frame (quadrat). We then counted the number of dandelion plants within this quadrat. We repeated this procedure for a total of 111 randomly placed quadrats.

We used a two-step procedure [2]. We first tested whether the distribution of dandelion was random or nonrandom. From the counts of the number of dandelions in our 111 quadrats, we used a log-likelihood ratio

Header contains a short title and the page number.

(G) test to examine the goodness of fit between our observed frequencies and those expected based on the Poisson series $e^{-\mu}$, $\mu e^{-\mu}$, $\mu^2/2!e^{-\mu}$, $\mu^3/3!e^{-\mu}$, . . . , where μ is the mean density of plants per quadrat. In carrying out this test, we grouped observed and expected frequencies so that no group had an expected frequency less than 1.0 [3]. We then determined whether the distribution was aggregated or uniform by calculating the coefficient of dispersion (ratio of the variance to the mean). A coefficient > 1 indicates an aggregated distribution whereas a coefficient < 1 indicates a more uniform distribution. Finally, we tested the significance of any departure of the ratio from a value of 1 by means of a t-test.

Specialized language of the field.

RESULTS

Table 1 shows the number of quadrats containing 0, 1, 2, . . . , 17 dandelion plants. More than two-thirds (67.6%) of the 111 quadrats contained no dandelion plants; almost 90% (89.2%) of the quadrats contained fewer than 3 dandelion plants. We observed a highly significant lack of fit between our observed frequencies and expected frequencies based on the Poisson distribution ($G = 78.4$, df = 3, $P < 0.001$). Thus, our data indicated that the distribution pattern of dandelion plants on the abandoned golf course was not random. The mean number of dandelion plants per quadrat was 1.05 (SD = 2.50), and the coefficient of dispersion was 5.95. A t-test showed that this value is significantly greater than 1.0 ($t = 36.7$, df = 110, $P < 0.001$), which strongly supports an aggregated distribution of the dandelion plants.

Headings organize the report into major sections.

DISCUSSION

An aggregated (clumped) distribution is the most commonly observed distribution type in natural populations [4]. Among plants, aggregated distributions often arise in species that have poorly dispersed seeds or vegetative reproduction [2]. In the dandelion, the seeds are contained in light, parachute-bearing fruits that are widely dispersed by the wind. This method of seed dispersal would tend to produce a random distribution. However, dandelion plants also reproduce vegetatively by producing new shoots from existing taproots, and what we considered as groups of closely spaced separate individuals probably represented

Writers interpret their results and compare them with results of other researchers.

Distribution Pattern of Dandelion 4

Table presents the data collected by the researchers in an accessible format.

Table 1 Frequency distribution of dandelion (*Taraxacum officinale*) plants in 1×1 m^2 quadrats positioned randomly over 6 ha on an abandoned golf course

Nr per quadrat	Observed frequency (f_i)	Expected frequency (f_i)[a]
0	75	38.68594
1	12	40.77707
2	12	21.49062
3	2	7.550757
4	3	1.989727
5	2	0.419456
6	0	0.073688
7	2	0.011096
8	0	0.001462
9	1	0.000171
10	0	1.8×10^{-5}
11	0	1.73×10^{-6}
12	0	1.52×10^{-7}
13	1	1.23×10^{-8}
14	0	9.27×10^{-10}
15	0	6.52×10^{-11}
16	0	4.29×10^{-12}
17	1	2.66×10^{-13}
Total 111		

[a] Expected frequencies were calculated from the successive terms of the Poisson distribution (see Methods).

shoots originating from the same plant. Thus, vegetative reproduction probably accounted for the observed aggregated distribution in this species.

REFERENCES

Sources are listed and numbered in the order in which they appear in the text.

1. Ketchum J. Lab manual for Botany 100; 2005.

2. Kershaw KA, Looney JHH. Quantitative and dynamic plant ecology. 3rd ed. London: Edward Arnold; 1985.

3. Zar JH. Biostatistical analysis. 5th ed. Englewood Cliffs (NJ): Prentice Hall; 2005.

4. Begon M, Harper JL, Townsend CR. Ecology: individuals, populations and communities. Oxford: Blackwell Science Limited; 1996.

D3 Writing in business

Communication, especially writing, is central to the business world. Because business writers generally aim to persuade or inform their audiences, they place a premium on clarity, brevity, and focus. When you write in business courses, your goal will be to communicate in a straightforward manner and with a clear purpose.

D3-a Determine your audience and their needs in business.

When you write in business, your audience may be varied. One type of audience might be executives, managers, and employees in various departments of a company—accounting, research and development, sales, and clerical support. Another audience might consist of stockholders, clients, and potential customers. Audiences within a business organization read to consider proposals for revising existing products, services, projects, policies, or procedures or for creating new ones. Business owners and executives may read to gather information to help them evaluate projects in progress, to assess sales, and to make decisions about changing product designs or adopting new marketing strategies. They read to understand whether a course of action would be feasible and profitable for the business. Managers, salespeople, and other employees read memos, e-mail, and other documents to help them conduct the daily transactions and activities of the organization, solve daily problems, and respond to customers. Customers read the publications of a business to learn about products and services and to determine whether it would benefit them to do business with a particular company.

For all of your readers, present empirical data such as sales figures or cost structures in easily readable formats such as tables, charts, and graphs. It might also be appropriate to give your readers opinions from questionnaires or surveys. A business owner deciding whether to adopt a marketing strategy might want to read feedback from potential customers, and a potential customer might want to read testimonials from satisfied customers. Respect your readers' time. Make sure your writing is clear, straightforward, focused, attractively presented on paper or a Web site, and as brief as possible. Because trust is essential in business transactions, maintain a respectful tone and project a credible image. Business writing should make personal connections and use inclusive language.

D3-b Recognize the forms of writing in business.

In business courses, you will be asked to create documents that mirror the ones written in professional settings. The different forms of business writing covered in this section are used for varied purposes, such as informing and persuading. Assignments in business courses may include the following:

- reports
- proposals
- executive summaries
- memos and correspondence
- presentations
- brochures, newsletters, and Web sites

Reports

Reports present factual information for a variety of purposes. If your company is considering the development of a new product, you may be asked to write a feasibility report that lays out the pros and cons. If you are asked to determine how your sales compare with those of a competitor, you will need to write an investigative report. A progress report updates a client or supervisor about the status of a project. A formal report details a major project and generally requires research.

Proposals

Proposals are written with the goal of convincing a specific audience to adopt a plan. A solicited proposal is directed to an audience that has requested it. An unsolicited proposal is written for an audience that has not indicated interest. An internal proposal is directed at others within an organization. An external proposal is directed at clients or potential clients. The length of a proposal will vary depending on your goals and your intended audience.

Executive summaries

An executive summary provides a concise summary of the key points in a longer document, such as a proposal or a report, with the goal of drawing the reader's attention to the longer document.

Memos and correspondence

In business, communication often takes place via letter, memo, or e-mail. Letters and e-mail are written to clients, customers, and colleagues. Memos convey information to others in the same organization for a variety of purposes. A memo might summarize the results of a study or project, describe policies or standards, put forth a plan, or assign tasks.

Presentations

Presentations are usually done orally, in front of a group, to instruct, persuade, or inform. Presenters often use presentation software or tools such as whiteboards to prepare and display visuals—graphs, tables, charts, transparencies, and so on.

Brochures, newsletters, and Web sites

Brochures generally convey information about products or services to clients, donors, or consumers. Newsletters generally provide information about an organization to clients, members, or subscribers. Web sites may either advertise products or provide information about an organization.

D3-c Know the questions business writers ask.

In business, your purpose and your understanding of your audience will determine the questions you ask.

- If you are writing a proposal to persuade a client to adopt a product, you will ask, "How will this product benefit my client?" and "What does my client need?"

- If you are asked to write a report informing your supervisor of your progress on a project, you will ask, "What does my supervisor need to know to authorize me to proceed?" You will also want to ask, "What does my supervisor already know?" and "How can I target this report to address my supervisor's specific concerns?"

- If you are applying for a job, you will ask, "What qualifications do I have for this job?"

D3-d Understand the kinds of evidence business writers use.

In business, your purpose for writing, your audience, and the questions you ask will determine the type of evidence you use. The following are some examples of the way you might use evidence in business writing:

- If you are writing a report or a proposal, you may need to gather data through interviews, direct observation, surveys, or questionnaires. The sources of data you choose will be determined by your audience. For example, if you are studying the patterns of customer traffic at a supermarket to recommend a new layout, you might go to the supermarket and observe customers or you might ask them to fill out surveys as they leave the store. If your audience is the store manager, you might focus on surveys at one store. If your audience is the owner of a large grocery chain, you would probably need to use data from several stores.

- If you are writing an investigative report in which you consider how to entice users to a health club, your evidence might include facts and statistics about the health benefits of exercise that you have drawn from published materials such as books, articles, and reports. You might also conduct research about the facilities of a competitor. In a long proposal or report, your evidence will probably come from a variety of sources rather than just one source.

- If you are applying for a job, your evidence will be your past experience and qualifications. For example, you might explain that you have worked in the industry for six years and held three management positions. You might also discuss how the skills you learned in those jobs will be transferable to the new position.

- If you are writing a brochure to promote a service, your evidence might be testimonials from satisfied users of the service. For example, a brochure advertising nanny services might quote a customer who says, "We found a full-time nanny who is both experienced and energetic—a perfect fit for our family."

D3-e Become familiar with writing conventions in business.

In business, writing should be straightforward and professional, but not too formal.

- Buzzwords (*value-added*, *win-win*, *no-brainer*) and clichés (*The early bird catches the worm*) should be used sparingly. This kind of vocabulary is imprecise and can sound phony or insincere.

- Use personal pronouns such as *you* and *I*. Where appropriate (in letters, e-mail, proposals), you can use the pronoun *you* to emphasize the interests of your readers. When you are addressing multiple readers, you might want to avoid using *you* unless it is clear that you are referring to all readers. When you are expressing your opinion, you should use the pronoun *I*. When you are speaking on behalf of your company, you should use the pronoun *we*.

- It is important to avoid language that could offend someone on the grounds of race, gender, sexual orientation, or disability. Use terms like *chair* or *chairperson* instead of *chairman* or *chairwoman*. Unless it is relevant to your point, avoid describing people by race or ethnicity. If you are describing someone with a disability, use phrases like *client with a disability* rather than *disabled client* to show that you recognize the disability as one trait rather than as a defining characteristic of the person. (Also see "appropriate language" in your handbook.)

- Business writing should always be concise. Avoid using words that are not essential to your point. Instead of writing *at this point in time*, just write *now*. Also avoid words that make a simple idea unnecessarily complicated. Using the passive voice often creates such complications. Instead of writing *This report was prepared to inform our customers*, write *We prepared this report to inform our customers*.

D3-f Use the APA or CMS (*Chicago*) system in business writing.

Business students typically use the style guidelines of the American Psychological Association (APA) or *The Chicago Manual of Style* (CMS) for formatting their paper, for citing sources in the text of their paper, and for listing sources at the end. The APA system is set forth in the *Publication Manual of the American Psychological Association*, 6th ed. (Washington, DC: APA, 2010). CMS style is found in *The Chicago Manual of Style*, 16th ed. (Chicago: University of Chicago Press, 2010). (For more details, see the documentation sections in your handbook.) In business courses, instructors will usually indicate which style they prefer.

D3-g Sample student papers: An investigative report and a proposal

Sample report

Different business situations require different types of reports. Formal reports are comprehensive discussions of a topic from multiple angles, while investigative reports often focus on a specific issue. If you are asked to write a report, you should always be sure that you understand the expectations of your audience.

The investigative report beginning on page D-21 was written for an introductory course in business writing. The student, Brian Spencer, was asked to research the problem of employee motivation at a small company. He used the style guidelines of the American Psychological Association (APA) to format the paper and to cite and list sources.

Sample proposal

Proposals are written to convince a specific audience to adopt a plan. If you are asked to write a proposal, you might start by identifying the purpose and the audience for the document.

The internal proposal beginning on page D-28 was written for a course in business writing. The student, Kelly Ratajczak, wrote her proposal in the form of a memorandum to the senior vice president of human resources at the medium-size company at which she was an intern. Her goal was to convince the vice president to adopt a wellness program for employees.

SAMPLE REPORT

Positively Affecting Employee Motivation

Prepared by Brian Spencer

Report Distributed March 9, 2006

Prepared for OAISYS

The title page of a business report is counted in the numbering, although a header and page number do not appear.

Title, writer's name, and date, centered on page; company name, centered at bottom.

Marginal annotations indicate business-style formatting and effective writing.

In a typical business report, the page header contains an abbreviated title and the page number.

Abstract

Corporate goals, such as sales quotas or increases in market share, do not always take into account employee motivation. Motivating employees is thus a challenge and an opportunity for firms that want to outperform their competitors. For a firm to achieve its goals, its employees must be motivated to perform effectively.

Empirical research conducted with employees of a subject firm, OAISYS, echoed theories published by leading authorities in journals, books, and online reports. These theories argue that monetary incentives are not the primary drivers for employee motivation. Clear expectations, communication of progress toward goals, accountability, and public appreciation are common primary drivers. A firm aiming to achieve superior performance should focus on these activities.

Abstract, on a separate page, provides a brief summary of the report.

While not strictly APA style, the formatting of the business report is consistent with the style typically used in businesses. Headings are flush with the left margin and boldface. Paragraphs are separated by an extra line of space, and the first line of each paragraph is not indented.

Employee Motivation 3

Introduction

All firms strive to maximize performance. Such performance is typically
defined by one or more tangible measurements such as total sales, earnings
per share, return on assets, and so on. The performance of a firm is created
and delivered by its employees. Employees, however, are not necessarily
motivated to do their part to maximize a firm's performance. Factors that
motivate employees can be much more complex than corporate goals. This
report will define the problem of employee motivation in one company and
examine potential solutions.

OAISYS is a small business based in Tempe, Arizona, that manufactures
business call recording products. Currently OAISYS employs 27 people. The
business has been notably successful, generating annual compound sales
growth of over 20% during the last three years. The company's management
and board of directors expect revenue growth to accelerate over the coming
three years to an annual compound rate of over 35%. This ambitious
corporate goal will require maximum productivity and effectiveness from all
employees, both current and prospective. OAISYS's management requested
an analysis of its current personnel structure focused on the alignment of
individual employee motivation with its corporate goal.

Background on Current Human Resources Program

OAISYS is currently structured departmentally by function. It has teams
for research and development, sales, marketing, operations, and
administration. Every employee has access to the same employment
benefits, consisting of medical insurance, a 401(k) plan, flexible spending
accounts, short- and long-term disability insurance, and the like.

Members of the sales team receive a yearly salary, quarterly commissions
tied to sales quotas, and quarterly bonuses tied to the performance of
specific tasks. These tasks can change quarterly to maintain alignment with
strategic initiatives.

All employees not in the sales department receive a yearly salary and profit
sharing at the end of the year. The formula for profit sharing is not

Introduction clearly
presents the problem
to be discussed and
sets forth the scope
of the report.

Heading announces
the purpose of each
section.

known by the employees, and specific information about profits is infrequently communicated. When profitability is discussed, it is only in general terms. Key employees, as determined by the management, are given stock option grants periodically. This process is informal and very confidential.

Disconnect Between Company and Employees

One common assumption is that a human resources program such as OAISYS's should be the platform for motivation. But monetary compensation is not the only driver of employee motivation (Dickson, 1973). In fact, studies have found that other factors are actually the primary drivers of employee motivation. Security, career advancement, the type of work, and pride in one's company are actually the highest-rated factors in employee satisfaction (Accel TEAM, 2005).

These conclusions drawn from the empirical research of others are supported by interviews conducted with current OAISYS employees. Justin Crandall, a current design engineer, stated that his primary motivation is the opportunity to work with leading-edge development tools to pursue results of the highest quality (personal communication, March 1, 2006). Crandall's strongest sense of frustration comes from a cluttered organizational structure because it restricts his ability to pursue innovative, high-quality results.

Todd Lindburg, the most senior design engineer on staff, had similar sentiments. His greatest motivator is the opportunity to create something lasting and important to the long-term success of the business (personal communication, March 2, 2006). Jack Wikselaar, vice president of sales, said he receives his strongest motivation from providing fulfilling job opportunities for others (personal communication, March 3, 2006).

These findings of what motivates employees tell only half the story. Other research (*Motivating*, 2006) suggests that businesses can actually demotivate employees through certain behaviors, such as the following:

Spencer presents evidence from research studies.

Spencer provides evidence from interviews with current employees.

Interviews are considered personal communication in APA style; they are cited in the text of the paper but not given in the reference list.

Employee Motivation 5

- company politics
- unclear expectations
- unnecessary rules and procedures
- unproductive meetings
- poor communication
- toleration of poor performance

Doug Ames, manager of operations for OAISYS, noted that some of these issues keep the company from outperforming expectations: "Communication is not timely or uniform, expectations are not clear and consistent, and some employees do not contribute significantly yet nothing is done" (personal communication, February 28, 2006).

Recommendations

It appears that a combination of steps can be used to unlock greater performance for OAISYS. Most important, steps can be taken to strengthen the corporate culture in key areas such as communication, accountability, and appreciation. Employee feedback indicates that these are areas of weakness or motivators that can be improved. This feedback is summarized in Figure 1.

A plan to use communication effectively to set expectations, share results in a timely fashion, and publicly offer appreciation to specific contributors will likely go a long way toward aligning individual motivation with corporate goals. Additionally, holding individuals accountable for results will bring parity to the workplace.

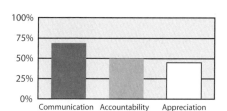

Figure 1. Areas of greatest need for improvements in motivation.

Employee Motivation 6

One technique that might be effective is basing compensation on specific responsibilities. Rather than tying compensation to corporate profit, tying it to individual performance will result in direct correlation between results and reward. Those who do what is necessary to achieve expected results will be rewarded. Those who miss the mark will be required to address the reasons behind their performance and either improve or take a different role. Professor of organizational behavior Jesper Sorenson (2002) has noted that "quantitative analyses have shown that firms with strong cultures outperform firms with weak cultures" (p. 70). Taking steps to strengthen the corporate culture is critical to the company's success.

Employee Motivation 7

References

Accel TEAM. (2005). *Employee motivation in the workplace*. Retrieved from
http://www.accel-team.com/motivation

Dickson, W. J. (1973). Hawthorne experiments. In C. Heyel (Ed.), *The
encyclopedia of management* (2nd ed., pp. 298-302). New York, NY:
Van Nostrand Reinhold.

Motivating employees without money. (2006). Retrieved from http://www
.employer-employee.com/howtomot.htm

Sorenson, J. B. (2002). The strength of corporate culture and the reliability
of firm performance. *Administrative Science Quarterly, 47*(1), 70-71.

Spencer provides a list of sources using APA style.

SAMPLE PROPOSAL

MEMORANDUM

Internal proposal is
structured in memo
format; subject is
identified in the
header.

To: Jay Crosson, Senior Vice President, Human Resources

From: Kelly Ratajczak, Intern, Purchasing Department

Subject: Proposal to Add a Wellness Program

Date: April 24, 2006

Ratajczak opens with
a clear, concise
statement of her
main point.

Health care costs are rising. In the long run, implementing a wellness program
in our corporate culture will decrease the company's health care costs.

Introductory section
provides supporting
background
information.

Research indicates that nearly 70% of health care costs are from common
illnesses related to high blood pressure, overweight, lack of exercise, high
cholesterol, stress, poor nutrition, and other preventable health issues
(Hall, 2006). Health care costs are a major expense for most businesses,
and they do not reflect costs due to the loss of productivity or
absenteeism. A wellness program would address most, if not all, of these
health care issues and related costs.

Headings clearly
define the sections
of the proposal.

Benefits of Healthier Employees

A wellness program would substantially reduce costs associated with
employee health care, and in addition our company would prosper through
many other benefits. Businesses that have wellness programs show a lower
cost in production, fewer sick days, and healthier employees ("Workplace
Health," 2006). Our healthier employees will help to cut not only our
production and absenteeism costs but also potential costs such as higher
turnover because of low employee morale.

While not strictly
APA style, the memo
format for a proposal
is consistent with the
style typically used
in businesses. A
header at the top of
each page contains
an abbreviated title
and an arabic page
number (the first
page is counted in
the numbering,
although a number
does not appear).
Headings are flush
with the left margin
and boldface.
Paragraphs are
separated by an
extra line of space,
and the first line of
each paragraph is
not indented.

Implementing the Program

Implementing a good wellness program means making small changes to the
work environment, starting with a series of information sessions. Simple
changes to our work environment should include healthier food selections
in vending machines and in the employee cafeteria. A smoke-free
environment, inside and outside the building, could be a new company
policy. An important step is to educate our employees through information
seminars and provide health care guides and pamphlets for work and home.
In addition, the human resources department could expand the current

Marginal annotations indicate business-style formatting and effective writing.

employee assistance program by developing online materials that help employees and their families to assess their individual health goals.

Each health program is different in its own way, and there are a number of programs that can be designed to meet the needs of our individual employees. Some programs that are becoming increasingly popular in the workplace are the following ("Workplace Health," 2006):

- health promotion programs
- subsidized health club membership
- return-to-work programs
- health-risk appraisals and screenings

Obstacles: Individual and Financial

The largest barrier in a wellness program is changing the habits and behaviors of our employees. Various incentives such as monetary bonuses, vacation days, merchandise rewards, recognition, and appreciation help to instill new habits and attitudes. Providing a healthy environment and including family in certain programs also help to encourage healthier choices and behaviors (Hall, 2006).

Ratajczak identifies and responds to potential concerns.

In the long run, the costs of incorporating a wellness program will be far less than rising costs associated with health care. An employee's sense of recognition, appreciation, or accomplishment is an incentive that has relatively low or no costs. The owner of Natural Ovens Bakery, Paul Sitt, has stated that his company gained financially after providing programs including free healthy lunches for employees (Springer, 2005). Sitt said he believes that higher morale and keeping valuable employees have helped his business tremendously.

It is important that our company be healthy in every way possible. Research shows that 41% of businesses already have some type of wellness program in progress and that 32% will incorporate programs within the next year ("Workplace Health," 2006). Our company should always be ahead of our competitors. I want to thank you for your time, and I look forward to discussing this proposal with you further next week.

The concluding paragraph summarizes the main point, provides support for being competitive, and indicates a willingness to discuss the proposal.

Ratajczak provides a list of the sources she used in her proposal. The reference list is formatted in APA style.

References

Hall, B. (2006). Good health pays off! Fundamentals of health promotion
    incentives. *Journal of Deferred Compensation 11*(2), 16-26. Retrieved
    from http://www.aspenpublishers.com/

Springer, D. (2005, October 28). Key to business success? *La Crosse*
    Tribune. Retrieved from http://lacrossetribune.com/

Workplace health and productivity programs lower absenteeism,
    costs. (2006). *Managing Benefit Plans 6*(2), 1-4. Retrieved
    from http://www.ioma.com/

D4 Writing in criminal justice and criminology

Criminal justice and criminology are part of the same broad field. Criminal justice refers to the application of policing practices and policies, and criminology is chiefly concerned with the theories that explain those practices and policies. The field of criminal justice and criminology draws from a diverse range of disciplines, including sociology, political science, public administration, psychology, history, and the law. Holding this multidisciplinary field together is its fundamental focus on justice. Whatever your specialization as a student—policing, law enforcement management, juvenile justice, corrections, law and the courts, or homeland security—you may be asked to write papers on topics such as policing practices and policies, the administration of justice, legal decision making, and the theories criminologists use to explain and analyze crime. Your instructors may also ask you to imagine different audiences and purposes for this writing to prepare you for the complexity of writing tasks and the readers you'll encounter in the workplaces you enter.

D4-a Determine your audience and their needs in criminal justice and criminology.

Criminal justice professionals write for diverse audiences, including peers and supervisors in an organization or members of other, related organizations, readers of professional and academic publications, and the general public. When you write in a criminal justice course, you might be asked to imagine that you are writing a memo to a new police chief explaining local crime trends and demographics. Or you might write a memo to the head of a law enforcement organization describing a policing practice or policy and making recommendations for change. You might write about the same practice or policy for an audience of public defenders or for public resources officers who must make sure that citizens understand what the policy means to them. You might be asked to write an article about the practice or policy for a magazine such as *Police Chief*, whose audience consists of many different kinds of practitioners in the field. Given these multiple and often overlapping audiences, you must analyze your readers' needs carefully.

D4-b **Recognize the forms of writing in criminal justice and criminology.**

When you take courses in criminal justice and criminology, you may be asked to write in a variety of forms for diverse audiences and purposes. These forms include the following:

- research papers
- analytical papers
- argument or position papers
- investigative and administrative reports
- policy memos
- case briefs and legal briefs
- case plans (or case notes)

Research papers

A research paper in a criminal justice course requires you to identify an issue or a topic and then to research what has been written about the topic or to explore the data that have been compiled about the topic (called *secondary sources*). You might also be expected to use *primary sources*—interviews or surveys that you conduct. In most cases, you'll be expected to find your own angle on the topic and to make an argument about it. You might also be required to apply a theory you've studied to your research findings. In a policing course, you might investigate whether police officers from different racial and ethnic backgrounds make decisions differently. To obtain information, you might conduct interviews and read published studies. In a social inequality and justice class, you might investigate whether the focus of racial profiling shifted from African Americans to Muslims after September 11, 2001, and what scholars are saying about possible trends. In a course on corrections, you might examine the punitive practice of solitary confinement and consider what this prison practice indicates about US law and society.

Analytical papers

Often you'll be given assignments that ask you to apply the theories you've studied to a situation, a legal case, or a personal account written by someone in the criminal justice system. For assignments like these, you will generally be expected to describe the theory and its main components and to use the theory to explain specific situations and people's behaviors and life choices. For example, you might

be asked to analyze how discretionary theory applies to street-level
policing or to critique a theory by comparing it with other theories
that attempt to explain the same behaviors and choices. Sometimes
analytical papers conclude with program or policy recommendations
based on the usefulness or persuasiveness of the theory.

Argument or position papers

In argument or position papers, you are expected to present both sides
of an issue in a balanced way and then to take a position. Your position
will be based on your analysis of the course readings and lectures or
on research you've conducted, not on your personal opinion. You might
also be asked to compare or contrast relevant theories and cases to
support your position. For example, an assignment might ask you to
argue for more or less discretionary power for street-level policing,
using as evidence cases in which that power has been used or abused.
Or, after investigating trends in racial profiling, you might take a position supporting or opposing changes in the current policies. Or you
might argue that the practice of long-term solitary confinement is or is
not justified as a crime control approach in US penal policy.

Investigative and administrative reports

Law enforcement professionals and criminologists write both investigative and administrative reports. Some common investigative reports
are crime and arrest reports, incident and accident reports, and pre-
sentencing reports. A typical crime or arrest report includes a clear
timeline of events, for both the crime and the investigation, such as
when the defendant was taken into custody, read his or her Miranda
rights, and interviewed. The report should also include other details
about the criminal investigation—for example, where the interview
with the defendant took place, who else was present, and whether any
other witnesses were interviewed. Administrative reports typically
include a description of a problem, supported by research and statistical data, and recommendations based on an analysis of the data. A
consultant's administrative report to a new police chief, for example,
may include a briefing about the demographics and crime problems in
the local area, an analysis of official crime statistics using the FBI's
Uniform Crime Reports, a summary of the findings, and recommendations based on the findings.

Both investigative and administrative reports may be formatted
as memos and written to specific audiences who need the information to make decisions, formulate policy, and implement recommendations. In all cases, accuracy, completeness, and objectivity are key
to an effective report.

Policy memos

Policy memos are written for many purposes—to inform, to explain, to document, to persuade, or to make a request. The format and style will vary from organization to organization, so you must be aware of the audience's expectations and the conventions set by the organization you're writing for. Typically, the purpose of a policy memo is to help the audience understand the issue and interpret the policy to make practical judgments. You might be asked to write a policy memo to the head of a criminal justice organization, such as the Transportation Security Administration, about the effects of racial profiling on a particular group. Your memo might include a description of the policies being used to address the problem; an argument, based on research, for changing the policies; and recommendations for policies or programs that would benefit the group about which you're concerned.

Case briefs and legal briefs

A brief is a document presented to interested members of a court of law. Briefs are addressed to a specific audience and typically include a short description of a legal case, highlighting key issues, relevant facts, and, if applicable, a history of related court decisions; an analysis and interpretation of how the case applies to a particular organization; and the legal principles and jurisdictional issues related to the desired outcome. For a case brief assignment, you might be asked to write to a public defender or a future judge on how to interpret issues involved in a specific case. A legal brief assignment might ask you to analyze documents submitted for a moot court exercise and to argue for one side.

Your instructor may ask you to follow the IRAC model when you write case and legal briefs. IRAC is an organizational approach used in legal writing as a method for problem solving and structuring an analysis. The acronym IRAC stands for the following steps:

Issue: State the legal issue of relevance.

Rules: List all the statutes and case law relevant to your brief.

Analysis or Application: Provide arguments in favor of and against the decision in this case.

Conclusion: Provide an answer to the legal issue raised.

Another organizational approach is based on the acronym PEAR:

Position: State a position.

Explanation: Explain the position.

Alternatives: Examine the alternative positions.

Response: Respond to potential objections.

NOTE: The explanations of the IRAC and PEAR models are adapted from the *Criminology, Law, and Society Writing Guide* from George Mason University at http://classweb.gmu.edu/WAC/adjguide/legal_briefs/case_briefs.html.

Case plans (or case notes)

Case plans, or case notes, may be written as memos or as part of pre-sentencing and postsentencing reports. They might be addressed to courtroom work groups, such as public defenders, prosecutors, judges, and probation officers. Case notes may be addressed to social workers and treatment providers in problem-solving courts such as drug and mental health courts. As the number of work groups expands, audience analysis becomes more complicated because each group may have different goals for its clients and constituencies. For example, a social worker might be interested in resources and treatment; lawyers, in justice; and judges, in the legal aspects of the case. Given the complexity of this writing task, there is no template to guide you. You will typically learn on the job or from models your instructor provides. In general, case notes and plans must be straightforward, clear, and well organized, with the goals and purpose carefully laid out in the introduction along with a preview of the main topics that you will cover. Be sure to include subheadings so that the various audiences can skim through the notes to identify information related to their concerns.

D4-c Know the questions criminal justice professionals and criminologists ask.

Generally, the questions that criminal justice professionals and criminologists ask can be divided into two broad areas of inquiry, one focused on legal systems, the other focused on justice organizations. Within these two broad areas are big-issue questions about crime, law enforcement, society, ethics, and social justice:

- What is deviance, and what is crime?
- What are the causes of crime?
- What is the difference between the law on the books and the law in action?
- What is effective policing?
- What are the theories and laws related to discretionary decision making for practitioners in the field?
- What policing, corrections, and court system policies and practices work to reduce crime and its social effects?

While most of your courses will take up these broad questions in one way or another, each course will have its own focusing questions. A course on policing in the United States, for example, will focus on the role of police in protecting the public against crime and disorder, influences on the decisions police make, the moral and ethical issues they confront, what good policing looks like, and the trends, innovations, and reforms that affect the policing profession. In a corrections course, the focus will be on postsentencing and postrelease issues, with questions about jail and prison management, probation and parole, and compliance with supervision and treatment follow-up requirements.

D4-d Understand the kinds of evidence criminal justice professionals and criminologists use.

Criminal justice professionals and criminologists use many different kinds of evidence—quantitative, qualitative, historical, and legal—to answer the questions they pose. Most practitioners rely on methods derived from the social sciences to gather evidence: interviews, direct observation, surveys, narrative analysis, natural setting experiments, and analysis of demographic, statistical, legal, geographic, and historical data. Criminologists also use theory-based evidence or the history of a theory or law enforcement policy.

As a student, you will probably be required to use both primary and secondary sources as evidence and to gather and analyze both quantitative and qualitative data. Quantitative data may include crime statistics, incarceration rates, racial profiling data from police stops, ticketing rates, and data on crime statistics linked to geographic areas. Qualitative data may include your own observations, others' responses to interviews and surveys, and the stories people tell about their encounters with crime and the criminal justice system.

Your instructors will also expect you to consult relevant secondary sources, including articles in scholarly and popular periodicals (such as *Police Chief*), news media, government and legal documents, statistical reports, and organizational Web sites, reports, and studies.

D4-e Become familiar with writing conventions in criminal justice and criminology.

Scholars and practitioners in the criminal justice field value independent thought; the ability to gather, synthesize, and analyze evidence from diverse sources; and the ability to interpret theory and to apply theory to practice and practice to theory. Beyond these broad goals, practitioners agree that writing in the field must be clear, concise, accurate, objective, and well organized, with a clear statement of the writer's purpose and main points. Writers must convey knowledge of the topic in a voice, tone, and format appropriate to the purpose and audience. They must present facts and evidence in an objective, balanced way to allow readers to draw their own conclusions.

To be objective, writers must strive for factual description. For example, in a crime report they should note the date, time, and location of a crime or suspected criminal behavior; they should also describe people and their actions as factually as possible, including identifying characteristics such as gender, race or ethnicity, age, height, weight, and distinctive features like facial hair, tattoos, scars, or physical mannerisms. Subjective descriptions such as "the perpetrator looked suspicious" are meaningless and unfair if not backed up with factual details. It is also important to avoid language that could be construed as offensive or that reveals biases toward gender, race, ethnicity, disabilities, and socioeconomic class.

In the criminal justice field, accuracy is crucial, whether in an arrest report, a briefing memo, a case plan, a researched report, or the application of a theory to an issue, practice, or policy. Errors and inaccuracies can cause readers to misinterpret a report, disregard a memo, or throw a case out of court.

First-person pronouns are rarely used in research papers, reports, policy memos, briefings, or analytical papers, in part because writers must present their views objectively, logically, and factually. While the writer of a memo or briefing report may use *I* on occasion, the content of the memo or report itself and the recommendations being made must be based on the writer's analysis of the evidence, not on personal opinions or biases. The diverse audiences for these documents also expect clear, concise writing, so writers typically use active voice and paraphrases rather than extensive quotations from their research. In some circumstances, however, it is important to include direct quotations as this information might be critical to an accurate interpretation of the problem, issue, or policy.

D4-f Use the APA or CMS (*Chicago*) system in writing in criminal justice and criminology.

While professionals in the field generally use the documentation style prescribed by the organization or academic journal for which they are writing, instructors typically ask students to use the style guidelines of the American Psychological Association (APA) or the name-year system of *The Chicago Manual of Style* (CMS) to format their paper, to document sources in the text of their paper, and to list sources at the end. Both systems call for in-text, parenthetical citations rather than footnotes or endnotes. The APA system is set forth in the *Publication Manual of the American Psychological Association*, 6th ed. (Washington, DC: APA, 2010). CMS style is found in *The Chicago Manual of Style*, 16th ed. (Chicago: University of Chicago Press, 2010). (For more details, see the documentation sections in your handbook.)

Sometimes students are asked to use *Bluebook* style (or, as it's sometimes called, modified Bluebooking) when they cite sources in case briefs and legal briefs. *Bluebook* format is used by courts, attorneys, and law schools; however, most instructors do not require students to learn this specialized style.

D4-g Sample student paper: Administrative report

Administrative reports are written for specific audiences, typically supervisors, to provide information about an issue or a problem of concern to an organization. When you are asked to write a report, you will be expected to identify the issue or problem, find and analyze relevant statistics and other research, and make recommendations for future actions.

The following administrative report was written for an introductory course on crime and crime policy. Students were asked to imagine that they had been hired as a consultant by the new police chief in their hometown. They were asked to brief the chief about crime in the area, to explain how crime statistics for their town compare with the national average using the FBI's Uniform Crime Reports, and to interpret the statistics so that the chief could decide how best to use the department's resources. The student writer, Chris Thompson, analyzed crime statistics for his hometown of Leesburg, Virginia. He used APA guidelines to format his paper and to cite and list his sources.

Running head: CRIME IN LEESBURG, VIRGINIA   1

The header consists of a shortened title in all capital letters at the left margin and the page number at the right margin; on the title page only, the shortened title is preceded by the words "Running head" and a colon.

Crime in Leesburg, Virginia

Chris Thompson

George Mason University

Full title, writer's name, and school, halfway down the page.

Author Note

This paper was prepared for Administration of Justice 305: Crime Policy, taught by Professor Devon Johnson.

An author's note lists specific information about the course or department and can provide acknowledgments and contact information.

Marginal annotations indicate APA-style formatting and effective writing.

Full title, repeated.

Crime in Leesburg, Virginia

Introduction establishes the purpose of the report and acknowledges the audience.

This report reviews crime statistics in Leesburg, Virginia, to familiarize the new police chief with the town and offer some suggestions about where to focus law enforcement resources. It analyzes local and national statistics from the FBI's Uniform Crime Reports (UCR) for the United States and for Leesburg and offers a basic assessment of the town's needs to provide a useful snapshot for the chief of police.

Description of Leesburg, Virginia

Centered headings define the major sections of the report.

Leesburg, Virginia, is a suburb of Washington, DC, 40 miles to the northwest. In 2008, its population was 39,899 (U.S. Department of Justice, 2009, Table 8). Like many northern Virginia and southern Maryland communities, it serves as a suburban bedroom community to those employed in the nation's capital. The town has grown significantly in the last three decades.

Thompson provides demographic information relevant to the crime statistics he will analyze.

Leesburg's population is predominantly middle and upper middle class, with a median household income 75% higher than the national average (Town of Leesburg, Virginia, 2009a). Leesburg is populated by young (median age 32.3), well educated (about 50% with a bachelor's degree, about 17% with an advanced degree) citizens; half are white-collar professionals (Town of Leesburg, Virginia, 2009a).

In-text citation from a Web site is in APA style.

The Leesburg Police Department has 77 sworn officers, operates 24 hours a day, and uses numerous special teams and modern law enforcement techniques. The department has divided the city into three patrol areas to address the specific needs of each zone (Town of Leesburg, Virginia, 2009b).

Nature and Extent of Crime in Leesburg, Virginia

Thompson points to the data tables, explaining their purpose and sources.

Tables 1 and 2 show the FBI's UCR statistics for 2008. Table 1 contains statistics for Leesburg and the United States, and Table 2 presents the crime rate in Leesburg as a percentage of the national average. A discussion of the accuracy of the UCR is on page 5.

Crime Rates in Leesburg Compared With the National Average

Thompson uses a major section of the report to analyze details from the tables.

The following list of index crimes compares their rates in Leesburg, Virginia (first value), with the national average (second value). In general, the crime rate in Leesburg is lower than it is across the country. This may be due in part to the demographics of the town's residents and the commuter-oriented suburban nature of the community.

CRIME IN LEESBURG, VIRGINIA   3

Table 1

Crime Rates, by Crime, in Leesburg, Virginia, and in the United States,
2008

	Leesburg		United States	
Offense type	No. reported offenses	Rate per 100,000 inhabitants	No. reported offenses	Rate per 100,000 inhabitants
Violent crime				
Forcible rape	7	17.5	89,000	29.3
Murder and nonnegligent manslaughter	1	2.5	16,272	5.4
Robbery	22	55.1	441,855	145.3
Aggravated assault	29	72.7	834,885	274.6
Total violent crime	59	147.8	1,382,012	454.5
Property crime				
Larceny theft	715	1,792	6,588,873	2,167
Burglary	62	155.4	2,222,196	730.8
Vehicle theft	25	62.7	956,846	314.7
Total property crime	802	2,010	9,767,915	3,212.5

Note. The data for Leesburg, Virginia, are from U.S. Department of
Justice (2009), Table 8. The data for the United States are from U.S.
Department of Justice (2009), Table 1.

Larceny Theft: 1,792 vs. 2,167 per 100,000

Larceny theft is one of the few index crimes found close to the same
level in Leesburg as in the entire nation and thus represents an area of
interest for the Leesburg police.

Forcible Rape: 17.5 vs. 29.3 per 100,000

The incidence of forcible rape is slightly more than half the national
average. Rape crimes may be an area of concern in Leesburg.

Murder and Nonnegligent Manslaughter: 2.5 vs. 5.4 per 100,000

The most serious crimes, those involving the loss of a human life, are
approximately half as prevalent in Leesburg as in the United States as a
whole. Murder is typically not a crime that can be countered through patrol.

Robbery: 55.1 vs. 145.3 per 100,000

Robbery (a direct, personal theft from an individual) in Leesburg
is approximately one-third the national average. Leesburg is not prone

The data tables are presented in APA style. The columns are clearly labeled, and the data categories reinforce the writer's purpose.

Thompson organizes his discussion of the crimes in Leesburg by most to least concerning.

Subheadings are flush left and boldface.

CRIME IN LEESBURG, VIRGINIA   4

Table 2

Crime Rates in Leesburg, Virginia, Compared With the National Average, 2008

Offense type	Crime rate in Leesburg per 100,000 inhabitants	Crime rate in the United States per 100,000 inhabitants	Crime rate in Leesburg compared with national average (%)
Violent crime			
Forcible rape	17.5	29.3	59.7
Murder and nonnegligent manslaughter	2.5	5.4	46.2
Robbery	55.1	145.3	37.9
Aggravated assault	72.7	274.6	26.4
Total violent crime	147.8	454.5	32.5
Property crime			
Larceny theft	1,792	2,167	82.6
Burglary	155.4	730.8	21.2
Vehicle theft	62.7	314.7	19.9
Total property crime	2,010	3,212.5	62.5

Note. The data for Leesburg, Virginia, are from U.S. Department of Justice (2009), Table 8. The data for the United States are from U.S. Department of Justice (2009), Table 1.

to the frequency of robberies found in urban areas, perhaps because most robberies are committed by residents of the same community, and the community of Leesburg is fairly homogeneous in terms of income levels.

Aggravated Assault: 72.7 vs. 274.6 per 100,000

The rate of felony assaults (attempts to commit or acts resulting in serious bodily harm) in Leesburg is roughly one-quarter that in the nation as a whole.

Burglary: 155.4 vs. 730.8 per 100,000

The incidence of burglary (breaking into the home of another person with the intent to commit a felony) in Leesburg is one-fifth the national average. The suburban nature of Leesburg may contribute to this low level.

Vehicle Theft: 62.7 vs. 314.7 per 100,000

Motor vehicle theft is uncommon in Leesburg, about one-fifth as likely as in the nation as a whole.

Areas of Interest for a New Police Chief

Overall, forcible rape and larceny theft are the two crimes of most interest to the Leesburg police because their frequency is closer to the national average than the frequency of other crimes. While overall crime is low in Leesburg, these two crimes stand out based solely on the FBI UCR statistics. The police may want to pay particular attention to these crimes for reasons not apparent in the UCR.

Forcible rape is typically an underreported crime because of victim-related factors such as shame and distrust of the system. This crime is of particular concern because even the UCR statistics may not reflect an accurate crime rate (Mosher, Miethe, & Phillips, 2002). The actual instances of rape may be significantly higher than those reported in the UCR. Policy implications may include an increased community policing focus on rape prevention as well as targeted police patrolling of areas where reported rapes occur.

The desire to file an insurance claim for larceny theft (which often requires a police report) may cause more citizens to come forward when they are victims of this particular crime. For this reason, the actual instances of larceny theft are likely closer to those captured in the UCR. Increased patrolling of residential neighborhoods during work hours may reduce burglary rates because most burglaries occur during the day when the occupants are at work.

Accuracy of UCR Statistics

The FBI's UCR, while useful in showing crime trends, is not without its faults. The UCR contains only crimes reported to or observed by law enforcement officers; therefore, it does not provide a complete portrait of crime. The National Crime Victimization Survey (NCVS) revealed that, in many cases, roughly half of the total crimes committed in the United States go unreported (Mosher et al., 2002). The reasons vary but include distrust or lack of faith in the police and the judicial system, shame about or apathy toward the crime, fear of reprisals, inability to recognize the perpetrator, and victim participation in illegal activities at the time of

Thompson interprets the crime statistics and makes recommendations for allocating department resources.

Thompson discusses issues related to the reporting of crime and the accuracy of the UCR. To analyze the strengths and weaknesses of the UCR, he draws on secondary sources.

victimization (Mosher et al., 2002). The new police chief should keep these limitations in mind when evaluating UCR statistics.

In addition, classifying crimes is often subjective. Mosher et al. (2002) pointed out that "political manipulation and fabrication of these data by police departments" can easily distort statistics related to an individual incident or a whole reporting agency (p. 84). Some of these distortions are a product of police officer discretion stemming from the "legal seriousness of the crime," "the complainant's preferences," any relationship between the police officer and the offender, the level of respect shown by the complainant, and the financial or social status of the complainant (p. 85).

Conclusion

The town of Leesburg, Virginia, is, in general, a safe place to live. Overall, it experiences a rate of crime considerably lower than the national average. The incidence of property crime is 62.5% of the national average, and the incidence of violent crime is 32.5% of the national average. Leesburg does, however, have two potential problem areas: forcible rape and larceny theft.

This report's initial examination of the data from the UCR is of limited value because of the UCR's lack of depth and breadth in exploring local crime. To obtain a better picture of crime in Leesburg, the new police chief should request a report that compares local, regional, and national crime statistics over several years using the FBI's UCR combined with NCVS data to develop an accurate picture of overall crime. Carefully weighing that information and evaluating it to reveal the big picture are both a means and an end in the law enforcement world: They allow policymakers to make decisions that may reduce the crime rate.

In APA style for a work with three to five authors, all authors are given the first time the source is cited; in subsequent citations, the first author is followed by "et al."

Thompson summarizes the findings in the report and provides a recommendation. He ends by explaining the importance of crime data analysis for policymaking and assessment.

CRIME IN LEESBURG, VIRGINIA   7

                              References

U.S. Department of Justice, Federal Bureau of Investigation. (2009). *Crime
        in the United States 2008*. Retrieved from http://www2.fbi.gov/ucr
        /cius2008/index.html

Mosher, C. J., Miethe, T. D., & Phillips, D. M. (2002). *The mismeasure of
        crime*. Thousand Oaks, CA: Sage.

Town of Leesburg, Virginia. (2009a). *Demographics*. Retrieved from http://
        www.leesburgva.gov/index.aspx?page=210

Town of Leesburg, Virginia. (2009b). *Field operations division*. Retrieved
        from http://www.leesburgva.gov/index.aspx?page=955

List of references is
in APA style.

List of references
begins on a new
page. The first line
of each entry is at
the left margin;
subsequent lines
indent ½".

D5 Writing in education

The field of education draws on the knowledge and the methods of a variety of disciplines. As you study to become a teacher, you will take courses that focus on such diverse topics as the history of education, the psychology of teaching and learning, the development of curriculum, and instructional methods. You will also learn how to navigate classrooms and schools through both course work and field placements. Depending on what you plan to teach, you may also take courses in a specific content area (such as history or mathematics) or courses that focus on children with special needs. The writing you do in education courses will be designed to help you become a successful teacher.

D5-a Determine your audience and their needs in education.

Audiences in the field of education may be school administrators, teachers, students, parents, or policymakers. Administrators read documents to evaluate faculty and assess programs, to revise or develop new programs and curricula, to create policy, to solve problems, to resolve student issues, and to communicate with parents. Teachers read scholarship in their fields to learn about new theoretical findings and methods. Because assessment is a major topic in academic institutions, teachers read reports on student and program assessment as well as informational documents that help them participate in making school policy for testing and placement. Students and parents read publications from their schools and school districts to learn about student performance and school policy. Policymakers such as school board members and state legislators expect information, assessment reports, and proposals about schools, curricula, and programs to be presented with numerical data in the form of graphs and tables.

When you write in education courses, be sure to give your readers empirical data, such as test scores, presented in an easily understandable format. You may need to provide direct observations of student performance as well. Always maintain student confidentiality. Because student groups are so diverse and because positive community relations are essential to every school, be sensitive to student backgrounds and respectful toward students and parents.

D5-b Recognize the forms of writing in education.

Although there are many paths you can take as you train to become
a teacher, you will encounter similar writing assignments in different
courses. These may include the following:

- reflective essays, journals, and field notes
- curriculum designs and lesson plans
- reviews of instructional materials
- case studies
- research papers
- self-evaluations
- portfolios

Reflective essays, journals, and field notes

Much of the writing you do in education courses will encourage you to
reflect on your own attitudes, beliefs, and experiences and how they
inform your thoughts about teaching and learning. In an introductory
course, for example, you may be asked to write an essay in which you
discuss your own education in the context of a theory that you are
studying. As a field observer or student teacher, you may be asked to
keep a journal or notes in which you reflect on your interaction with
students, teacher-student interactions, student-student interactions,
diversity issues, and student progress. These reflections might then
serve as the basis for an essay in which you connect your experiences
to course content.

Curriculum designs and lesson plans

In some courses, especially those focused on teaching methods, you
will be asked to design individual lessons or units in a particular content area. In an early childhood education course, for example, you
might be asked to read one or more children's books and write a plan
for a class activity that is related to the reading. In a science methods
course, you might be asked to design a unit about plant biology. In a
methods course for special education, you might be asked to design an
individualized education plan for a specific student. For any of these
courses, you might also be asked to integrate technology into your
curriculum design.

Reviews of instructional materials

In a review of materials, you assess the value of a set of instructional materials for classroom use. For example, you might be asked to look at several textbooks or software applications and explain which would be most useful in a particular classroom setting.

Case studies

Some education courses require students to conduct and write case studies. Case studies may involve observation and analysis of an individual student, a teacher, or classroom interactions. The goal of a case study may be to determine how the process of teaching or learning takes place or how an event can illuminate something about learning or classroom dynamics.

Research papers

In some education courses, you might be assigned papers that focus on broader educational issues or problems and that require you to conduct research and then formulate your own ideas about the topic. In a course about the history of education, you might be asked to research the evolution of literacy in the United States. In a developmental psychology course, you might be asked to research how students learn mathematics.

Self-evaluations

As a teacher candidate, you will be asked to evaluate your own teaching and learning. The format of the self-evaluation will vary depending on whether you are evaluating yourself as a learner or as a teacher. Sample questions of self-evaluation as a teacher may include the following:

- What were the strengths and weaknesses of your lesson or unit plan?
- How did your lesson further student learning?
- What have you learned about yourself and your students from teaching this class?
- How can you improve your teaching?

Portfolios

Most teacher education programs require you to assemble a teaching portfolio before you graduate. The purpose of the portfolio is to provide information about your teaching experience and your teaching philosophy. The contents of portfolios vary, but common documents include a statement of teaching philosophy, a statement of professional goals, a résumé, evaluations, and sample course materials. Education departments at some institutions will require you to assemble an electronic portfolio as well as a print version.

D5-c Know the questions educators ask.

Educators ask questions that are practical, theoretical, and self-reflective. Practical questions tend to focus on classroom and curriculum issues such as student progress and implementation of new approaches. Theoretical questions focus on how students should be educated and on the intellectual, political, and social contexts of learning. Self-reflective questions allow for discussion of the teacher's own role in the educational process. Any of the following questions could form the basis for a paper in an education course:

- How does this school's language arts curriculum prepare students to be information-literate?
- What are the effects of the use of standardized tests in economically disadvantaged districts in comparison with more affluent districts?
- How do my perceptions of my own education influence the way I approach teaching?

D5-d Understand the kinds of evidence educators use.

Educators and education students rely on evidence that is both quantitative (statistics, survey results, test scores) and qualitative (case studies, observation, personal experience). The following are some examples of evidence used in different situations:

- If you are writing a research paper that compares different approaches to social studies education, you might rely on quantitative evidence such as the results of standardized tests from different school districts.
- For a paper on child development, you might use a combination of personal observation and evidence from published case studies.
- If you are keeping a journal of your student teaching experiences, your evidence would come from your experiences in the classroom and from the changes in your attitudes over time.
- If you are creating a lesson plan, you will focus on your teaching objectives and explain how your plan will achieve those objectives.

D5-e Become familiar with writing conventions in education.

Educators agree on several conventions when they write:

- The personal pronoun *I* is commonly used in reflective writing. It is sometimes used to communicate observations and recommendations.

- Research papers and case studies are generally written in the third person (*he, she, it, they*) and in a formal, objective tone.

- Educators have a specialized vocabulary that includes terms such as *pedagogy* (teaching principles and methods), *practice* (actual teaching), *curriculum* (the written lesson plans followed by a class or school), *assessment* (the determination of whether students or teachers are successful), *achievement tests* (tests that measure what students have learned), and *NCLB* (the No Child Left Behind Act). You will likely use such terms in your writing.

Because the field of education draws on various disciplines, including psychology, history, and sociology, it is important to be aware of writing conventions in those disciplines as well. (See D7 and D10.)

D5-f Use the APA or CMS (*Chicago*) system in writing in education.

Writers in education typically use the style guidelines of the American Psychological Association (APA) or *The Chicago Manual of Style* (CMS) for formatting their paper, for citing sources in the text of their paper, and for listing sources at the end. The APA system is set forth in the *Publication Manual of the American Psychological Association*, 6th ed. (Washington, DC: APA, 2010). CMS style is found in *The Chicago Manual of Style*, 16th ed. (Chicago: University of Chicago Press, 2010). (For more details, see the documentation sections in your handbook.) In education courses, instructors will usually indicate which style they prefer.

D5-g Sample student paper: Reflective essay

In some education courses, you may be asked to write reflective essays in which you describe and analyze your own attitudes, beliefs, and experiences. Some reflective essays focus solely on personal observations while others integrate ideas from other sources as well.

The following reflective essay was written for a service learning course in which students explored issues of diversity, power, and opportunity in school settings. The writer, Onnalee Gibson, used a variety of professional sources to inform her own ideas about her experiences working with an eleventh-grade student. She formatted her paper and cited and listed her sources following the guidelines of the American Psychological Association (APA).

The header consists of a shortened title in all capital letters at the left margin and the page number at the right margin; on the title page only, the shortened title is preceded by the words "Running head" and a colon.

Running head: SERVICE LEARNING: ERIC   1

Full title, writer's name, and school halfway down the page.

A Reflection on Service Learning:

Working with Eric

Onnalee L. Gibson

Michigan State University

An author's note lists specific information about the course or department and can provide acknowledgments and contact information.

Author Note

This paper was prepared for Teacher Education 250, taught by Professor Carter. The author wishes to thank the guidance staff of Waverly High School for advice and assistance.

Marginal annotations indicate APA-style formatting and effective writing.

A Reflection on Service Learning:

Working with Eric

The first time I saw the beautiful yet simple architecture of Waverly High School, I was enchanted. I remember driving by while exploring my new surroundings as a transfer student to Michigan State University and marveling at the long front wall of reflective windows, the shapely bushes, and the general cleanliness of the school grounds. When I was assigned to do a service learning project in a local school district, I hoped for the opportunity to find out what it would be like to work at a school like Waverly—a school where the attention to its students' needs was evident from the outside in.

> Reflective essays may include descriptive passages.

Waverly High School, which currently enrolls about 1,100 students in grades 9 through 12 and has a teaching staff of 63, is extremely diverse in several ways. Economically, students range from poverty level to affluent. Numerous ethnic and racial groups are represented. And in terms of achievement, the student body boasts an assortment of talents and abilities.

> Background information about the school sets the scene for Gibson's personal experiences.

The school provides a curriculum that strives to meet the needs of each student and uses a unique grade reporting system that itemizes each aspect of a student's grade. The system allows both teachers and parents to see where academic achievement and academic problems surface. Unlike most schools, which evaluate students on subjects in one number or letter grade, Waverly has a report card that lists individual grades for tests, homework, exams, papers, projects, participation, community service, and attendance. Thus, if a student is doing every homework assignment and is still failing tests, this breakdown of the grades may effectively highlight how the student can be helped.

It was this unique way of evaluating students that led to my first meeting with Eric Johnson, an 11th grader to whom I was assigned as a tutor. Eric is an African American male who grew up in a nuclear middle-class family in a Lansing suburb. Teachers noticed over time that Eric's grades were dropping, yet his attendance, participation, and motivation were above average. Surprisingly, Eric himself was the one who asked for a tutor to help him raise his grades. What initially struck me about Eric was the level of responsibility he seemed to take for his own academic

> Transition leads from background information about the school to Gibson's personal experiences.

SERVICE LEARNING: ERIC   3

Journal entries are considered personal communication and are cited in the text but not included in the reference list.

achievement. At the time I wrote in my journal (January 31, 2006), "He appears to be a good student. He is trying his best to succeed in school. *He* came to *me* for help and realizes the need for a tutor."

While tutoring Eric, I paid attention to the way he talked about his classes and to the types of assignments he was being asked to complete. My impression was that Waverly High School was fostering student success by doing more than just placing posters in the hallways. Waverly's

Personal observations lead to broader insights.

curriculum encourages analytical thinking, requires group and individual projects that depend on creativity and research, and includes open-ended writing assignments designed to give students opportunities to form their own conclusions. I found this reality both difficult and inspiring; I had not expected an 11th grader's homework to be so challenging. I once said so to Eric, and he responded with a smile: "Yeah. My teachers say it's going to help us when we get to college to already know how to do some of these things."

What was surprising to me was the faculty's collective assumption that high school was not the end of a student's career. The fact that teachers talk with students about what will be expected *when* (not *if*) they

Gibson analyzes her evidence to draw a broader conclusion.

go to college is significant. That kind of positive language, which I heard many times at Waverly, most certainly affects students' sense of themselves as achievers. In this case, Eric was not preoccupied with worrying about whether he wanted to go to college or would be accepted; rather, he mentally prepared himself for the time when he would actually enroll.

This section bridges academic theory and personal experience.

According to education researcher Jean Anyon (1981), "Students from higher social class backgrounds may be exposed to legal, medical, or managerial knowledge . . . while those of the working classes may be offered a more 'practical' curriculum" (p. 5). I do not see this gravitation toward social reproduction holding true for most students at Waverly High School. Waverly's student body is a mix of social classes, yet the school's philosophy is to push each of its students to consider college. Through its curriculum, its guidance department literature, and its opportunities for career field trips, Waverly is opening doors for all of its students. In Eric's case, I also observed the beginnings of a break in social reproduction. From the start of our tutoring sessions, Eric frequently mentioned that neither of his parents went to college (O. Gibson, journal entry, March 14, 2006). This

made me wonder how his parents talk to him about college. Is the desire
to go to college something they have instilled in him? Have they given
him the message that if he works hard and goes to college he will be
successful? If that is the case, then Eric's parents are attempting to break
the cycle with their children—and they have the good fortune to live in a
school district that supports their desires. In contrast to the idea that most
people have nothing more than social reproduction to thank for their
socioeconomic status (Bowles & Gintis, 1976), Eric seems to believe that
hard work and a college education are keys to his success.

> Source is cited in APA in-text citation style.

Another key to Eric's success will be the resources he enjoys as a
student at Waverly. Abundance of or lack of resources can play an
important part in students' opportunities to learn and succeed. Because
nearly half of all school funding comes from local property taxes (D. Carter,
class lecture, April 4, 2006), areas with smaller populations or low property
values do not have the tax base to fund schools well. As a result, one
education finance expert has argued, some children receive substandard
education (Parrish, 2002). Waverly does not appear to have serious
financial or funding issues. Each student has access to current textbooks,
up-to-date computer labs, a well-stocked library, a full art and music
curriculum, and numerous extracurricular activities. While countless schools
are in desperate need of a better-equipped library, Waverly's library has a
rich collection of books, magazines and journals, computer stations, and
spaces in which to use all of these materials. It is a very user-friendly
library. This has shown me what the power of funding can do for a school.
Part of Waverly's (and its students') success results from the ample
resources spent on staff and curriculum materials. Adequate school funding
is one of the factors that drive school and student success.

> Class lecture (personal communication) is cited in the text only, not in the reference list.

> Gibson considers the larger implications of her personal observations.

Aside from funding, placement policies determine school and student
success. A major concern of both educators and critics of education policies
is that schools will place students into special education programs
unnecessarily. Too often students who do not need special education are
coded for special ed—even when they have a learning issue that can be
handled with a good teacher in a mainstream class (D. Carter, class lecture,
April 6, 2006). At Waverly High School, teachers and counselors are not so
quick to shuffle Eric into special ed. I agree with several of Eric's teachers

SERVICE LEARNING: ERIC   5

who feel that he may have a mild learning disability. I began to feel this
way when Eric and I moved from working in a private tutoring space to
working in the library. It was clear to me that he had difficulty paying
attention in a public setting. On February 9, I wrote in my journal:

A quotation longer
than forty words is
indented without
quotation marks.

> Eric was extremely distracted. He couldn't pay attention to what I was
> asking, and he couldn't keep his eyes on his work. There were other
> students in the library today, and he kept eavesdropping on their
> conversations and shaking his head when they said things he did not
> agree with. This is how he must behave in the classroom; he is easily
> distracted but he wants to work hard. I see that it is not so much that
> he needs a tutor because he can't understand what his teachers are
> telling him; it is more that he needs the one-on-one attention in a
> confined room free of distractions.

Even though Eric showed signs of distraction, I never felt as
if he should be coded for special education. I am pleased that the
administration and learning specialists did not decide to place Eric in a
special education track. Eric is exceedingly intelligent and shows promise
in every academic area. He seems to be able to succeed by identifying
problems on his own and seeking resources to help him solve those
problems. He is a motivated and talented student who simply seems like
a typical adolescent.

I came away from my service learning project with an even stronger
conviction about the importance of quality education for a student's
success. Unlike the high school I attended, Waverly pays close attention
to each child and thinks about how to get all its students to succeed
at their own level. Jean Patrice, an administrator, told me, "You have
to be able to reach a student where *they* are instead of making them
come to you. If you don't, you'll lose them" (personal communication,
April 10, 2006), expressing her desire to see all students get something
out of their educational experience. This feeling is common among
members of Waverly's faculty. With such a positive view of student
potential, it is no wonder that 97% of Waverly High School graduates go
on to a four-year university (Patrice, 2006). I have no doubt that Eric
Johnson will attend college and that he will succeed there.

As I look toward my teaching future, I know there is plenty that I have left to learn. Teaching is so much more than getting up in front of a class, reiterating facts, and requiring students to learn a certain amount of material by the end of the year. Teaching is about getting students—one by one—to realize and act on their potential. This course and this service learning experience have made me realize that we should never have a trial-and-error attitude about any student's opportunities and educational quality.

Conclusion raises questions for further reflection.

SERVICE LEARNING: ERIC   7

References

Anyon, J. (1981). Social class and school knowledge. *Curriculum Inquiry*, *11*(1), 5.

Bowles, S., & Gintis, H. (1976). *Schooling in capitalist America: Educational reform and contradictions of economic life*. New York, NY: Basic Books.

Parrish, T. (2002). Racial disparities in identification, funding, and provision of special education. In D. Losen & G. Orfield (Eds.), *Racial inequity in special education*. Cambridge, MA: Civil Rights Project and Harvard Education Press.

List of references, in APA style, begins on a new page.

List is alphabetized by authors' last names.

Double-spacing is used throughout.

D6 Writing in engineering

Engineers use the language of mathematics and the methods of science along with the experiences of society to design machines, tools, processes, and systems that will solve problems and accomplish tasks safely and efficiently. There are many different types of engineers: mechanical, chemical, electrical, civil, geological, environmental, and aerospace, to name a few. Each type of engineer addresses problems and tasks in a particular part of the physical world.

Writing plays a major role in the work of engineers, who write reports and recommendations based on their research and their design ideas. Engineers write technical reports addressed to manufacturers or the companies or agencies that hire them. Engineers also communicate their solutions to clients in their own organizations.

As a student of engineering, you will be challenged to devise solutions to real-world problems. Most of your assignments will be open-ended questions that will involve finding or proposing solutions to design challenges; you will be required to compose rationales for your solutions in writing. In laboratory experiments, you will maintain a lab notebook and write reports about your hands-on research. Because engineers usually work in teams, some writing assignments will involve working with other students to give you practice with collaboration.

D6-a Determine your audience and their needs in engineering.

Engineers usually write for readers who have a definite interest in what they have to say. Research and design in engineering never take place in isolation; these activities occur in universities, private industry, and government.

Sometimes your readers will be other engineers and decision makers working in your team or in other groups in your organization; they will expect you to provide a high level of technical detail and to use specialized vocabulary. They need to be able to replicate your work and confirm the results. Sometimes your audience will be a corporate client outside your organization in industry or government. Or your audience might be public-policy decision makers or the general public. Some of these audiences might not have your level of technical expertise, so your writing must be accessible and clear, with a minimum of technical language and jargon. For example, if you are writing a proposal to win a contract for your company or to receive funding for a project, your proposal will have to be written appropriately for an audience consisting of both specialists and nonspecialists.

When you write in engineering courses, keep in mind that you are learning to write for readers who probably have not done the study, research, or design work that you have done. When writing a report, for example, you will write for a reader who was not present in the laboratory or in the field. Even though your professor is in the laboratory with you, always describe your research and experimentation process carefully and thoroughly as if he or she is not familiar with your process. Add spreadsheets, drawings, plates, or illustrations to help your readers visualize your findings.

D6-b Recognize the forms of writing in engineering.

When you take courses in engineering, you may be asked to write any of the following:

- project notebooks
- laboratory reports
- technical reports
- proposals
- progress reports

Project notebooks

A project notebook is like a personal journal in which you record your work in progress. It is a log in which you can write your observations and data from the experimentation and design processes or brainstorm and explore explanations or interpretations of the data. You might describe the materials you use and the procedures you follow or draw sketches of your design and, later, its construction. A project notebook can be useful as you work through mathematical analysis of your data and your designs and as you pose questions and plan solutions to problems. It can also provide the space in which you make note of tests that work and those that do not. You can write reflections on articles you read, notes from meetings you attend, and logistics for projects you are working on. You might also record your instructor's and peers' comments and critiques.

Make your project notebook as complete and as neat as possible; sign and date entries daily. Remember that your notebook will be useful in your later research, design, and writing. If your notebook is part of an ongoing project that someone else will continue after you, then formality, thoroughness, and neatness will be critical. Notebooks are traditionally kept on paper, but you may keep one electronically to make it easier to record, update, and read. As you move into professional practice, these notebooks will become part of any project's formal records.

Laboratory reports

Engineers present the procedures, materials, and results of their experiments in laboratory reports. These reports are essential to the development of the discipline, as it is through these reports that new knowledge is recorded and communicated to researchers, teachers, and students. Laboratory reports for some assignments may have particular requirements. Generally, the laboratory reports you are assigned will follow the organization used in laboratory reports written by engineers working in industry and government.

Your report will need to accomplish the following:

- establish the main question or problem under investigation and provide some background

- state the objective of the laboratory work (to measure, to verify, to compare, and so on) and the exact methods and procedures step-by-step

- describe and comment on your results, explain what they mean, put any unexpected results in context, and compare your results with established knowledge in the discipline

- place your results in the context of your stated purpose; note patterns apparent in the results, implications for future consideration, and any questions that remain unanswered

- tell your reader if you achieved the predicted or anticipated results; account for any differences if possible

The structure of your laboratory report will function as "instructions" for anyone who wants to replicate your experiment, verify your results, or use your work as a foundation for his or her own research.

You can use the same method and structure to record and report on engineering design projects.

Technical reports

A technical report describes the structure and functions of a design. If the report's purpose is to investigate the failure of a design, tool, or machine, then it is a *forensic report*. The audience for a technical or design report is usually other engineers or a similar audience of experts; it can also be decision makers, regulators, and the courts.

A technical report usually has the following structure:

- executive summary, a one-page concise statement of the most important points in the report
- introduction
- purpose and goals
- methods
- data and findings
- recommendations and action items
- conclusion
- appendices if necessary

Use tables, charts, spreadsheets, maps, figures, and illustrations in the body of your report to present your data and findings or in appendices to support your conclusions. Your recommendations and conclusion should interpret your data, discuss any limitations or boundaries of your work, and suggest action items for this project or other, related projects. Document your work by citing your references in the style recommended by your instructor or the organization for which you are writing.

Proposals

Engineers write project proposals to seek funding from academic and government sources or to describe a project to potential clients. "Selling" a customer on a project is thus an important function of an engineer's job. Many proposals are written with cross-disciplinary teams including sales, marketing, production, and legal departments. A proposal for a client may include a price quote or estimate, also called a "bid."

For your classes, you may write proposals for laboratory projects or to suggest solutions for a hypothetical client (usually your professor) who has given you a technical problem or design problem. Prepare your proposals with sufficient research, appropriate graphics, careful organization, and neat presentation to assist your readers and show them that you are credible.

To make it easy for your readers to say yes to your proposal, give them clear, sufficient information about the project. Begin with an introduction that includes a brief project description and lays out the cost, completion date, and rate of return on investment. In the body of the proposal, provide the following:

- background and rationale for the project, describing the need to be met or the problem to be solved
- how the project will be accomplished

- expected outcomes
- materials and methods
- method of evaluation that will be used to determine that the objectives have been achieved
- timeline (sometimes presented in a Gantt chart, a graphical representation of the overlapping deadlines and milestones for all aspects of the project)
- budget, including deadlines and a list of items that must be funded

You can assume that your readers are receiving other proposals, so you might also provide a résumé or a section describing your skills and experiences that qualify you for the project.

Progress reports

Once a proposal is accepted and a project is under way, an engineer must write progress reports regularly to inform the client of the work accomplished. A progress report can be in the form of a business letter or a memo. It describes any milestones that have been achieved or tasks that have been completed. In engineering classes, your progress reports will be written to your professor to document your accomplishments and to describe the work still to be completed.

In your progress report, you might provide the following:

- a brief project description as a reminder of the scope of the project
- a summary of progress with a list of the tasks that have been completed
- a list of any problems that have arisen and solutions implemented or suggested
- any necessary alterations in deadlines or the budget
- a description of work remaining before the next progress report

Engineers frequently use spreadsheets to present data and provide a "snapshot" of the project at various stages. Spreadsheets can be converted into slides for PowerPoint presentations along with images of the work. Complete project reports will assure your readers that you are reliable, punctual, and in control of progress.

D6-c Know the questions engineers ask.

Engineers explore questions related to designing, repairing, and improving aspects of the physical world. Wherever people require a safer, faster, more effective, more efficient, more comfortable, or less expensive way to accomplish a task, engineers investigate and suggest solutions. The tasks might be related to transportation, to the construction of buildings and bridges, to the design of electrical grids and other city infrastructure, or to the invention of appliances and tools in the home or in the workplace.

Engineers explore questions such as these:

- An aging bridge in an area with heavy traffic must be replaced as soon as possible. What is the best design for a new bridge that can support a heavy payload but can also be built in a short period of time?

- Can a liquid laundry detergent be invented that will dissolve more quickly in water and flow more efficiently through the hoses of a new high-efficiency washing machine?

- What material would be best for resurfacing a parking lot in an area that often floods when it rains? What are the properties of different materials that might be used for this construction project?

- Two aerospace companies have proposed different configurations for the wings of a new fighter plane. Which of the two wing designs will allow the aircraft to achieve the highest possible speed with the lowest possible vibration at the most affordable cost?

- Is it possible to invent electronic devices that can be powered wirelessly rather than with batteries or electrical power?

- Because customers want more environmentally friendly equipment for the home, a manufacturer of lawn mowers asks whether it is possible to construct a new kind of engine, similar to the engines in hybrid cars, that would burn fuel more efficiently and more cleanly than current engines.

D6-d Understand the kinds of evidence engineers use.

Engineers use particular kinds of evidence:

- data from laboratory reports published by other engineers

- observations and measurements of apparatus and processes inside the laboratory

- observations and measurements from building models of proposed projects

- observations and measurements from computer simulations and models

- observations and measurements made in real-world settings

Engineers often begin the design process with computer simulations and analysis. Then they verify the simulated results with models and laboratory experiments. This process saves money for engineering firms and their clients. For example, car companies use multiple computer simulations of car crashes before they crash-test a real car. In your classes, your projects may be "pen and paper" designs: You design and test the project on the computer or with manual calculations but do not actually build the project.

Data in engineering are quantitative; they can be counted. Depending on the nature of the problem or experiment, some data can be qualitative, described without numbers. When a structure fails or displays flaws, forensic engineers perform physical tests and sometimes collect and analyze witness testimony as they seek the causes of the problem.

For example, after a passenger airplane exploded in midair in 1996, engineers spent months reconstructing the aircraft to locate the cause. They discovered that structural problems had resulted in small vibrations. Over a long period of time, the vibrations had caused two electrical wires located near a fuel tank to rub against each other. Eventually the insulation of one of the wires had rubbed away, and the electrical current in the wire caused a spark that ignited vapors from the fuel tank. The engineers arrived at this conclusion only after painstakingly examining numerous components, sometimes in microscopic detail, ruling out many of them, focusing on the relevant ones, and ultimately performing tests in the laboratory to replicate the effects of vibrations on the wires.

D6-e Become familiar with writing conventions in engineering.

Engineers agree on several conventions when they write:

- Engineers often work in teams on research and laboratory projects. In your classes, you will often collaborate with other students. Collaboration requires that team members delegate and accept responsibility, report to one another, share ideas, listen to one another, negotiate differences, and compromise on solutions. Usually one person on the team will be in charge of combining the individually written sections of a report into a single document. Some team members may not be engineers or engineering students. Developing relationships with nonengineering and nonscience students and professionals is essential to effective work and communication in engineering.

- Each type of writing should include standard sections. For example, a laboratory report is not complete if it does not include a section that interprets results.

- Engineers must be brief and clear. When describing a process or an apparatus you used, you will need to write exactly what you did and what resulted. You must present the order of the steps you followed in logical sequence.

- Engineers try to avoid ambiguous pronoun use so that readers will know exactly what a pronoun refers to. Instead of writing *This confirms the original results*, an engineer should write *This new set of data confirms the original results*.

- Engineers use headings and subheadings in their reports and proposals. Engineering reports can be long and detailed, and headings mark the important categories of information and help readers follow the organization. Engineers also divide their reports into clear parts with combinations of numbers and letters denoting major sections and their subsections.

- Engineering is a visual field. Readers expect writers to provide diagrams, illustrations, charts, tables, and graphs. Graphics should support the data and other information in a report; they should be easy to understand, with clear labels and captions.

- Engineers use verb tenses deliberately. They use past tense for laboratory reports (*These results demonstrated*). They use future tense in proposals (*This design will require*). They use both present tense and past tense in progress reports (*The design phase is on schedule* or *The foundation was poured during week 3*).

- Engineers usually use third-person pronouns (*he, she, it, they* rather than *I, me, we*). They use active voice where possible because it is more direct and concise. For instance, instead of writing *The viability of the instrument was demonstrated by the results*, they write *The results demonstrated the viability of the instrument*.

D6-f Use the CMS (*Chicago*), IEEE, or USGS system in writing in engineering.

Writers in different fields of engineering use different styles to cite sources in their papers and to list sources at the ends of their papers. Civil engineers, chemical engineers, industrial engineers, and mechanical engineers usually use the name-year system of *The Chicago Manual of Style*, 16th ed. (2010).

Electrical engineers, computer engineers, and mechanical engineers use the *IEEE Editorial Style Manual*, published by the Institute of Electrical and Electronics Engineers.

Engineers and scientists in geology usually use *Suggestions to Authors of the Reports of the United States Geological Survey*, 7th ed. (1991).

When you begin a project in an engineering class, check with your instructor about which style is required for your assignment.

D6-g Sample student paper: Proposal

A proposal recommends a solution to a design or technical problem posed by a client. A typical proposal includes details about how the project will be completed, the required materials and methods of construction, and the expected costs. It often includes alternatives for comparison. The following proposal was written in a junior-level geology engineering course. The student, Alice O'Bryan, explores the options that a fictional company called Ajax might consider for providing proper drainage for a planned park. O'Bryan presents descriptions of several alternatives, including costs, benefits, and overall effectiveness. She used the United States Geological Survey (USGS) guidelines to format her paper and to cite and list her sources.

O'Bryan 1

Full title, writer's name, course, and date, centered halfway down the page.

Site Stabilization Plan for Erosion Control

Alice O'Bryan

GLY 341

May 5, 2008

Marginal annotations indicate USGS-style formatting and effective writing.

O'Bryan 2

CONTENTS

The contents page lists all the major headings and subheadings; it can also list minor subheadings, as here. The indentation of headings in the contents indicates the hierarchy and organization of the paper.

A USGS proposal
often begins with an
executive summary
that briefly provides
background,
findings, and
recommendations.

O'Bryan 3

EXECUTIVE SUMMARY

Ajax is seeking to develop a 44-acre parcel of land into a recreational park and has requested proposals for erosion control. This proposal recommends a system of terraces and a grassed waterway culminating in a 1-acre constructed lake. While this is not the least expensive method of erosion control, it will be effective at preventing erosion and also will meet Ajax's goals for an aesthetically pleasing park that can attract human visitors as well as aquatic life and wildlife. Two less desirable plans are a system of terraces with a riprapped waterway and a buried pipeline. Both plans are less expensive, but both have drawbacks and do not meet all of Ajax's goals.

The recommended proposal (proposal A) will create a series of 13 vegetative terraces that flow into a grassed waterway approximately 1,200 feet long. The waterway will culminate in a 1-acre lake that will collect the drainage and provide a recreational fishing hole. This proposal has the advantage of not disrupting the open land and in fact enhancing it with planted vegetation along the terraces and waterway and with a lake that can attract wildlife and that can be used for recreational purposes. The cost of this proposal is as follows:

- Terraces: $15,034
- Grassed waterway: $4,000
- 1-acre lake: $18,000-60,000
- Total: $37,034-79,034

Additional costs will be incurred for recovery of the soil if more surface is disturbed than just the terrace and waterway construction areas. (See the summary of costs at the end of the proposal.)

The proposal for terraces and a riprapped waterway (proposal B) includes a riprapped channel that would disrupt the parklike atmosphere and that may not prevent off-site erosion. Its costs are as follows:

- Terraces: $15,034
- Riprapped waterway: $6,000
- Total: $21,034

The buried pipeline (proposal C) is the least desirable option because it is hard to maintain, requires an unattractive retaining wall, and is not suited for the soil type in this area. Its costs are as follows:

O'Bryan 4

- Buried pipeline: $6,000
- Gabion retaining wall: $25,000-50,000
- Total: $31,000-56,000

ANALYSIS OF PROPOSALS
PROPOSAL A: TERRACES AND GRASSED WATERWAY

Nonstructural and preventive erosion control provided by proposal A is the best choice for Ajax because the land is to be developed into a park. It is not the least expensive method, but it is likely to be most effective at meeting all the goals of the project. This proposal recommends a system of 7 terraces, each pair spaced 120 feet apart in the clayey silt soil, and 6 terraces, each pair spaced 150 feet apart in the silty clay soil. These terraces would have a 0.60% channel gradient, which would direct the water into a grassed waterway culminating in a 1-acre lake. A lake of this size is reasonable on a site of 44 acres and is more cost-effective than a smaller lake or a pond, which requires more specialized equipment to construct. The site is well suited for a lake because of its gently sloping topography. While a well-built lake can be expensive, Ajax can save money by using the excavated soil to build the terraces.

PROPOSAL B: TERRACES AND RIPRAPPED WATERWAY

Proposal B includes the same terraces as in proposal A, but the terraces flow into a riprapped channel going through the site and leading water beyond the boundaries of the property. A filter material must underlay the entire area that the riprap will cover (Minnesota Department of Transportation, 2005). Geotextile is the best material for this purpose. On top of this will be a 6-inch layer of granular filter material of uniform thickness over the prepared foundation. With geotextile, the foundation surface must be smooth and free of stones or other debris, and the fabric must not be torn during application. The riprap rocks should be placed from the bottom of the waterway to the top to achieve a uniform size distribution, with the smallest percent of void space possible. When completed, the riprap should not be less than 95% of the specified thickness.

PROPOSAL C: BURIED PIPELINE

A buried pipeline is the least optimal choice for the site. Methods

O'Bryan provides an analysis of three proposals, giving an overview of how each proposal would be implemented and recommending one.

First- and second-level headings are centered in all capital letters.

O'Bryan uses USGS style for citing sources in the text.

of erosion control that are constructed aboveground are preferred because it is much easier to perform maintenance on them. There is no room for error in the design and construction of a buried pipeline. Also, in the site area, clay makes up a large percentage of the soil; the shrink-swell potential of the soil could later damage the pipes. Pipelines are also just as expensive as riprap. For this method, a retaining wall would be constructed of gabion baskets, which are more flexible than concrete and allow for the possibility of establishing vegetation in the spaces. As with the riprap plan, an erosion control blanket is required under the gabion to prevent scouring. There are several drawbacks to the use of gabions. As Lynn Merill (2004) writes, quoting engineer Mark North, "'Gabions may not be appropriate for use in high-traffic areas' where people coming in contact with them run the risk of 'snagging their clothes on the wire.'" In addition, gabions can be very expensive.

GUIDELINES FOR CONSTRUCTION[1]

Geotextile material.—Geotextile material should be "woven, nonwoven, or knit fabric of polymeric filaments or yarns such as polypropylene, polyethylene, polyester, or polyamide formed into a stable network such that the filaments/yarns retain their relative position to each other" (Minnesota Department of Transportation, 2005, p. 907). If the geotextile is being used as an earth reinforcement or under riprap, all sewn seams on the fabric must meet strength requirements.

Erosion control blankets.—Erosion control blankets are designed to be used until vegetation can be established. There are nine different categories of blankets based on use longevity and flow velocity; use longevity ranges from 6-8 weeks through permanent. The category chosen should be specific to the method of construction and to the site. For example, if gabions are built and the flow velocity is calculated to be less than 6.5 ft/s, a category 6 erosion control blanket should be used. The blanket should be laid out parallel to the direction of flow, and adjacent blanket edges should overlap by at least 4 inches and should be stapled.

---

[1]All guidelines are based on Minnesota Department of Transportation, 2005, and Beasley and others, 1984, unless stated otherwise.

O'Bryan provides guidelines that should be followed for any of the three proposals. She uses a footnote to give the sources of her guidelines.

In USGS style, minor subheadings are indented and italicized, followed by a period and a dash.

O'Bryan uses a footnote for a general point related to the entire section.

O'Bryan 6

At the top of the slope, the blanket should be buried in a check slot, which should be backfilled and compacted. Within the channel, the blanket should be stapled every foot.

Silt fences.—No silt should be washed off-site, and the soil must be seeded if it is to be bare for more than 45 days. It is expected that silt fences will be required at some point during construction of any of the proposed plans. It is acceptable to use the standard machine-sliced silt fencing during site grading to keep sediment from moving. Each post of the silt fence should be secured by a minimum of five gun staples 1 inch long.

Excavation.—During excavation, a well-drained condition must be maintained through planned drainage facilities. Topsoil should be stockpiled and covered. If blasting is required, it must be conducted so that materials will not be thrown out of the area and will be easily recoverable. Excavations must have a secure uniformity in grade; if excavations fall below final grade, they must be done with the provision that they are subject to change.

Pipe installation.—Pipes should be installed to collect and discharge water infiltrating into the soil or accumulated in a subcut or to cut off or intercept groundwater flow. The pipes should be constructed of nonperforated threadless copper (TP) pipe. Minimum trench width should be the diameter of the pipe plus two times the diameter. All rocks within the trench should be removed. A fine filter aggregate layer of one pipe diameter should be laid in the bottom of the trench. If perforated pipe is used, it must be wrapped in geotextile. Pipes that will discharge at a constructed gabion wall should be installed so that small movements in the wall will not cause the pipes to separate.

Reseeding.—The purpose of reseeding the area is not just to beautify the landscape. Reseeding is also an effective erosion control method. The application of seed must be conducted with as much rigor and attention to detail as any construction project on the site will be carried out. The establishment of permanent vegetation requires soil tilling, liming, fertilizing, seeding, sodding, mulching, and any other work required to ensure that the plants survive to maturity. Proper planting times must be observed; until the time for seeding has arrived, previously

mentioned methods of erosion control must be used. The recommended
temporary seeding mixture is mixture number 130; its seeding date varies
because this seed has 40% of both winter wheat and oats. The optimal
time for planting winter wheat is Aug. 1-Oct. 1, and for oats it is May
1-Aug. 1. Other seed mixture numbers have different planting seasons, as
shown in table 1.

Tables are referred to in the text and are placed as close as possible to their text reference.

If rills or gullies have formed anywhere on the site, they should
be filled in prior to seeding and compacted so that they are approximately
the same density as the surrounding soil. The seed should be applied
according to the seed application rate for its mixture number (see
table 2). Hydroseeding is prohibited when wind speeds exceed 15 mph.
The traditional seed mixes (numbers 100-280) should be applied through
hydroseeding; native mixes, because of the shape of the seed, require a
native seed drill. In hydroseeding, seed must be uniformly distributed;
otherwise the area must be reseeded. The permanent seed mixture can be
applied to an area that is covered with a temporary seed mixture without
additional tillage or site preparation. The water-to-straw-bale ratio with
tackifier for mulch is 100 gallons to every 50-pound bale.

O'Bryan gives specific details about her recommended proposal.

PROPOSAL A: DETAILS AND GENERAL SPECIFICATIONS

Seeded terraces and waterway.—On this site, there will be 7 sets of
terraces 120 feet apart in the clayey silt soil and 6 sets of terraces 150 feet
apart in the silty clay soil. The terraces will have a 0.60% gradient. They
will begin at elevation 560 feet and will be 600 feet long, increasing by

Table number and title appear above the table. A headnote, in brackets, gives source information; it also can explain abbreviations or symbols.

Table 1. Planting seasons for seed
[From Minnesota Department of Transportation, 2005, table 2575-1, p. 712]

Seed mixture number	Spring	Fall
100	—	Aug. 1-Oct. 1
110	May 1-Aug. 1	—
150, 190	Apr. 1-July 20	July 20-Oct. 20
240, 250, 260, 270	Apr. 1-June 1	July 20-Sept. 20
280	Apr. 1-Sept. 1	—
310, 325, 328, 330, 340, 350	Apr. 15-July 20	Sept. 20-Oct. 20

O'Bryan 8

Table 2. Seed application rates
[From Minnesota Department of Transportation, 2005, table 2575-2, p. 716]

Seed mixture number	Application rate (lb/acre)
100, 110	100
159	40
190	60
240	75
250	70
260	100
270	120
280	50
310	82
325	84
328	88
330, 340, 350	84.5

28.5 feet at each terrace until they reach 1,000 feet in length at elevation 480 feet. Work should start at the base of the area and proceed upward. The terraces will flow into a larger grassed waterway approximately 1,200 feet long that intersects the site.

In USGS style, most numbers are expressed as numerals.

The terraces will be grassed with a native harvest. The waterway will be lined with something comparable to C350 riprap replacement and will also be seeded with a native harvest. The native harvest should consist of seed harvests from stands within 25 miles of the area. Approximately 70% of the mixture should consist of big bluestem and/or Indian grass, though 50% would be acceptable. There should be at least five species of native grasses and 3% (by mass) of native forbs. Since this is to be a recreational area, it will be best not to use a variety of grass that needs seasonal burning unless the park can be closed without financial repercussions and without the fire damaging any infrastructure erected at a later time. The application of herbicides seasonally (spring or summer) is acceptable though not encouraged, as runoff could harm fish and wildlife.

Erosion barrier.—The developer may not disturb more than 14,400 ft^2 at a time in the clayey silt soil or more than 22,500 ft^2 at a time in the silty clay soil without erecting an erosion barrier such as a silt fence on the downslope side. The bare soil above the work area should be stabilized by rocks and mulch at the end of each workday. The developer should create and maintain a covered stockpile of topsoil. If soil is going to be left bare for more than 45 days, it must be seeded. Idle areas should be seeded as soon as possible after grading or within 7 days. The seed should be mixture number 130, consisting of 40% oats, 40% winter wheat, 10% rye grass, and 10% alfalfa, annual. Compacted soils in the area should be deep-tilled to a depth of 18-24 inches to allow for deep root penetration. Six or more inches of organic compost should be laid on top of this and tilled into the top 10 inches of soil.

Lake.—Although a collection system for the runoff water was not a requirement for this proposal, a lake has several advantages and is not prohibitively expensive. It will collect drainage from the constructed waterway, it will attract wildlife to the area and enhance the appeal to visitors, and it can serve as a recreational fishing hole.

Other vegetation.—Revegetation should occur at the end of the major construction phase and should focus not only on establishing grasses in the area but also on planting other forms of vegetation. Some of the options for native plants that are readily available from nurseries are outlined in the "Shoreline Stabilization Handbook" (Northwest Regional Planning Commission, 2004). They include trees, shrubs, herbaceous plants, ferns, and vines. It is preferred that these be native to the area, such as Kentucky bluegrass, and not European or Asian in origin. While the European and Asian grasses have traditionally been used in American landscaping, they tend to have much smaller rooting zones and are not suitable for effective erosion control; they also require more effort to grow in this site soil. Native grasses would not have these problems and would be less expensive to maintain. Shrubs such as sumac, gray dogwood, wild rose, fragrant sumac, and hazelnut are also preferable because they have a dense, low-spreading growth pattern and are attractive.

Proposals usually provide itemized costs for the client.

Cost estimates.—The basic construction of Proposal A will cost Ajax $37,034-79,034. Additional costs of approximately $608,000 would provide

O'Bryan 10

for recovery of the runoff water and enhance the overall appearance and appeal of the area.

DIMENSIONS

Disturbed area	216,283.5 yd^2
Total area	333,330 yd^2
Undisturbed area	117,046.5 yd^2

BASIC COSTS

Terraces	$	15,034.00
Grassed waterway		4,000.00
1-acre lake		18,000.00-60,000.00
TOTAL BASIC COSTS............................$37,034.00-79,034.00		

ADDITIONAL COSTS (OPTIONAL)

Hydroseeding, tackifier not required	$175,570.00
Hydroseeding, tackifier required	432,567.00
TOTAL ADDITIONAL COSTS...............................$608,137.00	

CONCLUSION

While not the lowest-cost method of erosion control, proposal A meets all the goals of the project and creates an aesthetically pleasing and natural park atmosphere. The constructed appearance of the heavier erosion control options such as riprap and gabions would not mesh well with natural foliage. Such constructions also would not allow for aquatic life, one of the stated goals of the project. Heavy vegetation with the more aesthetic option of terraces is the correct choice in this situation. Native grasses not only will facilitate slope stabilization because of their deep rooting zones but also will attract birds and other wildlife, which would in turn draw wildlife enthusiasts into the park.

A good model for the proposed park is the Rachel Carson National Wildlife Refuge in Maine. While the type of land that is being protected in Maine is different from the land found on the Kentucky site, the Maine park combines the elements Ajax is seeking in its new park: a wildlife refuge, full of native plants, and a recreational area. The Maine park has trails throughout so that visitors have many different views of the beauty of the site. It also offers fishing and hunting and appeals to many different demographics. Ajax should consider this park as an ideal model.

In her conclusion, O'Bryan states again why she recommends proposal A. She ends with a paragraph that speaks plainly to connect with her readers.

O'Bryan 11

The writer uses USGS style to list the sources she consulted in preparing her proposal.

REFERENCES

Beasley, R.P., Gregory, J.M., and McCarty, T.R., 1984, Erosion and sediment pollution control (2d ed.): Ames, Iowa, Iowa State University Press, 354 p.

Merill, L., 2004, Multitalented and versatile—gabions in stormwater management and erosion control: Erosion Control, v. 11, no. 3, http://www.erosioncontrol.com/may-june-2004/gabions-cages -erosion.aspx.

Metropolitan Council, July 2001, Soil erosion control—vegetative methods, *in* Minnesota urban small sites BMP manual: St. Paul, Minn., Metropolitan Council Environmental Services, http://www .metrocouncil.org/environment/Watershed/BMP/CH3_RPPSoilVeget .pdf.

Minnesota Department of Transportation, 2005, Standard specifications for construction: St. Paul, Minn., Minnesota Department of Transportation, http://www.dot.state.mn.us/pre-letting/spec/2005 /2557-2582.pdf.

Northwest Regional Planning Commission, 2004, The shoreline stabilization handbook for Lake Champlain and other inland lakes: St. Albans, Vt., Northwest Regional Planning Commission, http://nsgd.gso.uri.edu /lcsg/lcsgh04001.pdf.

U.S. Fish and Wildlife Service, 2008, Rachel Carson National Wildlife Refuge: Wells, Maine, U.S. Fish and Wildlife Service, http://www.fws .gov/northeast/rachelcarson.

D7 Writing in history

Historians analyze the information available to them to develop theories about past events, experiences, ideas, and movements. Depending on their interests, historians may consider a variety of issues and sources related to economics, politics, social issues, science, the military, gender, the family, or popular culture.

Historians do not simply record what happened at a particular time; rather, they attempt to explain *why* or *how* events occurred as they did and to place those events in a larger context. For example, a historian writing about women in the British military during World War II would not simply describe the positions women held in the armed forces; through an analysis of the available information, the historian might develop a theory about why women were authorized to hold certain jobs and not others and how changes to women's roles affected the evolution of the women's rights movement in the decades that followed.

D7-a Determine your audience and their needs in history.

Historians write for diverse audiences. History scholars research and write books, articles, textbooks, Web sites, and film scripts for peers, teachers, and students. They also write for the general public, nonspecialists who are interested in history and may subscribe to history magazines or make frequent trips to museums. Amateur historians, often called "local historians," do genealogical or community research for a specific audience.

When you write in history, keep in mind that your audience appreciates an author who is knowledgeable and has done thorough research. Use multiple sources and cite your sources fully to assure your readers that your sources are credible. Because primary sources offer important evidence, include photos, maps, letters, or facsimiles. For example, if you are writing a newsletter article about a slave auction that occurred during the 1850s, you might add a picture of the poster that was used to advertise that auction.

D7-b Recognize the forms of writing in history.

Writing in history combines narrative (a description of what happened) and interpretation (an analysis of why events occurred). Historians ask questions that do not have obvious answers and analyze a variety of sources to draw conclusions.

When you take courses in history, you may be asked to write any of the following kinds of documents:

- critical essays
- book reviews
- research papers
- historiographic essays

Critical essays

For some assignments, you will be asked to write a short, critical essay in which you look at a document or group of documents—or perhaps a historical argument written by a scholar. For example, if you were studying the US decision to send troops to Vietnam, you might be asked to analyze one or more of John F. Kennedy's speeches and put forth a theory about why Kennedy chose to authorize the initial troop deployments. In the same course, you might be asked to read a journal article by a scholar analyzing Kennedy's decision and assess the way that scholar uses evidence to support his or her conclusion.

Book reviews

Because historians view their own work as part of an ongoing scholarly conversation, they value the serious discussion of the work of other scholars in the field. In some courses, you may be asked to write a book review analyzing the logic and accuracy of a scholarly work or of several works on the same topic. When you write a book review, you will have to make judgments about how much background information to provide about the book so that your readers will be able to understand and appreciate your critique.

Research papers

When you write a research paper in any course, you are expected to pose a question and examine the available evidence to find an answer to that question. In history courses, a research paper will generally focus on *why* and *how* questions that can be answered using a combination of sources. If you were studying the Vietnam War, you might ask how the rhetoric of the cold war shaped John F. Kennedy's early Vietnam policy. To answer this question, you might look at government documents from the Kennedy administration, press coverage of Kennedy's foreign policy, Kennedy's own writings, and interviews with those who were involved in policymaking. If you were interested in the role of women in the military during World War II, you might

critical essay • book review • research paper • analysis of
historians' methods • evidence • primary and secondary sources

D7-d   D-81

ask why the British government supported the expansion of women's roles in ways that the US government did not.

Historiographic essays

Historiography is the study by historians of how history is written. When you write a historiographic essay, you think about the methods by which other historians have drawn their conclusions. If you were writing a historiographic essay about how the cold war affected John F. Kennedy's policies, you would analyze how other historians have answered this question. What assumptions or biases influenced their choice and interpretation of sources? What methods shaped their work?

D7-c Know the questions historians ask.

Historians generally ask *how* and *why* questions. Other, more basic questions such as *What happened?* and *Who was involved?* will contribute answers to inform the broader, more controversial questions. Historians choose their questions by considering their own interests, the relevance to the ongoing discussions among scholars, and the availability of sources on the topic. The answer to any one of the following questions could form the basis of a thesis for a history paper:

- What role did nationalism play in the breakup of Yugoslavia in the early 1990s?
- Why did the US Congress decide to grant women the vote?
- How did the Salem witch trials (1692–93) differ from the Salzburg witch trials (1675–90)?
- Why did the Roman Empire collapse?

D7-d Understand the kinds of evidence historians use.

As investigators of the past, historians rely on both primary sources and secondary sources. Primary sources are materials from the historical period being studied—government documents, numerical data, speeches, diaries, letters, and maps. Secondary sources are materials produced after the historical period that interpret or synthesize historical events. The same source can function as either a primary or a secondary source depending on what you are writing about. For example, a newspaper article about Slobodan Milosevic's decision to defend himself during his war crimes trial would be a secondary source in an essay about why Milosevic made this decision. The same article, however, would be a primary source in an essay about newspaper coverage of Milosevic's war crimes trial.

Following are some of the ways historians use evidence:

- For a research paper about the role of women in the British military during World War II, you might find evidence in women's diaries and letters. If you were interested in how the government decided to create women's military services, you could consult records of parliamentary debates or correspondence between military and government leaders. You could also find numerous books by other scholars with information on the topic.

- For a research paper about attitudes toward Prohibition in different parts of the United States, you might consult regional newspapers or correspondence between politicians and their constituents. You might also find numerical data on liquor sales and Prohibition violations to support a hypothesis about regional attitudes.

- For a review of several books about the causes of the Tiananmen Square massacre, your evidence would come from the books themselves as well as other respected sources on the topic.

D7-e Become familiar with writing conventions in history.

No matter what topic they are writing about, historians agree on some general conventions:

- Historians value counterargument. To draw a conclusion about why or how something happened, historians must weigh conflicting theories and interpretations carefully and judiciously. In an essay answering the question of why the US Congress passed the Nineteenth Amendment, you might conclude that politicians truly believed that women should have the right to vote. But you would also need to account for the failure of the same legislation several years earlier. Did politicians change their minds? Or were other factors at work?

- Historians conduct research. Historians, like detectives or forensic specialists, look for explanations by assessing the available evidence rather than relying on assumptions or personal opinions. They look for multiple sources of evidence to confirm their theories, and they avoid value judgments.

- Historians write in the past tense when they are focusing on past events, ideas, and movements. They use the present tense

(*Goodman's book reveals new evidence*) or present perfect tense (*Olson has vividly depicted the political scene*) when talking about the contents of another writer's work.

- Historians credit the scholarship of others. Historians are aware that they are joining an existing scholarly conversation, and they place great importance on citing the ideas of other scholars.

D7-f Use the CMS (*Chicago*) system in writing in history.

Writers in history typically use the style guidelines of *The Chicago Manual of Style* (CMS) for formatting their papers, for citing sources in the text of their paper and in endnotes, and for listing sources in a bibliography at the end. CMS style is set forth in *The Chicago Manual of Style*, 16th ed. (Chicago: University of Chicago Press, 2010). (For more details, see the CMS documentation sections in your handbook.)

D7-g Sample student paper: Research essay

A history research paper generally focuses on a *how* or a *why* question, and it answers this question with an analysis of available sources. The student paper beginning on the next page was written for a course on the history of the industrial revolution in the United States. The student, Jenna Benjamin, used the style guidelines of *The Chicago Manual of Style* (CMS) to format her paper and to cite and list her sources.

Title page consists
of a descriptive title
and the writer's
name in the center
of the page and the
course number,
instructor, and date
at the bottom of the
page.

Wage Slavery or True Independence?

Women Workers in the Lowell, Massachusetts,

Textile Mills, 1820-1850

Jenna Benjamin

American History 200, Section 4

Professor Jones

May 22, 2010

Marginal annotations indicate CMS-style formatting and effective writing.

In 1813, New England merchant Francis Lowell introduced a new type of textile mill to Massachusetts that would have a permanent impact on family and village life. Over the next three decades, the transformation of home production to factory production of textiles would require a substantial labor force and would lead to the unprecedented hiring of thousands of women. The entrance of young women into the workforce sparked a passionate debate about whether factory work exploited young women and adversely affected society. The young women who worked in the mills received low pay for hard work and had little free time.[1] Were these women victims of the factory system? What was the long-term impact of their experiences? An analysis of the evidence reveals that rather than being exploited, these women workers shaped their experience for their own purposes and actively expanded the opportunities for women.

In the late eighteenth century, great changes in the production of textiles were taking place in England, with a transition from home production to factories using machines and employing children to do most of the work. Conditions in the factories were very bad, and stories of dark and dangerous mills reinforced Americans' prejudices against industrialization.[2] Meanwhile, New Englanders still spun yarn at home and some also wove their own cloth, mostly for their own families. Much of this work was done by women. A spinning wheel was a possession of almost every household.[3] But in the first two decades of the nineteenth century, a slow shift took place in New England from home to factory production.

Some American merchants, like Samuel Slater and Francis Cabot Lowell, began to envision an American textile industry. The first mills they built in the United States were in rural villages and employed whole families, not just children. Since the textile mills hired whole families who already lived in the villages, family and village life was not greatly altered.[4]

A dramatic change in textile production, however, came from a new machine, the power loom, and a new mechanized mill, built first in Waltham, Massachusetts, in 1813 by Francis Lowell and a small group of wealthy Boston merchants.[5] Waltham was not a village with a textile mill in it; it became a "mill town" in which the factory dominated the economic

Page header contains the writer's name followed by the page number. Since the title page is counted in the numbering, the first text page is numbered 2.

Introduction frames a debatable issue.

Research questions focus the essay.

Statement of thesis.

Section provides background about the historical period.

Historians write in the past tense when describing past events.

Benjamin 3

life of a rapidly growing city. Most significantly, the workers in Lowell's mill were not local families but individuals who came from great distances to live and work in the new mill town. When Lowell died in 1817, his business partners spread the new factory system to other places, notably a town on the Merrimack and Concord Rivers twenty-seven miles from Boston; in honor of their friend, they named the town Lowell. It soon became the biggest mill town in the nation, with more than a dozen large integrated mills using mechanical looms.[6]

Note numbers in text refer to endnotes at the end of the paper.

The growth of Lowell between 1821 and 1840 was unprecedented.[7] A rapidly developing textile industry like the one at Lowell needed more and more people to work the machines in the factories. The mill owners, aware of the negative view of English mill towns, decided to create a community where workers would live in solid, clean housing rather than slums. For their workers, they looked to a large group of people whose labor was not absolutely necessary to the New England farm economy— hundreds (later thousands) of young women who lived on the farms but who could be persuaded to come to Lowell and work in the mills.[8]

Topic sentence signals a transition to a specific discussion of the women workers.

Several factors in the social and economic history of New England made this group of workers available. Population growth and scarcity of land to pass down to younger generations of sons caused many New England farmers to send their sons to work on neighboring farms or as apprentices to craftsmen in towns or villages.[9] In addition, the position of women (wives and, especially, daughters) in the family was an inferior one. Adult, property-holding males were citizens with full civil rights, but the same was not true for women *of any age*. Wives had no legal rights, and daughters had no independence. Daughters were bound by social conventions to obey their fathers and rarely were able to earn money of their own. Even travel away from home was unusual. Although the family could not have functioned without the labor of wives and daughters at field work, food preparation, cleaning, washing, and so on, women gained no independent income or freedom as a result. For some young women, their subordinate position in family and society gave them an incentive to embrace the opportunities offered by mill work. Unlike the limited occupation of teaching, which was poorly paid and lasted for only a few months a year, the new mill work was steady, and it paid well.[10]

Benjamin 4

Hiring young women, of course, met strong resistance from fathers who saw their role as protecting their daughters and preparing them for marriage.[11] To confront this resistance, the mill owners created boardinghouses around the mills where groups of girls—ranging in age from fifteen to mid-twenties—lived and took their meals under the care of a housekeeper, usually an older woman. Strict boardinghouse rules were laid down by each company (see fig. 1). Moreover, the girls would never grow into a permanent working class, as it was expected that they

REGULATIONS

FOR THE

BOARDING HOUSES

OF THE

MIDDLESEX COMPANY.

THE tenants of the Boarding Houses are not to board, or permit any part of their houses to be occupied by any person except those in the employ of the Company.

They will be considered answerable for any improper conduct in their houses, and are not to permit their boarders to have company at unseasonable hours.

The doors must be closed at ten o'clock in the evening, and no one admitted after that time without some reasonable excuse.

The keepers of the Boarding Houses must give an account of the number, names, and employment of their boarders, when required; and report the names of such as are guilty of any improper conduct, or are not in the regular habit of attending public worship.

The buildings and yards about them must be kept clean and in good order, and if they are injured otherwise than from ordinary use, all necessary repairs will be made, and charged to the occupant.

It is indispensable that all persons in the employ of the Middlesex Company should be vaccinated who have not been, as also the families with whom they board; which will be done at the expense of the Company.

SAMUEL LAWRENCE, Agent.

JOEL TAYLOR, PRINTER, Daily Courier Office.

A primary source (a document) provides concrete evidence and adds historical interest.

Fig. 1. Each mill company established strict rules for the boardinghouses where its women workers lived. (American Textile History Museum, Lowell, Massachusetts.)

Benjamin 5

would return to their homes for visits and after a year or two would go back to their villages permanently.[12] The mill owners did not advertise for help. They sent recruiters into the countryside to assure parents that their daughters would live under strict supervision in the boardinghouses and at work and that their behavior would be monitored. The owners' efforts were successful: over the years, thousands of young women took the long trip by stagecoach or wagon from their rural homes to mill towns like Lowell.[13]

Benjamin introduces evidence that appears to contradict her thesis (counterargument).

Besides having to adjust to living in a city in a strange house with a dozen or more other girls, the young women had to get used to the rigorous rules and long hours at the mills.[14] Mill work was an opportunity, but it also was hard work. The girls worked an average of twelve hours a day. The mills operated six days a week, so the only day off was Sunday, part of which was usually spent at church. Thus free time was confined to two or three hours in the evening and to Sunday afternoon.[15] For many, however, this was still more leisure (and more freedom) than they would have had at home.

Despite a workday that took up fourteen hours, including time spent traveling to and from their houses for meals, most of the young women did not find the work very strenuous or particularly dangerous. As the mill owners had promised, Lowell did not resemble the grimy, packed mill towns of England.[16] Still, the work was tedious and confining, with the girls doing the same operation over and over again under the watchful eye of the overseer.[17]

Benjamin develops a response to the counterargument, with strong evidence for her thesis.

The young women earned an average of three to four dollars a week, from which their board of $1.25 a week was deducted. At that time, no other jobs open to women paid as well.[18] Three or four dollars a week was enough to pay board, send badly needed money home, and still have enough left over for new clothes once in a while. Many women mill workers even established savings accounts, and some eventually left Lowell with several hundred dollars, something they never could have done at home.[19]

Details about the beneficial effects on the young mill workers come from primary and secondary sources.

Even though their free time was very limited, the young women engaged in a variety of activities. In the evenings, they wrote letters home, entertained visitors (though there was little privacy), repaired their

Benjamin 6

clothing, and talked about friends and relatives and also about conditions in the mills. They could go out to the shops, especially clothing shops. The mill girls at Lowell prided themselves on a wardrobe that, at least on Sunday, was not inferior to that of the wives of prosperous citizens.[20] In addition, they attended evening courses that enabled them to extend their education beyond their few years of schooling. They also attended lectures and read novels and essays. So strong was the girls' interest in reading that many mills put up signs warning "No reading in the mills."[21] Some young women even began writing. Determined to challenge the idea that mill girls were mindless drones of the factory and lacked the refinement to ultimately be good wives, about seventy-five mill girls and women contributed in the 1840s to publications featuring stories and essays by the workers themselves.[22]

Benjamin paraphrases information from a secondary source, a late-nineteenth-century book.

The best known of these publications was the *Lowell Offering*. The *Offering* avoided sensitive issues about working conditions, but the women controlled the content of the publication and wrote on subjects (family, courtship, fashion, morality, nature) that interested them.[23] A few of the *Offering* writers even went on to literary careers, not the kind of future that most people expected of factory workers. Charles Dickens toured the mills in 1842 and later said of the girls' writing: "Of the merits of the *Lowell Offering*, as a literary production, I will only observe . . . that it will compare advantageously with a great many English annuals."[24]

Direct quotation provides evidence from the period.

Though the *Offering* was a sign that something unusual was happening in this factory town, the women still worked in an industry that caused them hardship. By the 1830s, tensions in the mills had begun to rise as the companies became more interested in profits and less concerned about their role as protectors of their young workers. Factory owners, observing a decline in the price of their cloth and an increase in unsold inventories, decided to lower their workers' wages.[25] When the reduction was announced in February 1834, the women workers circulated petitions among themselves pledging to stop work (or "turn out") if wages were lowered.[26] When the leader of the petition drive at one mill was fired, many of the women left work and marched to the other mills to call out their workers. It is estimated that one-sixth of all women mill workers walked out as a result. The strikers wrote another petition stating that "we will not go back into the mills to work until our wages are continued . . . as they have been."[27]

Although the "turn out" was brief and did not achieve its purpose, it demonstrated that the women workers did not accept the owners' view that they were minors under the owners' benevolent care. The sense of independence gained by factory work and cash wages led them to reject the idea that they were mere factory hands. Petitions referred to their "unquestionable rights" and to "the spirit of our patriotic ancestors, who preferred privation to bondage." One petition ended, "We are free, we would remain in possession of what kind providence has bestowed upon us, and remain *daughters of free men still*."[28] This language indicates that the women did not think of themselves as laborers complaining about low wages. They were free citizens of a republic and deserved respect as such. Many young women left the mills and went home when mill work came to seem more like "slavery" than independence (a comparison that appeared in the petitions). In 1836, another effort to lower wages led to an even larger "turn out."[29] The willingness of these young women to challenge the authority of the mill owners is a sign that their new lives had given them a feeling of personal strength and solidarity with one another.[30]

Economic recession in the late 1830s and early 1840s led to the layoff of hundreds more women workers. In the 1840s and 1850s, the mill owners tried to maintain profits by increasing the workload and abandoning paternalism toward their workers. To save money, the companies stopped building boardinghouses.[31] The look of Lowell changed as well. Mill buildings took up more of the green space that had been part of the original town plan. By 1850, Lowell did indeed look something like an English mill town.

As conditions in the mills and in the city declined, young New England women were replaced by young Irish immigrants escaping the famine and the poor living conditions in Ireland. Slowly, Lowell became just another industrial city. It was dirty and overcrowded, and its mills were beginning to look run-down.[32]

By 1850, an era had passed. But from the 1820s to the 1840s, the majority of the textile workers were young women who helped make possible the industrialization of New England at the same time as they expanded

---

Benjamin analyzes the quotation to show how it supports the paragraph's main point.

Strong evidence supports the paper's thesis.

Concluding paragraph opens with a brief restatement of part of the thesis.

Benjamin 8

their own opportunities. These early mill workers became models for later
women reformers and radicals who raised the banner for equal rights for
women in more and more areas of life. The independent mill girls of the
1830s and 1840s resisted pressures from their employers, gained both
freedom and maturity by living and working on their own, and showed an
intense desire for independence and learning.[33] Great fortunes were made
from the textile mills of that era, but within those mills a generation of
young women gained something even more precious: a sense of self-respect.

Conclusion considers
the broader
implications of the
thesis.

Benjamin 9

Notes

Endnotes begin on a new page. Sources are cited in CMS (*Chicago*) style. Complete source information is also listed in the bibliography.

1. Caroline F. Ware, *The Early New England Cotton Manufacture* (Boston: Houghton Mifflin, 1931), 4-8; Barbara M. Tucker, *Samuel Slater and the Origins of the American Textile Industry: 1790-1860* (Ithaca, NY: Cornell University Press, 1984), 38-41.

2. Tucker, *Samuel Slater*, 33-40.

3. Thomas Dublin, *Women at Work: The Transformation of Work and Community in Lowell, Massachusetts, 1826-1860* (New York: Columbia University Press, 1979), 14; Adrienne D. Hood, "The Gender Division of Labor in the Production of Textiles in Eighteenth-Century Rural Pennsylvania," *Journal of Social History* 27, no. 3 (1994), "Spinning as Women's Work" section, Academic OneFile (A15324645).

Citation of a journal article from a database. Section locator is used for unpaginated source.

4. Tucker, *Samuel Slater*, 79, 85, 99-100, 111; Barbara M. Tucker, "The Family and Industrial Discipline in Ante-Bellum New England," *Labor History* 21, no. 1 (1979): 56-60.

5. Robert F. Dalzell, *Enterprising Elite: The Boston Associates and the World They Made* (Cambridge, MA: Harvard University Press, 1987), 26-30; Tucker, *Samuel Slater*, 111-16.

Second reference to a source includes the author's name, a shortened title, and the page numbers.

6. Tucker, *Samuel Slater*, 116-17.

7. Dublin, *Women at Work*, 19-21, 133-35.

8. Ibid., 26, 76; Benita Eisler, ed., *The "Lowell Offering": Writings by New England Mill Women, 1840-1845* (Philadelphia: Lippincott, 1977), 15-16.

First line of each note is indented ½". All notes are single-spaced, with double-spacing between them. (Some instructors may prefer double-spacing throughout.)

9. Christopher Clark, "The Household Economy: Market Exchange and the Rise of Capitalism in the Connecticut Valley, 1800-1860," *Journal of Social History* 13, no. 2 (1979): 175-76, http://www.jstor.org/stable /3787339; Gail Fowler Mohanty, "Handloom Outwork and Outwork Weaving in Rural Rhode Island, 1810-1821," *American Studies* 30, no. 2 (1989): 42-43, 48-49.

10. Eisler, "*Lowell Offering*," 16, 193; Clark, "Household Economy," 178-79; Dalzell, *Enterprising Elite*, 33.

Primary source (Robinson) reprinted in a secondary source.

11. On the influence of patriarchy, see Tucker, *Samuel Slater*, 25-26; Harriet H. Robinson, *Loom and Spindle; Or, Life among the Early Mill Girls* (1898), reprinted in *Women of Lowell* (New York: Arno Press, 1974), 194; Barbara Welter, "The Cult of True Womanhood," *American Quarterly* 18, no. 2, pt. 1 (1966): 151, 170-71.

Benjamin 12

Bibliography

Bartlett, Elisha. *A Vindication of the Character and Condition of the Females Employed in the Lowell Mills.* 1841. Reprinted in *Women of Lowell.* New York: Arno Press, 1974.

A Citizen of Lowell. *Corporations and Operatives: Being an Exposition of the Condition [of] Factory Operatives and a Review of the "Vindication," by Elisha Bartlett, MD.* 1843. Reprinted in *Women of Lowell.* New York: Arno Press, 1974.

Clark, Christopher. "The Household Economy: Market Exchange and the Rise of Capitalism in the Connecticut Valley, 1800-1860." *Journal of Social History* 13, no. 2 (1979): 169-89. http://www.jstor.org /stable/3787339.

Dalzell, Robert F. *Enterprising Elite: The Boston Associates and the World They Made.* Cambridge, MA: Harvard University Press, 1987.

Dublin, Thomas. *Women at Work: The Transformation of Work and Community in Lowell, Massachusetts, 1826-1860.* New York: Columbia University Press, 1979.

Eisler, Benita, ed. *The "Lowell Offering": Writings by New England Mill Women, 1840-1845.* Philadelphia: Lippincott, 1977.

"Factory Rules from the Handbook to Lowell, 1848." Illinois Labor History Society. Center for Law and Computers, Chicago-Kent School of Law. Accessed May 12, 2006. http://www.kentlaw.edu/ilhs/lowell.html.

Hood, Adrienne D. "The Gender Division of Labor in the Production of Textiles in Eighteenth-Century Rural Pennsylvania." *Journal of Social History* 27, no. 3 (1994). Academic OneFile (A15324645).

Larcom, Lucy. "Among Lowell Mill-Girls: A Reminiscence." 1881. Reprinted in *Women of Lowell.* New York: Arno Press, 1974.

Mohanty, Gail Fowler. "Handloom Outwork and Outwork Weaving in Rural Rhode Island, 1810-1821." *American Studies* 30, no. 2 (1989): 41-68.

Robinson, Harriet H. *Loom and Spindle; Or, Life among the Early Mill Girls.* 1898. Reprinted in *Women of Lowell.* New York: Arno Press, 1974.

Sins of Our Mothers. Boston: PBS Video, 1988. Videocassette.

Stearns, Bertha Monica. "Early Factory Magazines in New England: The *Lowell Offering* and Its Contemporaries." *Journal of Economic and Business History* (1930): 685-705.

Bibliography begins on a new page and includes all the sources cited in the paper.

Online article with a stable URL.

Entries are listed alphabetically by authors' last names or by title for works with no author.

First line of each entry is at the left margin; subsequent lines are indented ½".

Entries are single-spaced, with double-spacing between entries. (Some instructors may prefer double-spacing throughout.)

D8 Writing in music

Musicians and musicologists—those who study, analyze, and interpret music—write about music for themselves or for larger audiences. Your instructor might ask you to keep a journal to record your impressions and ideas about concerts you attend. If you are a music student, you might write personal reflections about works that you are preparing for performance. Other kinds of writing are intended to inform or educate general audiences. They include reviews of performances and press releases that are published in newspapers, blogs, or other publications. More specialized publications are scholarly journals and concert program notes.

If you are a student learning how to write about music, you will need to train yourself to listen actively rather than passively. Passive listening means just enjoying a performance or recording. This kind of listening is certainly a valid way to hear music, but to write about music you must become more aware of what you are hearing. You must intentionally listen for certain qualities in the music. Active listening also involves learning about the background of a composer or musician to deepen your understanding of the music. As an active listener, you can observe how the audience responds during a performance, and you can analyze and critique the performance as you listen. To help you become a more active listener, your instructor might take your class on field trips to concerts so you can experience a variety of performances. You might attend a classical symphony concert, a chamber music performance, a recital showcasing the talents of a single performer, or a concert by a rock band or a jazz ensemble.

D8-a Determine your audience and their needs in music.

Audiences for music writers include professional musicians, music historians, and researchers, teachers, and students. They read scholarly or teaching journals to learn about new analyses or interpretations of musical compositions and about methods that other musicians, researchers, or teachers are using. Other audiences may include members of the general public, who read reviews of performances in newspapers or on Web sites to help them decide whether to attend concerts. Serious concertgoers read reviews after they attend a performance as a way of helping them think more about their experience at the concert. Audiences attending performances read the printed programs to learn about the biographies of composers and the histories of pieces they will hear. Some readers are in businesses, government agencies, or nonprofit organizations that fund musicians and arts groups. They read grant proposals written by researchers, musicians, teachers, and even students who are seeking funds to support their study or practice of music.

Readers in the field of music want to know the writer's opinion, but they expect the writing to contain more than just statements of personal taste. If the piece of writing is a music review, readers want the writer to evaluate the performance with specific details and examples to justify the writer's opinion. Because the discipline of music is a diverse field with a very long history, understanding one composer or work or performer requires making connections to others in the field. All readers expect writers about music to make references to other composers, styles, or musicians.

D8-b Recognize the forms of writing in music.

When you take courses in music, you may be asked to write any of the following:

- response papers
- program notes
- press releases
- concert reviews
- journal articles
- grant proposals

Response papers

A response paper is your personal reflection on a piece of music, a composer, a performance, or your own progress as a musician. Your instructor may ask you to write the paper as a brief assignment or as part of a journal that you keep during the course. The purpose of personal response is to brainstorm some initial ideas or to reflect on a work you are studying or a concert you attended. These writing activities will help you generate topics for larger, more formal projects. To help you focus your attention on particular elements of a performance, your instructor may provide questions you can use in forming your response. Your instructor might assign a response paper after you attend a concert and then later require a concert review using your response paper as a starting point. Thus a response paper can help you move from your immediate reactions to a more objective piece of writing. To be sure that your responses are useful for later assignments, make them detailed and thorough. Avoid simply writing that you like or dislike a particular work or performer. Instead, provide details that illustrate exactly why you have that particular reaction.

Program notes

When people attend a concert, they are usually given a program that lists the pieces they will hear and describes those pieces so they can understand and appreciate the music they will hear. Those descriptions are called *program notes.* A program note usually includes a biographical profile of the composer, background information about the composer's historical period, some mention of the first performance of the piece with a list or survey of major performances, and a description of the piece. The description will guide audience members through the performance, describing what they can expect to hear in each section of the piece. One kind of program note is a profile of each performer, describing the performer's major accomplishments and listing schools attended and major past performances. It may also give a brief discography, a listing of recordings that the performer has made professionally. Writing program notes will require you to do some research so you can provide the information readers expect to enhance their enjoyment and understanding of the performance. Think of program notes as small research papers that teach your readers about the music they are going to listen to.

Press releases

A press release is a brief document of no more than 250 words announcing an upcoming musical event to the general public. It is written by the event's organizers and distributed locally for publication in newspapers, in magazines, and on Web sites and as announcements on radio and television. Begin a press release with a one- or two-sentence statement giving the most important information about the event: what it is, who the main performers will be, and the time, date, and location of the event. Your press release can continue with a description of the composers and performers who will be featured. The press release should conclude with any other relevant information such as cost, parking, and a Web site or phone number where readers can get more information.

Concert reviews

Concert reviews might be the most popular kind of writing about music. The reviewer attends a concert, listens actively and intently, and tells readers about the experience. When you write a concert review, begin by engaging your audience with one or more sentences that capture the quality and mood of the entire performance. Tell readers what composers and works were featured and who the performers were. Then write about each part of the concert. Briefly describe what was played and how it was played, stating your opinions about the music and the performers, with examples to illustrate your opinions. You might also integrate historical information about the composer, the piece of music, or the performers. Vivid words and active sentences will give readers a sense of how it felt to attend the performance.

Journal articles

Musicologists research and write about the history and literature of music, and they analyze works of music. They publish their interpretations in scholarly journals and present their work at professional conferences. You may be assigned a paper that involves research and musical analysis. A typical assignment might ask you to explain how a composition reflects its historical period or to trace trends in music in a time period or region. You might explore larger issues such as music in mass media or how technology has changed music. Your assignment might ask you to focus on a less-known composer, performer, or work. If you are writing a journal article about the teaching of music, you might write a how-to paper that proposes an improved way to do something — how to rehearse a high school band more effectively, how to teach jazz improvisation, or how to start a school chamber music festival, for example. A paper of that type would involve reading articles, interviewing teachers and administrators, and using personal observations and experiences.

Grant proposals

Musicians and music teachers often apply for funding to support their projects. They might request money to purchase new equipment for their schools, to organize a summer workshop or camp, to travel to a library for research, or to attend a summer academy or workshop for intense study with well-known teachers. Whether you write a grant proposal on a form provided by the funding agency or draft your own, it typically includes several sections:

- an introduction that briefly describes the project and covers basic details about when, where, and how you expect the project to be achieved

- an outcomes section describing all the objectives you expect to attain with your project

- an itemized list of anticipated expenses

- a timeline section providing a schedule for completion, including deadlines for specific tasks
- a list of qualifications—the personal skills and experience that will enable you to complete the project
- a résumé

D8-c Know the questions musicians and musicologists ask.

Writers about music ask questions that guide them toward analysis and interpretation. The following are some questions that would lead to topics for research papers in music:

- In what ways do the symphonies of Brahms show the influence of earlier classical composers as well as the qualities of the Romantic period?
- How did rock and roll develop from earlier forms of music?
- How did changes in US society and mass media in the 1950s and 1960s influence the development of country music?
- What techniques of music composition and instrumentation has Alison Krauss used to create her unique bluegrass sound?
- What elements of blues and rock and roll does Green Day use most effectively in its hit single "September Song"?
- What challenges do symphony orchestras in the United States encounter, what are the causes of those challenges, and what are some effective strategies that cities have developed or could develop to build and sustain orchestras?

D8-d Understand the kinds of evidence musicians and musicologists use.

Musicians and musicologists use primary and secondary sources for evidence. A primary source is a music composition that the writer is analyzing or a concert or recording that the writer is reviewing. Secondary sources are books, articles, and Web sites about composers, musicians, or music.

The following are examples of the ways you might use evidence when you write about music:

- For program notes, you would use secondary sources for biographical material about the performer and historical

asking questions • evidence • primary sources •
secondary sources • conventions • specialized vocabulary
D8-e   D-99

information about the work of music to be performed. You might interview some of the performers (primary sources); for an original work, you might interview the composer, if possible.

- For a research paper tracing the development of Creole music in southern Louisiana, your primary sources could be songs representing different styles of Creole music and stages in the evolution of the music. Secondary sources would be books and other materials about the history of southern society and culture.

- For a review of a performance of Handel's *Messiah*, you would use specific moments from the concert itself as evidence to illustrate your opinions. You might mention how the conductor and the soloists interpreted particular parts of the piece and describe how sections of the orchestra and chorus performed. You might also note performers or moments from the performance that stood out because of their strengths or weaknesses.

D8-e Become familiar with writing conventions in music.

Musicians and musicologists agree on several conventions when they write:

- Musical compositions are known and categorized by detailed or specialized titles. For example, Beethoven's fifth symphony is Symphony no. 5 in C Minor, op. 67 (*op.* is the abbreviation for *opus*, or "work").

- Musicians and musicologists use a specialized vocabulary from music theory and history. Often that vocabulary includes words in Italian, German, or French. For example, movements of a symphony are known by their technical terms, such as the *adagio* section or the *allegro* movement.

- In reflective writing, the first-person pronoun *I* is acceptable. In a music review, it should be used sparingly so the review remains fair and analytical and does not seem to be merely a statement of personal taste. The first person can be used in grant proposals but not in press releases, program notes, or research papers in music.

- Writers use past tense to describe past events such as a composer's life or a performance. They use present tense when reviewing a recording or analyzing a work of music (for example, *In Nickel Creek's new song, the mandolin plays variations on an old folk tune*).

- Music writers use active voice and active verbs to keep their writing lively and engaging.

D8-f Use the MLA system in writing in music.

Writers in music typically use the style guidelines of the Modern Language Association (MLA), to format a paper, to document sources within the paper, and to cite sources at the end of the paper. Those guidelines are set forth in the *MLA Handbook for Writers of Research Papers*, 7th ed. (2009). (For more details, see the MLA documentation sections in your handbook.)

In addition, specific information about writing in music can be found in D. Kern Holoman, *Writing about Music: A Style Sheet*, 2nd ed. (2008), and Jonathan Bellman, *A Short Guide to Writing about Music*, 2nd ed. (2006).

D8-g Sample student paper: Concert review

A typical assignment in music courses is a review of a performance or a recording. Reviews appear in newspapers, in magazines, and on Web sites. The following student paper was written in a writing course for music majors and other students interested in music. The student, Tom Houston, attended a local concert for this assignment. He used the style guidelines in the *MLA Handbook* to format his paper and to cite and list his sources.

Tom Houston

Dr. Belland

MUS 291 W

27 February 2008

Concert Review: Cincinnati Symphony Orchestra

The Cincinnati Symphony Orchestra performed a stunning concert Saturday evening, February 23, 2008. Those who came, filling Music Hall to almost two-thirds capacity, were immersed in what became a soul-searching musical experience provided by Maestro John Adams. The program selections and the exquisite performances offered the audience an opportunity to expand their appreciation for contemporary music.

Opening this energetic program was *Tod und Verklärung* ("Death and Transfiguration"), a tone poem by Richard Strauss. Following the Strauss, Adams led the orchestra in *On the Transmigration of Souls* and, after the intermission, *The Dharma at Big Sur*, both composed by Adams.

Strauss wrote *Tod und Verklärung*, a lively musical stampede, when he was just twenty-five years old. This seems to be a relatively young age to tackle such a profoundly heavy subject. In his preconcert talk, Adams observed that at the time Strauss was "a bit overwhelmed at his own orchestral virtuosity." Very effective in the introduction of this tone poem is the motif played by the timpani suggesting the faltering heartbeat of a dying elderly man. Then the music grows to a galloping romp—a very young Strauss's concept of the old man's entrance into Glory Land. At least this is the generally accepted interpretation. Listening carefully, one can hear partway through the Glory Land section the faltering heart still beating. Strauss might be giving us pre-death hallucinations followed by a slightly subdued entrance into heaven.

The orchestra under Adams gave an intense interpretation of this Strauss masterpiece. The gentle, soft voice usually brought to this orchestra by music director Paavo Järvi would have added a welcome intensified dramatic contrast to what was a rendition with merely adequate drama under Adams's baton.

It is strange to think of the Strauss piece as whimsical. It is a heavyweight probe into heavyweight matter. However, in his preconcert talk to the early concertgoers, Adams said that he added it to the program

Writer's name and page number, flush right on every page.

Houston begins with the time and place of the concert and then gives his overall evaluation of the performance.

Houston provides context by listing the pieces on the program.

This section vividly describes the history and sound of the Strauss composition.

Houston evaluates how the orchestra performed the piece, giving supporting details from the performance.

Marginal annotations indicate MLA-style formatting and effective writing.

as "whimsy" but that it might not have been the most effective selection because it added more weight to an already heavy program. The truth of this comment became apparent during Adams's own *On the Transmigration of Souls.*

As the program notes by Richard E. Rodda indicate, *Transmigration* was originally written for and performed by the New York Philharmonic Orchestra in honor of the victims of the September 11, 2001, terrorist attacks. Adding to the orchestra the voices of the May Festival Chorus, the Cincinnati Children's Choir, and a prerecorded soundtrack, Adams transformed Music Hall into a cathedral. Adams's music avoids evoking the terrible scenes seen so many times, using as the text the simple, heartrending statements of both victims and their loved ones. Each poignant word was sung exquisitely, every phrase clearly understood through the appropriate musical dissonance of the orchestra.

The depth of the significance of this work cannot be overstated. Adams captured this event not only through the souls of the victims but also through the souls of the surviving loved ones and the souls of all whose lives were forever changed that morning. The performance began with Adams standing motionless in a silent hall, and it ended with him standing motionless in a silent hall. It seemed almost a sacrilege to clap, but that is all an audience can do. It was like clapping after Communion. Soon Robert Porco, director of the May Festival Chorus, and Robyn Lana, director of the Cincinnati Children's Choir, appeared with Adams to accept a well-deserved tribute from the audience. This seemed to make the extended applause more appropriate and a welcome emotional release.

Following the intermission, violinist Leila Josefowicz appeared with the orchestra to perform Adams's *The Dharma at Big Sur.* This is quintessential Adams at his compositional best. The entire work sounds improvisational, especially the solo violin. The instrument, made especially for Josefowicz, is a six-string electric violin with a very wide range, so different from a traditional violin that the performer is required to learn new technique to play it. The music, moving beyond traditional Western tones, employs quarter, or in-between, tones, which slide up or down, giving a sound that is strange to Western, classically trained ears.

Transition contrasts the first work on the program with the next work to be discussed.

Houston provides background, description, and an opinion about the performance of the second piece.

Houston uses vivid description to give readers a sense of what it was like to attend the concert.

Houston provides background about an instrument and music that might be unfamiliar to readers.

Houston 3

Josefowicz's enduring energy and technique, the controlled
orchestral dissonance and extraordinarily equipped percussion section, and
the leprechaunesque gyrations of Adams gave the audience an exciting
listening and viewing experience.

We Cincinnatians are traditionally a conservative people, preferring
an orchestra to have a traditionally "full" or lush sound, but Adams
composes on the leading crest of the wave of minimalism, a contemporary,
spare sound that can make an audience uncomfortable. The concert
Saturday night moved the Cincinnati audience a step or two forward.

Houston supports his opinion about the final piece with vivid details.

The conclusion summarizes the general impact of the performance on the audience.

Houston 4

Works cited list
begins on a new
page and is
formatted in MLA
style.

Works Cited

Adams, John. Preconcert talk. Cincinnati Symphony Orchestra. Music Hall,
Cincinnati. 23 Feb. 2008. Address.

Cincinnati Symphony Orchestra, perf. Concert. Cond. John Adams. Music
Hall, Cincinnati. 23 Feb. 2008. Performance.

Rodda, Richard E. "John Adams: *On the Transmigration of Souls*." Program
notes. Cincinnati Symphony Orchestra. 23 Feb. 2008. Print.

D9 Writing in nursing

Writing is an important tool in the education of nursing students as well as in the everyday workplaces of the profession. For students learning to become nurses, writing about specific nursing theories and practices, medical cases, and client experiences helps them better understand concepts and skills through research and analytical thinking.

For professional nurses, writing is a crucial means of communication with colleagues in the health care profession, communication that can improve the quality of care for patients, or *clients*, as they are increasingly called. Nurses write charts about their clients (a practice called *charting*), staff memos, patient education booklets, and policies for health care facilities. They may also contribute research articles to journals in the field or craft arguments to attempt to persuade decision makers to change or adopt a particular health care policy.

To write effectively in nursing, you need to support your claims with accurate client observations and current, researched evidence.

D9-a Determine your audience and their needs in nursing.

Nurses write for health care providers such as other nurses, patients or clients, and the staff and administrators of institutions such as clinics and hospitals. Health care providers read documents that inform them about a client's history and needs and a nurse's recommended interventions. Patients or clients read documents to learn about their health care options, home care needs, and nutrition and lifestyle choices. Administrators and staff read instructions, procedures, guidelines, reports, proposals, and policy recommendations that will enable them to make decisions and perform their functions effectively.

Your readers will expect your writing to be grounded in data, with a client's chart information and lab results clearly presented in an objective tone. You should describe your observations of a client's physical and emotional condition directly and thoroughly. You may present those observations using the first-person pronoun *I* or *we*, but be as objective as possible. Confidentiality and sensitivity to a client's background and diversity are essential.

Clients often feel anxious about their medical conditions, and many clients may not be familiar with medical terminology. When you write for clients, respect their right to understand their own medical

documents. Write in plain language that is direct and easy to understand, using a minimum of technical terminology and defining such
terms when it is necessary to use them. When you write for health
care professionals, be precise and use relevant specialized medical
terminology.

D9-b Recognize the forms of writing in nursing.

Students in nursing school are asked to write many different kinds
of papers. You might be required to write some of the following types
of documents:

- statements of philosophy
- nursing practice papers
- case studies
- research papers
- literature reviews
- experiential or reflective narratives
- position papers

Statements of philosophy

To help you articulate why you want to become a nurse, your instructor may ask you to write your personal philosophy of nursing at
the beginning of your professional schooling. This assignment is an
opportunity to explain what principles you value, what experiences
have shaped your career path, how you plan to put your principles
into practice, and perhaps what specialization you are interested in
pursuing.

Nursing practice papers

Assignments that ask you to apply your growing knowledge about
medicine and care practices can take different forms: a nursing care
plan, a concept map, or a nursing process paper. For these practice
papers, you provide

- a detailed client history and a nursing diagnosis of the client's
  health problems
- the interventions you recommend for the client
- your rationales for the interventions
- expected outcomes for the client
- actual, observed outcomes

A concept map is an important technique that students can use to understand how to approach client care or how to sort through possible solutions to a problem. Students create a diagram that shows the connections between the possible diagnoses, the client and medical research data that could support each diagnosis, and the plans for client care that follow from each diagnosis.

Case studies

When you are asked to do a case study, you are given detailed information about a hypothetical client's health issue and are instructed to analyze the data. Case studies help you develop a global view of the many elements that make up a client's health problems and shape the health care decisions you make for the client. In a case study, you might

- interpret laboratory results
- evaluate data from a chart that a nurse on the previous shift has completed
- prioritize the client's medical needs
- determine the necessary guidelines for carrying out any required procedures (such as wound care)
- consider, with sensitivity, how the client's personal history, including language and cultural background, might inform how you interact with the client, answer questions, and respond to his or her needs

Research papers

A research paper assignment calls on you to research and report on a topic relevant to the nursing field—perhaps a particular disease, such as Alzheimer's, or an issue that challenges medical professionals, such as maintaining quality care when the downsizing of nursing staffs leads to longer, more fatiguing shifts. Typically, you are required to use as sources as many as twenty-five scholarly articles published in peer-reviewed journals in medical fields. (Peer-reviewed journals publish manuscripts only after they have been carefully reviewed anonymously by experts in the field.)

In some cases, you will be asked to formulate a research question (such as *Is the use of animal-assisted therapy effective in managing behavioral problems of clients with Alzheimer's?*) and come to a conclusion based on a review of recently published research. In other cases, you may be expected to synthesize information from a number of published articles to answer questions about a nursing practice, such as medication administration, or about a disorder, such as muscular dystrophy.

Literature reviews

Review assignments ask you to read and synthesize published work on a nursing topic. Since as a nursing student you must read many scholarly articles about medical conditions and nursing practices, it is important to understand and stay current with the latest advances in the field. In a literature review, you summarize the arguments or findings of one or more journal articles or of a larger body of recent scholarship on a topic. In some cases, you may be asked more specifically to analyze the works critically, evaluating whether the findings seem justified by the data. Such an assignment may be called a *critical review*.

Experiential or reflective narratives

Some of the writing you do as a nursing student will be reflective. To begin to understand what clients are experiencing because of an illness, you might write a personal narrative about what happened to you while caring for a client or what happened to your client as he or she coped with an illness. For example, one student wrote about the increasing sense of isolation and hopelessness that an elderly woman suffered because of her late-stage glaucoma.

Position papers

In a position paper, you take a stance on a controversial issue in the field, such as whether the government should prohibit junk food commercials during children's television programming. You must support your argument with evidence from published research and show the evidence and reasoning that may support an opposing position. A good position paper makes clear why the issue is controversial and important to debate.

D9-c Know the questions nurses ask.

Nursing students ask questions in their writing that help them effectively care for clients. You might ask questions such as the following to understand the needs of clients:

- What information should you collect each day from a client with a particular condition?

literature review • narrative • position paper • asking questions •
evidence • lab results • vital signs • observations • conventions

D9-e   D-109

- Do the data in the client's chart indicate a normal or an abnormal status of his or her condition?
- What interventions should you take based on the diagnosis of the client's condition? Why are those interventions necessary?
- How do you care for a surgical patient with chronic pain?

D9-d Understand the kinds of evidence nurses use.

When you are writing a paper in nursing, sometimes your evidence will be quantitative (such as lab results or a client's vital signs), and sometimes it will be qualitative (such as your observations and descriptions of a client's appearance or state of mind). The following are examples of the kinds of evidence you might use:

- a client's lab test results
- data from a nurse's client chart
- research findings in a journal article
- direct observation of a client's physical or mental state

Because clients can have multiple medical problems that need to be prioritized for treatment, nurses use evidence to support more than one nursing diagnosis.

D9-e Become familiar with writing conventions in nursing.

Nurses agree on some conventions when they write:

- Nurses increasingly refer to the people in their care as "clients," not "patients."
- Evaluations and conclusions must be based on accurate and detailed information (*At the time of his diagnosis, the client had experienced a 20-lb weight loss in the previous 6 months. His CBC showed a WBC count of 32, an H & H of 13/38, and a platelet count of 34,000*).
- The first-person pronoun *I* is acceptable in reflective papers about your own experience, but you should use an objective voice in the third person for research papers, reviews, case studies, position papers, and papers describing nursing practices (*Post-operative findings: External fixation devices extend from the proximal tibia and fibular shafts of the left foot*).
- Nurses often use passive voice in describing procedures or recording their observations (*Inflammation was observed at the site of the incision*).

- The identity of clients whose cases are discussed in writing must remain confidential (nurses often make up initials to denote a client's name).

- Direct quotation of sources is rare; instead, nurses paraphrase to demonstrate their understanding of the source material and to convey information economically.

- The APA (American Psychological Association) system of headings and subheadings helps readers see the hierarchy of sections in a paper.

D9-f Use the APA system in writing in nursing.

Writers in nursing typically use the style guidelines of the American Psychological Association (APA) for formatting their paper, for citing sources in the text of their paper, and for listing sources at the end. The APA system is set forth in the *Publication Manual of the American Psychological Association*, 6th ed. (Washington, DC: APA, 2010). (For more details, see the APA documentation sections in your handbook.)

D9-g Sample student paper: Nursing practice paper

If you are asked to write a nursing practice paper, you will need to provide a detailed client history, a nursing diagnosis of the client's health problems, the interventions you recommend to care for the client and your rationales for those interventions, and the expected and actual outcomes for your client. The following student paper was written for a nursing course that focused on clinical experience. The writer, Julie Riss, used the style guidelines of the American Psychological Association (APA) to format her paper and to cite and list her sources.

1 The header consists
of a shortened title
in all capital letters
at the left margin
and the page
number at the right
margin; on the title
page only, the
shortened title is
preceded by the
words "Running
head" and a colon.

Acute Lymphoblastic Leukemia and Hypertension in One Client:

A Nursing Practice Paper

Julie Riss

George Mason University

Full title, writer's
name, and school
halfway down the
page.

Author Note

This paper was prepared for Nursing 451, taught by Professor
Durham. The author wishes to thank the nursing staff of Milltown General
Hospital for help in understanding client care and diagnosis.

An author's note lists
specific information
about the course
or department and
can provide
acknowledgments
and contact
information.

Marginal annotations indicate APA-style formatting and effective writing.

Full title, repeated.

Headings and subheadings, in APA style, mark the sections of the report and help readers follow the organization.

Riss begins by summarizing the client's history using information from his chart and her interview.

Riss respects the client's privacy by using only his initials in her paper.

Riss describes her detailed assessment of the client, using appropriate medical terminology.

Acute Lymphoblastic Leukemia and Hypertension in One Client:

A Nursing Practice Paper

Historical and Physical Assessment

Physical History

E.B. is a 16-year-old white male 5'10" tall weighing 190 lb. He was admitted to the hospital on April 14, 2006, due to decreased platelets and a need for a PRBC transfusion. He was diagnosed in October 2005 with T-cell acute lymphoblastic leukemia (ALL), after a 2-week period of decreased energy, decreased oral intake, easy bruising, and petechia. The client had experienced a 20-lb weight loss in the previous 6 months. At the time of diagnosis, his CBC showed a WBC count of 32, an H & H of 13/38, and a platelet count of 34,000. His initial chest X-ray showed an anterior mediastinal mass. Echocardiogram showed a structurally normal heart. He began induction chemotherapy on October 12, 2005, receiving vincristine, 6-mercaptopurine, doxorubicin, intrathecal methotrexate, and then high-dose methotrexate per protocol. He was diagnosed with hypertension (HTN) due to systolic blood pressure readings consistently ranging between 130s and 150s and was started on nifedipine. E.B. has a history of mild ADHD, migraines, and deep vein thrombosis (DVT). He has tolerated the induction and consolidation phases of chemotherapy well and is now in the maintenance phase, in which he receives a daily dose of mercaptopurine, weekly doses of methotrexate, and intermittent doses of steroids.

Psychosocial History

There is a possibility of a depressive episode a year previously when he would not attend school. He got into serious trouble and was sent to a shelter for 1 month. He currently lives with his mother, father, and 14-year-old sister.

Family History

Paternal: prostate cancer and hypertension in grandfather

Maternal: breast cancer and heart disease

Current Assessment

Client's physical exam reveals him to be alert and oriented to person, place, and time. He communicates, though not readily. His speech and vision are intact. He has an equal grip bilaterally and can move all

ALL AND HTN IN ONE CLIENT   3

extremities, though he is generally weak. Capillary refill is less than
2 s. His peripheral pulses are strong and equal, and he is positive for
posterior tibial and dorsalis pedis bilaterally. His lungs are clear to
auscultation, his respiratory rate is 16, and his oxygen saturation is 99%
on room air. He has positive bowel sounds in all quadrants, and his
abdomen is soft, round, and nontender. He is on a regular diet, but his
appetite has been poor. Client is voiding appropriately and his urine is
clear and yellow. He appears pale and is unkempt. His skin is warm, dry,
and intact. He has alopecia as a result of chemotherapy. His mediport site
has no redness or inflammation. He appears somber and is slow to comply
with nursing instructions.

Assessment uses a neutral tone.

Medical Diagnosis #1: Acute Lymphoblastic Leukemia

Leukemia is a neoplastic disease that involves the blood-forming
tissues of the bone marrow, spleen, and lymph nodes. In leukemia the
ratio of red to white blood cells is reversed. There are approximately
2,500 cases of acute lymphoblastic leukemia (ALL) per year in the United
States, and it is the most common type of leukemia in children—it
accounts for 75%-80% of childhood leukemias. The peak age of onset
is 4 years, and it affects whites more often than blacks and males more
often than females. Risk factors include Down syndrome or genetic
disorders; exposures to ionizing radiation and certain chemicals such as
benzene; human T-cell leukemia/lymphoma virus-1; and treatment for
certain cancers.

ALL causes an abnormal proliferation of lymphoblasts in
the bone marrow, lymph nodes, and spleen. As the lymphoblasts
proliferate, they suppress the other hematopoietic elements in the
marrow. The leukemic cells do not function as mature cells and so do not
work as they should in the immune and inflammatory processes. Because
the growth of red blood cells and platelets is suppressed, the signs and
symptoms of the disease are infections, bleeding, pallor, bone pain,
weight loss, sore throat, fatigue, night sweats, and weakness. Treatment
involves chemotherapy, bone marrow transplant, or stem cell transplant
(LeMone & Burke, 2004).

APA allows extra space above headings when it improves readability.

Riss paraphrases the source and uses an APA-style in-text citation.

ALL AND HTN IN ONE CLIENT   4

Medical Diagnosis #2: Hypertension

Primary hypertension in adolescence is a condition in which the blood pressure is persistently elevated to the 95th to 99th percentile for age, sex, and weight (Hockenberry, 2003). It must be elevated on three separate occasions for diagnosis to be made. Approximately 50 million people in the United States suffer from hypertension. It most often affects middle-aged and older adults and is more prevalent in black adults than in whites and Hispanics. In blacks the prevalence between males and females is equal, but in whites and Hispanics more males than females are affected. Risk factors include family history, age, race, mineral intake, obesity, insulin resistance, excess alcohol consumption, smoking, and stress. Hypertension results from sustained increases in blood volume and peripheral resistance. The increased blood volume causes an increase in cardiac output, which causes systemic arteries to vasoconstrict. This increased vascular resistance causes hypertension. Hypertension accelerates the rate of atherosclerosis, increasing the risk factor for heart disease and stroke. The workload of the heart is increased, causing ventricular hypertrophy, which increases risk for heart disease, dysrhythmias, and heart failure. Early hypertension usually exhibits no symptoms. The elevations in blood pressure are temporary at first but then progress to being permanent. A headache in the back of the head when awakening may be the only symptom. Other symptoms include blurred vision, nausea and vomiting, and nocturia. Treatment involves medications such as ACE inhibitors, diuretics, beta-adrenergic blockers, calcium channel blockers, and vasodilators as well as changes in diet, such as decreased sodium intake. An increase in physical activity is essential to aid in weight loss and to reduce stress (LeMone & Burke, 2004).

Chart Review

Active Orders

Vital signs q4h

Fall precautions

OOB as tolerated

Oximetry monitoring—continuous

Riss demonstrates her understanding of the medical condition.

ALL AND HTN IN ONE CLIENT   5

CBC with manual differential daily in am

Regular diet

Weight—daily

Strict intake and output monitoring

Type and cross match

PRBCs—2 units

Platelets—1 unit

Discharge after CBC results posttransfusion shown to MD

Rationale for Orders

Vital signs are monitored every four hours per unit standard. In
addition, the client's hypertension is an indication for close monitoring
of blood pressure. He has generalized weakness, so fall precautions should
be implemented. Though he is weak, ambulation is important, especially
considering the client's history of DVT. A regular diet is ordered—I'm not
sure why the client is not on a low-sodium diet, given his hypertension.
Intake and output monitoring is standard on the unit. His hematological
status needs to be carefully monitored due to his anemia and
thrombocytopenia; therefore he has a CBC with manual differential done
each morning. In addition, his hematological status is checked
posttransfusion to see if the blood and platelets he receives increase
his RBC and platelet counts. Transfused platelets survive in the body
approximately 1-3 days, and the peak effect is achieved about 2 hr
posttransfusion. Though platelets normally do not have to be
cross-matched for blood group or type, children who receive multiple
transfusions may become sensitized to a platelet group other than
their own. Therefore, platelets are cross-matched with the donor's
blood components. Blood and platelet transfusions may result in
hemolytic, febrile, or allergic reactions, so the client is carefully
monitored during the transfusion. Hospital protocol requires a set of
baseline vital signs prior to transfusion vital signs. After the blood and
platelets have been given, the physician is apprised of CBC results to
be sure that the client's thrombocytopenia has resolved before he is
discharged.

Riss uses specialized
medical terminology.

Riss shows how
physiology,
prescribed
treatments, and
nursing practices
are related.

D9-g   Writing in nursing

Pharmacological Interventions and Goals

Short tables, like those in this paper, are placed within the text. A longer table can be placed on a separate page.

Medications and Effects

ondansetron hydrochloride (Zofran) 8 mg PO PRN	serotonin receptor antagonist, antiemetic—prevention of nausea and vomiting associated with chemotherapy
famotidine (Pepcid) 10 mg PO ac	H2 receptor antagonist, antiulcer agent—prevention of heartburn
nifedipine (Procardia) 30 mg PO bid	calcium channel blocker, antihypertensive—prevention of hypertension
enoxaparin sodium (Lovenox) 60 mg SQ bid	low-molecular-weight heparin derivative, anticoagulant—prevention of DVT
mercaptopurine (Purinethol) 100 mg PO qhs	antimetabolite, antineoplastic—treatment of ALL
PRBCs—2 units leukoreduced, irradiated[a]	to increase RBC count
platelets—1 unit[a]	to treat thrombocytopenia

[a]Because these products are dispensed by pharmacy, they are considered a pharmacological intervention, even though technically not medications.

Laboratory Tests and Significance

Riss presents data in several tables for easy reference.

Complete Blood Count (CBC)[a]

Result name	Result	Abnormal	Normal range
WBC	3.0	*	4.5-13.0
RBC	3.73	*	4.20-5.40
Hgb	11.5		11.1-15.7
Hct	32.4	*	34.0-46.0
MCV	86.8		78.0-95.0
MCH	30.7		26.0-32.0
MCHC	35.4		32.0-36.0
RDW	14.6		11.5-15.5
Platelet	98	*	140-400
MPV	8.3		7.4-10.4

[a]*Rationale:* Client's ALL diagnosis and treatment necessitate frequent monitoring of his hematological status. WBC count, RBC, and hematocrit are decreased due to chemotherapy. The platelet count is low.

ALL AND HTN IN ONE CLIENT   7

Type and Cross-Match[a]

Result name	Result
ABORH	APOS
ANTIBODY SCR INTERP	NEGATIVE

[a]*Rationale:* To determine client's blood type and to screen for antibodies.

Vital Signs Before, During, and After Blood Transfusion[a]

Vital signs	Time	BP	Pulse	Resp	Temp (oral)
Pre	1705	113/74	92	18	98.7
15 min	1720	118/74	104	12	98.3
30 min	1735	121/74	96	16	99.3
45 min	1750	129/76	101	16	99.3
Post	1805	108/59	99	15	98.9

[a]*Rationale:* To monitor for reaction.

Nursing Diagnosis #1:
Injury, Risk for, Related to Decreased Platelet Count and Administration of Lovenox

Desired Outcome: Client will remain free of injury.

Interventions

Monitor vital signs q4h

Assess for manifestations of bleeding such as

- Skin and mucous membranes for petechiae, ecchymoses, and hematoma formation
- Gums and nasal membranes for bleeding
- Overt or occult blood in stool or urine
- Neurologic changes

Provide sponge to clean gums and teeth

Apply pressure to puncture sites for 3-5 min

Avoid invasive procedures when possible

Administer stool softeners as prescribed

Implement fall precautions

Monitor lab values for platelets

Administer platelets as prescribed

Measurable Outcomes

Mediport site will remain intact with no signs of bleeding.

Riss prioritizes her diagnoses and recommended interventions and gives a detailed description and rationales for each.

ALL AND HTN IN ONE CLIENT   8

Urine and stool will remain free of blood.

Lab values for anticoagulant therapy will remain in desired range.

Platelet count will remain in normal range.

Client Teaching

Riss uses specific examples.

Instruct client to avoid forcefully blowing nose, straining to have a bowel
movement, and forceful coughing or sneezing, all of which increase
the risk for external and internal bleeding

Discharge Planning

Instruct client to monitor for signs of decreased platelet count such as easy
bruising, petechiae, or inappropriate bleeding

Nursing Diagnosis #2:

Infection, Risk for, Related to Depressed Body Defenses

Desired Outcome: Client will remain free of infection.

Interventions

Screen all visitors and staff for signs of infection to minimize exposure to
infectious agents

Use aseptic technique for all procedures

Monitor temperature to detect possible infection

Evaluate client for potential sites of infection: needle punctures, mucosal
ulcerations

Provide nutritionally complete meals to support the body's natural
defenses

Monitor lab values for CBC

Administer G-CSF if prescribed

Measurable Outcomes

Mediport site will remain free of erythema, purulent drainage, odor, and
edema.

Client will remain afebrile.

Client Teaching

Instruct client and caregivers in correct hand-washing technique

Discharge Planning

Instruct client and caregivers to avoid live attenuated virus
vaccines

Instruct client to avoid large crowds

ALL AND HTN IN ONE CLIENT   9

Nursing Diagnosis #3:

Noncompliance, Related to HTN, as Evidenced by Lack of
Consistent Medication Regimen and Adherence to Dietary Plan

Desired Outcome: Client will follow treatment plan.

Interventions

Inquire about reasons for noncompliance

Listen openly and without judgment

Evaluate knowledge of HTN, its long-term effects, and treatment

Arrange for nutritional consult with dietitian

Measurable Outcomes

Client will take medication as prescribed.

Client's systolic blood pressure will remain in normal range.

Client Teaching

Instruct on medication regimen: appropriate administration and potential
   adverse effects

Provide information on hypertension and its treatment

Discharge Planning

Provide prescriptions

Nursing Diagnosis #4:

Health Maintenance, Ineffective, Related to
Unhealthy Lifestyle and Behaviors

Desired Outcome: Client will make changes in lifestyle.

Interventions

Assist in identifying behaviors that contribute to hypertension

Assist in developing a realistic health maintenance plan including
   modifying risk factors such as exercise, diet, and stress

Help client and family identify strengths and weaknesses in maintaining
   health

Measurable Outcomes

Client will verbalize ways to control his hypertension.

Client will identify methods to relieve stress.

Discharge Planning

Provide information on possible exercise programs

Analysis

In the margin:
Riss summarizes the client's conditions, treatments, and consequences for nursing and discusses client education in psychological and social contexts.

In the case of E.B., there are two separate disease processes at work—ALL and HTN. The ALL is the most immediately pressing of the two and is indirectly responsible for the client's current hospitalization. The chemotherapy treatment for his leukemia has caused thrombocytopenia. This condition places him at high risk for hemorrhage. The anticoagulant therapy for DVT increases this risk even further, not only because it may cause bleeding complications, but because in itself it may cause thrombocytopenia. Therefore, it is imperative to raise his platelet count as quickly as possible. Surprisingly, there were no lab tests ordered to determine his PT and INR, both of which are monitored when a client is on anticoagulant therapy. As his CBC demonstrates, not only is his platelet count low, but his red blood cells are decreased. That is why his physician ordered a transfusion of both PRBCs and platelets.

In terms of E.B.'s diagnosis of HTN, he has a positive family history, which is a major risk factor for developing the disease. Excess weight is also a risk factor, and the client has a history of obesity as well. Because exercise is an important factor in managing the excess weight and stress associated with the disease, his leukemia and the chemotherapy treatments aimed at curing E.B.'s leukemia actually negatively affect his ability to manage the hypertension: He is often too weak and fatigued to participate in much physical activity. Additionally, the steroids have resulted in added weight gain, increasing instead of decreasing the problem. To date, the client has failed to maintain a favorable diet regimen.

E.B.'s family circumstances must be taken into consideration when managing his treatment. Though he resides with both parents, there is some question as to the support and consistency of care he receives. He often appears very unkempt and is at times noncompliant with his hypertension medication. Due to his parents' inability to care for a central venous line (CVL) at home, he has a mediport that can be accessed as needed but requires care. On a positive note, the father is aware of their limitations and tries to work with the staff to make sure that E.B.'s ALL is managed appropriately.

ALL AND HTN IN ONE CLIENT   11

                               References

Hockenberry, M. (2003). *Wong's nursing care of infants and children.*

    St. Louis, MO: Mosby.

LeMone, P., & Burke, K. (2004). *Medical surgical nursing: Critical thinking in*

    client care. Upper Saddle River, NJ: Pearson Education.

Riss provides a reference list for sources she cited in her paper. The list is formatted in APA style.

D10 Writing in psychology

Psychologists write with various purposes in mind. They frequently publish articles about their research or present their work at professional conferences. They write proposals to convince funding agencies to award grants for their research. Sometimes psychologists write to influence the opinions held by the public or by decision makers in government, lending their expertise to discussions on issues such as the effects of racism, the challenges of aging, or children's mental health. Psychologists may write analyses for newspaper and magazine opinion pages as well as policy recommendations and advocacy statements.

D10-a Determine your audience and their needs in psychology.

Psychologists write for researchers, psychotherapists, teachers, students, clients, and sometimes members of the government or business community and the general public. Researchers or clinical psychologists may read to find out the results of an experiment, the analysis of new data, or information supporting or critiquing a theory. This information may be useful to readers in developing new research projects or providing services to their clients. Students read to learn about major concepts in the field. Researchers, teachers, and students expect data and findings to be communicated thoroughly in words and in graphics such as diagrams, tables, charts, and graphs. People working in government or academic settings may need information and support for decisions about funding proposed research projects.

In all cases, your readers will expect your writing to be completely objective and to present information as clearly as possible. When you are writing in psychology, you should make thorough use of others' research in the field to demonstrate your credibility. Readers are interested more in empirical data that can be presented quantitatively than in statements from experts. Qualitative information in the form of direct observations and statements from research subjects can help readers understand your conclusions or recommendations.

Your readers will appreciate your precise use of words and a scientific stance with an objective tone. When writing for clients of psychiatric or psychotherapy services, use straightforward language that respects the clients and their right to understand their conditions and needs. Such clients will also expect confidentiality and respect for diversity.

D10-b Recognize the forms of writing in psychology.

When you take courses in psychology, you may be asked to write any of the following:

- literature reviews
- research papers
- theoretical papers
- poster presentations

Literature reviews

You will likely write review papers early in your course work. In a review paper, you report on and evaluate the research that has been published in the field about a particular topic. A literature review does not merely summarize researchers' findings but argues a position with evidence that you assemble from the empirical (that is, experiment-based) studies that you review.

Sometimes a literature review stands alone as a paper, such as a survey of findings from research performed in the past century on what causes loss of memory in old age. In some cases, you will be asked to write a critical review, in which you will analyze the methods and interpretations of data in one or more journal articles. More often you will write a literature review as an introduction to a larger piece of writing, such as a report of your own empirical study. In that case, the literature review surveys previously published findings relevant to the question that your study investigates.

Research papers

When instructors refer to *research papers*, they may have different assignments in mind. A research paper might present your synthesis of many sources of information about, say, emotional responses to music. Your purpose would be to demonstrate your understanding of research findings and the ongoing debates emerging from researchers' investigations.

A research paper might also be a report on the results of an experiment you've conducted and on your interpretation of those results; in this case, your research paper would be an empirical study. A research paper might also relate your interpretations to what others in the field have concluded from their own experiments. Like other scientists, psychologists publish research papers in journals after the papers have undergone rigorous and impartial review by other psychologists (called *peer review*) to make sure that the scientific process used by the researchers is sound.

Whether published in a journal or written for a college course, research papers based on original experiments have the following standard elements:

- the question you set out to research and why your question is important
- a review of research relevant to your question
- your hypotheses (tentative, plausible answers to the research question that your experiment will test) and your predictions that follow from the hypotheses
- the method you used to conduct your experiment
- the results from the experiment
- your analysis of those results

Writers of research reports also use tables and figures to present experimental data in easy-to-grasp visual form.

Theoretical papers

Psychologists often write theoretical papers in which they propose their own theories or extend existing theories about a research problem in the field. For example, in one journal article, a psychologist argues that the field needs to combine attachment theory and social network theory to understand child and adolescent development.

If you are asked to write a theoretical paper for a course, you will be expected to support the theory you propose by pointing to evidence and counterevidence from the literature in the field, to compare your theory with other theories, and possibly to suggest experiments that could test your theory.

Poster presentations

At professional gatherings such as annual conventions, psychologists have the opportunity to present their work in the form of a poster rather than as a formal talk. Conference attendees approach presenters in an exhibit area to talk about the presenters' research, which the posters concisely summarize. A poster typically features an introduction to the project, the method, information about the research or the subjects of an experiment, the results, and the presenter's conclusions.

Poster presentations also feature graphs and tables since it is important to convey information to conference attendees quickly and concisely as they walk through the exhibit area. An effective poster presentation will encourage the audience to ask questions and carry on an informal conversation with the presenter.

Your instructor may ask you to create a poster presentation about an experiment you or other researchers have conducted both to help you understand complex concepts and to practice your communication skills.

NOTE: Some presenters use presentation software to create a slide show that they can click through for a small audience or project on a screen for a larger group. Presenters generally include the same kinds of information in slide presentations as they do in poster presentations.

D10-c Know the questions psychologists ask.

Psychologists generally investigate human behavior and perceptions. Their questions range widely across the different specializations that make up the field, such as animal cognition, personality, social interactions, and infant development, to name a few. The following are questions that specialists in psychology might ask:

- What personality characteristics might affect employees' personal use of work computers?
- When adult learners return to school, what is the impact on their families and working lives?
- Do variations in cerebral blood flow in different areas of the brain predict variations in performance of different imagery tasks?

D10-d Understand the kinds of evidence psychologists use.

To back up their conclusions, psychologists look for evidence in case studies and the results of experiments. They do not use expert opinion as evidence; direct quotations of what other psychologists have written are rare in psychology papers. Instead, papers focus on data (the results of experiments) and on the analysis of the results that the writer has collected.

Depending on their specialization, psychologists may ask questions that require quantitative or qualitative evidence. Quantitative evidence involves numerical measurement; qualitative evidence involves examples and illustrations.

- Quantitative evidence might be facts and statistics: *Regional cerebral blood flow in a total of 26 areas predicted performance, and 20 of these areas predicted performance only in a single task. In a study on what motivates adolescents to quit smoking, 44.7% of the participants reported that they wanted to quit because their parents wanted them to.* Or it might be results of original experiments: *Fraudulent excuse scores were correlated with cheating scores (r = .37, n = 211, p < .0001).*

- Qualitative evidence might be descriptions of interviews or statements of the researcher's observations: *Many of the respondents believed that girls' tendency either to address indirectly or to avoid conflict was supported by adults, who expected them to be* ladylike; *when asked to define this term, they used such descriptors as "mature" and "calm."*

D10-e Become familiar with writing conventions in psychology.

Psychologists use straightforward and concise language and depend on special terms to explain their findings.

- Specialized vocabulary may include terms such as *methods, results, double-blind study, social identity perspective,* and *nonverbal emotions.*

- Often researchers use specific, technical definitions of terms that nonspecialists use differently. For example, if a psychologist asks whether adults with eating disorders are "depressed," the term refers to a specific mental disorder, not to a general mood of sadness.

- When reporting conclusions, writers in psychology use the past tense (*Berkowitz found*) or the present perfect tense (*Berkowitz has found*). When discussing results, they use the present tense (*The results confirm*). They avoid using subjective expressions like *I think* and *I feel.*

D10-f Use the APA system in writing in psychology.

Writers in psychology typically use the style guidelines of the American Psychological Association (APA) for formatting their papers, for citing sources in the text of their papers, and for listing sources at the end. The APA system is set forth in the *Publication Manual of the American Psychological Association,* 6th ed. (Washington, DC: APA,

2010). (For more details, see the APA documentation sections in your handbook.)

D10-g Sample student paper: Literature review (excerpt)

A psychology literature review assignment usually asks you both to survey published research on a topic in the field and to argue your own position with evidence that you assemble from your survey. The student paper excerpted beginning on the next page was written for a second-year developmental psychology course. The student, Valerie Charat, used the style guidelines of the American Psychological Association (APA) to format her paper and to cite and list her sources.

The header consists of a shortened title in all capital letters at the left margin and the page number at the right margin; on the title page only, the shortened title is preceded by the words "Running head" and a colon.

Running head: ADHD IN BOYS VS. GIRLS   1

Full title, writer's name, and school halfway down the page.

Always out of Their Seats (and Fighting):

Why Are Boys Diagnosed with ADHD More Often Than Girls?

Valerie Charat

Harvard University

An author's note lists specific information about the course or department and can provide acknowledgments and contact information.

Author Note

This paper was prepared for Psychology 1806, taught by Professor Korfine.

Marginal annotations indicate APA-style formatting and effective writing.

ADHD IN BOYS VS. GIRLS 2

Abstract

Until the early 1990s, most research on attention deficit hyperactivity disorder (ADHD) focused on boys and did not explore possible gender differences. Recent studies have suggested that gender differences do exist and are caused by personality differences between boys and girls, by gender bias in referring teachers and clinicians, or by the diagnostic procedures themselves. But the most likely reason is that ADHD is often comorbid—that is, it coexists with other behavior disorders that are not diagnosed properly and that do exhibit gender differences. This paper first considers studies of gender differences only in ADHD and then looks at studies of gender differences when ADHD occurs with comorbid disorders. Future research must focus more specifically on how gender differences are influenced by factors such as referrals, family history, and comorbid conditions.

Abstract, a 100-to-150-word overview of the paper, appears on a separate page.

D10-g Writing in psychology

ADHD IN BOYS VS. GIRLS   3

Full title, repeated.

Charat gives abbreviations in parentheses the first time she uses common psychology terms.

Introduction provides background to the topic and establishes why a literature review on ADHD is necessary.

Thesis states what Charat will argue by describing and analyzing the sources she has reviewed.

Charat uses APA style to cite her sources. Two sources in one parenthetical citation are separated with a semicolon.

Headings, centered, divide the paper into two main sections.

Always out of Their Seats (and Fighting):

Why Are Boys Diagnosed with ADHD More Often Than Girls?

Attention deficit hyperactivity disorder (ADHD) is a commonly diagnosed disorder in children that affects social, academic, or occupational functioning. As the name suggests, its hallmark characteristics are hyperactivity and lack of attention as well as impulsive behavior. For decades, studies have focused on the causes, expression, prevalence, and outcome of the disorder, but until recently very little research investigated gender differences. In fact, until the early 1990s most research focused exclusively on boys (Brown, Madan-Swain, & Baldwin, 1991), perhaps because many more boys than girls are diagnosed with ADHD. Researchers have speculated on the possible explanations for the disparity, citing reasons such as true sex differences in the manifestation of the disorder's symptoms, gender biases in those who refer children to clinicians, and possibly even the diagnostic procedures themselves (Gaub & Carlson, 1997). But the most persuasive reason is that ADHD is often a comorbid condition—that is, it coexists with other behavior disorders that are not diagnosed properly and that do exhibit gender differences.

It has been suggested that in the United States children are often misdiagnosed as having ADHD when they actually suffer from a behavior disorder such as conduct disorder (CD) or a combination of ADHD and another behavior disorder (Disney, Elkins, McGue, & Iancono, 1999; Lilienfeld & Waldman, 1990). Conduct disorder is characterized by negative and criminal behavior in children and is highly correlated with adult diagnoses of antisocial personality disorder (ASPD). This paper first considers research that has dealt only with gender difference in the occurrence of ADHD and then looks at research that has studied the condition along with other behavior disorders.

Gender Differences in Studies of ADHD

Most of the research on ADHD has lacked a comparative component. Throughout the 1970s and 1980s, most research focused only on boys. If girls were included, it was often in such low numbers that gender-based comparisons were unwarranted (Gaub & Carlson, 1997). One of the least debated differences is the dissimilarity in male and female prevalence

ADHD IN BOYS VS. GIRLS   4

rates. Some studies have claimed a 3:1 ratio of boys with ADHD to girls with ADHD (American Psychiatric Association, 1987), while others have cited ratios as high as 9:1 (Brown et al., 1991). The differences in prevalence have been attributed to a variety of causes, one of which is that girls may have more internalized symptoms and may be overlooked in ADHD diagnoses (Brown et al., 1991).

> *Charat summarizes key research findings about the paper's central question.*

A study conducted by Breen (1989) sought to test the differences in cognition, behavior, and academic functioning for boys and girls. Past research had indicated that boys with ADHD showed more aggressive behavior while girls showed more learning problems, but the results were often conflicting. To clarify the existing information, Breen conducted a study on 39 children aged 6 to 11, from a group of children referred to a pediatric psychology clinic. All subjects were white, with varying socioeconomic status. He broke the subjects into three groups: boys with ADHD, girls with ADHD, and a control group of girls without any psychiatric or family history of behavioral or emotional problems. Each group was given a battery of tests to assess cognitive functioning. All children were also observed in a playroom while they worked math problems, and all were coded for a variety of behaviors including fidgeting, vocalizing, being out of their seats, and so on.

> *A signal phrase names the author and gives the date of the source in parentheses.*
>
> *Charat examines an important study in detail. She summarizes experimental methods used by researchers.*

The results showed that while both groups with ADHD performed nearly equally across most measures, ADHD boys were generally viewed as more deviant than normal girls. Girls with ADHD were closer behaviorally to girls in the control group than to ADHD boys. This finding indicates that it may be difficult to distinguish girls with ADHD from girls without the disorder based solely on behavior. This conclusion was corroborated by the later finding (Brown et al., 1991) that girls with ADHD are often not clinically referred unless they demonstrate a more severe form of the disorder than boys do. A contradictory finding (Breen, 1989) was that ADHD boys and girls displayed rates of disruptive behavior that were not significantly different from each other, although Breen did not indicate what forms the disruptive behavior took and whether the girls were less aggressive than the boys. But as Brown et al. (1991) later pointed out, it was easier to differentiate ADHD in externalized behaviors—aggression, inattention, and overactivity—than in internalized behaviors—depression,

> *Charat uses the specialized language of the field.*
>
> *Source first mentioned on page 3. In subsequent citations, for a source with three to five authors "et al." is used after the first author's name in the text and in parentheses.*

anxiety, and withdrawal. It is striking, however, that the distinction in Breen's study was clearer not between boys and girls but between girls with and girls without ADHD. Breen concluded that differences between boys and girls with the disorder do not seem significant.

A few drawbacks to Breen's study include a lack of screening for comorbid conduct disorders, which were no doubt present in some of the subjects. The small sample size could have hindered the results, with only 13 subjects in each group. Another limitation is the small cross section: All subjects were white and clinically referred. Therefore, the findings cannot be generalized to a nonclinical, racially diverse population. Finally, the lack of male controls is surprising, given the usual trend to overrepresent boys when studying ADHD. A reasonable comparison would have been between girls with ADHD and boys in a control group to see if the girls' range of antisocial behavior was beyond that of control boys.

Another study (Maughan, Pickles, Hagell, Rutter, & Yule, 1996) investigated the association between reading problems and antisocial behavior. The researchers cited a connection that had previously been made (Hinshaw, 1992, as cited in Maughan et al., 1996) between antisocial behavior and underachievement in early childhood, while aggression and antisocial behavior became salient in later years. Maughan et al. looked specifically at reading because research has shown that children who develop reading problems have higher rates of behavioral problems even before they learn to read (Jorm, Share, Matthews, & Mclean, 1986). It had also been shown that reading problems can affect behavioral development (Pianta & Caldwell, 1992, as cited in Maughan et al., 1996). However, since most studies had been done with boys, the researchers also compared gender differences.

Subjects were selected from a previously conducted study in a population of children who were 10 years old in 1970. The majority were British-born Caucasians of low socioeconomic status. The analysis used two subsamples, one with poor reading scores, the other a randomly sampled control group with average IQ and no reading difficulties. Poor readers were rated as either "backward" or "retarded." The subjects in the backward group were 28 months below average in reading level for their age and IQ. At age 10, children had received psychometric testing, and the study

Charat analyzes the study's shortcomings.

Topic sentence states paragraph's main point.

An indirect source (work quoted in another source) is indicated with the words "as cited in."

An ampersand separates the authors' names in parentheses.

Charat describes the study's methods in detail.

ADHD IN BOYS VS. GIRLS   6

accounted for parental occupation, the child's government benefits status, and the ranking of the child's state school in terms of economic adversity. There were follow-ups at ages 14, 17, and early 20s.

Poor readers demonstrated high rates of behavior problems by age 10. About 40% of the girls and almost 50% of the boys in the retarded reading group exhibited antisocial behavior at age 10. Interestingly, reading-retarded girls showed high rates of conduct problems, while the boys did not. Also, among girls there were much higher rates of antisocial behavior in the lowest socioeconomic category than in slightly higher socioeconomic categories. In boys, the differences were not as pronounced. For boys, poor performance in school was the only predictor of antisocial behavior, while for girls poor school performance and reading level were predictors. This finding suggests that for boys, learning difficulties do not increase the risk of behavior problems, while for girls they do. Inattentiveness and overactivity were also related to reading problems and were highly related to antisocial behavior. When inattentiveness and overactivity were factored in, there were no direct links between reading difficulties and antisocial behavior. This absent connection means that reading problems do not cause antisocial behavior. It is when they cannot pay attention or sit long enough to read that both boys and girls exhibit elevated rates of antisocial behavior.

By age 14, girls still showed a significant correlation between reading problems and antisocial behavior, while boys showed no association. In early adulthood (ages 17 and early 20s), criminality, alcohol problems, aggression, and personality disorders were found in low rates in girls. In the sample of girls interviewed in their 20s, 1.9% had juvenile offense records and 5.4% had records of adult crime. In boys, poor readers did not show any significant rates of antisocial personality disorders.

The study had several drawbacks. Subject responses at follow-up periods were not uniformly gathered, and the lack of analysis of female juvenile offenders made it harder to understand the results in terms of gender differences and antisocial behavior. The sample consisted only of inner-city children of low socioeconomic status because they had higher rates of reading difficulty than other children. But because economic adversity was found to be a predictor for poor conduct in girls, this group

> In APA style, the numbers 10 and above are expressed in numerals; percentages are expressed in numbers with a percent symbol.

> After presenting the study's findings, Charat analyzes the study's weaknesses.

ADHD IN BOYS VS. GIRLS 7

of subjects may have contained a disproportionate number of female subjects with more severe antisocial behavior.

Charat speculates on possible explanations for the results of the study.

Of particular interest was that for girls but not for boys, reading level and low socioeconomic status predicted antisocial behavior. However, when the children were followed into adulthood, the females who had originally displayed antisocial behavior did not show elevated rates of juvenile offenses or adult crime. Perhaps the results indicate that girls with antisocial and hyperactive behavior in childhood are different from boys in that they are responding to passing learning impairments rather than permanent personality problems. Or girls may have continued to have ADHD, but with internalized rather than externalized symptoms. Another possibility is that the girls had more severe forms of ADHD because of sampling bias for socioeconomic status but that they eventually grew out of the disorder in adolescence while the boys did not.

Another study (Brown et al., 1991) looked specifically at the cognitive and academic performance of children with ADHD and compared internalizing versus externalizing features of the disorder across genders. As in Breen (1989), Brown et al. (1991) found there were few gender differences on measures of attention, concentration, and distractibility. However, some significant differences were found. Parent and teacher ratings of internalizing and externalizing characteristics described boys as more aggressive and girls as more unpopular. Girls were also more commonly held back one or two grades, a finding the researchers interpreted as evidence of female academic difficulties and possible neurological disorders or impairments. This would correlate with the findings of Maughan et al. (1996) of an association between reading impairment and antisocial behaviors in ADHD girls. However, the data must

If a source is cited in the text of the paragraph, only the authors' names are given when the source is cited later in the text of the same paragraph. (The date is required in all parenthetical citations.)

also be regarded cautiously. Brown et al. did not use a control group and thus did not have a standard by which to measure the differences. Any implication of a neurological impairment in females with ADHD should be viewed skeptically. The historical perception of women as the weaker or more defective sex should make any researcher reluctant to postulate . . .

[Charat continues to describe and analyze researchers' studies and findings.]

ADHD IN BOYS VS. GIRLS   11

Conclusion

Although the studies presented here are filled with flaws and contradictory findings, they have a unifying thread. Through direct findings or indirect lack of information, all suggest that the higher rate of male diagnoses of ADHD does not necessarily mean that the disorder actually occurs in boys more often than in girls. Although boys are more commonly diagnosed, this phenomenon could reflect a long-standing history of misperceptions. Since hyperactive and inattentive boys are also often aggressive and disruptive, girls who do not demonstrate similar behaviors may be overlooked.

It is important to reevaluate the way boys and girls are observed and understood when attention and hyperactivity are being assessed. Males and females may display different behaviors, and parents and teachers may interpret their behaviors differently. But when rated by trained researchers, boys and girls identified as having ADHD are rated similarly. However, it is easier to identify externalizing, aggressive behavior than it is to identify internalizing behavior, and this difference may be one of the main factors at the root of the perceived gender differences in the prevalence of ADHD. There is not enough concrete evidence to rule out the possibility that a gender difference does exist, regardless of the fact that boys and girls seem to show equal rates and degrees of symptoms. Until more studies look at population samples, exclude conduct disorders, and take into account possible differences in the ways the symptoms are manifested, it is impossible to conclude that gender differences are the result of social and clinical biases and stereotypes. Further research on genetics and familial rates of the disorder are also necessary to help clarify the relationship between adult antisocial personality disorder and ADHD. Also, until a clear distinction is made between conduct disorder and ADHD, not only in the text of the *DSM-IV* but also in the minds of laypeople and clinicians, it will be difficult to separate children with comorbid disorder and those without it and to assess gender differences as well.

Conclusion presents a synthesis of the paper's points.

Charat raises questions about the research she reviews but adopts a balanced tone in summarizing the sources.

Charat suggests areas for future research.

Conclusion affirms the necessity of continuing investigation.

ADHD IN BOYS VS. GIRLS   12

List of references
begins on a new
page. The first line
of an entry is at the
left margin;
subsequent lines
indent ½".

If an online source
has a DOI (digital
object identifier), no
URL is given.

A work with up to
seven authors lists
all authors' names. A
work with more than
seven authors lists
the first six followed
by three ellipsis dots
and the last author's
name.

List is alphabetized
by authors' last
names. All authors'
names are inverted;
an ampersand
separates the last
two authors.

References

American Psychiatric Association. (1987). *Diagnostic and statistical manual of mental disorders* (3rd ed., rev.). Washington, DC: Author.

American Psychiatric Association. (1994). *Diagnostic and statistical manual of mental disorders* (4th ed.). Washington, DC: Author.

Breen, M. J. (1989). Cognitive and behavioral differences in AdHD boys and girls. *Journal of Child Psychology and Psychiatry, 30,* 711-716. doi:10.1111/j.1469-7610.1989.tb00783.x

Breen, M. J., & Altepeter, T. S. (1990). Situational variability in boys and girls identified as ADHD. *Journal of Clinical Psychology, 46,* 486-490.

Brown, R. T., Madan-Swain, A., & Baldwin, K. (1991). Gender differences in a clinic-referred sample of attention-deficit-disordered children. *Child Psychiatry and Human Development, 22,* 111-127.

Disney, E. R., Elkins, J. J., McGue, M., & Iancono, W. G. (1999). Effects of ADHD, conduct disorder, and gender on substance use and abuse in adolescence. *American Journal of Psychiatry, 156,* 1515-1521.

Faraone, S. V., Biederman, J., Chen, W. J., Milberger, S., Warburton, R., & Tsuang, M. T. (1995). Genetic heterogeneity in attention-deficit hyperactivity disorder (ADHD): Gender, psychiatric comorbidity, and maternal ADHD. *Journal of Abnormal Psychology, 104,* 334-345.

Gaub, M., & Carlson, C. L. (1997). Gender differences in ADHD: A meta-analysis and critical review. *Journal of the American Academy of Child and Adolescent Psychiatry, 36,* 1036-1045.

Jorm, A. F., Share, D. L., Matthews, R., & Mclean, R. (1986). Behaviour problems in specific reading retarded and general reading backward children: A longitudinal study. *Journal of Child Psychology and Psychiatry, 27,* 33-43. doi:10.1111/j.1469-7610.1986.tb00619.x

Lahey, B. B., Piacentini, J. C., McBurnett, K., Stone, P., Hartdagen, S., & Hynd, G. (1988). Psychopathology in the parents of children with conduct disorder and hyperactivity. *Journal of the American Academy of Child and Adolescent Psychiatry, 27,* 163-170.

Lilienfeld, S. O., & Waldman, I. D. (1990). The relation between childhood attention-deficit hyperactivity disorder and adult antisocial behavior reexamined: The problem of heterogeneity. *Clinical Psychology Review, 10,* 699-725.

ADHD IN BOYS VS. GIRLS 13

Maughan, B., Pickles, A., Hagell, A., Rutter, M., & Yule, W. (1996). Reading
    problems and antisocial behavior: Developmental trends in
    comorbidity. *Journal of Child Psychology and Psychiatry, 37,* 405-418.
    doi:10.1111/j.1469-7610.1996.tb01421.x

Oltmanns, T. F., & Emery, R. E. (1998). Psychological disorders of
    childhood. In *Abnormal psychology* (2nd ed., pp. 572-607). Upper
    Saddle River, NJ: Prentice Hall.

Sprock, J., Blashfield, R. K., & Smith, B. (1990). Gender weighting of
    DSM-III-R personality disorder criteria. *American Journal of
    Psychiatry, 147,* 586-590.

Index

Revision Symbols

Letter-number codes refer to sections of this book.

abbr	faulty abbreviation **P9**		*p*	error in punctuation
adj	misuse of adjective **G4**		$\stackrel{\wedge}{;}$	comma **P1**
add	add needed word **S2**		*no ,*	no comma **P2**
adv	misuse of adverb **G4**		*;*	semicolon **P3**
agr	faulty agreement **G1, G3-a**		*:*	colon **P3**
appr	inappropriate language **W4**		$\stackrel{\vee}{?}$	apostrophe **P4**
art	article **M2**		" "	quotation marks **P5**
awk	awkward		. ?	period, question mark,
cap	capital letter **P8**		!	exclamation point,
case	error in case **G3-c, G3-d**		— ( )	dash, parentheses,
cliché	cliché **W5-e**		[ ] ...	brackets, ellipsis mark,
coh	coherence **C4-d**		/	slash **P6**
coord	faulty coordination **S6-c**		*pass*	ineffective passive **W3**
cs	comma splice **G6**		*pn agr*	pronoun agreement **G3-a**
dev	inadequate development **C4-b**		*proof*	proofreading problem **C3-d**
dm	dangling modifier **S3-e**		*ref*	error in pronoun reference **G3-b**
-ed	error in *-ed* ending **G2-d**		*run-on*	run-on sentence **G6**
emph	emphasis **S6**		*-s*	error in *-s* ending **G2-c**
ESL	ESL grammar **M1, M2, M3, M4, M5**		*sexist*	sexist language **W4-e**
exact	inexact language **W5**		*shift*	distracting shift **S4**
frag	sentence fragment **G5**		*sl*	slang **W4-c**
fs	fused sentence **G6**		*sp*	misspelled word **P7**
gl/us	see glossary of usage **W1**		*sub*	faulty subordination **S6-d**
hyph	error in use of hyphen **P7**		*sv agr*	subject-verb agreement **G1, G2-c**
idiom	idiom **W5-d**			
inc	incomplete construction **S2**		*t*	error in verb tense **G2-f**
irreg	error in irregular verb **G2-a**		*trans*	transition needed **C4-d**
			usage	see glossary of usage **W1**
ital	italics **P10**		*v*	voice **W3**
jarg	jargon **W4-a**		*var*	sentence variety **S6-b, S6-c, S7**
lc	lowercase letter **P8**			
mix	mixed construction **S5**		*vb*	verb error **G2**
mm	misplaced modifier **S3-b**		*w*	wordy **W2**
mood	error in mood **G2-g**		*//*	faulty parallelism **S1**
nonst	nonstandard usage **W4-c**		∧	insert
num	error in use of number **P9**		x	obvious error
om	omitted word **S2**		#	insert space
¶	new paragraph **C4**		⌣	close up space

Detailed Menu